CW00351007

CONCISE *World* ATLAS

Sphere Reference

First Published in the UK by Sphere Books Ltd 1987
Sphere Books Ltd, 27 Wrights Lane, London W8 5T2.

THE CONCISE WORLD

STATISTICS

The World 6- 7
Europe 8-15
Asia 16-25
Australia 24-27
Africa 28-38
North-America 38-42
South-America 42-47

READER INFORMATION

Reader information 48
Legend 49

EUROPE

Europe, environment, flags 50-51

British Isles and Central Europe 52-53
Belgium, Czechoslovakia, Federal Republic of Germany, German Democratic Republic, Luxembourg, Netherlands, Poland

Northern Europe 54-55
Denmark, Finland, Iceland, Norway, Sweden

Spain, Italy, France 56-57

The Balkans 58-59
Bulgaria, Cyprus, Greece, Hungary, Romania, Turkey

The Middle East 60-61
Bahrain, Iran, Iraq, Israel, Jordan, Kuwait, Lebanon, Qatar, Syria, United Arab Emirates

Western Soviet Union 62-63
European USSR, Western Siberia

ASIA

Asia, environment, flags 64-65

South West Asia 66-67
Afghanistan, Iran, Pakistan

Eastern Soviet Union 68-69
Eastern Siberia, Mongolia

China and Japan 70-71
incl. Mongolia, North Korea, South Korea, Taiwan

India and South East Asia 72-73
incl. Bangladesh, Bhutan, Burma, Kampuchea, Laos, Nepal, Sri Lanka, Thailand, Vietnam

The East Indies 74-75
Brunei, Indonesia, Malaysia, Philippines

AUSTRALIA

Australasia, environment, flags 76-77

Australia 78-79

New Guinea and New Zealand 80-81

Oceania 82-83
Melanesia, Micronesia, Polynesia

AFRICA

Africa, environment, flags 84-85

North-West Africa 86-87
Algeria, Libya, Morocco, Mauretania, Niger, Tunisia

The Nile Valley and Arabia 88-89
Bahrain, Egypt, Iraq, Israel, Jorda, Kuwait, Lebanon, Oman, Qatar, Saudi-Arabia, Southern Yemen, Sudan, Syria, United Arab Emirates, Yemen

West Africa 90-91
Benin, Burkina, Cameroon, Chad, Congo, Equatorial Guinea, Gabon, Ghana, Guinea, Guinea-Bissau, Ivory Coast, Liberia, Mali, Niger, Nigeria, São Tomé and Príncipe, Senegal, Sierra Leone, The Gambia, Togo

East Africa 92-93
Central Africa, Ethiopia, Kenya, Sudan, Tanzania, Uganda, Zaire

Southern Africa 94-95
Angola, Botswana, Comores, Madagascar, Malawi, Mauritius, Mozambique, Namibia, Lesotho, South Africa, Swaziland, Zambia, Zimbabwe

NORTH AMERICA

North America, environment, flags 96-97

Alaska and Western Canada 98-99
incl. the Aleutian islands

Eastern Canada 100-101

The United States 102-103
incl. Mexico

Central America and the West Indies 104-105
Belize, The Caribbean Archipelago, Costa Rica, Cuba, El Salvador, Guatemala, Honduras, Mexico, Nicaragua

SOUTH AMERICA

South America, environment, flags 106-107

South America, northern part 108-109
Brazil, Colombia, Ecuador, Guyana, Panama, Peru, Surinam, Venezuela

South America, central part 110-111
Bolivia, Brazil, Chile, Peru

South America, southern part 112-113
Argentina, Bolivia, Brazil, Chile, Paraguay, Uruguay

POLAR REGIONS

The Arctic, environment 114

The Antarctica, environment 115

THE WORLD

The World, environment 116-117

The World, political 118-119

The World, Time Zones 120-121

Animals on the Edge of Extinction 120-123

INDEX

Index 124-183

THE WORLD'S longest, greatest, highest, largest

Area: 150.243.000 km²
(Land: 26%, Water: 71%, Ice: 3%)
Population: 4,025,281,000

World's Longest Rivers

1.	Nile (Africa)	6.690 km
2.	Amazon (South America)	6.570 km
3.	Mississippi-Missouri (North America)	6.020 km
4.	Yangtze (Asia)	5.980 km
5.	Yenisey (Asia)	5.870 km

Greatest Depth in each ocean

Arctic: North Polar Basin	5.500 m
Atlantic: Milwaukee Depth (Puerto Rico Trench)	9.219 m
Indian: Java Trench	7.450 m
Pacific: Challenger Deep (Mariana Trench)	11.034 m

Highest Mountain in each continent

Africa: Kilimanjaro	5.89
(Antarctica Vinson Massif)	5.14
Asia: Mt. Everest	8.84
Europe: Mont Blanc	4.81
North America: Mount McKinley	6.194
Oceania: Puncak Jaya	5.03
South America: Cerro Aconcagua	6.95

Largest Island in each continent

Africa: Madagascar	587.000 km
(Antarctica: Alexander 1)	43.200 km
Asia: Borneo	737.000 km
Europe: Great Britain	219.000 km
North America: Greenland	2.131.000 km
Oceania: New Guinea	790.000 km
South America: Grande de Tierra del Fuego	48.000 km

argest Natural Lake in each continent	
frica: Lake Victoria	62.940 km²
sia: Caspian Sea	371.000 km²
urope: Ladoga	18.130 km²
orth America: Lake Superior	82,260 km²
ceania: Lake Eyre	7.690 km²
outh America: Lago Titicaca	8.030 km²

Comparison of population to area by continent

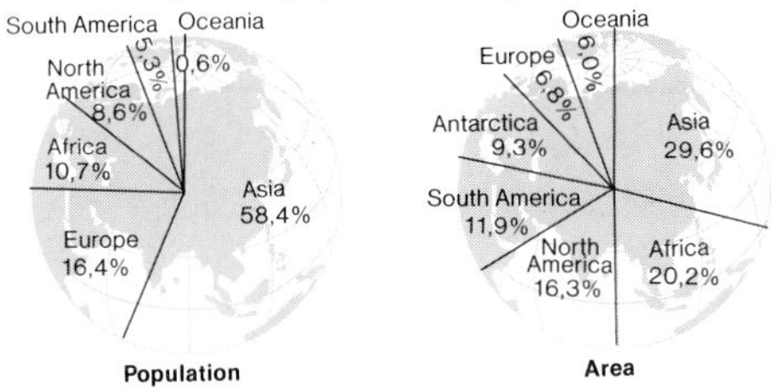

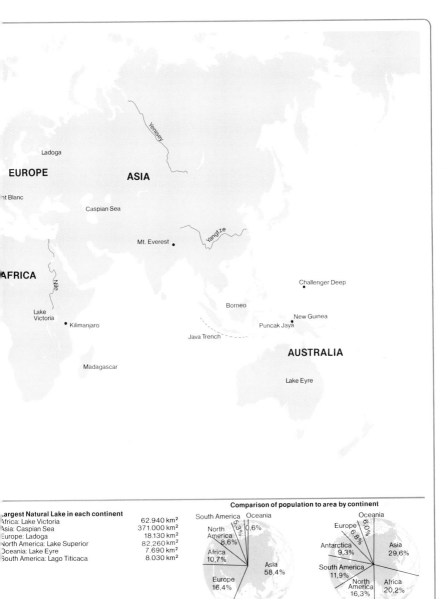

EUROPE

Area: 10,245,000 km²
Population: 660,476,000
Density of population per km²: 64

The North Atlantic West Wind Drift together with prevailing westerly winds gives Northern Europe a climate about 5° C. warmer than the average for these latitudes.

The European mainla[nd] most northerly point [is] Nordkinn at 71° 8′ N [.] latitude. North Cape i[s an] impressive rocky pro[-] montory on the neighbouring island [of] Magerøy which has it[s] most northerly point a[t] Knivskjellodden.

① ICELAND

All the world's geysers are named after Geysir in Haukadalur, Europe's largest geyser which at ir- regular intervals, but usually once a day, throws a column of boil- ing water some 30 m. in the air (maximum height 70m.)

Vatnajökull is Europe's largest glacier with an area of about 8,400 km²

② NORWAY

Sognefjorden (220 km. in length) is Europe's longest inlet.

③ SWEDEN

④ FINLAND

Ladoga with an ar[ea] 18,130 km² is Eu[rope's] largest lake.

⑧ UNIO[N]

Europe's largest island is Great Britain which, with an area of 219,000 km², ranks seventh in the world.

⑤ REPUBLIC OF IRELAND

⑦ DENMARK

⑥ UNITED KINGDOM

Agricultural land cover[s] 40% of Europe. No oth[er] continent is so intensi[ve-] ly utilized.

Europe lies on the Prime Meridian, which divides the earth into Eastern and Western hemispheres.

⑨ NETHER- LANDS

⑩

⑪ GERMAN DEMOCRATIC REPUBLIC

⑫ POLAND

⑬ BELGIUM

FEDERAL REPUBLIC

OF GERMANY

⑮ CZECHOSLOVAKIA

At St. Malo the difference betwêen ebb and flow is 15 m., the greatest tidal range in Europe.

⑭ LUXEMBOURG

Cabo da Roca at 9° 31′ W. longitude is the westernmost point on the European mainland.

⑰ FRANCE

⑲ LIECHTEN STEIN

⑱ SWITZERLAND

⑳ AUSTRIA

HUNGARY ⑯

⑳

Mont Blanc is Europe's highest mountain.

㉔ ROMANIA

PORTUGAL ㉕

ANDORRA ㉗

㉑ MONACO

㉘ SAN MARINO

㉓ YUGOSLAVIA

㉖ SPAIN

㉙ VATICAN STATE

㉒ ITALY

BULGARIA

㉛

TURKEY

㉜

Europe's highest temperature, 51° C., has been recorded at Sevilla.

㉚ ALBANIA

Punta Marroqui at 36° 0′ N. latitude is the most southerly point on the European mainland.

㉞ GREECE

The highest active volcano in Europe is Etna which last erupted in 1984.

㉝ MALTA

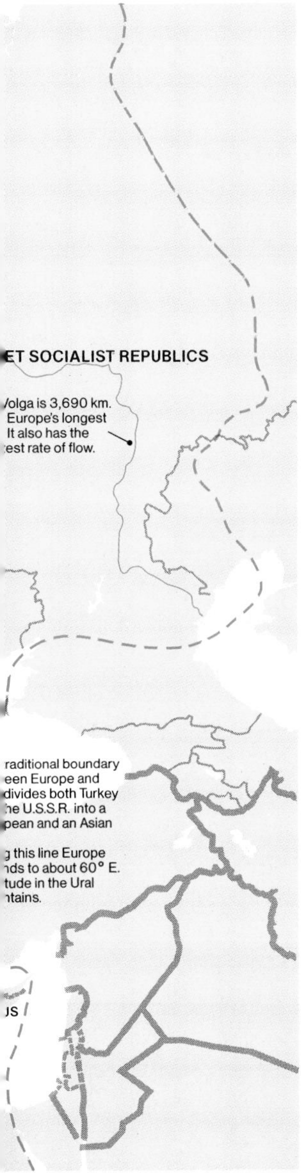
ET SOCIALIST REPUBLICS
/olga is 3,690 km.
Europe's longest
It also has the
est rate of flow.
raditional boundary
een Europe and
divides both Turkey
he U.S.S.R. into a
pean and an Asian
g this line Europe
nds to about 60° E.
tude in the Ural
ntains.

30 ALBANIA
27 ANDORRA
20 AUSTRIA
13 BELGIUM
31 BULGARIA
35 CYPRUS
15 CZECHOSLOVAKIA
7 DENMARK
10 FEDERAL REPUBLIC OF GERMANY
4 FINLAND
17 FRANCE
11 GERMAN DEMOCRATIC REPUBLIC
34 GREECE
16 HUNGARY
1 ICELAND
22 ITALY
19 LIECHTENSTEIN
14 LUXEMBOURG
33 MALTA
21 MONACO
9 NETHERLANDS
2 NORWAY
12 POLAND
25 PORTUGAL
5 REPUBLIC OF IRELAND
24 ROMANIA
28 SAN MARINO
26 SPAIN
3 SWEDEN
18 SWITZERLAND
32 TURKEY
8 UNION OF SOVIET SOCIALIST REPUBLICS
6 UNITED KINGDOM AND NORTHERN IRELAND
29 VATICAN STATE
23 YUGOSLAVIA

① ICELAND

Lýðveldið Island
(Republic of Iceland)

Area: 102,819 km²
Population: 240,000
Population growth per annum: 1.1%
Life expectancy at birth: males 73 years, females 79 years
Literacy: 99,9%
Capital with population: Reykjavik 87,000
Other important cities with population: Akureyri 14,000
Language: Icelandic
Religion: Protestant
Currency: Króna = 100 aurar

The Island of the Norse sagas, Iceland's "althingi" claims to be the world's oldest parliament, enacting laws since 930. The Icelanders kept the old Norse myths and sagas alive by oral tradition until Snorri Sturluson collected them in his epic Edda. A sight to be seen is the world famous Geysir. Independent 930, JUN 17, 1944.

② NORWAY

Kongeriket Norge
(Kingdom of Norway)

Area: 386,974 km² (including Svalbard and Jan Mayen)
Population: 4,130,000
Population growth per annum: 0.4%
Life expectancy at birth: males 72 years, females 78 years
Literacy: 99%
Capital with population: Oslo 447,000
Other important cities with population: Bergen 207,000, Trondheim 134,000
Language: Norwegian
Religion: Protestant
Currency: Norwegian krone = 100 öre

Norway, proclaimed 'The land of the Midnight Sun" might rather be called the Land of Fiords. These spectacular inlets between vertical mountain walls dissect Norway, and have made the Norwegians a people who sail and fish. The Sogne Fiord is 220 km. long — the Europe's longest bay. Independent 1905.

③ SWEDEN

Konungariket Sverige
(Kingdom of Sweden)

Area: 449,964 km²
Population: 8,350,000
Population growth per annum: 0.2%
Life expectancy at birth: males 72 years, females 79 years
Literacy: 99%
Capital with population: Stockholm 651,000 (metropolitan area 1,409, 000)
Other important cities with population: Göteborg 424,000 Malmö 230,000
Language: Swedish
Religion: Protestant
Currency: Swedish krona = 100 öre

The metallurgical industry that gave the world "Swedish steel" has traditions that reach beyond the Viking Age. The world's oldest company, Stora, chartered in 1280, is still working the mine of Falun, that produced the copper that once made Sweden a great power.

④ FINLAND

Suomen Tasavatta — Republiken Finland
(Republic of Finland)

Area: 337,032 km²
Population: 4,870 000
Population growth per annum: 0.6%
Life expectancy at birth: males 69 years, females 77 years
Literacy: 99%
Capital with population: Helsinki (Helsingfors) 484,000
Other important cities with population: Tampere (Tammerfors) 170.000, Turku (Åbo) 165,000
Language: Finnish, Swedish
Religion: Protestant
Currency: Markka (mark) = 100 penniä (penni)

The "land of a thousand lakes" (actually almost a hundred thousand) has also become known as "the land that pays its debts" — by repaying not only U.S. loans but also a huge war indemnity to the Soviet Union after World War II. Exporting high quality manufactured goods to East and West has brought prosperity to the Finns. Independent MAR 29, 1809, DEC 6, 1917

⑤ REPUBLIC OF IRELAND

Poblacht na L'Éireann
(Eire)

Area: 70,283 km²
Population: 3,440,000
Population growth per annum: 1.1%
Life expectancy at birth: males 70 years, females 75 years
Literacy: 99%
Capital with population: Dublin 526,000
Other important cities with population: Cork 150,000, Limerick 76,000
Language: Irish, English
Religion: Roman Catholic
Currency: Irish pound (punt Eirenmach) = 100 pighne

"The Emerald Isle" is perhaps most famous for its people — for boisterous bards, for poets and playwrights and Irish Eyes — but also for Irish coffee, whiskey and Guinness beer. Ireland justly prides itself also on the Book of Kells — and maybe more reluctantly for the Blarney Stone, kissed by many. Independent 1916, 1922.

⑥ UNITED KINGDOM AND NORTHERN IRELAND

Area: 244,104 km²
Population: 56,780,000
Population growth per annum: — 0.1%
Life expectancy at birth: males 70 years, females 76 years
Literacy: 99%
Capital with population: London 6,755,000
Other important cities with population: Birmingham 1,013,000, Leeds 714,000, Sheffield 543,000
Language: English
Religion: Protestant, Roman Catholic, Moslem
Currency: British pound = 100 pence

Britannia ruled the waves for over three hundred years, and finally gracefully resigned from the role of "peacekeeper" after the Pax Britannica had been broken by two world wars. The sun may have set over the Empire, but it still shines on the Union Jack in many places all over the world.

⑦ DENMARK

Kongeriget Danmark
(Kingdom of Denmark)

Area: 43,069 km²
Population: 5,112,000
Population growth per annum: 0.2%
Life expectancy at birth: males 71 years, females 77 years
Literacy: 99%
Capital with population: Köbenhavn (Copenhagen) 483,000, (Greater Copenhagen 1,400,000)
Other important cities with population: Aarhus 250,000, Odense 170,000
Language: Danish
Religion: Protestant (Lutherans)
Currency: Danish krone = 100 øre

Danish kings have ruled not only all of Scandinavia but also England. Today no other country has larger overseas territories. They include the world's largest island, Greenland. Friendly Denmark now serves as an important link between the Nordic countries and the rest of Europe, especially the E.E.C.

⑧ UNION OF SOVIET SOCIALIST REPUBLICS

Soyuz Sovyetskikh
Sotsialisticheskikh Respublik

Area: 22,402,200 km²
Population: 276,300,000
Population growth per annum: 0.9 %
Life expectancy at birth: males 65 years, females 74 years
Literacy: 99%
Capital with population: Moskva (Moscow) 8,537,000
Other important cities with population: Leningrad 4,800,000, Baku 1,660,000, Kuybyshev 1,250,000
Language: Slavic (Russian, Ukrainian, Byelorussian, Polish), Altaic (Turkish , etc.) Other Indo-European, Uralian, Caucasian.
Religion: Orthodox, Moslem
Currency: Rubel = 100 kopek

The U.S.S.R. is a country that is almost a continent not only in size, but also in diversity. It covers 1/6 of the Earth's land area, and is larger than South America. 75% is traditionally considered to be part of Asia, but 75% of its people live in the European part. In comprises 120 different peoples, dominated by the Russians.

⑨ NETHERLANDS

Koninkrijk der Nederlanden
(Kingdom of the Netherlands)

Area: 41,548 km²
Population: 14,395,000
Population growth per annum: 0.6%
Life expectancy at birth: males 72 years, females 78 years
Literacy: 99%
Capital with population: Amsterdam 994,000
Other important cities with population: Rotterdam 1,025,500, S-Gravenhage (The Hague) (672,000)
Language: Dutch
Religion: Roman Catholic (40%), Protestant (35%)
Currency: Guilder = 100 cents

More than one third of the country lies below sealevel. Some Dutch say that 'God created the world, except the Netherlands, which we had to create ourselves'. This task was begun in the 15th century, when they learned to reclaim their slowly sinking land from the encroaching sea. Independent APR 19, 1839.

⑩ FEDERAL REPUBLIC OF GERMANY

Bundesrepublik Deutschland

Area: 248,687 km²
Population: 61,420,000
Population growth per annum: — 0.3 %
Life expectancy at birth: males 69 years, females 75 years
Literacy: 99%
Capital with population: Bonn 293,000
Other important cities with population: Berlin 1,860,000, Hamburg 1,620,000, Munich 1,285,000
Language: German
Religion: Protestant (49%), Roman Catholic (45%)
Currency: D-mark = 100 pfennig

Like the mythical Phoenix, West Germany has miraculously sprung from the pyre of total defeat and destruction since 1945. In economic and industrial importance the western half of divided Germany now ranks fourth in the world. The Grand Tour must include the Rhine valley with its castles and vineyards. Independent SEP 6, 1949.

⑪ GERMAN DEMOCRATIC REPUBLIC

Deutsche Demokratische Republik

Area: 108,333 km²
Population: 16,700,000
Population growth per annum: 0%
Life expectancy at birth: males 69 years, females 75 years
Literacy: 99%
Capital with population: Berlin 1,185,000
Other important cities with population: Leipzig 560,000, Dresden 525,000, Karl-Marx-Stadt 320,000
Language: German
Religion: Protestant (80%)
Currency: Mark (of the GDR) = 100 pfennig

The republic is divided nation with a divided capital. The fears and the rivalries of the victorious powers after World War II prevented the reestablishment of a German "Reich". Thus part of the old capital, Berlin, is now a West German enclave, by road and railway over 150 km. (100 miles) inside East Germany. Independent OCT 7, 1949.

⑫ POLAND

Polska Rzeczpospolita Ludowa
(Polish Peoples Republic)

Area: 312,683 km²
Population: 36,400,000
Population growth per annum: 1.0 %
Life expectancy at birth: males 67 years, females 75 years
Literacy: 98%
Capital with population: Warszawa (Warsaw) 1,630,000
Other important cities with population: Lódź 850,000 Kraków 725,000
Language: Polish
Religion: Roman Catholic
Currency: Zloty = 100 groszy

The Polish people do not give up. Time and again conquering armies have swept over Poland and divided the spoils. After World War II the Soviet Union pushed the land westwards over former German land, annexing 1/3 of pre-war Poland in the east. Independent 966, NOV 10, 1918.

⑬ BELGIUM

Royaume de Belgique —
Koninkrijk België
(Kingdom of Belgium)

Area: 30,519 km²
Population: 9,850 000
Population growth per annum: 0.1%
Life expectancy at birth: males 69 years, females 75 years
Literacy: 98%
Capital with population: Bruxelles 980,000 (Brussels)
Other important cities with population: Antwerpen 490,000, Gent 240,000
Language: Flemish (Dutch), French, German
Religion: Roman Catholic
Currency: Belgian franc = 100 centimes

The country at "the crossroads of Western Europe" is dominated by the capital Brussels, Brussels is also the capital of the E.E.C. The difficulties in uniting Europe are mirrored in the Belgian nation. The Dutch-speaking Flemings and French-speaking Walloons stick together against others, but often quarrel amongst themselves. Independent OCT 4, 1830.

⑭ LUXEMBOURG

Grand-Duché Luxembourg
(Grand Duchy of Luxembourg)

Area: 2,586 km²
Population: 366,000
Population growth per annum: —0.04%
Life expectancy at birth: males 68 years, females 75 years
Literacy: 100%
Capital with population: Luxembourg 79,000
Other important cities with population: none
Language: Luxemburgish, French, German
Religion: Roman Catholic (94%)
Currency: Luxembourg franc = 100 centimes

Historically Luxembourg has always had strong ties with one or another of its neighbours while maintaining independence in form if not in fact. It also formed some sort of a nucleus for the Coal and Steel Union that evolved into the E.E.C. Indep. 1866.

⑮ CZECHOSLOVAKIA

Československá Socialistická Republika
(Czechoslovak Socialist Republic)

Area: 127,869 km²
Population: 15,400 000
Population growth per annum: 0.7%
Life expectancy at birth: males 67 years, females 74 years
Literacy: 99%
Capital with population: Praha (Prague) 1,185,000
Other important cities with population: Bratislava 395,000, Brno 380,000
Language: Czech, Slovak
Religion: Roman Catholic (55%), Protestant (10%)
Currency: Koruna = 100 haléřu

Haseks fictionary "Good soldier Schweik" in many ways epitomizes the survival instincts of his fellow citizens. Both Czechs and Slovaks have always striven for freedom, but throughout the centuries have been forced to bow to foreign rule. Mining and manufacturing have a long history in Czechoslovakia. Independent OCT 28, 1918.

⑯ HUNGARY

Magyar Nepköztársaság
(Hungarian People's Republic)

Area: 93,032 km²
Population: 10,680,000
Population growth per annum: 0.4%
Life expectancy at birth: males 67 years, females 73 years
Literacy: 98%
Capital with population: Budapest 2,064,000
Other important cities with population: Debrecen 205,000, Miskolc 212,000
Language: Hungarian (Magyar)
Religion: Roman Catholic (65%), Protestant (25%)
Currency: Forint = 100 fillér

Hungary is in many ways an enclave in Eastern Europe — a Finno-Ugric nation surrounded by Slav neighbors, a land of plains, the famous puszta, and rolling hills, encircled by higher mountain lands — and, within limits, more prosperous and "capitalistic" than the other Soviet satellites. Independent 1001.

⑰ FRANCE

République Française
(French Republic)

Area: 547,026 km²
Population: 54,539,000
Population growth per annum: 0.3%
Life expectancy at birth: males 70 years, females 78 years
Literacy: 99%
Capital with population: Paris 2,320,000 (Greater Paris 8,550,000)
Other important cities with population: Marseille 915,000, Lyon 465,000
Language: French
Religion: Roman Catholic (90%) Islam (4%)
Currency: French franc = 100 centimes

France is one of the great powers of the world. The French language is still the language of diplomacy. France is culturally the world's leading nation, and most former French colonies remain members of the French Commonwealth. France is also the leading European nation on the space frontier. National day: JULY 14, (1789)

⑱ SWITZERLAND

Schweiz - Suisse - Svizzera
(Swiss Confederation)

Area: 41,293 km²
Population: 6,400,000
Population growth per annum: 0.2 %
Life expectancy at birth: males 72 years, females 78 years
Literacy: 99%
Capital with population: Bern 144,000
Other important cities with population: Zürich 363,000, Basel 180,000
Language: German, French, Italian, Romansch
Religion: Roman Catholic (49%), Protestant (48%)
Currency: Swiss franc = 100 centimes (rappen)

The Financial Pole of the world is claimed to be in situated in some undefined spot in Zürich. Through centuries of neutrality and economic stability, Switzerland has grown into a global center of banking. Besides quality watches, tourism somehow seems to have been invented in this land of few natural resources. Independent AUG 1, 1291.

⑲ LIECHTENSTEIN

Fürstentum Liechtenstein
(Principality of Liechtenstein)

Area: 160 km²
Population: 27,000
Population growth per annum: 7.0%
Life expectancy at birth: not available
Literacy: 100 %
Capital with population: Vaduz 5,000
Other important cities with population: none
Language: German
Religion: Roman Catholic
Currency: Swiss franc = 100 centimes

Liechtenstein epitomizes the notion "postage stamp state" — because of its size and its fame among collectors of stamps. It is also an anomaly surviving principality from the times when Europe was divided among many princes and kings, before their realms were united into nations. Independent MAY 3, 1342.

⑳ AUSTRIA

Republik Österreich
(Republic of Austria)

Area: 83,853 km²)
Population: 7,550,000
Population growth per annum: —0.1%
Life expectancy at birth: males 68 years, females 75 years
Literacy: 98%
Capital with population: Wien (Vienna) 1,530,000
Other important cities with population: Graz 243,000, Linz 200,000
Language: German
Religion: Roman Catholic (89%), Protestant (6%)
Currency: Schilling = 100 groschen

Austria is the only state pledged both by law and treaties to neutrality. Vienna, for centuries the capital of the "Holy Roman Empire", the seat of the Habsburg Emperors, still bears the imprint of bygone greatness, and remains the cultural capital of Central Europe. Indep. 1276, 1804, 1918, APR 27, 1945.

㉑ MONACO

Principauté de Monaco
(Principality of Monaco)

Area: 1,95 km²
Population: 27,000
Population growth per annum: —3.0%
Life expectancy at birth: males 70 years, females 78 years
Literacy: 99%
Capital with population: Monaco-Ville 1,700
Other important cities with population: none
Languages: French, Monegasque
Religion: Roman Catholic
Currency: French-or Monegasque franc = 100 centimes

Monaco proves that gambling can pay provided you run the bank! The Monte Carlo Casino has been the Mecca of gamblers since 1858 and also made Monaco a fashionable tourist resort. The citizens of microscopic Monaco do not pay income tax. Independent 1297.

㉒ ITALY

Repubblica Italiana
(Italian Republic)

Area: 301,268 km²
Population: 56,930,000
Population growth per annum: 0.4%
Life expectancy at birth: males 70 years, females 76 years
Literacy: 98%
Capital with population: Roma (Rome) 2,830,000
Other important cities with population: Milano 1,500,000, Napoli 1,200,000
Language: Italian
Religion: Roman Catholic
Currency: Lira = 100 centesimi

All roads lead to Rome, still the Eternal City — the city of the Pope, of the Sistine Chapel, of the Colosseum and innumerable monuments of Imperial Rome. But Italy is also the land of Saint Francis and Leonardo, of Pisa, Venice and Florence — and today of Milan, Torino and Cortina d'Ampezzo. Independent FEB 18, 1861.

㉓ YUGOSLAVIA

Socijalistička Federativna Republika Jugoslavija
(Socialist Federal Republ. of Yogoslavia)

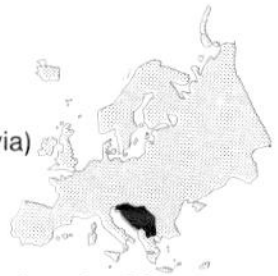

Area: 255,804 km²
Population: 22,850,000
Population growth per annum: 0.9%
Life expectancy at birth: males 67 years, females 72 years
Literacy: 85%
Capital with population: Beograd (Belgrade) 1,407,000
Other important cities with population: Zagreb 1,175,000, Skopje 507,000, Ljubljana 305,000
Language: Serbo-Croatian, Macedonian, Slovenian, Albanian
Religion: Orthodox (41%), Roman Catholic (32%), Moslem (12%)
Currency: Yugoslavian dinar = 100 para

Few would in 1918 have placed any money on the survival of any country in the Balkan Peninsula and least of them all Yugoslavia with its mosaic of quarrelling religions — three — and combative peoples — five — speaking four different languages. Independent DEC 1, 1918.

㉔ ROMANIA

Republica Socialistâ România
(Socialist Republic of Romania)

Area: 237,500 km²
Population: 22,600,000
Population growth per annum: 0.9%
Life expectancy at birth: males 68 years, females 73 years
Literacy: 98%
Capital with population: Bucuresti (Bucharest) 1,835,000
Other important cities with population: Constanța 285,000, Cluj-Napoca 271,000
Language: Romanian
Religion: Orthodox (70%), Roman Catholic (14%)
Currency: Leu = 100 bani

A land that is still Roman after almost two thousand years! Rome sett-led fertile Dacia and made an everlasting imprint. In spite of that, the frontier province was lost less than two centuries after conquest. The people today speak a language based on Latin. Transylvania is known for fictitious Count Dracula. Independent 1877.

㉕ PORTUGAL

República Portuguesa
(Republic of Portugal)

Area: 92,082 km²
Population: 9,930,000
Population growth per annum: 0.9%
Life expectancy at birth: males 66 years, females 74 years
Literacy: 80%
Capital with population: Lisboa (Lisbon) 818,000
Other important cities with population: Porto 330,000
Language: Portuguese
Religion: Roman Catholic
Currency: Escudo = 100 centavos

In spite of its small size, Portugal managed to become one of the world's great powers, and to acquire and retain a global empire for half a millennium. Portugal produces famous wines, such as madeira and port (from Oporto), and every second wine bottle in the world is sealed with Portuguese cork.

㉖ SPAIN

Reino de España
(Kingdom of Spain)

Area: 504,782 km²
Population: 38,220,000
Population growth per annum: 1.0 %
Life expectancy at birth: males 70 years, females 76 years
Literacy: 97%
Capital with population: Madrid 3,188,000
Other important cities with population:
Barcelona 1,755,000, Sevilla 654,000,
Zaragoza 600,000
Language: Spanish, Catalan, Basque
Religion: Roman Catholic
Currency: Spanish peseta = 100 céntimos

Proud Spain, once one of the world's great powers that sent the Great Armada to England in a bid to become master of the oceans, is today still the cultural leader in the Iberic World. It gave the world people such as Cervantes, Loyola, Goya, and Picasso.

㉗ ANDORRA

Principat d'Andorra
(Principality of Andorra)

Area: 453 km²
Population: 41,600
Population growth per annum: not available
Life expectancy at birth: males 70 years, females 76 years
Literacy: 100%
Capital with population: Andorra la Vella 10,500
Other important cities with population: none
Language: Catalan
Religion: Roman Catholic
Currency: French franc, Spanish peseta

Conducting trade between Spain and France is and has been the main business of this Pyrenean principality, jointly ruled by the Spanish Bishop of Urgel and the Head of State of France. Outside Andorra some call it smuggling. Tourism also benefits from the absence of customs duties. Independent 1278.

㉘ SAN MARINO

Repubblica di San Marino
(Republic of San Marino)

Area: 61 km²
Population: 22,000
Population growth per annum: not available
Life expectancy at birth: not available
Literacy: not available
Capital with population: San Marino 5,000
Other important cities with population: none
Language: Italian
Religion: Roman Catholic
Currency: Italian lira = 100 centesimi

The only surviving city state of medieval Italy, San Marino is still governed by two Capitani Reggenti, democratically elected for a period of only six months. Sale of postage stamps was an important industry, but is now dwarfed by the tourist trade. Over 3.5 million visit San Marino each year. Independent 1263.

㉙ VATICAN CITY STATE

Stato della Citta del Vaticano

Area: 0,44 km²
Population: 1,000
Population growth per annum: —
Life expectancy at birth: —
Literacy: —
Capital with population: —
Other important cities with population: —
Language: Italian
Religion: Roman Catholic
Currency: Vatican City lira, Italian lira = 100 centesimi

The spiritual importance of the Pope is inversely proportionate to the size of his worldly domains, the world's smallest state. Relative to its size it certainly contains greater treasures of art than any other state in the world, such as the Sistine Chapel and the Pietà. Independent FEB 11, 1929.

㉚ ALBANIA

Rebublika Popullore
Socialiste e Shqipërisë

Area: 28,748 km²
Population: 2,850 000
Population growth per annum: 2.4%
Life expectancy at birth: males 68 years, females 71 years
Literacy: 75%
Capital with population: Tirana 198,000
Other important cities with population: Shkodra 63,000
Language: Albanian
Religion: Religions are not allowed since 1967
Currency: Lek = 100 qindarka

A desire for self-sufficiency has turned Albania into a virtually unknown "white spot" on the map. This nation is Europe's only Moslem country, but has declared itself "the world's first atheist state". It is so dogmatically communist, that it has broken all ties with other communist countries. Independent NOV 11,1912.

㉛ BULGARIA
Narodna Republika Bâlgarija
(Peoples Republic of Bulgaria)

Area: 110,912 km²
Population: 8,930,000
Population growth per annum: 0.6%
Life expectancy at birth: males 69 years, females 75 years
Literacy: 95%
Capital with population: Sofiya 1,080,000
Other important cities with population: Plovid 310,000, Varna 260,000
Language: Bulgarian
Religion: Orthodox (85%), Moslem (13%)
Currency: Lev = 100 stótinki

The Bulgarians do not forget that Russia helped to liberate their country from Turkish rule that lasted for over five centuries. Today it is counted among the most loyal allies of the Soviet Union. Europe's "vegetable and fruit garden" is also the tourist "Riviera" of Eastern Europe. Independent SEPT 22, 1908.

㉜ TURKEY
Türkiye Cumhuriyeti
(Republic of Turkey)

Area: 779,452 km²
Population: 48,000,000
Population growth per annum: 2.5%
Life expectancy at birth: males 58 years, females 63 years
Literacy: 70%
Capital with population: Ankara 1,877,000
Other important cities with population: Istanbul 2,773,000, Izmir 758,000,
Language: Turkish
Religion: Moslem
Currency: Turkish lira = 100 kuruş

The land that for centuries served as a link between Europe and Asia now also provides the two continents with a physical link, the huge bridge over the Bosporus. The world famous cathedral of Hagia Sofia, built by emperor Justinian 532-537, was turned into a mosque after the fall of Constantinople in 1453.

㉝ MALTA
Repubblika ta'Malta
(Republic of Malta)

Area: 316 km²
Population: 330,000
Population growth per annum: 0.9%
Life expectancy at birth: males 69 years, females 73 years
Literacy: 83%
Capital with population: Valletta 14,000
Other important cities with population: none
Language: Maltese, English
Religion: Roman Catholic
Currency: Lira Maltija (Maltese Lira) = 100 cents = 1000 mils

For unprecedented valour during World War II the people of Malta were collectively awarded the George Cross, Britaini's highest civilian decoration. Malta still proudly carries the cross in its national flag. From 1530 to 1798 Malta was ruled by the Knights Hospitallers — since Known as the Knights of Malta. Independent SEP 21, 1964.

㉞ GREECE
Elleniki Dimokratia
(Hellenic Republic)

Area: 131,944 km²
Population: 9,750,000
Population growth per annum: 0.6%
Life expectancy at birth: males 71 years, females 75 years
Literacy: 95%
Capital with population: Athínai (Athens) 900,000 (Greater Athens 3,000,000)
Other important cities with population: Thessaloníki 400,000, Pátrai 140,000
Language: Greek
Religion: Greek Orthodox (97%)
Currency: Drachma = 100 lepta

The cradle of European civilization is now a member of the E.E.C. and thus takes an active part in shaping the Europe of the future. Greece may well have the world's largest merchant fleet — even if few sail under Greek flag. Venerable Parthenon, temple of Pallas Athena, still crowns Athen's Acropolis. Independent FEB 3, 1830.

㉟ CYPRUS
Kypriaki Dimokratia —
Kibris Cumhuriyeti
(Republic of Cyprus)

Area: 9,251 km²
Population: 655,000
Population growth per annum: 0.4%
Life expectancy at birth: males 70 years, females 74 years
Literacy: 89%
Capital with population: Nicosia 161,000
Other important cities with population: Limassol 107,000, Famagusta 40,000
Language: Greek, Turkish
Religion: Orthodox (77%)
Currency: Cyprus pound = 100 cents

The very name of the metal copper is derived from the island's original name, Kypros, as it in ancient times was the world's leading producer of copper. The Greek goddess of love, Aphrodite, was said to have been born here out of the surf. Actually Cyprus itself is a child of the sea, a part of former deep ocean crust lifted high above sealevel. Indep. AUG 16, 1960.

ASIA

Area: 44,493,000 km²
Population: 2,349,048,000
Density of population per km²: 53

The Asian mainland's northernmost point is Cape Chelyuskin at 77° 44′ N. latitude.
Lowest surface temperature in the thern hemisphere, C., was recorded a Oymyakon.
Northeastern Siberia has the most extreme continental climate in the world. The variation between the warmest month of Summer (average temperature of up to 17°C.) and the coldest month of Winter (below —50°C.) is greater than anywhere else. Winter here is colder than in any other populated spot.
The coniferous forests of Siberia, the Taiga, are the most extensive in the world. The wide-stretched lowlands rank second after those of the Amazon Basin.
There is no clear, natural boundary between Asia and Europe which together form the Eurasian mainland. The boundary is usually drawn along the crest of the Ural Mountains then follows the Ural River to the Caspian Sea then to the Black Sea via the Manych Depression and the Sea of Azov.
① UNION OF SOVIET SOCIALIST REPUBLIC
The Ob drainage system of 3 million km² is the largest in Asia
The deepest lake in the world is Lake Baykal, 1940 m.
Baba Burun at 26° 3′ E. longitude is the Asian mainland's westernmost cape.
The Caspian Sea (371,000 km²) is the largest lake in the world.
The deserts and steppes of Central Asia are the most extensive area of inland drainage in the world. They cover about a third of the continent.
TURKEY⑤
② MONGOLIA
⑥ LEBANON
⑦ SYRIA
⑬ ISRAEL
Asia's highest surface temperature, 50°C., has been recorded at Baghdad.
JORDAN ⑭
⑧ IRAQ
⑨ IRAN
The Fedchenko Glacier is Asia's largest, 1,350 km² in size.
Asia's and the world's deepest depression is the Dead Sea in the Jordan Valley, —402 m.
Tibet is the Roof of the World, 2 million km² above 4,000 m. high.
The earth's largest v ty of grass — bamb can reach up to 40 length and up tom 3 in thickness in Chin
⑮ KUWAIT
AFGHANISTAN ⑩
⑰ SAUDI ARABIA
⑱ BAHRAIN
C H I N A ⑪
Mount Everest (Qomolangma Feng) is the world's highest mountain, 8,848 m.
The Arabian Peninsula is the world's largest and extends over 2,5 million km² (larger than Greenland).
⑲ QATAR ⑳ UNITED ARAB EMIRATES
PAKISTAN ⑯
NEPAL ㉕
BHUTAN ㉖
The world's heavies fall, 26,461 mm., wa recorded at Cherrap in 1860-61.
㉑ YEMEN
SOUTH YEMEN ㉒
㉓ OMAN
Himalaya is the world's highest mountain range with nine of the world's ten highest peaks and altogether fourteen reaching above 8,000 m.
BANGLA-DESH ㉗
㉘ BURMA
INDIA ㉔
㉚ LAOS
THAILAND ㉙
VIET ㉛
KAMPUCHEA ㉟
In Summer the eastbound Southwest Monsoon Current replaces the westerly North Equatorial Current in the Indian Ocean, just as the South West Monsoon replaces the Northeast Trade Winds.
㉞ SRI LANKA
㉝ MALDIVES
MALAYSIA ㊲
Cape Buru at 1° 25′N. latitude is the southernmost point of the Asian mainland.
SINGAPOR ㊳

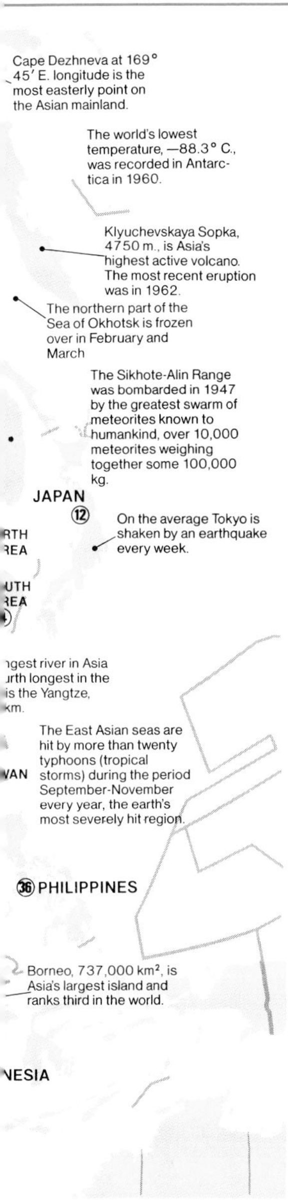
Cape Dezhneva at 169° 45′ E. longitude is the most easterly point on the Asian mainland.
The world's lowest temperature, —88.3° C., was recorded in Antarctica in 1960.
Klyuchevskaya Sopka, 4750 m., is Asia's highest active volcano. The most recent eruption was in 1962.
The northern part of the Sea of Okhotsk is frozen over in February and March
The Sikhote-Alin Range was bombarded in 1947 by the greatest swarm of meteorites known to humankind, over 10,000 meteorites weighing together some 100,000 kg.
JAPAN
⑫
On the average Tokyo is shaken by an earthquake every week.
RTH
REA
UTH
REA
ngest river in Asia
rth longest in the
is the Yangtze,
km.
The East Asian seas are hit by more than twenty typhoons (tropical storms) during the period September-November every year, the earth's most severely hit region.
WAN
㊱ PHILIPPINES
Borneo, 737,000 km², is Asia's largest island and ranks third in the world.
NESIA

⑩ AFGHANISTAN
⑱ BAHRAIN
㉗ BANGLADESH
㉖ BHUTAN
㊴ BRUNEI
㉘ BURMA
⑪ CHINA
㉔ INDIA
㊵ INDONESIA
⑨ IRAN
⑧ IRAQ
⑬ ISRAEL
⑫ JAPAN
⑭ JORDAN
㉟ KAMPUCHEA
⑮ KUWAIT
㉚ LAOS
⑥ LEBANON
㊲ MALAYSIA
㉝ MALDIVES
② MONGOLIA
㉕ NEPAL
③ NORTH KOREA
㉓ OMAN
⑯ PAKISTAN
㊱ PHILIPPINES
⑲ QATAR
⑰ SAUDI ARABIA
㊳ SINGAPORE
④ SOUTH KOREA
㉒ SOUTH YEMEN
㉞ SRI LANKA
⑦ SYRIA
㉙ THAILAND
㉜ TAIWAN
⑤ TURKEY
① UNION OF SOVIET SOCIALIST REPUBLICS
⑳ UNITED ARAB EMIRATES
㉛ VIETNAM
㉑ YEMEN

① UNION OF SOVIET SOCIALIST REPUBLICS

Soyuz Sovyetskikh Sotsialisticheskikh Respublik

Area: 22,402,200 km²
Population: 276,300,000
Population growth per annum: 0.9%
Life expectancy at birth: males 65 years, females 74 years
Literacy: 99%
Capital with population: Moskva (Moscow) 8,537,000
Other important cities with population: Leningrad 4,800,000, Baku 1,660,000, Kuybyshev 1,250,000
Language: Altaic (Turkish etc.), other Indo-European, Uralian Caucasian
Religion: Orthodox, Moslem
Currency: Rubel = 100 kopek

The U.S.S.R. is a country that is almost a continent not only in size, but also in diversity. It covers 1/6 of the Earth's land area, and is larger than South America. 75% is traditionally considered to be part of Asia, but 75% of its people live in the European part. In comprises 120 different peoples, dominated by the Russians.

② MONGOLIA

Bügd Nayramdakh Mongol Ard Uls
(Mongolian People's Republic)

Area: 1,565,000 km²
Population: 1,820,000
Population growth per annum: 2.9%
Life expectancy at birth: males 61 years, females 65 years
Literacy: 80%
Capital with population: Ulaanbaatar (Ulan Bator) 400,000
Other important cities with population: Darkhan 52,000
Language: Mongol, Russian, Chinese
Religions: Buddhist
Currency: Tugrik = 100 möngö

The home of Genghis Khan is now as then a land of unbroken horizons where trees are as rare as people on the windswept grasslands. The Mongols have now exchanged their horses for motor bikes and so only disappear faster out of view. One third of Mongolia is part of the mighty Gobi Desert. Independent JAN 5, 1946.

③ NORTH KOREA

Chosun Minchu-chui Inmin Konghwa-guk
(Democratic People's Republic of Korea)

Area: 122,098 km²
Population: 18,490,000
Population growth per annum: 3.2%
Life expectancy at birth: males 70 years, females 78 years
Literacy: 85%
Capital with population: P'yŏngyang 1,280,000
Other important cities with population: Hamhŭng 420,000, Ch'ŏngjin 265,000
Languages: Korean
Religion: Buddhist (activities discouraged)
Currency: Won = 100 chon

Korea is a victim of the 20th century. During the scramble for colonies it was annexed by Japan, and after the Japanese capitulation in 1945 it was divided into two zones of occupation by the U.S.A. and the U.S.S.R. along 38° N lat. The cold war began here and grew into a real war 1950-53. Korea remains divided. Independent NOV 9, 1948.

④ SOUTH KOREA

Han Kook
(Republic of Korea)

Area: 98,992 km²
Population: 39,950,000
Population growth per annum: 1.6%
Life expectancy at birth: 68 years
Literacy: 92%
Capital with population: Sŏul (Seoul) 8,367,000
Other important cities with population: Pusan 3,160,000, Taegu 1,607,000
Language: Korean
Religion: Buddhist, Confucianist, Christian
Currency: Won = 100 chon

In the shadow of China, the Korean people have managed to maintain a national identity — and true independence during most of their history — and also to achieve great cultural feats of their own. Here books were being printed as early as a thousand years ago. Independent AUG 15, 1948.

⑤ TURKEY

Türkiye Cumhuriyeti
(Republic of Turkey)

Area: 779,452 km²
Population: 48,000,000
Population growth per annum: 2.5%
Life expectancy at birth: males 58 years, females 63 years
Literacy: 70%
Capital with population: Ankara 1,877,000
Other important cities with population: Istanbul 2,773,000, Izmir 758,000
Language: Turkish
Religion: Moslem
Currency: Turkish lira = 100 kurş

The land that for centuries served as a link between Europe and Asia now also provides the two continents with a physical link, the huge bridge over the Bosporus. The world famous cathedral of Hagia Sofia, built by emperor Justinian 532-537, was turned into a mosque after the fall of Constantinople in 1453.

⑥ LEBANON

Al-Jumhouriya al-Lubnaniya
(Republic of Lebanon)

Area: 10,452 km²
Population: 3,500,000
Population growth per annum: 0.8%
Life expectancy at birth: males 63 years, females 67 years
Literacy: 75%
Capital with population: Bayrút (Beirut) 702,000
Other important cities with population: Tarábulus (Tripoli) 175,000
Language: Arabaic
Religion: Moslem (50%), Christian (50%)
Currency: Lebanese pound = 100 piastres

Since Phoenician times international trade has been the blood of life here at the crossroads of the Levant, populated by fiercely proud clans from all over the Middle East. The lone cedar tree of the flag is almost the last remnant of the mighty forests that once covered Mt. Lebanon. Independent JUN 1, 1944.

⑦ SYRIA

Al-Jamhouriya al Arabia as-Souriya
(Syrian Arab republic)

Area: 185,180 km²
Population: 9,840,000
Population growth per annum: 3.8%
Life expectancy at birth: males 63 years, females 66 years
Literacy: 65%
Capital with population: Dimashq (Damascus) 1,251,000
Other important cities with population:
Halab (Aleppo) 1,525,000 Hims (Homs) 630,000
Language: Arabic
Religion: Moslem (88%), Christian
Currency: Syrian pound = 100 piaster

Long before Rome was founded all caravan trails and trade routes "of the world" converged on the capital of Syria, Damascus. Herod, St. Paul and Ibn Battuta as well as Alexander the Great, Julius Caesar and Genghis Khan have all passed through Damascus. Independent JAN 1, 1944.

⑧ IRAQ

Al Jumhouriya al 'Iraqia
(Republic of Iraq)

Area: 434,924 km²
Population: 14,000,000
Population growth per annum: 3.4%
Life expectancy at birth: males 54 years, females 57 years
Literacy: 70%
Capital with population: Baghdad 3,200,000
Other important cities with population: Al Basrah 400,000, Al Mawsil (Mosul) 350,000
Language: Arabic, Kurdish
Religion: Moslem (95%)
Currency: Iraqi dinar = 20 dirham = 1000 fils

The ancient "Land Between the Rivers", Mesopotamia, is today known as Iraq. The name is said to be derived from a word meaning "origin", a very apt name. Here the wheel and the plow were invented. Here the oldest maps and written records have been found as well as the oldest Codes of Law. Independent 1932.

⑨ IRAN

Jomhori-e-Islami-e-Irân
(Islamic Republic of Iran)

Area: 1,648,100 km²
Population: 43,830,000
Population growth per annum: 3.0%
Life expectancy at birth: males 53 years, females 54 years
Literacy: 48%
Capital with population: Tehrān 4,500,000
Other important cities with population: Esfahān 700,000, Mashhad 700,000
Language: Farsi (persian), Turkic languages, Kurdish
Religion: Shiá Moslems (93%)
Currency: Rial = 100 dinars

Through milennia Iran previously called Persia — has influenced the history and culture of all people. Iran has nurtured Cyrus, Darius and Xerxes, Zoroaster, Firdawsi and Omar Khayyam — and ayatollah Khomeini. Iranians invented polo and developed chess.

⑩ AFGHANISTAN

De Afghanistan Democrateek
Jamhuriat
(Democratic Republic of Afganistan)

Area: 647,497 km²
Population: 17,500,000 (of which 23% are refugees outside the country)
Population growth per annum: 2.5%
Life expectancy at birth: males 40 years, females 41 years
Literacy: 10%
Capital with population: Kabul 900,000
Other important cities with population: Kandahar 180,000 Herat 140,000
Language: Pushtu, Dari (Persian)
Religion: Islam (90% Sunni Moslems)
Currency: Afghani = 100 puls

The crossroads of Asia — and once more, a theater of war. Throughout history, conquering armies have marched through the green valleys beneath Afghanistan's forbidding mountains, but no one has ever been able to subjugate its warlike tribes, so fiercely independent, that they were not even united into an emirate before 1747. Independent 1747.

⑪ CHINA

(Peoples Republic of China)

Area: 9,561,000 km²
Population: 1,008,175,000
Population growth per annum: 1.4%
Life expectancy at birth: males 62 years, females 69 years
Literacy: 75%
Capital with population: Beijing (Peking) 5,550,000
Other important cities with population: Shanghai 6,300,000, Tianjin 5,200,000, Shenuang 4,000,000
Language: Mandarin Chinese, Shanghai-, Canton-, Fukien-, Hakka- dialects, Tibetan, Vigus (Turkic)
Religion: Officially atheist, Confucanist, Buddhist, Taoist.
Currency: Yuan = 10 jiap = 100 fen

The length of the historical records of China are paralleled only by the Great Wall one of the greatest human-made structures 4,000 kms, 2,500 miles). China is the world's most populous nation, human-made, and will without doubt be one of the superpowers of the future. Independent OCT 1, 1949.

⑫ JAPAN

Nippon (or Nihon)

Area: 377,765 km²
Population: 119,500,000
Population growth per annum: 0.9%
Life expectancy at birth: males 73 years, females 78 years
Literacy: 99%
Capital with population: Tōkyō 8,150,000
Other important cities with population:
Yokohama 2,870,000 Nagoya 2,060,000, Kyōto 1,460,000
Language: Japanese
Religion: Buddhist, Shinto, Roman Catholic
Currency: Yen = 100 sen

Japan has learned to live with earthquakes. Minor tremors are registered more than twice a day, and on average the earth here trembles perceptibly once a week. Only a few cause damage to buildings, as houses here are either very light structures or built to resist even severe shocks.

⑬ ISRAEL
Medinat Israel — State of Israel

Area: 20,770 km²
Population: 4,150,000
Population growth per annum: 2.6%
Life expectancy at birth: males 71 years, females 73 years
Literacy: 88%
Capital with population: Yerushalayim (Jerusalem) 430,000
Other important cities with population:
Tel Aviv-Yafo 330,000, Hefa (Haifa) 226,000
Language: Hebrew, Arabic
Religion: Judaism (85%), Moslem (11%)
Currency: Shekel = 100 agorot

The unprecedented rebirth of a land and a language after almost two thousand years must be considered a miracle. This fulfillment of an cient prophecies is due to the tenacity and spirit of the Jewish people. A majority of human kind considers Jerusalem Holy. Independent MAY 14, 1948.

⑭ JORDAN
Al Mamlaka al Urduniya al Hashemiyah
(The Hashemite Kingdom of Jordan)

Area: 97,740 km²
(incl. 5,880 km² on the West Bank)
Population: 3,500,000
Population growth per annum: 3.7%
Life expectancy at birth: males 58 years, females 62 years
Literacy: 58%
Capital with population: 'Ammãn 1,230,000
Other important cities with population: Az Zarqã 270,000, Irbid 140,000
Language: Arabic
Religion: Moslem (80% Sunni Moslems)
Currency: Jordan dinar = 1000 fils

Once the rulers of the arid lands east of River Jordan controlled the trade routes across the desert, and accumulated wealth from the incense trade, as can be seen from the glory of the rose-red ruins of Petra. Independent MAR 22, 1946.

⑮ KUWAIT
Dowlat al Kuwait
(State of Kuwait)

Area: 17,818 km²
Population: 1,910,,000
Population growth per annum: 6.0%
Life expectancy at birth: males 67 years, females 72 years
Literacy: 71%
Capital with population: Al Kuwayt (Kuwait) 280,000
Other important cities with population: none
Language: Arabic
Religion: Moslem (70% Sunni Moslems)
Currency: Kuwait dinar = 1000 fils

The name Kuwait today associates with oil and wealth. Once sturdy dhows sailing to far away African and East Indian ports brought renown to Kuwait. The real Sindbad the Sailor may have lived here. Independent JUN 19, 1961.

⑯ PAKISTAN
(Islamic Republic of Pakistan)

Area: 887,747 km²
Population: 89,000,000
Population growth per annum: 2.8%
Life expectancy at birth: males 52 years, females 50 years
Literacy: 23%
Capital with population: Islamabad 201,000
Other important cities with population: Karachi 5,103,000, Lahore 2,920,000, Faisalabad 1,092,000
Language: Urdu, Punjabi
Religion: Moslem (sunni Moslems)
Currency: Pakistani rupie = 100 paisa

By peaceful agreement, but through tumultuous upheaval the Islamic nation of Pakistan was created out of parts of former British India. Until 1971 it also comprised Bangladesh 2,000 km. away, then known as East Pakistan. Independent AUG 14, 1947.

⑰ SAUDI ARABIA
Al-Mamlaka-al-Arabiya as-Sa'udiya
(Kingdom of Saudi Arabia)

Area: 2,149,690 km²
Population: 8,400,000
Population growth per annum: 4.2%
Life expectancy at birth: males 52 years, females 55 years
Literacy: 15%
Capital with population: Ar Riyád (Riyadh) 670,000
Other important cities with population: Jiddah 561,000, Makkah (Mecca) 370,000
Language: Arabic
Religion: Moslem
Currency: Rial = 100 halalas

Like the genie released from Aladdin's oil lamp, the wealth of oil released from the rocks of the desert have brought fabulous palaces and gardens to its owners. Modern cities, industries, universities and motorways have been created overnight. Independent SEP 20, 1932.

⑱ BAHRAIN
Mashyaka al Bahrayn
(State of Bahrain)

Area: 622 km²
Population: 380,000
Population growth per annum: 2.8%
Life expectancy at birth: males 64 years, females 68 years
Literacy: 40%
Capital with population: Al Manãmah 122,000
Other important cities with population: Al Muharraq 62,000
Language: Arabic
Religion: Islam (Sunni Moslems)
Currency: Bahrain dinar = 100 fils

The popular joke, that Bahrain gas stations should give free fuel to every buyer of water for coolant, is of course not true. It reflects the lack of water that troubles oil-rich Bahrain. It will be solved by a pipeline following the giant causeway to the mainland. Independent AUG 15, 1971.

⑲ QATAR

Dawlat Qatar
(State of Qatar)

Area: 11,437 km²
Population: 260 000
Population growth per annum: 6.5%
Life expectancy at birth: males 55 years, females 58 years
Literacy: 40%
Capital with population: Ad Dawhah 190,000
Other important cities with population: none
Language: Arabic
Religion: Moslem
Currency: Riyal = 100 dirham

A black underground sea of oil has become the source of wealth to Qatar, instead of the Gulf's warm blue waters and its pearl oysters. Independent SEP 1, 1971.

⑳ UNITED ARAB EMIRATES

Al Imarat al Arabiya al Muttahida

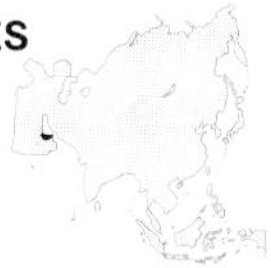

Area: 92,100 km²
Population: 1,175,000
Population growth per annum: 7.3%
Life expectancy at birth: males 60 years, females 74 years
Literacy: 53%
Capital with population: Alu Zaly (Abu Dhabi) 240,000
Other important cities with population: Dubayy 278,000
Language: Arabic
Religion: Islam
Currency: UAE dirham = 100 fils

Pearl-fishing and clandestine trade (by some called smuggling) sustained the people on the Trucial Coast after the more lucrative slave trade was abolished by the Perpetual Maritime Truce Treaty, signed by Great Britain and the seven sheiks 1853. Oil has now brought prosperity. Independent DEC 2, 1971.

㉑ YEMEN

Al Jamhuriyah al Arabiya al Yamaniya
(Yemen Arab Republic)

Area: 195,000 km²
Population: 7,160,000
Population growth per annum: 2.3%
Life expectancy at birth: males 37 years, females 39 years
Literacy: 12%
Capital with population: San'a 278,000
Other important cities with population: Hodeida 130,000, Taż 120,000
Language: Arabic
Religion: Moslem
Currency: Yemen paper riyal = 100 rial

The Roman name for Yemen "Arabia Felix" or Lucky Arabia was more apt then than today. The old great dams filled up with silt and were destroyed by floods, and incense no longer fetches its weight in silver or gold.

㉒ SOUTH YEMEN

Jumhurijah al-Yemen al Dimuqratiya al Sha'abijah
(Peoples Democratic)

Area: 287,682 km²
Population: 2,030,000
Population growth per annum: 1.8%
Life expectancy at birth: males 40 years, females 42 years
Literacy: 25%
Capital with population: Baladıyat 'Adan (Aden) 295,000
Other important cities with population: Al Mukallá 100,000
Language: Arabic
Religion: Moslem
Currency: South Yemen dinar = 1000 fils

This is the land of ancient skyscrapers. The high-rise buildings that form the skyline of Hadramaut are mainly built of mud bricks. They are 6-7 stories high, but seem higher as every story has 2 rows of windows.

㉓ OMAN

(Sultanate of Oman)

Area: 212,457 km²
Population: 1,500 000
Population growth per annum: 3.0%
Life expectancy at birth: males 46 years, females 48 years
Literacy: 20%
Capital with population: Masqat 50,000
Language: Arabic
Religion: Moslem
Currency: Rial = 1000 biazas

Like his rival, the King of Portugal, the Sultan of Oman once ruled over a far-flung transocean empire. The red flag of the Sultan flew over forts and trading posts on Asian and African coasts, such as Mombasa and Zanzibar.

㉔ INDIA

Bharat
(Republic of India)

Area: 3,184,290 km²
Population: 683,810,000
Population growth per annum: 2.0%
Life expectancy at birth: males 50 years, females 49 years
Literacy: 36%
Capital with population: Delhi 5,720,000
Other important cities with population:
Bombay 8,230,000, Calcutta 9,170,000, Madras 4,280,000
Language: Hindi, English
Religion: Hindu (83%), Moslem (11%)
Currency: Rupee = 100 Paise

Like the images of Hindu gods that have several eyes, heads and arms (symbolizing their paradoxical nature), the subcontinent and nation of India has many diverse and contradictory features. India is the serene Taj Mahal in cool white marble, and Calcutta with its teeming millions, holy cows and also nuclear power. Independent JAN 26, 1950.

㉕ NEPAL

Sri Nepala Sarkar
(Kingdom of Nepal)

Area: 145,391 km²
Population: 16,100,000
Population growth per annum: 2.3%
Life expectancy at birth: males 43 years, females 44 years
Literacy: 20%
Capital with population: Katmandu 195,000
Other important cities with population: Patan 50,000
Language: Nepali, Indian Languages
Religion: Hindu (90%), Buddist (7%)
Currency: Nepalese Rupee = 2 mohur = 100 paisa

By avoiding involvement in the affairs of the outside world the mountain kingdom of Nepal has like Switzerland managed to remain independent. Nepal shares with China the world's highest peak, Chomolungma, the "Goddess Mother of the World" to the Tibetans, since 1865 also known as Mt. Everest.

㉖ BHUTAN

Druk Gaykhab
(Kingdom of Bhutan)

Area: 46,600 km²
Population: 1,250,000
Population growth per annum: 2.2%
Life expectancy at birth: males 44 years, females 43 years
Literacy: 5%
Capital with population: Thimphu 21,000
Other important cities with population: none
Language: Dzongka, Nepali
Religion: Buddhist (70%), Hindu
Currency: Ngultrum = 100 chetrums (Indian rupee also used)

Bhutan's official name Druk Yul translates Land of the Dragon. This is an apt name, as the mountainous former hermit kingdom has many fairy-tale qualities . The only real dragons to be found are those on the national flags.

㉗ BANGLADESH

(Peoples Republic of Bangladesh)

Area: 143,998 km²
Population: 96,000,000
Population growth per annum: 2.8%
Life expectancy at birth: males 46 years, females 46 years
Literacy: 25%
Capital with population: Dakha 3,500,000
Other important cities with population:
Ghittagong 1,390,000, Khulna 650,000
Language: Bengali, English
Religion: Islam (80%), Hindu
Currency: Taka = 100 poisha

The fertile delta lands of Ganges and Brahmaputra, created by floods, have long been more than overpopulated. Troubled by alternating droughts and torrential rains, poor Bangladesh is frequently plagued by hurricanes and devastating tidal floods. Independent DEC 20, 1971.

㉘ BURMA

Pyidaungsu Socialist Thammada
Myanma Naingngandaw
(Socialist Republic of the Union of Burma)

Area: 676,552 km²
Population: 35,310,000
Population growth per annum: 2.4%
Life expectancy at birth: males 51 years, females 54 years
Literacy: 78%
Capital with population: Rangoon 2,460,000
Other important cities with population: Mandalay 420,00C
Bassein 360,000
Language: Burmese
Religions: Buddhist (85%)
Currency: Kyat = 100 pyas

Burma is still the land of the gilded pagodas, where time flows a slowly as the mighty Irrawaddy. In this land of yesterday veterar cars are in everyday use, and elephants haul teak logs to the rivers. Burma's socialists have governed the country since 1948. Independent JAN 4, 1948.

㉙ THAILAND

Prathes Thai
(Kingdom of Thailand)

Area: 514,000 km²
Population: 50,000,000
Population growth per annum: 2.3%
Life expectancy at birth: males 58 years, females 63 years
Literacy: 84%
Capital with population: Krung Thep (Bangkok) 5,470,000
Other important cities with population: Chiang Mai 105,000
Language: Thai
Religion: Buddhist (93%), Moslem (4%)
Currency: Baht = 100 Satang

Thailand has throughout history managed to survive and maintain independence by deft diplomacy and careful observation of prevailing wind directions. Internally the king retains power in much the same way.

㉚ LAOS

(The Lao People's Democratic Republic)

Area: 236,800 km²
Population: 3,500,000
Population growth per annum: 2.4%
Life expectancy at birth: males 42 years, females 45 years
Literacy: 28%
Capital with population: Vientiane 120,000
Other important cities with population:
Luang Prabang 45,000
Language: Lao
Religion: Buddhist
Currency: Kip = 100 at

Reverence for royalty has always transcended life in Laos. A royal prince led the communists to victory in 1975 and abolished monarchy. Several hundred huge carved burial urns, presumably containing royal remains from prehistoric times, still dot the Plain of Jars. Independent JUN 20, 1954.

㉛ VIETNAM

Công Hòa Xã Hôi Chu Nghĩa Viêt Nam
(Socialist Republic of Vietnam)

Area: 329,566 km²
Population: 60,000,000
Population growth per annum: 2.3%
Life expectancy at birth: males 51 years, females 54 years
Literacy: 73%
Capital with population: Hanoi 2,570,000
Other important cities with population:
Ho Chi Minh 3,500,000, Hai Phong 1,300,000
Language: Vietnamese, French, English
Religion: Buddhist
Currency: Dong = 10 hao = 10 xu

The proud and martial Vietnamese of the Red River basin have been called the Prussians of Indo-China. With military aid from the U.S.S.R and captured U.S. arms they have now become the strongest military power of South East Asia. Independent JUL 20, 1954.

㉜ TAIWAN

(Republic of China)

Area: 36,174 km²
Population: 18,800,000
Population growth per annum: 1.8%
Life expectancy at birth: males 70 years, females 75 years
Literacy: 89%
Capital with population: Taipei 2,400,000
Other important cities with population:
Kaohsiung 1,260,000
Language: Chinese
Religion: Confucianist, Buddist, Taoist
Currency: New Taiwan dollar = 100 cents

The Chinese governments in Peking and Taipei do agree in one important respect: There is only one China, and Taiwan is no more than a Chinese province. The main difference is that the authority of the rulers in Taipei does not extend to any part of ancient, mainland China proper.

㉝ MALDIVES

Divehi Jumhuriya
(Republic of Maldives)

Area: 298 km²
Population: 168,000
Population growth per annum: 2.9%
Life expectancy at birth: not available
Literacy: 36%
Capital with population: Malé 40,000
Other important cities with population: none
Languages: Divehi
Religion: Moslem (Sunni Moslems)
Currency: Rufiyaa = 100 laaris

In the days when the dhows carried carpets, ivory and slaves over the Indian Ocean, the thousand coral islands of the Maldives lay at the crossroads of the ocean. Now even the names of the atolls, Tiladummati, Fadiffolu, Miladummadulu sound of long lost fame and tales of far away lands. Independent NOV 11, 1968.

㉞ SRI LANKA

(Democratic Socialist
Republic of Sri Lanka)

Area: 65,610 km²
Population: 14,850,000
Population growth per annum: 1.7%
Life expectancy at birth: males 64 years, females 67 years
Literacy: 84%
Capital with population: Colombo 586,000
Other important cities with population:
Dehiwela-Mt. Lavinia 175,000, Moratuwa 136,000
Language: Sinhala, Tamil
Religion: Buddhist (70%), Hindu (17%), Christian, Moslem
Currency: Sri Lanka rupee = 100 cents

Ceylon is even today a land of legends. On the top of Adam's Peak there is a 1.5 m. (5 ft.) long foot print, claimed to be left in the rock by Adam (or by Buddha, or Sheva, or St. Thomas according to preference). Independent 1947.

㉟ KAMPUCHEA

(Cambodian People's Republic)

Area: 181,035 km²
Population: 6,680,000
Population growth per annum: 2.9%
Life expectancy at birth: males 44 years, females 47 years
Literacy: 48%
Capital with population: Phnom Penh 500,000
Other important cities with population:
Battambang 50,000
Language: Khmer
Religion: Buddhist
Currency: Riel = 100 sen

Clashing radical ideologies have once more made life only worse for everyone. Pleasant Kampuchea now lies in ruins like mighty remains from its glorious past. Famous Angkor, for over 500 years the capital of all Indochina, has so far been spared further destruction. Independent OCT 9, 1970.

㊱ PHILIPPINES

República de Filipinas
Republika ng Pilipinas
(Republic of the Philippines)

Area: 300,000 km²
Population: 53,350,000
Population growth per annum: 2.7%
Life expectancy at birth: males 59 years, females 62 years
Literacy: 88%
Capital with population: Manila 1,600,000
Other important cities with population:
Quezon City 1,200,000, Davao 620,000, Cebu 500,000
Language: Pilipino, English, Spanish
Religion: Roman Catholic (80%), Islam (7%)
Currency: Philippine pesó = 100 centavos

East and west meet in this island nation, east of the Asian mainland, yet west of the Pacific. The people of this fomer colony of Spain (1521-1899) and the United States (1899-1942) are of Malayo-Polynesian stock but speak Spanish, English and Pilipino. Most are Roman Catholics but some are Moslems. Independent JUL 4, 1946.

㊲ MALAYSIA

Area: 329,749 km²
Population: 15,070,000
Population growth per annum: 2.5%
Life expectancy at birth: males 62 years, females 65 years
Literacy: 75%
Capital with population: Kuala Lumpur 450,000
Other important cities with population:
George Town 300,000, Ipoh 250,000
Language: Bahasa Malaysia, Chinese
Religion: Moslem 50%, Buddhist (26%), Hindu (9%)
Currency: Ringgit = 100 sen

In this land reigning rajahs (and sultans) each in turn serve five years as 'Supreme Head of State'. This unusual system of royal rotation has brought unity and stability to the geographically divided nation. In Sarawak the world's largest cave (700×300 m.) has been found. Independent SEP 16, 1963.

㊳ SINGAPORE

(Republic of Singapore)

Area: 618 km²
Population: 2,530,000
Population growth per annum: 1.2%
Life expectancy at birth: males 69 years, females 73 years
Literacy: 84%
Capital with population: Singapore 2,350,000
Other important cities with population: none
Language: Chinese, Malay, Tamil, English
Religion: Buddhist, Taoist, Moslem, Hindu, Christian
Currency: Singapore-dollar = 100 cents

A modern City state, living off free entrepot trade and local manufacturing industries requiring skilled labour, Singapore survives without hinterland. Independent AUG 9, 1965.

AUSTRALIA

Area: 8,945,000 km²
Population: 23,446,000
Density of population per km²: 2,6

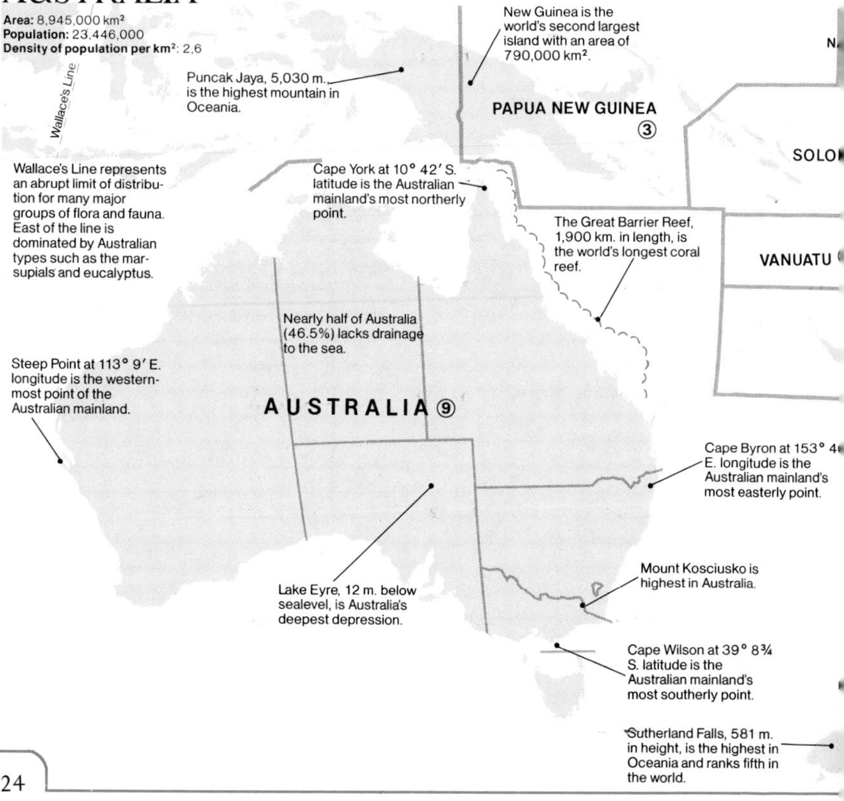
Wallace's Line
Puncak Jaya, 5,030 m. is the highest mountain in Oceania.
New Guinea is the world's second largest island with an area of 790,000 km².
PAPUA NEW GUINEA
③
SOLO
VANUATU
Wallace's Line represents an abrupt limit of distribution for many major groups of flora and fauna. East of the line is dominated by Australian types such as the marsupials and eucalyptus.
Cape York at 10° 42′ S. latitude is the Australian mainland's most northerly point.
The Great Barrier Reef, 1,900 km. in length, is the world's longest coral reef.
Nearly half of Australia (46.5%) lacks drainage to the sea.
Steep Point at 113° 9′ E. longitude is the westernmost point of the Australian mainland.
AUSTRALIA ⑨
Cape Byron at 153° 4 E. longitude is the Australian mainland's most easterly point.
Mount Kosciusko is highest in Australia.
Lake Eyre, 12 m. below sealevel, is Australia's deepest depression.
Cape Wilson at 39° 8¾ S. latitude is the Australian mainland's most southerly point.
Sutherland Falls, 581 m. in height, is the highest in Oceania and ranks fifth in the world.

㊴ BRUNEI

Area: 5,765 km²
Population: 213,000
Population growth per annum: not available
Life expectancy at birth: not available
Literacy: not available
Capital with population: Bandar Seri Begawan 51,000
Other important cities with population: none
Language: Malay, English
Religion: Moslem (64%), Buddhist, Christian
Currency: Brunei dollar = 100 cents

A land flowing with oil — where the citizens can use their own money to buy "milk and honey" — as they do not have to pay any income taxes! No wonder the Sultan of Brunei can continue to rule — with broad popular support. Independent DEC 31, 1983.

㊵ INDONESIA

Republik Indonesia
(Republic of Indonesia)

Area: 1,919,400 km²
Population: 158,000,000
Population growth per annum: 1.7%
Life expectancy at birth: males 46 years, females 49 years
Literacy: 64%
Capital with population: Jakarta 6,500,000
Other important cities with population:
Surabaya 2,000,000 Bandung 1,500,000,
Medan 1,400,000
Language: Bahasa Indonesia
Religion: Moslem (92%)
Currency: Rupiah = 100 sen

Panta rei (all flows) ought to be the motto of this nation of over 13,000 islands. No other state has so many active volcanoes. On Java alone there are 27. Here the island volcano of Krakatoa, 1,800 m. (6,000 ft.) high, disintegrated in 1883 in the most catastrophic eruption in history. Independent DEC 27, 1949.

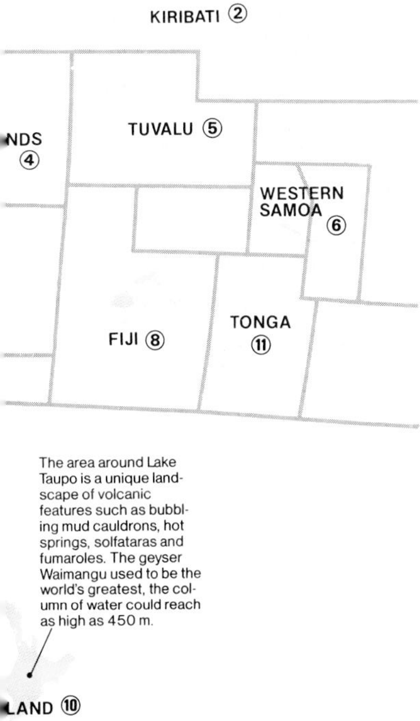

KIRIBATI ②
TUVALU ⑤
NDS ④
WESTERN SAMOA ⑥
TONGA ⑪
FIJI ⑧
The area around Lake Taupo is a unique landscape of volcanic features such as bubbling mud cauldrons, hot springs, solfataras and fumaroles. The geyser Waimangu used to be the world's greatest, the column of water could reach as high as 450 m.
LAND ⑩

⑨ AUSTRALIA
⑧ FIJI
② KIRIBATI
① NAURU
⑩ NEW ZEALAND
③ PAPUA NEW GUINEA
④ SOLOMON ISLANDS
⑪ TONGA
⑤ TUVALU
⑦ VANUATU
⑥ WESTERN SAMOA

① NAURU
(Republic of Nauru)

Area: 21,3 km²
Population: 8,400
Population growth per annum: 1.5%
Life expectancy at birth: not available
Literacy: 99%
Capital with population: Yaren
Other important cities with population: none
Language: Nauruan, English
Religion: Protestant (60%), Roman Catholic (30%)
Currency: Australian dollar = 100 cents

It is easy to drive around all of Nauru in a car in less time that it takes for an astronaut to circle the Earth, as the total circumference is only 34 km. (21 miles). Independent JUN 31, 1970.

② KIRIBATI
(Republic of Kiribati)

Area: 886 km²
Population: 60,000
Population growth per annum: not available
Life expectancy at birth: not available
Literacy: not available
Capital with population: Bairiki 20,000
Other important cities with population: none
Language: Kiribati, English
Religion: Protestant (50%), Roman Catholic (50%)
Currency: Australian dollar = 100 cents

No other nation is spread so thinly as Kiribati, with land size — smaller than New York City scattered over an area wider than the contiguous United States! Kiribati always has two days, as it is divided by the dateline. Independent JUL 12, 1979.

③ PAPUA NEW GUINEA

Area: 461,691 km²
Population: 3,260,000
Population growth per annum: 2.7%
Life expectancy at birth: males 51 years, females 50 years
Literacy: 32%
Capital with population: Port Moresby 124,000
Other important cities with population: Lae 62,000
Language: English, numerous, local languages
Religions: Animist, Protestant, Roman Catholic
Currency: Kina = 100 toe

The official "Pidgin English" developed here during the last hundred years is quite a new language, using mainly English words. E.g. "Ars bilong diwai" means "roots" (Diwai is a melanesian word for tree, belong equals of — and ars is just the very bottom of anything. Independent SEP 16, 1975.

④ SOLOMON ISLANDS

Area: 29,785 km²
Population: 258,000
Population growth per annum: 3.0%
Life expectancy at birth: not available
Literacy: not available
Capital with population: Honiara 24,000
Other important cities with population: none
Language: English, numerous local languages
Religion: Protestant (75%), Roman Catholic (19%)
Currency: Solomon Island dollar = 100 cents

The Solomon Islands suffered heavily during World War II during the battles of Guadalcanal and the Coral Sea. Yet some islands still profit from the spoils of war by exporting scrap iron. Independent JUL 7, 1978.

⑤ TUVALU

Area: 24,6 km²
Population: 7,300
Population growth per annum: 1.6%
Life expectancy at birth: males 57 years, females 59 years
Literacy: not available
Capital with population: Funafuti 2,100
Other important cities with population: none
Language: Samoan, English
Religion: Protestant
Currency: Australian dollar = 100 cents

Tuvalu comprises nine low coral atolls (formerly also called Lagoon or Ellice islands) in the very centre of the island world of the South Pacific. In spite of the fact that an atoll can measure 10-20 km. across its land area is almost negligible. Independent OCT 1, 1978.

⑥ WESTERN SAMOA
Samoa i Sisifo
(Independent State of Western Samoa)

Area: 2,831 km²
Population: 156,000
Population growth per annum: 1.3%
Life expectancy at birth: 63%
Literacy: 90%
Capital with population: Apia 33,200
Other important cities with population: none
Language: Samoan, English
Religion: Protestant (75%), Roman Catholic (22%)
Currency: Tala = 100 sene

Truly Polynesian Samoa is in many ways an incarnation of the South Sea Islands — complete with beaches and palms and friendly people, but it is at the same time a modern society with TV, colleges, and all the rest. Independent JAN 1, 1962.

⑦ VANUATU
(Republic of Vanuatu)

Area: 14,763 km²
Population: 117,000
Population growth per annum: 2.7%
Life expectancy at birth: not available
Literacy: not available
Capital with population: Vila 14,000
Other important cities with population: none
Language: Bislama, English, French
Religion: Protestant (68%), Roman Catholic (16%)
Currency: Vatu

Two colonial powers, France and Great Britain ruled the former Condominium of the New Hebrides in quaint harmony with strict and sometimes silly division of authority 1906-80. Independent JUL 30, 1980.

⑧ FIJI
(Dominion of Fiji)

Area: 18,376 km²
Population: 670,000
Population growth per annum: 1.8%
Life expectancy at birth: males 70%, females 73%
Literacy: 75%
Capital with population: Suva 71,000
Other important cities with population: Lautoka 26,000
Language: English, Fijian, Hindustani
Religion: Christian (49%), Hindu (40%)
Currency: Fijian dollar = 100 cents

Volcanic soil, tropical sunshine and gentle trade winds bringing regular rainfall favour sugar cane cultivation. Sugar has become the major product of Fiji. Independent OCT 10, 1970.

⑨ AUSTRALIA
(Commonwealth of Australia)

Area: 7,686,848 km²
Population: 15,450,000
Population growth per annum: 1.2%
Life expectancy at birth: males 70 years, females 76 years
Literacy: 99%
Capital with population: Canberra 256,000
Other important cities with population: Sydney 3,281,000, Melbourne 2,804,000, Brisbane 1,090,000
Language: English, aboriginal languages
Religion: Christian Protestant (61%), Catholic (27%)
Currency: Australian dollar = 100 cents

The only land that is quite different, Australia comprises an entire continent with a quite different fauna and flora — eucalyptus trees and kangaroos, egg-laying mammals and koalas, the living teddy bears. The 1,900 km. long Great Barrier Reef is the world's longest coral reef. Independent JAN 1, 1901.

⑩ NEW ZEALAND

Area: 268,704 km²
Population: 3,200,000
Population growth per annum: 1.1%
Life expectancy at birth: males 70 years, females 76 years
Literacy: 99%
Capital with population: Wellington 342,000
Other important cities with population: Auckland 864,000, Christchurch 322,000
Language: English, Maori
Religion: Protestant
Currency: New Zealand dollar = 100 cents

Far from being the opposite of England, green and civilized New Zealand is at the Antipodes seen from Britain — that is exactly at the other side of the Earth. New Zealand England is rich in beautiful scenery. Independent 1931.

⑪ TONGA
(Kingdom of Tonga)

Area: 748 km²
Population: 99,000
Population growth per annum: not available
Life expectancy at birth: not available
Literacy: not available
Capital with population: Niku'alofa 20,000
Other important cities with population: none
Language: English
Religion: Protestant (85%), Roman Catholic (15%)
Currency: Pa'anga = 100 seniti

The "Friendly Islands", Captain Cook's name for Tonga, are not easy to reach due to lack of good harbours. The island of Niuafo'ou has become known among philatelists as "Tin Can Island" because of the method used to collect and deliver mail. Independent JUN 4, 1970.

AFRICA

Area: 30,293,000 km²
Population: 431,209,,000
Density of population per km²: 14

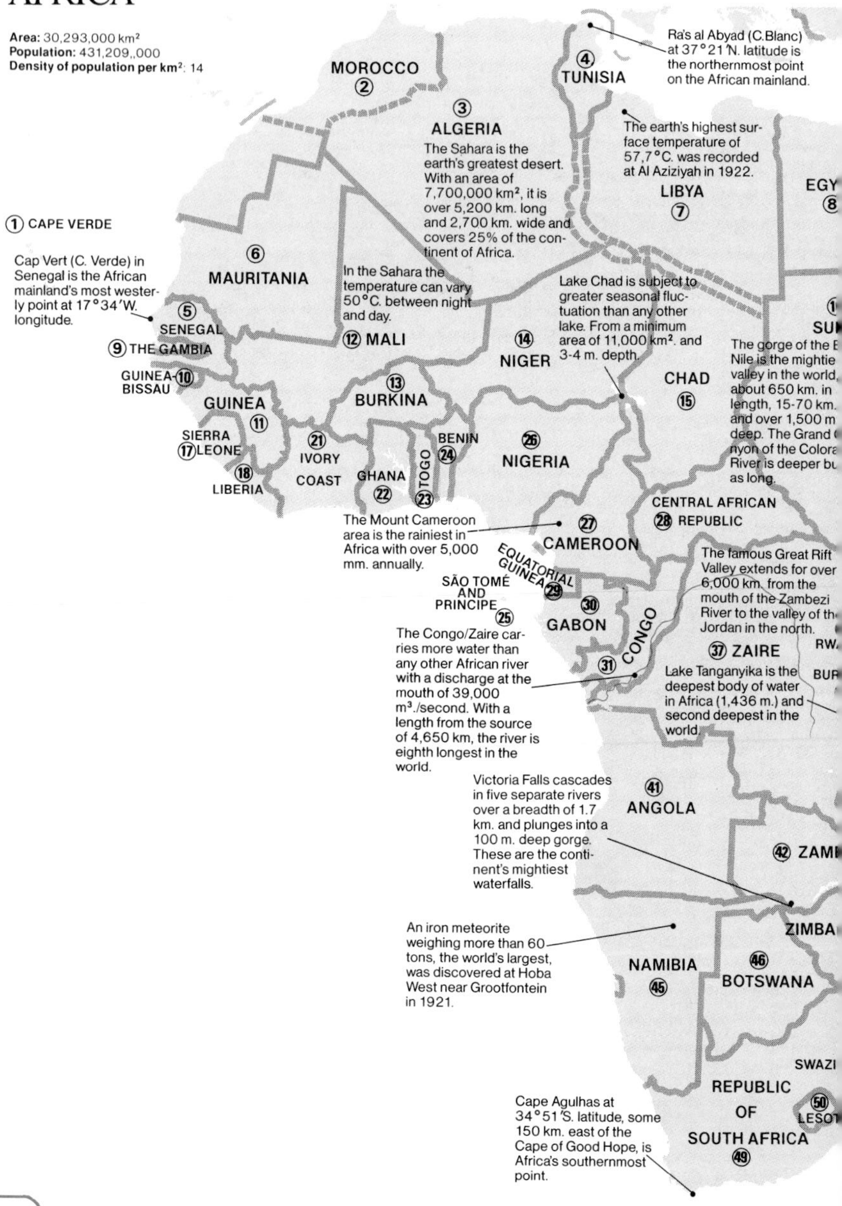

MOROCCO
②
TUNISIA
④
Ra's al Abyad (C.Blanc) at 37°21'N. latitude is the northernmost point on the African mainland.
③
ALGERIA
The Sahara is the earth's greatest desert. With an area of 7,700,000 km², it is over 5,200 km. long and 2,700 km. wide and covers 25% of the continent of Africa.
The earth's highest surface temperature of 57,7°C. was recorded at Al Aziziyah in 1922.
LIBYA
⑦
EGY
⑧
① CAPE VERDE
Cap Vert (C. Verde) in Senegal is the African mainland's most westerly point at 17°34'W. longitude.
⑥
MAURITANIA
In the Sahara the temperature can vary 50°C. between night and day.
Lake Chad is subject to greater seasonal fluctuation than any other lake. From a minimum area of 11,000 km². and 3-4 m. depth.
⑤
SENEGAL
⑨ THE GAMBIA
⑫ MALI
⑭
NIGER
CHAD
⑮
The gorge of the Blue Nile is the mightiest valley in the world, about 650 km. in length, 15-70 km. and over 1,500 m deep. The Grand Canyon of the Colorado River is deeper but not as long.
GUINEA-⑩
BISSAU
GUINEA
⑪
⑬
BURKINA
SIERRA
⑰LEONE
㉑
IVORY
COAST
BENIN
㉔
㉖
NIGERIA
TOGO
⑱
LIBERIA
GHANA
㉒
㉓
CENTRAL AFRICAN
㉘ REPUBLIC
The Mount Cameroon area is the rainiest in Africa with over 5,000 mm. annually.
㉗
CAMEROON
EQUATORIAL GUINEA ㉙
SÃO TOMÉ AND PRINCIPE
㉕
㉚
GABON
CONGO
㉛
The famous Great Rift Valley extends for over 6,000 km. from the mouth of the Zambezi River to the valley of the Jordan in the north.
㊲ ZAIRE
The Congo/Zaire carries more water than any other African river with a discharge at the mouth of 39,000 m³./second. With a length from the source of 4,650 km, the river is eighth longest in the world.
Lake Tanganyika is the deepest body of water in Africa (1,436 m.) and second deepest in the world.
Victoria Falls cascades in five separate rivers over a breadth of 1.7 km. and plunges into a 100 m. deep gorge. These are the continent's mightiest waterfalls.
㊶
ANGOLA
㊷ ZAM
An iron meteorite weighing more than 60 tons, the world's largest, was discovered at Hoba West near Grootfontein in 1921.
ZIMBA
NAMIBIA
㊺
㊻
BOTSWANA
SWAZI
REPUBLIC OF SOUTH AFRICA
㊾
㊿
LESO
Cape Agulhas at 34°51'S. latitude, some 150 km. east of the Cape of Good Hope, is Africa's southernmost point.

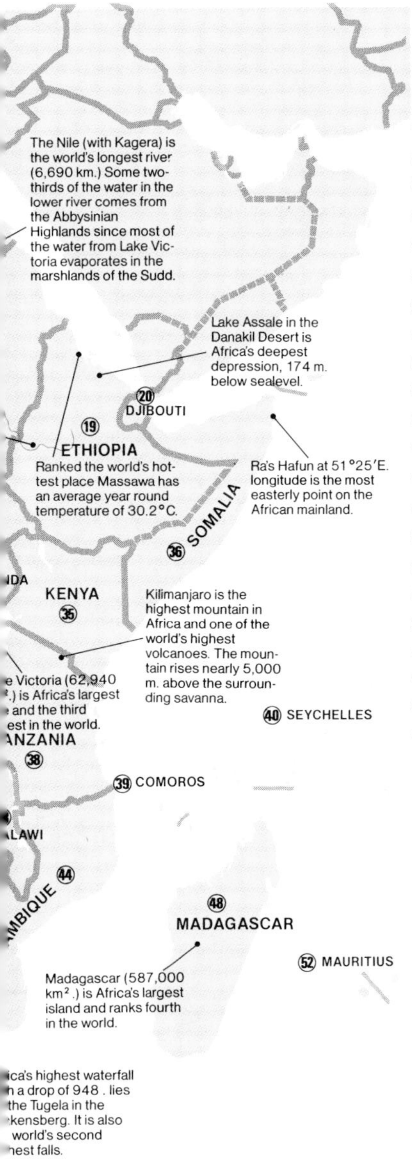
The Nile (with Kagera) is the world's longest river (6,690 km.) Some two-thirds of the water in the lower river comes from the Abbysinian Highlands since most of the water from Lake Victoria evaporates in the marshlands of the Sudd.
Lake Assale in the Danakil Desert is Africa's deepest depression, 174 m. below sealevel.
20 DJIBOUTI
19 ETHIOPIA
Ranked the world's hottest place Massawa has an average year round temperature of 30.2°C.
Ra's Hafun at 51°25′E. longitude is the most easterly point on the African mainland.
36 SOMALIA
IDA
KENYA 35
Kilimanjaro is the highest mountain in Africa and one of the world's highest volcanoes. The mountain rises nearly 5,000 m. above the surrounding savanna.
e Victoria (62,940
².) is Africa's largest
and the third
est in the world.
NZANIA 38
40 SEYCHELLES
39 COMOROS
LAWI
44
MBIQUE
48 MADAGASCAR
52 MAURITIUS
Madagascar (587,000 km².) is Africa's largest island and ranks fourth in the world.
ica's highest waterfall
h a drop of 948 . lies
the Tugela in the
kensberg. It is also
world's second
hest falls.

(3) ALGERIA
(41) ANGOLA
(24) BENIN
(46) BOTSWANA
(13) BURKINA
(34) BURUNDI
(27) CAMEROON
(1) CAPE VERDE
(28) CENTRAL AFRICAN REP.
(15) CHAD
(39) COMOROS
(31) CONGO
(20) DJIBOUTI
(8) EGYPT
(29) EQUATORIAL GUINEA
(19) ETHIOPIA
(30) GABON
(22) GHANA
(11) GUINEA
(10) GUINEA-BISSAU
(21) IVORY COAST
(35) KENYA
(50) LESOTHO
(18) LIBERIA
(7) LIBYA
(48) MADAGASCAR
(43) MALAWI
(12) MALI
(6) MAURITANIA
(52) MAURITIUS
(2) MOROCCO
(44) MOZAMBIQUE
(45) NAMIBIA
(14) NIGER
(26) NIGERIA
(49) REPUBLIC OF SOUTH AFRICA
(33) RWANDA
(25) SÃO TOMÉ AND PRINCIPE
(5) SENEGAL
(40) SEYCHELLES
(17) SIERRA LEONE
(36) SOMALIA
(16) SUDAN
(51) SWAZILAND
(38) TANZANIA
(9) THE GAMBIA
(23) TOGO
(4) TUNISIA
(32) UGANDA
(37) ZAIRE
(42) ZAMBIA
(47) ZIMBABWE

① CAPE VERDE

República de Cabo Verde
(Republic of Cape Verde)

Area: 4,033 km²
Population: 296,000
Population growth per annum: 1.7%
Life expectancy at birth: males 58 years, females 62 years
Literacy: 37%
Capital with population: Praia 38,000
Other important cities with population: Mindelo 40,000
Language: Portuguese, Crioulo
Religion: Roman Catholic
Currency: Escudo = 100 centavos

Heat and drought are two words that characterize the volcanic islands, named after a cape on the mainland, 580 km. to the east. Salt is produced by evaporation an industry with good natural prospects. Independent JUL 5, 1975.

② MOROCCO

Al-Mamlaka al-Maghrebia
(Kingdom of Morocco)

Area: 458,730 km²
Population: 21,160,000
Population growth per annum: 3.2%
Life expectancy at birth: males 54 years, females 57 years
Literacy: 24%
Capital with population: Rabat 440,000
Other important cities with population: Dar el Beida (Casablanca) 1,400,000, Marrakech 330,000
Language: Arabic, Berber
Religion: Moslem, (Sunni Moslems)
Currency: Dirham = 100 centimes

East and West meet in Morocco. For the "western" world it is a land of the Near East — and for the "eastern", Islamic world it is a land of the Maghreb, The West. The mosques and palaces of cities such as Marrakech and Fez are famous in the west as well as in the east. Independent MAR 28, 1956.

③ ALGERIA

al-Jumhuriya al -Jazairia
ad-Dimuqratiya ash-Shabiya
(Democratic and Popular Republ. of Algeria)

Area: 2,381,740 km²
Population: 21,460,000
Population growth per annum: 3.3%
Life expectancy at birth: males 54 years, females 56 years
Literacy: 46%
Capital with population: Al Jazair (Algiers) 2,500,000
Other important cities with population: Oran 630,000, Constantine 385,000
Language: Arabic
Religion: Islam (Sunni Moslems)
Currency: Algerian dinar = 100 centimes

Four-fifths of the land is desert. The prosperous and fertile coastal area is just a thin gilt edge along the northern rim of the majestic Sahara. Covering 7.7 million km².(5,200 by 2,700 km.), the Sahara is the world's greatest desert, so that the barren wastes of Algeria comprise only 25% of the Sahara! Independent JUL 3, 1962.

④ TUNISIA

Al-Djoumhouria Attunisia
(Republic of Tunisia)

Area: 164,150 km²
Population: 6,970,000
Population growth per annum: 2.5%
Life expectancy at birth: males 57 years, females 58 years
Literacy: 62%
Capital with population: Tunis 557,000
Other important cities with population: Sfax 232,000, Sousse 85,000
Language: Arabic
Religion: Moslem
Currency: Tunisian dinar = 100 millimes

A nation with many ties. Ties of history and culture link it forever to all its Mediterranean neighbours, and very strongly to France. Ties of language and blood bind it to the Arabic West, Maghreb. This is also the land of Carthage, that fought Rome for the hegemony of "the world". Independent MAR 20, 1956.

⑤ SENEGAL

République du Sénégal
(Republic of Senegal)

Area: 196,192 km²
Population: 6,270,000
Population growth per annum: 2.6%
Life expectancy at birth: males 41 years, females 44 years
Literacy: 10%
Capital with population: Dakar 800,000
Other important cities with population: Thies 130,000 Kaolack 116,000
Language: French, Tribal languages
Religion: Moslem (80%), Christian (10%), Animist
Currency: CFA-franc = 100 centimes

The Gateway to West Africa. The leading metropolis of the area, Dakar, is favoured by a magnificent natural harbour. The location near Cap Vert, the most westerly point of the mainland made Dakar the natural staging post for transatlantic flights to South America until the 1960's. Independent AUG 20, 1960.

⑥ MAURITANIA

République Islamique de Mauritanie
(Islamic Republic of Mauritania)

Area: 1,030,700 km²
Population: 1,830,000
Population growth per annum: 2.8%
Life expectancy at birth: males 41 years, females 44 years
Literacy: 17%
Capital with population: Nouakchott 135,000
Other important cities with population: none
Language: French, Arabic
Religion: Moslem
Currency: Ouguiya = 5 khoum

For the Arabs and the Islamic World, Mauretania is the Far West, the Land of the Sunset. Only a fraction of the vast country is habitable, and the lack of water is a severe handicap to any development. Independent NOV 28, 1960.

⑦ LIBYA

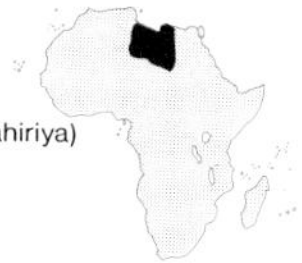

Al-Jamahiriya Al-Arabiya-Al Libya
Al-Shabiya Al-Ishitrakiya
(Socialist People's Libyan Arab jamahiriya)

Area: 1,759,540 km²
Population: 3,500,000
Population growth per annum: 4.1%
Life expectancy at birth: males 54 years, females 57 years
Literacy: 40 %
Capital with population: Tripoli (Tarabulus) 860,000
Other important cities with population: Beghasi 300,000
Language: Arabic
Religion: Moslem
Currency: Libyan dinar = 1000 dirham

Elusive Libya retains in our times some of the enigmatic features of Africa. The central volcanic area, the Black Hills that are clearly visible on space images of Africa, were recently mapped with the aid of satellite photos.

⑧ EGYPT

Jumhuriyat Misr al-Arabiya
(Arab Republic of Egypt)

Area: 1,001,449 km²
Population: 46,000,000
Population growth per annum: 2.6%
Life expectancy at birth: males 54 years, females 56 years
Literacy: 40%
Capital with population: Al Qahirah (Cairo)9,000,000
Other important cities with population: Al Iskandariyah (Alexandria) 3,000,000, Al Jızah (Giza) 2,000,000
Language: Arabic
Religion: Islam (Sunni Moslems 90%)
Currency: Egyptian pound = 100 piastres

The whole of inhabitable Egypt is nothing but an oasis — totally dependent on the water of the Nile. In general the width of the cultivated and settled land is only 3-15 km. Of the seven wonders of the ancient world, Egypt had two, and even if the Pharos has been destroyed, the Pyramids still stand. Independent FEB 28. 1922.

⑨ THE GAMBIA

(Republic of The Gambia)

Area: 11,295 km²
Population: 700,000
Population growth per annum: 2.8%
Life expectancy at birth: males 39 years, females 43 years
Literacy: 12 %
Capital with population: Banjul 45,000
Other important cities with population: none
Language: English, Mandinka, Wolof
Religion: Moslem (85%), Christian, Animist
Currency: Dalasi = 100 bututs

The land that is a river. This former British colonial enclave inside Senegal is now joined with Senegal in the Confederation of Senegambia. Here Alex Haley found his roots, as described in his bestseller. Independent FEB 18, 1965.

⑩ GUINEA-BISSAU

(Republic of Guinea-Bissau)

Area: 36,125 km²
Population: 830,000
Population growth per annum: 1.7%
Life expectancy at birth: males 39 years, females 43 years
Literacy: 9%
Capital with population: Bissau 110,000
Other important cities with population: none
Language: Portuguese, Criolo
Religion: Tribal (50%), Moslem (38%), Christian (5%)
Currency: Guinea-Bissau peso = 100 centavos

A new name heralds a new era. For more than 500 years this land was known as Portuguese Guinea. No other land has been a colony for so many years. Guinea Bissau has an exceptional un-African archipelago coast. Independent SEP 24, 1973.

⑪ GUINEA

République populaire
et révolutionnaire de Guinée
(Republic of Guinea)

Area: 245,857 km²
Population: 5,410,000
Population growth per annum: 2.5%
Life expectancy at birth: males 42 years, females 45 years
Literacy: 48 %
Capital with population: Conakry
Other important cities with population: Kankan 100,000
Language: French, tribal languages
Religion: Moslems (75%), Tribal
Currency: Syli = 100 cauris

The name Guinea rings with a chink of gold — since 1663, when coins were struck in England out of pure 22 carat gold from Guinea. In Britain prices can still be quoted in guineas. Guinea still has natural resources that could bring prosperity to this very poor country. Independent OCT 2, 1958.

⑫ MALI

République du Mali
(Republic of Mali)

Area: 1,240,142 km²
Population: 7,720,000
Population growth per annum: 2.7%
Life expectancy at birth: males 44 years, females 44 years
Literacy: 10%
Capital with population: Bamako 405,000
Other important cities with population: Ségou 65,000
Language: French, Bambara
Religion: Moslem (65%), Animist (30%), Christian (5%)
Currency: Mali franc = 100 centimes

Half Sahara and half Sahel, half desert and half savanna land, Mali has been hard hit by years of drought. Once the kings of Mali controlled the trade routes of the Sahara and the minarets of fabled Timbuktu attracted both traders and adventurers to cross the sand seas. Independent SEP 22, 1960.

⑬ BURKINA

République de Burkina Faso
(People's Democratic Republic
of Burkina)

Area: 274,122 km²
Population: 6,700,000
Population growth per annum: 2.6%
Life expectancy at birth: males 42 years, females 45 years
Literacy: 7%
Capital with population: Ouagadougou 286,000
Other important cities with population:
Bobu Dioulasso 165,000
Language: French, Sudanic tribal languages
Religion: Animist (50%), Moslem (20%)
Currency: CFA-franc = 100 centimes

A land at the mercy of the winds. The dreaded dry Harmattan blowing from Sahara is a harbinger of death — the blessed Guinea Monsoon from the south an angel of life with its seasonal rain. The savanna lands here depend on a precarious balance between precipitation and evaporation. Independent AUG 5, 1960.

⑭ NIGER

République du Niger
(Republic of Niger)

Area: 1,267,000 km²
Population: 6,270,000
Population growth per annum: 2.9%
Life expectancy at birth: males 41 years, females 44 years
Literacy: 5%
Capital with population: Niamey 225,000
Other important cities with population: Zinder 60,000,
Language: French, Hausa, Djerma
Religion: Moslem (85%), Animist
Currency: CFA-franc = 100 centimes

A name that is more of an incantation than a description. This is a land-locked, dry and infertile part of Sahara, and the mighty Niger crosses only a narrow corner. The Tuaregs still cross the desert with salt caravans. Independent AUG 3, 1960.

⑮ CHAD

République du Tchad
(Republic of Chad)

Area: 1,284,000 km²
Population: 5,120,000
Population growth per annum: 2.0%
Life expectancy at birth: males 39 years, females 41 years
Literacy: 15%
Capital with population: N'djamena 303,000
Other important cities with population: Moundou 66,000
Language: French, Arabic, Sudanese languages
Religion: Animist, Moslem (45%), Christian (5%)
Currency: CFA-franc = 100 centimes

Land-locked Chad can be called a coastal land, as it is part of the Sahel, "the coast" of the sand sea of Sahara. It is drained to the shallow central basin of Lake Chad, the ever changing lake that varies from 10,000-50,000 km². and from 1 to 4 m. in average depth. Independent AUG 11, 1960.

⑯ SUDAN

Jamhuryat es-Sudan Al Democratia
(The Democratic Republic of Sudan)

Area: 2,505,813 km²
Population: 21,440,000
Population growth per annum: 2.8%
Life expectancy at birth: males 46 years, females 48 years
Literacy: 20 %
Capital with population: Al Khartum (Khartoum) 476,000, (Metropolitanarea 1,350,000)
Other important cities with population: Bur Sudan 207,000
Language: Arabic, various tribal languages
Religion: Moslem (70%) Christian, Animist
Currency: Sudanese pound = 100 piaster

In Sudan there are two countries in one. There are the Islamic, Arabic-speaking northern desert lands, and there are the Christian, Nilotic southern savanna lands. In spite of the name, most of the world's gum arabic comes from the acacia forests of Sudan. Independent JAN 1, 1956.

⑰ SIERRA LEONE

(Republic of Sierra Leone)

Area: 73,326 km²
Population: 3,350,000
Population growth per annum: 2.6%
Life expectancy at birth: males 44 years, females 48 years
Literacy: 15 %
Capital with population: Freetown 300,000
Other important cities with population: Makeni 1,000,000, Kenema 775,000
Language: English, Tribal languages
Religion: Animist, Moslem (30%)
Currency: Leone = 100 cents

A new homeland for freed slaves. Under British protection repatriated slaves from Great Britain founded Freetown at one of the few good natural harbours of West Africa back in 1787. Later it was used as a settlement for Africans rescued from slaveships. Sierra Leone became independent in APR 27, 1961.

⑱ LIBERIA

(Republic of Liberia)

Area: 111,369 km²
Population: 1,900,000
Population growth per annum: 3.5%
Life expectancy at birth: males 52 years, females 54 years
Literacy: 24%
Capital with population: Monrovia 425,000
Other important cities with population: none
Language: English
Religion: Moslem (21%), Christian (35%), Traditional (43%)
Currency: Liberian dollar = 100 cents

As the name implies, Liberia is a free nation, and has been since it was established in 1822 for freed slaves from the USA. In 1847 it became the continent's first independent republic and remained so during the days of the "Scramble for Africa" when this was divided into colonies.

19 ETHIOPIA
Hebretesbawit Ityopia
(Socialist Ethiopia)

Area: 1,221,900 km²
Population: 42,020,000
Population growth per annum: 1.8%
Life expectancy at birth: males 38 years, females 41 years
Literacy: 8%
Capital with population: Addis Ababa 1,400,000
Other important cities with population: Asmara 45,000, Gondar 80,000
Language: Amharic, other Semitic and Hamitic languages, Arabic, English
Religion: Orthodox Christian (40%), Moslem (40%)
Currency: Ethiopian birr = 100 cents

The nation that is an archipelago on dry land. For centuries Ethiopia was a Christian island in a Moslem sea. It is still an archipelago of densely populated islands of high plateaus, separated by deep river gorges and hot lowlands — and a linguistic archipelago of over 70 ethnic groups.

20 DJIBOUTI
Jumhouriyya Djibouti
(Republic of Djibouti)

Area: 23,000 km²
Population: 340,000
Population growth per annum: 2.2%
Life expectancy at birth: 50 years
Literacy: 20%
Capital with population: Djibouti 150,000
Other important cities with population: Tadjourah
Language: French, Arabic
Religion: Islam
Currency: Djibouti franc = 100 centimes

The nation is a railway terminal — and vice versa. The entrepôt port would not and could not exist as an independent unity without the railway to Addis-Ababa. This railway was built in 1915 and has since served as the major link between central Ethiopia and the world. Independent JUN 27, 1977.

21 IVORY COAST
République de la Côte d'Ivoire
(Republic of Ivory Coast)

Area: 322,464 km²
Population: 8,500,000
Population growth per annum: 3.5%
Life expectancy at birth: males 44 years, females 48 years
Literacy: 24%
Capital with population: Abidjan 1,850,000
Other important cities with population: Bouaké 640,000, Man-Danané 450,000
Language: French, tribal languages
Religion: Moslem (15%), Christian (12%), Indigenous (63%)
Currency: CFA-franc = 100 centimes

The Cocoa Coast would be more apt but less poetic name for this land. Cocoa and coffee long ago replaced ivory and slaves as the staples of the Ivory Coast. No nation produces more cocoa. Other agricultural products are pineapples, bananas and palm oil. Independent AUG 7, 1960.

22 GHANA
(Republic of Ghana)

Area: 238,305 km²
Population: 12,210,000
Population growth per annum: 3.1%
Life expectancy at birth: males 47 years, females 50 years
Literacy: 30%
Capital with population: Accra 750,000
Other important cities with population: Sekondi-Takoradi 300,000,
Language: English, 50 tribal languages
Religion: Christian (42%), Traditional beliefs, Moslem (12%)
Currency: Cedi = 100 pesewas

The former Gold Coast is at the same time a historic truth and a fitting description. One man and his dreams brought first independence and then financial ruin to his once — prosperous country. Many foreign flags have flown over Gold Coast — Portuguese, Swedish, Danish, Dutch and British. Independent MAR 6, 1957.

23 TOGO
République Togolaise
(Republic of Togo)

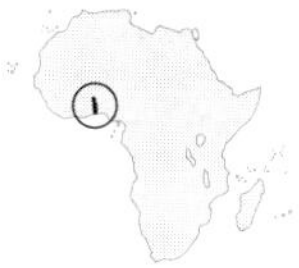

Area: 56,785 km²
Population: 2,890,000
Population growth per annum: 2.7%
Life expectancy at birth: males 44 years, females 48 years
Literacy: 10%
Capital with population: Lomé 283,000
Other important cities with population: none
Language: French, Tribal languages
Religion: Animist, Christian (25%), Moslem (10%)
Currency: CFA-franc = 100 centimes

An artificial nation. During the scramble for Africa, the Germans, like all other colonial powers just grabbed as much land as they could regardless of tribal, linguistic and other natural boundaries. Part of their colonial patchwork finally emerged as free Togo. Independent APR 27, 1960.

24 BENIN
République Populaire du Benin
(Peoples Republic of Benin)

Area: 112,622 km²
Population: 3,830 000
Population growth per annum: 3.0%
Life expectancy at birth: males 44 years, females 48 years
Literacy: 20%
Capital with population: Porto Novo 105,000
Other important cities with population: Cotonou 490,000
Language: French, local dialects
Religion: Roman Catholic, Islam, Animist
Currency: CFA-franc = 100 centimes

Coastal Benin is a country apart island — studded lagoons that are neither sea nor land. Here the fishing villages were built on stilts to escape occasional floods and to give some protection against slavers. Independent AUG 1, 1960.

㉕ SÃO TOMÉ AND PRINCIPE

São Tomé e Principe
(Democratic Republic of Sao Tome and Principe)

Area: 964 km²
Population: 102,000
Population growth per annum: 3.4%
Life expectancy at birth: not available
Literacy: 50 %
Capital with population: São Tomé 20,000
Other important cities with population: none
Language: Portuguese
Religion: Roman Catholic
Currency: Dobra = 100 centimos

These tropical islands in the cool Benguela current are favoured by fertile volcanic soil. At the turn of the century they were the world's leading producers of cocoa — but now others produce more. Coconuts and coffee are also grown. Independent JUL 12, 1975.

㉖ NIGERIA

(Federal Republic of Nigeria)

Area: 923,768 km²
Population: 82,390,000
Population growth per annum: 3.2%
Life expectancy at birth: males 46 years, females 49 years
Literacy: 25%
Capital with population: Lagos 1,061,000
Other important cities with population: Ibadan 850,000, Ogbomosho 435,000, Kano 400,000
Language: English, Hausa, Yoruba, Ibo
Religion: Moslem (55%), Christian (25%)
Currency: Naira = 100 kobo

Nigeria is Africa's most populous country in more than one sense. No other can match its over 80 millions and its over 250 linguistic groups (and tribes). It is hard to believe that this prosperous nation once was justly called "The White Man's Grave" (due to the coastal malaria swamps). Independent OCT 1, 1960.

㉗ CAMEROON

République du Cameroun
(United Republic of Cameroon)

Area: 475,442 km²
Population: 9,060,000
Population growth per annum: 2.3%
Life expectancy at birth: males 44 years, females 48 years
Literacy: 34%
Capital with population: Yaoundé 314,000
Other important cities with population: Douala 460,000
Language: English, French, Bantu, Sudanic
Religion: Moslem (25%), Roman Catholic (20%), Protestant (15%), Animist
Currency: CFA-franc = 100 centimes

An ethnic kaleidoscope, the country was a German colony, then two separate League of Nations mandates (French and British) before becoming a unitary republic. There are some two hundred different African ethnic groups. The famous Mt. Cameroon, that rises 4,070 m. up from the sea, serves at times as a natural lighthouse. The volcano erupted as recently as 1959. Indep.JAN 1, 1960.

㉘ CENTRAL AFRICAN REPUBLIC

République Centralafricaine

Area: 622,984 km²
Population: 2,520 000
Population growth per annum: 2.7%
Life expectancy at birth: 44 years
Literacy: 20%
Capital with population: Bangui 390,000
Other important cities with population: Berbérati 95,000
Language: French, local dialects
Religion: Animist (57%), Roman Catholic (20%), Protestant (15%)
Currency: CFA-franc = 100 centimes

At this crossroads of Africa the savannas meet the rain forests and the Bantu peoples mingle with the nilo-saharan groups and others. Even the rivers are running in opposite directions: the Ubangi towards Congo, the Shari to Lake Chad. Indep. AUG 13, 1960.

㉙ EQUATORIAL GUINEA

República de Guinea Ecuatorial
(Republic of Equatorial)

Area: 28,051 km²
Population: 398,000
Population growth per annum: 2.3%
Life expectancy at birth: males 44 years, females 48 years
Literacy: 20%
Capital with population: Malabo 27,000
Other important cities with population: none
Language: Spanish, Fang, English
Religion: Roman Catholic (60%)
Currency: Ekuele = 100 céntimos

As an antithesis, a part of the mainland of Africa belongs to the main island of Equatorial Guinea. On Bioko the lingua franca has been pidgin English and on Pagalu Portuguese patois in spite of the fact that Spanish was the official language! Indep. OCT 12, 1968.

㉚ GABON

République Gabonaise
(Gabonese Republic)

Area: 267,667 km²
Population: 1,370,000
Population growth per annum: 1.0%
Life expectancy at birth: males 42 years, females 45 years
Literacy: 65%
Capital with population: Libreville 350,000
Other important cities with population: Port Gentil 78,000
Language: French, Bantu dialects
Religion: Roman Catholic (42%), Animist, Protestant
Currency: CFA-franc = 100 centimes

Like some brand names Gabon has become almost a household word, because of the widespread use of mahogany plywood for furniture and doors. In addition to timber, Gabon produces oil, manganese and uranium. Independent AUG 17, 1960.

31 CONGO

République Populaire du Congo
(Peoples Republic of the Congo)

Area: 342,000 km²
Population: 1,740 000
Population growth per annum: 2.6%
Life expectancy at birth: males 44 years, females 48 years
Literacy: 80%
Capital with population: Brazzaville 422,000
Other important cities with population:
Pointe Noire 185,000
Language: French, bantu dialects
Religion: Animist (47%), Roman Catholic (40%), Protestant (12%)
Currency: CFA-franc = 100 centimes

Without the Congo River there wouldn't be any Congo. The sole reason for establishing the French colony north of the great river was to explore and exploit as much as possible of the basin (in competition with the Belgians). The name of the capital still honours the founding explorer de Brazza. Independent AUG 15, 1960.

32 UGANDA

(Republic of Uganda)

Area: 236,860 km²
Population: 14,000,000
Population growth per annum: 3.0%
Life expectancy at birth: males 51 years, females 54 years
Literacy: 25%
Capital with population: Kampala 340,000
Other important cities with population: none
Language: English, Swahili, Tribal languages
Religion: Roman Catholic (35%), Protestant (25%), Moslem (10%), Animist
Currency: Uganda shilling = 100 cents

Once and future Pearl of Africa? Here people has demonstrated once more that they are their own worst enemy in their lust for power. The setting of the gem remains: fertile lands wity an abundance of water, and magnificent scenery: The fabled Mountains of the Moon, the Ruwenzori, and the source lakes of the Nile. Independent SEP 9, 1962.

33 RWANDA

Republika y'u Rwanda
(Republic of Rwanda)

Area: 26,338 km²
Population: 5,650,000
Population growth per annum: 3.0%
Life expectancy at birth: males 44 years, females 48 years
Literacy: 37%
Capital with population: Kigali 157,000
Other important cities with population: none
Language: French, Kinyarwandu, Swahili
Religion: Animist, Roman Catholic (40%)
Currency: Rwanda franc = 100 centimes

This tiny nation contains some spectacular features: some of the true sources of the Nile, some of the last mountain gorillas and some active volcanoes in the Virunga Mountains. Independent JUL 7, 1962.

34 BURUNDI

(Republic of Burundi)

Area: 27,834 km²
Population: 4,560 000
Population growth per annum: 2.2%
Life expectancy at birth: males 39 years, females 43 years
Literacy: 25%
Capital with population: Bujumbura 160,000
Other important cities with population: none
Language: French, Kirundi
Religion: Roman Catholic 78%
Currency: Burundi franc = 100 centimes

A free colony. The hamitic Tutsi established colonial rule over the Hutu — the Bantu majority of the people as early as the 17th century. The Europeans came over two hundred years later and left after seventy years. The Tutsi still rule Burundi. Independent JUL 1, 1962.

35 KENYA

Jamhuri ya Kenya
(Republic of Kenya)

Area: 582,646 km²
Population: 19,500,000
Population growth per annum: 4.0%
Life expectancy at birth: males 51 years, females 56 years
Literacy: 40 %
Capital with population: Nairobi 1,200,000
Other important cities with population: Mombasa 340,000, Kisumu 155,000
Language: Swahili, English
Religion: Protestant (37%), Roman Catholic (22%), Moslem (5%), Others
Currency: Kenya Shilling = 100 cents

If there is a Safari Land in the world, it must be Kenya. The word safari (from the Arabic word for travel) rings with adventure. Here the adventurer's dreams may still be realized. In parks such as famous Amboseli close-ups of lions can be taken against the background of snow-capped Kilimanjaro. Independent DEC 12, 1963.

36 SOMALIA

Jamhuryadda Dimugradiga Somaliya
(Somali Democratic Republic)

Area: 637,657 km²
Population: 3,860,000
Population growth per annum: 7.9%
Life expectancy at birth: males 41 years, females 45 years
Literacy: 5%
Capital with population: Muqdisho 600,000
Other important cities with population: Hargeysa 150,000
Language: Somali
Religion: Moslem
Currency: Somali shilling = 100 centesimi

The land of frankincense and myrrh — today as in the days of ancient Egypt. Incense resins and carvings of aromatic resinous wood are still an important product of this droughtridden land of semideserts and dry savannas. Some of its proud camel herders now farm irrigated lands. Independent JUL 1, 1960.

(37) ZAIRE

République du Zaïre
(Republic of Zaire)

Area: 2,344,885 km²
Population: 31,940,000
Population growth per annum: 2.8%
Life expectancy at birth: males 44 years, females 48 years
Literacy: males 40%, females 15%
Capital with population: Kinshasa 2,450,000
Other important cities with population: Kananga 705,000, Lubumbashi 455,000
Language: French, Bantu-an Sudan dialects
Religion: Roman Catholic 48%, Animist, Protestant (12%)
Currency: Zaire = 100 makuta

The heart of Africa. Within Zaire (former Belgian Congo) can be found sophisticated Kinshasa and rain forests with pygmy tribes, uranium and diamond mines as well as leaking river steamers, steaming rain forests but also prosperous farmland — and some 200 different ethnic groups. Independent JUN 30, 1960.

(38) TANZANIA

(United Republic of Tanzania)

Area: 945,050 km²
Population: 19,730,000
Population growth per annum: 2.9%
Life expectancy at birth: 52 years
Literacy: 66%
Capital with population: Dar es Salaam 757,000
Other important cities with population: Zanzibar (Town) 111,000, Mwanza 111,000
Language: Swahili, English, local dialects
Religion: Animist, Christian (30%), Moslem (30%)
Currency: Tanzanian shilling = 100 cents

Arid Tanzania is full of natural wonders: The snow-capped, perfect volcanic cone on Mt Kilimanjaro, highest in Africa; Lake Victoria, third largest in the World; Lake Tanganyika, second deepest; the Serengeti Plains with the last prim of eval herds wild animals; the serene Ngorongoro Crater.

(39) COMOROS

Republique fédérale islamique des Comores
(Federal Islamic Republic of the Comoros)

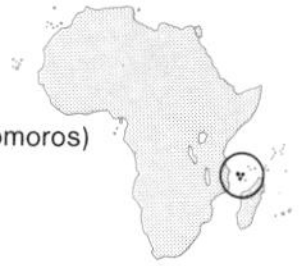

Area: 1,862 km²
Population: 370,000
Population growth per annum: 2.2%
Life expectancy at birth: males 47 years, females 45 years
Literacy: 15%
Capital with population: Moroni 25,000
Other important cities with population: none
Language: French, Arabic
Religion: Islam
Currency: CFA-franc = 100 centimes

Essence is the very essence of the economy of the Comoro Islands that produce exotic ilang-ilang, citronella and jasmine essences as well as vanilla extract and cloves. Independent JUL 6, 1975.

(40) SEYCHELLES

(Republic of Seychelles)

Area: 443 km²
Population: 65,000
Population growth per annum: 3.1%
Life expectancy at birth: 66 years
Literacy: 60%
Capital with population: Victoria 14,000
Other important cities with population: none
Language: English, French, Creole
Religion: Roman Catholic (91%), Protestant (8%)
Currency: Seychelles rupee = 100 cents

The islands of the love fruit — the world's largest, the sea (or double) coconut. This gigantic fruit, that may weigh 20-25 kg. (50 pounds), contains 3-4 smooth bilobed nuts with unavoidable associations to the human body. They grow only on the Seychelles, and their origin was long a mystery. Independent JUN 29, 1976.

(41) ANGOLA

República Popular de Angola
(People's Republic of Angola)

Area: 1,246,700 km²
Population: 7,770,000
Population growth per annum: 2.5%
Life expectancy at birth: males 40 years, females 43 years
Literacy: 20 %
Capital with population: Luanda 475,000
Other important cities with population: Huambo 62,000
Language: Portuguese, various Bantu languages
Religion: Roman Catholic, Animist
Currency: Kwanza = 100 lwei

Accessibility shaped the destiny of Angola. In contrast to other parts of Africa there are good harbours here and neither forbidding deserts nor feverish swamps bar the routes to the interior. Thus Angola became one of the first European colonies on the African mainland. Independent NOV 11, 1975.

(42) ZAMBIA

(Republic of Zambia)

Area: 752,620 km²
Population: 6,240,000
Population growth per annum: 3.2%
Life expectancy at birth: males 47 years, females 50 years
Literacy: 54%
Capital with population: Lusaka 538,000
Other important cities with population: Kitwe 315,000, Ndola 285,000
Language: English, Bantu dialects
Religion: Christian (60%), Animist
Currency: Kwacha = 100 ngwee

A colony for less than 40 years! Here colonial rule was not established until 1924 (as the result of Cecil Rhode's dream of extending British rule from the Cape to Cairo) but by 1964 the winds of change brought freedom to Zambia. The Victoria Falls are Zambia's most famous sight. Independent OCT 24, 1964.

MALAWI
(Republic of Malawi)

Area: 118,484 km²
Population: 6,100 000
Population growth per annum: 3.2%
Life expectancy at birth: males 44 years, females 48 years
Literacy: 25%
Capital with population: Lilongwe 103,000
Other important cities with population: Blantyre 220,000
Language: English, Chichewa
Religion: Animist, Christian (30%), Moslem (15%)
Currency: Kwacha = 100 tambala

A self-sufficient land of farmers, striving to build a better future. This is expressed also in their names for the units of currency. One kwacha (dawn) is divided into 100 tambalas (cockerels).

MOZAMBIQUE
República Popular de Moçambique
(People's Republic of Mozambique)

Area: 799,380 km²
Population: 13,140,000
Population growth per annum: 2.6%
Life expectancy at birth: males 44 years, females 48 years
Literacy: 14%
Capital with population: Maputo 755,000
Other important cities with population: Nampula 156,000
Beira 230,000
Language: Portuguese, Bantu languages
Religion: Roman Catholic (18%), Moslem (10%), Animist
Currency: Metical = 100 centavos

Geographical facts force "all-black" Mozambique to live in an uneasy partnership with "all-white" South Africa. Mozambique has water-power (Cabora Bassa, 1.4 GW.) and people-power but few minerals. South Africa needs contract workers and electricity in its mines. Independent JUN 15, 1975.

45 NAMIBIA (SOUTH-WEST AFRICA)
Namibia (Suidwes-Afrika)
(U.N. trusteeship, ruled by South Africa)

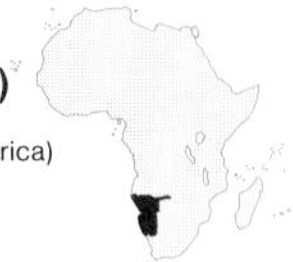

Area: 823,168 km²
Population: 1,040,000
Population growth per annum: not available
Life expectancy at birth: not available
Literacy: not available
Capital with population: Windhoek 89,000
Other important cities with population: none
Language: Afrikaans, English, German
Religion: Protestant (40%)
Currency: South African rand = 100 cents

Poor but potentially rich, a nation but yet kept in colonial bondage, Namibia awaits full freedom. This former German colony was given as a mandate under the auspices of the League of Nations in 1919. South Africa refuses to set Namibia free.

46 BOTSWANA
(Republic of Botswana)

Area: 600,372 km²
Population: 940,000
Population growth per annum: 2.8%
Life expectancy at birth: males 47 years, females 50 years
Literacy: 30%
Capital with population: Gaborone79,000
Other important cities with population:
Francistown 36,000
Language: English, Setswana
Religion: Indigenous beliefs (majority), Christian (15%)
Currency: Pula = 100 thebe

Land-locked Botswana lies in the center of the mountainbowl of southern Africa. Here lies the Kalahari desert and here the Cubango River loses itself in a maze of salt swamps and shallow lakes without outlet, such as famed Lake Ngami. Independent SEP 30, 1966.

47 ZIMBABWE

Area: 390,308 km²
Population: 7,530,000
Population growth per annum: 3.4%
Life expectancy at birth: males 52 years, females 55 years
Literacy: 45 %
Capital with population: Harare 656,000
Other important cities with population: Bulawayo 414,000, Chitungwiza 175,000
Language: English, Bantu dialects
Religion: Christian, Animist
Currency: Zimbabwe dollar = 100 cents

A nation with well-deserved pride. Zimbabwe is named after the impressive ruin-city that also is the firm foundation of the national spirit. These massive stone walls and towe‿ were built more than a thousand years ago by Bantu kings — ancestors to the people of today's Zimbabwe. Independent APR 18, 1980.

48 MADAGASCAR
Repoblika Demokratika n'i
Madagascar
(Democratic Republic of Madagascar)

Area: 587,041 km²
Population: 9,740,000
Population growth per annum: 2.6%
Life expectancy at birth: males 44 years, females 48 years
Literacy: 53%
Capital with population: Antananarivo 500,000
Other important cities with population: Toamasina 60,000
Language: Merina, French
Religion: Animist, Christian (40%), Moslem (10%)
Currency: Malagasy franc = 100 centimes

The fourth largest island of all — and in most aspects an Asian island. Geologically it is a segment of the same block as India, and the population is of Indo-Melanesian stock. The endemic wildlife comprises rare species, such as the bug-eyed aye-aye and the hedgehog-like tenrec.

㊾ REPUBLIC OF SOUTH AFRICA

Area: 1,225,824 km²
Population: 31,850,000
Population growth per annum: 2.8%
Life expectancy at birth: males 59 years, females 62 years
Literacy: Whites 98%, Asians 85%, Coloureds 75%
Capital with population: Cape Town 1,108,000
Pretoria 528,000
Other important cities with population:
Johannesburg 1,540,000 Durban 506,000
Language: Afrikaans, English
Religion: Protestant, Roman Catholic
Currency: Rand = 100 cents

Humans are their own enemies in rich South Africa. The original natives, the bushmen, fled into the Kalahari desert at the arrival of the Bantu tribes and the original Dutch Boers. The peoples of South Africa are now torn apart by worsening racial conflicts, aggravated by the in famous Apartheid ideology. Independent MAY 31, 1910, 1931.

㊿ LESOTHO
(Kingdom of Lesotho)

Area: 30,355 km²
Population: 1,470,000
Population growth per annum: 2.4%
Life expectancy at birth: males 49 years, females 51 years
Literacy: 55%
Capital with population: Maseru 45,000
Other important cities with population: none
Language: Sesotho, English
Religion: Roman Catholic (40%), Protestant (40%)
Currency: Lote = 100 lisente

An encircled nation, but not a subjugated land. This free black enclave in "white" South Africa is a reminder to its neighbours that all people are created equal. Independent OCT 4, 1966.

NORTH AMERICA

Area: 24,454,000 km²
Population: 346,418,000
Density of population per km²: 14

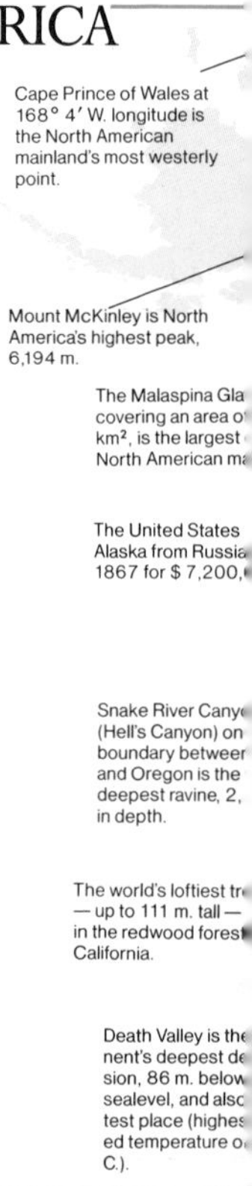

Cape Prince of Wales at 168° 4′ W. longitude is the North American mainland's most westerly point.
Mount McKinley is North America's highest peak, 6,194 m.
The Malaspina Gla covering an area o km², is the largest North American ma
The United States Alaska from Russia 1867 for $ 7,200,
Snake River Cany (Hell's Canyon) on boundary betwee and Oregon is the deepest ravine, 2, in depth.
The world's loftiest tr — up to 111 m. tall — in the redwood fores California.
Death Valley is th nent's deepest de sion, 86 m. below sealevel, and als test place (highes ed temperature o C.).

⑩ BELIZE
① CANADA
⑭ COSTA RICA
⑤ CUBA
⑧ DOMINICAN REPUBLIC
⑪ EL SALVADOR
⑨ GUATEMALA
⑦ HAITI
⑫ HONDURAS
⑥ JAMAICA
③ MEXICO
⑬ NICARAGUA
⑮ PANAMA
④ THE BAHAMAS
② UNITED STATES

51 SWAZILAND
(Kingdom of Swaziland)

Area: 17,365 km²
Population: 630,000
Population growth per annum: 2.8%
Life expectancy at birth: males 44 years, females 48 years
Literacy: 65%
Capital with population: Mbabane 23,000
Other important cities with population: none
Language: Swazi, English
Religion: Protestant (60%), Roman Catholic, Animist
Currency: Lilangeni = 100 cents

The proud Swazi people claim a history of five hundred years, but in their country their 'rights' are not older than those of their white neighbours on the other side of the Drakensberg Mountains. British protection kept Swaziland out of the Boer's hands. Independent SEP 6, 1968.

52 MAURITIUS

Area: 2,045 km²
Population: 990,000
Population growth per annum: 1.6%
Life expectancy at birth: males 61 years, females 67 years
Literacy: 61%
Capital with population: Port-Louis 150,000
Other important cities with population: Beau-Bassin (Rose Hill) 90,000
Language: English, French, Creole
Religion: Hindu (53%), Roman Catholic (25%), Moslem (16%)
Currency: Mauritius rupee = 100 cents

In relation to size no land on Earth has as many different languages — spoken by so many diverse ethnic groups: English (official), Hindi, Creole, Urdu, Tamil, French, Chinese, Arabic and a few African languages. Indep. MAR 12, 1968.

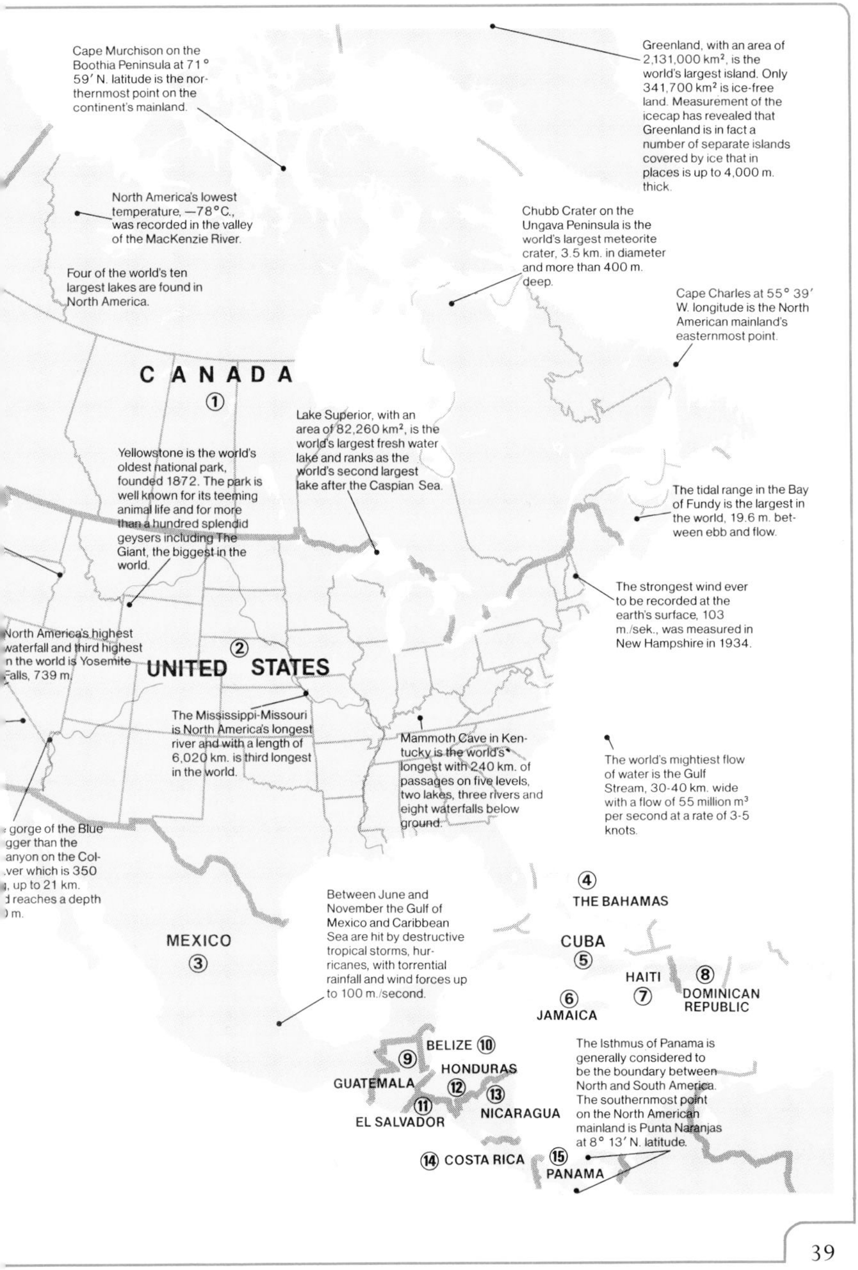
Cape Murchison on the Boothia Peninsula at 71° 59′ N. latitude is the northernmost point on the continent's mainland.
Greenland, with an area of 2,131,000 km², is the world's largest island. Only 341,700 km² is ice-free land. Measurement of the icecap has revealed that Greenland is in fact a number of separate islands covered by ice that in places is up to 4,000 m. thick.
North America's lowest temperature, −78°C., was recorded in the valley of the MacKenzie River.
Chubb Crater on the Ungava Peninsula is the world's largest meteorite crater, 3.5 km. in diameter and more than 400 m. deep.
Four of the world's ten largest lakes are found in North America.
Cape Charles at 55° 39′ W. longitude is the North American mainland's easternmost point.
CANADA
①
Lake Superior, with an area of 82,260 km², is the world's largest fresh water lake and ranks as the world's second largest lake after the Caspian Sea.
Yellowstone is the world's oldest national park, founded 1872. The park is well known for its teeming animal life and for more than a hundred splendid geysers including The Giant, the biggest in the world.
The tidal range in the Bay of Fundy is the largest in the world, 19.6 m. between ebb and flow.
The strongest wind ever to be recorded at the earth's surface, 103 m./sek., was measured in New Hampshire in 1934.
North America's highest waterfall and third highest n the world is Yosemite Falls, 739 m.
②
UNITED STATES
The Mississippi-Missouri is North America's longest river and with a length of 6,020 km. is third longest in the world.
Mammoth Cave in Kentucky is the world's longest with 240 km. of passages on five levels, two lakes, three rivers and eight waterfalls below ground.
The world's mightiest flow of water is the Gulf Stream, 30-40 km. wide with a flow of 55 million m³ per second at a rate of 3-5 knots.
gorge of the Blue
gger than the
anyon on the Col-
ver which is 350
, up to 21 km.
reaches a depth
m.
Between June and November the Gulf of Mexico and Caribbean Sea are hit by destructive tropical storms, hurricanes, with torrential rainfall and wind forces up to 100 m./second.
④ THE BAHAMAS
MEXICO ③
CUBA ⑤
HAITI ⑦
⑧ DOMINICAN REPUBLIC
⑥ JAMAICA
BELIZE ⑩
⑨ GUATEMALA
HONDURAS ⑫
⑬ NICARAGUA
⑪ EL SALVADOR
⑭ COSTA RICA
⑮ PANAMA
The Isthmus of Panama is generally considered to be the boundary between North and South America. The southernmost point on the North American mainland is Punta Naranjas at 8° 13′ N. latitude.

① CANADA

Area: 9,976,139 km²
Population: 25,130,000
Population growth per annum: 1.5%
Life expectancy at birth: males 70 years, females 77 years
Literacy: 99%
Capital with population: Ottawa 295,000
Other important cities with population:
Montréal 1,000,000, Toronto 600,000, Calgary 595,000
Language: English, French
Religion: Roman Catholic (46%), Protestant (36%)
Currency: Canadian dollar = 100 cents

A nation that spans a continent, Canada is the world's second largest country. Halifax on the Atlantic is closer to Great Britain than to Vancouver on the Pacific. When the sun rises over Newfoundland it is still midnight in Yukon. The 19.6 m (55 ft) tides in the Bay of Fundy are the world's greatest. Independent JUL 1, 1867.

② UNITED STATES OF AMERICA

Area: 9,363,123 km²
Population: 234,250,000
Population growth per annum: 0.9%
Life expectancy at birth: males 69 years, females 77 years
Literacy: 99%
Capital with population: Washington 638,000
Other important cities with population:
New York 7,100,000, Chicago 3,000,000, Los Angeles 3,000,000
Language: English
Religion: Protestant (33%), Roman Catholic (23%), Judaism (3%)
Currency: US dollar = 100 cents

U.S.A. is a powerful nation. The economic strength and military might of the nation can hardly be overestimated. It is the world's leading producer of most important commodities: oil, gas, coal, steel, paper. It is also found at the top of most lists of world records and extremes — and especially those of engineering feats. Independent JUL 4, 1776.

③ MEXICO
Estados Unidos Mexicanos
(United Mexican States)

Area: 1,972,547 km²
Population: 76,790,000
Population growth per annum: 3.0%
Life expectancy at birth: males 62 years, females 67 years
Literacy: 74 %
Capital with population: Mexico City 13,000,000
Other important cities with population:
Guadalajara 2,300,000, Monterrey 2,000,000
Language: Spanish
Religion: Roman Catholic
Currency: Mexican peso = 100 centavos

The centre of power in Central America lies as before in Mexico. In the early 19th century, the Spanish viceroy ruled half of Northern America from here, and today the nation is ranked high among the powers of the Third World. The famous pyramids of Teotihuacán manifest the greatness of Mexico. Independent SEP 16, 1810.

④ THE BAHAMAS
(Commonwealth of the Bahamas)

Area: 13,935 km²
Population: 230,000
Population growth per annum: 3.7%
Life expectancy at birth: males 64 years, females 69 years
Literacy: 89 %
Capital with population: Nassau 139,000
Other important cities with population: Freeport 16,000
Language: English
Religion: mainly Protestant
Currency: Bahamian dollar = 100 cents

A thousand coral reefs and not one but 700 coral islands in the sun. For the industrial eastern USA the beaches of the Bahamas are conveniently close — as Mediterranean shores are to northwestern Europe. Blue underwater caves attract scuba divers. Independent JUL 10, 1973.

⑤ CUBA
República de Cuba
(Republic of Cuba)

Area: 121,046 km²
Population: 10,000 000
Population growth per annum: 0.8%
Life expectancy at birth: males 71 years, females 74 years
Literacy: 96%
Capital with population: La Habana (Havana) 1,950,000
Other important cities with population:
Santiago de Cuba 565,000, Camagüey 480,000
Language: Spanish
Religion: Roman Catholic
Currency: Cuban peso = 100 centavos

The Sugar Island. Sugar and Cuba are now almost synonymous words, but it is a fact that the sugar cane was imported to Cuba from the Old World by the Spaniards. The Cubans themselves are also descendants of immigrants from the Old World: the Spaniards and their negro slaves. Independent DEC 10, 1898.

⑥ JAMAICA

Area: 10,991 km²
Population: 2,310,000
Population growth per annum: 1.4%
Life expectancy at birth: males 68 years, females 73 years
Literacy: 82%
Capital with population: Kingston 650,000
Other important cities with population:
St. Catherine 220,000, Clarendon 195,000
Language: English
Religion: Protestant (75%), Roman Catholic
Currency: Jamaica dollar = 100 cents

Pirate Island has become Island in the Sun and Land of the Rasta — as Fifteen men on a dead man's chest has been replaced by the inspired music of the Rastafarians. The bottle of rum is still available. Only scuba divers can today visit infamous Port Royal on the bottom of Kingston Bay. Independent AUG 6, 1962.

⑦ HAITI

République d'Haiti
(Republic of Haiti)

Area: 27,750 km²
Population: 5,200,000
Population growth per annum: 2.4%
Life expectancy at birth: males 49 years, females 52 years
Literacy: 23%
Capital with population: Port-au-Prince 460,000
Other important cities with population: Cap Haïtien 55,000
Language: French, Creole
Religion: Roman Catholic (66%), Protestant (11%)
Currency: Guorde = 100 centimes

Historically the land of voodo, of mystery and magic. Officially all are Roman catholics, but the undercurrent of ancient African religions is still strong here. Slaves who won their freedom against Spanish, British and French armies created here the world's first Negro republic. Independent JAN 1, 1804.

⑧ DOMINICAN REPUBLIC

Repb̆lica Dominicana

Area: 48,442 km²
Population: 5,980,000
Population growth per annum: 2.6%
Life expectancy at birth: males 58 years, females 62 years
Literacy: 62%
Capital with population: Santo Domingo 1,300,000
Other important cities with population: Santiago (de los Caballeros) 280,000, La Romana 90,000
Language: Spanish
Religion: Roman Catholic
Currency: RD peso = 100 centavos

This is in all but name Columbu's country. Here lie his mortal remains in a lead casket in the cathedral of Santo Domingo. The city that he founded is the oldest European city in the New World, and the island itself carries the name he gave it, Hispaniola — "the Spanish (Island)". Independent FEB 27, 1844.

⑨ GUATEMALA

República de Guatemala
(Republic of Guatemala)

Area: 108,889 km²
Population: 6,580,000
Population growth per annum: 3.0%
Life expectancy at birth: males 57 years, females 59 years
Literacy: 47%
Capital with population: Guatemala 1,300,000
Other important cities with population: Quezaltenango 66,000
Language: Spanish, Indian dialects
Religion: Roman Catholic
Currency: Quetzal = 100 centavos

A land of awe inspiring ruins and memories of its brilliant past during the reign of the Mayas — of once glorious cities like Tikal and Uaxactún. It is also a land of melodious place names like Chichicastenango (a famous market town) and Sololá. Independent 1821, 1839.

⑩ BELIZE

Area: 22,965 km²
Population: 158 000
Population growth per annum: not available
Life expectancy at birth: 60 years
Literacy: 80%
Capital with population: Belmopan 2,900
Other important cities with population: Belize City 40,000
Language: English, Spanish
Religion: Roman Catholic (60%), Protestant
Currency: Belize dollar = 100 cents

Belize is an anomaly — the only British enclave in Latin America. The forests yield valuable timber — mahogany and rosewood — and chicle latex, the original "gum" used for making chewing gum before the development of synthetic gum. Independent SEP 21, 1981.

⑪ EL SALVADOR

República de El Salvador
(Republic of El Salvador)

Area: 21,393 km²
Population: 5,300,000
Population growth per annum: 2.9%
Life expectancy at birth: males 60 years, females 65 years
Literacy: 40%
Capital with population: San Salvador 884,000
Other important cities with population: Santa Ana 210,000, San Miguel 160,000
Language: Spanish
Religion: Roman Catholic
Currency: Colón = 100 centavos

This is truly the land of volcanoes. The average distance between active volcanoes here is less than 30 km. (19 miles)! Politically the nation is disrupted by even more serious eruptions of violence, aggravated by outside interference. Independent 1839, 1841.

⑫ HONDURAS

República de Honduras
(Republic of Honduras)

Area: 112,088 km²
Population: 4,090,000
Population growth per annum: 3.8%
Life expectancy at birth: males 55 years, females 59 years
Literacy: 47%
Capital with population: Tegucigalpa 534,000
Other important cities with population: San Pedro Sula 398,000, El Progreso 105,000
Language: Spanish
Religion: Roman Catholic
Currency: Lempira = 100 centavos

The word banana republic must have been coined with Honduras in mind. Bananas thrive in the fertile volcanic soil and the warm, humid climate of the tropical coastlands. The forest covers impressive Maya ruins, such as Copán. Independent 1821, NOV 5, 1838.

⑬ NICARAGUA

República de Nicaragua
(Republic of Nicaragua)

Area: 148,000 km²
Population: 2,910,000
Population growth per annum: 3.3%
Life expectancy at birth: males 54 years, females 57 years
Literacy: 87%
Capital with population: Managua 615,000
Other important cities with population: León 160,000
Language: Spanish
Religion: Roman Catholic
Currency: Córdoba = 100 centavos

Nicaragua could be called a land of turmoil. Plagued by earthquakes, revolutions, and counter-revolutions the people today are certainly longing for peace and quiet. Lake Nicaragua is said to contain people-eating sharks, trapped there when the former bay became a fresh water lake. Indep. 1821, 1838.

⑭ COSTA RICA

República de Costa Rica

Area: 50,700 km²
Population: 2,450,000
Population growth per annum: 2.4%
Life expectancy at birth: males 68 years, females 72 years
Literacy: 90%
Capital with population: San José 245,000
Other important cities with population: Alajuela 35,000
Language: Spanish
Religion: Roman Catholic
Currency: Colón = 100 céntimos

Costa Rica is known as the country that has no army, but the police are one of the world's best equipped! The lack of generals and colonels is in any case not the only cause for the peaceful, democratic development of the country during the last twenty-five years. Independent 1821, 1838.

⑮ PANAMA

República de Panamá
(Republic of Panamá)

Area: 78,046 km²
Population: 1,970,000
Population growth per annum: 2.5%
Life expectancy at birth: males 68 years, females 72 years
Literacy: 85%
Capital with population: Panamá 389,000
Other important cities with population: Colón 80,000
Language: Spanish
Religion: Roman Catholic
Currency: Balboa = 100 centimes

Panama is known all over the Seven Seas. Few know that the word means 'abundance of fish' but many know the quartered tricolor flag that is flown over many ships (as a flag of 'convenience') — and all know of the Canal that every year carries over 10,000 large ships between the Atlantic and the Pacific. Independent 1819, NOV 3, 1903.

SOUTH AMERICA

Area: 17,838,000 km²
Population: 214,684,000
Density of population per km²: 12

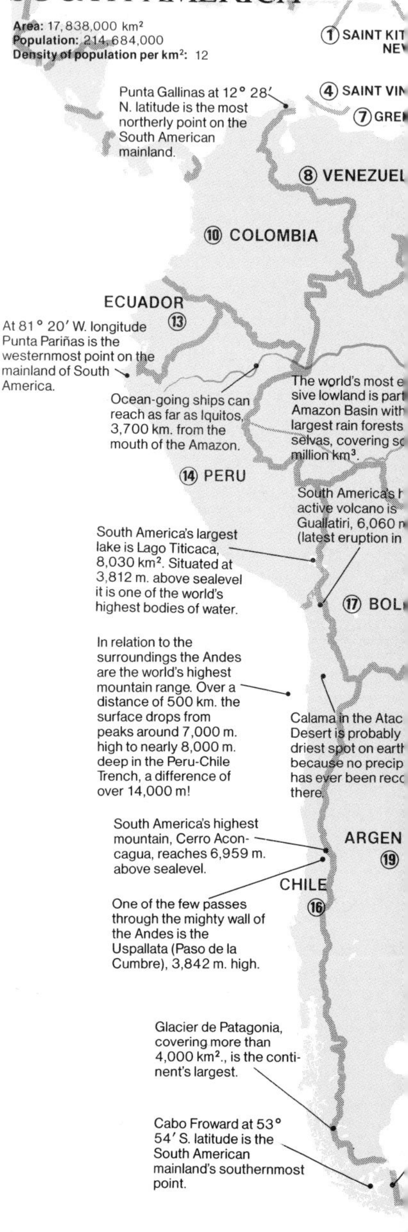
① SAINT KIT
NE
④ SAINT VIN
⑦ GRE
Punta Gallinas at 12° 28′ N. latitude is the most northerly point on the South American mainland.
⑧ VENEZUEL
⑩ COLOMBIA
ECUADOR
⑬
At 81° 20′ W. longitude Punta Pariñas is the westernmost point on the mainland of South America.
Ocean-going ships can reach as far as Iquitos, 3,700 km. from the mouth of the Amazon.
The world's most e
sive lowland is part
Amazon Basin with
largest rain forests
selvas, covering so
million km³.
⑭ PERU
South America's h
active volcano is
Guallatiri, 6,060 m
(latest eruption in
South America's largest lake is Lago Titicaca, 8,030 km². Situated at 3,812 m. above sealevel it is one of the world's highest bodies of water.
⑰ BOL
In relation to the surroundings the Andes are the world's highest mountain range. Over a distance of 500 km. the surface drops from peaks around 7,000 m. high to nearly 8,000 m. deep in the Peru-Chile Trench, a difference of over 14,000 m!
Calama in the Atac
Desert is probably
driest spot on eart
because no precip
has ever been reco
there.
South America's highest mountain, Cerro Aconcagua, reaches 6,959 m. above sealevel.
ARGEN
⑲
CHILE
⑯
One of the few passes through the mighty wall of the Andes is the Uspallata (Paso de la Cumbre), 3,842 m. high.
Glacier de Patagonia, covering more than 4,000 km²., is the continent's largest.
Cabo Froward at 53° 54′ S. latitude is the South American mainland's southernmost point.

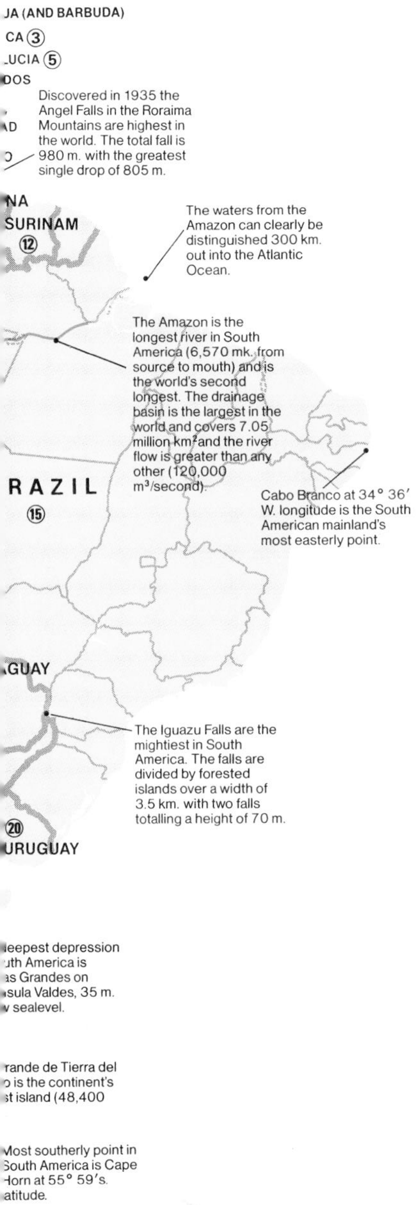
Discovered in 1935 the Angel Falls in the Roraima Mountains are highest in the world. The total fall is 980 m. with the greatest single drop of 805 m.
SURINAM
12
The waters from the Amazon can clearly be distinguished 300 km. out into the Atlantic Ocean.
The Amazon is the longest river in South America (6,570 mk. from source to mouth) and is the world's second longest. The drainage basin is the largest in the world and covers 7.05 million km² and the river flow is greater than any other (120,000 m³/second).
15
Cabo Branco at 34° 36′ W. longitude is the South American mainland's most easterly point.
The Iguazu Falls are the mightiest in South America. The falls are divided by forested islands over a width of 3.5 km. with two falls totalling a height of 70 m.
20
URUGUAY

② ANTIGUA (AND BARBUDA)
⑲ ARGENTINA
⑥ BARBADOS
⑰ BOLIVIA
⑮ BRAZIL
⑯ CHILE
⑩ COLOMBIA
③ DOMINICA
⑬ ECUADOR
⑦ GRENADA
⑪ GUYANA
⑱ PARAGUAY
⑭ PERU
① SAINT KITTS-NEVIS
⑤ SAINT LUCIA
④ SAINT VINCENT
⑫ SURINAM
⑨ TRINIDAD AND TOBAGO
⑳ URUGUAY
⑧ VENEZUELA

① SAINT ST. KITTS-NEVIS

(Sovereign Democratic Federal State)

Area: 261 km²
Population: 45,000
Population growth per annum: not available
Life expectancy at birth: not available
Literacy: not available
Capital with population: Basseterre 15,000
Other important cities with population: none
Language: English
Religion: Protestant (76%), Roman Catholic (8%)
Currency: EC-dollar = 100 cents

St. Kitts cultivates tourists and sugar. The pleasant climate in the trade wind tropics favours both of the main industries. Palms and beaches correspond to the common "image" of the Caribbean. Independent SEP 19, 1983.

② ANTIGUA (AND BARBUDA)

Area: 442 km²
Population: 79,000
Population growth per annum: not available
Life expectancy at birth: not available
Literacy: not available
Capital with population: Saint Johns 25,000
Other important cities with population: none
Language: English
Religion: Christian (predominantly Church of England)
Currency: East Caribbean dollar = 100 cents

Antigua and Barbuda are names known to collectors of stamps, to naval strategy planners, some students of colonial history and a few in the sugar trade, and of course, to the proud and independent islanders of the Lesser Antilles. Ind. NOV 1, 1981.

③ DOMINICA

(Commonwealth of Dominica)

Area: 751 km²
Population: 82,000
Population growth per annum: 2.7%
Life expectancy at birth: males 57 years, females 59 years
Literacy: not available
Capital with population: Roseau 20,000
Other important cities with population: none
Language: English, French patois
Religion: Roman Catholic
Currency: French franc = 100 centimes

Dominica can be called the only Caribbean country among all the Caribbean lands. Only here still lives a sizeable remnant of the once dreaded Carib Indians — whose name is perpetuated in the equally dreadful word cannibal. Indep. NOV 3, 1978.

④ SAINT VINCENT (AND THE GRENADINES)

Area: 389 km²
Population: 123,000
Population growth per annum: 5.9%
Life expectancy at birth: males 59 years, females 60 years
Literacy: 95 %
Capital with population: Kingstown 33,000
Other important cities with population: none
Language: English
Religion: Protestant (75%), Roman Catholic (13%)
Currency: EC-dollar = 100 cents

Many different kinds of fruit are grown on the islands — coconuts, mangoes, avocados, guavas just to mention a few, but not the pomegranates used for making grenadine syrup (an ingredient of many cocktails). Most of the 600 volcanic Grenadine Islands belong to St. Vincent. Ind. OCT 27, 1979.

⑤ SAINT LUCIA

Area: 616 km²
Population: 127,000
Population growth per annum: 1.8%
Life expectancy at birth: males 65 years, females 70 years
Literacy: 78%
Capital with population: Castries 45,000
Other important cities with population: none
Language: English, French patois
Religion: Roman Catholic
Currency: EC-dollar = 100 cents

Bananas, cocoa and coconuts are the chief products of St. Lucia instead of sugar as on most other Antillean Islands. A growing number of tourists are discovering the pleasant beaches of St. Lucia. Independent FEB 22, 1979.

⑥ BARBADOS

Area: 431 km²
Population: 250,000
Population growth per annum: 1.4%
Life expectancy at birth: males 68 years, females 73 years
Literacy: 97%
Capital with population: Bridgetown 7,500
Other important cities with population: none
Language: English
Religion: Protestant
Currency: Barbados dollar = 100 cents

Tourists and sugar cane thrive here on the most easterly of the Windward Islands. The gentle trade winds blow with a constant 5-6 m./s. to keep the surf rolling in and the sky clear of clouds. Independent NOV 30, 1966.

⑦ GRENADA
(State of Grenada)

Area: 344 km²
Population: 115,000
Population growth per annum: 1.0%
Life expectancy at birth: 69 years
Literacy: 85%
Capital with population: Saint George's 7,500
Other important cities with population: none
Language: English
Religion: Roman Catholic
Currency: E C dollar = 100 cents

Grenada is one of the "spice islands" of the world. It produces more than one third of the nutmeg on the world market. In the world of the super powers Grenada has also had an importance without relation to its tiny size. Independent FEB 7, 1974.

⑧ VENEZUELA
Republica de Venezuela
(Republic of Venezuela)

Area: 912,050 km²
Population: 15,260,000
Population growth per annum: 3.5%
Life expectancy at birth: males 64 years, females 69 years
Literacy: 86%
Capital with population: Caracas 2,700,000
Other important cities with population:
Maracaibo 845,000, Barquismeto 459,000
Language: Spanish
Religion: Roman Catholic
Currency: Bolivar = 100 céntimos

Venice has been called a floating city, and Venezuela — "little Venice" — a land floating on oil. Over 4,000 oil drilling derricks stand now in the shallow waters of the Maracaibo lagoon like the houses on stilts that gave the country its name. In the southeast the Angel Falls, highest in the world, plunge 980 m. down (805 m. uninterrupted). Independent 1821, 1830.

⑨ TRINIDAD AND TOBAGO

Area: 5,128 km²
Population: 1,160,000
Population growth per annum: 1.5%
Life expectancy at birth: males 66 years, females 72 years
Literacy: 92%
Capital with population: Port of Spain 56,000
Other important cities with population:
San Fernando 40,000
Language: English, Spanish
Religion: Roman Catholic (31%), Protestant (26%), Hindu (23%), Moslem (6%)
Currency: Trinidad and Tobago dollar = 100 cents

A melting pot where everything is transformed. Cultures traditions, and people from five continents have been mixed and combined under the sun of Trinidad. A different melting pot an "inexhaustible" lake of asphalt, Pitch Lake, is unique in the world. Independent AUG 31, 1962.

⑩ COLOMBIA
República de Colombia
(Republic of Colombia)

Area: 1,141,748 km²
Population: 27,410,000
Population growth per annum: 2.1%
Life expectancy at birth: males 60 years, females 65 years
Literacy: 82%
Capital with population: Bogotá 4,900,000
Other important cities with population:
Medellín 1,800,000, Cali 1,200,000, Barranquilla 900,000
Language: Spanish
Religion: Roman Catholic
Currency: Colombian peso = 100 centavos

Colombia may have been the legendary land of El Dorado — the gold-covered king. Today it could be called the land of green gold — as 90% of all emeralds in the world come from mines in Colombia. However high quality coffee is the country's main export product. Independent DEC 17, 1819.

⑪ GUYANA
(Cooperative Republic of Guyana)

Area: 215,000 km²
Population: 830,000
Population growth per annum: 2.2%
Life expectancy at birth: males 67 years, females 72 years
Literacy: 85%
Capital with population: Georgetown 187,000
Other important cities with population: none
Language: English, Hindi, Creole
Religion: Hindu (37%), Protestant (32%), Roman Catholic (13%), Islam (9%)
Currency: Guyana dollar = 100 cents

Guyana is an East Indian country in the West Indies, as the major part of the inhabitants are descendants of immigrants from India. Of all the world's waterfalls only nine are higher than the near 500 m. high uninterrupted cascades of the King George VI Falls, north of the Roraima Plateau. Indep. MAY 26, 1966.

⑫ SURINAM

Area: 163,820 km²
Population: 370,000
Population growth per annum: 1.3%
Life expectancy at birth: males 65 years, females 70 years
Literacy: 80%
Capital with population: Paramaribo 68,000
Other important cities with population: none
Language: Dutch
Religion: Hindu (29%), Protestant (20%), Moslem (19%), Roman Catholic (18%)
Currency: Suriname guilder or florin = 100 cents

A country för $ 24? In a deal with Britain in the 15th century the Dutch acquired this British colony in exchange for New Amsterdam — later better known as the city of New York — in turn bought for $24. 90% of today's Surinam is covered with dense rainforest. Independent NOV 25, 1975.

⑬ ECUADOR

República del Ecuador
(Republic of Ecuador)

Area: 283,561 km², (disputed area 190,807 km² not included)
Population: 8,810,000
Population growth per annum: 3.0%
Life expectancy at birth: males 58 years, females 62 years
Literacy: 84%
Capital with population: Quito 920,000
Other important cities with population: Guaqaquil 1,300,000, Cuenca 270,000
Language: Spanish, Quechuan, Jivaroan
Religion: Predominantly Roman Catholic
Currency: Sucre = 100 centavos

A "heavy" item in Ecuador's export statistics is featherweight balsa timber. The Spanish word balsa denotes both raft and the timber, lighter than cork. The Indians used it for building sailing rafts as early as prehistoric times. The logs for Heyerdahl's famous Kon-Tiki were cut in Ecuador in 1947. Independent MAY 13, 1830.

⑭ PERU

República del Perú
(Republic of Peru)

Area: 1,285,216 km²
Population: 18,300,000
Population growth per annum: 2.7%
Life expectancy at birth: males 56 years, females 59 years
Literacy: 72%
Capital with population: Lima 3,100,000
Other important cities with population: Callao 300,000
Language: Spanish, Quechua, Aymará
Religion: Roman Catholic
Currency: Sol = 100 centavos

The Inca's land of gold and silver was turned into a land of guano and fishmeal. The conquistadores stripped the land of its immense treasures of golden artwork. The stone buildings of Machu Picchu's breath-taking eagle's nest-city still remain — hidden and forgotten for five centuries until discovered by Hiram Bingham in 1911. Independent JUL 28, 1821.

⑮ BRAZIL

Repuiblica Federativa do Brasil
(Federative Republic of Brazil)

Area: 8,511,965 km²
Population: 120,000,000
Population growth per annum: 2.4%
Life expectancy at birth: males 60 years, females 64 years
Literacy: 68%
Capital with population: Brasília 410,000, (Federal district 1,200,000)
Other important cities with population: São Paulo 7,000,000, Río de Janeiro 5,100,000
Language: Portuguese
Religion: Roman Catholic (89%), Protestant (7%)
Currency: Cruzeiro = 100 centavos

Only four countries in the world are larger than Brazil, The mighty Amazon carries more water than any other river (120 000 m²/s at the mouth) and is navigable for ocean-going ships up to Iquitos, 3 700 km from the sea. Brasília, created by president Kubitscheck and architects Oscar Niemeyer and Lúcio Costa, became capital in 1960. Independent SEP 7, 1822.

⑯ CHILE

República de Chile
(Republic of Chile)

Area: 756,945 km²
Population: 11,490,000
Population growth per annum: 1.7%
Life expectancy at birth: males 62 years, females 69 years
Literacy: 90%
Capital with population: Santiago 3,450,000
Other important cities with population: Viña del Mar 300,000, Varparíso 270,000
Language: Spanish
Religion: Predominantly Roman Catholic
Currency: Chilean peso = 100 centavos

The "narrowest" country in the world, Chile, is nearly twenty-five times longer than it is wide (175 by 4 300 km) and stretches from the tropics down to the stormy Cape Horn in the "Furious Fifties". At Calama in the Atacama Desert no rainfall has ever been recorded. Independent SEP 18, 1810.

⑰ BOLIVIA

República de Bolivia
(Republic of Bolivia)

Area: 1,098,580 km²
Population: 5,900 000
Population growth per annum: 2.6%
Life expectancy at birth: males 47 years, females 51 years
Literacy: 75%
Capital with population: La Paz 650,000 and Sucre 65,000
Other important cities with population: Santa Cruz 260,000, Cochabamba 200,000
Language: Spanish, Quechua (34%), Aymará (25%)
Religion: Roman Catholic
Currency: Bolivian peso = 100 centavos

Tin mining is the main source of wealth in land-locked Bolivia. Most of the population live on the dry, cold tablelands, higher than many peaks in the European Alps. Lake Titicaca, shared with Peru, is the, worlds highest (3 812 m) navigable body of water. Independent AUG 6, 1825.

⑱ PARAGUAY

República del Paraguay
(Republic of Paraguay)

Area: 406,752 km²
Population: 3,000,000
Population growth per annum: 3.3%
Life expectancy at birth: males 62 years, females 66 years
Literacy: 82%
Capital with population: Asunción 460,000
Other important cities with population: Caaguazu 73,000
Language: Spanish, Guarani (90%)
Religion: Roman Catholic
Currency: Guarani = 100 céntimos

Here one man's will is, and has been, law — by unbroken tradition from Jesuit times. The pope was replaced by the King of Spain, he in turn by the founding dictator "El Supremo" and so on. General Alfredo Stroessner seized power in 1954. The Iguaçu falls of the Parana cascade 82 m. over a width of four km. between hundreds of forest islands. Independent MAY 14, 1811.

19 ARGENTINA

República Argentina
(Argentine Republic)

Area: 2,777,815 km²
Population: 27,950,000
Population growth per annum: 1.3%
Life expectancy at birth: males 66 years, females 73 years
Literacy: 94 %
Capital with population: Buenos Aires 2,900,000, (Greater Buenos Aires 9,900,000)
Other important cities with population: Córdoba 970,000, Rosario 880,000, Mendoza 600,000
Language: Spanish
Religion: Roman Catholic
Currency: Arg. peso = 100 centavos

The home of the tango and the gaucho, Argentina is a Europe in miniature. It is situated on southern latitudes, and it, was populated by settlers from all over Europe. It has the continents highest peak, Aconcagua, and its lowest spot, Salinas Grandes on the Peninsula Valdés, 35 m. below sea level. Independent MAR 25, 1810.

20 URUGUAY

República Oriental del Uruguay
(Oriental Republic of Uruguay)

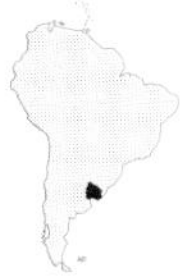

Area: 186,926 km²
Population: 2,990,000
Population growth per annum: 0.6%
Life expectancy at birth: males 66 years, females 73 years
Literacy: 94%
Capital with population: Montevideo 1,362,000
Other important cities with population: Salto 80,000, Paysandá 80,000
Language: Spanish
Religion: Roman Catholic
Currency: Nuevo peso (new peso) = 100 centésimos

A country of rolling grasslands with grazing cattle and cultivated fields. As in other agricultural lands, more people live in the capital than in all the other towns put together. Independent AUG. 25, 1825.

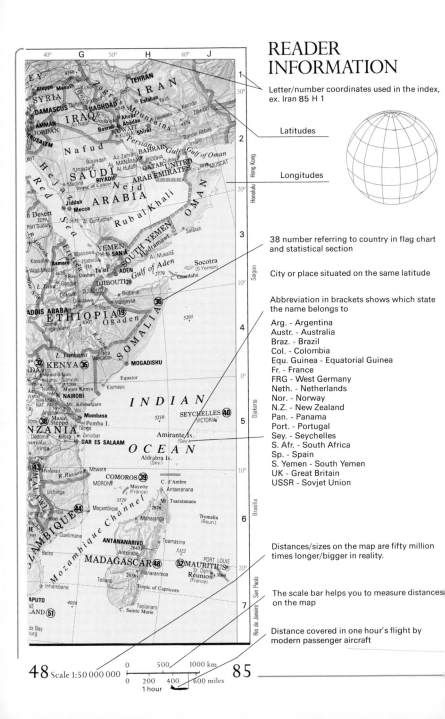

READER INFORMATION

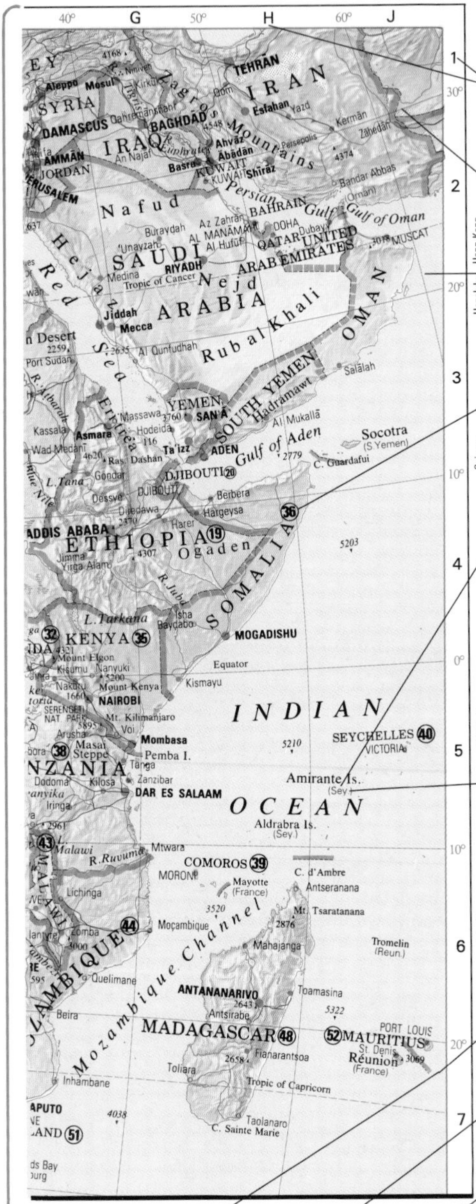

Letter/number coordinates used in the index, ex. Iran 85 H 1

Latitudes

Longitudes

38 number referring to country in flag chart and statistical section

City or place situated on the same latitude

Abbreviation in brackets shows which state the name belongs to

Arg. - Argentina
Austr. - Australia
Braz. - Brazil
Col. - Colombia
Equ. Guinea - Equatorial Guinea
Fr. - France
FRG - West Germany
Neth. - Netherlands
Nor. - Norway
N.Z. - New Zealand
Pan. - Panama
Port. - Portugal
Sey. - Seychelles
S. Afr. - South Africa
Sp. - Spain
S. Yemen - South Yemen
UK - Great Britain
USSR - Sovjet Union

Distances/sizes on the map are fifty million times longer/bigger in reality.

The scale bar helps you to measure distances on the map

Distance covered in one hour's flight by modern passenger aircraft

 Scale 1:50 000 000

0 500 1000 km
0 200 400 600 miles
1 hour

85

Symbols Scale 1:10 000 000, 1:20 000 000

Bombay	More than 5 000 000 inhabitants	Major road	4807 Height above sea-level in metres
Milano	1 000 000-5 000 000 inhabitants	Other road	3068 Depth in metres
Zürich	250 000-1 000 000 inhabitants	Road under construction	National park
Dijon	100 000-250 000 inhabitants	Railway	Niniveh Ruin
Dover	25 000-100 000 inhabitants	Railway under construction	Pass
Torquay	Less than 25 000 inhabitants	Train ferry	KAINJI DAM Dam
Tachiumet	Small sites	National boundary	Wadi
WIEN	National capital	Disputed national boundary	Canal
Atlanta	State capital	State boundary	Waterfalls
		Disputed state boundary	Reef
		Undefined boundary in the sea	

Symbols Scale 1:30 000 000 1:50 000 000 1:54 000 000 1:60 000 000 1:75 000 000

Shanghai	More than 5 000 000 inhabitants	Major road	8848 Height above sea-level in metres
Barcelona	1 000 000-5 000 000 inhabitants	Railway	11034 Depth in metres
Venice	250 000-1 000 000 inhabitants	Railway under construction	2645 Thickness of ice cap
Aberdeen	50 000-250 000 inhabitants	National boundary	Thebes Ruin
Beida	Less than 50 000 inhabitants	Disputed national boundary	Dam
Mawson	Scientific station	State boundary	Wadi
CAIRO	National capital	Disputed state boundary	Canal
		Undefined boundary in the sea	Waterfalls
			Reef

Colour Key

Tundra	Tropical rain forest	Steppe, semi-desert	Salt lake
Glacier	Chacos	Sand desert	Intermittent lake
Coniferous forest	Arable land	Other desert	Salt desert, salt pan, dry lake
Mixed forest	Grassland, pasture	Mountain	Lava plateau
Deciduous forest	Savanna	Marshland	

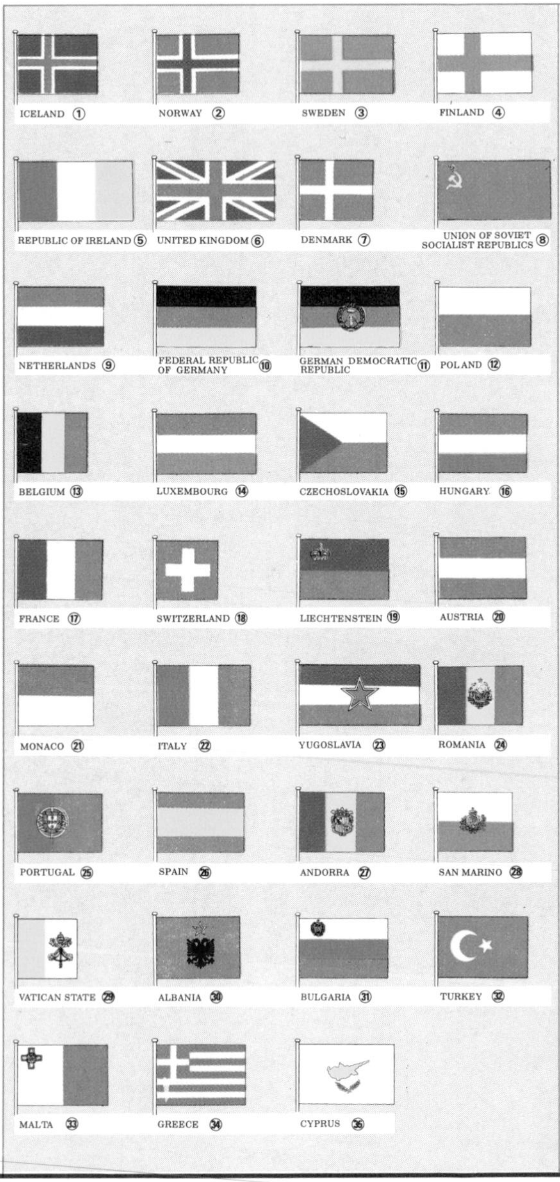
ICELAND ①
NORWAY ②
SWEDEN ③
FINLAND ④
REPUBLIC OF IRELAND ⑤
UNITED KINGDOM ⑥
DENMARK ⑦
UNION OF SOVIET SOCIALIST REPUBLICS ⑧
NETHERLANDS ⑨
FEDERAL REPUBLIC OF GERMANY ⑩
GERMAN DEMOCRATIC REPUBLIC ⑪
POLAND ⑫
BELGIUM ⑬
LUXEMBOURG ⑭
CZECHOSLOVAKIA ⑮
HUNGARY ⑯
FRANCE ⑰
SWITZERLAND ⑱
LIECHTENSTEIN ⑲
AUSTRIA ⑳
MONACO ㉑
ITALY ㉒
YUGOSLAVIA ㉓
ROMANIA ㉔
PORTUGAL ㉕
SPAIN ㉖
ANDORRA ㉗
SAN MARINO ㉘
VATICAN STATE ㉙
ALBANIA ㉚
BULGARIA ㉛
TURKEY ㉜
MALTA ㉝
GREECE ㉞
CYPRUS ㉟

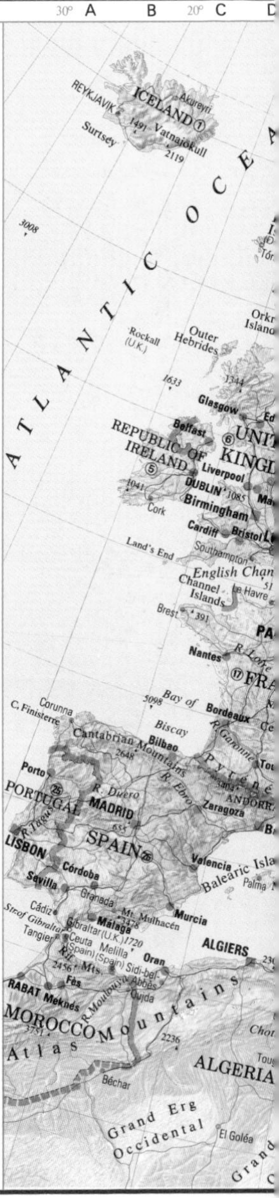
30° A
B
20° C
ICELAND ①
REYKJAVIK
Akureyri
Vatnajökull
1491
2119
Surtsey
ATLANTIC OCEAN
3008
Rockall (U.K.)
Outer Hebrides
1633
1344
Glasgow
Belfast
REPUBLIC OF IRELAND ⑤
⑥ UNITED KINGDOM
Liverpool
DUBLIN
1085
1041
Cork
Birmingham
Cardiff
Bristol
Land's End
Southampton
English Channel
Channel Islands
Le Havre
Brest
391
Nantes
R. Loire
⑰ FRANCE
Bay of Biscay
5098
Bordeaux
R. Garonne
Corunna
C. Finisterre
Cantabrian Mountains
2648
Bilbao
R. Ebro
Pyrénées
ANDORRA
Porto
PORTUGAL ㉕
R. Duero
MADRID
Zaragoza
R. Tagus
655
SPAIN ㉖
LISBON
Valencia
Balearic Islands
Palma
Córdoba
Sevilla
Granada
Murcia
Mt. Mulhacén
3478
Cádiz
Málaga
Str. of Gibraltar
Gibraltar (U.K.)
Tangier
Ceuta (Spain)
Melilla (Spain)
1720
Oran
ALGIERS
Sidi-bel-Abbès
Oujda
2456
Fès
RABAT
Meknès
R. Moulouya
MOROCCO
3751
Atlas Mountains
2236
ALGERIA
Béchar
Grand Erg Occidental
El Goléa

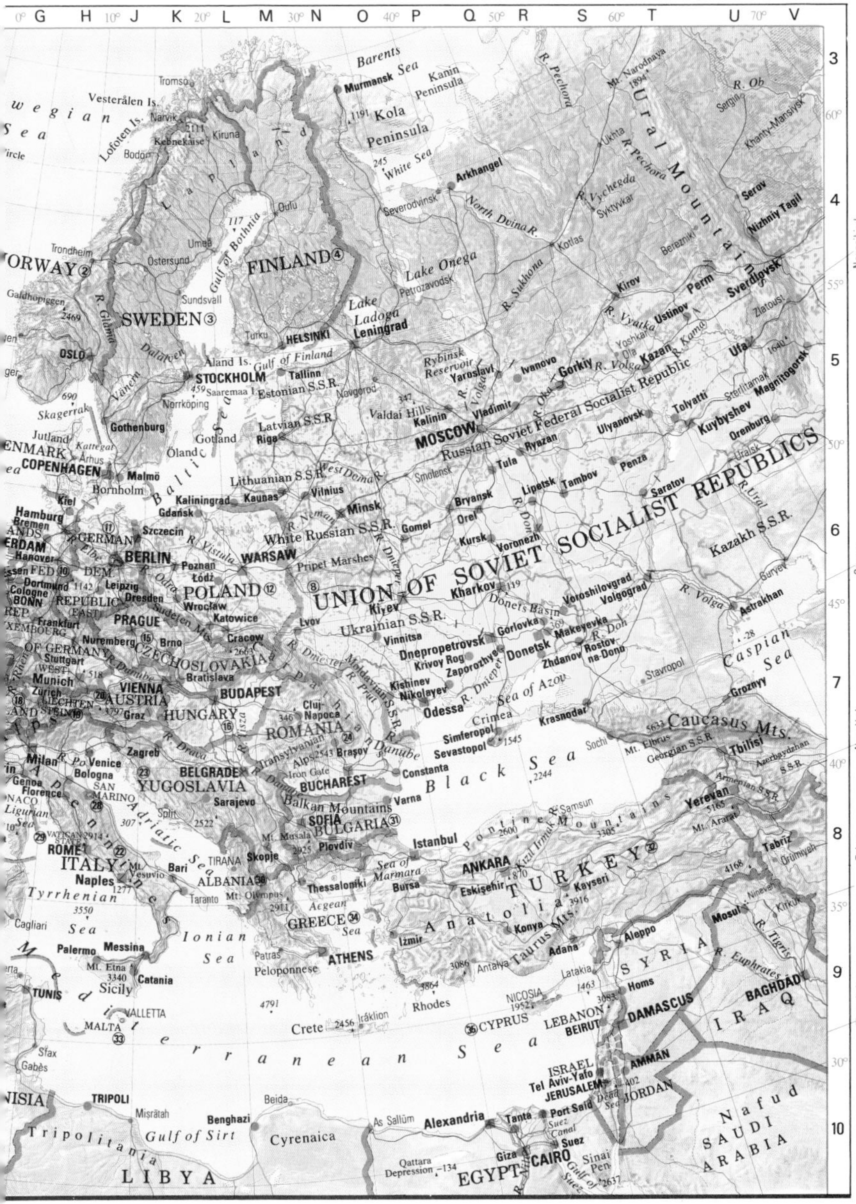

Scale 1:30 000 000

0 500 1000 km

0 250 500 miles

1 hour

A
B
C
D
1
3
4
5
Faeroe Is
(Denmark)
Norðoyar
Streymoy
Vàgar
Eysturoy
Sandoy
Tuðroyri
Suðuroy
Unst
Mainland
Shetland Is
(U.K.)
Lerwick
Sumburgh Head
Fair Isle
Orkney Islands
Kirkwall
Hoy
John o' Groats
Wick
Butt of Lewis
Cape Wrath
Stornoway
Lewis
Outer Hebrides
North Uist
South Uist
Barra
Barra Head
Skye
North Minch
Ullapool
North West Highlands
Moray Firth
Inverness
Kinnaird's Head
Ben Macdui
1309
Grampian Mountains
Aberdeen
Scotland
Fort William
Ben Nevis
1344
Mallaig
Inner Hebrides
Mull
Oban
Perth
Dundee
Jura
Islay
Greenock
Glasgow
Paisley
Glenrothes
Firth of Forth
Edinburgh
Kilmarnock
Arran
Ayr
Southern Uplands
North Channel
Malin Head
Londonderry
Northern Ireland
Ulster
Larne
Lisburn
Newtownabbey
Bangor
Belfast
Lough Neagh
852
Stranraer
Dumfries
Carlisle
Newcastle-upon-Tyne
Pennine Chain
South Shields
Sunderland
Hartlepool
Teesside
Darlington
Scarborough
UNITED KINGDOM
Whitehaven
Scafell Pike
977
Isle of Man
Douglas
Lancaster
Irish Sea
Blackpool
Preston
Bradford
Leeds
York
Kingston-upon-Hull
Bolton
Manchester
Sheffield
Grimsby
Anglesey
Holyhead
Birkenhead
Liverpool
Snowdon
1085
Stoke-on-Trent
Derby
Lincoln
Nottingham
The Wash
Wales
Shrewsbury
Stafford
Leicester
Wolverhampton
Dudley
Birmingham
Coventry
Cambrian Mts
Cardigan Bay
Aberystwyth
Norwich
Lowestoft
England
Hereford
Worcester
Northampton
Cambridge
Ipswich
Gloucester
Oxford
Luton
Rhondda
Swansea
Newport
Cardiff
Bristol
Bristol Channel
Reading
Thames
LONDON
Southend-on-Sea
Ramsgate
Dover
Strait of Dover (Pas de Calais)
Folkestone
Brighton
Guildford
Southampton
Taunton
Exeter
Dartmoor
Torbay
Plymouth
Poole
Bournemouth
Portsmouth
Isle of Wight
St. Austell
Falmouth
Lizard
Land's End
Isles of Scilly
English Channel
(La Manche)
Donegal Bay
Donegal Mountains
Mullet Peninsula
Mountains of Mayo
Sligo
Monaghan
Dundalk
Dundalk Bay
Carrick-on-Shannon
Connaught
REPUBLIC OF IRELAND
(EIRE)
Galway
(Gaillimh)
Boyne
DUBLIN
(BAILE ATHA CLIATH)
Dún Laoghaire
Shannon
Port Laoise
Mouth of the Shannon
Munster
Limerick
(Luimneach)
Barrow
Arklow
Killarney
Rosslare
Waterford
(Port Láirge)
Boggeragh Mts.
Cork
(Corcaigh)
Mizen Head
St George's Channel
Fishguard
Milford Haven
Celtic Sea
2300
1600
2487
722
120
294
140
15
10
150
ATLANTIC OCEAN
North Sea
Dogger Bank
Great Fisher Bank
NORWAY
Fensfjorden
Bergen
Sotra
Korsfj
Stord
Haugesund
Karmøy
Stavanger
Sandnes
Nærbø
Egersund
Frisian
Leeuwarden
NETHERLANDS
Den Helder
AMSTERDAM
Haarlem
Leiden
's-Gravenhage
(The Haag)
Rotterdam
Utrecht
Dordrecht
Breda
Vlissingen
Tilburg
Brugge
Antwerpen
Oostende
Gent
Dunkerque
BRUXELLES
Maastricht
BELGIUM
Tourcoing
Lille
Béthune
Mons
Charleroi
Namur
Calais
Boulogne
Plaine des Flandres
Arras
Maubeuge
Cambrai
Somme
Fourmies
Saint-Quentin
Sedan
Abbeville
Dieppe
Amiens
Picardie
Laon
LUXEMBOURG
Cap de la Hague
Cherbourg
Guernsey
Jersey
Channel Islands
(U.K.)
Golfe de Saint-Malo
Le Havre
Rouen
Beauvais
Compiègne
Creil
Reims
Châlons-sur-Marne
Caen
Lisieux
Normandie
Ile de France
Saint-Denis
Seine
Marne
Épernay
Ile d'Ouessant
Brest
Saint-Brieuc
Saint-Malo
Forêt d'Écouves
Évreux
Dreux
Versailles
PARIS
Meaux
Collines du Perche
Bretagne
Fougères
Quimper
Rennes
Bassin de Rennes
Laval
Alençon
Chartres
Melun
Troyes
Champagne
Saint-Dizier
Pointe de Penmarch
Lorient
Vannes
Le Mans
Orléans
Sens
Chaumont
Yonne
Angers
Blois
Loire
Auxerre
Belle-Ile
Saint-Nazaire
Nantes
Anjou
Tours
Bourgogne
Dijon
Vierzon
Bourges
Ile de Ré
Bocage Vendéen
Rezé
Cholet
Touraine
FRANCE
Ile d'Yeu
La Roche-sur-Yon
Châtellerault
Châteauroux
Nevers
Chalon-sur-Saône
5°
0°
62°
55°
50°

Scale 1:10 000 000

0 100 200 300 400 500 km

0 100 200 300 miles

1/2 hour

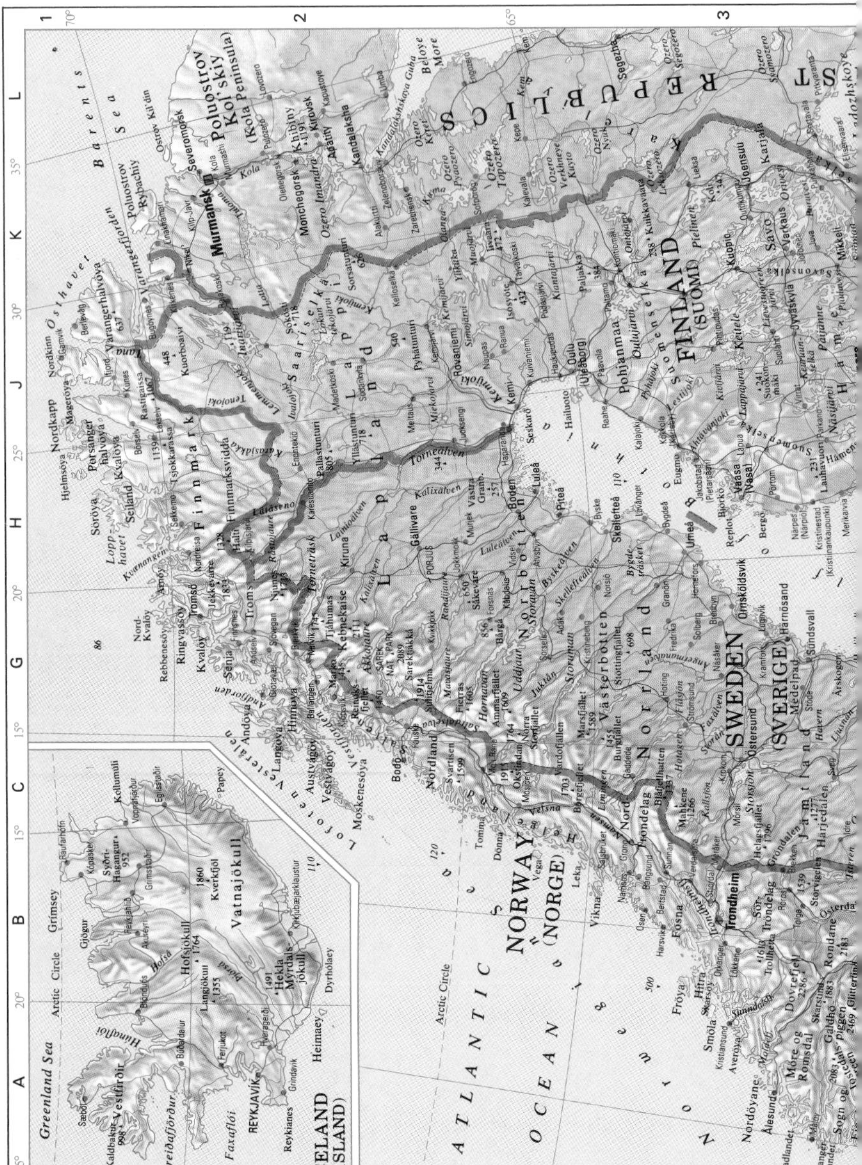

ICELAND
(ÍSLAND)
Greenland Sea
Arctic Circle
Grímsey
Vatnajökull
Hofsjökull
Hekla
Mýrdalsjökull
REYKJAVÍK
Faxaflói
Breiðafjörður
Vestfirðir
Heimaey
Papey
NORWAY
(NORGE)
SWEDEN
(SVERIGE)
FINLAND
(SUOMI)
ATLANTIC
OCEAN
Barents Sea
Murmansk
Poluostrov Kol'skiy
(Kola Peninsula)
Poluostrov Rybachiy
Varangerfjorden
Varangerhalvöya
Nordkapp
Magerøya
Porsanger halvöya
Finnmarksvidda
Finnmark
Troms
Tromsø
Lofoten
Vesterålen
Hinnöya
Andöya
Austvågöy
Vestvågöy
Moskenesöya
Bodø
Nordland
Lappland
Kiruna
Gällivare
Kebnekaise
Luleå
Boden
Piteå
Skellefteå
Umeå
Norrbotten
Västerbotten
Norrland
Östersund
Jämtland
Härjedalen
Medelpad
Sundsvall
Härnösand
Örnsköldsvik
Trondheim
Trøndelag
Nord-Trøndelag
Sör-Tröndelag
Dovrefjell
Rondane
Galdhøpiggen
Möre og Romsdal
Ålesund
Nordöyane
Smöla
Hitra
Fröya
Kristiansund
Oulu
(Uleåborg)
Pohjanmaa
Kemi
Rovaniemi
Vaasa
(Vasa)
Kokkola
Kuopio
Jyväskylä
Joensuu
Savo
Karjala
Päijänne
Kandalaksha
Kirovsk
Apatity
Monchegorsk
Khibiny
Severomorsk
Kola
Beloye More
Ozero Imandra
Ozero Topozero
Tornealven
Kalixälven
Storuman
Saariselkä
Lokan tekojärvi
Hailuoto
Arctic Circle

Scale 1:10 000 000

0	100	200	300	400	500 km
0	100	200	300 miles		

1/2 hour

A
B
C
D
2
3
4
10°
5°
0°
45°
40°
ATLANTIC
OCEAN
Bay of Biscay
English Channel
(La Manche)
UNITED KINGDOM
St. Austell
Land's End
Isles of Scilly
Lizard
Falmouth
Dartmoor
Torbay
Plymouth
Poole
Bournemouth
Portsmouth
Isle of Wight
Brighton
Calais
Boulogne
Béthune
Tourcoing
Abbeville
Dieppe
Amiens
Cambrai
Arras
Plaine des Flandres
Picardie
Cap de la Hague
Cherbourg
Guernsey
Jersey
Channel Islands
(U.K.)
Le Havre
Rouen
Beauvais
Compiègne
Caen
Lisieux
Creil
Seine
Somme
Normandie
Golfe de Saint-Malo
Ile d'Ouessant
Brest
Saint-Brieuc
Saint-Malo
Forêt d'Ecouves
Evreux
Saint-Denis
Meaux
Dreux
Versailles
PARIS
Collines du Perche
Bretagne
Quimper
Pointe de Penmarch
Rennes
Bassin de Rennes
Fougères
Laval
Alençon
Chartres
Melun
Lorient
Vannes
Le Mans
Orléans
Belle-Ile
Saint-Nazaire
Angers
Anjou
Blois
Loire
Auxerre
150
Nantes
Tours
Vierzon
Bourges
Ile de Ré
Bocage Vendéen
Rezé
Cholet
Touraine
FRANCE
Ile d'Yeu
La Roche-sur-Yon
Châtellerault
Châteauroux
Nevers
Niort
Poitiers
Plateaux de la Marche
Moulins
Poitou
La Rochelle
Montluçon
Ile d'Oléron
Rochefort
Vichy
Saintes
Limoges
Riom
Pointe de Grave
Gironde
Angoulême
Plateau de Millevaches
Limousin
1886
Puy de Sancy
Périgueux
Creuse
Vézère
5100
Mérignac
Pessac
Brive
Massif Central
Cap Ferret
Bordeaux
Bergerac
Aurillac
Talence
Guyenne
Monts d'Aubrac
1440
Côte d'Argent
Les Landes
Lot
Rodez
Agen
Garonne
Millau
Mont-de-Marsan
Montauban
Gascogne
Tarn
Albi
Cévennes
Biarritz
Bayonne
Toulouse
Montpellier
Irún
Gave de Pau
Canal du Midi
Castres
Béziers
Pau
Tarbes
Carcassonne
Narbonne
Aude
Petites Pyrénées
Pyrénées
1632
Puerto Somport
Pico de Aneto
3404
ANDORRA LA VELLA
ANDORRA
Perpignan
Golfe du Lion
Col de Perthus
Cabo
2647
Sierra del Cadí
Rías Altas
Cabo Ortegal
La Coruña
(Corunna)
El Ferrol del Caudillo
Costa Verde
Avilés
Gijón
Santander
Cabo de Ajo
Portugalete
Cabo de Finisterre
Carballo
Oviedo
Pola de Siero
Torrelavega
Santiago de Compostela
Navia
Asturias
Mieres
Baracaldo
Basauri
San Sebastián
Villagarcía de Arosa
Lugo
Cordillera Cantábrica
(Cantabrian Mts.)
Bilbao
Rías Bajas
Pontevedra
Galicia
La Estrada
Embalse del Ebro
Vitoria
Pamplona
Vigo
Orense
Ponferrada
2188
Ebro
Miranda de Ebro
Navarra
Minho
Sierra de la Cabrera
León
Burgos
Logroño
La Rioja
La Ribera
Póvoa de Varzim
Braga
Chaves
Serra do Mogadouro
Tierra del Pan
Tierra de Campos
Castilla la Vieja
Palencia
2305
Sistema Ibérico
Huesca
Matozinhos
Serra do Marão
1415
Bragança
Cataluña
Porto
(Oporto)
Zamora
Valladolid
1140
Soria
Aragón
Alagón
Cinca
Gerona
Vila Nova de Gaia
Douro
Embalse de Almendra
Duero
Zaragoza
Lérida
Manresa
PORTUGAL
Salamanca
Eresma
Duratón
Calatayud
Jalón
Sabadell
Badalona
Segovia
Coimbra
1991
Serra da Estrela
Guarda
Ciudad-Rodrigo
Puerto de Villatoro
1356
Ávila
1511
Sierra de Guadarrama
2430
Alcolea del Pinar
Embalse de Mequinenza
Villanueva-y-Geltrú
Reus
Tarrasa
Barcelona
Hospitalet
Tarragona
Costa Dorada
Sierra de Gata
2291
Serrota
El Escorial
Guadalajara
Monreal del Campo
1259
Ebro
Tortosa
Nazaré
Batalha
Zêzere
1910
2592
Sierra de Gredos
Leganés
Alcalá
MADRID
Sierra de Gúdar
2204
El Maestrazgo
Plasencia
Getafe
Castilla
Montes Universales
Costa del Azahar
Estremadura
Tejo
Abrantes
Embalse de Alcántara
624
Talavera de la Reina
Toledo
Aranjuez
Cuenca
2020
Castellón
Tajo
Cáceres
Castelo de Vide
Alto-Alentejo
SPAIN
(ESPAÑA)
La Nueva
Vall de Uxó
Sagunto
LISBOA
(LISBON)
Guadalupe
Montes de Toledo
Alcázar de San Juan
Villarreal de los Infantes
Islas Baleares
(Balearic Islands)
(Spain)
Cabo de Formentor
Pollensa
1445
Almada
Barreiro
Elvas
Mérida
Guadiana
Campo de Calatrava
900
Torrente
Valencia
Golfo de Valencia
Palma
Baía de Setúbal
Setúbal
Évora
Badajoz
Extremadura
Don Benito
La Serena
Tomelloso
La Mancha
Júcar
Alcira
Mallorca
Cabrera
Zújar
Valdepeñas
Puertollano
Albacete
Gandía
Ibiza
Baixo-Alentejo
Santiago do Cacém
Beja
Barragem da Rocha de Galé
Sierra Morena
Santa Cruz de Mudela
Sierra de Alcaraz
Villena
Alcoy
Cabo de la Nao
Benidorm
Formentera
Serpa
Sierra de Aracena
Córdoba
Guadalquivir
Linares
Segura
Cieza
Elda
Elche
Alicante
Andalucía
Andújar
Ubeda
Orihuela
Costa Blanca
Sagres
Algarve
Faro
Sevilla
Écija
Jaén
Murcia
Cabo de São Vicente
Golfo de Cádiz
Cabo de Santa Maria
Huelva
Alcalá
Lucena
Sistemas Béticos
Lorca
Guardal
Cabo de Palos
Sanlúcar de Barrameda
Utrera
Morón
Puente-Genil
Granada
Cartagena
El Puerto de Santa María
Arcos
Antequera
865
Mulhacén
3478
Sierra Nevada
Vera
Mediterranean
Cádiz
Jerez de la Frontera
Vélez-Málaga
Costa Blanca
Costa de la Luz
Cabo Trafalgar
San Fernando
Ronda
Málaga
Motril
Almería
AL JAZĀ'IR
(ALGIERS)
Marbella
Costa del Sol
Cabo de Gata
Algeciras
La Línea
Gibraltar (U.K.)
Estrecho de Gibraltar
(Str. of Gibraltar)
1700
Ténès
Cherchell
Tanger
Punta Almina
Ceuta (Sp.)
Alborán
(Spain)
Ech Cheliff
Cheliff
Blida
Khemis Miliana
Tétouan

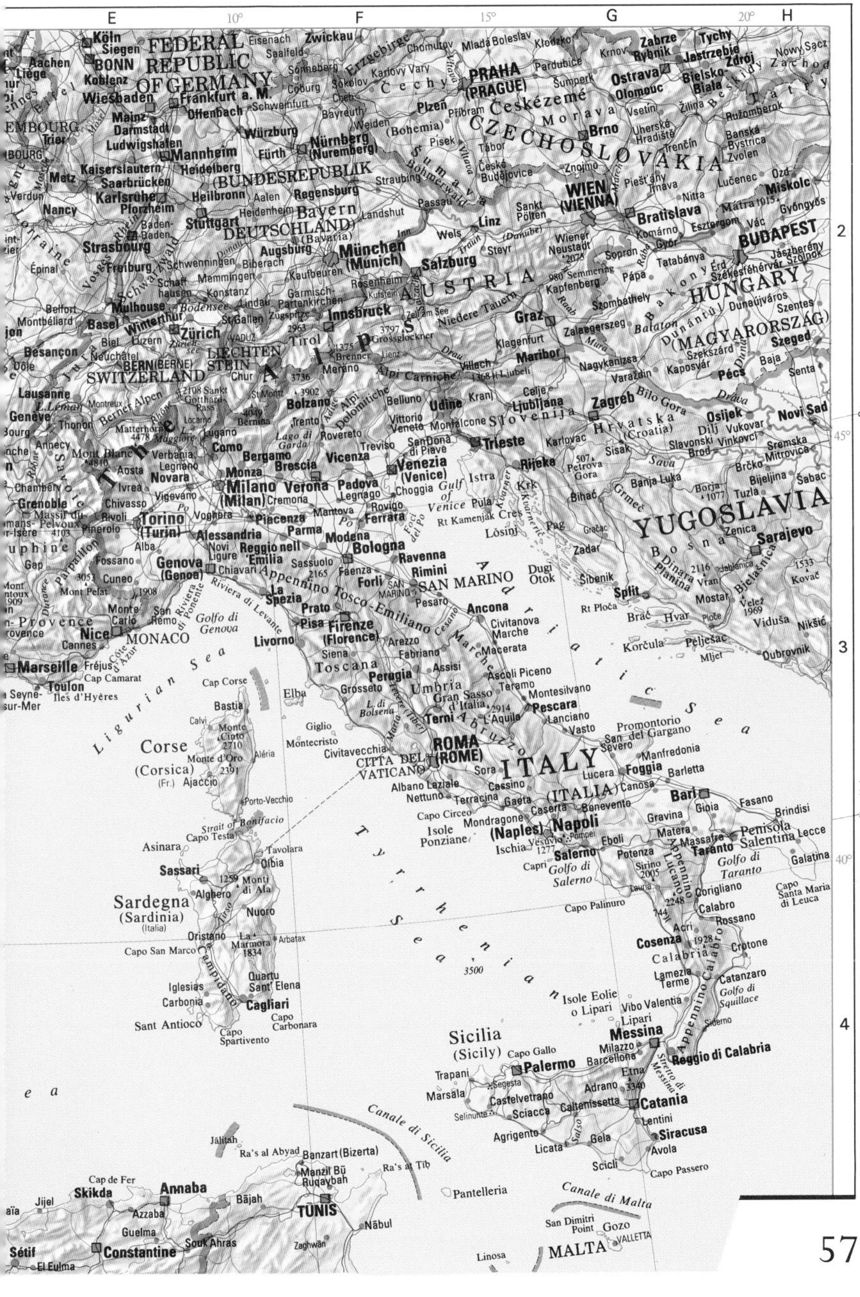
E
F
G
H
10°
15°
20°
2
3
4
45°
40°
Ottava
New York
FEDERAL REPUBLIC OF GERMANY
(BUNDESREPUBLIK DEUTSCHLAND)
Köln
Siegen
BONN
Aachen
Liège
Koblenz
Wiesbaden
Frankfurt a. M.
Offenbach
Mainz
Darmstadt
Trier
Ludwigshafen
Mannheim
Heidelberg
Kaiserslautern
Saarbrücken
Metz
Karlsruhe
Heilbronn
Nancy
Pforzheim
Stuttgart
Baden-Baden
Strasbourg
Freiburg
Épinal
Mulhouse
Belfort
Montbéliard
Basel
Besançon
Eisenach
Saalfeld
Zwickau
Erzgebirge
Sonneberg
Coburg
Schweinfurt
Würzburg
Fürth
Nürnberg
(Nuremberg)
Bayreuth
Weiden
Regensburg
Aalen
Heidenheim
Bayern
(Bavaria)
Landshut
Augsburg
München
(Munich)
Schwenningen
Biberach
Memmingen
Kaufbeuren
Rosenheim
Konstanz
Lindau
Bodensee
Garmisch-Partenkirchen
Kufstein
Zugspitze
Winterthur
Zürich
St. Gallen
LIECHTENSTEIN
VADUZ
BERN (BERNE)
SWITZERLAND
Luzern
Biel
Neuchâtel
Chur
Lausanne
Genève
Thonon
Annecy
Montreux
Berner Alpen
Matterhorn 4478
Mont Blanc 4810
Sankt Gotthard-Pass
St. Moritz
Bernina 4049
Lugano
Locarno
Como
Maggiore
Bergamo
Brescia
Monza
Milano
(Milan)
Verona
Vicenza
Padova
Venezia
(Venice)
Treviso
San Donà di Piave
Trento
Rovereto
Lago di Garda
Bolzano
Merano
Innsbruck
Tirol
Brenner 1375
Grossglockner 3797
Zell am See
Salzburg
AUSTRIA
Linz
Wels
Steyr
Passau
Sankt Pölten
WIEN (VIENNA)
Wiener Neustadt
Semmering 980
Kapfenberg
Graz
Klagenfurt
Villach
Maribor
Niedere Tauern
Drau
Alpi Carniche
Alpi Dolomitiche
Belluno
Udine
Vittorio Veneto
Monfalcone
Trieste
Ljubljana
Celje
Kranj
Slovenija
THE ALPS
Savoie
Chambéry
Grenoble
Aosta
Ivrea
Novara
Vigevano
Verbania
Legnano
Chivasso
Rivoli
Torino
(Turin)
Pinerolo
Massif du Pelvoux 4103
Alba
Alessandria
Voghera
Piacenza
Cremona
Mantova
Legnago
Rovigo
Ferrara
Chioggia
Parma
Reggio nell'Emilia
Modena
Bologna
Ravenna
Rimini
SAN MARINO
Forlì
Faenza
Sassuolo
Novi Ligure
Genova
(Genoa)
Chiavari
La Spezia
Fossano
Cuneo
Gap
Mont Pelat
Durance
Provence
Nice
MONACO
Cannes
Sanremo
Monte Carlo
Côte d'Azur
Riviera di Ponente
Riviera di Levante
Golfo di Genova
Marseille
Fréjus
Toulon
Cap Camarat
Îles d'Hyères
Ligurian Sea
Appennino Tosco-Emiliano
Prato
Pisa
Firenze
(Florence)
Livorno
Arezzo
Siena
Toscana
Fabriano
Perugia
Assisi
Umbria
Grosseto
Pesaro
Ancona
Civitanova Marche
Macerata
Marche
Ascoli Piceno
Teramo
Montesilvano
Pescara
Gran Sasso d'Italia 2914
L'Aquila
Abruzzo
Terni
Lanciano
Vasto
L. di Bolsena
Tevere (Tiber)
Elba
Cap Corse
Bastia
Calvi
Monte Cinto 2710
Corse
(Corsica)
(Fr.)
Monte d'Oro 2391
Aléria
Ajaccio
Porto-Vecchio
Strait of Bonifacio
Giglio
Montecristo
Civitavecchia
CITTÀ DEL VATICANO
ROMA
(ROME)
Albano Laziale
Nettuno
Sora
Cassino
Terracina
Gaeta
Capo Circeo
Isole Ponziane
Mondragone
Caserta
Benevento
ITALY
(ITALIA)
Napoli
(Naples)
Ischia
Vesuvio 1277
Pompei
Capri
Salerno
Golfo di Salerno
Eboli
Potenza
Lucera
Foggia
Canosa
Manfredonia
Barletta
Promontorio del Gargano
San Severo
Bari
Gioia
Fasano
Gravina
Matera
Massafra
Taranto
Brindisi
Penisola Salentina
Lecce
Galatina
Golfo di Taranto
Capo Santa Maria di Leuca
Appennino Lucano
Sirino 2005
Capo Palinuro
Corigliano
Calabro
Rossano
Acri
Cosenza
Crotone
Calabria
Lamezia Terme
Catanzaro
Golfo di Squillace
Vibo Valentia
Isole Eolie o Lipari
Lipari
Messina
Stretto di Messina
Reggio di Calabria
Sicilia
(Sicily)
Capo Gallo
Palermo
Trapani
Segesta
Marsala
Castelvetrano
Selinunte
Sciacca
Agrigento
Caltanissetta
Licata
Gela
Adrano
Etna 3340
Catania
Lentini
Siracusa
Avola
Scicli
Capo Passero
Milazzo
Barcellona
Tyrrhenian Sea
3500
Asinara
Capo Testa
Tavolara
Olbia
Sassari
Monti di Alà
Alghero
Nuoro
Sardegna
(Sardinia)
(Italia)
Oristano
La Marmora 1834
Arbatax
Capo San Marco
Campidano
Iglesias
Carbonia
Quartu Sant' Elena
Cagliari
Capo Carbonara
Sant Antioco
Capo Spartivento
Canale di Sicilia
Pantelleria
Canale di Malta
Linosa
Gozo
MALTA
VALLETTA
San Dimitri Point
Jalitah
Ra's al Abyad
Banzart (Bizerta)
Ra's at Tib
Manzil Bū Ruqaybah
Cap de Fer
Skikda
Annaba
Jijel
Bājah
TŪNIS
Azzaba
Guelma
Nābul
Zaghwān
Sétif
El Eulma
Constantine
Souk Ahras
Čechy
Plzeň
(Bohemia)
Příbram
Písek
Tábor
České Budějovice
Šumava
Böhmerwald
Vltava
PRAHA
(PRAGUE)
Chomutov
Mladá Boleslav
Karlovy Vary
Sokolov
Cheb
Pardubice
Kłodzko
Šumperk
České zemé
Morava
CZECHOSLOVAKIA
Brno
Znojmo
Krnov
Zabrze
Rybnik
Tychy
Jastrzębie Zdrój
Bielsko-Biała
Nowy Sącz
Ostrava
Olomouc
Vsetín
Uherské Hradiště
Žilina
Ružomberok
Trenčín
Banská Bystrica
Zvolen
Piešťany
Trnava
Nitra
Lučenec
Ózd
Miskolc
Bratislava
Komárno
Esztergom
Mátra 1015
Gyöngyös
Vác
BUDAPEST
Jászberény
Szolnok
Győr
Sopron
Tatabánya
Pápa
Bakony
Érd
Székesfehérvár
HUNGARY
(MAGYARORSZÁG)
Dunaújváros
Szentes
Szombathely
Zalaegerszeg
Balaton
Dunántúl
Szekszárd
Szeged
Nagykanizsa
Kaposvár
Baja
Pécs
Senta
Varaždin
Drava
Zagreb
Bilo Gora
Hrvatska
(Croatia)
Osijek
Novi Sad
Vukovar
Vinkovci
Slavonski Brod
Sremska Mitrovica
Karlovac
Sisak
Sava
Rijeka
Krk
Istra
Pula
Kvarner
Cres
Lošinj
Pag
Petrova Gora 507
Bihać
Banja Luka
Brčko
Bijeljina
Šabac
Tuzla
Zenica
Sarajevo
YUGOSLAVIA
Bosna
Gračac
Zadar
Dugi Otok
Šibenik
Dinara Planina
2116
Split
Brač
Hvar
Mostar
Jablanica
Vran
Bjelašnica
Kovač 1533
Velež 1969
Nikšić
Korčula
Pelješac
Mljet
Dubrovnik
Ploče
Vidusa
Rt Ploča
Rt Kamenjak
Gulf of Venice
Foci del Po
Adriatic Sea

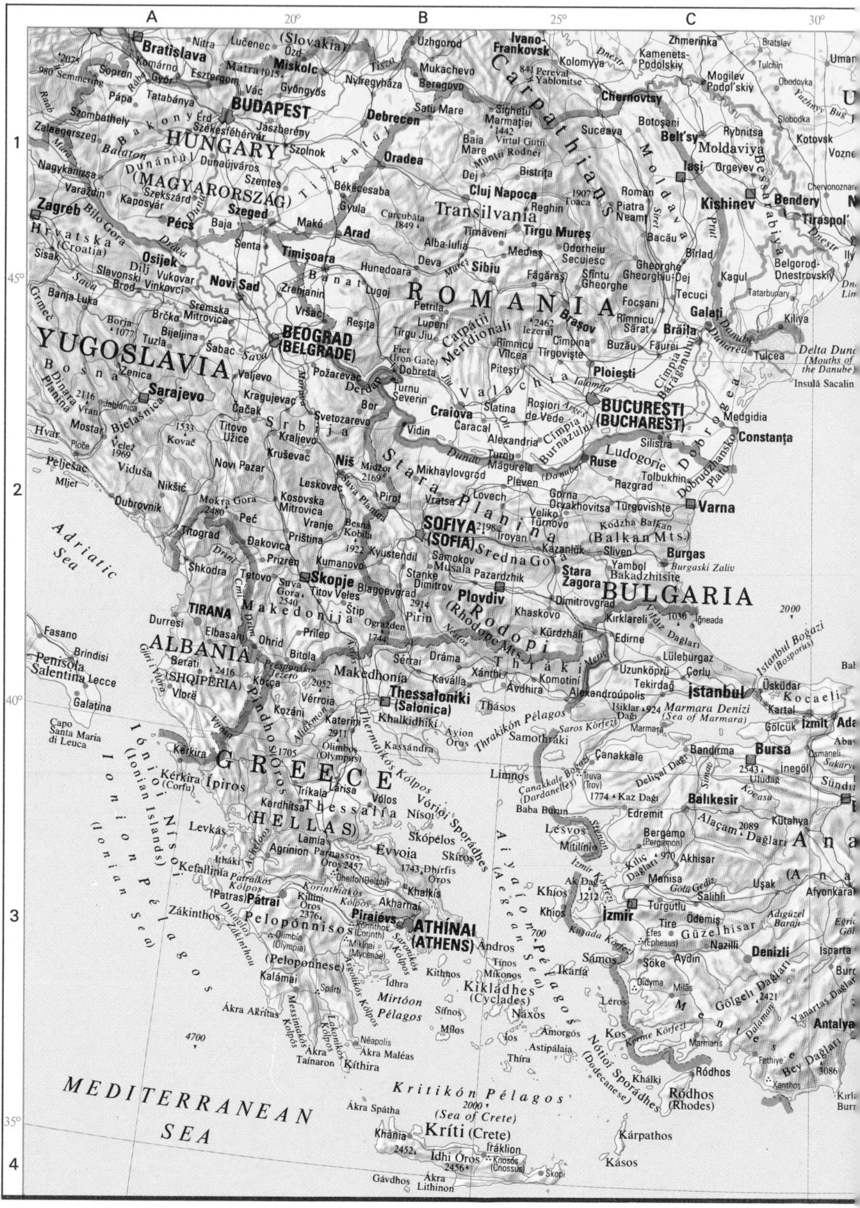
A
B
C
20°
25°
30°
45°
40°
35°
1
2
3
4
Bratislava
Nitra
Lučenec
(Slovakia)
Ózd
Miskolc
Uzhgorod
Ivano-Frankovsk
Zhmerinka
Kamenets-Podolskiy
Bratslav
Tulchin
Uman
Sopron
Komárno
Győr
Esztergom
Mátra 1015
Vác
Gyöngyös
Tisza
Nyíregyháza
Mukachevo
Beregovo
Kolomyya
Dnestr
Pereval Yablonitse
Mogilev Podol'skiy
Obodovka
Semmering
Pápa
Tatabánya
BUDAPEST
Debrecen
Satu Mare
Sighetu Marmaţiei
Chernovtsy
Szombathely
Bakony
Érd
Székesfehérvár
Jászberény
Botoşani
Rybnitsa
Slobodka
Zalaegerszeg
HUNGARY
Szolnok
Oradea
Baia Mare
Virtul Gutii
Munţii Rodnei
Suceava
Bel'tsy
Moldaviya
Kotovsk
Balaton
Dunántúl
Dunaújváros
(MAGYARORSZÁG)
Tiszántúl
Bistriţa
Iaşi
Orgeyev
Nagykanizsa
Szentes
Békéscsaba
Dej
Cluj Napoca
Carpathians
Moldava
Bessarabiya
Varaždin
Szekszárd
Kaposvár
Szeged
Gyula
Curcubăta 1849
Transilvania
Toaca
Reghin
Roman
Piatra Neamţ
Kishinev
Bendery
Tiraspol'
Zagreb
Bilo Gora
Pécs
Baja
Makó
Arad
Tîrnăveni
Tîrgu Mureş
Siret
Prut
Hrvatska (Croatia)
Drava
Senta
Alba Iulia
Mediaş
Odorheiu Secuiesc
Bacău
Bîrlad
Sisak
Osijek
Timişoara
Hunedoara
Deva
Mureş
Sibiu
Făgăraş
Sfîntu Gheorghe
Gheorghe Gheorghiu-Dej
Belgorod-Dnestrovskiy
Slavonski Brod
Dilj
Vukovar
Vinkovci
Novi Sad
Banat
Lugoj
Kagul
Sava
Zrenjanin
ROMANIA
Tecuci
Tatarbunary
Banja Luka
Sremska Mitrovica
Vršac
Petrila
Focşani
Galaţi
Kiliya
Borja 1077
Brčko
Bijeljina
BEOGRAD (BELGRADE)
Reşiţa
Lupeni
Carpaţii Meridionali
Iezerul
Braşov
Rîmnicu Sărat
Brăila
Danube
YUGOSLAVIA
Tuzla
Šabac
Tîrgu Jiu
Rîmnicu Vîlcea
Cîmpina
Tîrgovişte
Buzău
Făurei
Dunărea
Tulcea
Delta Dunării (Mouths of the Danube)
Bosna
Zenica
Valjevo
Fier (Iron Gate)
Dobreta
Piteşti
Ploieşti
Insulă Sacalin
Dinara Planina
Sarajevo
Kragujevac
Požarevac
Morava
Derdap
Turnu Severin
Jiu
Valachia
Ialomiţa
Cîmpia Bărăganului
Vran
Jablanica
Bjelašnica
Čačak
Bor
Craiova
Slatina
Olt
Roşiori de Vede
BUCUREŞTI (BUCHAREST)
Dobrogea
Medgidia
Mostar
Titovo Užice
Srbija
Svetozarevo
Caracal
Alexandria
Argeş
Cîmpia Burnazului
Hvar
Ploče
Velež 1969
Kovač
Kraljevo
Vidin
Silistra
Constanţa
Pelješac
Kruševac
Niš
Turnu Măgurele
Dunav
Ruse
Ludogorie
Dobrudzhansko Plato
Mljet
Viduša
Novi Pazar
Midžor 2169
Mikhaylovgrad
Pleven
Tolbukhin
Razgrad
Nikšić
Leskovac
Stara Planina
Lovech
Gorna Oryakhovitsa
Varna
Dubrovnik
Mokra Gora 2480
Kosovska Mitrovica
Suva Planina
Pirot
Vratsa
Veliko Tŭrnovo
Tŭrgovishte
Adriatic Sea
Titograd
Peć
Vranje
Besna Kobila
SOFIYA (SOFIA)
Troyan
Kodzha Balkan
(Balkan Mts.)
Priština
Sredna Gora
Kazanlŭk
Sliven
Burgas
Drini
Đakovica
Prizren
Kyustendil
Samokov
Musala
Yambol
Burgaski Zaliv
Shkodra
Kumanovo
Stanke Dimitrov
Pazardzhik
Stara Zagora
Bakadzhitsite
Tetovo
Skopje
Suva Gora 2540
Titov Veles
Blagoevgrad
Plovdiv
BULGARIA
TIRANA
Makedonija
Štip
Pirin
Rodopi (Rhodope Mts.)
Dimitrovgrad
Khaskovo
Kirklareli
Iğneada
2000
Durresi
Elbasani
Ohrid
Prilep
Ograzhden
Kŭrdzhali
Yıldız Dağları
Fasano
ALBANIA
Bitola
Nestos
Edirne
İstanbul Boğazi (Bosporus)
Brindisi
Berati
Prespansko Jezero
Sérrai
Dráma
Thráki
Lüleburgaz
Penisola Salentina
Lecce
(SHQIPERIA)
Korça
Makedhonía
Xánthi
Komotiní
Uzunköprü
Çorlu
Üsküdar
Vlorë
Pindhos Óros
Vérroia
Thessaloniki (Salonica)
Kavála
Ávdhira
Aléxandroúpolis
Tekirdağ
İstanbul
Kocaeli
Galatina
Kozáni
Kateríni
Khalkidhikí
Thásos
Evros
İşiklar 924 Dağı
Marmara Denizi (Sea of Marmara)
Kartal
İzmit
Capo Santa Maria di Leuca
Vijosë
Aliákmon
Thermaïkós Kólpos
Áyion Óros
Thrakikón Pélagos
Saros Körfezi
Samothráki
Marmara
Gölcük
Kérkira
Ólimbos (Olympus)
Kassándra
Çanakkale
Bandırma
Bursa
GREECE
Límnos
Çanakkale Boğazi (Dardanelles)
Truva (Troy)
Delicai Dağı
Uludağ
İnegöl
Kérkira (Corfu)
Ípiros
Tríkala
Lárisa
Vólos
Kaz Dağı
Balıkesir
Ionioi Nísoi (Ionian Islands)
Kardhítsa
Thessalía
Vórioi Sporádhes
Baba Burnu
Edremit
Kocasu
Kütahya
HELLAS
Nísoi
Lésvos
Alaçam Dağları
Levkás
Lamía
Skópelos
Mitilíni
Bergamo (Pergamon)
Agrínion
Parnassós Óros 2457
Evvoia
Skíros
Aiyaíon Pélagos (Aegean Sea)
Kılıç Dağları
Akhisar
Ithákí
Dhírfis Óros
İzmir Körfezi
Kefallinía
Patraikós Kólpos
Dhelfoi (Delphi)
Ak Dağ
Manisa
Gölü Gediz
Salihli
Uşak
Afyonkarahisar
Pátrai
Korinthiakós Kólpos
Khalkís
Khíos
Izmir
Turgutlu
Ionion Pélagos (Ionian Sea)
Zákinthos
Killini Óros
Akharnaí
Ödemiş
Adıgüzel Barajı
Pelopónnisos
Piraiévs
ATHÍNAI (ATHENS)
Efes (Ephesus)
Tire
Güzelhisar
Dhiavlos Zákinthou
Olimbía (Olympia)
Kórinthos (Corinth)
Mikínai (Mycenae)
Saronikós Kólpos
Ándros
Kuşada Körfezi
Nazilli
Denizli
Isparta
Argolikós Kólpos
Tínos
Sámos
Ikaría
Söke
Aydın
(Peloponnese)
Míkonos
Kíthnos
Kalámai
Spárti
Ídhra
Kikládhes (Cyclades)
Didyma
Milâs
Gölgeli Dağları
Mirtóon Pélagos
Léros
Mentese
Ákra Akritas
Messiniakós Kólpos
Lakonikós Kólpos
Sífnos
Náxos
Dalaman
Mílos
Amorgós
Nótioi Sporádhes (Dodecanese)
Kos
Kerme Körfezi
Antalya
4700
Néapolis
Ákra Maléas
Íos
Astipálaia
Marmaris
Ákra Taínaron
Kíthira
Thíra
Fethiye
Bey Dağları
Ródhos
Xanthos
MEDITERRANEAN SEA
Kritikón Pélagos
Khálki
Ródhos (Rhodes)
Ákra Spátha
2000
(Sea of Crete)
Khaniá
Kríti (Crete)
Kárpathos
Iráklion
Idhi Óros
Knosós (Cnossus)
Kásos
Gávdhos
Ákra Líthinon
Skopi

Scale 1:10 000 000

0 100 200 300 400 500 km

0 100 200 300 miles

1/2 hour

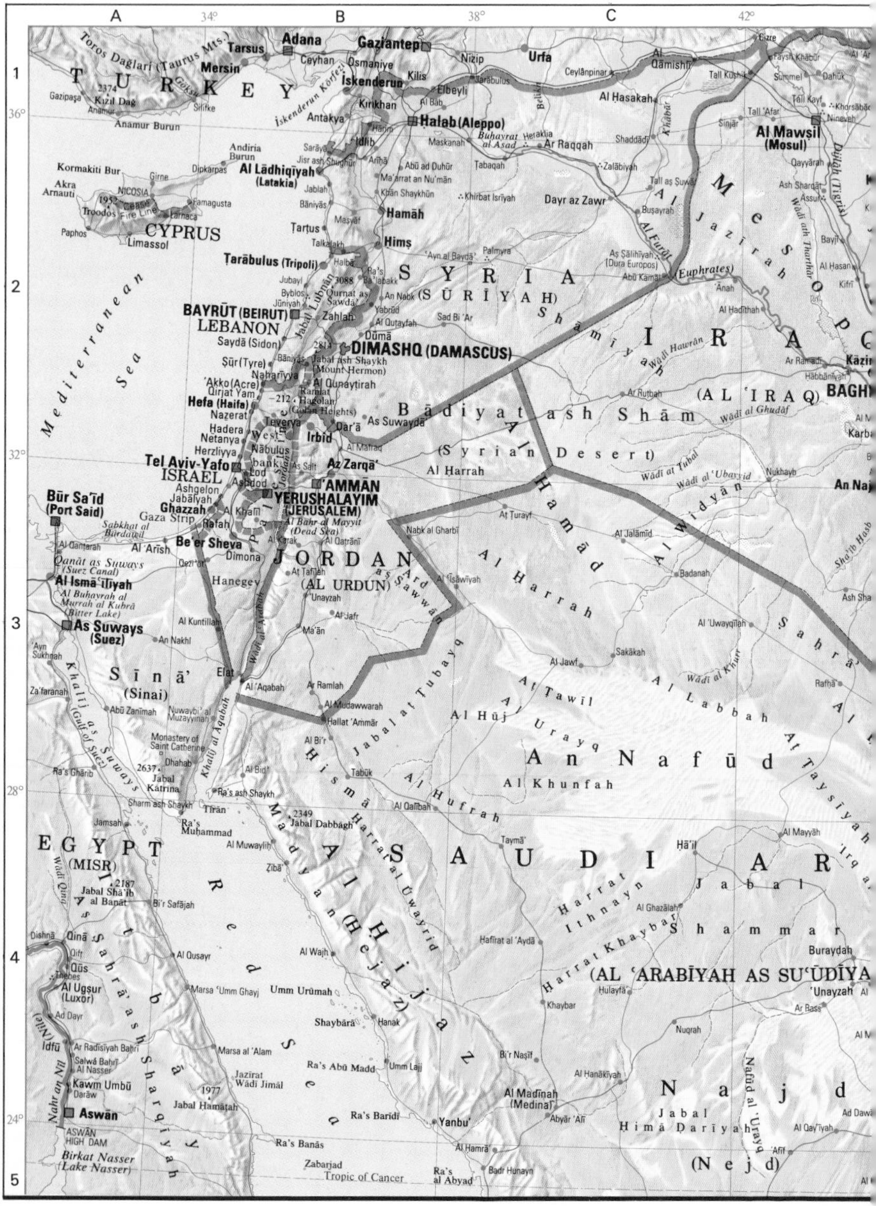
A
B
C
34°
38°
42°
36°
32°
28°
24°
1
2
3
4
5
TURKEY
Toros Dağlari (Taurus Mts.)
Tarsus
Adana
Gaziantep
Mersin
Ceyhan
Osmaniye
İskenderun
İskenderun Körfezi
Kilis
Nizip
Urfa
Ceylânpinar
Al Qāmishlī
Cizre
Fayşh Khābūr
Tall Kūshik
Summel
Dahūk
Tall Kayf
Khorsābād
Nineveh
Tall 'Afar
Sinjār
Al Mawşil (Mosul)
Qayyārah
Ash Sharqāţ
Āssur
Dijlah (Tigris)
Wādī ath Tharthār
Bayjī
Al Ḩasan
Kifrī
Gazipaşa
2374
Kızıl Dağ
Anamur
Silifke
Göksu
Anamur Burun
Elbeyli
Ţarābulus
Al Bāb
Kırıkhan
Antakya
Ḩalab (Aleppo)
Ḩārim
Idlib
Sarāyā
Jisr ash Shughūr
Arīḩā
Abū ad Duḩūr
Maskanah
Buḩayrat al Asad
Heraklia
Ar Raqqah
Balīkh
Al Ḩasakah
Khābūr
Shaddādī
Zalābiyah
Ţabaqah
Andiria Burun
Kormakiti Bur
Akra Arnauti
Girne
Dipkarpas
Al Lādhiqīyah (Latakia)
Jablah
Ma'arrat an Nu'mān
Khān Shaykhūn
Khirbat Isrīyah
Dayr az Zawr
Tall aş Şuwar
Buşayrah
Al Furāt
NICOSIA
1952
Cease Fire Line
Larnaca
Famagusta
Troodos
Paphos
CYPRUS
Limassol
Bāniyās
Maşyāf
Ḩamāh
Ţarţūs
Talkalakh
Ḩimş
Palmyra
'Ayn al Bayḑā'
Aş Şāliḩīyah (Dura Europos)
Abū Kamāl
Euphrates
'Ānah
Al Ḩadīthah
Ţarābulus (Tripoli)
Ḩalbā
Ra's Ba'labakk
Jubayl
Byblos
Jūniyah
3088
Qurnat as Sawdā'
Jabal Lubnān
SYRIA
(SŪRĪYAH)
An Nabk
Yabrūd
Al Quţayfah
Sad Bi 'Ar
Shāmīyah
Wādī Ḩawrān
BAYRŪT (BEIRUT)
LEBANON
Zaḩlah
Dūmā
Saydā (Sidon)
2814
DIMASHQ (DAMASCUS)
Şūr (Tyre)
Bāniyās
Jabal ash Shaykh (Mount Hermon)
Nahariyya
'Akko (Acre)
Qiryat Yam
Al Qunayţirah
Hefa (Haifa)
-212
Ramlat Hagolan (Golan Heights)
Nazerat
Teverya
As Suwaydā'
Dar'ā
Hadera
Netanya
West
Irbid
Al Mafraq
Herzliyya
Nābulus
bank
Jordan
Tel Aviv-Yafo
Lod
As Salt
Az Zarqā'
ISRAEL
Ashdod
'AMMĀN
Ashqelon
YERUSHALAYIM (JERUSALEM)
Jabālyah
Ghazzah
Gaza Strip
Al Khalīl
Rafah
Al Baḩr al Mayyit (Dead Sea)
Be'er Sheva
Al Karak
Al Qaţrānī
Dimona
JORDAN
(AL URDUN)
Aţ Ţafīlah
Ard aş Şawwān
'Unayzah
Al Jafr
Ma'ān
Hanegev
Wādī al 'Arabah
Al Kuntillah
An Nakhl
Elat
Al 'Aqabah
Ar Ramlah
Al Mudawwarah
Ḩallat 'Ammār
Jabal aţ Ţubayq
Al Bi'r
Ḩismā
Tabūk
Al Bid'
Ra's ash Shaykh
Tīrān
Būr Sa'īd (Port Said)
Sabkhat al Bardawīl
Al Qanţarah
Al 'Arīsh
Quşaymah
Qanāt as Suways (Suez Canal)
Al Ismā'īlīyah
Al Buḩayrah al Murrah al Kubrá (Bitter Lake)
As Suways (Suez)
'Ayn Sukhnah
Khalīj as Suways (Gulf of Suez)
Sīnā' (Sinai)
Za'farānah
Abū Zanīmah
Nuwaybi' al Muzayyinah
Monastery of Saint Catherine
2637
Jabal Kātrīnā
Dhahab
Khalīj al 'Aqabah
Ra's Ghārib
Sharm ash Shaykh
Ra's Muḩammad
Jamsah
Al Muwaylīḩ
EGYPT
(MISR)
Wādī Qinā
2187
Jabal Shā'ib al Banāt
Būr Safājah
Aş Şaḩrā' ash Sharqīyah
Dishnā
Qinā
Qifţ
Qūş
Thebes
Al Uqşur (Luxor)
Ad Dayr
Nahr an Nīl (Nile)
Idfū
Ar Radīsīyah Baḩrī
Salwá Baḩrī
Al Nasser
Kawm Umbū
Darāw
Aswān
ASWĀN HIGH DAM
Birkat Nasser (Lake Nasser)
Al Quşayr
Marsa 'Umm Ghayj
Marsa al 'Alam
Jazīrat Wādī Jimāl
1977
Jabal Ḩamāţah
Red Sea
Ḑibā
2349
Jabal Dabbāgh
Madyan
Al Ḩijāz (Hejaz)
Ḩarrat al 'Uwayrid
Al Wajh
Umm Urūmah
Shaybārā
Hanak
Ra's Abū Madd
Umm Lajj
Ra's Barīdī
Yanbu'
Ra's Banās
Zabarjad
Tropic of Cancer
Ra's al Abyaḑ
Al Ḩamrā'
Badr Ḩunayn
Ar Ruţbah
Bādiyat ash Shām
(Syrian Desert)
Al Ḩamād
Al Ḩarrah
Al Widyān
Wādī al Ghudāf
Wādī aţ Ţubal
Wādī al 'Ubayyid
Nukhayb
Aţ Ţurayf
Nabk al Gharbī
Al Jalāmīd
Badanah
Al 'Īsāwīyah
Al 'Uwayqīlah
Sakākah
Al Jawf
Wādī al Khurr
Aţ Ţawīl
Al Ḩūj
Al 'Urayq
An Nafūd
Al Khunfah
Al Ḩufrah
Al Qalībah
Taymā'
Ḩā'il
Al Labbah
Aţ Taysīyah
Al Mayyāh
SAUDI ARABIA
Jabal Shammar
Ḩarrat Ithnayn
Al Ghazālah
Ḩarrat Khaybar
Ḩafīrat al 'Aydā
(AL 'ARABĪYAH AS SU'ŪDĪYA
Ḩulayfā'
Khaybar
'Unayzah
Ar Rass
Buraydah
Nuqrah
Bi'r Naşīf
Al Ḩanākīyah
Al Madīnah (Medina)
Abyār 'Alī
Najd
Jabal Ḩimā Ḑarīyah
Nafūd al 'Urayq
'Afīf
(Nejd)
Ad Dawā
Al Qay'īyah
IRAQ
(AL 'IRAQ)
Mesopotamia
Al Jazīrah
Ar Ramādī
Ḩabbānīyah
Kāzimīyah
BAGHDAD
Karbalā'
An Najaf
Sha'īb Ḩasb
Ash Shabakah
Rafḩā
Şaḩrā' al Ḩijārah
Mediterranean Sea

Scale 1:10 000 0

46°
E
50°
F
54°
G
1
2
3
4
5
38°
32°
28°
24°
Caspian Sea
Rasht
Lāhījān
Mīaneh
Darvācheh-ye Orūmīyeh
Miāndowāb
Mahābād
Sā'īn Dezh
3285
Bandar Shāh
Zanjān
Nīkpey
Qezel Owzan
Khamseh
Manjil
Sakht Sar
Tonekābon
Chālūs
4805 Takht-e Soleimān
Mahmūdābād
Babol Sar
Bābol
Behshahr
Kord Kūy
Gorgān (Gurgān)
Āzādshahr
Meyāmey
Dāvarzan
Sad Kharv
Abbāsābād
Kavīr-e Namak
Emāmrūd
Qā'emshahr
Āmol
Now Shahr
Reshteh-ye Kūhhā-ye Alborz (Elburz Mts.)
Qazvīn
Gardaneh-ye Kandovān
3000
Qolleh-ye Damāvand (Mt Demavend)
5671
Dāmghān
Shahmīrzād
Dazjā
Ebrāhīm
Saqqez
Takāb
Abhar
Tākestān
Ābyek
Sar Dasht
Dīvāndarreh
Beyānlū
Nehāvand
Karaj
Tajrīsh
Fīrūz Kūh
Semnān
TEHRĀN
Rey
Torūd
Sorkheh
Garmsar
3171 Kūh-e Khvojeh
Zāgheh-ye Bālā
Gardaneh-ye Āvej
Āvej
2356
Kordestān
Sanandaj
Razan
Kabūd Rāhang
Nowbarān
Zarand
Sāveh
Hājjīābād-e Māsīleh
Kūh-e Gūgerd
Dasht-e Kavīr
Nowdesheh
Dow Sar
Şālehābād
Hamadān
Qom
Darvācheh-ye Namak
Khvor
Ravānsar
Sonqor
3571 Kūh-e Alvand
Sarafjagān
Qasr-e Shīrīn
Kangāvar
Malāyer
Kūh-e 'Alīābād
3356
Germī
Tabas
Qahremānshahr (Kermanshāh)
Nahāvand
Arāk
Kāshān
Eslāmābād
3638
3638
Kūh-e Garrī
Tūreh
Delījān
Bayāzeh
Robāt-e-Khān
Naftshahr
Kūh-e Safīd
Borūjerd
Bād
Posht-e Badam
Khomeyn
Meymeh
Kūh-e Karkas
3896
Ardestān
Ilām
Rāzān
Khorramābād
Aznā
Alīgūdarz
Dasht-e Lūt
Zurbātīyah
Lorestān
Dow Rūd
Oshtorān Kūh
4328
IRAN
(PERSIA)
Kūh-e Sorkh
Godār-e Sorkh
1490
Malāwī
Nā'īn
Kabīr Kūh
Jelow Gīr
Dārān
Homāyūnshahr
Chādegān
4294
Kūh-e Garbosh
Najafābād
Esfahān
Anārak
Kharānaq
Sāqand
Al Kūt
Shaykh Sa'd
Mūsīān
Andīmeshk
Dezfūl
Bābā Heydar
4548
Zard Kūh
Shahr Kord
Bātlāq-e Gāvkhūnī
Ardakān
3197
Kūh-e Kharānaq
Hawr as S'adīyah
Al Hayy
Susa
Shūshtar
Borūjen
Qomsheh
Yazd
Al Kumayt
Sūsangerd
Masjed Soleymān
4297
Kūh-e Kūkalār
Bāfq
Dīwānīyah
Qal'at Sukkar
Al 'Amārah
Khūzestān
Dehdez
3723
Kūh-e Alījūq
Yazd-e Khvāst
Kavīr-e Abarqu
4074
Shīr Kūh
Mehrīz
Rāvar
Qal'at Sālih
Ahvāz
Āsh Shatrah
Rāmhormoz
Kūh-e Dīnār
Ābādeh
Abarqu
Kermānshāhān
Al Khidr
An Nāsirīyah
Al 'Uzayr
Kūh-e Būl
3965
Shams
Anār
Zarand
Al Qurnah
Arabestān
Hoseynīyeh
Ur
Ur Suq ash Shuyūkh
Hawr al Hammār
Khorramshahr (Khurramshahr)
Agha Jārī
4276
Qer Gerd
Deh Bīd
Heydarābād
Rafsanjān
3472
Kūh-e Masāhim
Bandar-e Khomeynī
Behbehān
Kūh-e Khāīz
Al Basrah (Basra)
Shatt al Arab
Ābādān
Khosrowābād
3189
Gach Sārān
Ardakān
Sa'ādatābād
Bāghīn
Jalībah
Safwān
Hendījān
Mashīz
Gardaneh-ye Khāneh Sorkh
2629
Ar Rawdatayn
Qosbeh-ye Nassār
Bandar-e Deylam
Kūh-e Tābask
3219
Persepolis
Darvācheh-ye Tashk
Qulbān Layyah
Al Bahrah
Būbiyān
Ganāveh
Kāzerūn
Shīrāz
Darvācheh-ye Bakhtegān
Sa'īdābād
Bāft
KUWAIT
Al Jahrah
AL KUWAYT (KUWAIT)
As Sālimīyah
Qalīb ash Shuyūkh
Hawallī
Al Fuhayhīl
Bandar-e Rīg
Khārk
Būshehr
Borāzjān
Sarvestān
Qatrūyeh
Tang-e Karam
Neyrīz
Fārs
Kūh-e Khabr
3862
Alīābād
Mīnā' 'Abd Allāh
Mīnā' Sa'ūd
Khvormūj
Fasā
Dārāb
Jahrom
Zagros Mts.
Kūh-hā-ye Zāgros
Wādī al Bātin
Al Qaysūmah
Ad Dibdibah
Ra's al Khafjī
Ra's al Mish'āb
Ra's as Saffānīyah
Kākī
Mand
Gahkom
Jūyom
Kangān
Shīb Kūh
Qotbābād
Lār
Lārestān
Thumāmī
Ra's az Zawr
Abū 'Alī
An Nu'ayrīyah
Ra's-e Nāy Band
Nāy Band
Bastak
Bandar Abbas
Qeshm
Qeshm
ARABIA
As Summān
Khursanīyah
Al Jubayl
Bandar-e Māqām
Lāvān
Lāzeh
Bandar-e Moghūyeh
Bāsa'īdū
Bandar-e Lengeh
Strait of Hormuz
Musandam Pen. (Oman)
Al Artāwīyah
Ash Shumlūl
As Sulb
Al Qatīf
Ad Dammām
BAHRAIN
Al Muharraq
AL MANAMAH (MANAMA)
The Gulf (Persian Gulf)
Qeys
Abū Mūsā (Mubarak)
Al Khasab
Al Khubar
Az Zallāq
Ar Ruways
Al Fuwayrit
Ra's al Khaymah
Dahnā
Al 'Armah
Buqayq
QATAR
Hālūl
Abū al Bukhush
'Umm Qam'ul
'Ajmān
Khawr al Fakkān
'Ushayrah
Al Hasā
Dukhān
AD DAWHAH (DOHA)
Dubayy
Al Fujayrah
Al Mubarraz
Al Hufūf
Dawhat as Salwā
Al Kir'ānah
Az Zarqā'
As Sadr
Al Tuwayq
Al Jubaylah
Khurays
Al Shagra
Salwā
Trucial Coast
Mahdah
AR RIYĀD (RIYADH)
Durmā
Abū Jifān
Sauda Nathīl
Ra's Abū Qumayyis
Dalmā'
ABŪ ZABY (ABU DHABI)
Al Maqtā'
Al 'Ayn
Mushāsh al 'Ashāwī
Tarīf
Ar Ruways
Hafīt
As Salamīyah
Sha'ib Nisāh
Haradh
As Silā'
UNITED ARAB EMIRATES
Az Zāhirah
Al Rayhānī
Ad Dilam
Al Kharj
Al Jāfūrah
Al Manādir
Ad Dafrah
Al Hillah
Tropic of Cancer
Marīyyah
OMAN
'Arādah
Al Majan
Al Jiwā'
100
200
300
400
500 km
100
200
300 miles
1/2 hour

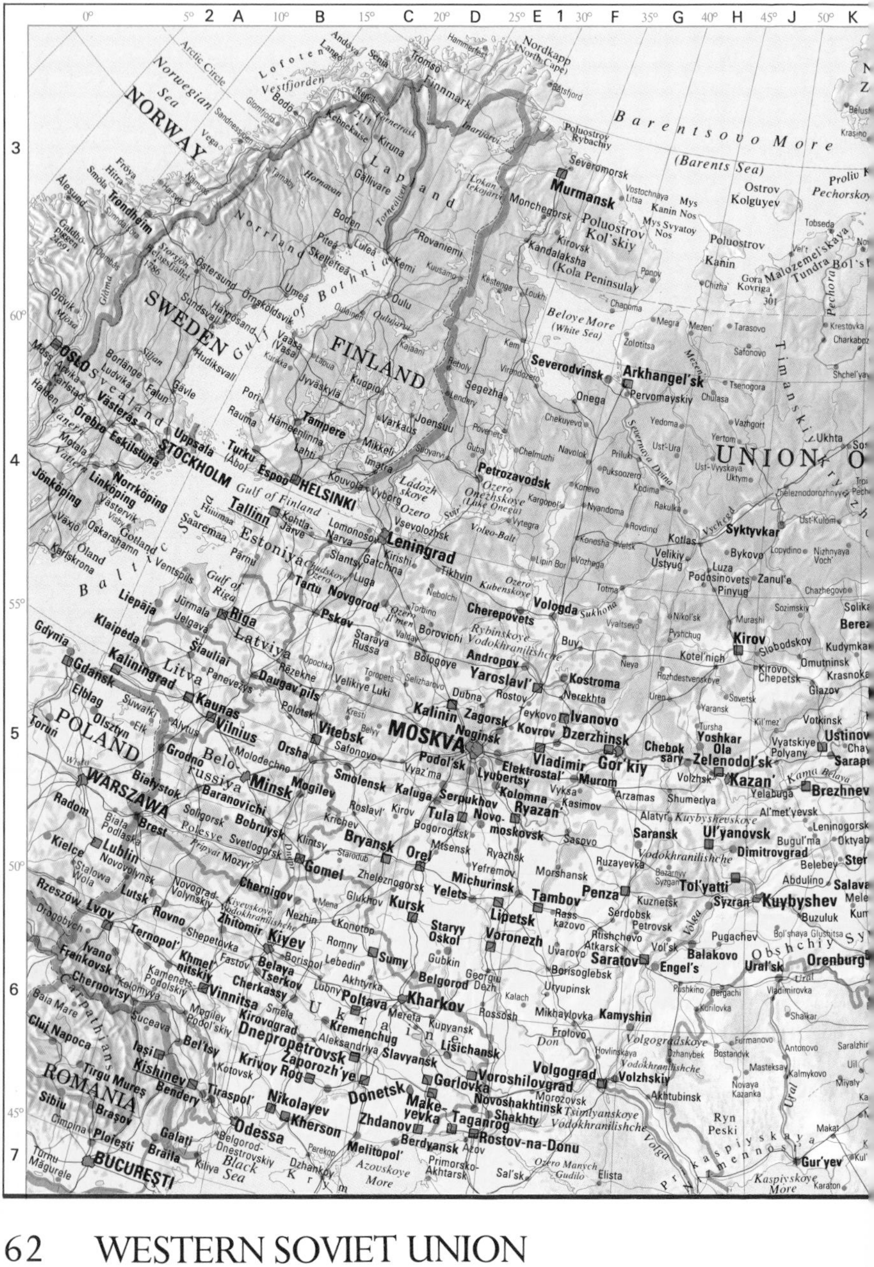
0°
5°
2
A
10°
B
15°
C
20°
D
25°
E
1
30°
F
35°
G
40°
H
45°
J
50°
K
3
4
5
6
7
60°
55°
50°
45°
Arctic Circle
Norwegian Sea
NORWAY
Lofoten
Andøya
Senja
Tromsø
Hammerfest
Nordkapp (North Cape)
Vestfjorden
Bodø
Narvik
Kebnekaise
Kiruna
Finnmark
Båtsfjord
Barentsovo More
(Barents Sea)
Poluostrov Rybachiy
Severomorsk
Murmansk
Lapland
Gällivare
Inarijärvi
Monchegorsk
Poluostrov Kol'skiy
Kirovsk
Kandalaksha
(Kola Peninsula)
Mys Kanin Nos
Mys Svyatoy Nos
Ostrov Kolguyev
Proliv Pechorskoy
Poluostrov Kanin
Gora Kovriga 301
Malozemel'skaya Tundra
Pechora
Trondheim
Ålesund
Galdhøpiggen 2469
Storsjön
Östersund
Örnsköldsvik
Umeå
Skellefteå
Piteå
Luleå
Boden
Kemi
Rovaniemi
Oulu
Gulf of Bothnia
Norrland
SWEDEN
Sundsvall
Härnösand
Vaasa (Vasa)
FINLAND
Kajaani
Kuopio
Jyväskylä
Joensuu
Segezha
Beloye More (White Sea)
Kem
Severodvinsk
Arkhangel'sk
Onega
Pervomayskiy
Mezen'
Timanskiy Kryazh
Ukhta
UNION OF
Gjøvik
OSLO
Hudiksvall
Gävle
Falun
Borlänge
Ludvika
Karlstad
Västerås
Örebro
Eskilstuna
Uppsala
STOCKHOLM
Pori
Rauma
Tampere
Hämeenlinna
Lahti
Mikkeli
Imatra
Varkaus
Turku (Åbo)
Espoo
HELSINKI
Kouvola
Vyborg
Ladozhskoye Ozero
Petrozavodsk
Onezhskoye Ozero (Lake Onega)
Kotlas
Syktyvkar
Velikiy Ustyug
Jönköping
Norrköping
Linköping
Västervik
Växjö
Oskarshamn
Öland
Karlskrona
Gotland
Gulf of Finland
Tallinn
Kohtla-Järve
Narva
Lomonosov
Leningrad
Kirishi
Gatchina
Tikhvin
Vologda
Cherepovets
Baltic Sea
Estoniya
Saaremaa
Hiiumaa
Pärnu
Ventspils
Gulf of Riga
Tartu
Novgorod
Pskov
Rybinskoye Vodokhranilishche
Liepāja
Klaipėda
Riga
Jūrmala
Jelgava
Latviya
Šiauliai
Staraya Russa
Borovichi
Bologoye
Andropov
Yaroslavl'
Kostroma
Kirov
Gdynia
Gdańsk
Kaliningrad
Litva
Panevėžys
Daugavpils
Rēzekne
Velikiye Luki
Dubna
Rostov
Ivanovo
Elbląg
Olsztyn
Kaunas
Vilnius
Polotsk
Vitebsk
Kalinin
Zagorsk
MOSKVA
Noginsk
Kovrov
Dzerzhinsk
Gor'kiy
Cheboksary
Yoshkar Ola
Zelenodol'sk
Kazan'
Toruń
POLAND
Grodno
Belorussiya
Orsha
Molodechno
Minsk
Smolensk
Mogilev
Podol'sk
Elektrostal'
Vladimir
Murom
Lyubertsy
Kolomna
Ryazan'
Arzamas
WARSZAWA
Białystok
Baranovichi
Radom
Bobruysk
Kaluga
Serpukhov
Tula
Novomoskovsk
Saransk
Ul'yanovsk
Dimitrovgrad
Brest
Lublin
Gomel
Bryansk
Orel
Tambov
Penza
Tol'yatti
Syzran
Kuybyshev
Chernigov
Kursk
Michurinsk
Lipetsk
Voronezh
Yelets
Saratov
Engel's
Balakovo
Ural'sk
Orenburg
Lutsk
Rovno
Zhitomir
Kiyev
Lvov
Ternopol'
Sumy
Belgorod
Kharkov
Poltava
Khmel'nitskiy
Vinnitsa
Belaya Tserkov
Cherkassy
Kremenchug
Dnepropetrovsk
Zaporozh'ye
Krivoy Rog
Ukraine
Lisichansk
Kamyshin
Volgograd
Volzhskiy
Voroshilovgrad
Gorlovka
Donetsk
Makeyevka
Shakhty
Novoshakhtinsk
Taganrog
Rostov-na-Donu
Zhdanov
Ivano Frankovsk
Chernovtsy
Carpathians
Cluj Napoca
Iaşi
Bel'tsy
Kishinev
Bendery
Tiraspol'
Nikolayev
Kherson
Odessa
Melitopol'
Berdyansk
ROMANIA
Tirgu Mureş
Sibiu
Braşov
Ploieşti
Galaţi
Brăila
BUCUREŞTI
Black Sea
Azovskoye More
Krym
Tsimlyanskoye Vodokhranilishche
Elista
Astrakhan
Ryn Peski
Prikaspiyskaya Nizmennost'
Gur'yev
Kaspiyskoye More

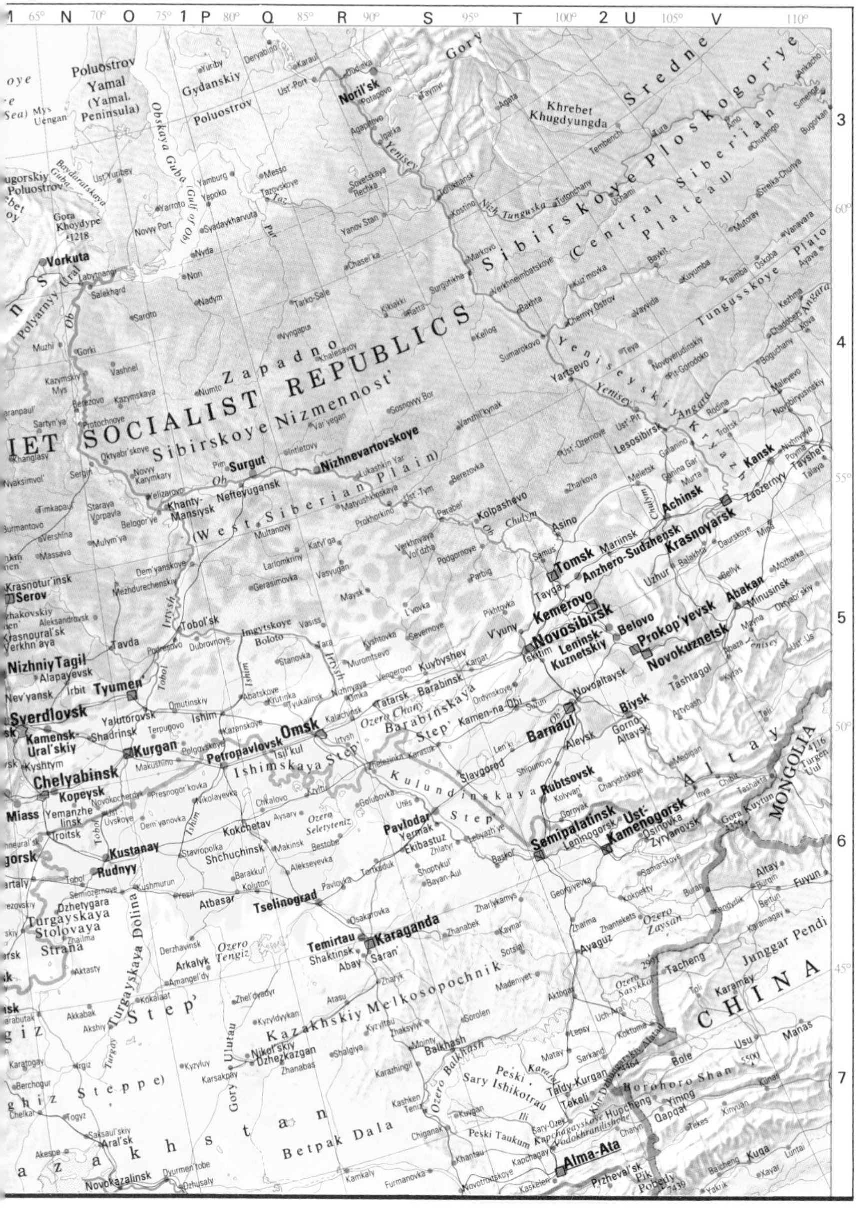

Scale 1:20 000 000

0 200 400 600 800 1000 km

0 200 400 600 miles

1 hour

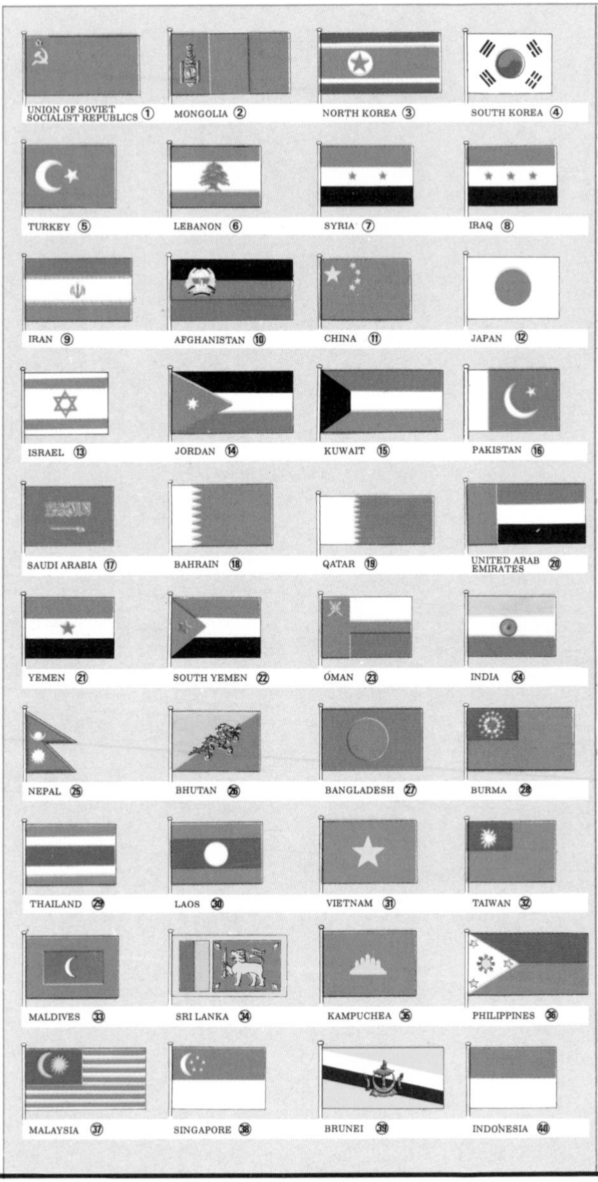
UNION OF SOVIET SOCIALIST REPUBLICS ①
MONGOLIA ②
NORTH KOREA ③
SOUTH KOREA ④
TURKEY ⑤
LEBANON ⑥
SYRIA ⑦
IRAQ ⑧
IRAN ⑨
AFGHANISTAN ⑩
CHINA ⑪
JAPAN ⑫
ISRAEL ⑬
JORDAN ⑭
KUWAIT ⑮
PAKISTAN ⑯
SAUDI ARABIA ⑰
BAHRAIN ⑱
QATAR ⑲
UNITED ARAB EMIRATES ⑳
YEMEN ㉑
SOUTH YEMEN ㉒
OMAN ㉓
INDIA ㉔
NEPAL ㉕
BHUTAN ㉖
BANGLADESH ㉗
BURMA ㉘
THAILAND ㉙
LAOS ㉚
VIETNAM ㉛
TAIWAN ㉜
MALDIVES ㉝
SRI LANKA ㉞
KAMPUCHEA ㉟
PHILIPPINES ㊱
MALAYSIA ㊲
SINGAPORE ㊳
BRUNEI ㊴
INDONESIA ㊵

5
50°
4
60°
ATLANTIC OCEAN
LONDON
AMSTERDAM
BRUSSELS
PARIS
DUBLIN
COPENHAGEN
BERLIN
STOCKHOLM
Glasgow
Bordeaux
Nantes
Bilbao
Barcelona
ROME
Naples
Palermo
Milan
Turin
VIENNA
PRAGUE
WARSAW
BUDAPEST
BELGRADE
BUCHAREST
SOFIA
ATHENS
Kiyev
Odessa
Simferopol
Istanbul
Izmir
ANKARA
Yerevan
Mediterranean Sea
Black Sea
Alexandria
CAIRO
Giza
Suez
BEIRUT
DAMASCUS
Aleppo
BAGHDAD
AMMAN
JERUSALEM
TEHRAN
Basra
Abadan
Shiraz
Nafud
SAUDI ARABIA
RIYADH
Medina
Jiddah
Mecca
Red Sea
Rub al Khali
SAN'A
ADEN
Gulf of Aden
Al Mukalla
Salalah
Socotra
DJIBOUTI
ADDIS ABABA
Berbera
Hargeysa
Ogaden
SOMALIA
MOGADISHU
Kismayu
Equator
VICTORIA
SEYCHELLES
COMOROS
MORONI
MADAGASCAR
ANTANANARIVO
Antseranana
Mahajanga
Toamasina

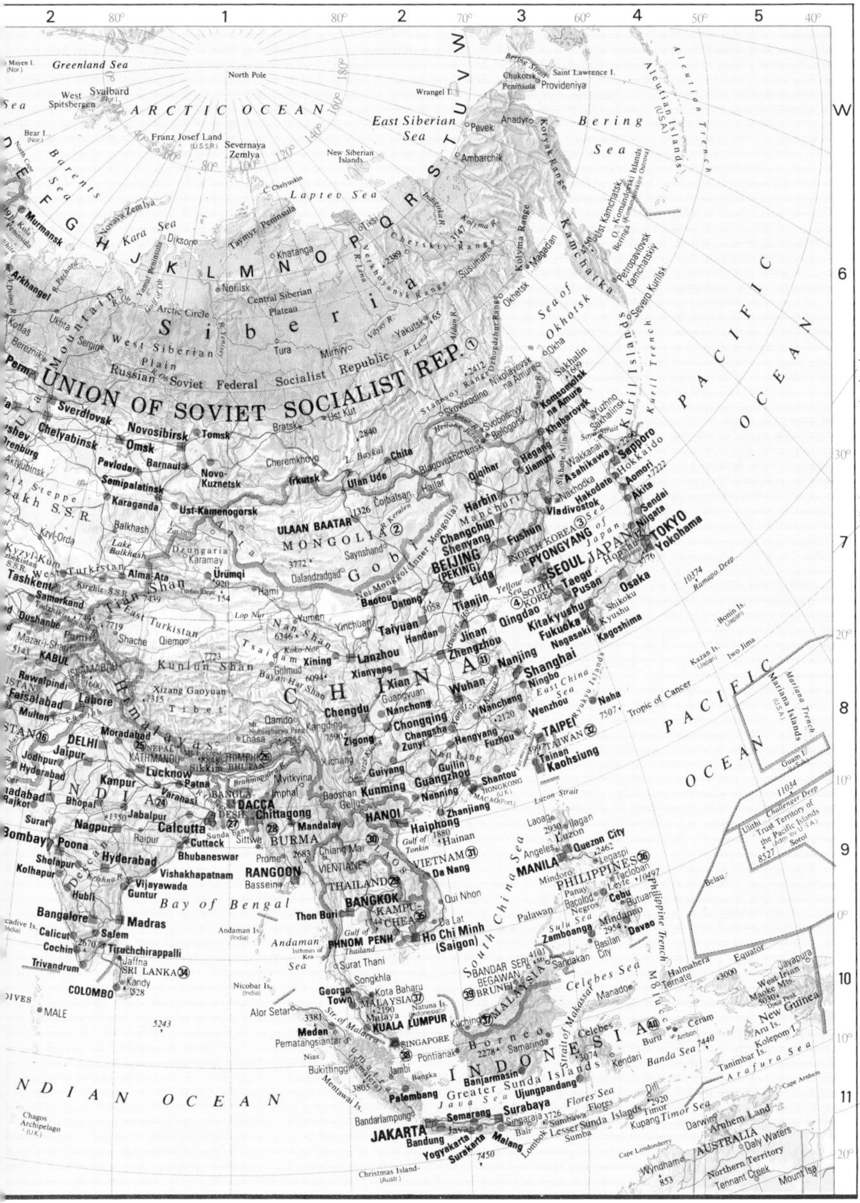

Scale 1:75 000 000

0 1000 2000 km

0 400 800 1200 miles

1 hour

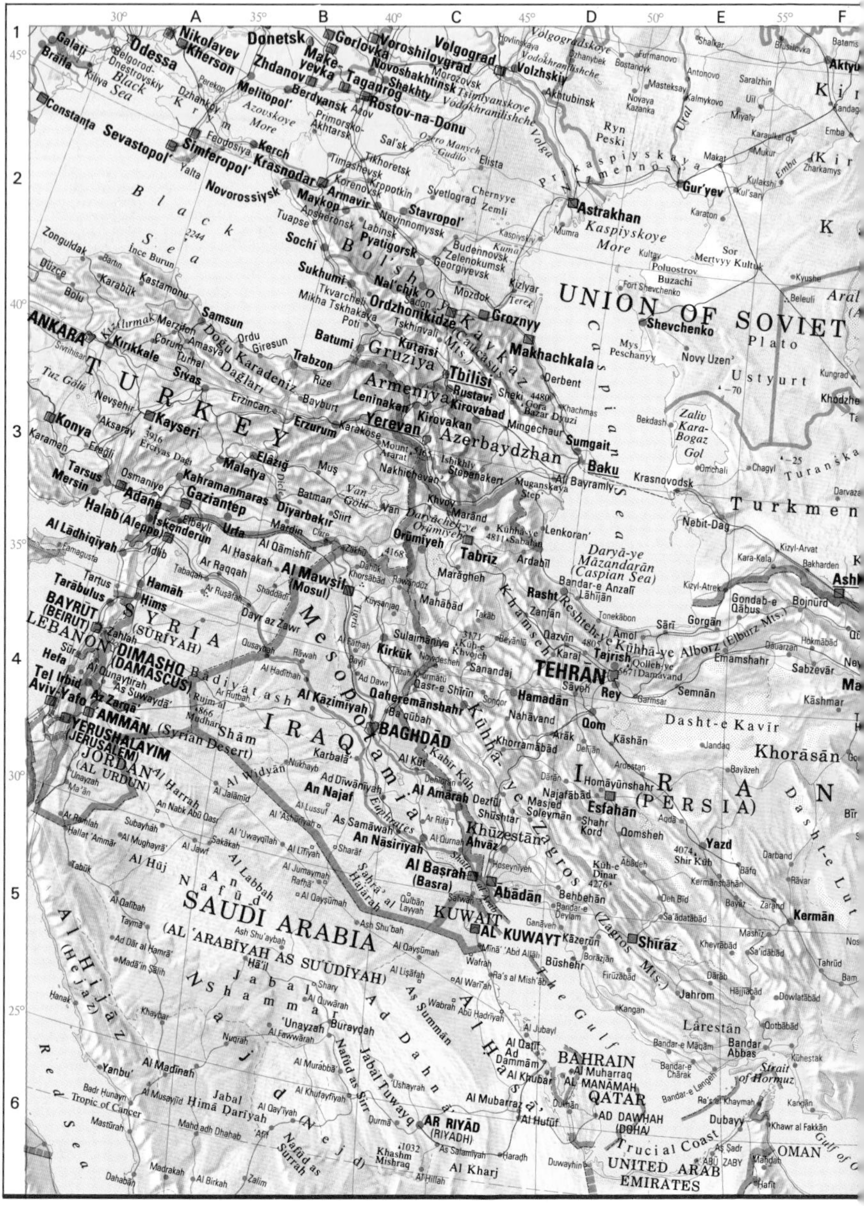
30°
A
35°
B
40°
C
45°
D
50°
E
55°
F
1
2
3
4
5
6
45°
40°
35°
30°
25°
Galați
Brăila
Odessa
Nikolayev
Kherson
Donetsk
Gorlovka
Voroshilovgrad
Volgograd
Makeyevka
Zhdanov
Novoshakhtinsk
Shakhty
Taganrog
Volzhskiy
Melitopol'
Berdyansk
Rostov-na-Donu
Constanța
Sevastopol'
Simferopol'
Kerch
Krasnodar
Black Sea
Azovskoye More
Novorossiysk
Armavir
Maykop
Stavropol'
Astrakhan
Kaspiyskoye More
Gur'yev
Elista
Chernyye Zemli
Ryn Peski
Akhtubinsk
Volga
Ural
Emba
Pyatigorsk
Sochi
Sukhumi
Nal'chik
Ordzhonikidze
Groznyy
Makhachkala
Derbent
Batumi
Kutaisi
Gruziya
Tbilisi
Rustavi
Kirovabad
Armeniya
Leninakan
Yerevan
Kirovakan
Azerbaydzhan
Sumgait
Baku
Krasnovodsk
Shevchenko
UNION OF SOVIET
Plato Ustyurt
Novy Uzen'
Zaliv Kara-Bogaz Gol
Turkmen
Nebit-Dag
Kizyl-Arvat
Ashkhabad
Zonguldak
Samsun
ANKARA
Kırıkkale
Sivas
Trabzon
Erzurum
TURKEY
Konya
Kayseri
Elâzığ
Malatya
Tarsus
Mersin
Adana
Kahramanmaraş
Gaziantep
Diyarbakır
Urfa
İskenderun
Halab (Aleppo)
Al Lādhiqīyah
Ḥamāh
Ḥimş
Ṭarābulus
BAYRŪT (BEIRUT)
LEBANON
SYRIA (SŪRĪYAH)
DIMASHQ (DAMASCUS)
Hefa
Tel Aviv-Yafo
Az Zarqā'
'AMMĀN
YERUSHALAYIM (JERUSALEM)
JORDAN (AL URDUN)
Al Mawṣil (Mosul)
Dayr az Zawr
Mesopotamia
Kirkūk
IRAQ
BAGHDĀD
Karbalā'
An Najaf
Al 'Amārah
An Nāṣirīyah
Al Başrah (Basra)
Ābādān
KUWAIT
AL KUWAYT
Orūmīyeh
Tabrīz
Rasht
TEHRĀN
Qom
Hamadān
Eşfahān
IRAN (PERSIA)
Shīrāz
Yazd
Kermān
Dasht-e Kavīr
Dasht-e Lut
Khorāsān
Kūhhā-ye Zāgros (Zagros Mts.)
Reshteh-ye Kūhhā-ye Alborz (Elburz Mts.)
Daryā-ye Māzandarān (Caspian Sea)
Bandar Abbas
Strait of Hormuz
The Gulf
BAHRAIN
Al Manāmah
QATAR
AD DAWḤAH (DOHA)
SAUDI ARABIA (AL 'ARABĪYAH AS SU'ŪDĪYAH)
AR RIYĀḌ (RIYADH)
Al Hufūf
Ad Dammām
Trucial Coast
UNITED ARAB EMIRATES
Dubayy
OMAN
Al Hijāz (Hejaz)
Al Madīnah
Nafūd
Najd (Nejd)
Red Sea
Tropic of Cancer

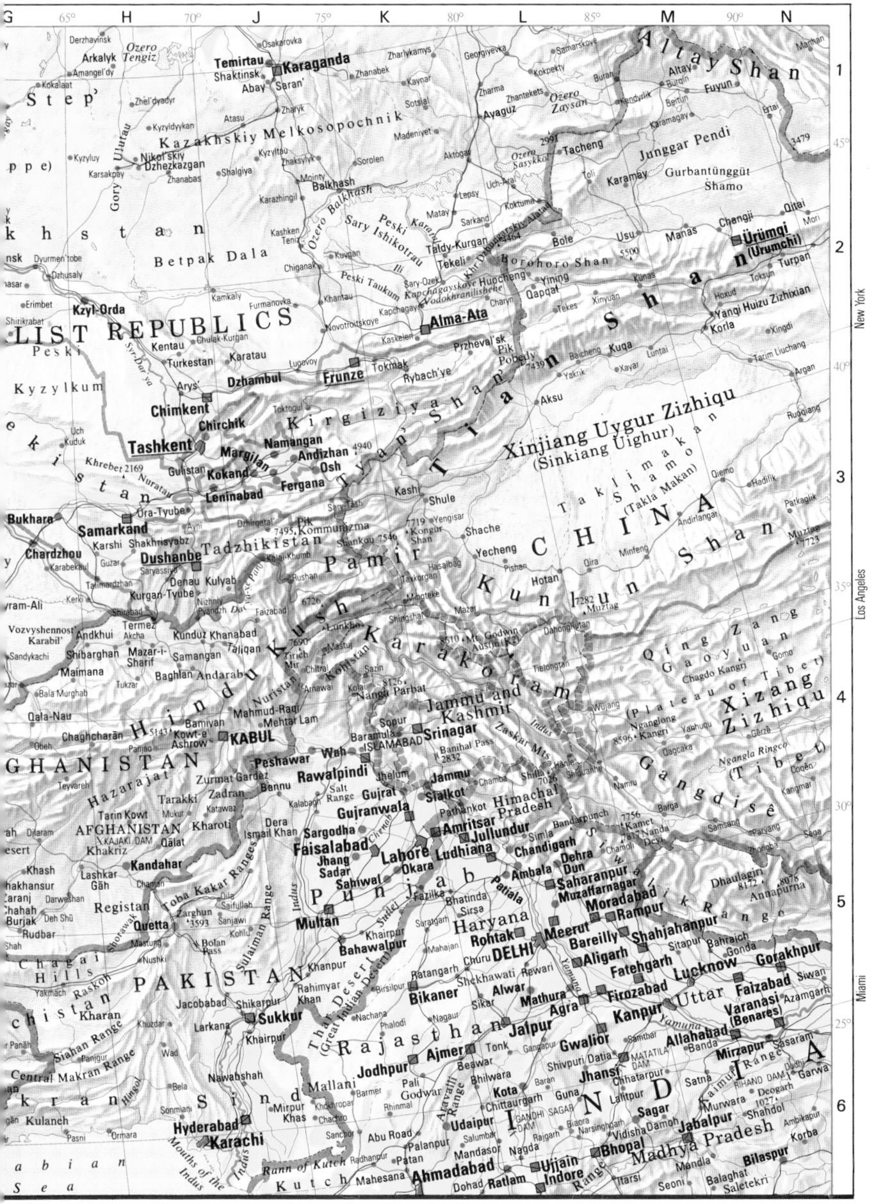

Scale 1:20 000 000

0	200	400	600	800	1000 km	
0		200		400		600 miles

1 hour

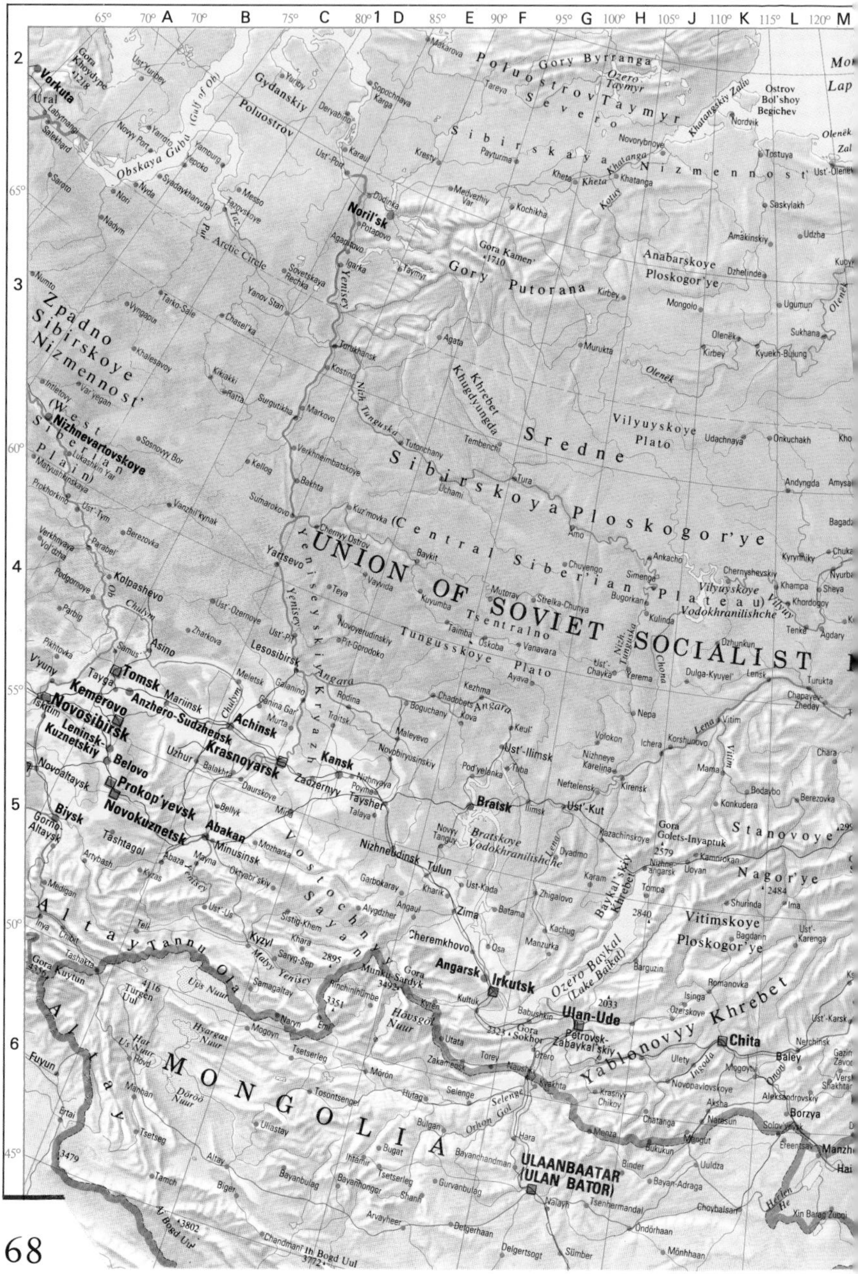
A
B
C
1
D
E
F
G
H
J
K
L
M
65°
70°
75°
80°
85°
90°
95°
100°
105°
110°
115°
120°
2
3
4
5
6
55°
60°
50°
45°
Vorkuta
Ural
Labytnangi
Salekhard
Obskaya Guba (Gulf of Ob')
Gydanskiy Poluostrov
Nadym
Nori
Nyda
Yamburg
Tazovskiy
Messo
Arctic Circle
Pur
Taz
Yenisey
Noril'sk
Dudinka
Igarka
Karaul
Ust'-Port
Dikson
Makarova
Poluostrov Taymyr
Gory Byrranga
Ozero Taymyr
Severo Sibirskaya Nizmennost'
Khatangskiy Zaliv
Ostrov Bol'shoy Begichev
Khatanga
Kheta
Kotuy
Gora Kamen' 1710
Gory Putorana
Anabarskoye Ploskogor'ye
Olenëk
Ust'-Olenëk
Saskylakh
Zpadno Sibirskoye Nizmennost' (West Siberian Plain)
Tarko-Sale
Nizhnevartovskoye
Surgutikha
Turukhansk
Nizh. Tunguska
Khrebet Khugdyungda
Sredne Sibirskoya Ploskogor'ye (Central Siberian Plateau)
Vilyuyskoye Plato
Tura
Udachnaya
UNION OF SOVIET SOCIALIST
Tsentralno Tungusskoye Plato
Yeniseyskiy Kryazh
Vilyuyskoye Vodokhranilishche
Vilyuy
Kolpashevo
Ob
Chulym
Asino
Tomsk
Kemerovo
Novosibirsk
Leninsk-Kuznetskiy
Belovo
Prokop'yevsk
Novokuznetsk
Biysk
Gorno-Altaysk
Anzhero-Sudzhensk
Achinsk
Krasnoyarsk
Kansk
Tayshet
Lesosibirsk
Yartsevo
Angara
Bratsk
Bratskoye Vodokhranilishche
Ust'-Ilimsk
Ust'-Kut
Lena
Vitim
Kirensk
Abakan
Minusinsk
Vostochnyy Sayan
Nizhneudinsk
Tulun
Zima
Cheremkhovo
Angarsk
Irkutsk
Ozero Baykal (Lake Baikal)
Baykal'skiy Khrebet
Stanovoye Nagor'ye
Vitimskoye Ploskogor'ye
Ulan-Ude
Yablonovyy Khrebet
Chita
Borzya
Altay
Tannu Ola
Kyzyl
Malyy Yenisey
Uvs Nuur
Hövsgöl Nuur
Hyargas Nuur
Khar Us Nuur
Hovd
MONGOLIA
Selenge
Orhon Gol
Kyakhta
ULAANBAATAR (ULAN BATOR)
Ih Bogd Uul 3772
Choybalsan
Herlen He
Manzhouli
Hailar

P
140°
Q
145°
R
150°
S
155°
T
1
160°
U
165°
V
170°
W
175°
2
X
180°
65°
Y
3
4
5
6
60°
55°
160°
50°
45°
Ostrov Kotel'nyy
O. Malyy Lyakhovskiy
Ostrov Bol'shoy Lyakhovskiy
Lyakhovskiye Ostrova
Mys Svatoy Nos
Mys Buorkhaya
Yanskiy Zaliv
Guba Buorkhaya
Yano-Indigirskaya Nizmennost'
Indigirskaya Nizmennost'
Kolymskaya Nizmennost'
Severnyy Anyuyskiy Khrebet
Anadyrskoye Ploskogor'ye
Arctic Circle
Anadyrskaja Nizmennost
Anadyrskiy Zaliv
Mys Navarin
Yukagirskoye Ploskogor'ye
Oloyskiye Gory
Penzhinskiy Khrebet
Koryakskiy Khrebet
Khrebet Cherskogo (Cherskiy Range)
Momskiy Khrebet
Gora Pobeda 3147
Khrebet Kolymskiy (Kolyma Range)
Kolymskoye Nagor'ye
Gora Ezop 2038
Khrebet Suntar Khayata
Gora Nelkuchan
Gora Taklaun
Zaliv Shelikhova
Gizhiginskaya Guba
Penzhinskaya Guba
Mys Taygonos
Bering Sea
Sredinnyy Khrebet
Magadan
Poluostrov Koni
Ostrov Zav'yalova
Mys Tolstoy
Mys Yuzhnyy
Yakutsk
Aldan
Amga
Sopka Shiveluch 3283
Mys Kronotskiy
Kronotskaya Sopka 3528
Ichinskaya Sopka 3621
Poluostrov Kamchatka
Okhotskoye More (Sea of Okhotsk)
Petropavlovsk-Kamchatskiy
Yelizovo
Mys Shipunskiy
Mys Lopatka
Okhotsk
Mys Duga-Zapadnaya
Khrebet Dzhugdzhur (Dzhugdzhur Range)
Khr. Sette-Daban
Ayan
Shantarskiye Ostrova
Ostrov Bol'shoy Shantar
Ostrov Feklistova
Mys Yelizavety
Sakhalinskiy Zaliv
Zaliv Akademii
Okha
Khrebet Dzhagdy
Nikolayevsk-na-Amure
Sakhalin
Proliv Nevel'skogo
Khrebet Turana
Bureinskiy Khrebet
Komsomol'sk-na-Amure
Tatarskiy Proliv
Zaliv Terpeniya
Mys Terpeniya
Sikhote Alin
Khabarovsk
Birobidzhan
Blagoveshchensk
Belogorsk
Svobodnyy
Xiao Hinggan Ling
Heilong Jiang
Amur
Yuzhno-Sakhalinsk
Korsakov
Kholmsk
Mys Aniva
Mys Kril'on
Ostrov Paramushir
Ostrov Onekotan
Ostrov Shiashkotan
O. Matua
O. Rasshua
O. Ketoy
Ostrov Simushir
Ostrova Chernyye Brat'ya
Ostrov Urup
Ostrov Iturup
Kuril'skiye Ostrova (Kuril Is) (USSR)
Kambal'naya Sopka 2156
Hegang
Jiamusi
Qiqihar
Fujin
Yichun
INA
LICS

MONGOLIA
Ürümqi (Urumchi)
Turpan
Korla
Hami
Xinjiang Uygur Zizhiqu (Sinkiang Uighur)
Lop Nur
Altun Shan
Kunlun Shan
Qaidam Pendi
Qinghai
Golmud
Xining
Lanzhou
Qilian Shan
Bei Shan
Gobi
Nei Monggol (Inner Mongolia)
Ömnögovĭ
Dornogovĭ
Dundgovĭ
Baotou
Hohhot
Datong
Yinchuan
Ningxia Huizu Zizhiqu
Mu Us Shamo
Shanxi
Taiyuan
Shaanxi
Xianyang
Xi'an
Qinling Shan
Henan
Luoyang
Zhengzhou
CHINA
Sichuan
Chengdu
Chongqing
Nanchong
Neijiang
Zigong
Yibin
Luzhou
Wutunghliao
Hengduan Shan
Hubei
Wuhan
Yichang
Hunan
Changsha
Xiangtan
Zhuzhou
Guizhou
Guiyang
Zunyi
Yunnan
Kunming
Dukou
Guangxi Zhuangzu Zizhiqu
Nanning
Liuzhou
Guilin
Guangdong
Guangzhou (Canton)
Foshan
Kowloon
Victoria
HONG KONG (U.K.)
Macao (Port.)
Zhanjiang
Haikou
Hainan Dao
BURMA
Mandalay
RANGOON
Pegu
Kachin
Nagaland
Arunachal Pradesh
Imphal
LAOS
THAILAND
Chiang Mai
HA NOI
Hai Phong
Beibu Wan (Gulf of Tonkin)
Nan Hai (South China Sea)

Scale 1:20 000 000

0 200 400 600 800 1000 km

0 200 400 600 miles

1 hour

65° A 70° B 75° C 80° D 85° E
1 2 3 4 5 6
30° 25° 20° 15° 10°
AFGHANISTAN
Tarin Kowt
Tarakki
Zurmat
Gardez
Zadran
Mukur
Katawaz
KAJAKI DAM
Khakriz
Qalat
Kharoti
Lashkar Gah
Kandahar
Chaman
Registan
Shorawak
Toba Kakar Range
Quetta
Zarghun 3593
Qila Saifullah
Sanjawi
Mastung
Nushki
Bolan Pass
Kohlu
Sulaiman Range
PAKISTAN
Khuzdar
Jacobabad
Larkana
Shikarpur
Sukkur
Khairpur
Wad
Bela
Nawabshah
Sonmiani
Sind
Hyderabad
Karachi
Mouths of the Indus
Mirpur Khas
Peshawar
Wah
Bannu
Rawalpindi
ISLAMABAD
Kalabagh
Salt Range
Dera Ismail Khan
Jhelum
Gujrat
Gujranwala
Sargodha
Faisalabad
Chenab
Jhang Sadar
Lahore
Sahiwal
Okara
Punjab
Multan
Indus
Sutlej
Fazilka
Khairpur
Bahawalpur
Khanpur
Rahimyar Khan
Thar Desert (Great Indian Desert)
Baramula
Sopur
Srinagar
Jammu and Kashmir
Banihal Pass 2832
Jammu
Sialkot
Chamba
Zaskar Mts
Pathankot
Amritsar
Himachal Pradesh
Jullundur
Ludhiana
Simla
Chandigarh
Bhatinda
Sirsa
Patiala
Ambala
Dehra Dun
Saharanpur
Muzaffarnagar
Haryana
Rohtak
Meerut
Moradabad
Rampur
DELHI
Suratgarh
Mahajan
Birsilpur
Ratangarh
Churu
Bikaner
Shekhawati
Nachana
Phalodi
Rewari
Alwar
Nagaur
Sikar
Rajasthan
Mallani
Jodhpur
Ajmer
Jaipur
Mathura
Agra
Barmer
Khokhropar
Chachro
Pali
Beawar
Tonk
Godwar
Rhinmal
Sanchor
Bhilwara
Gangapur
Aravalli Range
Rann of Kutch
Kutch
Abu Road
Radhanpur
Palanpur
Patan
Udaipur
Chittaurgarh
Kota
Baran
Tropic of Cancer
Mandvi
Gulf of Kutch
Mahesana
Surendranagar
Jamnagar
Nadiad
Ahmadabad
Salumbar
Mandasor
GANDHI SAGAR DAM
Guna
Dwarka
Rajkot
Gujarat
Kathiawar
Porbandar
Dhoraji
Junagadh
Veraval
Mahuva
Diu
Vadodara
Bharuch
Bhavnagar
Surat
Gulf of Khambhat
Daman
Dohad
Ratlam
Ujjain
Indore
Nagda
Rajgarh
Biaora
Narsinghgarh
Bhopal
Vidisha
Vindhya Range
Narmada
Satpura R.
Khandwa
Jalgaon
Dhule
Burhanpur
Bhusawal
Khamgaon
Nasik
Malegaon
Manmad
Deolali 1646
Kalsubai
Thana
Ulhasnagar
Bombay
Aurangabad
Ahmadnagar
Maharashtra
Pune
Janjira
Dapoli
Phaltan
Pandharpur
Ratnagiri
Konkan
Western Ghats
Sholapur
Barsi
Osmanabad
Udgir
Sangli
Bijapur
Gulbarga
Kolhapur
Belgaum
Bagalkot
Yadgir
Raichur
Panaji
Goa
Dharwar
Karnataka
Gadag
Hubli
Hospet
Bellary
Karwar
Honavar
Shimoga
Davangere
Bhadravati
Udipi
Mangalore
Hassan
Bangalore
Kolar Gold Fields
Cannanore
Hunsur
Mysore
Amindivi Islands
Lakshadweep (Laccadive Islands)
Calicut
2339 Kunda Hills
Malabar Coast
Trichur
Coimbatore
Anaimalai Hills 2670
Cochin
Alleppey
Madurai
Dindigul
Rajapalaiyam
Aruppukkottai
Quilon
Trivandrum
Tirunelveli
Tuticorin
Nagercoil
Cape Comorin
Arabian Sea
4000
MALDIVES
1900
Tielongtan
Qing Zang Gaoyuan
(Plateau of Tibet)
Chagdo Kangri
Gomo
Wujiang
Nganglong Kangri 8596
Xizang Zizh
Shiquanhe
Shipki 7026
Hanle
Qagcaka
Yanhuqu
Gangdisê
Ngangla Ringco
Gêrzê
6300
Nyima
Lhazhong 6371
Namru
Bandarpunch
Kamet 7756
Nanda Devi 7817
Chamoli
Barga
Coqên
Ombu
Kangmar
Samsang
Paryang
Zhongba
Saga
Tibe Shan
Himalaya
NEPAL
Dhaulagiri 8172
Annapurna 8078
8156
Gya La
Ngamring
Tingri
Siwalik Range
Bareilly
Aligarh
Shahjahanpur
Sitapur
Bahraich
Gonda
Fatehgarh
Firozabad
Lucknow
Mt Everest 8848
KATMANDU 8598
Kang
Sikkim
Patan
Mahabharat Range
Yamuna
Kanpur
Uttar Pradesh
Faizabad
Gorakhpur
Motihari
Siwan
Muzaffarpur
Biratnagar
Darbhanga
Gwalior
Shivpuri
Datia
Samthar
MATATILA DAM
Jhansi
Chhatarpur
Banda
Allahabad
Azamgarh
Varanasi (Benares)
Chapra
Baruni
Katihar
Purnia
Patna
Ganga
Lalitpur
INDIA
Mirzapur
Sasaram
Bihar
Monghyr
Bhagalpur
Gaya
Deoghar
Satna
Kaimur Range
RIHAND DAM
Dudhi
Garwa
Sagar
Damoh
Jabalpur
Murwara
Deogarh 1027
Shahdol
Daltenganj
Ranchi
Berhampur
Asansol
Durgapur
Madhya Pradesh
Itarsi
Mandla
Ambikapur
Chotanagpur
Burdwan
Jamshedpur
Howrah
Bengal
Korba
Seoni
Balaghat
Bilaspur
Betul
Nagpur
Gondia
Saletekri
Raurkela
Kharagpur
Raigarh
Megasani Hill
Bhandara
Durg
Raj Nandgaon
Sambalpur
Balasore
Amravati
Akola
Buldana
Raipur
Orissa
Bhadrakh
Dhamtari
Borasambar
Patnagarh
Bhuban
Kaintragarh
Palmyras Point
Hinganghat
Adilabad
Chandrapur
Cuttack
Bhubaneshwar
Nander
Parlakote
Makri
Bhawanipatna
Eastern Ghats
Jagdalpur
Jeypore
Berhampur
1500
Nizamabad
Deccan
Warangal
Bidar
Godavari
Parlakimidi
1646
Srikakulam
Vizianagaram
Anakapalle
Vishakhapatnam
Hyderabad
Mahbubnagar
Rajahmundry
Eluru
Kakinada
Andhra Pradesh
Krishna
Vijayawada
Guntur
Machilipatnam
Tenali
Bay
3900
Kurnool
Nandyal
Ongole
Anantapur
Cuddapah
Nellore
Chik Ballapur
Gudur
Chittoor
Tirupati
Vellore
Madras
Ambur
Kanchipuram
Tiruvannamalai
Pondicherry
Tamil Nadu
Salem
Erode
Cuddalore
Coromandel Coast
Kumbakonam
Karikal
Thanjavur
Tiruchchirappalli
Karaikkudi
Palk Strait
Kankesanturai
Jaffna
Mullaittivu
Adams Bridge
Gulf of Mannar
Trincomalee
Anuradhapura
Negombo
Kurunegala
Kandy
SRI LANKA (CEYLON)
COLOMBO
Pidurutalagala
Badulla
Ratnapura
Moratuwa
Yala
Galle
Matara
Dondra Head
INDIAN OCEAN
3600

F
95°
G
100°
H
105°
J
110°
K
115°
1
2
3
4
5
6
30°
25°
20°
15°
10°
Miami
Mexico C.
C H I N A
Qinling Shan
Kunlun Shankou
Yagradagze Shan
Bayan Har Shankou
Tanggula Shankou
Tongtian He
(Yangtze Kiang)
Baoji
Wugong
Min Xian
Funiu Shan
Nanyang
Queshan
Biyang
Xinyang
Huaibin
Wudu
Lueyang
Yang Xian
Ankang
Jun Xian
Tanghe
Zaoyang
Xiangfan
Shangcheng
Xixiang
Zhushan
Guanghua
Nanzhang
Anlu
Guangyuan
Bazhong
Hubei
Wuhan
Jiangyou
Langzhong
Xuanhan
Kai Xian
Fengjie
Yichang
Hankou
Huangshi
Mianyang
Nanchong
Wanxian
Chang Jiang
Yidu
Shashi
Deyang
Dazhu
Enshi
Li Xian
Shishou
Chengdu
Guan Xian
Qionglai
Danba
Dianjiang
Hechuan
Zhong Xian
Dayong
Anxiang
Dongting Hu
Yueyang
Changde
Sichuan
Neijiang
Chongqing
Yiyang
Changsha
Kangding
Wutunghliao
Zigong
Luzhou
Qijiang
Wuchuan
Jishou
Anhua
Xiangtan
Zhuzhou
Yibin
Chishui
Tongzi
Chenxi
Hunan
Pingxiang
Shaoyang
Yuexi
Zhaojue
Xuyong
Gulin
Zunyi
Tongren
Zhijiang
Hengyang
Hengduan Shan
Xichang
Zhenxiong
Jinsha
Zhenyuan
Wugang
Qiyang
Leiyang
Zhaotong
Guizhou
Kaili
Jing Xian
Dao Xian
Chenzhou
Lijiang
Huili
Weining
Shuicheng
Guiyang
Anshun
Duyun
Rongjiang
Jianghua
Dukou
Xuanwei
Zhenning
Dushan
Guilin
Lian Xian
Shaoguan
Jinsha Jiang
Dongchuan
Fuyuan
Pan Xian
Xingren
Rongan
Pingle
Yingde
Dali
Kunming
Qujing
Anlong
Luzhai
Liuzhou
He Xian
Guangzhou
(Canton)
Xiaguan
Chuxiong
Xingyi
Hechi
Guangxi Zhuangzu Zizhiqu
Wuzhou
Deqing
Foshan
Jiangmen
Yunnan
Yiliang
Luxi
Yuxi
Mile
Tonghai
Bose
Tiandong
Heng Xian
Gui Xian
Yulin
Rong Xian
Fengqing
Shiping
Kaiyuan
Wenshan
Nanning
Bobai
Yangjiang
Lincang
Gejiu
Mengzi
Longzhou
Qinzhou
Gaozhou
Lianjiang
Maoming
Lancang Jiang
(Mekong)
Song Hong
Lang Son
Pingxiang
Beihai
Zhanjiang
Haikang
Xuwen
Haikou
HA NOI
Hoa Binh
Hai Phong
Nam Dinh
Beibu Wan
(Gulf of Tonkin)
Dan Xian
Qionghai
Hainan Dao
Wuzhi Shan
1880
Dongfang
Thanh Hoa
Ya Xian
Vinh
South China Sea
Ha Tinh
Hue
Da Nang
Paracel Islands
(China)
Quang Ngai
VIETNAM
Qui Nhon
Pleiku
Nha Trang
Cam Ranh
Da Lat
Ban Me Thuot
Ho Chi Minh (Saigon)
Cu Lao Hon
Catwick Islands
Vung Tau
Can Tho
My Tho
Phu Vinh
Vinh Loi
Con Son
Mouths of the Mekong
LAOS
Luang Prabang
Pou Bia
VIENTIANE
Nong Khai
Udon Thani
Khon Kaen
Khorat Plateau
Savannakhet
Phu Set
Pakse
Muang Ubon
Mekong
THAILAND
Chiang Mai
Doi Inthanon
Lampang
Phitsanulok
Nakhon Sawan
Three Pagodas Pass
Lop Buri
Nakhon Ratchasima
Sara Buri
KRUNG THEP (BANGKOK)
Thon Buri
Samut Prakan
Chon Buri
Rat Buri
Phet Buri
Bight of Bangkok
KAMPUCHEA
(CAMBODIA)
Tonle Sap
Battambang
Kompong Chhnang
Kompong Cham
PHNOM PENH
Chau Phu
Rach Gia
Khanh Hung
Gulf of Thailand
Ko Chang
Ko Kut
Kas Kong
Kompong Som
Quan Phu Quoc
Hon Panjang
Mui Bai Bung
Ko Phangan
Surat Thani
Nakhon Si Thammarat
Thung Song
Khao Luang
Songkhla
Hat Yai
Yala
Phuket
Trang
Ko Phuket
Butang Group
MALAYSIA
South China Sea
Isthmus of Kra
Chumphon
Mergui
Mergui Archipelago
Tavoy
Tenasserim
Andaman Sea
Moulmein
Thaton
Gulf of Martaban
Pegu
RANGOON
Bassein
Henzada
Prome
Toungoo
Kayah
Karen
Salween
Pegu Yoma
Magwe
Arakan Yoma
Mandalay
Sagaing
Shan
BURMA
Chin
Mount Victoria
3053
Myitkyina
Kachin
Bhamo
Lashio
Irrawaddy
Chindwin
Sittwe
Ramree
Cheduba
Combermere Bay
Cape Negrais
Mouths of the Irrawaddy
Coco Islands
North Andaman
Middle Andaman
South Andaman
Andaman Islands
(India)
Barren
Port Blair
Little Andaman
Car Nicobar
Teressa
Camorta
Nicobar Islands
(India)
Little Nicobar
Great Nicobar
Chittagong
Imphal
Manipur
Mizoram
Nagaland
Naga Hills
Arunachal Pradesh
Tinsukia
Dibrugarh
Sibsagar
Jorhat
Tezpur
Nowgong
Lumding
Shillong
Silchar
Tripura
Agartala
Cox's Bazar
Namjagbarwa Feng
7755
Yarlung Zangbo Jiang
Nagqu
Lhari
Qamdo
Dêgê
Yalong Jiang
Yunling Shan
Wuliang Shan

Scale 1:20 000 000

A
B
C
D
100°
105°
110°
115°
1
2
3
4
5
10°
5°
0°
5°
10°
BURMA
Tavoy
Nakhon Pathom
Thon Buri
BANGKOK
Rat Buri
Samut Songkhram
Samut Prakan
Chon Buri
Phet Buri
Sisophon
Tabeng
ANGKOR
Mekong
Stung Treng
Pleiku
Hoai Nhon
Phu My
Qui Nhon
KAMPUCHEA
Battambang
Tonle Sap
Kompong Chhnang
Kompong Thom
Sambor
Ban Me Thuot
Sattahip
Mergui
Mergui Archipelago
Kui Nua
Trat
1813
Phnom Aural
VIETNAM
Nha Trang
Cam Ranh
PHNOM PENH
Kompong Cham
Snoul
Chon Thanh
Da Lat
Di Linh
Bokpyin
Thap Sakae
Takeo
Gulf of Thailand
Kompong Som
Kampot
Ca Na
Andaman Sea
Isthmus of Kra
Chumphon
Sa Dec
Ho Chi Minh (Saigon)
Rach Gia
My Tho
Vung Tau
Ko Phangan
Phu Vinh
Khanh Hung
Surat Thani
Takua Pa
THAILAND
Vinh Loi
Mouths of the Mekong
Nakhon Si Thammarat
Mui Bai Bung
Nam Can
Thung Song
Ko Phuket
Phuket
Trang
South China Sea
Kantang
Songkhla
Hat Yai
Butang Group
Yala
Kangar
Alor Setar
Kota Baharu
Banda Aceh
George Town
Kuala Terengganu
Kota Kinabalu
Sabah
Taiping
Peureulak
Gunung Tahan
2189
G. Abong Abong
2985
Ipoh
Kampar
G. Batu Puteh
2130
MALAYSIA
BRUNEI
BANDAR SERI BEGAWAN
Miri
Telok Anson
Kepulauan Natuna
2371
Gunung Mulu
Seumanyam
G. Leuser
3381
Binjai
Medan
Kuantan
Tebingtinggi
Pematangsiantar
Strait of Malacca
Kelang
KUALA LUMPUR
Seremban
Bintulu
Tambalan
P. Simeulue
Tanjungbalai
Kepulauan Anambas
Matu
Sibu
Sarawak
2012
Melaka
Muar
Keluang
Tarutung
Rantauprapat
Hose Mountains
Tanjung Api
Saratok
2988
Sibolga
Padangsidempuan
Johor Baharu
SINGAPORE
Pemangkat
Kuching
Simanggang
Pulau Padang
Pulau Bintan
Peg. Muller
Pulau Nias
Sumatera
2145
G. Sorikmerapi
Pekanbaru
Kepulauan Riau
Monterado
Kalimantan
(Borneo)
Semitau
1744
Mandor
Equator
Bukittinggi
Payakumbuh
Kepulauan Lingga
Pontianak
Sintang
Padangpanjang
1758
2278
Selat Mentawai
Gunung Saran
Peg. Schwaner
Padang
Telukbatang
Muara Teweh
Pulau Siberut
Gunung Kerinci
3805
Batang Hari
Jambi (Telanaipura)
Tanjung Samak
Nangatayap
Palangkaraya
Bangko
Kepulauan Mentawai
Pulau Bangka
Selat Karimata
Pangkalpinang
Kendawangan
Sukaraja
Sampit
Amuntai
2933
Bukit Masurai
G. Besar
1892
Pegunungan Barisan
Tebingtinggi
Palembang
Pulau Belitung
Kandangan
Banjarmasin
Muaraenim
Teluk Kumai
Bengkulu
3159
G. Dempo
Tanjung Jabung
Tanjung Selatan
Laut Jawa (Java Sea)
Kotabumi
Bandar Lampung
Pulau Enggano
Kotaagung
Serang
JAKARTA
Indramayu
Tangerang
Bogor
Cirebon
Tegal
Pekalongan
Kudus
Rembang
Pulau Madura
Kepulauan Kangean
Rangkasbitung
Cianjur
Pamekasan
INDIAN OCEAN
Sukabumi
Bandung
Magelang
Semarang
Surabaya
Laut Bali
Kediri
Tasikmalaya
Surakarta
Bondowoso
Cilacap
Madiun
Singaraja
Bali
Yogyakarta
Tulungagung
Malang
Jawa (Java)
Banyuwangi
Denpasar
Praya
Christmas Island (Austr.)

Scale 1:20 000 000

0 200 400 600 800 1000 km

0 200 400 600 miles

1 hour

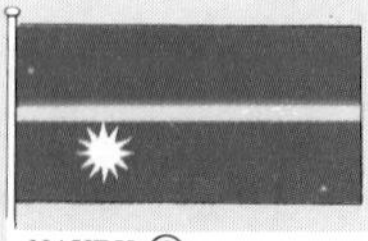

NAURU ①

KIRIBATI ②

PAPUA NEW GUINEA ③

SOLOMON ISLANDS ④

TUVALU ⑤

WESTERN SAMOA ⑥

VANUATU ⑦

FIJI ⑧

AUSTRALIA ⑨

NEW ZEALAND ⑩

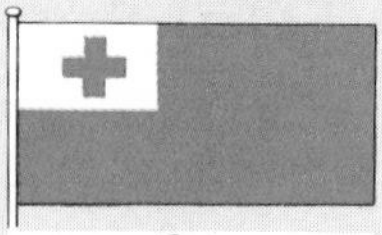

TONGA ⑪

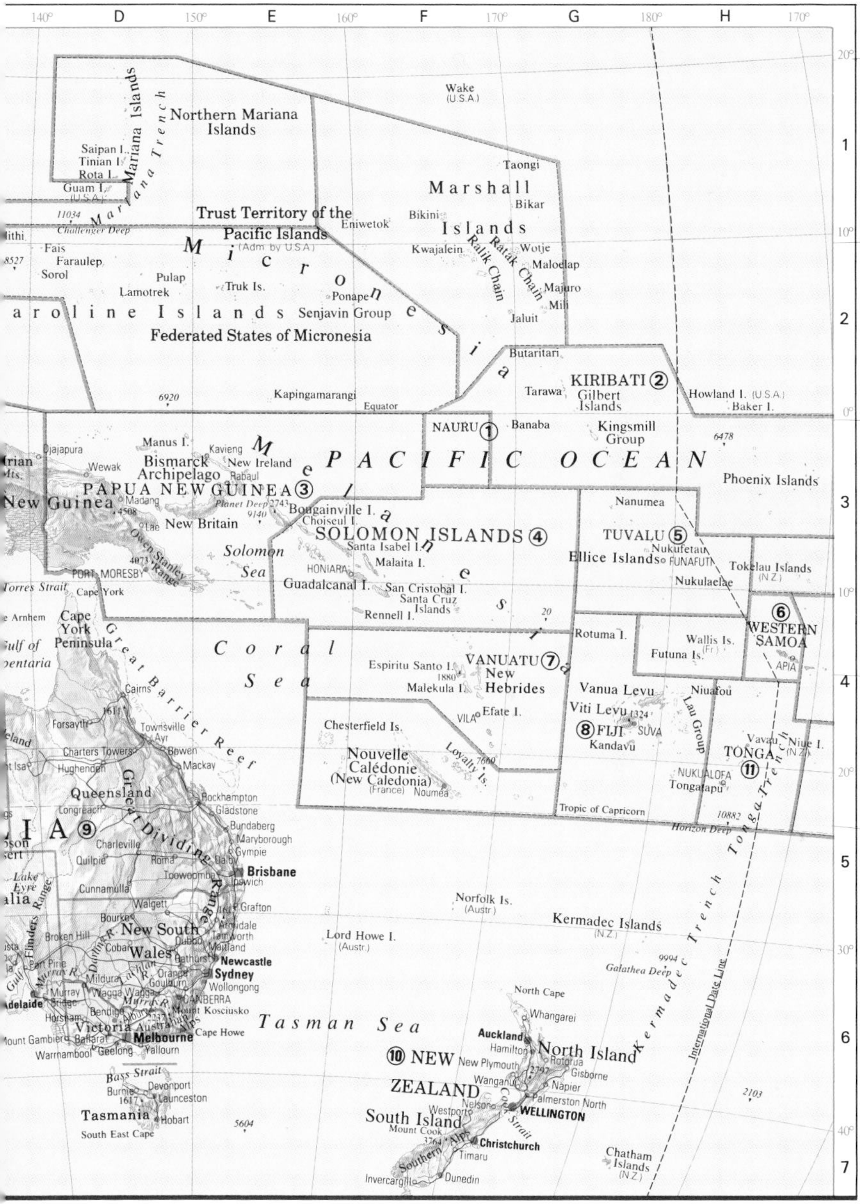

Scale 1:50 000 000

0 500 1000 km
0 200 400 600 miles
1 hour

A
B
C
D
E
115°
120°
125°
130°
15°
20°
25°
30°
35°
1
2
3
4
5
6
INDIAN
OCEAN
INDONESIA
Baing
Kupang
Pulau Roti
Timor Sea
Cape Van Diemen
Bathurst Island
Melville Island
Cape Croker
Croker Island
Van Diemen Gulf
Port Darwin
Darwin
Rum Jungle
Adelaide River
Arnhem
Cape Scott
Cape Londonderry
Joseph Bonaparte Gulf
Daly River
Port Keats
KATHERINE GORGE N.P.
Katherine
Beswick
Roper
Mataranka
Scott Reef
Bonaparte Archipelago
Kalumburu
DRYSDALE RIVER NATIONAL PARK
Wyndham
Legune
Kununurra
Newry
Bradshaw
Willeroo
Victoria River
Ord R.
Kimberley
Collier Bay
Durack Range
Lake Argyle
Daly Waters
Cape Lévêque
King Sound
King Leopold Ranges
Mount Ord 936
Kimberley Plateau
Montejinnie
Dunmarra
Dampier Land
Derby
Yeeda River
Fitzroy Crossing
Wave Hill
Newcastle
Elliot
Broome
Roebuck Bay
Thangoo
Fitzroy River
Halls Creek
Northern
Gordon Downs
Tanami Des
Eighty Mile Beach
Anna Plains
Bohemia Downs
Canning Basin
Larrey Point
Tanami
Port Hedland
Goldsworthy
Great Sandy Desert
TANAMI DESERT WILDLIFE SANCTUARY
The Granites
436
Dampier
Roebourne
Barrow Island
Territo
North West Cape
Exmouth
Onslow
Hamersley Range
Mount Bruce 1235
RUDALL RIVER NATIONAL PARK
AUSTRA
Roy Hill
Lake Mackay
HAMERSLEY RANGE NATIONAL PARK
Newman
Lake Disappointment
Narwietooma
Macdonnell
Western
FINKE GORGE NATIONAL PARK
Lake Amadeus
Henbury
Lake McLeod
Mount Augustus 1106
COLLIER RANGES NATIONAL PARK
Mount Essendon 910
Gibson Desert
BROWNE RANGE NATURE RESERVE
Mount Deering 1219
Giles
Carnarvon
KENNEDY RANGE N.P.
Gascoyne Junction
Milgun
AYERS ROCK – MOUNT OLGA NATIONAL PARK
Kulge
Shark Bay
Macadam Plains
Carnegie
Warburton Mission
Musgrave Ranges
Dirk Hartog Island
Wooramel
Byro
Mount Hale 732
Karalundi
Tomkinson Ranges
Lake Carnegie
Edel Land
Hamelin Pool
Meekatharra
Birksgate Range 773
S
Australia
KALBARRI NATIONAL PARK
Murchison R.
Lake Austin
Mount Shenton 594
Great Victoria Desert
Aus
Yalgoo
Mount Magnet
Mullewa
Leonora
Lake Carey
Geraldton
Morava
Paynes Find
Dongara
Lake Barlee
Lake Ballard
GREAT VICTORIA DESERT NATURE RESERVE
Lake Maurice
Lake Moore
Menzies
Lake Rebecca
Cook
Ooldea
Watheroo
Dalwallinu
Mount Jackson
Forrest
Jurien Bay
Kondut
Kalgoorlie Boulder
Rawlinna
Nullarbor Plain
Southern Cross
Lake Lefroy
Zanthus
Colona
Gingin
Northam
Merredin
Cocklebiddy
Wilson Bluff
Fowlers Bay
Perth
York
Eyre
Brookton
The Johnston Lakes
Hyden
Norseman
Balladonia
Darling Range
Mandurah
Jarrahdale
Kondinin
658
Charles Peak
Point Culver
Great Australian Bight
Narrogin
Wagin
Bunbury
FITZGERALD RIVER N.P.
Esperance Bay
CAPE ARID NATIONAL PARK
Cape Naturaliste
Cape Arid
Margaret River
Bridgetown
STIRLING RANGE N.P. 1042
Cranbrook
Hood Point
Bluff Knoll
Cape Leeuwin
Albany
Point D'Entrecasteaux
Bald Head

Scale 1:20 000 000

0 200 400 600 800 10
0 200 400 60
1 hour

Coral Sea
PACIFIC OCEAN
PAPUA NEW GUINEA
Louisiade Archipelago
Coral Sea Islands Territory (Austr.)
Great Barrier Reef
Queensland
New South Wales
Victoria
Great Dividing Range
Great Artesian Basin
Cape York Peninsula
Gulf of Carpentaria
Torres Strait
Bass Strait
Brisbane
Sydney
Melbourne
CANBERRA
Newcastle
Wollongong
Adelaide
Geelong
Rockhampton
Townsville
Cairns
Mackay
Tropic of Capricorn
Lord Howe Island
Rio de Janeiro

A
B
C
D
E
130°
135°
140°
145°
0°
5°
10°
35°
40°
45°
150°
155°
160°
165°
1
2
3
4
7
8
9
10
K
L
M
N
O
Halmahera
Buli
1508
Bukit Sulat
Wosi
Laut Halmahera
Pulau Waigeo
Equator
Sorong
Mega
3000
Gunung Kwoka
Waibumi
Cendrawasih
P. Salawati
Pulau Biak
Biak
Pulau Yapen
Serui
Teba
Sarmi
Fluk
Pulau Misool
Arandai
Teluk Cendrawasih
Waren
Laut Seram
Teluk Berau
Babo
Irian Jaya
Jayapura
Wahai
Piru
3055
Gunung Binaiya
Masohi
Bomberai
Selassi
Ambon
Seram
Angar
Murana
Hamuku
Karufa
New Guinea
Aitape
Schouten Islands
Wewak
Green River
Pegunungan Maoke
5030
Puncak Jaya
Umari
Sepik River
Bismarck Range
Karkar
PAPUA
INDONESIA
Kepulauan Kai
P. Kai Besar
Centra Range
Madang
Long Island
Vitiaz Strait
Mount Wilhelm
4508
Laut Banda
(Banda Sea)
Pulau Wokam
Pulau Kobroor
Kepulauan Aru
Agats
Atsy
Kiunga
Doma Peaks
3962
Goroka
Kainantu
Mount Bangeta
4107
Okapa
3384
Lae
Huon
Pulau Trangan
Keketa
Tenggara
Pulau Yamdena
Kepulauan Tanimbar
Laut Arafura
(Arafura Sea)
Mapi
Baimuru
NEW GUINEA
(NIUGINI)
Kepulauan Babar
Pulau Selaru
Pulau Jos Sodarso
Okaba
Kerema
Fly River
Wasua
Gesoa
Kepulauan Leti
Tanjung Vals
Merauke
Gulf of Papua
PORT MORESBY
Mari
Laut Timor
(Timor Sea)
Mulgrave Island
Banks Island
Torres Strait
Prince of Wales Island
Cape York
Somerset
Coral Sea
AUSTRALIA
Cape Croker
Croker Island
Cape Wessel
JARDINE RIVER NATIONAL PARK
Cape Van Diemen
Melville Island
Bathurst Island
Van Diemen Gulf
Buckingham Bay
Admiralty Islands
Manus
Bismarck
Ivanhoe
Lachlan River
Forbes
Bathurst
West Wyalong
Cowra
KANANGRA BOYD N.P.
Sydney
Wollongong
Shellharbour
Young
Hay
Murrumbidgee R.
Balranald
Goulburn
Nowra
Junee
Riverina
Wagga Wagga
CANBERRA
Swan Hill
Australian Capital Territory
Batemans Bay
Albury
Mount Kosciusko
2230
Charlton
Shepparton
Benalla
Australian Alps
Saint Arnaud
Bendigo
1922
Mount Feathertop
Bega
AUSTRALIA
Delegate
Cape Howe
Ballarat
Cann River
Melbourne
Ninety Mile Beach
Geelong
Morwell
Sale
Warragul
Warrnambool
Wonthaggi
Yarram
Tasman Sea
Cape Otway
Wilsons Promontory
King
North Point
Bass Strait
Furneaux Group
Banks Strait
Cape Grim
Burnie
Scottsdale
Devonport
Launceston
Saint Marys
Mount Ossa
1617
Freycinet Peninsula
Queenstown
Triabunna
HARTZ MOUNTAINS NATIONAL PARK
Hobart
Port Arthur
5604
South East Cape
Tasmania
South
Mount Aspiring
FIORDLAND NATIONAL PARK
Cape Providence
Foveaux Strait
Stewart Island
Southwest Cape

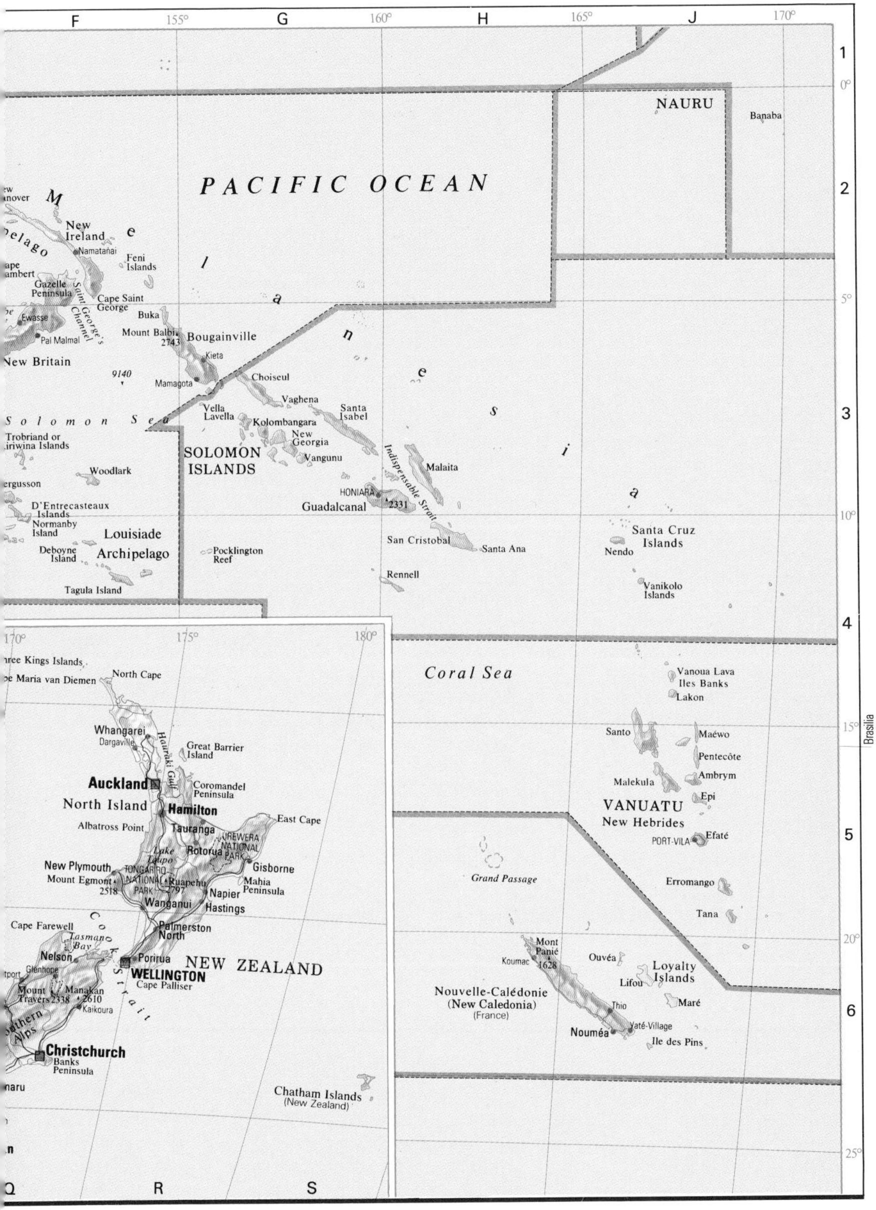

Scale 1:20 000 000

0 200 400 600 800 1000 km

0 200 400 600 miles

1 hour

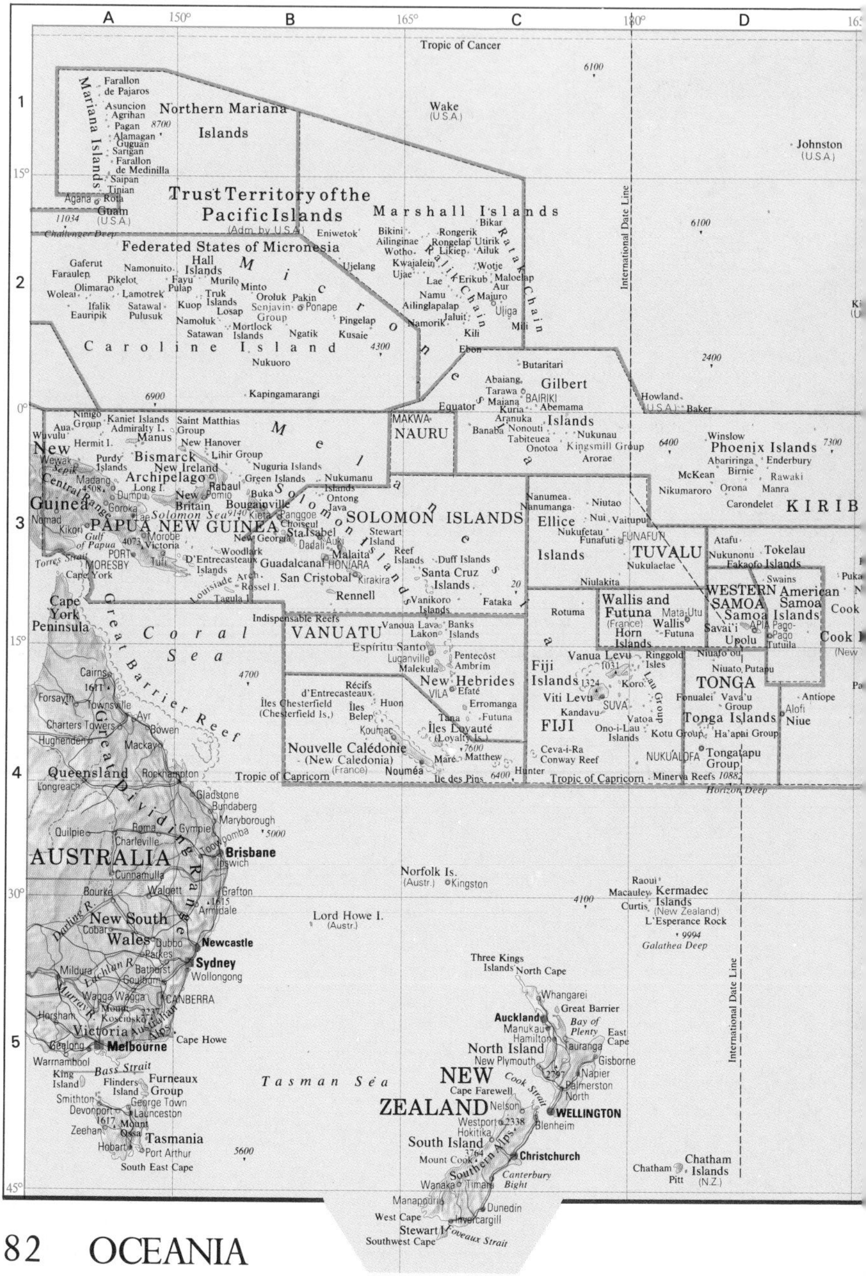

Tropic of Cancer
Farallon de Pajaros
Mariana Islands
Asuncion
Agrihan
Pagan
Alamagan
Guguan
Sarigan
Farallon de Medinilla
Saipan
Tinian
Rota
Agana
Guam (U.S.A.)
Northern Mariana Islands
Wake (U.S.A.)
Johnston (U.S.A.)
Trust Territory of the Pacific Islands (Adm. by U.S.A.)
Marshall Islands
Challenger Deep
Federated States of Micronesia
Micronesia
Eniwetok
Bikini
Ailinginae
Wotho
Rongerik
Rongelap
Utirik
Bikar
Likiep
Ailuk
Kwajalein
Ujae
Ujelang
Lae
Erikub
Wotje
Maloelap
Aur
Namu
Majuro
Ailinglapalap
Jaluit
Namorik
Kili
Mili
Uliga
Ebon
Ralik Chain
Ratak Chain
International Date Line
Gaferut
Faraulep
Namonuito
Hall Islands
Pikelot
Fayu
Pulap
Murilo
Minto
Olimarao
Woleai
Lamotrek
Truk Islands
Oroluk
Pakin
Senjavin Group
Ponape
Ifalik
Eauripik
Satawal
Pulusuk
Kuop
Losap
Namoluk
Mortlock Islands
Satawan
Pingelap
Kusaie
Ngatik
Caroline Islands
Nukuoro
Kapingamarangi
Butaritari
Abaiang
Tarawa
BAIRIKI
Maiana
Kuria
Abemama
Gilbert Islands
Aranuka
Banaba
Nonouti
Tabiteuea
Onotoa
Nukunau
Kingsmill Group
Arorae
Equator
MAKWA
NAURU
Howland
Baker (U.S.A.)
Winslow
Phoenix Islands
Abariringa
Enderbury
Birnie
McKean
Rawaki
Nikumaroro
Orona
Manra
Carondelet
KIRIB
Ninigo Group
Aua
Wuvulu
Kaniet Islands
Admiralty I.
Manus
Saint Matthias Group
Hermit I.
New Hanover
Melanesia
New Guinea
Wewak
Sepik
Purdy Islands
Bismarck Archipelago
Lihir Group
New Ireland
Nuguria Islands
Madang
Central Range
Long I.
Rabaul
Green Islands
Nukumanu Islands
Dumpu
Pomio
New Britain
Buka
Bougainville
Ontong Java
Goroka
Lae
Solomon Sea
Kieta
Panggoe
Choiseul
Nomad
Kikori
PAPUA NEW GUINEA
SOLOMON ISLANDS
Morobe
Victoria
New Georgia
Santa Isabel
Stewart Island
Gulf of Papua
PORT MORESBY
Woodlark
D'Entrecasteaux Islands
Dadali
Auki
Malaita
Reef Islands
Duff Islands
Torres Strait
Cape York
Guadalcanal
HONIARA
San Cristobal
Kirakira
Santa Cruz Islands
Louisiade Arch.
Rossel I.
Rennell
Tagula I.
Vanikoro Islands
Fataka
Nanumea
Nanumanga
Niutao
Nui
Vaitupu
Ellice Islands
Nukufetau
Funafuti
FUNAFUTI
TUVALU
Nukulaelae
Niulakita
Atafu
Nukunonu
Fakaofo
Tokelau Islands
Swains
Cape York Peninsula
Great Barrier Reef
Coral Sea
Indispensable Reefs
VANUATU
Vanoua Lava
Banks Islands
Lakon
Espiritu Santo
Luganville
Malekula
Pentecost
Ambrim
New Hebrides
VILA
Efate
Erromanga
Tana
Futuna
Rotuma
Wallis and Futuna (France)
Mata-Utu
Wallis
Horn Islands
WESTERN SAMOA
Savai'i
APIA
Upolu
American Samoa
Samoa Islands
Pago-Pago
Tutuila
Cook
Cairns
Forsayth
Townsville
Charters Towers
Ayr
Bowen
Hughenden
Mackay
Récifs d'Entrecasteaux
Îles Chesterfield (Chesterfield Is.)
Îles Belep
Huon
Koumac
Îles Loyauté (Loyalty Is.)
Nouvelle Calédonie (New Caledonia) (France)
Nouméa
Maré
Matthew
Hunter
Île des Pins
Fiji Islands
Vanua Levu
Viti Levu
Kandavu
SUVA
Koro
Ringgold Isles
Lau Group
Vatoa
Ono-i-Lau Islands
FIJI
Ceva-i-Ra
Conway Reef
Niuafo'ou
Niuato Putapu
TONGA
Fonualei
Vava'u Group
Tonga Islands
Kotu Group
Ha'apai Group
NUKU'ALOFA
Tongatapu Group
Minerva Reefs
Horizon Deep
Antiope
Alofi
Niue
Tropic of Capricorn
Queensland
Rockhampton
Longreach
Great Dividing Range
Gladstone
Bundaberg
Maryborough
Roma
Gympie
Quilpie
Charleville
Toowoomba
Brisbane
Ipswich
AUSTRALIA
Cunnamulla
Norfolk Is. (Austr.)
Kingston
Raoul
Macauley
Kermadec Islands (New Zealand)
Curtis
L'Esperance Rock
Galathea Deep
Bourke
Walgett
Grafton
Armidale
Lord Howe I. (Austr.)
Darling R.
New South Wales
Cobar
Dubbo
Newcastle
Parkes
Sydney
Wollongong
Mildura
Lachlan R.
Bathurst
Goulburn
Murray R.
Wagga Wagga
CANBERRA
Mount Kosciusko
Australian Alps
Horsham
Victoria
Geelong
Melbourne
Cape Howe
Warrnambool
Bass Strait
King Island
Flinders Island
Furneaux Group
Smithton
Devonport
George Town
Launceston
Zeehan
Mount Ossa
Tasmania
Hobart
Port Arthur
South East Cape
Tasman Sea
Three Kings Islands
North Cape
Whangarei
Great Barrier
Auckland
Manukau
Hamilton
Bay of Plenty
East Cape
Tauranga
North Island
New Plymouth
Gisborne
Napier
NEW ZEALAND
Cook Strait
Palmerston North
Cape Farewell
Nelson
WELLINGTON
Westport
Blenheim
Hokitika
South Island
Mount Cook
Southern Alps
Christchurch
Canterbury Bight
Wanaka
Timaru
Chatham
Chatham Islands (N.Z.)
Pitt
Manapouri
Dunedin
West Cape
Invercargill
Stewart I.
Foveaux Strait
Southwest Cape

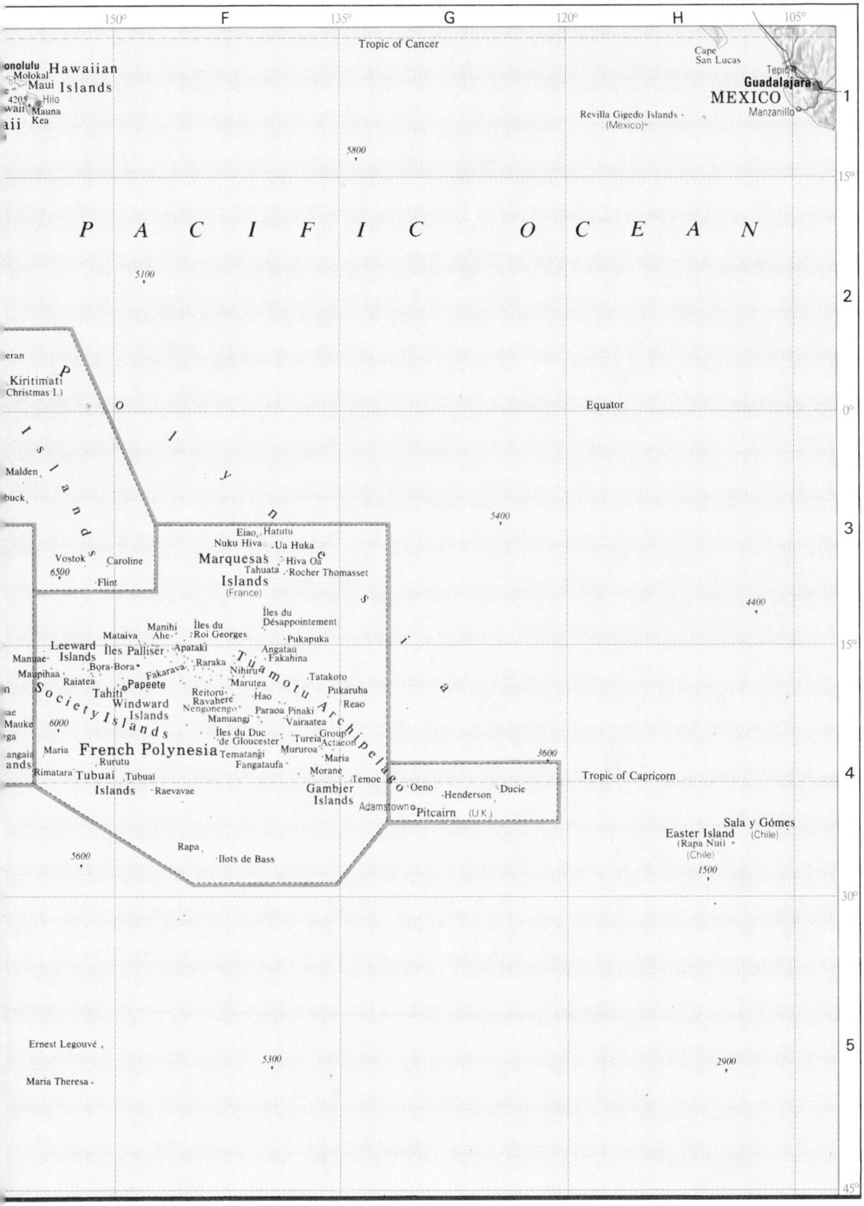

Scale 1:54 000 000

0 1000 2000 km

0 400 800 1200 miles

1 hour

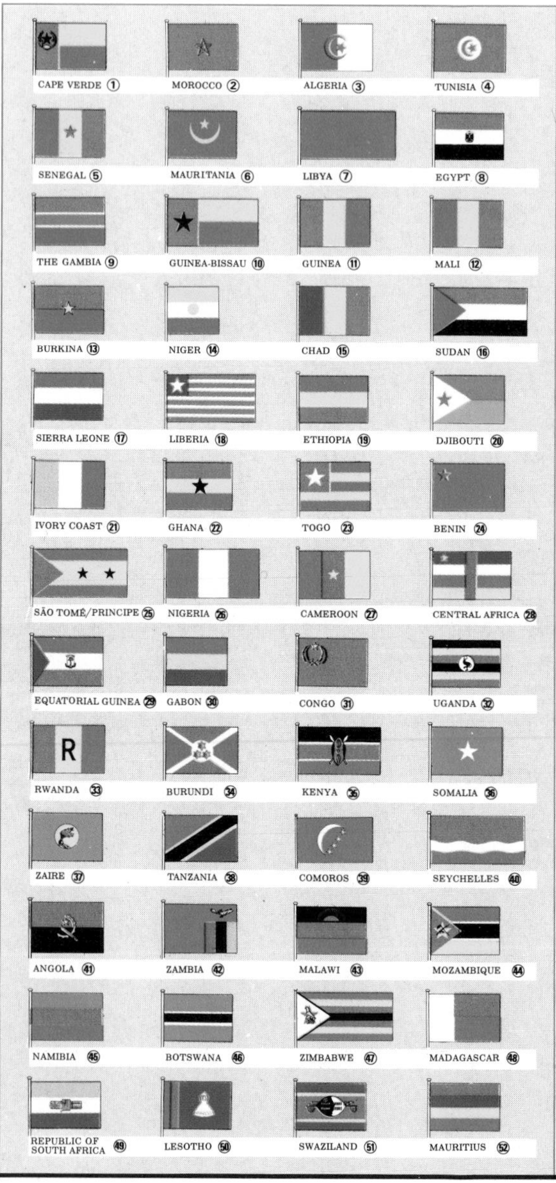
CAPE VERDE ①
MOROCCO ②
ALGERIA ③
TUNISIA ④
SENEGAL ⑤
MAURITANIA ⑥
LIBYA ⑦
EGYPT ⑧
THE GAMBIA ⑨
GUINEA-BISSAU ⑩
GUINEA ⑪
MALI ⑫
BURKINA ⑬
NIGER ⑭
CHAD ⑮
SUDAN ⑯
SIERRA LEONE ⑰
LIBERIA ⑱
ETHIOPIA ⑲
DJIBOUTI ⑳
IVORY COAST ㉑
GHANA ㉒
TOGO ㉓
BENIN ㉔
SÃO TOMÉ/PRINCIPE ㉕
NIGERIA ㉖
CAMEROON ㉗
CENTRAL AFRICA ㉘
EQUATORIAL GUINEA ㉙
GABON ㉚
CONGO ㉛
UGANDA ㉜
RWANDA ㉝
BURUNDI ㉞
KENYA ㉟
SOMALIA ㊱
ZAIRE ㊲
TANZANIA ㊳
COMOROS ㊴
SEYCHELLES ㊵
ANGOLA ㊶
ZAMBIA ㊷
MALAWI ㊸
MOZAMBIQUE ㊹
NAMIBIA ㊺
BOTSWANA ㊻
ZIMBABWE ㊼
MADAGASCAR ㊽
REPUBLIC OF SOUTH AFRICA ㊾
LESOTHO ㊿
SWAZILAND 51
MAURITIUS 52

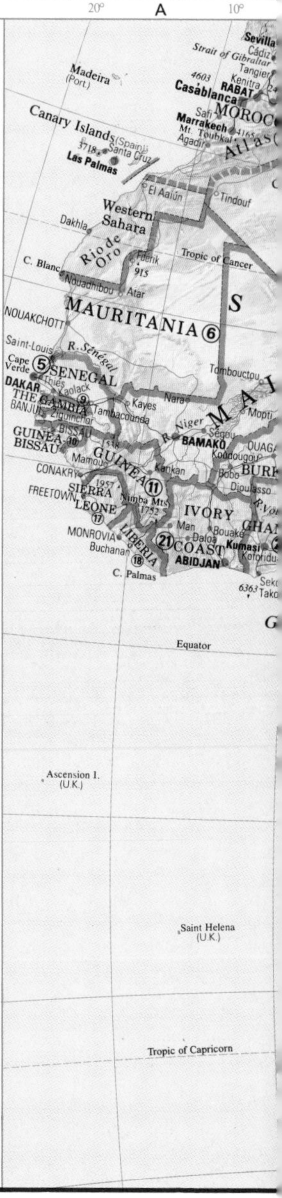
20°
A
10°
Strait of Gibraltar
Madeira (Port.)
Canary Islands (Spain)
Las Palmas
Santa Cruz
Casablanca
RABAT
Marrakech
Mt. Toubkal
Agadir
El Aaiún
Tindouf
Western Sahara
Dakhla
Rio de Oro
Tropic of Cancer
C. Blanc
Nouadhibou
Atar
MAURITANIA ⑥
NOUAKCHOTT
Saint-Louis
R. Sénégal
Cape Verde
DAKAR
SENEGAL
THE GAMBIA
BANJUL
Kaolack
Tambacounda
Kayes
Nara
Tombouctou
Mopti
R. Niger
BAMAKO
Ségou
GUINEA-BISSAU
BISSAU
GUINEA ⑪
Mamou
Kankan
CONAKRY
FREETOWN
SIERRA LEONE ⑰
Nimba Mts.
MONROVIA
Buchanan
LIBERIA ⑱
C. Palmas
IVORY COAST ㉑
Man
Bouaké
Daloa
ABIDJAN
Kumasi
Bobo
Dioulasso
Equator
Ascension I. (U.K.)
Saint Helena (U.K.)
Tropic of Capricorn

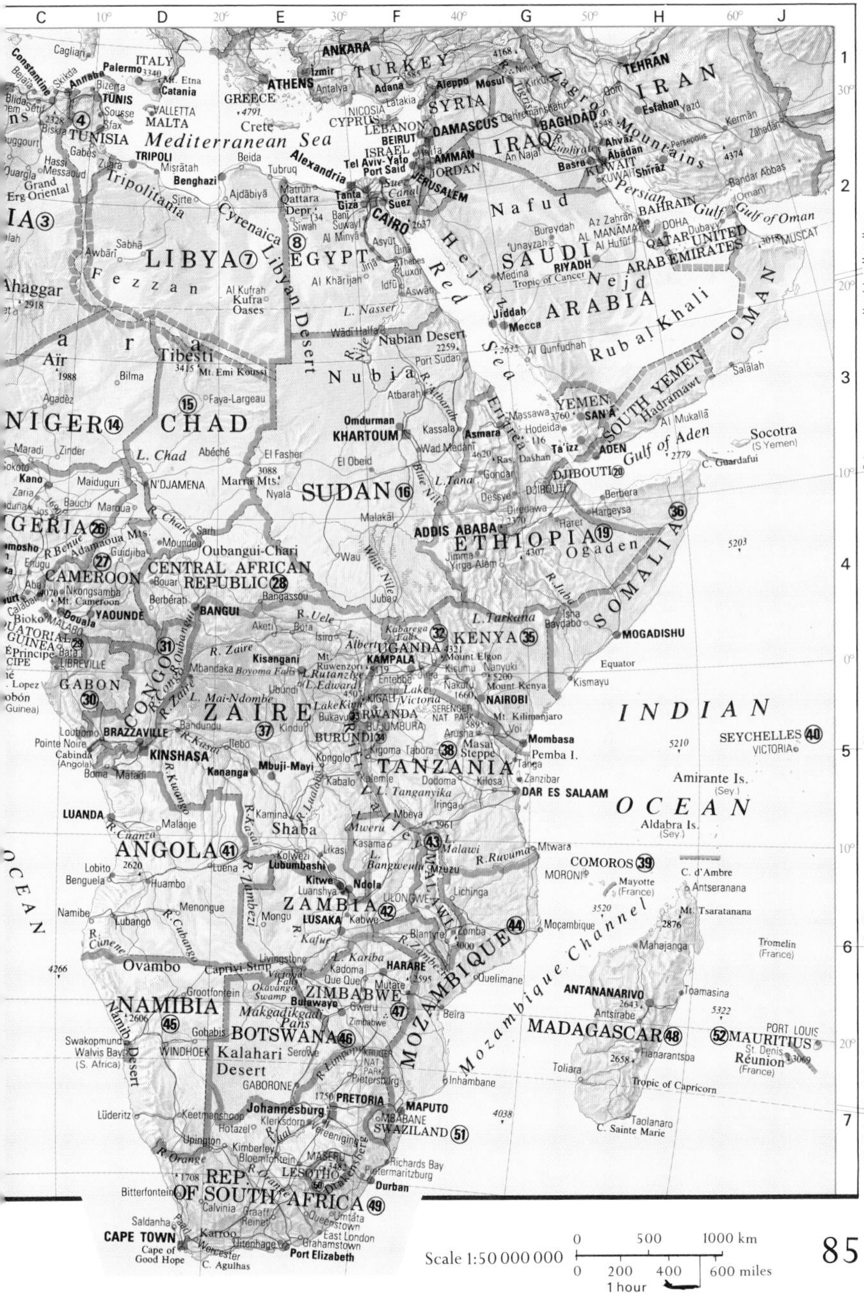

Scale 1:50 000 000

0 500 1000 km

0 200 400 600 miles

1 hour

A
C
D
E
30°
25°
15°
10°
5°
38°
30°
25°
20°
15°
1
2
3
4
5
6
Azores
(Port.)
Flores
Terceira
Angra do Heroismo
San Antonio
Pico
São Miguel
1105
Ponta Delgada
Santa Maria
2600
PORTUGAL
Algarve
Cabo de São Vicente
Huelva
Sevilla
Cordoba
Murcia
Lorca
Granada
Jerez de la Frontera
Cádiz
Malaga
Almeria
Marbella
Algeciras
Gibraltar (U.K.)
Ceuta (Spain)
Tanger
Tétouan
Mosta
Oran
Larache
Melilla (Spain)
Nador
Oujda
Ouezzane
Fès
Taza
Jerada
Kenitra
Salé
RABAT
Meknès
Sefrou
Dar el Beida (Casablanca)
El Jadida
Settat
Khenifra
Safi
Khouribga
Oued Zem
Beni Mellal
Bou Arfa
Marrakech
MOROCCO
Essaouira
Béchar
Abadla
4165
Jbel Toubkal
Ouarzazate
Agadir
Taroudant
Tiznit
Tagounite
Oglat Beraber
Goulimime
Bou Izakarn
Tabelbala
Kerzaz
Tinfouchy
Assa
Zag
Ksabi
Tindouf
4100
2600
Madeira
(Port.)
Pôrto Santo
Funchal
Ilhas Selvagens
(Port.)
Islas Canarias
(Canary Islands)
(Spain)
La Palma
Santa Cruz de Tenerife
Lanzarote
Gomera
Hierro
Tenerife
Las Palmas
Fuerteventura
Gran Canaria
Tarfaya
El Aaiún
Mahbès
Cabo Bojador
Semara
Bu Craa
Bordj Fly Sainte Marie
680
Eglab Dersa
Chenachane
Ain ben Tili
Guelta Zemmur
Bir Moghrein
Chegga
Tropic of Cancer
Sebkha Oumm ed Droûs Telli
Sebkhet Oumm ed Droûs Guebli
Dakhla
Western Sahara
Terhazza
El Mreiti
Cabo Barbas
Rio de Oro
Fdérik
Kediat Idjil
915
Tourine
Taoudenni
Tichla
Nouadhibou
Güera
Boulanouar
Choum
Ksar Torchane
Ouadane
Bir Ounane
Taguenout Hagguerét
Atar
Chinguetti
E l D j o u f
Ile Tidra
Cap Timiris
M A U R I T A N I A
Monts Timétrine
Bou Rjeima
NOUAKCHOTT
Ouad Naga
Tidjikdja
Araouane
Bou Djéhiba
2200
Moudjéria
554
Aoudaghost
Tiguent
Tamchaket
H o d h
Rkiz
Aleg
Bamba
Rosso
Bogué
Aioun el Atrouss
Néma
Tombouctou
Gourma-Rharous
Saint-Louis
Kaédi
Kiffa
Niger
Louga
Fouta
Matam
Kankossa
Kobenni
Niout
Koumbi-Saleh
Diré
Cap Vert
Dahra
Ferlo
Sénégal
Boulouli
Nioro du Sahel
Nara
Nampala
Lac Débo
1155
Hombori Tondo
DAKAR
Thiès
Diourbel
Bakel
Sandaré
Kona
Douentza
Rufisque
Mbour
SENEGAL
Kidira
Diéma
Mopti
Kaolack
Koungheul
Bondou
Kayes
THE GAMBIA
BANJUL
Gambia
Tambacounda
PARC NATIONAL DE LA BOUCLE DE BAOULÉ
Djidiéni
Sansanding
Ké Macina
Ouahigouya
Georgetown
Ségou
Kaya
Fouladou
P. N. DU NIOKOLO KOBA
Badoumbé
Kita
Fana
Kimparana
Ziguinchor
Kédougou
Kéniéba
BAMAKO
Dédougou
OUAGA
GUINEA-BISSAU
BISSAU
Bafatá
Koundara
Gaoual
Koudougou
Arquipélago dos Bijagós
Fouta Djallon
Labé
BURKINA
Bougouni
Sikasso
Bobo Dioulasso
G U I N E A
Siguiri
Boké
Mont 1421
Dinguiraye
Mandiana
Banfora
Gaoua
Bolgatanga
Lawra
Boffa
Kavendou
Mamou
Dabola
Kankan
Niellé
Ouangolodougou
MOLE GAME RESERVE
Ferkéssédougou
PARC NATIONAL DE LA KOMOÉ
Odienné
Boundiali
Korhogo
Bole
IVORY COAST
A T L A N T I C O C E A N
Sierra Morena
Atlas Mountains
Atlas el Kebir
Erg Iguidi
Erg Chech
ALGERIA
MALI

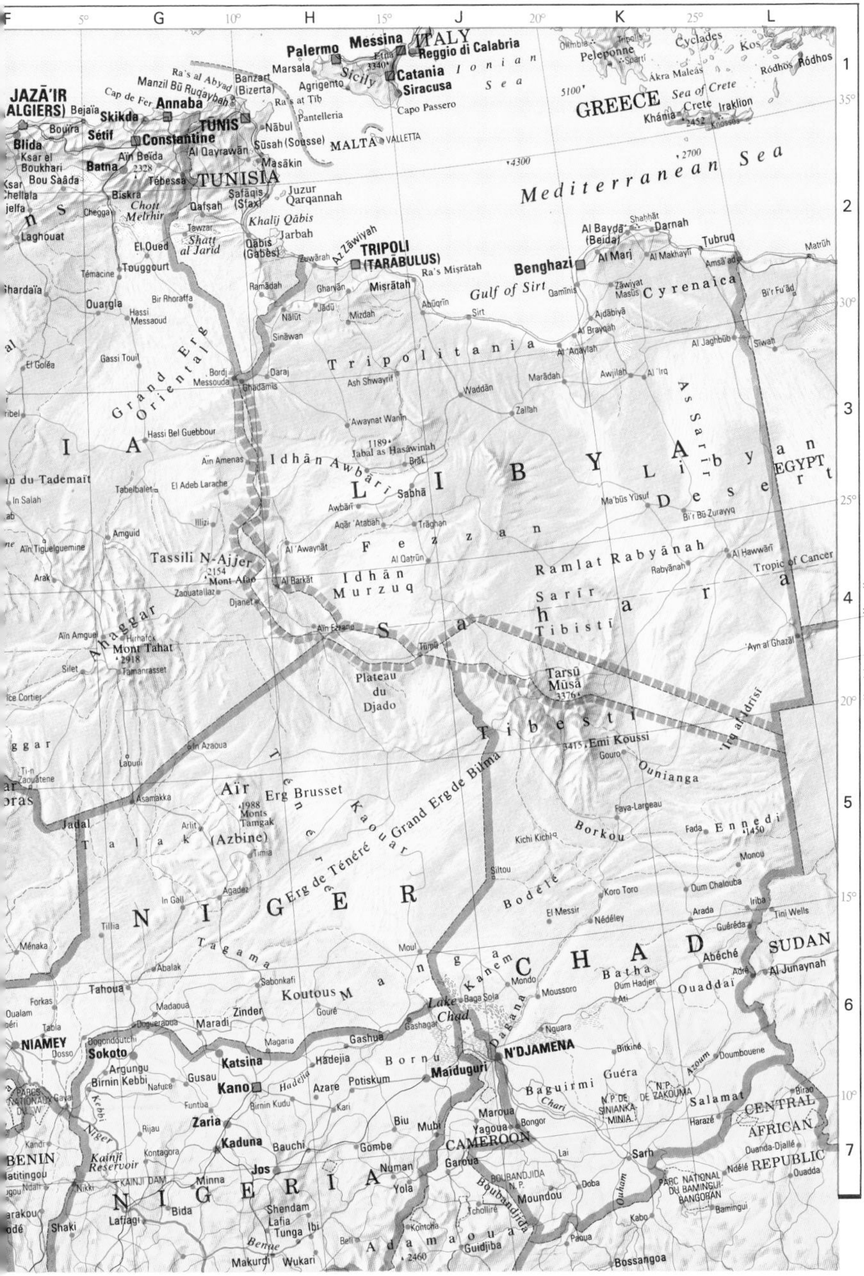
F
G
H
J
K
L
5°
10°
15°
20°
25°
35°
30°
25°
20°
15°
10°
1
2
3
4
5
6
7
Hong Kong
Honolulu
ITALY
Palermo
Messina
Reggio di Calabria
Marsala
Sicily
Catania
Siracusa
Agrigento
Capo Passero
Ionian Sea
Pantelleria
MALTA
VALLETTA
GREECE
Peloponnese
Cyclades
Kos
Ródhos
Sea of Crete
Crete
Khánia
Iraklion
Ákra Maleás
Mediterranean Sea
JAZĀ'IR
(ALGIERS)
Bejaïa
Skikda
Annaba
Sétif
Blida
Constantine
Batna
Biskra
Bou Saâda
Laghouat
Touggourt
Ouargla
Hassi Messaoud
Ghardaïa
El Goléa
Témacine
Chott Melrhir
El Oued
Ra's al Abyad
Manzil Bū Ruqaybah
Cap de Fer
Banzart (Bizerta)
TŪNIS
Al Qayrawān
Sūsah (Sousse)
Masākin
TUNISIA
Tébessa
Safāqis (Sfax)
Qafşah
Tawzar
Shaţţ al Jarīd
Jarbah
Qābis (Gabès)
Jazur Qarqannah
Khalīj Qābis
Ra's at Tib
Nābul
Zuwārah
Az Zāwiyah
TRIPOLI (TARĀBULUS)
Ra's Mişrātah
Mişrātah
Gharyān
Jādū
Mizdah
Nālūt
Sīnāwan
Darāj
Ghadāmis
Bordj Messouda
Grand Erg Oriental
Gassi Touil
Hassi Bel Guebbour
Aïn Amenas
In Salah
El Adeb Larache
Tabelbalet
Amguid
Illizi
Tassili N-Ajjer
Mont Afao
Djanet
Zaouatallaz
Arak
Aïn Tiguelguemine
Ahaggar
Mont Tahat
2918
Tamanrasset
Silet
Aïn Amguel
Hirhafok
In Azaoua
Laouni
Tin Zaouâtene
Asamakka
Abūqrīn
Sirt
Gulf of Sirt
Benghazi
Qamīnis
Al Bayḑā (Beida)
Shaḩḩāt
Darnah
Al Marj
Al Makhaylī
Ţubruq
Amsā'ad
Maţrūḩ
Bi'r Fu'ād
Cyrenaica
Zāwiyat Masūs
Ajdābiyā
Al Brayqah
Al 'Aqaylah
Al Jaghbūb
Sīwah
Tripolitania
Ash Shwayrif
Waddān
Marādah
Awjilah
Al 'Irq
Zallah
As Sarir
'Awaynat Wanīn
Jabal as Hasāwinah
1189
Brāk
Idhān Awbārī
Sabhā
Awbārī
LIBYA
Libyan Desert
EGYPT
Ma'būs Yūsuf
Bi'r Bū Zurayyq
Aqār 'Atabah
Trāghan
Fezzan
Al 'Awaynāt
Al Qaţrūn
Ramlat Rabyānah
Rabyānah
Al Hawwārī
Tropic of Cancer
Al Barkāt
Idhān Murzuq
Sahara
Sarīr Tibistī
Aïn Ezzane
Tūmū
'Ayn al Ghazāl
Plateau du Djado
Tarsū Mūsā
3376
'Irq al Idrīsī
Tibesti
3415
Emi Koussi
Gouro
Ounianga
Faya-Largeau
Borkou
Fada
Ennedi
1450
Kichi Kichi
Monou
Aïr
Erg Brusset
1988
Monts Tamgak
Arlit
(Azbine)
Timia
Ténéré
Kaouar
Grand Erg de Bilma
Erg de Ténéré
Talak
Jadal
Agadez
In Gall
NIGER
Tillia
Ménaka
Tagama
Abalak
Tahoua
Siltou
Bodélé
Koro Toro
Oum Chalouba
El Messir
Nédéley
Arada
Iriba
Tiné Wells
Guéréda
SUDAN
Moul
Manga
Kanem
CHAD
Abéché
Adré
Al Junaynah
Mondo
Batha
Oum Hadjer
Ati
Ouaddaï
Moussoro
Lake Chad
Baga Sola
Dagana
Koutous
Gouré
Zinder
Madaoua
Maradi
Forkas
Dogueraoua
Gashagar
Gashua
Magaria
Hadejia
N'DJAMENA
Nguara
Bitkine
Doumbouene
Azoum
NIAMEY
Dosso
Bogondoutchi
Sokoto
Argungu
Birnin Kebbi
Nafuce
Gusau
Katsina
Kano
Hadejia
Azare
Potiskum
Bornu
Maiduguri
Baguirmi
Guéra
N.P. DE ZAKOUMA
N.P. DE SINIANKA-MINIA
Salamat
Chari
Birao
CENTRAL AFRICAN REPUBLIC
PARC NATIONAL DU "W"
Kebbi
Niger
Funtua
Birnin Kudu
Kari
Zaria
Biu
Mubi
Maroua
Yagoua
Bongor
Harazé
Rijau
Kandi
BENIN
Kainji Reservoir
KAINJI DAM
Kontagora
Kaduna
Bauchi
Gombe
CAMEROON
Lai
Sarh
Ouanda-Djallé
Ndélé
Ouadda
Natitingou
Nikki
Ndali
Minna
Jos
Numan
Yola
Garoua
BOUBANDJIDA N.P.
Boubandjida
Moundou
Doba
Ouham
PARC NATIONAL DU BAMINGUI-BANGORAN
Bamingui
NIGERIA
Bida
Lafiagi
Shaki
Shendam
Lafia
Tunga
Ibi
Benue
Makurdi
Wukari
Beli
Adamaoua
2460
Kontcha
Tcholliré
Guidjiba
Paoua
Kabo
Bossangoa

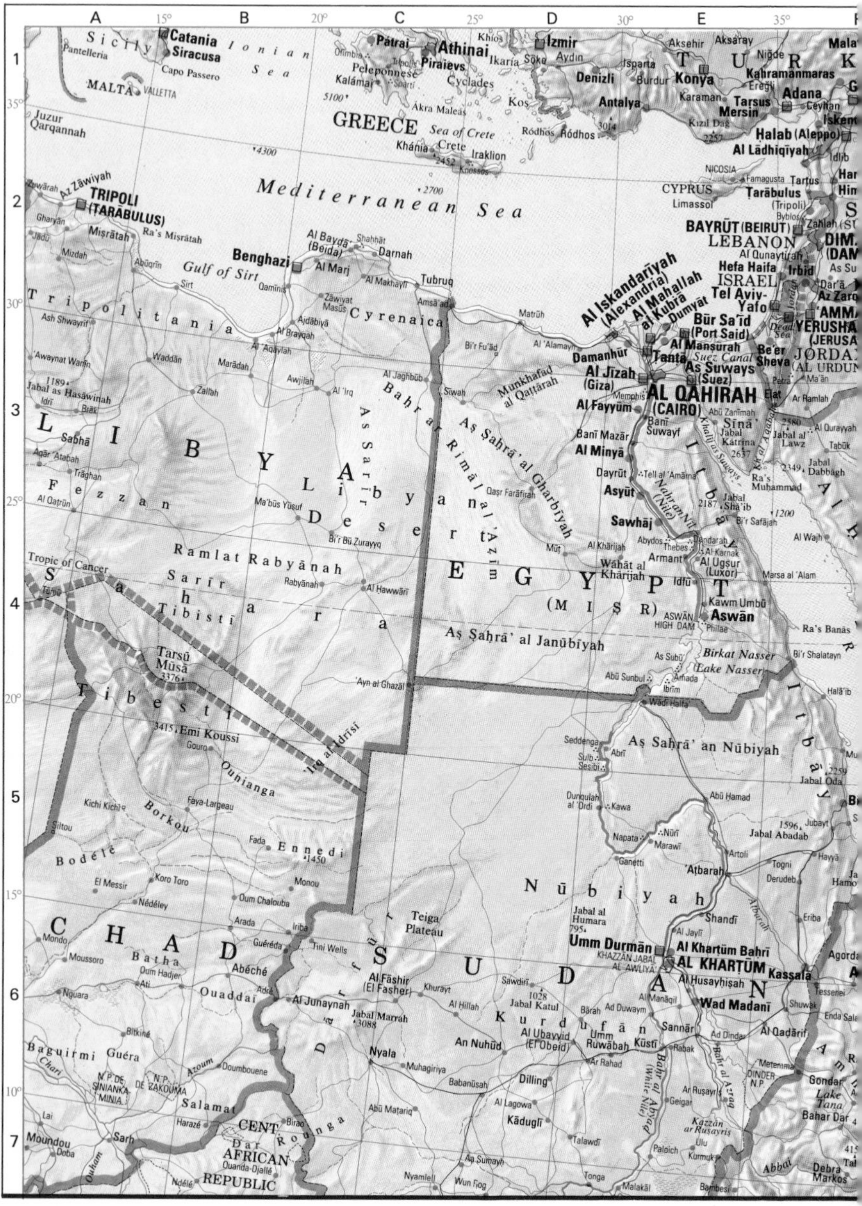

A
B
C
D
E
15°
20°
25°
30°
35°
35°
30°
25°
20°
15°
10°
1
2
3
4
5
6
7
Sicily
Catania
Siracusa
Pantelleria
Capo Passero
MALTA
VALLETTA
Ionian Sea
Pátrai
Athinai
Piraievs
Peloponnese
Kalámai
Cyclades
Khios
Ikaría
Izmir
Aydın
Söke
Kos
Denizli
Isparta
Burdur
Konya
Aksehir
Aksaray
Niğde
Kahramanmaras
Ereğli
Karaman
Tarsus
Adana
Mersin
Antalya
Kızıl Dağ
Ceyhan
Halab (Aleppo)
Al Lādhiqīyah
Ákra Maleas
GREECE
Sea of Crete
Crete
Khánia
Iraklion
Ródhos
Juzur Qarqannah
Mediterranean Sea
NICOSIA
Famagusta
CYPRUS
Limassol
Tartus
Tarābulus
(Tripoli)
Byblos
BAYRŪT (BEIRUT)
LEBANON
Zahlah
Al Qunaytirah
Irbid
Hefa Haifa
ISRAEL
Tel Aviv-Yafo
Az Zawiyah
TRIPOLI (TARĀBULUS)
Gharyān
Misrātah
Ra's Misrātah
Mizdah
Abūqrīn
Gulf of Sirt
Sirt
Benghazi
Al Bayḍā' (Beida)
Shaḥḥāt
Darnah
Al Marj
Al Makhayli
Tubruq
Qamīnis
Zāwiyat Masūs
Cyrenaica
Amsā'ad
Tripolitania
Ash Shwayrif
Ajdābiyā
Al Brayqah
Al 'Aqaylah
Waddān
Marādah
Awjilah
Al Jaghbūb
Al 'Irq
Sīwah
Bi'r Fu'ād
Matrūh
Al 'Alamayn
Munkhafad al Qaṭṭārah
Al Iskandarīyah (Alexandria)
Al Maḥallah al Kubrā
Dumyāt
Būr Sa'īd (Port Said)
Al Manṣūrah
Damanhūr
Tanṭā
Suez Canal
As Suways (Suez)
Al Jīzah (Giza)
Memphis
AL QAHIRAH (CAIRO)
Al Fayyūm
Banī Suwayf
Banī Mazār
Al Minyā
Dayrūt
Tell al 'Amārna
Asyūt
Sawhāj
Nahr an Nīl (Nile)
Abydos
Thebes
Dandarah
Al Karnak
Al Uqṣur (Luxor)
Armant
Idfū
Kawm Umbū
Aswān
ASWĀN HIGH DAM
Philae
Be'er Sheva
Elat
Sīnā'
Jabal Kātrina
Abū Zanīmah
Khalīj as Suways
'Awaynat Wanīn
Jabal as Hasāwinah
Idrī
Brāk
Zallah
Sabhā
Aqār 'Atabah
Trāghan
Fezzan
Al Qatrūn
LIBYA
Libyan Desert
As Sarīr
Baḥr ar Rimāl al 'Aẓīm
Aṣ Ṣaḥrā' al Gharbīyah
Qaṣr Farāfirah
Ma'būs Yūsuf
Bi'r Bū Zurayyq
Ramlat Rabyānah
Rabyānah
Al Hawwārī
Mūt
Al Khārijah
Wāḥāt al Khārijah
EGYPT
(MISR)
Tropic of Cancer
Sarīr Tibistī
Sahara
Aṣ Ṣaḥrā' al Janūbīyah
As Subū'
Birkat Nasser (Lake Nasser)
Abū Sunbul
Amada
Ibrīm
'Ayn al Ghazāl
Wādī Halfā
Tarsū Mūsā
3376
Tibesti
3415 Emi Koussi
Gouro
'Irq ar Idrīsī
Ounianga
Kichi Kichi
Faya-Largeau
Borkou
Siltou
Bodélé
Fada
Ennedi
1450
El Messir
Koro Toro
Monou
Nédéley
Oum Chalouba
Arada
Iriba
CHAD
Mondo
Moussoro
Batha
Oum Hadjer
Ati
Guéréda
Tini Wells
Abéché
Adré
Ouaddaï
Nguara
Bitkiné
Baguirmi
Guéra
Chari
Azoum
Doumbouene
N.P. DE SINIANKA-MINIA
N.P. DE ZAKOUMA
Salamat
Lai
Harazé
Birao
Moundou
Doba
Sarh
CENTRAL AFRICAN REPUBLIC
Dar Rounga
Ouanda-Djallé
Ndélé
Ouham
Seddenga
Abrī
Sulb
Sesibi
Aṣ Ṣaḥrā' an Nūbiyah
Abū Ḥamad
Dunqulah al 'Ordi
Kawa
Napata
Nūrī
Marawī
Ganetti
Nūbiyah
Aṭbarah
Artoli
Jabal al Humara
795
Teiga Plateau
Shandī
Al Jaylī
Umm Durmān
KHAZZĀN JABAL AL AWLIYĀ'
Al Khartūm Bahrī
AL KHARṬŪM
SUDAN
Al Fāshir (El Fasher)
Khurayt
Darfur
Al Junaynah
Jabal Marrah
3088
Nyala
Muhagiriya
Babanūsah
Al Ḥillah
Sawdirī
1028
Jabal Katul
Kurdufān
Al Ubayyid (El Obeid)
Umm Ruwābah
An Nuhūd
Bārah
Ad Duwaym
Al Ḥusayḥiṣah
Al Manāqil
Wad Madanī
Sannār
Kūstī
Rabak
Ad Dindar
Ar Rahad
Dilling
Al Lagowa
Kādugli
Abū Matāriq
Talawdī
Aq Sumayh
Nyamlell
Wun Rog
Tonga
Malakāl
Baḥr al Abyaḍ (White Nile)
Baḥr al Azraq
Ar Ruṣayriṣ
Geigar
Khazzān ar Ruṣayriṣ
Ulu
Paloich
Kurmuk
Bambesi
Abbai
Kassalā
Tessenei
Shuwak
Al Qaḍārif
Metenma
DINDER N.P.
Gondar
Lake Tana
Bahar Dar
Debra Markos
Atbarah
Eriba
Derudeb
Togni
Jabal Abadab
1596
Jubayt
Ḥalā'ib
Jabal Oda
2259
Bi'r Shalatayn
Ra's Banās
Marsa al 'Alam
Bi'r Safājah
Jabal Sha'ib
2187
Ra's Muḥammad
Jabal Dabbāgh
2349
Jabal al Lawz
2580
Al Qurayyah
Tabūk
Ar Ramlah
Ma'ān
Al Wajh
1200
DIM. (DAM
As Su
'AMMA
YERUSHA (JERUSA
JORDA (AL URDUN
Dead Sea
Petra

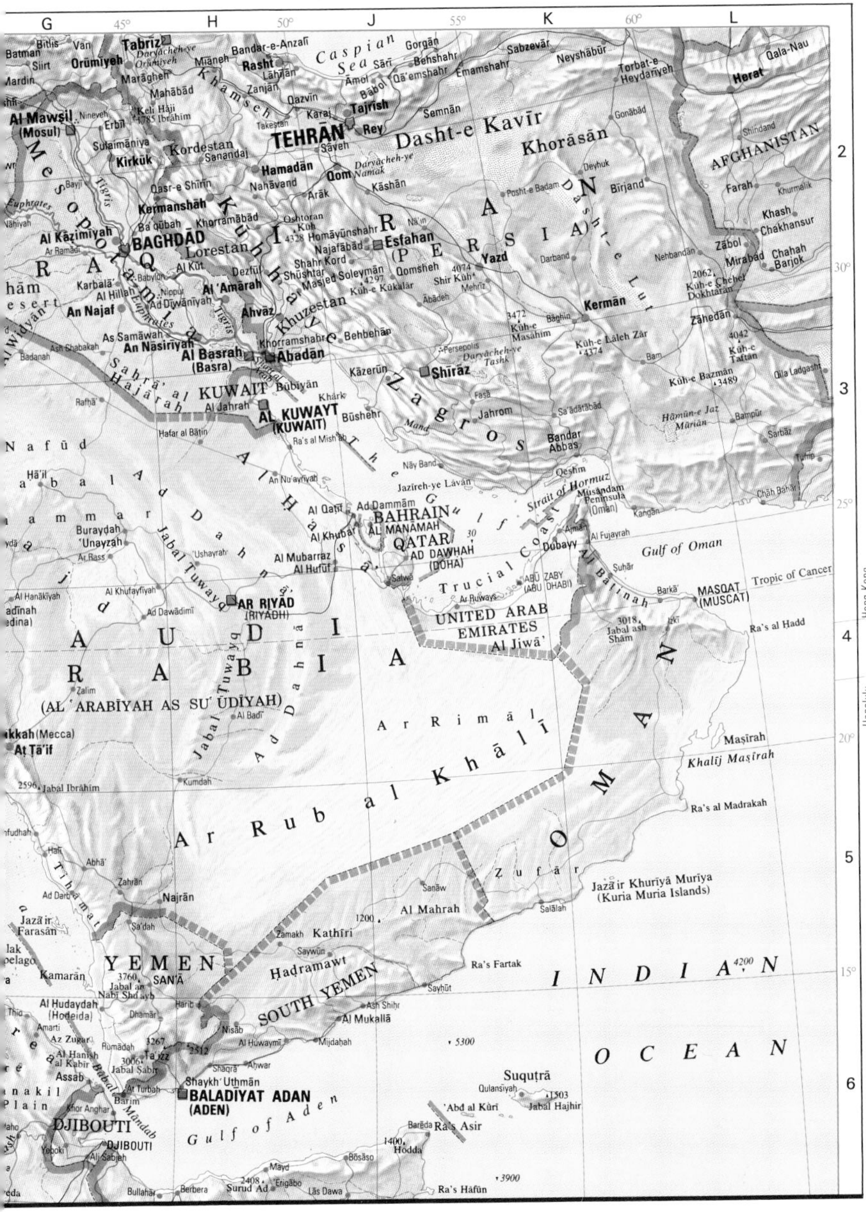

Scale 1:20 000 000

0 200 400 600 800 1000 km

0 200 400 600 miles

1 hour

MAURITANIA
El Djouf
NOUAKCHOTT
Nouadhibou
Atar
Tidjikdja
Hodh
Saint-Louis
DAKAR
SENEGAL
THE GAMBIA
BANJUL
GUINEA-BISSAU
BISSAU
Arquipélago dos Bijagós
GUINEA
Fouta Djallon
CONAKRY
FREETOWN
SIERRA LEONE
Sherbro Island
MONROVIA
LIBERIA
Grain Coast
Cape Palmas
MALI
BAMAKO
Ségou
Mopti
Tombouctou
Gao
Niger
Kayes
Bobo Dioulasso
BURKINA
OUAGADOUGOU
IVORY COAST
ABIDJAN
Bouaké
Yamoussoukro
Ivory Coast
GHANA
Kumasi
Tamale
ACCRA
Sekondi-Takoradi
Gold Coast
TOGO
LOMÉ
PORTO NOVO
Cotonou
Bight
ATLANTIC OCEAN
Equator
CAPE VERDE
(CABO VERDE)
Santo Antão
São Vicente
Mindelo
Sal
São Nicolau
Boa Vista
São Tiago
Maio
Fogo
PRAIA

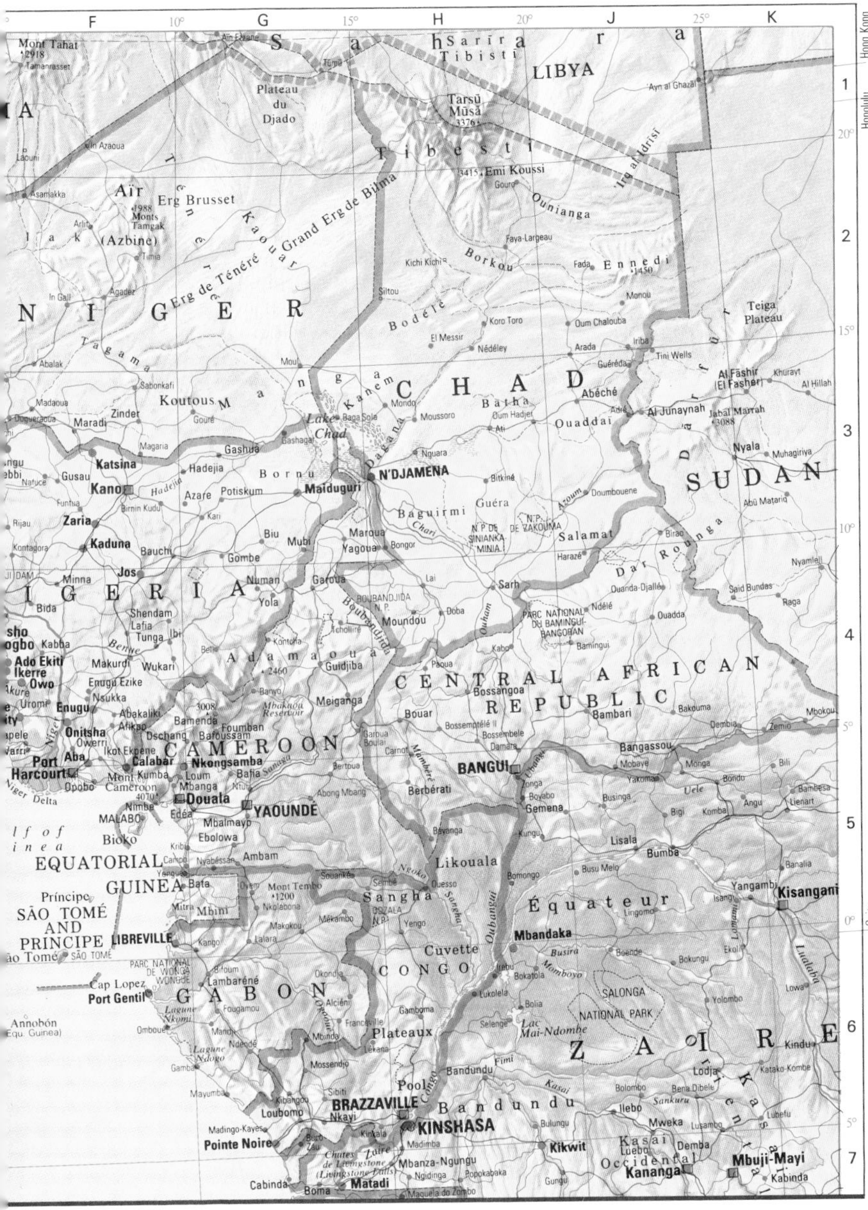

Scale 1:20 000 000

km	0	200	400	600	800	1000 km
miles	0	200	400	600 miles		

1 hour

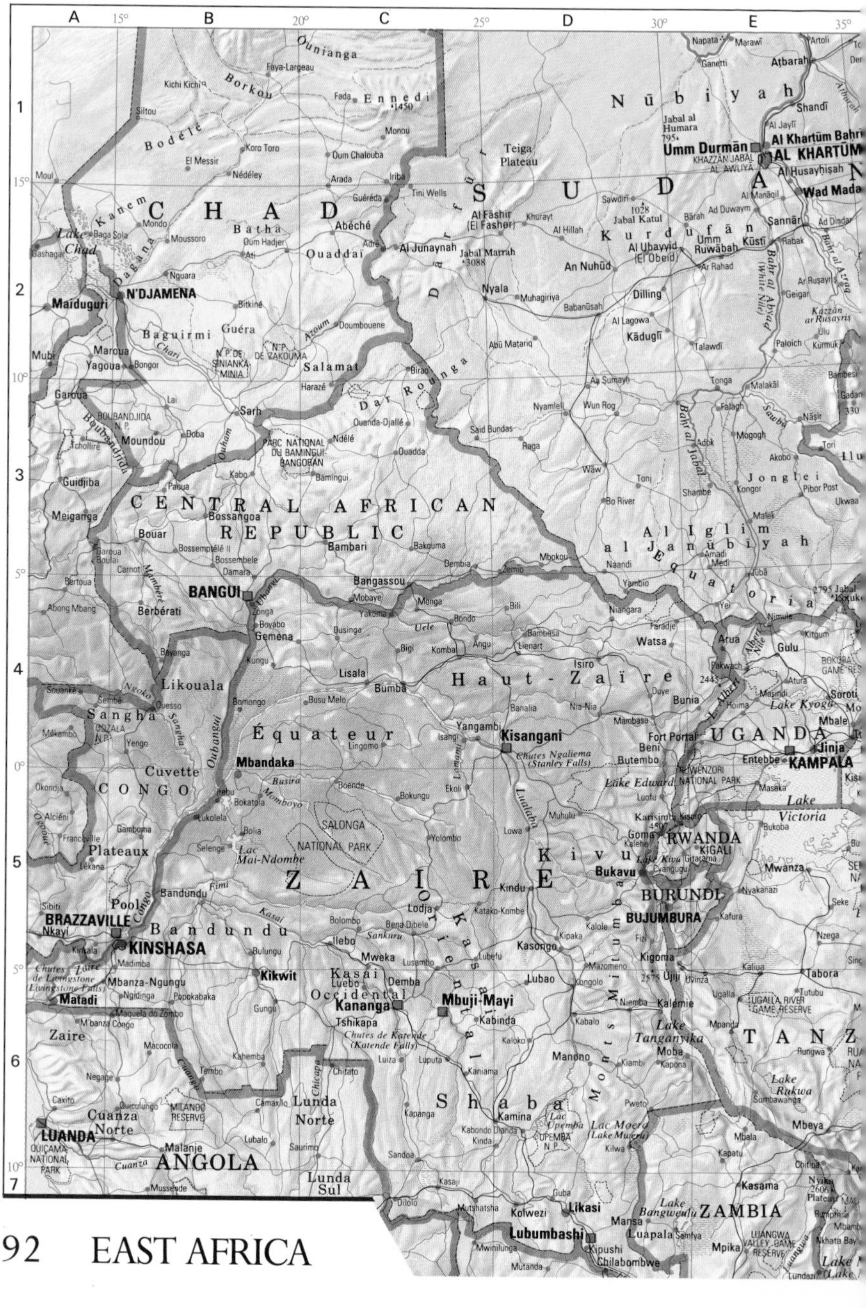
A
B
C
D
E
15°
20°
25°
30°
35°
1
2
3
4
5
6
7
10°
5°
0°
CHAD
SUDAN
CENTRAL AFRICAN REPUBLIC
CONGO
ZAIRE
UGANDA
RWANDA
BURUNDI
ANGOLA
ZAMBIA
Ounianga
Faya-Largeau
Borkou
Kichi Kichi
Siltou
Bodélé
Koro Toro
El Messir
Nédéley
Fada
Ennedi
1450
Monou
Oum Chalouba
Arada
Iriba
Tini Wells
Guéréda
Moul
Kanem
Mondo
Baga Sola
Lake Chad
Moussoro
Batha
Oum Hadjer
Ati
Abéché
Adré
Ouaddaï
Gashaga
Dagana
Nguara
N'DJAMENA
Maiduguri
Bitkine
Baguirmi
Guéra
Azoum
Doumbouene
Mubi
Maroua
Yagoua
Bongor
Chari
N.P. DE SINIANKA-MINIA
N.P. DE ZAKOUMA
Salamat
Haraze
Birao
Garoua
Lai
Sarh
Dar Rounga
Ouanda-Djallé
BOUBANDJIDA N.P.
Doba
Moundou
Tcholliré
Ouham
PARC NATIONAL DU BAMINGUI-BANGORAN
Ndélé
Ouadda
Kabo
Bamingui
Guidjiba
Paoua
Meiganga
Bossangoa
Bouar
Bambari
Bakouma
Bossemptélé II
Bossembele
Garoua Boulai
Carnot
Damara
Mambéré
Dembia
Zemio
Bertoua
BANGUI
Ubangi
Bangassou
Mobaye
Abong Mbang
Berbérati
Zongo
Yakoma
Monga
Bondo
Bili
Boyabo
Gemena
Busingo
Uele
Bambesa
Bayanga
Bigi
Komba
Angu
Lienart
Kungu
Lisala
Bumba
Souanké
Sembé
Ngoko
Likouala
Ouesso
Sangha
ODZALA N.P.
Mékambo
Yengo
Bomongo
Busu Melo
Équateur
Lingomo
Oubangui
Mbandaka
Cuvette
Okondja
Irebu
Busira
Boende
Bokatola
Momboyo
Bokungu
Lukolela
Bolia
SALONGA NATIONAL PARK
Alcléni
Ogooué
Franceville
Gamboma
Plateaux
Lékana
Selenge
Lac Mai-Ndombe
Yolombo
Fimi
Bandundu
Pool
Congo
Sibiti
BRAZZAVILLE
Nkayi
KINSHASA
Kinkala
Zaire
Chutes Livingstone (Livingstone Falls)
Madimba
Mbanza-Ngungu
Ngidinga
Matadi
Kasai
Bulungu
Kikwit
Popokabaka
Gungu
Maquela do Zombo
M'banza Congo
Zaire
Macocola
Kahemba
Tembo
Cuango
Negage
Caxito
Quiculungo
MILANDO RESERVE
Cuanza Norte
LUANDA
QUIÇAMA NATIONAL PARK
Cuanza
Malanje
Lubalo
Saurimo
Camaxilo
Lunda Norte
Lunda Sul
Chicapa
Chitato
Musserede
Ilebo
Mweka
Bolombo
Bena Dibele
Sankuru
Lodja
Kasai Occidental
Luebo
Demba
Kananga
Tshikapa
Chutes de Katende (Katende Falls)
Luiza
Luputa
Mbuji-Mayi
Kabinda
Kaniama
Kasai Oriental
Lusambo
Lubefu
Katako-Kombe
Kindu
Kasongo
Kipaka
Kalole
Lubao
Kongolo
Kaloko
Kabalo
Manono
Kiambi
Shaba
Kamina
Kapanga
Kabondo Dianda
Kinda
Sandoa
Kasaji
Dilolo
Mutshatsha
Kolwezi
Likasi
Lubumbashi
Kipushi
Chilabombwe
Mwinilunga
Mutanda
Lac Upemba
UPEMBA N.P.
Lac Moero (Lake Mweru)
Kilwa
Pweto
Monts Mitumba
Kivu
Bukavu
Cyangugu
Goma
Kalehe
Lake Kivu
Gitarama
KIGALI
Karisimbi
4507
Kisoro
BUJUMBURA
Fizi
Mazomeno
Kigoma
Ujiji
Uvinza
2575
Niemba
Kalemie
Lake Tanganyika
Moba
Kapona
Nūbiyah
Napata
Marawī
Ganetti
Atbarah
Artoli
Shandī
Jabal al Humara
795
Al Jaylī
Umm Durmān
Al Khartūm Bahrī
AL KHARTŪM
KHAZZĀN JABAL AL AWLIYA
Al Husayhisah
Wad Madanī
Teiga Plateau
Darfūr
Al Fāshir (El Fasher)
Khurayt
Al Hillah
Sawdirī
Jabal Katul
1028
Bārah
Ad Duwaym
Al Manāqil
Sannār
Kurdufān
Al Junaynah
Jabal Marrah
3088
Al Ubayyid (El Obeid)
Umm Ruwābah
Kūstī
Rabak
Ar Rahad
Bahr al Abyad (White Nile)
Bahr al Azraq
An Nuhūd
Nyala
Muhagiriya
Babanūsah
Dilling
Ar Ruṣayriṣ
Geigar
Kazzān ar Ruṣayriṣ
Al Lagowa
Kādugli
Abū Matariq
Talawdī
Paloich
Kurmuk
Aa Sumayh
Tonga
Malakāl
Nyamlell
Wun Rog
Bahr al Jabal
Falagh
Sawba
Nāsir
Said Bundas
Raga
Adok
Mogogh
Akobo
Waw
Tonj
Jonglei
Kongor
Shambe
Pibor Post
Bo River
Malek
Al Iglīm al Janūbīyah
Mbokou
Naandi
Amadi
Medi
Equatoria
Yambio
Jūbā
Yei
Nimule
2795 Jabal Kinyeti
Niangara
Faradje
Kitgum
Watsa
Arua
Gulu
Albert Nile
Isiro
Pakwach
BOKORA GAME RESERVE
Haut-Zaïre
Duye
Bunia
2445
Atura
Masindi
Soroti
L. Albert
Hoima
Lake Kyoga
Banalia
Nia-Nia
Mambasa
Mbale
Yangambi
Isangi
Kisangani
Fort Portal
Beni
Jinja
Chutes Ngaliema (Stanley Falls)
Butembo
Entebbe
KAMPALA
Lomami
RUWENZORI NATIONAL PARK
Lake Edward
Masaka
Ekoli
Lualaba
Luofu
Lake Victoria
Muhulu
Lowa
Bukoba
Mwanza
Nyakanazi
Kafura
Seke
Nzega
Kaliua
Tabora
Ugalla
UGALLA RIVER GAME RESERVE
Tutubu
Mpanda
TANZ
Rungwa
Lake Rukwa
Sumbawanga
Mbeya
Mbala
Kapatu
Chitipa
Kasama
Nyika 2606 Plateau
Lake Bangweulu
Mansa
Luapala
Samfya
Mpika
LUANGWA VALLEY GAME RESERVE
Luangwa
Lundazi
Mbambi
Rumphi
Nkhata Bay

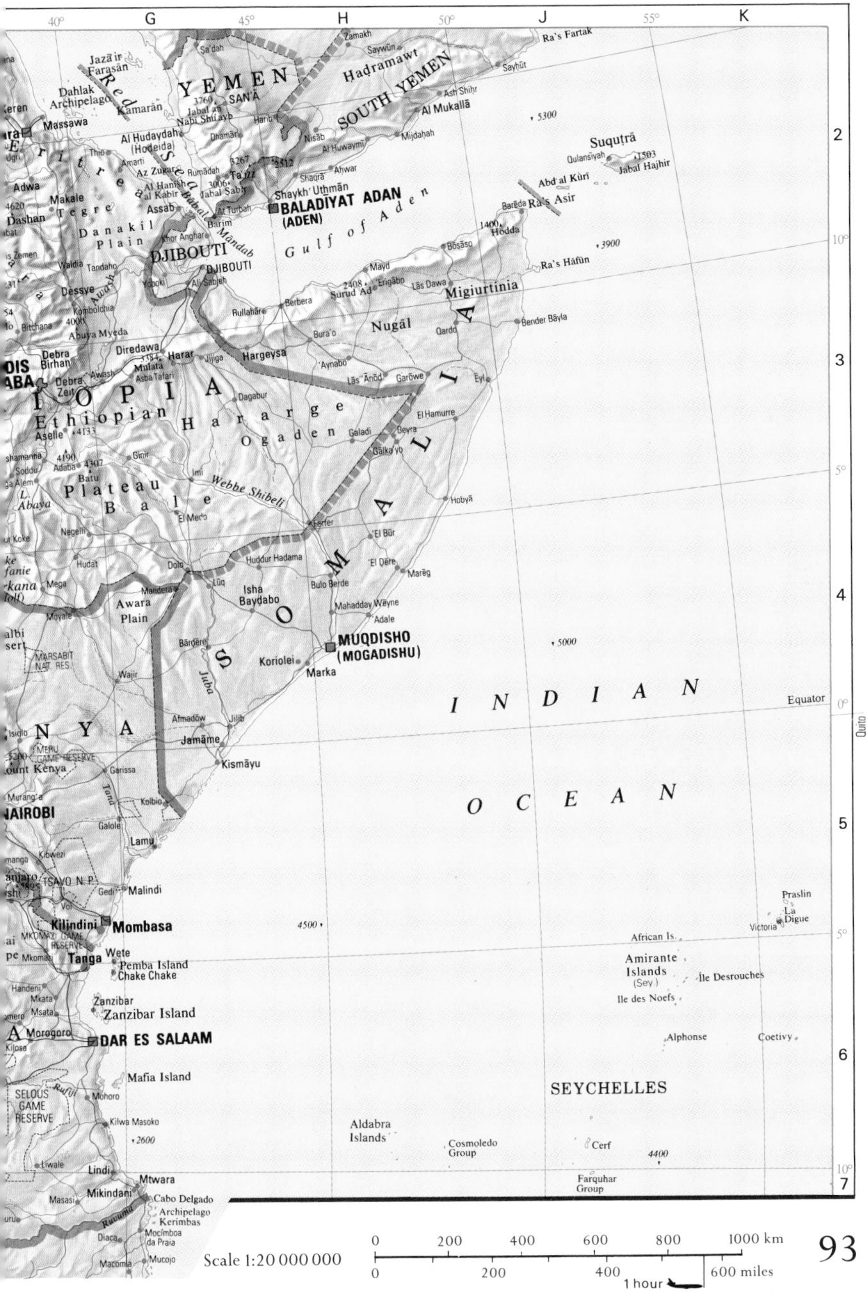
YEMEN
SOUTH YEMEN
SAN'A
BALADIYAT ADAN
(ADEN)
Gulf of Aden
Red Sea
DJIBOUTI
SOMALIA
ETHIOPIA
KENYA
MUQDISHO
(MOGADISHU)
INDIAN OCEAN
Suquṭrā
SEYCHELLES
DAR ES SALAAM
Mombasa
Zanzibar Island
Pemba Island
Mafia Island
Hargeysa
Kismāyu
Equator
Scale 1:20 000 000
0 200 400 600 800 1000 km
0 200 400 600 miles
1 hour

A
B
C
D
10°
15°
20°
25°
30°
1
2
3
4
5
6
Ponta do Padrão
Maquela do Zombo
M'banza Congo
Zaire
Macocola
Kahemba
Tembo
Cuango
Negage
Caxito
Quiculungo
MILANDO RESERVE
LUANDA
Cuanza Norte
Malanje
QUIÇAMA NATIONAL PARK
Cuanza
Porto Amboim
Gabela
Sumbe
Cuanza Sul
Quibala
Mussende
LUANDO RESERVE
Luando
Huambo
Bailundo
Lobito
Benguela
Morro de Moco
2620
Kuito
Munhango
Luena
A N G O L A
Bié
Moxico
Quembo
Mount Tama
2490
Caconda
Bentiaba
Huíla
Cacula
Kuvango
Dongo
Menongue
Cangombe
Cangamba
Lumbala N'guimbo
Lubango
Namibe
NAMIBE RESERVE
BICUARI NATIONAL PARK
MUPA NATIONAL PARK
Caiundo
Cuito Cuanavale
Cubango
Cunene
Cuando Cubango
Neriquinha
IONA NATIONAL PARK
Monte Negro Falls
Xangongo
Ruacana Falls
Chitado
Kunene
Tshikapa
Chutes de Katende (Katende Falls)
Chicapa
Chitato
Camaxilo
Lunda Norte
Lubalo
Saurimo
Lunda Sul
Dala
Dilolo
Luacano
CAMEIA NATIONAL PARK
Lucusse
Lumbala Kaquengue
Lumbala
Kabinda
Kaloko
Z A I R E
Luiza
Luputa
Kaniama
Manono
Kiambi
Shaba
Kapanga
Kamina
Lac Upemba
UPEMBA N.P.
Kabondo Dianda
Kinda
Lac Moero (Lake Mweru)
Pweto
Kilwa
Sandoa
Kasaji
Mutshatsha
Kolwezi
Likasi
Guba
Lubumbashi
Mansa
Mwinilunga
Kipushi
Chilabombwe
Mutanda
Chingola
Kitwe
Luanshya
Copperbelt
Kabompo
Kafue
Kabwe
Zambezi
Kaoma
Mongu
Barotseland
Z A M B
KAFUE NATIONAL PARK
Mazabuka
Kafue
Batoka
Mulobezi
Sesheke
Zimba
Livingstone (Maramba)
Lake Kariba
Oshakati
Ondangwa
Nkurenkuru
Rundu
Okavango
Dirico
Luiana
Kongola
CAPRIVI GAME PARK
Caprivi Strip
Linyanti
Victoria Falls
Wankie
Ohopoho
Ovamboland
Etosha Pan
ETOSHA NATIONAL PARK
Cape Fria
SKELETON COAST PARK
Sesfontein
Kamanjab
Tsumeb
Kanovlei
Otavi
Grootfontein
Tsumkwe
Tsodilo Hills
1805
Okavango Swamp
Ngamiland
Maun
CHOBE NATIONAL PARK
Pandamatenga
WANKIE NATIONAL PARK
Lupane
Matabe
Outjo
Waterberg
1887
N A M I B I A
Nata
Maitengwe
Botletle
Makgadikgadi Pan (Makarikari)
Dukwe
Tshesebe
Francistown
Orapa
2606
Brandberg
Uis Mine
2289
Mt. Amatako
Erongo Mts.
2350
Erongo
Otjozondu
Okorukambe
Karibib
Okahandja
Cape Cross
3700
Damaraland
Gobabis
Mamuno
Ghanzi
CENTRAL KALAHARI GAME RESERVE
B O T S W A N A
Serule
Serowe
Palapye
Takatshwane
Kalahari
Mahalapye
Dinokwe
Limpopo
Swakopmund
WINDHOEK
2484
Auas Mountains
Walvis Bay (S. Africa)
NAMIB DESERT PARK
Rehoboth
Leonardville
Tropic of Capricorn
Solitaire
Hoachanas
Aranos
Tshane
Mariental
Gochas
Namib Desert
Molepolole
Sekoma
Khakhea
GABORONE
Kanye
Mochudi
Nylstroom
Pietersburg
Potgietersrus
GEMSBOK NATIONAL PARK
KALAHARI GEMSBOK N.P.
Namaland
1586
Mount Brukkaros
Helmeringhausen
Nossob
Koës
Rustenburg
Witwatersrand
Krugersdorp
Carletonville
Vanderbijlpark
Klerksdorp
Orkney
Vereeniging
Parys
Bophuthatswana
Keetmanshoop
Lüderitz
Aus
Seeheim
Aroab
Kuruman
Hotazel
Vryburg
Kuruman
Gakarosa
1855
Warrenton
Odendaalsrus
Kroonstad
Welkom
Virginia
Orange Free State
Grünau
Karasburg
Molopo
Upington
Postmasburg
Vaal
Oranje
Keimoes
Griquatown
Kimberley
Namaqualand
Steinkopf
Port Nolloth
Pofadder
Bushman Land
Kenhardt
REP. OF SOUTH AFRICA
Bloemfontein
LESOTHO
MASERU
Springbok
Groot Vloer
Prieska
Orange
Wepener
Mafeteng
Brandvlei
Britstown
De Aar
Zastron
Aliwal North
Carnarvon
Colesberg
Burgersdorp
Bitterfontein
Nieuwoudtville
Victoria West
Hanover
Elliot
Vanrhynsdorp
Williston
Kompas Berg
2504
Middelburg
Drakensberg
Umtata
Cape Province
Lamberts Bay
Clanwilliam
Graaff Reinet
Cradock
Queenstown
2371 Groot Winter Berg
Ciskei
King Williams Town
East London
Beaufort West
Great Karroo
Cape Columbine
Saldanha
Tulbagh
Worcester
2325
Willowmore
Grahamstown
Paarl
Stellenbosch
Oudtshoorn
Uitenhage
CAPE TOWN
Table Mountain
Strand
Swellendam
Port Elizabeth
Cape of Good Hope
Mosselbaai
Cape Saint Francis
Cape Agulhas
ATLANTIC OCEAN

94 SOUTHERN AFRICA

Scale 1:20 000 000

0 200 400 600 800 1000 km

0 200 400 600 miles

1 hour

CANADA (1)

UNITED STATES (2)

MEXICO (3)

THE BAHAMAS (4)

CUBA (5)

JAMAICA (6)

HAITI (7)

DOMINICAN REPUBLIC (8)

GUATEMALA (9)

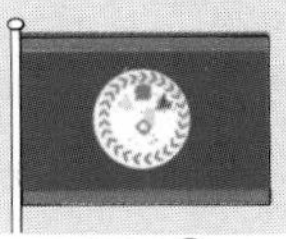

BELIZE (10)

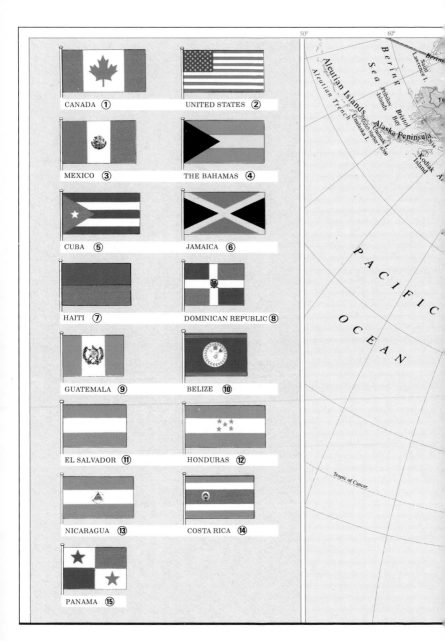

EL SALVADOR (11)

HONDURAS (12)

NICARAGUA (13)

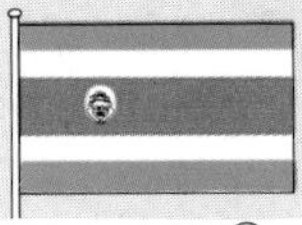

COSTA RICA (14)

PANAMA (15)

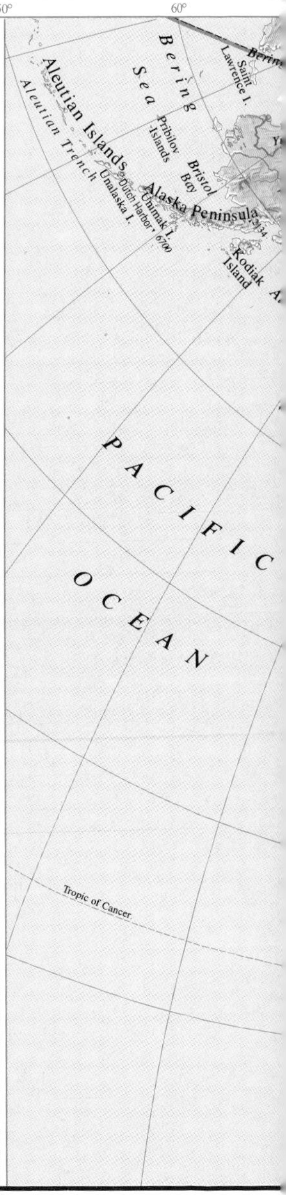

Scale 1:50 00

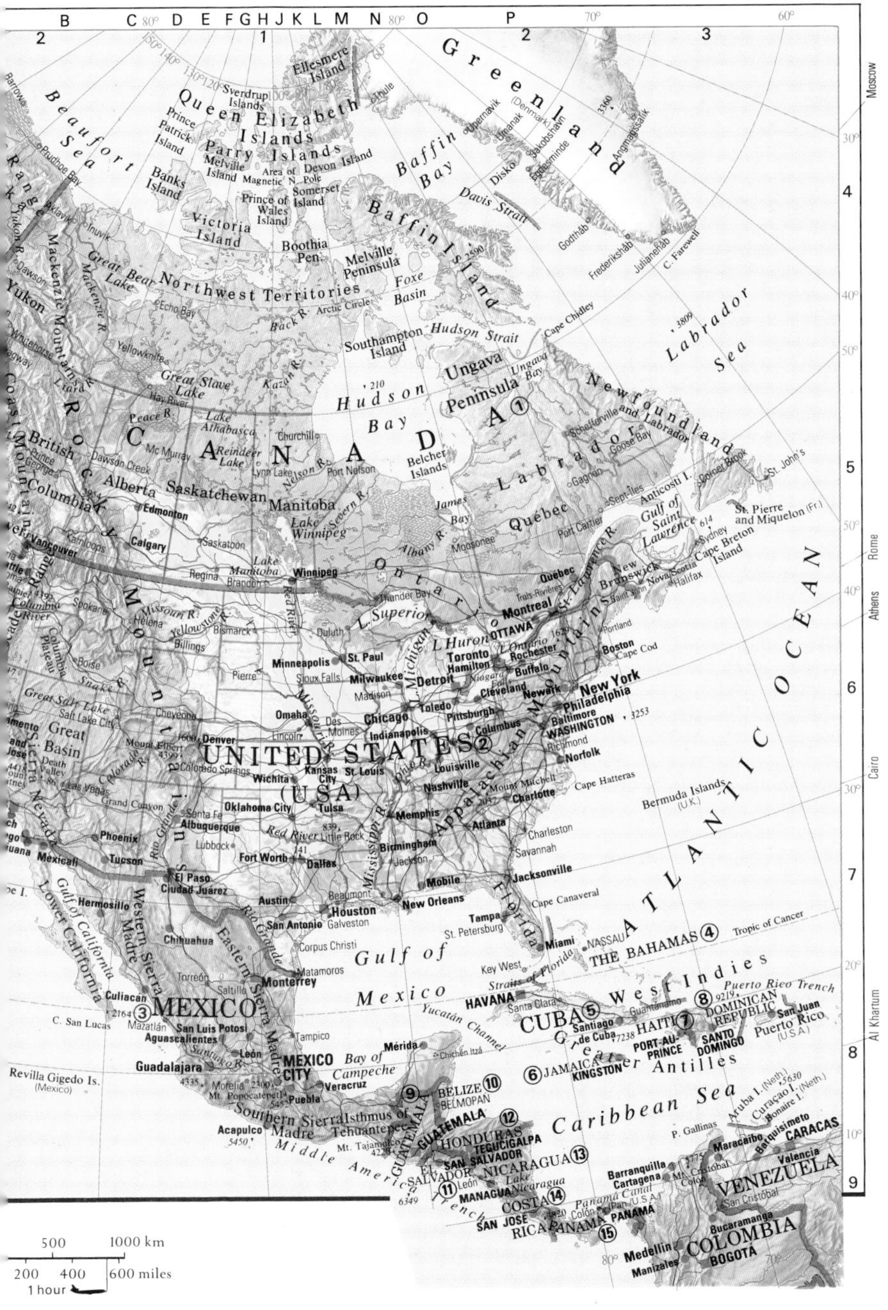

B C D E F G H J K L M N O P
1 2 3 4 5 6 7 8 9
Greenland
(Denmark)
Ellesmere Island
Queen Elizabeth Islands
Parry Islands
Sverdrup Islands
Prince Patrick Island
Melville Island
Banks Island
Victoria Island
Prince of Wales Island
Somerset Island
Devon Island
Area of Magnetic N. Pole
Boothia Pen.
Thule
Upernavik
Umanak
Jakobshavn
Egedesminde
Disko
Angmagssalik
Godthåb
Frederikshåb
Julianehåb
C. Farewell
Baffin Bay
Davis Strait
Baffin Island
Beaufort Sea
Prudhoe Bay
Barrow
Aklavik
Inuvik
Dawson
Yukon
Whitehorse
Mackenzie Mountains
Mackenzie R.
Great Bear Lake
Northwest Territories
Arctic Circle
Echo Bay
Back R.
Melville Peninsula
Foxe Basin
Southampton Island
Hudson Strait
Cape Chidley
Labrador Sea
Ungava Peninsula
Ungava Bay
Hudson Bay
Yellowknife
Great Slave Lake
Hay River
Liard R.
Kazan R.
Lake Athabasca
Peace R.
Mc Murray
Reindeer Lake
Churchill
Lynn Lake
Nelson R.
Port Nelson
Belcher Islands
CANADA
Newfoundland and Labrador
Schefferville
Goose Bay
Gagnon
Corner Brook
St. John's
Anticosti I.
Sept-Îles
Port Cartier
Gulf of Saint Lawrence
St. Pierre and Miquelon (Fr.)
Sydney
Cape Breton Island
Nova Scotia
Halifax
New Brunswick
Saint John
Québec
Moosonee
James Bay
Albany R.
Severn R.
Ontario
Rocky Mountains
Coast Mountains
British Columbia
Prince George
Dawson Creek
Alberta
Edmonton
Calgary
Saskatchewan
Saskatoon
Regina
Brandon
Manitoba
Lake Winnipeg
Lake Manitoba
Winnipeg
Vancouver
Kamloops
Red River
Thunder Bay
L. Superior
Duluth
Trois-Rivières
Québec
Montreal
OTTAWA
St. Lawrence R.
Portland
Boston
Cape Cod
Spokane
Columbia River
Columbia Plateau
Helena
Missouri R.
Yellowstone R.
Billings
Bismarck
Boise
Snake R.
Minneapolis
St. Paul
Sioux Falls
Pierre
L. Michigan
L. Huron
L. Ontario
Toronto
Hamilton
Rochester
Buffalo
Niagara Falls
Milwaukee
Madison
Detroit
Cleveland
Newark
New York
Philadelphia
Baltimore
WASHINGTON
Richmond
Norfolk
Great Salt Lake
Salt Lake City
Cheyenne
Great Basin
Sierra Nevada
Death Valley
Las Vegas
Grand Canyon
Mount Elbert
Denver
Colorado Springs
Colorado R.
Omaha
Des Moines
Lincoln
Chicago
Toledo
Pittsburgh
Columbus
Indianapolis
UNITED STATES (USA)
Wichita
Kansas City
St. Louis
Ohio R.
Louisville
Nashville
Appalachian Mountains
Mount Mitchell
Charlotte
Cape Hatteras
Bermuda Islands (U.K.)
Santa Fe
Albuquerque
Oklahoma City
Tulsa
Memphis
Little Rock
Atlanta
Charleston
Savannah
Phoenix
Tucson
Lubbock
Fort Worth
Dallas
Red River
Mississippi R.
Birmingham
Jackson
Mobile
Jacksonville
Cape Canaveral
Mexicali
El Paso
Ciudad Juárez
Rio Grande
Austin
Beaumont
Houston
Galveston
New Orleans
San Antonio
Corpus Christi
Tampa
St. Petersburg
Florida
Miami
Key West
Straits of Florida
NASSAU
THE BAHAMAS
Tropic of Cancer
ATLANTIC OCEAN
Gulf of California
Lower California
Hermosillo
Chihuahua
Western Sierra Madre
Eastern Sierra Madre
Torreón
Saltillo
Monterrey
Matamoros
Gulf of Mexico
Culiacán
C. San Lucas
MEXICO
Mazatlán
San Luis Potosí
Aguascalientes
Tampico
León
Guadalajara
Santiago R.
MEXICO CITY
Morelia
Mt. Popocatepetl
Puebla
Veracruz
Bay of Campeche
Mérida
Chichén Itzá
Yucatán Channel
Revilla Gigedo Is. (Mexico)
Southern Sierra Madre
Isthmus of Tehuantepec
Acapulco
Middle America Trench
Mt. Tajamulco
HAVANA
Santa Clara
CUBA
Santiago de Cuba
Guantánamo
West Indies
Greater Antilles
HAITI
PORT-AU-PRINCE
DOMINICAN REPUBLIC
SANTO DOMINGO
Puerto Rico Trench
San Juan
Puerto Rico (U.S.A.)
JAMAICA
KINGSTON
BELIZE
BELMOPAN
GUATEMALA
HONDURAS
TEGUCIGALPA
EL SALVADOR
SAN SALVADOR
NICARAGUA
León
MANAGUA
Lake Nicaragua
COSTA RICA
SAN JOSÉ
PANAMA
Panama Canal
Colón
Caribbean Sea
Aruba I. (Neth.)
Curaçao I. (Neth.)
Bonaire I. (Neth.)
P. Gallinas
Maracaibo
Barquisimeto
CARACAS
Valencia
Barranquilla
Cartagena
VENEZUELA
San Cristóbal
Bucaramanga
COLOMBIA
Medellín
Manizales
BOGOTÁ
Moscow
Rome
Athens
Cairo
Al Khartum
500 1000 km
200 400 600 miles
1 hour

U.S.S.R.
Chukchi Sea
ARCTIC OCEAN
Beaufort Sea
Point Barrow
Barrow
Icy Cape
Cape Lisburne
Point Hope
Point Lay
Harrison Bay
Prudhoe Bay
Kaktovik
Mackenzie Bay
North Slope
Brooks Range
Mount Isto
Endicott Mts
Arctic Circle
Bering Strait
Cape Prince of Wales
Anadyrskiy Zaliv
Saint Lawrence Island
Seward Peninsula
Kotzebue Sound
Nome
Norton Sound
Bering Sea
Alaska
(UNITED STATES)
Yukon Flats
Fairbanks
Yukon
Nunivak Island
Nelson Island
Kuskokwim Mts
Kuskokwim Bay
Pribilof Islands
Alaska Range
Mount McKinley
Mount Kimball
Anchorage
Cook Inlet
Kenai Peninsula
Bristol Bay
Alaska Peninsula
Aleutian Range
Kodiak Island
Afognak
Shumagin Islands
Unimak
Aleutian Is
Gulf of Alaska
Mount Marcus Baker
Mount Blackburn
Mount Bona
Mount Logan
Yukon Territory
Ogilvie Mts
Pelly Mountains
Whitehorse
Chichagof
Alexander Archipelago
Baranof
Prince of Wales I.
Dixon Entrance
Queen Charlotte Islands
Graham
Moresby
Hecate Strait
Bering Sea
Pribilof Islands
Shishaldin Volcano
Unimak
Fox Is
Umnak
Unalaska
Islands of Four Mountains
Atka I.
Amlia
Adak
Tanaga
Andreanof Is
Rat Islands
Kiska
Near Islands
Attu
Agattu
Aleutian Islands
(U.S.A.)
PACIFIC OCEAN

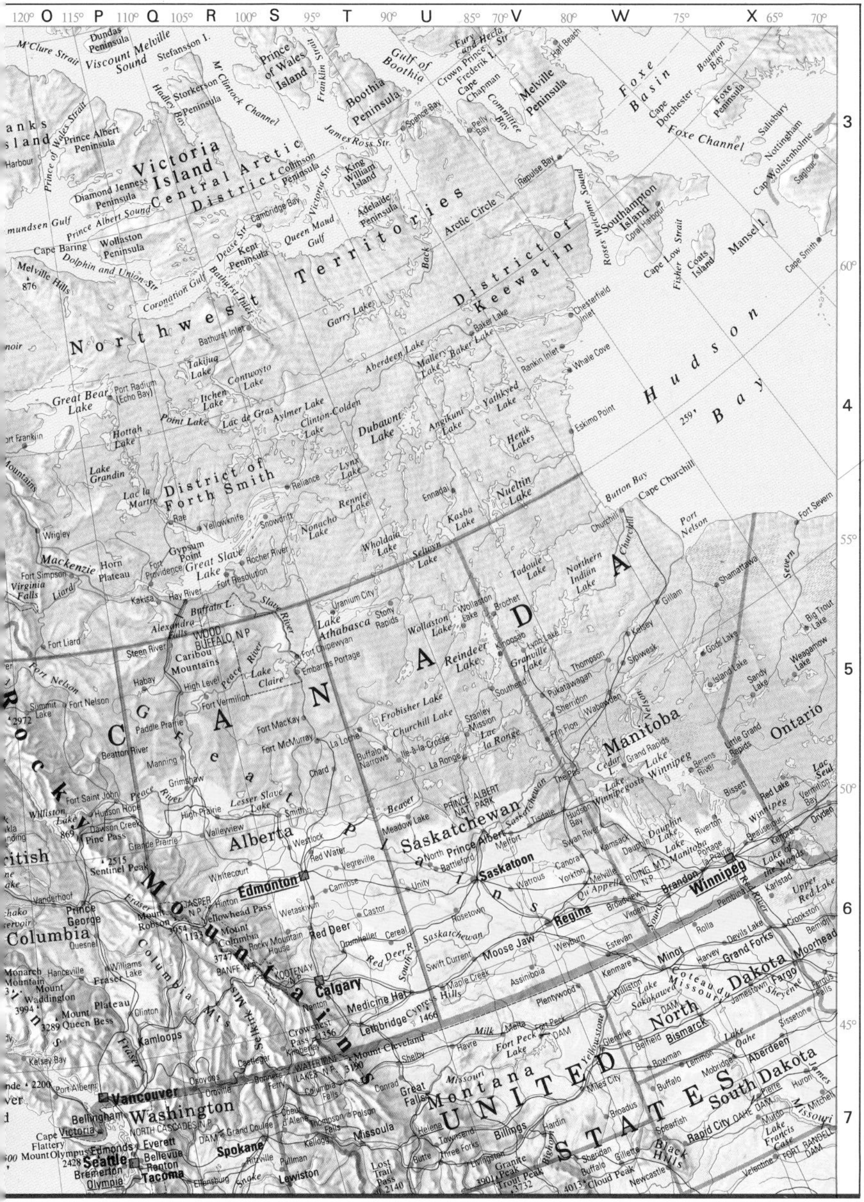

Scale 1:20 000 000

0 200 400 600 800 1000 km

0 200 400 600 miles

1 hour

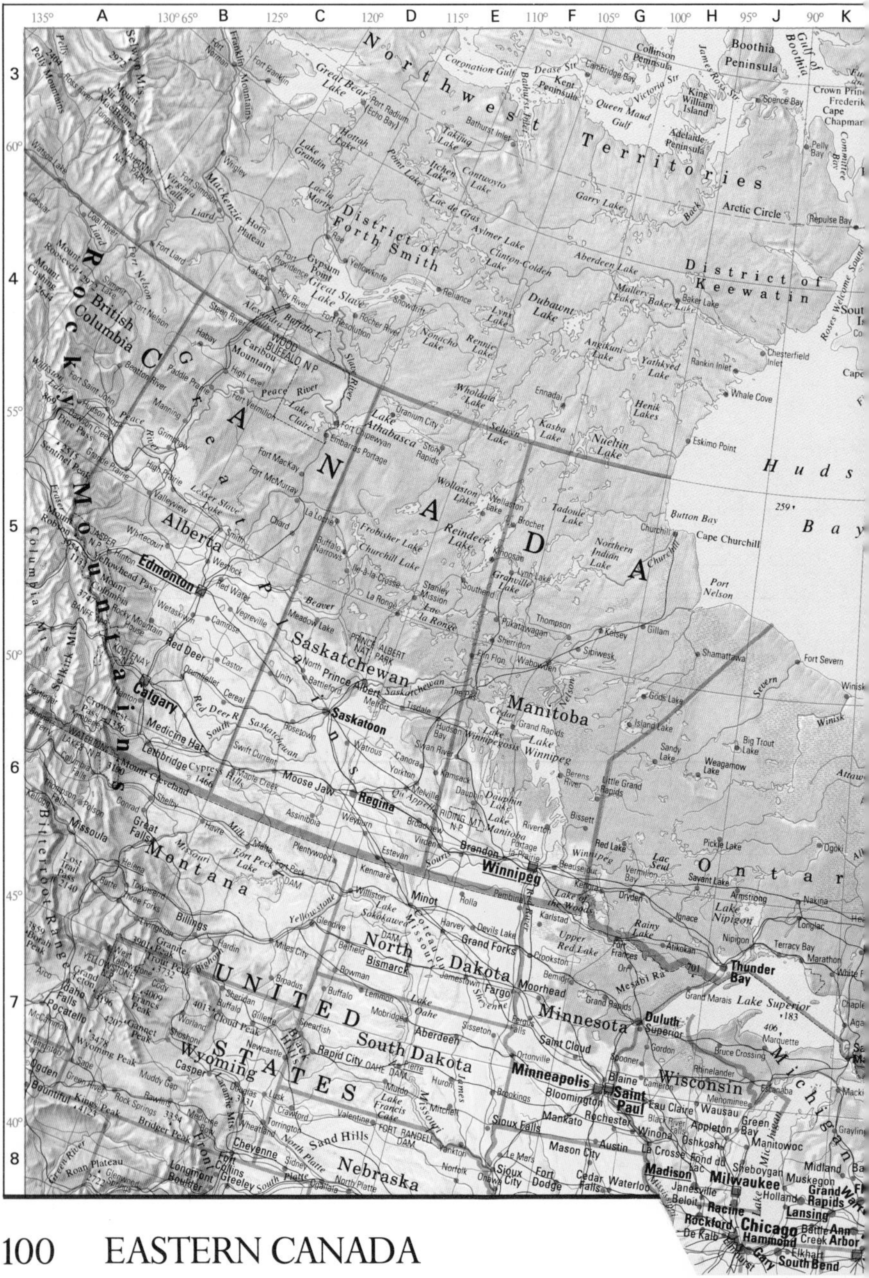
Northwest Territories
District of Forth Smith
District of Keewatin
Arctic Circle
Coronation Gulf
Queen Maud Gulf
Boothia Peninsula
Gulf of Boothia
Collinson Peninsula
Kent Peninsula
Adelaide Peninsula
King William Island
Great Bear Lake
Great Slave Lake
Lake Athabasca
Wollaston Lake
Reindeer Lake
Dubawnt Lake
Aberdeen Lake
Baker Lake
Yathkyed Lake
Nueltin Lake
Hudson Bay
Button Bay
Cape Churchill
Port Nelson
Chesterfield Inlet
Rankin Inlet
Whale Cove
Eskimo Point
Churchill
Fort Severn
CANADA
Rocky Mountains
Great Plains
British Columbia
Alberta
Saskatchewan
Manitoba
Ontario
Edmonton
Calgary
Saskatoon
Regina
Winnipeg
Thunder Bay
Lake Winnipeg
Lake Winnipegosis
Lake Manitoba
Lake of the Woods
Lake Nipigon
Lake Superior
Lake Michigan
Red Deer
Lethbridge
Medicine Hat
Moose Jaw
Prince Albert
Brandon
Flin Flon
Yellowknife
Fort Nelson
Fort McMurray
UNITED STATES
Montana
North Dakota
South Dakota
Wyoming
Nebraska
Minnesota
Wisconsin
Michigan
Bismarck
Pierre
Cheyenne
Minneapolis
Saint Paul
Madison
Milwaukee
Chicago
Lansing
Duluth
Fargo
Sioux Falls
Billings
Missoula
Great Falls
Casper
Rapid City
Minot
Grand Forks
Rockford
Gary
South Bend
Grand Rapids
Ann Arbor
Sand Hills
Bitterroot Range
Selkirk Mts.
Columbia Mts.
135°
130°
125°
120°
115°
110°
105°
100°
95°
90°
65°
60°
55°
50°
45°
40°
A
B
C
D
E
F
G
H
J
K
3
4
5
6
7
8

M
N
O
P
Q
R
S
T
U
75°
70°
65°
60°
55°
50°
45°
40°
35°
3
4
5
6
7
60°
55°
50°
45°
Moscow
Baffin Island
Barnes Ice Cap
1127
Cape Raper
2100
Home Bay
Bray
Spicer Islands
Prins Charles I.
Taverner Bay
Kangeeak Point
Auyuittuq N.P.
Penny Ice Cap
Merchants Bay
Cape Dyer
Cumberland Peninsula
Angijak Island
Hoare Bay
Nettilling Lake
Cumberland Sound
Cape Mercy
Lemieux Islands
Bowman Bay
Amadjuak Lake
Foxe Peninsula
Foxe Channel
Frobisher Bay
Hall Peninsula
Brevoort Island
Salisbury
Nottingham
Loks Land
Meta Incognita Peninsula
Everett Mts
Resolution I.
Cap Wolstenholme
Hudson Strait
Gabriel Strait
Saglouc
Maricourt
Button Islands
Cap Hopes Advance
Killinek
Cape Chidley
Akpatok
Cape Smith
Lac Klotz
Bellin
Ungava Bay
1676
Cirque Mountain
Peninsule d'Ungava
Baie aux Feuilles
Port-Nouveau-Québec
Hebron
Okak Islands
Promontoire Portland
Inoucdjouac
Fort-Chimo
Koksoak
George
Nutak
Nain
Davis Inlet
Coast of Labrador
Lac Minto
Aillik
Cape Harrison
Indian Harbour
Sanikiluaq
Lac Champdore
Lac à l'Eau-Claire
Lac d'Iberville
Labrador
Attikamagen Lake
Smallwood Réservoir
Newfoundland
Hawke Harbour
Poste-de-la-Baleine
Lac Bienville
Schefferville
Melville
Menihek Lakes
Churchill Falls
Goose Bay
Port Hope Simpson
Lac Caniapiscau
Livingston
Cape Bauld
Saint Anthony
Strait of Belle Isle
Radisson
Kanaaupscow
Polaris
Keyano
Labrador City
Ashuanipi
Atikonak Lake
Laurentien
Fort-George
David
Lac Naococane
Ashuanipi Lake
Joseph Lake
Lac Sakami
La Sarcelle
Eric
Baie-des-Moutons
Port Saunders
Monts Otish
1135
Gagnon
Eastmain
Québec
Harrington Harbour
Long Range Mts
Notre Dame Bay
Cape Freels
Wesleyville
Bonavista Bay
Fort Rupert
Rupert
Manicouagan
Natashquan
Romaine
Bishop's Falls
Trout River
Deer Lake
Port Blandford
Bay de Verde
Lac Mistassini
Lac Albanel
Plateau
Havre Saint-Pierre
Sept-Îles
Île d'Anticosti
Corner Brook
Newfoundland
Saint John's
Lac au Goéland
Chibougamau
Chute-des-Passes
Détroit d'Honguedo
Ramea
Saint Alban's
Avalon Peninsula
Matagami
Réservoir Pipmouacan
Hauterive
Cap de Gaspé
Burgeo
Marystown
Trepassey
Cape Race
Miquelon
St. Lawrence R.
Péninsule de Gaspé
Gaspé
Gulf of Saint Lawrence
Cape Ray
Fortune Bay
Burin Peninsula
Placentia Bay
Lake Abitibi
Amos
Réservoir Gouin
Jonquière
Rimouski
Chandler
Cabot Strait
Île de la Madeleine
Saint Pierre et Miquelon (France)
Senneterre
Saint Jérôme
Chicoutimi
Campbellton
Bathurst
Val-d'Or
Réservoir Decelles
Trois-Pistoles
Monts Notre Dame
Miramichi Bay
Prince Edward Island
Cape Breton Island
600
Réservoir Cabonga
Charlesbourg
Saint Léonard
Acadie
Sydney
Charlottetown
Northumberland Strait
Québec
Lévis
Peaked Mountain
689
New Brunswick
Moncton
New Glasgow
Canso
Temiscaming
Réservoir Baskatong
Shawinigan
Cap-de-la-Madeleine
Saint-Georges
North Bay
Laurentian Scarp
Sainte-Thérèse
Trois-Rivières
Drummondville
Fredericton
Truro
Nova Scotia
ATLANTIC OCEAN
20
Laval
Montreal
Sherbrooke
Saint John
Bay of Fundy
Dartmouth
Halifax
2600
Renfrew
Hull
Huntsville
Bancroft
St-Jean
Granby
Maine
Bingham
Eastport
OTTAWA
Cornwall
Bangor
Sable Island
Orillia
Peterborough
Kingston
Burlington
Adirondack Mountains
1629
Montpelier
New England
Augusta
Lewiston
Yarmouth
Shelburne
Barrie
Belleville
Watertown
Verm
NH
Auburn
Portland
250
Toronto
Ontario
Concord
Portsmouth
Gulf of Maine
Cape Sable
70
Hamilton
Rochester
Niagara Falls
Syracuse
Ithaca
Buffalo
Erie
New York
Jamestown
Elmira
Davis Strait
300
Agto
Frederik IX Land
Arctic Circle
Itivdleq
Sukkertoppen
Atangmik
Godthåb
Kapisigdlit
Greenland (Denmark)
2850
Kong Frederik VI Kyst
Skjoldungen
Tingmiarmiut
Cape Herluf Trolle
1890
J.A.D. Jensens Nunatakker
Fiskenæsset
Frederikshåb
Arsuk
Ivigtut
Julianehåb
Narssaq
2300
Frederiksdal
Kap Farvel
4000
3100
Labrador Sea
4100
300
0
200
400
600
800
1000 km
0
200
400
600 miles
1 hour

Scale 1:20 000 000

A
B
C
D
E
F
125°
120°
115°
110°
105°
100°
45°
40°
35°
30°
25°
2
3
4
5
6
7
Vancouver
Victoria
Washington
Seattle
Tacoma
Olympia
Spokane
Br. Col.
Alberta
Medicine Hat
Lethbridge
Saskatchewan
Regina
Moose Jaw
Swift Current
Portland
Salem
Eugene
Oregon
Medford
Boise
Idaho
Lewiston
Missoula
Helena
Great Falls
Montana
Billings
Bismarck
North
Dakota
South Dakota
Rapid City
Pierre
Wyoming
Casper
Cheyenne
Nebraska
North Platte
Salt Lake City
Ogden
Provo
Great Salt Lake
Utah
Nevada
Great Basin
Reno
Carson City
Las Vegas
Sacramento
San Francisco
Oakland
Berkeley
Stockton
San Jose
Fresno
California
Los Angeles
Long Beach
Pasadena
San Bernardino
Riverside
Santa Ana
San Diego
Tijuana
Mexicali
Mojave Desert
Arizona
Phoenix
Tucson
Flagstaff
Grand Canyon
Colorado
Colorado Plateau
Denver
Aurora
Lakewood
Colorado Springs
Pueblo
Grand Junction
New Mexico
Albuquerque
Santa Fe
Amarillo
Lubbock
El Paso
Ciudad Juárez
Texas
Midland
Odessa
San Angelo
San Antonio
Rocky Mountains
UNITED
Great Plains
Sonora
Hermosillo
Chihuahua
Coahuila
Monterrey
Saltillo
Torreón
Durango
Victoria de Durango
Culiacán
Los Mochis
Ciudad Obregón
Nuevo Laredo
Nuevo León
Altiplanicie Mexicana
MEXICO
Baja California Norte
Baja California Sur
Golfo de California
La Paz
Cabo San Lucas
Tropic of Cancer
PACIFIC OCEAN
Isla de Guadalupe (Mexico)
Isla Cedros
Channel Islands
Point Conception
Cape Mendocino
Mount Whitney 4418
Mount Shasta 4317
Mt. Rainier 4392

Scale 1:20 000 00

H
J
K
L
M
N
90°
85°
80°
50°
75°
70°
65°
45°
40°
35°
30°
25°
2
3
4
5
6
7
Rome
Cairo
Delhi
CANADA
Ontario
Québec
Thunder Bay
Lake Superior
Lake Nipigon
Duluth
Superior
Sault Sainte Marie
Sudbury
North Bay
OTTAWA
Montreal
Québec
Laval
Toronto
Hamilton
Kitchener
London
Windsor
Lake Huron
Lake Michigan
Lake Erie
Lake Ontario
Georgian Bay
Wisconsin
Minneapolis
Saint Paul
Milwaukee
Madison
Chicago
Gary
Detroit
Toledo
Cleveland
Akron
Buffalo
Rochester
Syracuse
Albany
Boston
Worcester
Providence
Hartford
New Haven
Bridgeport
Stamford
Yonkers
New York
Newark
Paterson
Trenton
Philadelphia
Allentown
Pittsburgh
Youngstown
Baltimore
WASHINGTON
Arlington
Alexandria
Richmond
Norfolk
Virginia Beach
Portsmouth
Pennsylvania
New York
Maine
New England
Mass
Conn
RI
NH
NJ
Delaware
Maryland
Fredericton
Saint John
Gulf of Maine
Cape Cod
Iowa
Des Moines
Davenport
Cedar Rapids
Peoria
Illinois
Springfield
Indiana
Indianapolis
Ohio
Columbus
Dayton
Cincinnati
Fort Wayne
South Bend
Louisville
Lexington
Kentucky
Evansville
Saint Louis
Missouri
Kansas City
Independence
West Virginia
Charleston
Virginia
UNITED STATES
Tennessee
Nashville
Knoxville
Memphis
Chattanooga
Huntsville
Arkansas
Little Rock
Tulsa
Oklahoma
Mississippi
Jackson
Alabama
Birmingham
Montgomery
Mobile
Atlanta
Georgia
Columbus
Macon
Savannah
Augusta
South Carolina
Columbia
Charleston
North Carolina
Charlotte
Greensboro
Winston-Salem
Durham
Raleigh
Cape Hatteras
Cape Lookout
Cape Fear
Wilmington
Shreveport
Baton Rouge
Metairie
New Orleans
Houston
Beaumont
Galveston
Port Arthur
Mississippi Delta
Jacksonville
Tallahassee
Orlando
Tampa
Saint Petersburg
Florida
Fort Lauderdale
Hollywood
Hialeah
Miami
Miami Beach
Cape Canaveral
Key West
Florida Keys
Straits of Florida
Gulf of Mexico
ATLANTIC OCEAN
Tropic of Cancer
THE BAHAMAS
NASSAU
Grand Bahama Island
Andros Island
LA HABANA (HAVANA)
CUBA
Santa Clara
Cienfuegos
Camagüey
Holguín
Santiago de Cuba
Guantánamo
Naval station (USA)
Isla de la Juventud
Cayman Islands (U.K.)
200
400
600
800
1000 km
200
400
600 miles
1 hour

A
B
C
D
E
105°
100°
95°
90°
30°
25°
20°
15°
10°
5°
2
3
4
5
6
MEXICO
Gulf of Mexico
PACIFIC OCEAN
Tropic of Cancer
Chihuahua
Monterrey
Saltillo
Torreón
Victoria de Durango
Mazatlán
Zacatecas
Aguascalientes
San Luis Potosí
Guadalajara
León
Querétaro
Morelia
Toluca
MEXICO CITY
Cuernavaca
Puebla
Veracruz
Acapulco
Oaxaca de Juárez
Tampico
Poza Rica de Hidalgo
Ciudad Victoria
Matamoros
Reynosa
Nuevo Laredo
Monclova
Mérida
Campeche
Villahermosa
Coatzacoalcos
Minatitlán
Tapachula
Yucatán Peninsula
Bahía de Campeche
Golfo de Tehuantepec
Golfo de Honduras
BELIZE
Belize City
GUATEMALA
EL SALVADOR
SAN SALVADOR
HONDURAS
TEGUCIGALPA
San Pedro Sula
NICARAGUA
MANAGUA
COSTA RICA
SAN JOSÉ
Houston
San Antonio
Austin
Corpus Christi
Galveston
Beaumont
Shreveport
Jackson
Baton Rouge
New Orleans
Mobile
Montgomery
Birmingham
Mississippi
Alabama
Sierra Madre Occidental
Sierra Madre Oriental
Sierra Madre del Sur
Altiplanicie Mexicana
Rio Grande
Lago de Nicaragua
Península de Nicoya

G
H
J
K
L
80°
75°
70°
65°
60°
1
2
3
4
5
6
Cairo
Delhi
Al Khartum
30°
25°
20°
15°
10°
Sumter
Wilmington
South Carolina
Cape Fear
Myrtle Beach
Beaufort
Charleston
Savannah
Jacksonville
Daytona Beach
Titusville
Cape Canaveral
Merritt Island
Melbourne
Palm Bay
Fort Pierce
Florida
West Palm Beach
Boca Raton
Fort Lauderdale
Hollywood
Miami
Miami Beach
Bermuda Islands (U.K.)
5500
600
ATLANTIC
OCEAN
5300
5200
Sargasso Sea
4700
Grand Bahama Island
Little Abaco Island
Marsh Harbour
Abaco Island
Northeast Providence Channel
Eleuthera Island
NASSAU
New Providence I.
THE BAHAMAS
Andros Island
Cat Island
Kemps Bay
San Salvador (Watling I.)
Bahama Islands
6300
Tropic of Cancer
West Indies
(Indias Occidentales)
Great Exuma Island
Long Island
Crooked Island
Crooked Island Passage
Old Bahama Channel
Mayaguana Island
6900
Turks and Caicos Islands
(U.K.)
Acklins Island
Caicos Islands
Great Inagua I.
Turks Islands
Cárdenas
Sagua la Grande
Caibarién
Placetas
Morón
Ciego de Ávila
Florida
Sancti Spíritus
Trinidad
CUBA
Camagüey
Banes
Holguín
Victoria de las Tunas
Bayamo
Manzanillo
Palma Soriano
Guantánamo
Naval Station (U.S.A.)
Santiago de Cuba
20
DOMINICAN REPUBLIC
8300
7600
Greater Antilles
Paso de los Vientos
Cap-Haïtien
Montecristi
Puerto Plata
Gonaïves
Mao
Santiago
Puerto Rico (U.S.A.)
Virgin Island (U.K.)
Leeward Is.
HAITI
La Vega
San Francisco de Macorís
Ile de la Gonâve
3175
Hispaniola
La Romana
Arecibo
San Juan
Anegada Passage
Anguilla (U.K.)
Montego Bay
Lucea
2347
PORT-AU-PRINCE
San Juan
SANTO DOMINGO
Mayagüez
Caguas
Ponce
Netherlands Antilles
BASSETERRE
ANTIGUA AND BARBUDA
JAMAICA
KINGSTON
Spanish Town
May Pen
Barahona
San Cristóbal
Cabo Beata
Canal de la Mona
Saint Croix
SAINT KITTS AND NEVIS
SAINT JOHN'S
15
(Antillas Mayores)
Montserrat (U.K.)
Guadeloupe Passage
Guadeloupe (Fr.)
Pointe-à-Pitre
Basse-Terre
ROSEAU
DOMINICA
Caribbean Sea
Fort-de-France
Martinique (Fr.)
400
Windward Is.
Lesser Antilles
SAINT LUCIA
CASTRIES
Saint Vincent Passage
5600
4200
KINGSTOWN
SAINT VINCENT
BRIDGETOWN
BARBADOS
Netherland Antilles
Aruba
Curaçao
Willemstad
GRENADA
SAINT GEORGE'S
Tobago
Punta Gallinas
Puerto Estrella
Carrizal
Uribia
Punta Fijo
Golfo de Venezuela
Puerto Cumarebo
Puerto Cabello
Valencia
Maracay
CARACAS
Petare
Isla de Margarita
Porlamar
PORT OF SPAIN
TRINIDAD AND TOBAGO
Santa Marta
Barranquilla
Puerto Colombia
Ciénaga
5775 Pico Cristóbal Colón
Maracaibo
Coro
San Felipe
Guarenas
Los Teques
Cumaná
Trinidad
San Fernando
Sabanalarga
Soledad
Valledupar
Cabimas
Carora
Puerto la Cruz
Cartagena
Lago de Maracaibo
Ciudad Ojeda (Lagunillas)
Barquisimeto
San Juan de los Morros
Barcelona
Anaco
Cantaura
Maturín
Tucupita
Mouths of the Orinoco
Istmo de Panamá
Panama Canal (U.S.A.)
Colón
San Onofre
El Difícil
Chiriguaná
Trujillo
Acarigua
Sincelejo
Valera
Guanare
Calabozo
Zaraza
PANAMÁ
Golfo del Darién
Magangué
San Carlos del Zulia
Mérida
Valle de la Pascua
El Tigre
Ciudad Guayana
Barrancas
Santo Tomé de Guayana
PANAMÁ
Montería
Barinas
Aspurito
Santa Rita
Upata
La Palma
Turbo
Ocaña
Puerto Villamizar
La Fría
Guayabal
Orinoco
Ciudad Bolívar
GURI DAM
Guasipati
Las Tablas
Golfo de Panamá
COLOMBIA
San Cristóbal
Apure
Mantecal
San Fernando de Apure
Cabruta
Represa Raúl Leoni
Tumeremo
Azuero
Mariato
Chigorodó
Puerto Wilches
Pamplona
Cúcuta
La Urbana
La Paragua
El Dorado
Jurado
Bucaramanga
Arauca
Llanos
VENEZUELA
Yarumal
Barrancabermeja
Floridablanca
Cupica
Atrato
Puerto Rondón
Tame
Meta
Puerto Páez
Caura
Angel Falls
El Valle
Bello
Medellín
Itagüí
Envigado
Puerto Carreño
Cerro Yavi
2241
Scale 1:20 000 000
0
200
400
600
800
1000 km
0
200
400
600 miles
1 hour

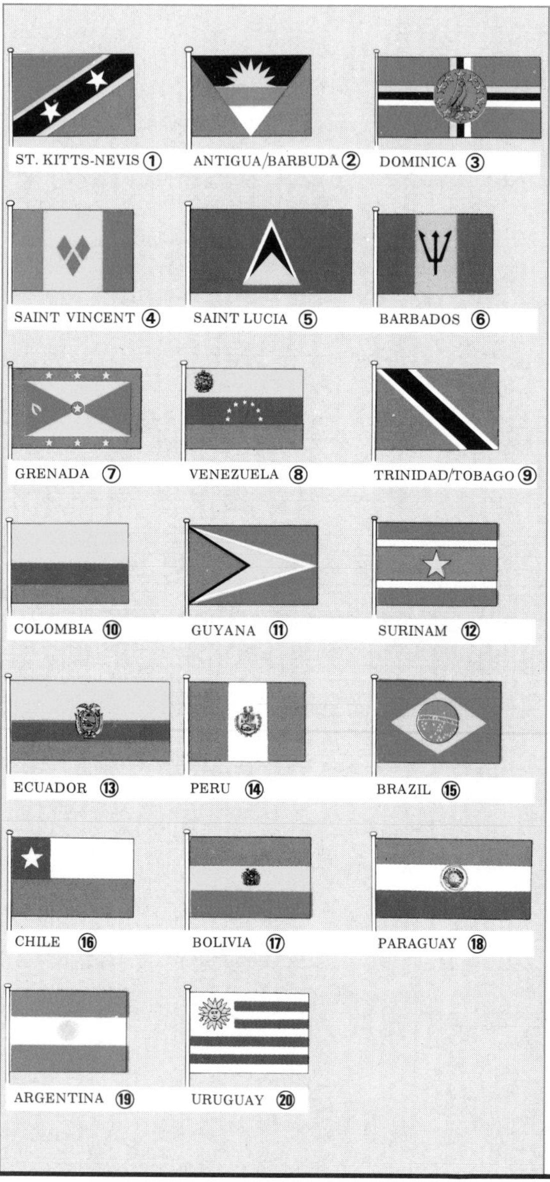
ST. KITTS-NEVIS ①
ANTIGUA/BARBUDA ②
DOMINICA ③
SAINT VINCENT ④
SAINT LUCIA ⑤
BARBADOS ⑥
GRENADA ⑦
VENEZUELA ⑧
TRINIDAD/TOBAGO ⑨
COLOMBIA ⑩
GUYANA ⑪
SURINAM ⑫
ECUADOR ⑬
PERU ⑭
BRAZIL ⑮
CHILE ⑯
BOLIVIA ⑰
PARAGUAY ⑱
ARGENTINA ⑲
URUGUAY ⑳

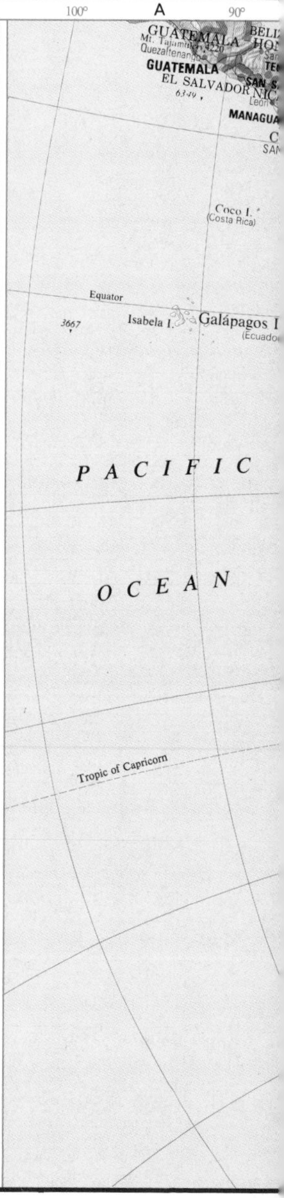
100°
A
90°
GUATEMALA
Quezaltenango
GUATEMALA
EL SALVADOR
MANAGUA
Coco I.
(Costa Rica)
Equator
3667
Isabela I.
PACIFIC
OCEAN
Tropic of Capricorn

Scale 1:50 00

C
D
E
F
G
H
70°
60°
50°
40°
30°
Puerto Rico
(U.S.A.)
ST. KITTS-NEVIS
ANTIGUA AND BARBUDA
Guadeloupe (France)
Pointe-à-Pitre
DOMINICA
Martinique (France)
Fort-de-France
ST. LUCIA
BRIDGETOWN
BARBADOS
ST. VINCENT
GRENADA
TRINIDAD AND TOBAGO
PORT OF SPAIN
Caribbean Sea
Lesser Antilles
Aruba I.
Curaçao I.
P. Gallinas
Maracaibo
Barquisimeto
Maracay
CARACAS
Valencia
Cumaná
Barcelona
Ciudad Bolívar
Ciudad Guayana
VENEZUELA
GUYANA
GEORGETOWN
PARAMARIBO
SURINAM
French Guiana
Cayenne
Angel Falls
Kaieteur Falls
Mt. Roraima
Boa Vista
Roraima
Orinoco R.
Guaviare R.
Meta R.
Llanos
Medellín
Bucaramanga
Cúcuta
BOGOTÁ
Ibagué
COLOMBIA
Amapá
Macapá
Marajó I.
Belém
São Luís
Manaus
Amazon R.
Negro R.
Branco R.
Xingu R.
Tocantins R.
Tapajós R.
Santarém
Madeira R.
Purus R.
Juruá R.
Fonte Boa
Amazonas
Leticia
Iquitos
Putumayo R.
Selvas
Pará
Maranhão
Parnaíba
Fortaleza
Sobral
Ceará
Teresina
Mossoró
Rio Grande do Norte
Natal
C. São Roque
João Pessoa
Paraíba
Campina Grande
Pernambuco
Recife
Caruaru
Garanhuns
Alagoas
Maceió
Sergipe
Aracaju
Caatingas
Piauí
Juazeiro do Norte
Juazeiro
BRAZIL
Acre
Pôrto Velho
Rio Branco
Guajará Mirim
Rondônia
Guaporé R.
Mato Grosso
Goiás
Barreiras
Bahía
Feira
Alagoinhas
Salvador
Campos
São Francisco R.
Araguaia R.
Xingu R.
Distrito Federal
BRASÍLIA
Anápolis
Goiânia
Cuiabá
Jequié
Itabuna
Ilhéus
Vitória da Conquista
Montes Claros
Brazilian Highlands
Minas Gerais
Belo Horizonte
Uberlândia
Uberaba
Teófilo Otoni
Governador Valadares
Espírito Santo
Vitória
Mato Grosso do Sul
Paranaíba R.
São Paulo
Campo Grande
Presidente Prudente
Bauru
Ribeirão Prêto
Juiz de Fora
Campinas
Sorocaba
Santos
Niterói
Rio de Janeiro
C. Frio
Londrina
Paraná
Ponta Grossa
Curitiba
Joinville
Santa Catarina
Blumenau
Florianópolis
Passo Fundo
Caxias do Sul
Rio Grande do Sul
Pôrto Alegre
L. dos Patos
Pelotas
Rio Grande
Lake Mirim
Santa Maria
Uruguaiana
Salto
Paysandú
URUGUAY
MONTEVIDEO
River Plate
La Plata
BUENOS AIRES
Mar del Plata
Tandil
Azul
Santa Rosa
Bahía Blanca
Pampas
Colorado R.
ARGENTINA
PARAGUAY
ASUNCIÓN
Ponta Porã
Iguazú Falls
Posadas
Encarnación
Formosa
Resistencia
Corrientes
Paraná R.
Paraguay R.
Pilcomayo R.
Bermejo R.
Gran Chaco
Salado R.
Uruguay R.
Santa Fe
Paraná
Rosario
Córdoba
Río Cuarto
Zárate
Junín
San Luis
Mendoza
San Juan
La Rioja
Santiago del Estero
Salinas Grandes
Catamarca
Tucumán
Salta
Jujuy
Mt. Llullaillaco
Mt. Ojos del Salado
Mt. Galán
Mt. Aconcagua
BOLIVIA
Trinidad
Beni R.
Lake Titicaca
Mt. Ancohuma
Mt. Illimani
LA PAZ
Cochabamba
Santa Cruz
Oruro
Llallagua
Lake Poopó
SUCRE
Potosí
Tarija
Andes Mountains
PERU
Huánuco
Huascarán
Cajamarca
Ucayali R.
La Oroya
Huancayo
Huancavelica
Ayacucho
Pisco
Ica
Machu Picchu
Cuzco
Mt. Coropuna
Arequipa
Puno
Mollendo
Tacna
Arica
Peru Current
Iquique
Tocopilla
Antofagasta
Atacama Desert
Chile Current
Copiapó
La Serena
CHILE
Viña del Mar
Valparaíso
SANTIAGO
Rancagua
Talca
Chillán
Concepción
Talcahuano
Temuco
Valdivia
Osorno
Puerto Montt
Chiloé I.
San Ambrosio I.
Juan Fernández Islands
(Chile)
Plaza Huincul
Neuquén
San Carlos de Bariloche
Viedma
Gulf of San Matías
Rawson
Gulf of San Jorge
Comodoro Rivadavia
Puerto Aisén
Cerro San Valentín
Puerto Deseado
Patagonia
Río Gallegos
Strait of Magellan
Punta Arenas
Tierra del Fuego
Ushuaia
Cape Horn
Falkland Islands
(U.K.)
Stanley
South Georgia
(U.K.)
ATLANTIC OCEAN
St. Peter and St. Paul Rocks
(Braz.)
Equator
Fernando de Noronha I.
(Braz.)
Trindade I.
(Braz.)
Martin Vaz Is.
(Braz.)
Tropic of Capricorn
Bangkok
Brazzaville
Darwin
Antananarivo
Cape Town
Melbourne
POLAR PROJECTION
500
1000 km
400
600 miles

NICARAGUA
MANAGUA
Matagalpa
León
Masaya
Granada
Cabo Santa Elena
Islas del Maíz
Bluefields
Punta Gorda
San Carlos
San Juan del Norte
Liberia
Puntarenas
Alajuela
COSTA RICA
SAN JOSÉ
Limón
Cartago
Golfo de los Mosquitos
Colón
PANAMÁ
PANAMA
La Chorrera
David
Golfo de Chiriquí
Santiago
Las Tablas
Golfo de Panamá
Punta Mariato
San Andrés (Col.)
Darién
Caribbean Sea
Neth. Antilles
Aruba
Curaçao
Willemstad
Punta Gallinas
Barranquilla
Santa Marta
Cartagena
Sabanalarga
Soledad
Valledupar
Sincelejo
Montería
Magangué
Maracaibo
Lago de Maracaibo
Golfo de Venezuela
Coro
Cabimas
Barquisimeto
Valencia
Acarigua
Guanare
Barinas
Valera
Mérida
San Cristóbal
Cúcuta
Ocaña
Bucaramanga
Floridablanca
Barrancabermeja
San Fernando de Apure
Apure
Medellín
Bello
Envigado
Itagüí
Quibdó
Cabo Corrientes
Duitama
Sogamoso
Tunja
Manizales
Pereira
Armenia
Ibagué
La Dorada
BOGOTÁ
Fusagasuga
Villavicencio
Buenaventura
Tuluá
Buga
Cali
Palmira
Neiva
COLOMBIA
Malpelo (Col.)
PACIFIC OCEAN
Popayán
Tumaco
Pasto
Ipiales
Tulcán
Florencia
Esmeraldas
Ibarra
QUITO
Cotopaxi
Portoviejo
Manta
Ambato
ECUADOR
Chimborazo
Riobamba
Milagro
Guayaquil
Cuenca
Golfo de Guayaquil
Machala
Tumbes
Loja
Talara
Sullana
Piura
Desierto de Sechura
Punta Negra
Chiclayo
Cajamarca
Trujillo
Chimbote
PERU
Iquitos
Amazonas
Marañón
Ucayali
Putumayo
Napo
Caquetá
Pucallpa
Huánuco
Cerro de Pasco
La Oroya
Callao
LIMA
Huancayo
Huancavelica
Ayacucho
Cuzco
Chincha Alta
Acre
Rio Branco
Tabatinga
Leticia
Archipiélago de Colón (Galápagos Islands) (Ecuador)
Isabela
Santa Cruz
San Cristóbal
BOL

Scale 1:20 000 000

0 200 400 600 800 1000 km

0 200 400 600 miles

1 hour

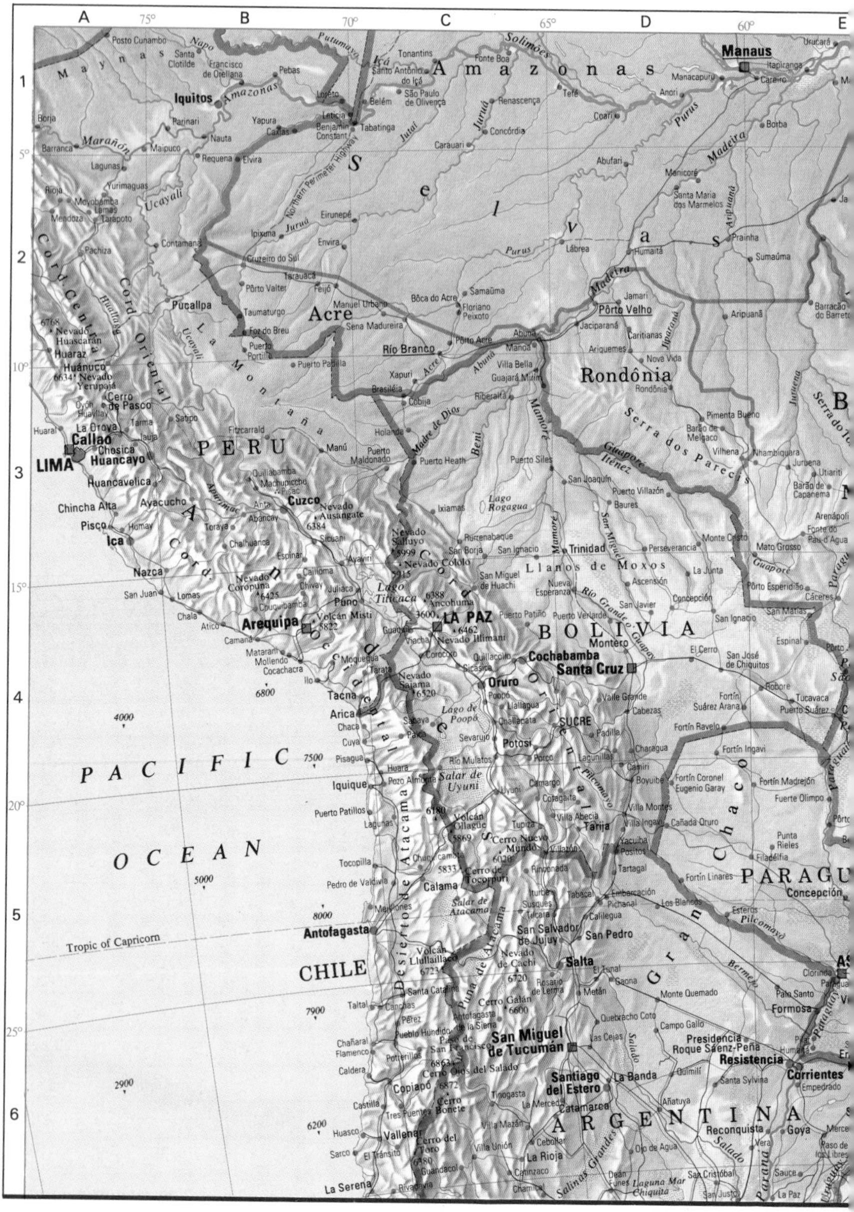
A
B
C
D
E
75°
70°
65°
60°
5°
10°
15°
20°
25°
1
2
3
4
5
6
Manaus
Amazonas
Solimões
Putumayo
Napo
Iquitos
Amazonas
Maynas
Marañón
Ucayali
Tonantins
Fonte Boa
Tefé
Coari
Manacapuru
Leticia
Benjamin Constant
Tabatinga
Pebas
Borja
Barranca
Lagunas
Yurimaguas
Rioja
Moyobamba
Lamas
Tarapoto
Mendoza
Contamana
Pachiza
Jutaí
Juruá
Renascença
Concórdia
Carauari
Purus
Borba
Madeira
Abufari
Manicoré
Santa Maria dos Marmelos
Aripuanã
Prainha
Sumaúma
Humaitá
Lábrea
Eirunepé
Envira
Ipixuna
Cruzeiro do Sul
Tarauacá
Feijó
Pôrto Valter
Manuel Urbano
Acre
Sena Madureira
Bôca do Acre
Samaúma
Floriano Peixoto
Selvas
Northern Perimeter Highway
Pucallpa
Taumaturgo
Foz do Breu
Puerto Portillo
Puerto Pardilla
Río Branco
Pôrto Acre
Xapuri
Brasiléia
Cobija
Abunã
Mamoré
Manoa
Villa Bella
Guajará Mirim
Riberalta
Pôrto Velho
Jamari
Jaciparaná
Caritianas
Ariquemes
Nova Vida
Rondônia
Serra dos Parecis
Pimenta Bueno
Barão de Melgaço
Vilhena
Nhambiquara
Juruena
Aripuanã
Barracão do Barreto
Cord. Central
Cord. Oriental
La Montaña
Huallaga
Nevado Huascarán
6768
Huaraz
Huánuco
Nevado Yerupajá
6634
Cerro de Pasco
Oyón
Huayllay
La Oroya
Tarma
Jauja
Satipo
Huaral
Callao
LIMA
Chosica
Huancayo
PERU
Huancavelica
Chincha Alta
Pisco
Ica
Ayacucho
Nazca
San Juan
Lomas
Chala
Atico
Camaná
Arequipa
Volcán Misti
5822
Mollendo
Cocachacra
Ilo
Moquegua
Tacna
Arica
Cuzco
Nevado Ausangate
6384
Machupicchu
Quillabamba
Abancay
Sicuani
Puno
Juliaca
Lago Titicaca
Nevado Coropuna
6425
Madre de Dios
Manú
Puerto Maldonado
Puerto Heath
Beni
Ixiamas
Lago Rogagua
Rurrenabaque
San Borja
San Ignacio
Trinidad
Llanos de Moxos
Nevado Illimani
6462
LA PAZ
Ancohuma
6388
Cochabamba
Santa Cruz
BOLIVIA
Montero
Oruro
Lago de Poopó
Potosí
SUCRE
Salar de Uyuni
Camargo
Tarija
Villa Montes
Yacuiba
Cord. Occidental
Cord. Oriental
Guaporé
Itenez
San Joaquín
Puerto Villazón
Mato Grosso
Cáceres
San Matías
San José de Chiquitos
Roboré
Tucavaca
Puerto Suárez
Gran Chaco
Charagua
Camiri
Boyuibe
Fortín Ravelo
Fortín Ingavi
Fortín Madrejón
Fuerte Olimpo
Punta Rieles
Filadélfia
PARAGU
Concepción
Pilcomayo
Bermejo
PACIFIC OCEAN
4000
7500
5000
8000
7900
2900
6200
6800
Tropic of Capricorn
CHILE
Iquique
Pisagua
Tocopilla
Calama
Antofagasta
Taltal
Chañaral
Caldera
Copiapó
Vallenar
Huasco
La Serena
Desierto de Atacama
Salar de Atacama
Puna de Atacama
Volcán Llullaillaco
6723
Nevado de Cachi
6720
Cerro Galán
6600
Ojos del Salado
6863
Cerro Bonete
San Salvador de Jujuy
Salta
San Pedro
San Miguel de Tucumán
Santiago del Estero
La Banda
Catamarca
La Rioja
ARGENTINA
Salinas Grandes
Salado
Laguna Mar Chiquita
Presidencia Roque Sáenz-Peña
Resistencia
Corrientes
Formosa
Reconquista
Goya
Paraná
Uruguay
Paraguay

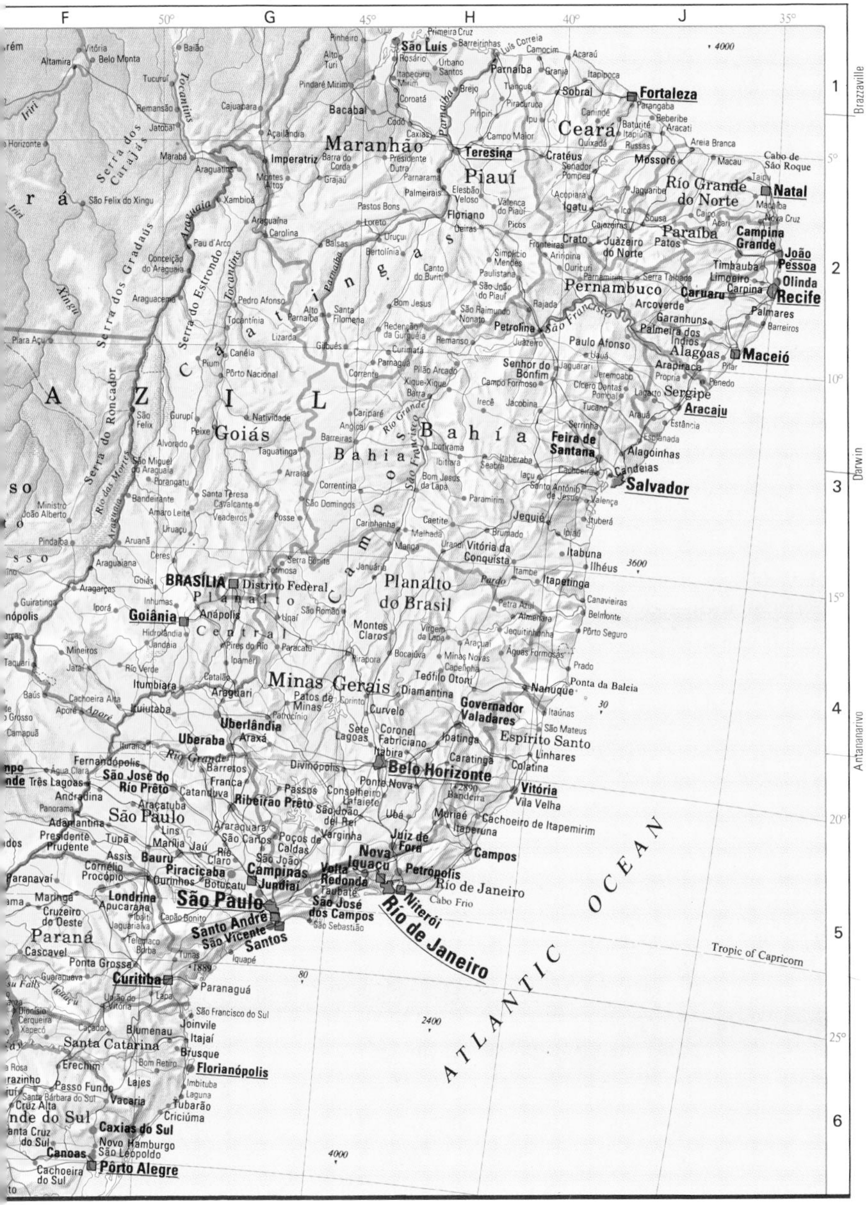

Scale 1:20 000 000

0 200 400 600 800 1000 km

0 200 400 600 miles

1 hour

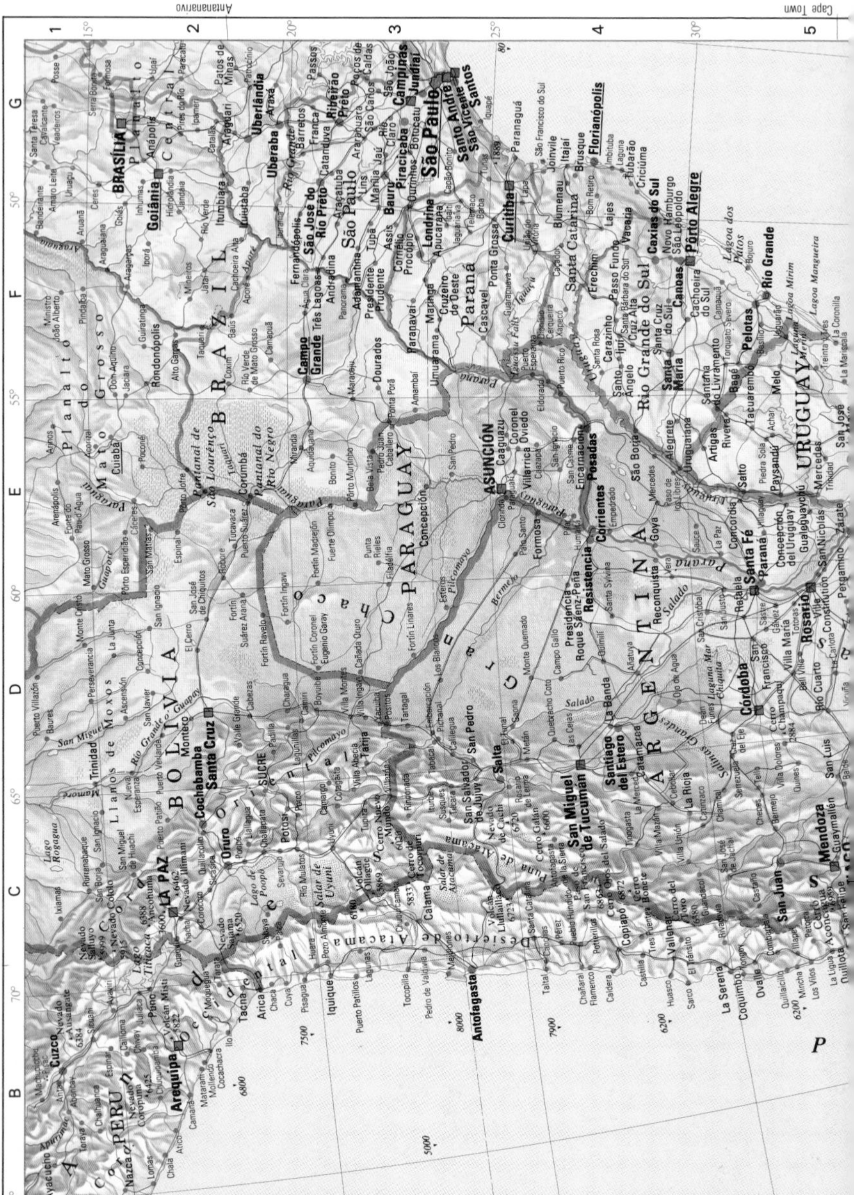

Antananarivo
Cape Town
BRAZIL
BOLIVIA
PARAGUAY
URUGUAY
ARGENTINA
PERU
BRASÍLIA
LA PAZ
SUCRE
ASUNCIÓN
São Paulo
Santos
Curitiba
Florianópolis
Porto Alegre
Rio Grande
Pelotas
Campo Grande
Cuiabá
Goiânia
Uberlândia
Uberaba
Londrina
Santa Cruz
Cochabamba
Oruro
Potosí
Tarija
Salta
San Miguel de Tucumán
Santiago del Estero
Córdoba
Rosario
Santa Fé
Paraná
Corrientes
Resistencia
Posadas
Mendoza
San Juan
Antofagasta
Iquique
Arica
Tacna
Arequipa
Cuzco
Nazca
Copiapó
La Serena
Coquimbo
Ovalle
Lago Titicaca
Salar de Uyuni
Desierto de Atacama
Gran Chaco
Planalto do Mato Grosso
Llanos de Moxos
Lagoa dos Patos
Pantanal de São Lourenço

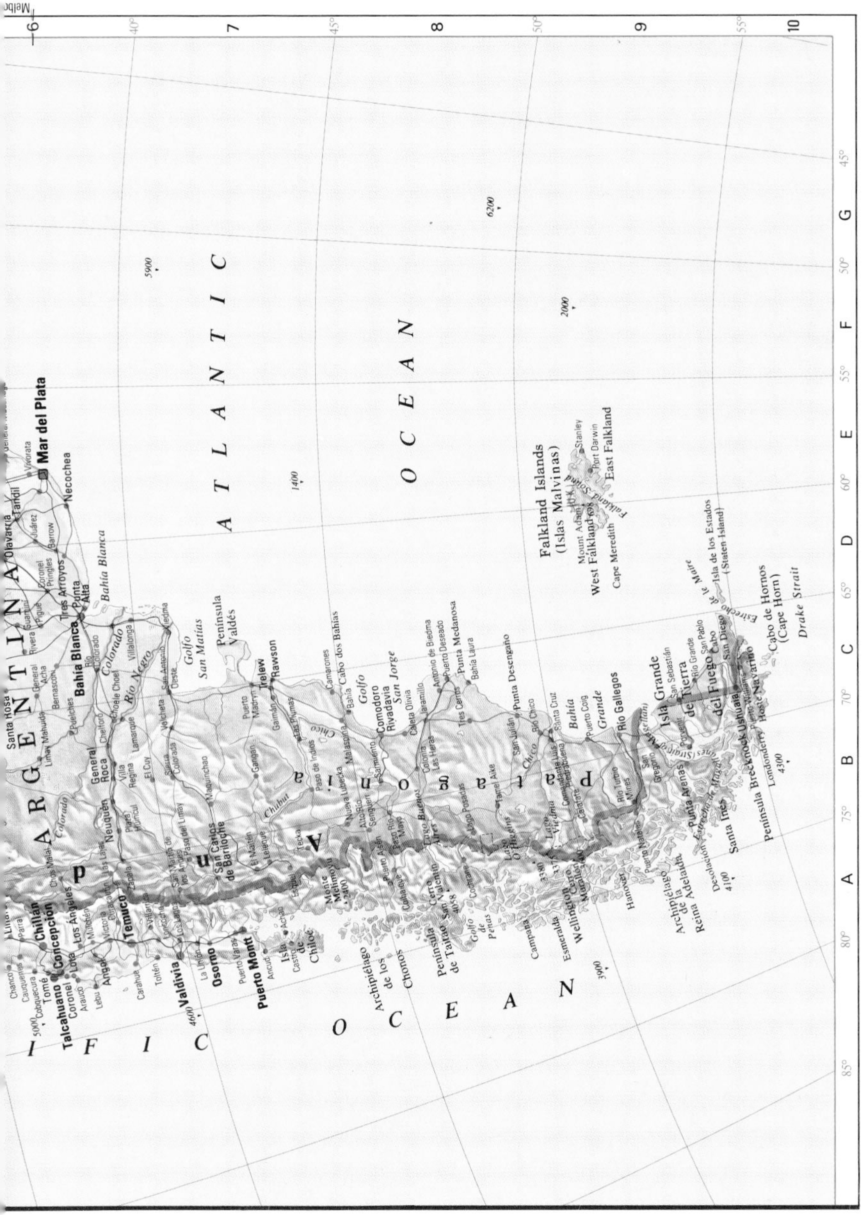

Scale 1:20 000 000

0 200 400 600 800 1000 km

0 200 400 600 miles

1 hour

PACIFIC OCEAN
Andreanof Islands
Aleutian Islands
Near Is. (U.S.A.)
Kuril Is.
JAPAN
Umnak
Unalaska
Dutch Harbor
Unimak
Bering Sea
Commander Is. (U.S.S.R.)
Paramushir
Petropavlovsk-Kamchatskiy
Iturup
Asahikawa
Yuzhno-Sakhalinsk
Sakhalin
Kamchatka Peninsula
Ust'Kamchatsk
Alaska Pen.
Maximum extent of drift ice
Sea of Okhotsk
Sovetskaya Gavan
Okha
Khabarovsk
Komsomolsk
Amur
Kodiak
Nunivak
Gulf of Alaska
St. Lawrence Island
Koryak Range
Magadan
Nikolayevsk-na-Amure
Queen Charlotte Is.
Kenai Pen.
Anchorage
Alaska Range
Alaska (U.S.A.)
Nome
Seward Pen.
Bering Strait
Chukotsk Pen.
Anadyr
Arctic Circle
Kolyma Range
UNION OF SOVIET SOCIALIST REPUBLICS
Okhotsk
Dzhugdzhur Ra.
Vancouver Island
Alexander Arch.
Valdez
6194 Mt.McKinley
Prince Rupert
Coast Mountains
Skagway
6050 Mt.Logan
Juneau
Fairbanks
Yukon River
Chukchi Sea
Chukotsk Range
Pevek
Susuman
Stanovoy Range
Fraser R.
Whitehorse
Dawson
Brooks Range
Wrangel I.
Zvezdnyy
Kolyma
Ambarchik
Cherskiy Range
Aldan
Skovorodino
Mackenzie Mts.
Barrow
Point Barrow
Prudhoe Bay
East Siberian Sea
Indigirka
Yakutsk
Mackenzie R.
Franklin Mts.
Inuvik
Beaufort Sea
Verkhoyansk
Verkhoyansk Range
Lena
Peace R.
Athabasca R.
Hay River
Great Slave Lake
Great Bear Lake
C. Bathurst
Amundsen Gulf
New Siberian Islands
Sannikova
Tiksi
Olenek
Mirnyy
Lensk
McMurray
Yellowknife
Echo Bay
Tempa
L. Athabasca
Coppermine
Banks Island
Central Siberian Plateau
Northwest Territories
CANADA
Reindeer L.
Dubawnt Lake
M'Clure Strait
Prince Patrick
Victoria Island
ARCTIC OCEAN
Laptev Sea
3800
Lynn Lake
Garry L.
Melville I.
Mackenzie King
Parry Islands
Queen Elizabeth Islands
Ellef Ringnes I.
Bathurst I.
Prince of Wales I.
Cape Chelyuskin
Taymyr Peninsula
Khatanga
Lower Tunguska
Churchill
Back R.
Boothia Pen.
North Magnetic Pole
Axel Heiberg I.
Severnaya Zemlya
North Pole
Siberia
Hudson Bay
Southampton Island
Melville Pen.
Devon I.
Ellesmere Island
Yenisey
Noril'sk
Igarka
Foxe Basin
Bylot I.
Nares Strait
Lincoln Sea
5220
Dikson
North Geomagnetic Pole
Thule
Knud Rasmussen Land
Peary Land
Cape Morris Jesup
Franz Josef Land (U.S.S.R.)
Cape Zhelaniya
Belcher Is.
Baffin Island
Melville Bay
1390 Camp Century (U.S.A.)
2170
Wandel Sea
Nordostrundingen
Gulf of Ob
Yamal Peninsula
West Siberian Plain
Ungava Peninsula
Hudson Strait
Baffin Bay
Novaya Zemlya
Kara Sea
Smidovich
Nordaustlandet
Vorkuta
Khanty-Mansiysk
Cumberland Sound
Upernavik
2836
King Frederik VIII Land
Svalbard
Spitsbergen (Nor.)
Edgeöya
Ob
Ungava Bay
Disko
Disko Bugt
Umanak
1742
1795
Greenland (Denmark)
Greenland Sea
Danmarks Havn
Belush'ya Guba
Berezovo
Tobolsk
Ural Mountains
Labrador
C. Chidley
Davis Strait
Jakobshavn
Barents Sea
Schefferville
3270
3410
King Christian X Land
Bear Island
Björnöya (Nor.)
Kolguyev
Pechora
Serov
Tyumen
Godthåb
Söndre Strömfjord
3075
King Christian IX Land
Mesters Vig
North Cape
Murmansk
Ukhta
Sverdlovsk
2140
2240 Mt Forel
J. A. D. Jensens Nunatakker
1680
3360
Blosseville Coast
Scoresbysund
Kap Brewster
Scoresby Sound
Kolskiy Poluostrov
White Sea
Arkhangel
Perm
Goose Bay
3809
King Frederik VI-Coast
Angmagssalik
Jan Mayen Island (Nor.)
Tromsö
Kotlas
Izhevsk
Magnitogorsk
Julianehåb
Denmark Strait
Narvik
Kiruna
Kirov
C. Farewell
Maximum extent of drift ice
Norwegian Sea
NORWAY
SWEDEN
FINLAND
Oulu
Lake Onega
Kazan
Newfoundland
ICELAND
Arctic Circle
Akureyri
REYKJAVIK
Hekla
Vestmannaeyjar
Surtsey
1491
Vatnajökull
L. Ladoga
Petrozavodsk
Gorki
Ulyanovsk
Leningrad
Yaroslavl
Trondheim
HELSINKI
Kalinin
Penza
Sundsvall
Turku
Novgorod
Faeroe Is. (Denmark)
STOCKHOLM
Tallinn
MOSCOW
Tula
ATLANTIC OCEAN
Bergen
Smolensk
Bryansk
Voronezh
Shetland Is.
OSLO
Riga
Volgograd
Orkney Is.
Stavanger
Norrköping
Minsk
Kursk
Kharkov
Aberdeen
North Sea
Gothenburg
Vilnius
Gomel
Rostov
DENMARK
Baltic Sea
Gdańsk
Dnepropetrovsk
REP. OF IRELAND
UNITED KINGDOM
Glasgow
Edinburgh
Belfast
COPENHAGEN
Hamburg
POLAND
Donetsk
Leeds
EAST GER.
WARSAW
Kiev
DUBLIN
Manchester
AMSTERDAM
BERLIN
Cracow
Lvov
Odessa
Krasnodar
Birmingham
Rotterdam
NETHERLANDS
Crimea
Sevastopol
LONDON
BONN
PRAGUE
Carpathians
Kishinev
Black Sea
BELGIUM
BRUSSEL
W. GER.
CZECH.
BUDAPEST
ROMANIA
Channel Is. (U.K.)
PARIS
Munich
VIENNA
HUNGARY
BUCHAREST
TURKEY
FRANCE
BERNE
AUSTRIA
Zagreb
BULGARIA
Varna
ANKARA
Nantes
Loire
SWITZ.
LIECHT.
Venice
BELGRADE
SOFIA
Istanbul
150°
165°
180°
165°
150°
135°
120°
105°
90°
75°
60°
45°
30°
15°

Scale 1:60 000

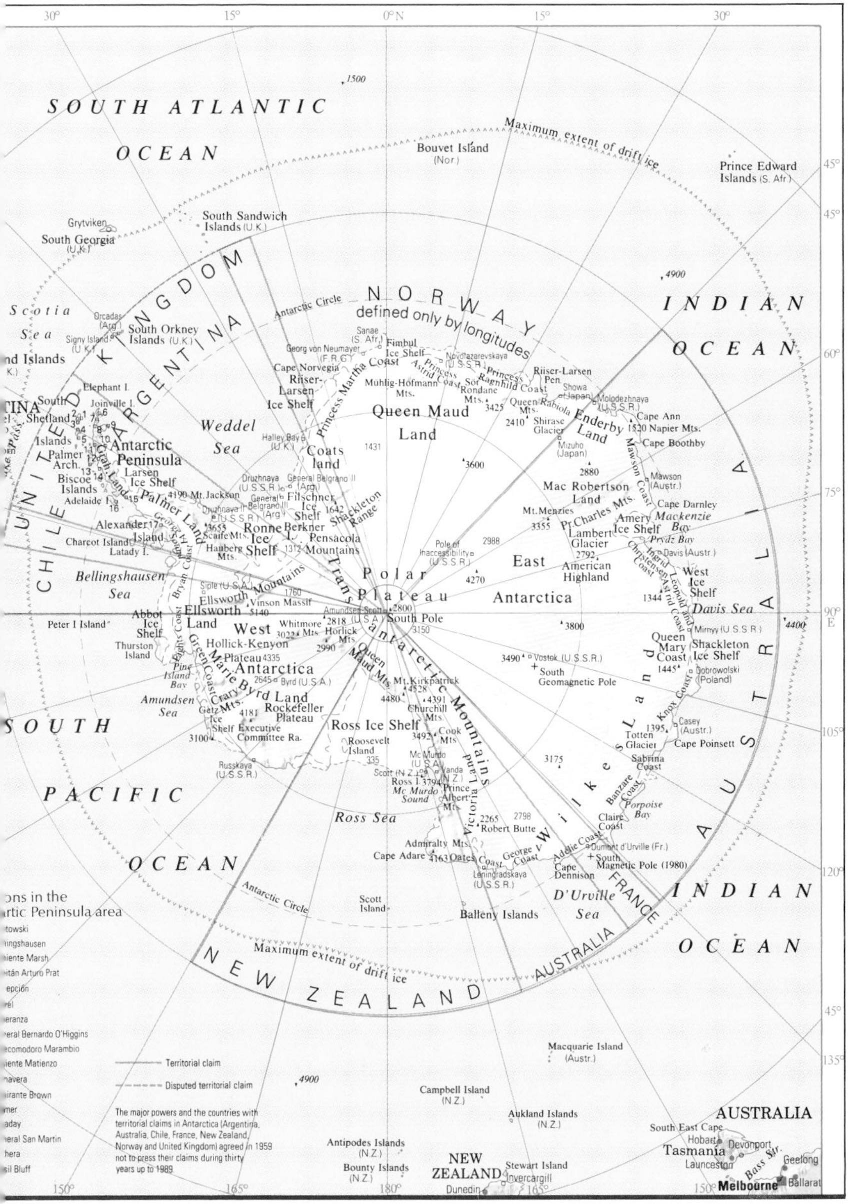
SOUTH ATLANTIC OCEAN
Maximum extent of drift ice
Bouvet Island (Nor.)
Prince Edward Islands (S. Afr.)
South Sandwich Islands (U.K.)
Grytviken
South Georgia (U.K.)
UNITED KINGDOM
ARGENTINA
CHILE
NORWAY defined only by longitudes
Antarctic Circle
INDIAN OCEAN
Scotia Sea
South Orkney Islands (U.K.)
Signy Island (U.K.)
Orcadas (Arg.)
Elephant I.
Joinville I.
South Shetland Islands
Antarctic Peninsula
Palmer Arch.
Biscoe Islands
Adelaide I.
Larsen Ice Shelf
Palmer Land
Alexander I. Island
Charcot Island
Latady I.
Weddel Sea
Halley Bay (U.K.)
Coats Land
Queen Maud Land
Sanae (S. Afr.)
Georg von Neumayer (F.R.G.)
Fimbul Ice Shelf
Cape Norvegia
Riiser-Larsen Ice Shelf
Princess Martha Coast
Princess Astrid Coast
Princess Ragnhild Coast
Mühlig-Hofmann Mts.
Sör Rondane Mts.
Novolazarevskaya (U.S.S.R.)
Riiser-Larsen Pen.
Showa (Japan)
Molodezhnaya (U.S.S.R.)
Queen Maud Mts.
Shirase Glacier
Enderby Land
Cape Ann
Napier Mts.
Cape Boothby
Mizuho (Japan)
Mawson Coast
Mawson (Austr.)
Mac Robertson Land
Mt. Menzies
Pr. Charles Mts.
Lambert Glacier
Amery Ice Shelf
Cape Darnley
Mackenzie Bay
Prydz Bay
Davis (Austr.)
Ingrid Christensen Coast
Leopold and Astrid Coast
West Ice Shelf
Davis Sea
American Highland
East Antarctica
Pole of Inaccessibility (U.S.S.R.)
Polar Plateau
Druzhnaya (U.S.S.R.)
General Belgrano II (Arg.)
Filchner Ice Shelf
Berkner I.
Shackleton Range
Pensacola Mountains
Ronne Ice Shelf
Scaife Mts.
Hauberg Mts.
Mt. Jackson
Bellingshausen Sea
Siple (U.S.A.)
Ellsworth Mountains
Vinson Massif
Ellsworth Land
Amundsen-Scott (U.S.A.)
South Pole
Trans Antarctic Mountains
Abbot Ice Shelf
Peter I Island
Thurston Island
West Antarctica
Whitmore Mts.
Horlick Mts.
Hollick-Kenyon Plateau
Marie Byrd Land
Byrd (U.S.A.)
Pine Island Bay
Amundsen Sea
Crary Mts.
Getz Ice Shelf
Rockefeller Plateau
Executive Committee Ra.
Ross Ice Shelf
Roosevelt Island
Mt. Kirkpatrick
Churchill Mts.
Cook Mts.
Mc Murdo (U.S.A.)
Scott (N.Z.)
Vanda (N.Z.)
Ross I.
Mc Murdo Sound
Prince Albert Mts.
Victoria Land
Russkaya (U.S.S.R.)
Ross Sea
Robert Butte
Admiralty Mts.
Cape Adare
Oates Coast
George V Coast
Leningradskaya (U.S.S.R.)
Scott Island
Balleny Islands
Adelie Coast
Dumont d'Urville (Fr.)
South Magnetic Pole (1980)
Cape Dennison
D'Urville Sea
FRANCE
AUSTRALIA
NEW ZEALAND
Wilkes Land
Vostok (U.S.S.R.)
South Geomagnetic Pole
Queen Mary Coast
Shackleton Ice Shelf
Mirnyy (U.S.S.R.)
Dobrowolski (Poland)
Knox Coast
Casey (Austr.)
Cape Poinsett
Totten Glacier
Sabrina Coast
Banzare Coast
Porpoise Bay
Claire Coast
SOUTH PACIFIC OCEAN
Territorial claim
Disputed territorial claim
The major powers and the countries with territorial claims in Antarctica (Argentina, Australia, Chile, France, New Zealand, Norway and United Kingdom) agreed in 1959 not to press their claims during thirty years up to 1989
Macquarie Island (Austr.)
Campbell Island (N.Z.)
Aukland Islands (N.Z.)
Antipodes Islands (N.Z.)
Bounty Islands (N.Z.)
NEW ZEALAND
Stewart Island
Invercargill
Dunedin
AUSTRALIA
South East Cape
Tasmania
Hobart
Devonport
Launceston
Bass Str.
Geelong
Melbourne
Ballarat

1000 2000 km
500 1000 miles

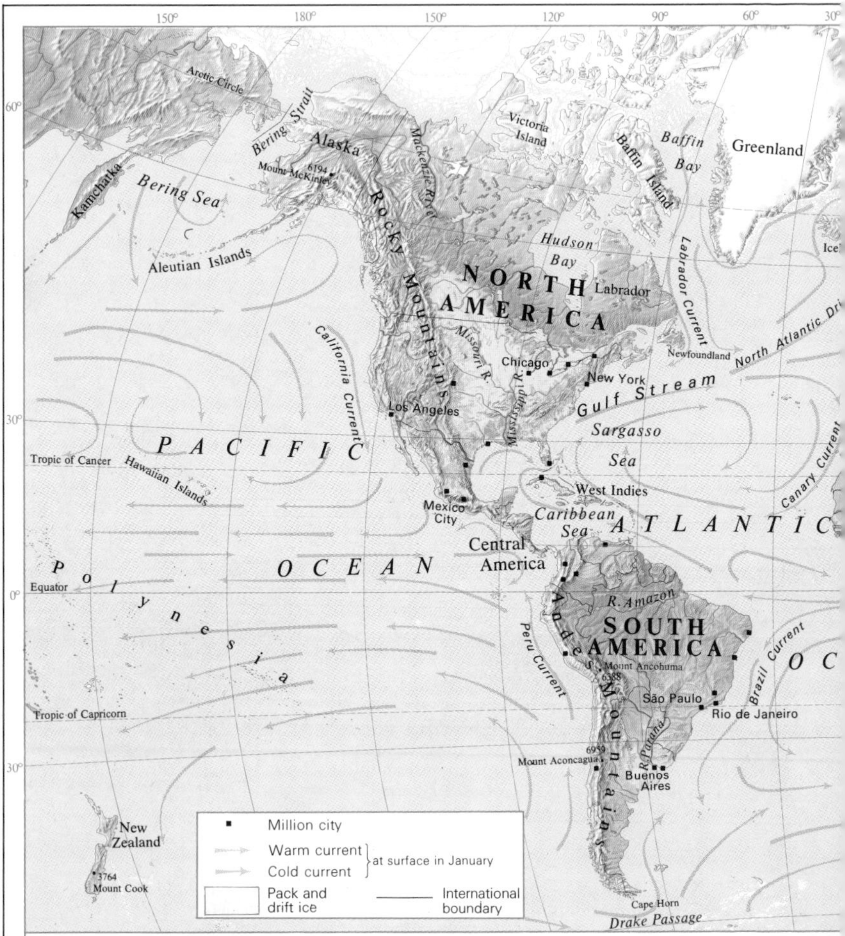

Glacier, ice cap

Tundra

Coniferous forest

Rain forest

Cultivated land | Savanna | Steppe | Desert

ER GRINTEN'S PROJECTION

e 1:180 000 000
e equator

0° 0 400 800 km
30°
60°
200 600 1000 km

0° 0 200 600 miles
30°
60°
100 300 500 miles

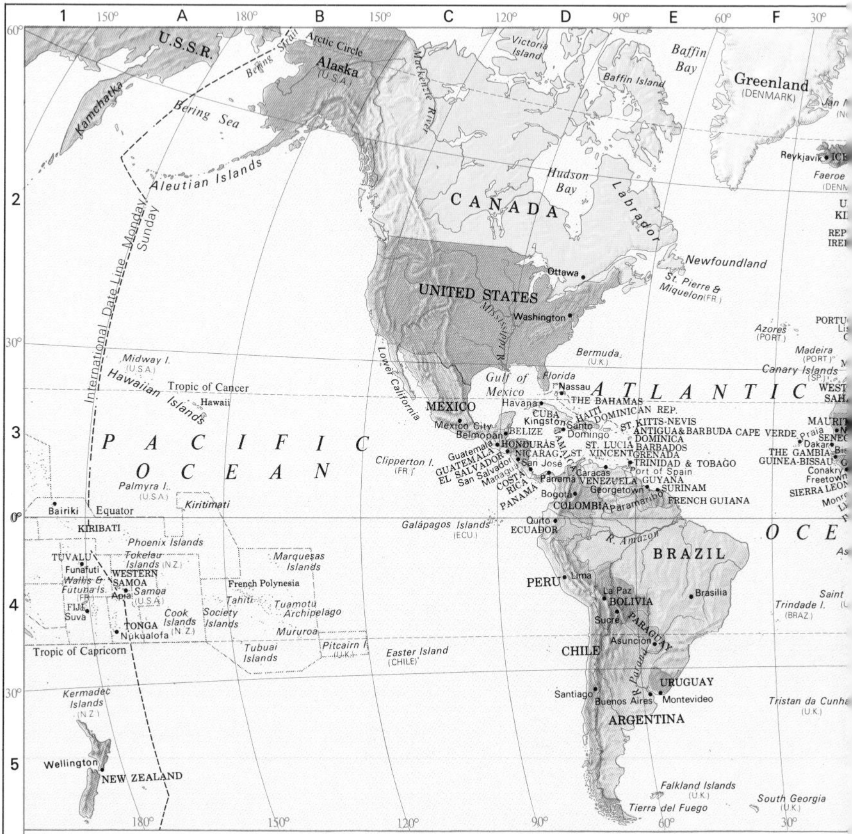
1
A
B
C
D
E
F
150°
180°
150°
120°
90°
60°
30°
60°
30°
0°
30°
2
3
4
5
U.S.S.R.
Kamchatka
Bering Strait
Arctic Circle
Alaska
(U.S.A.)
Bering Sea
Aleutian Islands
Mackenzie River
Victoria Island
Baffin Bay
Baffin Island
Greenland
(DENMARK)
Reykjavik
Faeroe
Hudson Bay
Labrador
CANADA
International Date Line
Monday
Sunday
Newfoundland
St. Pierre & Miquelon (FR.)
Ottawa
UNITED STATES
Mississippi R.
Washington
Azores
(PORT.)
Madeira
Canary Islands
Midway I.
(U.S.A.)
Hawaiian Islands
Tropic of Cancer
Hawaii
Lower California
Bermuda
(U.K.)
Gulf of Mexico
Florida
Nassau
THE BAHAMAS
ATLANTIC
MEXICO
Havana
CUBA
HAITI
DOMINICAN REP.
Kingston
Santo Domingo
ST. KITTS-NEVIS
ANTIGUA & BARBUDA
DOMINICA
CAPE VERDE
ST. LUCIA
BARBADOS
ST. VINCENT
GRENADA
TRINIDAD & TOBAGO
Port of Spain
Mexico City
Belmopan
BELIZE
HONDURAS
Guatemala
GUATEMALA
EL SALVADOR
San Salvador
Managua
NICARAGUA
San José
COSTA RICA
PANAMA
Panamá
Caracas
VENEZUELA
GUYANA
Georgetown
SURINAM
Paramaribo
FRENCH GUIANA
Bogotá
COLOMBIA
THE GAMBIA
GUINEA-BISSAU
Conakry
Freetown
SIERRA LEONE
PACIFIC OCEAN
Clipperton I.
(FR.)
Palmyra I.
(U.S.A.)
Kiritimati
Bairiki
Equator
KIRIBATI
Galápagos Islands
(ECU.)
Quito
ECUADOR
R. Amazon
OCE
BRAZIL
Phoenix Islands
TUVALU
Funafuti
Tokelau Islands (N.Z.)
Marquesas Islands
WESTERN SAMOA
Apia
Wallis & Futuna Is.
(FR.)
Samoa
(U.S.A.)
French Polynesia
PERU
Lima
La Paz
BOLIVIA
Brasília
FIJI
Suva
Tahiti
Tuamotu Archipelago
Society Islands
Cook Islands
(N.Z.)
TONGA
Nukualofa
Mururoa
Sucre
PARAGUAY
Asunción
Trindade I.
(BRAZ.)
Tropic of Capricorn
Tubuai Islands
Pitcairn I.
(U.K.)
Easter Island
(CHILE)
CHILE
R. Paraná
URUGUAY
Kermadec Islands
(N.Z.)
Santiago
Buenos Aires
Montevideo
ARGENTINA
Tristan da Cunha
(U.K.)
Wellington
NEW ZEALAND
Falkland Islands
(U.K.)
Tierra del Fuego
South Georgia
(U.K.)

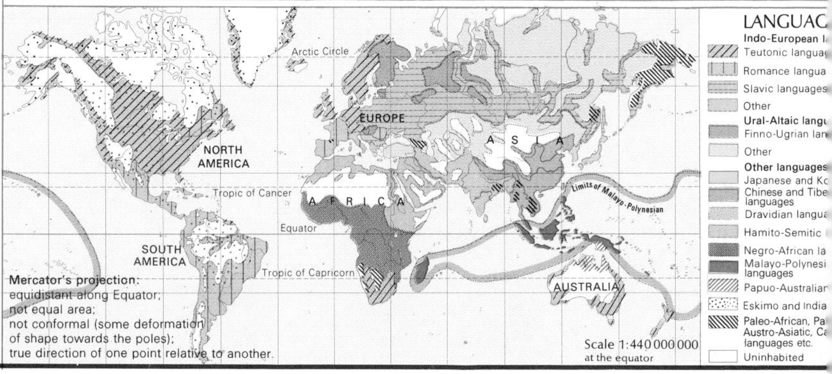
Arctic Circle
EUROPE
ASIA
NORTH AMERICA
Tropic of Cancer
AFRICA
Limits of Malayo-Polynesian
Equator
SOUTH AMERICA
Tropic of Capricorn
AUSTRALIA
Mercator's projection:
equidistant along Equator;
not equal area;
not conformal (some deformation
of shape towards the poles);
true direction of one point relative to another.
Scale 1:440 000 000
at the equator
LANGUAG
Indo-European l
Teutonic langua
Romance langua
Slavic languages
Other
Ural-Altaic lang
Finno-Ugrian lan
Other
Other languages
Japanese and Ko
Chinese and Tibe
languages
Dravidian langua
Hamito-Semitic
Negro-African la
Malayo-Polynesi
languages
Papuo-Australian
Eskimo and India
Paleo-African, Pa
Austro-Asiatic, Ca
languages etc.
Uninhabited

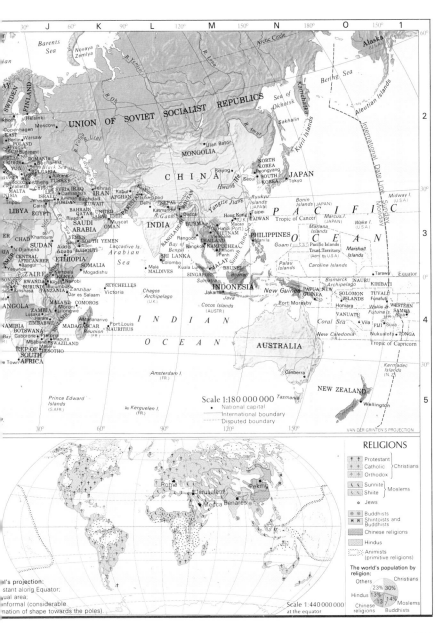

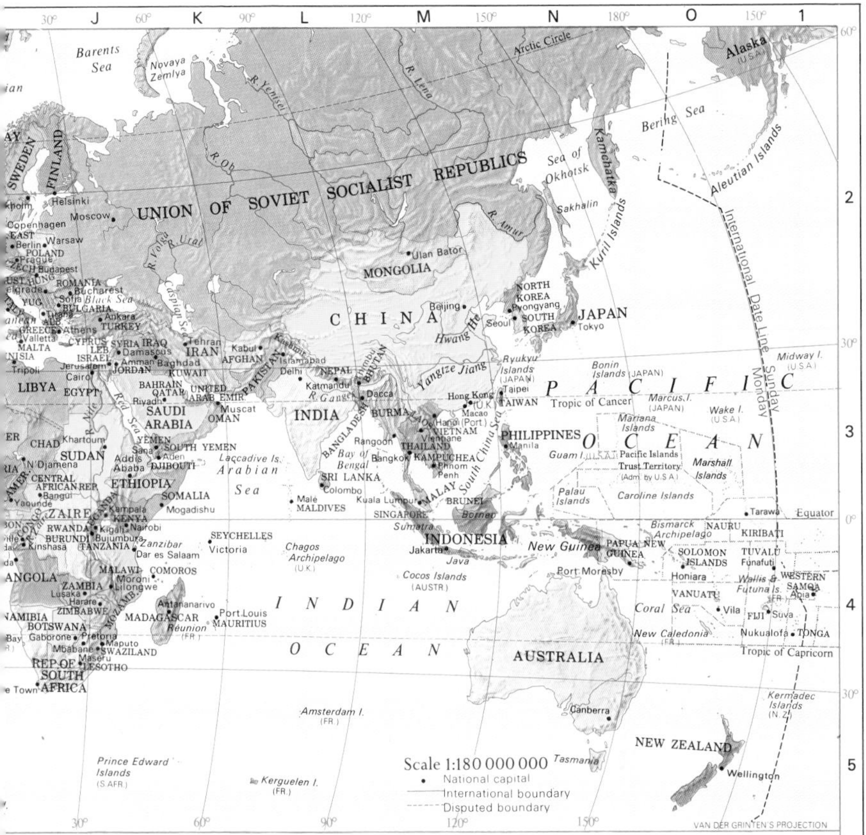

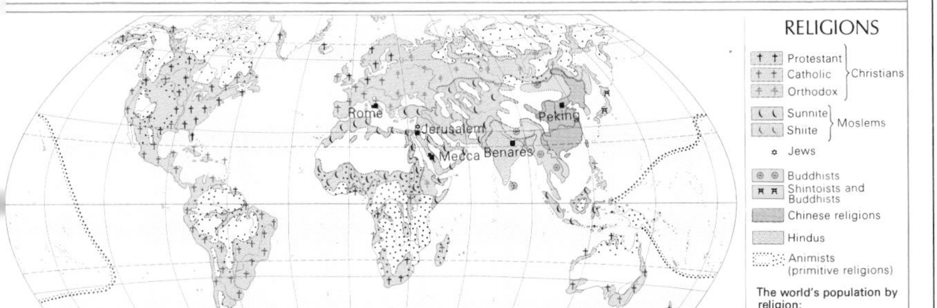

…l's projection:
…stant along Equator;
…ual area;
…nformal (considerable
…nation of shape towards the poles).

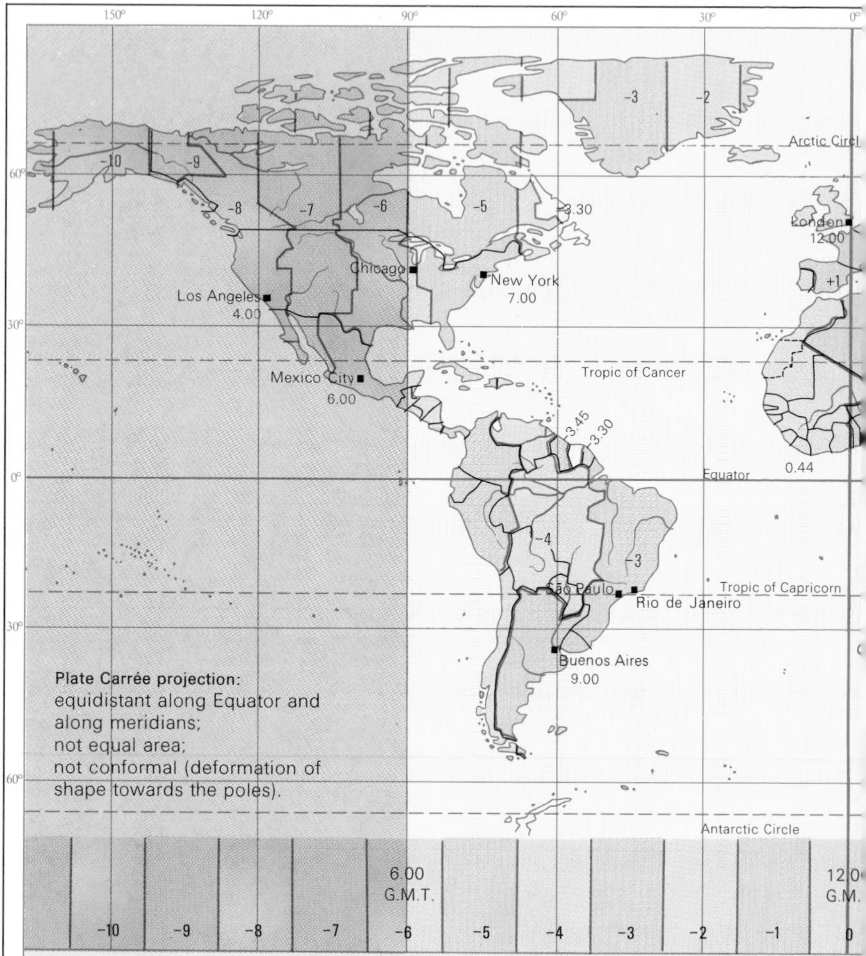

About December 22 at 12.00 G.M.T.

Daylight:
north of Arctic Circle; 0 h.
London (51°30′N.); 8 h.
at the Equator 12 h.

About June 21 at 12.00 G.M.T.

Daylight:
north of Arctic Circle; 24 h.
London (51°30′N.); 17 h.
at the Equator 12 h.

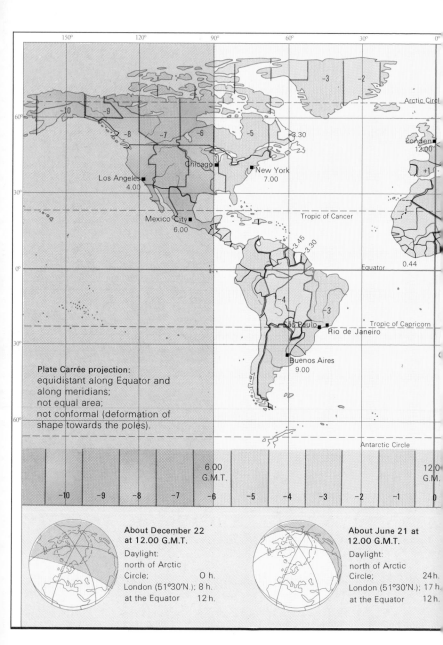

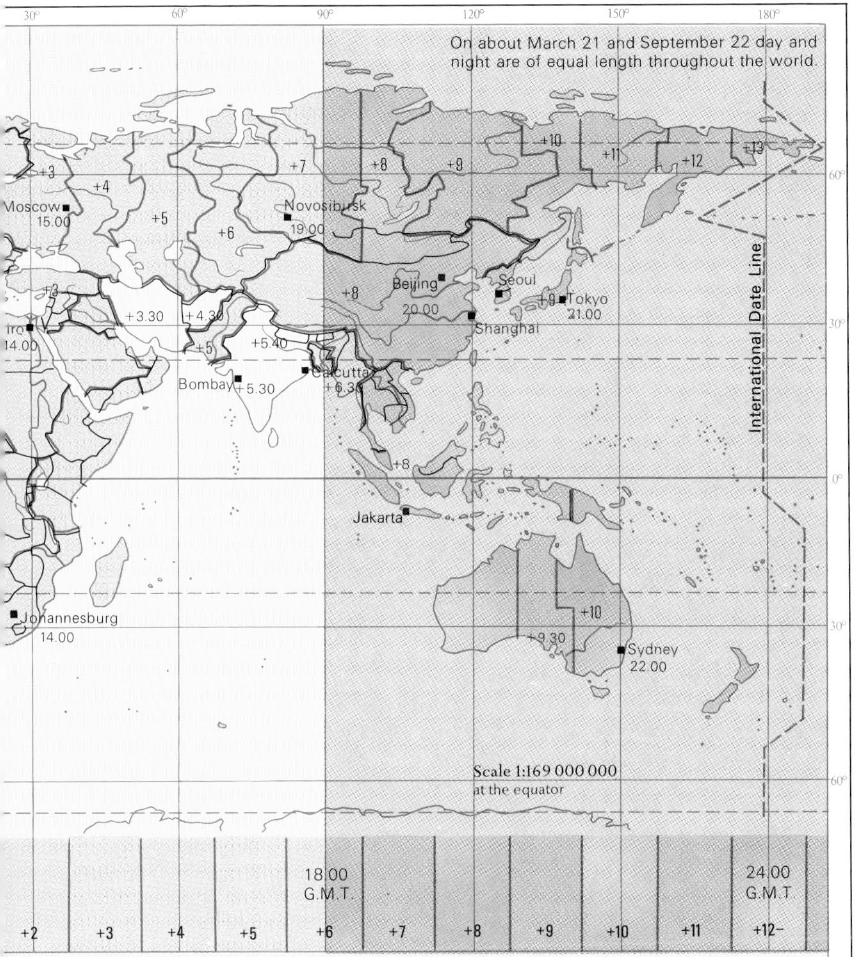

Direction of Earth's rotation. The Earth rotates on its axis from west to east and completes one rotation in about 24 hours. The Earth has been divided into 24 Standard Time Zones. The lines separating these Zones on land mostly follow country or province boundaries. Many countries however use a different standard, eg. British Summer Time.

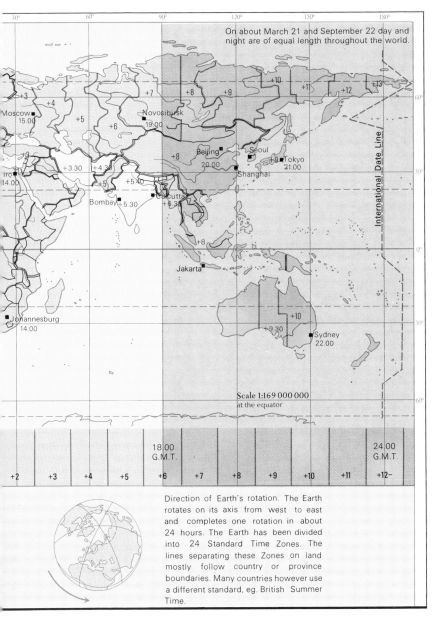

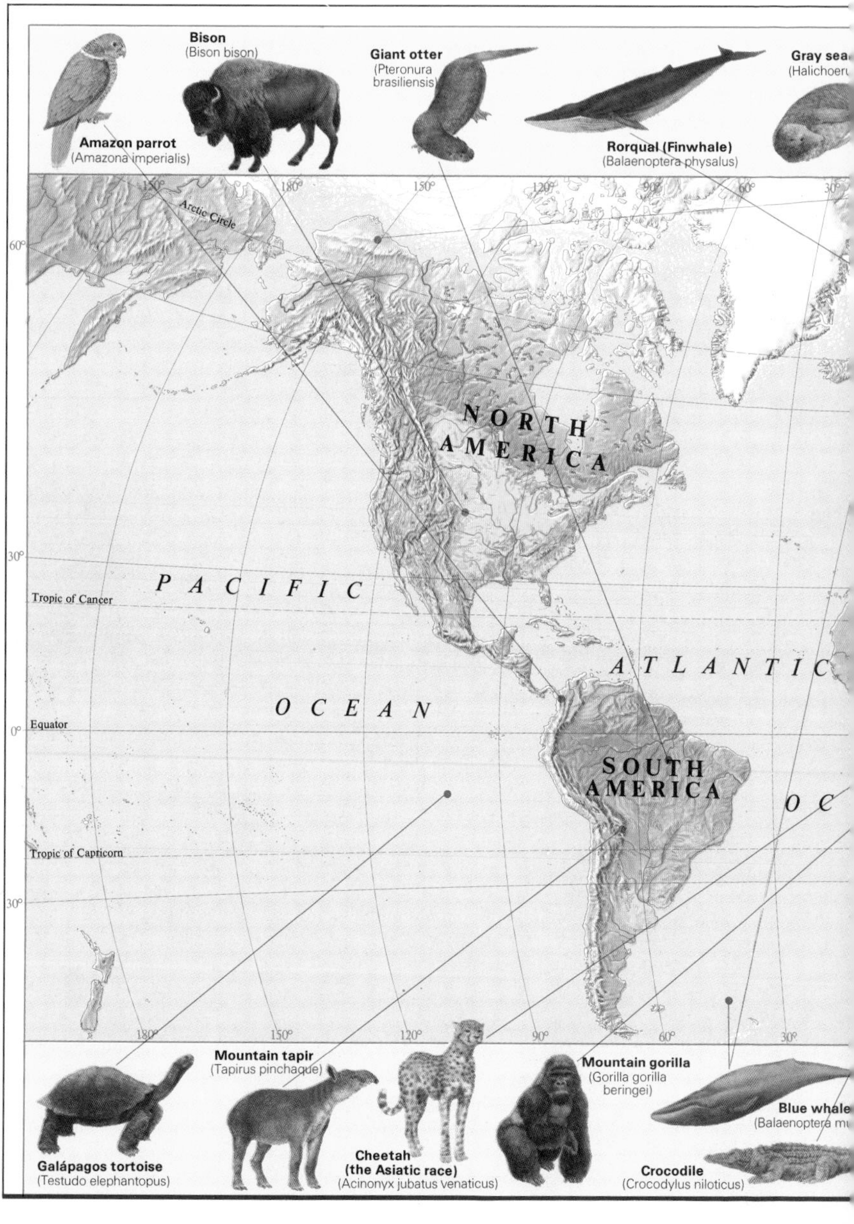

Bison
(Bison bison)
Giant otter
(Pteronura brasiliensis)
Amazon parrot
(Amazona imperialis)
Rorqual (Finwhale)
(Balaenoptera physalus)
Gray sea
(Halichoer
Arctic Circle
NORTH AMERICA
PACIFIC
OCEAN
ATLANTIC
SOUTH AMERICA
OC
Tropic of Cancer
Equator
Tropic of Capricorn
60°
30°
0°
30°
150°
180°
150°
120°
90°
60°
30°
180°
150°
120°
90°
60°
30°
Mountain tapir
(Tapirus pinchaque)
Mountain gorilla
(Gorilla gorilla beringei)
Blue whale
(Balaenoptera m
Galápagos tortoise
(Testudo elephantopus)
Cheetah
(the Asiatic race)
(Acinonyx jubatus venaticus)
Crocodile
(Crocodylus niloticus)

n rhinoceros
ceros unicornis)
Ounce
(Snow leopard)
(Panthera unica)
Walrus
(Odobenus rosmarus)
Giant panda
(Ailuropoda melanoleuca)
Orangutan
(Pongo pygmaeus)
30°
60°
90°
120°
150°
180°
150°
OCEAN
Arctic Circle
60°
UROPE
ASIA
PACIFIC
30°
Tropic of Cancer
OCEAN
RICA
Equator
0°
INDIAN
OCEAN
AUSTRALIA
Tropic of Capricorn
30°
30°
60°
90°
120°
150°
180°
Aye-aye
(Daubentonia
madagascariensis)
Arabian oryx
(Oryx leucoryx)
Tiger
(Leo tigris)
Tasmanian wolf
(Thylacinus cynocephalus)
Kiwi
(Apteryx australis)

DER GRINTEN'S PROJECTION

ale 1:180 000 000

A

Aachen 52 E 4
Aalen 53 F 5
Aạ Sumayḥ 92 D 3
Aba (Nigeria) 91 F 4
Abaco Island 105 G 2
Abadab, Jabal 88 F 5
Ābādān (Iran) 61 E 3
Ābādān (Iran) 66 D 4
Ābādeh (Iran) 61 F 3
Ābādeh (Iran) 66 E 4
Abadla 86 E 2
Abaetetuba 109 J 4
Abagnar Qi 71 G 2
Abaiang 82 C 2
Abakaliki 91 F 4
Abakan 68 F 5
Abalak 91 F 2
Abancay 110 B 3
Abant Silsilesi 58 D 2
Abariringa 82 D 3
Abarqu (Iran) 61 F 3
Abarqu, Kavir-e (Iran) 61 F 3
Abatskoye 63 O 4
Abay 63 O 6
Abaya, Lake 93 F 3
Abaza 68 F 5
Abbai 92 F 2
Abbāsābād (Iran) 61 G 1
Abbeville (France) 56 D 1
Abbot Ice Shelf 115
'Abd al Kūrī 93 J 2
Abdulino 62 K 5
Abéché 91 J 3
Abemama 82 C 2
Abengourou 90 D 4
Abeokuta 90 E 4
Aberdeen (Andaman Is.) 73 F 5
Aberdeen (S.D., U.S.A.) 102 G 2
Aberdeen (U.K.) 52 C 3
Aberdeen Lake 99 RS 3
Aberystwyth 52 C 4
Abhā' 89 G 5
Abhar (Iran) 61 E 1
Abidjan 90 CD 4
Abilene 102 FG 5
Abkit 69 T 3
Åbo 55 H 3
Abong Abong, Gunung 74 A 3
Abong Mbang 91 G 5
Abrantes 56 B 4
'Abrī 88 E 4
Abruzzo 57 F 3
Abū ad Duhūr (Syria) 60 B 2
Abū al Bukhush (United Arab Emirates) 61 F 4
Abū 'Alī (Saudi Arabia) 61 E 4
Abu Dhabi 89 J 4
Abu Dhabī (United Arab Emirates) 61 FG 4
Abufari 109 F 5
Abū Ḥadrīyah 66 D 5
Abū Ḥamad 88 E 5
Abū Jifān (Saudi Arabia) 61 E 4
Abū Kamāl (Syria) 60 C 2
Abū Maṭariq 88 D 6
Abū Mūsa' (Iran) 61 G 4
Abunã (Brazil) 110 C 3
Abuqasr 66 BC 4
Abūqrīn 87 J 2
Abū Qumayyis, Ra's (United Arab Emirates) 61 F 4
Abu Road 72 B 3
Abū Sunbul 88 E 4
Abuya Myeda 93 FG 2
Abū Ẓaby 89 J 4
Abū Ẓaby (United Arab Emirates) 61 FG 4
Abū Zanīmah (Egypt) 60 A 3
Abyad, Ra's al (Saudi Arabia) 60 BC 5
Abyār 'Alī (Saudi Arabia) 60 C 4
Abydos 88 E 3
Ābyek (Iran) 61 F 2
Açailândia 109 J 4
Acaponeta 104 AB 3
Acapulco 104 B 4
Acarai, Serra 109 G 3
Acaraú 111 HJ 1
Acari (Brazil) 111 J 2
Acarigua 108 E 2
Accomac 103 L 4
Accra 90 DE 4
Achao 113 B 7
Achar 112 E 5
Achayvayam 69 VW 3
Achelóos 58 B 3
Achinsk 68 F 4
Acklins Island 105 H 3
Acongagua, Cerro 112 BC 5
Acorizal 110 E 3–4
Acre (Brazil) 108 D 5
Acre (Brazil) 110 C 3
Acre (Israel) 60 B 2
Acri 57 G 4
Adaba 93 F 3
Adak (AK, U.S.A.) 98 B 5
Adak (Sweden) 54 G 2
'Adale 93 H 4
Adam, Mount 113 DE 9
Adamantina 111 F 5
Adamaoua 91 G 4
Adams Bridge 72 CD 6
Adamstown 83 G 4
Adana (Turkey) 59 E 3
Adana (Turkey) 60 B 1
Adapazarı 58 D 2
Adare, Cape 115
Adavale 79 GH 4
Aḍ Ḍafrah (United Arab Emirates) 61 F 5
Ad Dahnā' (Saudi Arabia) 61 DE 4
Ad Dahnā' (Saudi Arabia) 89 GH 3
Ad Dammām (Saudi Arabia) 61 EF 4
Ad Dammām (Saudi Arabia) 89 J 3
Ad Dār al Ḥamrā' 66 B 5
Ad Darb 89 G 5
Ad Dawādimī (Saudi Arabia) 60 D 4
Ad Dawḥah 89 J 3
Ad Dawḥah (Qatar) 61 F 4
Ad Dawr (Iraq) 60 D 2
Ad Dawr (Iraq) 66 C 4
Ad Dayr (Egypt) 60 A 4
Ad Dibdibah (Saudi Arabia) 61 E 3
Ad Dilam (Saudi Arabia) 61 E 5
Ad Dindar 88 E 6
Addis Ababa 93 F 3
Addis Zemen 93 F 2
Ad Dīwānīyah 89 H 2
Ad Dīwanīyah (Iraq) 61 D 3
Ad Duwaym 88 E 6
Adelaide Island 115
Adelaide Peninsula 99 S 2
Adelaide River 78 E 1
Adélie Coast 115
Adige 57 F 2
Adıgüzel Barajı 58 C 3
Adirondack Mountains 103 M 3
Adi Ugri 93 F 2
Adıyaman 59 E 3
Admiralty 98 L 4
Admiralty Islands 80 E 2
Admiralty Mountains 115
Ado 90 E 4
Ado Ekiti 91 F 4
Adok 92 E 3
Adrano 57 F 4
Adrar (Algeria) 86 E 3
Adrar des Iforas 90 E 1–2
Adré 91 J 3
Adriatic Sea 57 FG 3
Adwa 93 F 2
Adzhar 59 F 2
Adzopáe 90 D 4
Aegean Sea 58 C 3
Afao, Mont 87 G 3
Afghanistan 67 GH 4
'Afīf 66 C 6
Afif (Saudi Arabia) 60 D 4–5
Afikpo 91 F 4
Afmadōw 93 G 4
Afognak 98 G 4
African Islands 93 J 5
Afyonkarahisar 58 D 3
Agabah, Khalij al 60 B 3
Agadez 91 F 2
Agadir 86 CD 2
Agana 82 A 2
Agapitovo 63 R 2
Agartala 73 F 3
Agata 68 F 2
Agats 75 J 5
Agattu 98 A 5
Agawa Bay 100 L 6
Agboville 90 CD 4
Agdary 68 L 3
Agen 56 D 3
Agepsta 59 F 2
Agha Jārī (Iran) 61 EF 3
Agordat 93 F 1
Agra 72 C 2
Ağrı 59 F 3
Agrigento 57 F 4
Agrihan 82 A 1
Agrinion 58 B 3
Agto 101 R 2
Água Clara 111 F 5
Aguadulce 108 BC 2
Águas Formosas 111 HJ 4
Agulhas, Cape 94 C 6
Aguscalientes 104 B 3
Ahaggar 87 FG 4
Ahe 83 F 3
Ahmadabad 72 B 3
Ahmadnagar 72 BC 4
Ahome 102 E 6
Ähtävänjoki 54 H 3
Ahvāz (Iran) 61 E 3
Ahvāz (Iran) 66 D 4
Ahvenanmaa (Åland) 55 GH 3
Aḥwar 89 H 6
Aihui 69 N 6
Ailinginae 82 BC 2
Ailinglapalap 82 C 2
Aillik 101 Q 4
Ailuk 82 C 2
Aim 69 O 4
Aïn Amenas 87 G 3
Aïn Amguel 87 FG 4
Aïn Beïda 87 G 1
Aïn Ezzane 87 H 4
Aïn Tiguelguemine 87 F 3
Aioun el Atrouss 86 D 5
Aïr 91 F 2
Airao 109 F 4
Aitape 80 D 2
Aitutaki 83 E 4
Aix-en-Provence 57 DE 3
Aiyaion Pélagos 58 C 3
Aizuwakamatsu 71 M 3
Ajaccio 57 E 3
Aj Bogd Uul 70 BC 2
'Ajmān (United Arab Emirates) 61 G 4
Ajmer 72 B 2
Ajo, Cabo de 56 C 3
Akademii, Zaliv 69 P 5
Ak Dağ 58 C 3
Akespe 66 G 1
Akharnai 58 B 3
Akhisar 58 C 3
Akhtubinsk 62 J 6
Akhtyrka 62 FG 5
Akimiski 101 L 5
Akita 71 L 3
Akkabak 67 G 1
Akkajaure 54 G 2
'Akko (Israel) 60 B 2
Aklavik 98 K 2
Akmenrags 55 H 4
Akobo 92 E 3
Akola 72 C 3
Akosombo Dam 90 E 4
Akpatok 101 O 3
Ákra Akritas 58 B 3
Akra Arnauti (Cyprus) 60 A 2
Ákra Maleás 58 B 3
Ákra Spátha 58 B 3
Ákra Taínaron 58 B 3
Akritas, Ákra 58 B 3
Akron 103 K 3
Aksaray 59 D 3
Aksay Kazakzu Zizhixian 70 B 3
Aksehir 58 D 3
Aksha 68 K 5
Akshiy 67 G 1
Aksu (China) 67 L 2
Aksu (Turkey) 58 D 3
Aktash 67 H 3
Aktasty 63 M 5
Aktogay 63 P 6
Aktyubinsk 63 L 5
Akure 91 F 4

Akureyri **54** B 2
Ala, Monti di **57** E 3
Alabama **103** J 5
Alabama River **103** J 5
Al Abyaḍ, Ra's **87** G 1
Alaçam Dağları **58** C 3
Alachakh **69** P 4
Aladağ (Turkey) **59** DE 3
Aladağ (Turkey) **59** F 3
Alagoas **111** J 2
Alagoinhas **111** J 3
Alagon (Spain) **56** C 3
Alajuela **104** F 5
Alakurtti **54** K 2
Al 'Alamayn **88** D 2
Al Amādīyah (Iraq) **60** D 1
Alamagan **82** A 1
Al 'Amārah (Iraq) **61** E 3
Al 'Amārah (Iraq) **89** H 2
Alamogordo **102** E 5
Alamos **102** E 6
Ålands hav **55** G 3–4
Alanya **59** D 3
Alaotra, Lac **95** H 3
Alapayevsk **63** M 4
Al' Aqabah (Jordan) **60** B 3
Al 'Aqaylah **87** J 2
Al Arabīyah as Su'ūdīyah → Saudi Arabia **89** GH 4
Al 'Arīsh (Egypt) **60** A 3
Al 'Armah (Saudi Arabia) **61** DE 4
Al Arṭāwīyah (Saudi Arabia) **61** D 4
Al 'Āshūrīyah **66** C 4
Alaska **98** FH 2
Alaska, Gulf of **98** HJ 4
Alaska Peninsula **98** E 4
Alaska Range **98** GH 3
Alatyr' **62** J 5
Al 'Awaynāt **87** H 3
Al'Awsajīyah (Saudi Arabia) **60** D 4
Al 'Ayn (United Arab Emirates) **61** G 4
Alazani **59** G 2
Alba **57** E 3
Al Bāb (Syria) **60** B 1
Albacete **56** C 4
Al Badī' (Saudi Arabia) **89** H 4
Al Bahrah (Kuwait) **61** E 3
Al Baḥr al Mayyit (Jordan) **60** B 3
Alba Iulia **58** B 1
Albanel, Lac **101** N 5
Albania **58** AB 2
Albano Laziale **57** F 3
Albany (Australia) **78** B 5
Albany (GA, U.S.A.) **103** K 5
Albany (N.Y., U.S.A.) **103** M 3
Albany (Ontario, Can.) **100** L 5
Al Barkāt **87** H 4
Al Basrah (Iraq) **61** E 3
Al Baṣrah (Iraq) **89** H 2
Al Batin (Iraq) **61** E 3
Al Bāṭinah **89** K 4
Albatross Point **81** Q 8
Al Bayḍā' (Libya) **87** K 2
Albert, Lake (Uganda/Zaire) **92** E 4
Alberta **99** OP 5
Albert Nile **92** E 4
Albi **56** D 3
Al Bid' (Saudi Arabia) **60** B 3
Albina **109** H 2
Al Bi'r (Saudi Arabia) **60** B 3
Al Birkah **66** C 6
Alborán **56** C 4
Ålborg **55** F 4
Al Brayqah **87** JK 3
Albu Ali **59** F 4
Al Buḥayrah al Murrah al Kubrā (Egypt) **60** A 3
Albuquerque **102** E 4–5
Albury **79** H 6
Alcalá **56** C 3
Alcalá **56** B 4
Alcântara **109** K 4
Alcántara, Embalse de **56** B 4
Alcaraz, Sierra de **56** C 4
Alcázar de San Juan **56** C 4
Alciéni **91** G 6
Alcira **56** C 4
Alcolea del Pinar **56** C 3
Alcoy **56** C 4
Aldabra Islands **93** H 6
Aldan **69** O 3
Aldan **69** N 4
Aldanskoye Nagor'ye **69** MN 4
Aleg **86** C 5
Alegrete **112** E 4
Aleksandriya (Ukraine, U.S.S.R.) **62** FG 6
Aleksandrovsk **63** M 4
Aleksandrovskiy **68** L 5
Aleksandrovsk-Sakhalinskiy **69** Q 5
Alekseyevka (Kazakhstan, U.S.S.R.) **63** O 5
Alekseyevo **69** R 1
Alençon **56** D 2
Aleppo (Syria) **60** B 1
Aleppo (Syria) **88** F 1
Aléria **57** E 3
Alès **56** D 3
Alessandria **57** E 3
Ålestrup **55** E 4
Ålesund **54** E 3
Aleutian Islands **98** AC 4
Aleutian Range **98** F 4
Alexander Archipelago **98** K 4
Alexander Island **115**
Alexandra **80** PQ 10
Alexandra Falls **99** O 3
Alexandria (Egypt) **88** DE 2
Alexandria (LA, U.S.A.) **103** H 5
Alexandria (MD, U.S.A.) **103** L 4
Alexandria (Romania)**58** BC 2
Alexandroúpolis **58** C 2
Aleysk **63** Q 5
Al Fāshir **88** D 6
Al Fatḥah **66** C 3
Al Fayyūm **88** DE 3
Al Fuḥayhīl (Kuwait) **61** E 3
Al Fujayrah (United Arab Emirates) **61** G 4
Al Fujayrah (United Arab Emirates) **89** K 3
Al Furat (Iraq) **59** F 3–4
Al Furāt (Iraq) **60** C 2
Al Fuwayrit (Qatar) **61** F 4
Algama **69** N 4
Alganskaya **69** WX 3
Algarve **56** B 4
Algeciras **56** B 4
Algeria **86–87** EF 3
Al Ghazālah (Saudi Arabia) **60** C 4
Alghero **57** E 3
Algiers **87** F 1
Al Ḥadhālīl (Saudi Arabia) **60–61** D 3
Al Ḥadīthah **66** C 4
Al Hadīthah (Iraq) **60** CD 2
Al Hamād **60** C 2–3
Al Hamrā' (Saudi Arabia) **60** C 5
Al Ḥanākīyah **89** G 4
Al Ḥanākīyah (Saudi Arabia) **60** C 4
Al Ḥanīsh al Kabīr **89** G 6
Al Harrah (Saudi Arabia) **60** C 3
Al Ḥarrah (Saudi Arabia) **66** B 4
Al Ḥarrah (Syria) **60** BC 2
Al Ḥasa (Jordan) **60** B 3
Al Hasā' (Saudi Arabia) **61** E 4
Al Ḥasā' (Saudi Arabia) **89** H 3
Al Hasakah (Syria) **60** C 1
Al Ḥasakah (Syria) **89** FG 1
Al Ḥasan (Iraq) **60** D 2
Al Ḥawwārī **87** K 4
Al Ḥayy (Iraq) **61** DE 2
AlḤijāz **88** F 3
Al Hijaz (Saudi Arabia) **60** B 4
Al Ḥillah (Iraq) **61** D 2
Al Ḥillah (Iraq) **89** G 2
Al Ḥillah (Saudi Arabia) **61** E 5
Al Ḥillah (Saudi Arabia) **66** D 6
Al Ḥillah (Sudan) **88** D 6
Al Ḥudaydah **89** G 6
Al Hufrah (Saudi Arabia) **60** BC 3–4
Al Hufūf (Saudi Arabia) **61** E 4
Al Hufūf (Saudi Arabia) **89** H 3
Al Hūj (Saudi Arabia) **60** C 3
Al Hūj (Saudi Arabia) **66** B 5
Al Ḥusayḥiṣah **88** E 6
Al Ḥuwaymī **89** H 6
Alīābād (Iran) **61** G 3
Aliákmon **58** B 2
Ali Bayramly **66** DE 3
Alicante **56** C 4
Alice River **79** H 3
Alice Springs **78** E 3
Aligarh **72** C 2
Al Iglim al Janūbīyah **92** DE 3
Alīgūdarz (Iran) **61** E 2
Alījūq, Kūh-e (Iran) **61** F 3
Al 'Iraq **60** D 2
Al 'Irq **87** K 3
Ali Sabjeh **93** G 2
Al 'Isāwīyah (Saudi Arabia) **60** B 3
Al' Īsāwīyah (Saudi Arabia) **60** BC 3
Al Iskandarīyah **88** DE 2
Aliskerovo **69** U 2
Al Ismā'īlīyah (Egypt) **60** A 3
Aliwal North **94** D 6
Al Jafr (Jordan) **60** B 3
Al Jāfūrah (Saudi Arabia) **61** F 4–5
Al Jaghbūb **87** K 3
Al Jahrah (Kuwait) **61** E 3
Al Jahrah (Kuwait) **89** H 3
Al Jalāmīd (Saudi Arabia) **60** C 3
Al Jalāmīd (Saudi Arabia) **89** FG 2
Al Jawf (Saudi Arabia) **60** C 3
Al Jawf (Saudi Arabia) **89** F 3
Al Jaylī **88** E 5
Al Jazā'ir **87** F 1
Al Jazīrah (Iraq) **59** F 3–4
Al Jazīrah (Iraq) **60** CD 2
Al Jiwā' (United Arab Emirates) **61** FG 5
Al Jiwā' (United Arab Emirates) **89** J 4
Al Jīzah **88** DE 2
Al Jubayl **66** DE 5
Al Jubaylah (Saudi Arabia) **61** E 4
Al Jumaymah **66** C 5
Al Junaynah **88** C 6
Al Karak (Jordan) **60** B 3
Al Karnak **88** E 3
Al Kāzimīyah (Iraq) **60** D 2
Al Khalīl **60** B 3
Al Khāliṣ (Iraq) **61** D 2
Al Kharj (Saudi Arabia) **61** E 5
Al Kharj (Saudi Arabia) **66** D 6
Al Kharṭūm **88** EF 5
Al Kharṭūm Baḥrī **88** EF 5
Al Khaṣab (Oman) **61** G 4
Al Khidr (Iraq) **61** D 3
Al Khubar (Saudi Arabia) **61** F 4
Al Khubar (Saudi Arabia) **89** HJ 3
Al Khufayfīyah (Saudi Arabia) **61** D 4
Al Khufayfīyah (Saudi Arabia) **89** G 4
Al Khunfah (Saudi Arabia) **60** C 3
Al Kir'ānah (Qatar) **61** F 4
Al Kūfah (Iraq) **60** D 2
Al Kumayt (Iraq) **61** E 2–3
Al Kuntillah (Egypt) **60** B 3
Al Kūt (Iraq) **61** D 2
Al Kūt (Iraq) **89** H 2
Al Kuwayt (Kuwait) **61** E 3
Al Kuwayt (Kuwait) **89** H 3
Al Labbah (Saudi Arabia) **60** C 3
Al Labbah (Saudi Arabia) **66** C 5
Al Lādhiqīyah (Syria) **88** EF 1
Al Lādhiqīyan (Syria) **60** B 2
Al Lagowa **88** D 6
Allahabad **72** D 2
Allakh-Yun' **69** P 3
Allentown **103** L 3
Alleppey **72** C 6
Al Līfīyah **66** C 4
Al Liṣāfah **66** D 5
Al Lussuf **66** C 4
Alma-Ata **67** K 2
Almada **56** B 4
Al Madīnah **89** FG 4

Al Madīnah (Saudi Arabia) **60** C 4
Al Mafraq (Jordan) **60** B 2
Al Maḥallah al Kubrā **88** E 2
Al Mahrah **89** J 5
Al Majann (Saudi Arabia) **61** F 5
Al Makhaylī **87** K 2
Al Manadīr (Oman) **61** G 5
Al Manāmah **89** J 3
Al Manāmah (Bahrain) **61** F 4
Al Manāqil **88** E 6
Al Manṣūrah **88** E 2
Al Maqṭā' (United Arab Emirates) **61** G 4
Al Marj **87** K 2
Al Mawṣil (Iraq) **60** D 1
Al Mawṣil (Iraq) **89** G 1
Al Mayyāh (Saudi Arabia) **60** D 4
Almeirim **109** H 4
Almenara **111** HJ 4
Almendra, Embalse de **56** B 3
Almeria **56** C 4
Al'met'yevsk **62** K 4–5
Al Minyā **88** DE 3
Almirante Brown **115**
Almoustarat **90** D 2
Al Mubarraz (Saudi Arabia) **61** E 4
Al Mubarraz (Saudi Arabia) **89** H 3
Al Mudawwarah (Saudi Arabia) **60** B 3
Al Mughayrā' **66** B 5
Al Muharraq (Bahrain) **61** F 4
Al Mukallā **89** HJ 6
Al Murabbā' (Saudi Arabia) **60** D 4
Al Murabbā' (Saudi Arabia) **66** C 5
Al Musayjīd **66** BC 6
Al Musayyib (Iraq) **60** D 2
Al Muwaylih (Saudi Arabia) **60** B 4
Al Nasser (Egypt) **60** A 4
Alofi (Cook Is.) **82** D 4
Alongshan **69** M 5
Alor, Pulau **75** F 5
Alor Setar **74** AB 2
Alpena **103** K 2
Alphonse **93** J 6
Alpi Carniche **57** F 2
Alpi Dolomitiche **57** F 2
Alpine (TX, U.S.A.) **102** F 5
Al Qaḍārif **88** F 6
Al Qaḍīmah **89** F 4
Al Qāhirah **88** E 2
Al Qalībah (Saudi Arabia) **60** B 3
Al Qalībah (Saudi Arabia) **88** F 3
Al Qāmishlī (Syria) **60** C 1
Al Qāmishlī (Syria) **89** FG 1
Al Qanṭarah (Egypt) **60** A 3
Al Qatīf (Saudi Arabia) **61** E 4
Al Qatif (Saudi Arabia) **89** H 3
Al Qaṭrānī (Jordan) **60** B 3
Al Qatrūn **87** H 3
Al Qayʿīyah (Saudi Arabia) **60** D 4
Al Qayrawān **87** GH 1
Al Qayṣūmah **66** C 5
Al Qayṣūmah (Saudi Arabia) **61** E 3
Al Qayṣūmah (Saudi Arabia) **66** D 5
Al Qunaytirah (Syria) **60** B 2
Al Qunayṭirah (Syria) **88** EF 2
Al Qunfudhah **89** FG 5
Al Qurayyah **88** F 3
Al Qurnah (Iraq) **61** E 3
Al Qurnah (Iraq) **66** D 4
Al Qusayr (Egypt) **60** B 4
Al Qūṣūrīyah (Saudi Arabia) **60** D 5
Al Qutayfah (Syria) **60** B 2
Al Quwārah **66** C 5
Al Quwayīyah (Saudi Arabia) **61** D 4
Al Shagra (Qatar) **61** F 4
Altamira **109** H 4
Altamont **102** B 3
Alta Shany **67** M 1
Altay (China) **67** M 1
Altay (Mongolia) **68** G 6
Altay (U.S.S.R.) **63** RS 5
Altiplanicie Mexicana **104** AB 2
Altmark **53** F 4
Alto - Alentejo **56** B 4
Alto Garças **111** F 4
Alton (IL, U.S.A.) **103** H 4
Alto Parnaíba **109** J 5
Alto Río Senguerr **113** BC 7–8
Alto Turi **109** J 4
Altun Shan **70** AB 3
Alturas **102** B 3
Altus **102** FG 5
Altynasar **67** G 1
Al Ubayyid **88** DE 6
Al Ugṣur (Egypt) **60** A 4
Al Ugṣur (Egypt) **88** E 3
Al Urayq (Saudi Arabia) **60** C 3
Al Urdun **60** B 3
Al Urdun **88** F 2
Al 'Uwayqīlah (Saudi Arabia) **60** CD 3
Al 'Uwayqīlah (Saudi Arabia) **66** C 4
Al 'Uzayr (Iraq) **61** E 3
Alva (OK, U.S.A.) **102** G 4
Alvano, Kūh-e (Iran) **61** E 2
Alvorado **111** G 3
Älvsbyn **54** H 2
Al Wajh (Saudi Arabia) **60** B 4
Al Wajh (Saudi Arabia) **88** F 3
Alwar **72** C 2
Al Warīʿah **89** H 3
Al Widyān (Iraq) **60** C 3
Al Widyān (Iraq) **89** G 2
Alxa Zuoqi **70** DE 3
Alygdzher **68** G 5
Alys-Khaya **69** P 2
Alytus **55** H 5
Amada **88** E 4
Amadjuak Lake **101** NO 2–3
Amakinskiy **68** K 1
Amambaí **111** EF 5
Amami-ō-shima **71** JK 5
Amangel'dy **63** N 5
Amanzimtoti **95** E 6
Amapá **109** H 3
Amarillo **102** F 4
Amaro Leite **111** G 3
Amarti **93** G 2
Amasya **59** E 2
Amazar **68** LM 5
Amazonas **108–109** EF 4
Amazonas **109** H 4
Ambala **72** C 1
Ambam **91** G 5
Ambarchik **69** U 2
Ambato **108** C 4
Ambikapur **72** D 3
Ambilobe **95** H 2
Ambohitralanana **95** J 3
Ambon **75** G 4
Ambositra **95** H 4
Ambovombe **95** H 5
Ambre, Cap d' **95** HJ 2
Ambrim **82** C 4
Ambrym **81** J 5
Ambur **72** C 5
Amchitka Pass **98** AB 5
Amdo **70** B 4
American Highland **115**
American Samoa **82** D 3
Amery Ice Shelf **115**
Ames **103** H 3
Amga **69** O 3
Amguema **98** B 2
Amguid **87** G 3
Amhara **93** F 2
Amiens **56** D 2
Amindivi Islands **72** B 5
Amirante Islands **93** J 6
Amlia **98** C 5
'Amman (Jordan) **60** B 3
'Ammān (Jordan) **88** F 2
Ammarfjället **54** G 2
Amo **68** H 3
Āmol (Iran) **61** F 1
Āmol (Iran) **66** E 3
Amorgos **58** C 3
Amos **101** M 6
Amoy **71** G 6
Amravati **72** C 3
Amritsar **72** C 1
Amsā'ad **87** K 2
Amsterdam (Netherlands) **52** DE 4
Amsterdam (N.Y., U.S.A.) **103** M 3
Amu-Dar'ya **67** G 2
Amukta Pass **98** C 5
Amundsen Gulf **99** N 1
Amundsen-Scott **115**
Amundsen Sea **115**
Amuntai **74** E 4
Amur **69** P 5
Amysakh **68** L 2
Anabarskoye Ploskogor'ye **68** J 1–2
Anaco **109** F 2
Anadoli **58–59** CD 3
Anadyr **69** WX 3
Anadyrskaja Nīzmennost **69** X 2
Anadyrskiy Zaliv **69** Y 3
Anadyrskiy Zaliv **98** BC 3
Anadyrskoye Ploskogor'ye **69** VW 2
Ānah (Iraq) **60** C 2
Anaimalai Hills **72** C 5
Anakapalle **72** D 4
Anamur (Turkey) **60** A 1
Anamur Burun (Turkey) **60** A 2
Anamuryum **59** D 3
Anantapur **72** C 5
Anapa **59** E 2
Anápolis **111** G 4
Anār (Iran) **61** G 3
Anatolia **58–59** CD 3
Añatuya **112** D 4
Anchorage **98** H 3
Ancohuma **110** C 4
Ancona **57** F 3
Ancud **113** B 7
Anda **71** J 1
Andalucía **56** BC 4
Andaman Islands **73** F 5
Andaman Sea **73** G 5–6
Andarab **67** H 3
Anderson (IN, U.S.A.) **103** J 3–4
Anderson (N.W.T., Can.) **98** M 2
Anderson (S.C., U.S.A.) **103** K 5
Andes Mountains **107** C 2–6
Andfjorden **54** G 2
Andhra Pradesh **72** C 4
Andīmeshk (Iran) **61** E 2
Andiria Burun (Cyprus) **59** D 3
Andiria Burun (Cyprus) **60** B 2
Andirlangar **67** L 3
Andiyskiy Khrebet **59** G 2
Andizhan **67** J 2
Andkhui **67** GH 3
Andong **71** J 3
Andorra **56** D 3
Andorra la Vella **56** D 3
Andöya **54** G 2
Andradina **111** F 5
Andreanof Islands **98** BC 5
Andriba **95** H 3
Andropov **62** G 4
Ándros **58** BC 3
Andros Island **105** G 3
Andselv **54** G 2
Andújar **56** C 4
Andyngda **68** L 2
Anéfis **90** E 2
Anegada Passage **105** K 4
Aneto, Pico de **56** D 3
Angar **75** H 4
Angara **68** F 4
Angarsk **68** H 5
Angatau **83** F 4
Angaul **68** GH 5
Angeles **75** HJ 1
Angel Falls **109** F 2
Ängelholm **55** F 4
Ångermanälven **54** G 3
Angers **56** C 2
Angical **111** GH 3
Angijak Island **101** P 2
Angikuni Lake **99** RS 3
Angkor **73** H 5
Anglesey **52** BC 4
Angmagssalik **114**
Angoche **95** G 3
Angol **113** B 6
Angola **94** BC 2
Angoulême **56** D 2

Angu **92** C 4
Anguilla **105** K 4
Anhua **70** F 5
Anhui **71** G 4
Aniak **98** F 3
Aniakchak National Monument and Preserve **98** F 4
Animas Peak **102** E 5
Anjou **56** CD 2
Anjouan **95** GH 2
Ankang **70** E 4
Ankara **59** D 2
Ankazobe **95** H 3
Anlong **70** E 5–6
Anlu **70** F 4
Ann, Cape **115**
Annaba **87** G 1
An Nabk (Syria) **60** B 2
An Nabk (Syria) **66** B 4
An Nafūd (Saudi Arabia) **60** C 3
An Nafūd (Saudi Arabia) **89** FG 3
An Nāḥiyah **89** G 2
Annai **109** G 3
An Najaf (Iraq) **60** D 2–3
An Najaf (Iraq) **89** G 2
An' Nakhi (Egypt) **60** AB 3
Annam **73** J 4–5
Annandale **79** H 3
Anna Plains **78** C 2
Annapolis **103** L 4
Annapurna **72** D 2
Ann Arbor **103** K 3
An Nāsirīyah (Iraq) **61** E 3
An Nāsirīyah (Iraq) **89** GH 2
Annecy **57** E 2
Annobón **91** F 6
An Nu'ayrīyah (Saudi Arabia) **61** E 4
An Nu'ayrīyah (Saudi Arabia) **89** H 3
An Nuhūd **88** D 6
Anori **109** F 4
Anqing **71** G 4
Anshan **71** H 2
Anshun **70** DE 5
Ansongo **90** DE 2
Anta **110** B 3
Antakya **59** E 3
Antakya (Turkey) **60** B 1
Antalya (Turkey) **58** D 3
Antalya Kőrfezi **58** D 3
Antananarivo **95** H 3
Antarctic Peninsula **115**
Antequera **56** C 4
Antigua and Barbuda **105** K 4
Antillas Mayores **105** HJ 4
Antiope **82** D 4
Antipodes Islands **115**
Antlāt **87** K 2
Antofagasta **110** B 5
Antofagasta de la Sierra **112** C 4
Antongil, Baie d' **95** HJ 3
Antonio de Biedma **113** CD 8
Antonovo **66** E 1
Antseranana **95** HJ 2
Antsirabe **95** H 3
Antsohihy **95** H 2
Antwerpen **52** D 4
Anuradhapura **72** D 6
Anxi (Gansu, China) **70** C 2
Anxiang **70** F 5
Anyang **70** FG 3
Anzhero-Sudzhensk **63** RS 4
Aomori **71** M 2
Aosta **57** E 2
Aoudaghost **86** CD 5
Aouinat Legraa **86** D 3
Aoulef el Arab **86–87** F 3
Apaporis **108** DE 3–4
Apataki **83** F 4
Apatity **54** K 2
Apatzingán **104** B 4
Apeldoorn **52** E 4
Api, Tanjung **74** C 3
Apia **82** D 3
Aporé **111** F 4
Appalachian Mountains **103** KM 2–4
Appenno Lucano **57** G 3–4
Appenno Tosco-Emiliano **57** F 3
Appleton **103** J 3
Apsheronsk **59** E 2
Apucarana **111** F 5
Apure **108** E 2
Apurimac **110** B 3
Aqār 'Atabah **87** H 3
Aqdā (Iran) **61** F 2
Aqdā (Iran) **66** E 4
Aquidauana **110** E 5
ʿArabah, Wādi al (Jordan) **60** B 3
Arabestān (Iran) **61** E 3
Arabian Sea **117**
Arabiyah as Su'udiyah (Saudi Arabia) **60** CD 4
Aracaju **111** J 3
Aracati **111** J 1
Araçatuba **111** FG 5
Aracena, Sierra de **56** B 4
Araçuai **111** H 4
Arad **58** B 1
Arada **91** J 2
'Arādah (United Arab Emirates) **61** F 5
Arafura Sea **75** HJ 5
Aragarças **111** F 4
Aragon **56** C 3
Araguacema **109** HJ 5
Aragua de Maturín **109** F 2
Araguaia **109** J 5
Araguaiana **111** F 4
Araguaína **109** J 5
Araguari (Minas Gerais, Brazil) **111** G 4
Araguatins **109** J 5
Arak (Algeria) **87** F 3
Arāk (Iran) **61** E 2
Arāk (Iran) **66** DE 4
Arakaka **109** G 2
Arakan Yoma **73** FG 3–4
Aral'sk **67** G 1
Aral'skoye More **66–67** FG 2
Aramac **79** H 3
Arandai **75** H 4
Aranjuez **56** C 3–4
Aranos **94** B 4
Aranuka **82** C 3
Araouane **90** D 2
Arapiraca **111** J 2–3
Araquara **111** G 5
Arauá **111** J 3
Arauca **108** D 2
Arauco **113** B 6
Aravalli Range **72** B 2–3
Araxá **111** G 4
Arbatax **57** E 4
Archer River National Park **79** G 1
Archipelago Kerimbas **95** G 2
Archipiélago de Colón **108** B 6
Archipiélago de la Reina Adelaida **113** A 9
Archipiélago de los Chonos **113** AB 7–8
Arco **102** D 3
Arcos **56** B 4
Arctic Ocean **114**
Arctic Red River **98** L 2
Arctowski **115**
Ardabīl **66** D 3
Ardakān (Iran) **61** F 2
Ardakān (Iran) **61** F 3
Ard as Sawwān (Jordan) **60** B 3
Ardennes **52** E 4
Ardestan (Iran) **61** F 2
Ardestan (Iran) **66** E 4
Arecibo **105** J 4
Areia Branca **111** J 1
Arenápolis **110** E 3
Arequipa **110** B 4
Arere **109** H 4
Arezzo **57** F 3
Arga **69** R 2
Argan **70** A 2
Argentina **113** CD 6
Arges **58** C 2
Argolíkós Kólpos **58** B 3
Argungu **91** EF 3
Argyle, Lake **78** D 2
Ar Horqin Qi **71** H 2
Århus **55** F 4
Arica (Chile) **110** B 4
Arica (Colombia) **108** D 4
Ariguaní **108** C 1
Arīhā (Syria) **60** B 2
Arinos(Mato Grosso, Brazil) **110** E 3
Arinos (Mato Grosso, Brazil) **110** E 3
Aripuanã **109** F 5
Aripuanã **109** FG 5
Ariquemes **109** F 5
Ariripina **111** HJ 2
Arizona (Argentina) **113** C 6
Arizona (U.S.A.) **102** D 5
Arjona **108** C 1
Arka **69** Q 3
Arkalyk **63** N 5
Arkansas **103** H 4
Arkansas City **103** G 4
Arkansas River **102–103** FH 4–5
Arkhangel'sk **62** H 3
Arkhara **69** O 6
Arklow **52** B 4
Arles **57** D 3
Arlington (OR, U.S.A.) **102** C 2
Arlington (TX, U.S.A.) **103** G 5
Arlington (VA, U.S.A.) **103** L 4
Arlit **91** F 2
Arly **90** E 3
Armant **88** E 3
Armavir **59** F 1
Armenia **108** C 3
Armeniya **59** F 2
Armidale **79** J 5
Armstrong **100** K 5
Armyansk **59** D 1
Arnauti, Akra (Cyprus) **60** A 2
Arnawai **67** J 3
Arnhem **52** E 4
Arnhem, Cape **79** F 1
Aroab **94** B 5
Arorae **82** C 3
Arquipélago dos Bijagós **90** A 3
Ar Radīsīyah Baḥrī (Egypt) **60** A 4
Ar Rahad **88** E 6
Arraias **111** G 3
Ar Ramādī (Iraq) **60** D 2
Ar Ramādī (Iraq) **89** G 2
Ar Ramlah (Jordan) **60** B 3
Ar Ramlah (Jordan) **88** F 3
Arran **52** B 3
Ar Raqqafi **89** F 1
Ar Raqqah (Syria) **60** C 2
Arras **56** D 1
Ar Rass (Saudi Arabia) **60** D 4
Ar Rass (Saudi Arabia) **89** G 3
Ar Rawḍatayn (Kuwait) **61** E 3
Ar Rayḥānī (Oman) **61** G 5
Ar Rifāʿī **66** D 4
Ar Rimāl **89** J 4
Ar Riyād (Saudi Arabia) **61** E 4
Ar Riyād (Saudi Arabia) **89** H 4
Ar Rubʿ al Khālī **89** HJ 4–5
Ar Ruṣāfah **66** B 3
Ar Ruṣayriṣ **88** E 6
Ar Ruṭbah (Iraq) **60** C 2
Ar Ruṭbah (Iraq) **66** BC 4
Ar Ruways (Qatar) **61** F 4
Ar Ruways (Quatar) **89** J 4
Ar Ruways (United Arab Emirates) **61** F 4
Års **55** E 4
Arsen'yev **71** K 2
Årskogen **54** G 3
Arsuk **101** S 3
Arteaga **104** B 4
Artem **71** K 2
Artemisa **104** F 3
Artic Circle **54** AB 2
Artigas **112** E 5
Artoli **88** E 5
Artybash **63** R 5
Artyk **69** R 3
Arua **92** E 4
Aruanã **111** F 3
Aruba, Isla **108** E 1
Arunachal **73** F 2
Arun Qi **69** M 6
Aruppukkottai **72** C 6
Arusha **93** F 5
Arvada **102** E 4
Arvayheer **70** D 1
Arvika **55** F 4
Arys' **67** H 2
Arzamas **62** H 4
Asahikawa **71** LM 2

Asamakka **91** F 2
Asansol **72** E 3
Asba Tafari **93** G 3
Ascensión (Bolivia) **110** D 4
Ascoli Piceno **57** F 3
Aselle **93** F 3
Asha **63** L 5
Ashdod (Israel) **60** B 3
Asheville **103** K 4
Ashgelon (Israel) **60** B 3
Ashkhabad **66** FG 3
Ash Shabakah (Iraq) **60** D 3
Ash Shabakah (Iraq) **89** G 2
Ash Sharqāt (Iraq) **60** D 2
Ash Shatrah (Iraq) **61** E 3
Ash Shiḥr **89** HJ 6
Ash Shinafiyah (Iraq) **61** D 3
Ash Shu'aybah **66** C 5
Ash Shu'bah (Saudi Arabia) **61** D 3
Ash Shu'bah (Saudi Arabia) **66** CD 5
Ash Shumlūl (Saudi Arabia) **61** E 4
Ash Shwayrif **87** H 3
Ashtabula **103** KL 3
Ashuanipi **101** O 5
Ashuanipi Lake **101** O 5
Asinara **57** E 3
Asino **63** RS 4
Asir, Ra's **93** J 2
Asmara **93** F 1
Aspermont **102** F 5
Aspiring, Mount **80** P 9
Assab **93** G 2
Aş Şadr (United Arab Emirates) **61** G 4
Aş Şaḥrā' al Gharbīyah **88** D 3
Aş Şaḥrā' al Janūbīyah **88** DE 4
Aş Saḥrā' an Nūbiyah **88** EF 4
Aş Şahrā' ash Sharqīyah (Egypt) **60** AB 4
As Salamīyah (Saudi Arabia) **61** E 4
As Salamīyah (Saudi Arabia) **66** D 6
Aş Şāliḥīyah (Syria) **60** C 2
As Sālimīyah (Kuwait) **61** E 3
As Salmān (Iraq) **61** D 3
As Salt (Jordan) **60** B 2
Assam **73** F 2
As Samāwah (Iraq) **61** D 3
As Samāwah (Iraq) **89** GH 2
As Sarir **87** K 3
As Silā (United Arab Emirates) **61** F 4
Assiniboia **99** Q 6
Assis **111** F 5
Assisi **57** F 3
As Subū' **88** E 4
Aş Şulb (Saudi Arabia) **61** E 4
Aş Şummān (Saudi Arabia) **61** DE 4
Aş Şummān (Saudi Arabia) **66** D 5
Assur (Iraq) **60** D 2
As Suwaydā' (Syria) **60** B 2
As Suways (Egypt) **60** A 3
Astakh **69** P 2
Astipálaia **58** C 3
Astrakhan **66** DE 1
Asturias **56** B 3
Asuncion (Mariana Is.) **82** A 1
Asunción (Paraguay) **112** E 3–4
Aswān (Egypt) **60** A 4
Aswan High Dam (Egypt) **60** A 5
Asyūţ **88** E 3
Atacama, Desierto de **110** C 5
Atacama, Salar de **110** C 5
Atafu **82** D 3
Atambua **75** F 5
Atangmik **101** R 3
Atar **86** C 4
Atas Bogd Uul **70** C 2
Atasu **63** O 6
'Aţbarah **88** E 5
Aţbarah **88** EF 5
Atbasar **63** N 5
Athens (GA, U.S.A.) **103** K 5
Athens → Athínai **58** B 3
Athínai **58** B 3
Ath Thumāmī (Saudi Arabia) **61** D 4
Ati **91** H 3
Atico **110** B 4
Atikokan **100** J 6
Atikonak Lake **101** P 5
Atka (AK, U.S.A.) **98** C 5
Atka (U.S.S.R.) **69** S 3
Atkarsk **62** H 5
Atlanta **103** JK 5
Atlantic City **103** M 4
Atlantic Ocean **116**
Atlas el Kebir **86** D 2
Atlas Mountains **86** DF 2
Atlin **98** L 4
Ätran **55** F 4
Atrato **108** C 2
Atsy **75** J 5
At Tafīlah (Jordan) **60** B 3
Aţ Ţā'if **89** G 4
Attawapiskat **100** KL 5
Attawapiskat **100** L 5
At Tawīl (Saudi Arabia) **60** C 3
Aţ Ţaysīyah (Saudi Arabia) **60** D 3–4
Aţ Ţīb, Ra's **87** H 1
Attikamagen Lake **101** O 5
Attu **98** A 5
At Turayf (Saudi Arabia) **60** C 3
At Turbah **89** G 6
Atuel **113** C 6
Atura **92** E 4
Aua **82** A 3
Auas Mountains **94** B 4
Auburn (ME, U.S.A.) **103** LM 3
Auckland **81** Q 8
Auckland **82** C 5
Auckland Islands **115**
Aude **56** D 3
Augathella **79** H 4
Augsburg **53** F 5
Augusta (AR, U.S.A.) **103** H 4
Augusta (GA, U.S.A.) **103** K 5
Augusta (ME, U.S.A.) **103** N 3
Augustus, Mount **78** B 3
Auki **82** B 3
Aur **82** C 2
Aurangaband **72** C 4
Aurillac **56** D 3
Aurora (CO, U.S.A.) **102** F 4
Aus **94** B 5
Ausangate, Nevado **110** B 3
Aust-Agder **55** E 4
Austin (MN, U.S.A.) **103** H 3
Austin (TX, U.S.A.) **102** G 5
Austin, Lake **78** B 4
Australia **78–79** CG 3
Australian Alps **79** H 6
Australian Capital Territory **79** H 6
Austria **57** F 2
Austvågöy **54** F 2
Auvézère **56** D 2
Auxerre **56** D 2
Auyuittuq National Park **101** OP 2
Avalon Peninsula **101** R 6
Avanavero **109** G 3
Avarua **83** E 4
Avaz **66** FG 4
Avdhira **58** C 2
Āvej (Iran) **61** E 2
Avellaneda **112** E 5
Averöya **54** E 3
Avesta **55** G 3
Avignon **57** DE 3
Ávila **56** C 3
Avilés **56** B 3
Avola **57** G 4
Awara Plain **93** G 4
Awash **93** G 2
Awash **93** G 3
'Awaynat Wanīn **87** H 3
Awbārī **87** H 3
Awjilah **87** K 3
Axel Heiberg Island **114**
Axios **58** B 2
Ayabaca **108** BC 4
Ayacucho (Peru) **110** AB 3
Ayaguz **63** Q 6
Ayan **69** P 4
Ayanaka **69** V 3
Ayava **68** H 4
Ayaviri **110** BC 3
Aydın **58** C 3
Ayers Rock – Mount Olga National Park **78** E 4
Áyion Óros **58** B 2
Aylmer Lake **99** Q 3
'Aynabo **93** H 3
'Ayn al Baydā' (Syria) **60** BC 2
'Ayn al Ghazāl **87** K 4
Ayni **67** H 3
'Ayn Sukhnah (Egypt) **60** A 3
Ayon **69** V 1
Ayr (Australia) **79** H 2
Ayr (U.K.) **52** C 3
Aysary **63** O 5
Āzādshahr (Iran) **61** G 1
Azamgarh **72** D 2
Azare **91** G 3
Azbine **91** F 2
Azerbaydzhan **66** D 2
Aznā (Iran) **61** E 2
Azores **86** A 1
Azoum **91** J 3
Azov **59** E 1
Azovskoye More **59** E 1
Aztec ruins **102** E 4
Azul **113** E 6
Az Zallāq (Bahrain) **61** F 4
Az Zargā' (United Arab Emirates) **61** F 4
Az Zarqā' (Jordan) **60** B 2
Az Zāwiyah **87** H 2
Az Zilfī (Saudi Arabia) **61** D 4
Az Zugar **89** G 6

B

Baba Burnu **58** D 2
Baba Burun **58** C 3
Bābā Heydar (Iran) **61** F 2
Babahoyo **108** BC 4
Babai Gaxun **70** D 2
Bāb al Māndab **89** G 6
Babanūsah **88** D 6
Babar, Kepulauan **75** G 5
Babine Lake **99** M 5
Babo **75** H 4
Bābol (Iran) **61** F 1
Babol Sar (Iran) **61** F 1
Babushkin **68** J 5
Babylon (Iraq) **60** D 2
Babylon (Iraq) **89** GH 2
Bacabal (Maranhão, Brazil) **111** GH 1
Bacan, Pulau **75** G 4
Bacău **58** C 1
Back **99** S 2
Bād (Iran) **61** F 2
Badajoz **56** B 4
Badalona **56** D 3
Badanah (Saudi Arabia) **60** C 3
Baden-Baden **53** E 5
Badiyat ash Shām **60** BC 2
Badoumbé **90** B 3
Badr Ḥunayn (Saudi Arabia) **60** C 5
Badr Ḥunayn (Saudi Arabia) **66** B 6
Badulla **72** D 6
Badzhal **69** OP 5
Bafatá **90** B 3
Baffin Bay **114**
Baffin Island **101** NO 2
Bafia **91** G 5
Bafoussam **91** G 4
Bāfq (Iran) **61** G 3
Bāfq (Iran) **66** F 4
Bafra **59** E 2
Bāft (Iran) **61** G 3
Bagadzha **68** L 3
Bagalkot **72** C 4
Baga Sola **91** GH 3
Bagdarin **68** K 5
Bagé **112** F 5
Baghdād (Iraq) **60** D 2
Baghdād (Iraq) **89** GH 2
Bāghin (Iran) **61** G 3
Baghlan **67** H 3
Bagua **108** C 5
Baguio **75** J 1
Baguirmi **91** H 3
Bahama Islands **105** H 3
Bahar Dar **93** F 2
Bahawalpur **67** J 5
Bahía (Argentina) **113** C 8
Bahía (Brazil) **111** H 3
Bahía Blanca **113** D 6
Bahía Blanca **113** D 6
Bahía de Campeche **104** CD 4

Bahía de Caráquez **108** B 4
Bahía Grande **113** C 9
Bahía Kino **102** D 6
Bahía Laura **113** CD 8
Bahía Rosario **102** C 6
Bahías, Cabo dos **113** CD 8
Bahía Sebastián Vizcaíno **102** D 6
Bahrain **61** F 4
Baḥr al Abyaḍ **88** E 6
Baḥr al Azraq **88** E 6
Baḥr al Jabal **92** E 3
Baḥr ar Rimāl al 'Aẓīm **88** CD 3
Baía de Setúbal **56** B 4
Baia Mare **58** B 1
Baião **109** J 4
Baicheng **67** L 2
Baicheng **71** H 1
Baie aux Feuilles **101** O 4
Baie d'Antongil **95** HJ 3
Baie-des-Moutons **101** Q 5
Bailang **68** M 6
Baile Átha Cliath **52** B 4
Bailundo **94** B 2
Baimuru **80** D 3
Baing **75** F 6
Baingoin **72** E 1
Baiquan **69** N 6
Bairiki **82** C 2
Bairin Zuoqi **71** GH 2
Baixo-Alentejo **56** B 4
Baiyü **70** C 4
Baja **58** A 1
Baja California Norte **102** C 5
Baja California Sur **102** CD 6
Bakadzhitsite **58** C 2
Bakel **90** B 3
Baker (Pacific Ocean, U.S.A.) **82** D 2
Baker Lake **99** S 3
Baker Lake (N.W.T., Can.) **99** S 3
Bakersfield **102** C 4
Bakhta **63** RS 3
Bakhta **63** RS 3
Bakhtegān, Daryācheh-ye (Iran) **61** FG 3
Bakony **58** A 1
Bakouma **92** C 3
Baku **66** DE 2
Balabac Strait **74** E 2
Balabakk, Ra's (Syria) **60** B 2
Baladīyat 'Adan **89** H 6
Balaghat **72** D 3
Balakhta **68** F 4
Balakovo **62** J 5
Bala Murghab **67** G 3
Balasore **72** E 3
Balaton **58** A 1
Balclutha **80** PQ 10
Balde **112** C 5
Bald Head **78** B 6
Baldy Peak **102** E 5
Bale **93** G 3
Balearic Islands **56** D 3
Baleia, Ponta da **111** J 4
Baley **68** L 5
Bali **74** D 5
Balıkesir **58** C 3
Balintang Channel **75** J 1
Balkan Mountains **58** C 2
Balkhash **63** OP 6
Balkhash, Ozero **63** P 6
Balladonia **78** C 5
Ballarat **79** G 6
Ballard, Lake **78** C 4
Balleny Islands **115**
Ballina (Australia) **79** J 4
Balranald **79** G 5
Balsas **109** J 5
Balsas, Rio **104** B 4
Baltic Sea **55** GH 4
Baltimore (MD, U.S.A.) **103** L 4
Baltiskaja Grjada **55** HJ 4–5
Baluchistan **66–67** G 5
Bam **66** F 5
Bamako **90** C 3
Bamba (Mali) **90** D 2
Bambari **92** C 3
Bambesa **92** D 4
Bambesi **92** E 3
Bamenda **91** FG 4
Bamingui **92** C 3
Bamingui-Bangoran, Parc National du **92** BC 3
Bamiyan **67** H 4
Bampūr **67** G 5
Banaba **81** J 2
Banaba **82** C 3
Banalia **92** D 4
Banana **79** J 3
Banās, Ra's **88** F 4
Banās, Ra's (Egypt) **60** B 5
Bancroft **101** M 6
Banda **72** D 2
Banda **72** C 3
Banda Aceh **74** A 2
Bandar Abbas (Iran) **61** G 4
Bandar Abbas (Iran) **66** F 5
Bandar-e-Anzalī **66** DE 3
Bandar-e Chārak **66** E 5
Bandar-e Deylam **66** E 4–5
Bandar-e Deylam (Iran) **61** F 3
Bandar-e Khomeynī (Iran) **61** E 3
Bandar-e Lengeh (Iran) **61** G 4
Bandar-e Lengeh (Iran) **66** E 5
Bandar-e Māqām (Iran) **61** F 4
Bandar-e Māqām (Iran) **66** E 5
Bandar-e Moghūyeh (Iran) **61** FG 4
Bandar-e Rig (Iran) **61** F 3
Bandarlampung **74** C 5
Bandarpunch **72** C 1
Bandar Seri Begawan **74** D 3
Bandar Shāh (Iran) **61** E 1
Banda Sea **75** GH 5
Bandau **74** E 2
Band Bonī **66** F 5
Bandeira **111** H 5
Bandeirante **111** FG 3
Bandırma **58** C 2
Bandundu **92** B 5
Bandundu **92** B 5
Bandung **74** C 5
Banes **105** GH 3
Banff National Park **99** O 5
Banfora **90** CD 3
Bangalore **72** C 5
Bangassou **92** C 4
Bangeta, Mount **80** E 3
Banggai, Kepulauan **75** F 4
Bangko **74** B 4
Bangkok **73** H 5
Bangkok, Bight of **73** H 5
Bangladesh **73** F 3
Bangor (ME, U.S.A.) **103** N 3
Bangor (N. Ireland, U.K.) **52** B 4
Bangsund **54** F 3
Bangui **92** B 4
Bangui Mogadishu **93** H 4
Banhine National Park **95** E 4
Banihal Pass **67** K 4
Banī Mazār **88** DE 3
Banī Suwayf **88** E 3
Bāniyās (Lebanon) **60** B 2
Bāniyās (Syria) **60** B 2
Banja Luka **57** G 3
Banjarmasin **74** DE 4
Banjul **90** A 3
Ban Kniet **73** J 5
Banks Island (N.W.T., Can.) **99** N 1
Banks Island (Queensland, Austr.) **79** G 1
Banks Islands **81** J 4
Banks Islands (Vanuatu) **82** C 3
Banks Peninsula **81** Q 9
Banks Strait **80** L 9
Ban Me Thuot **73** J 5
Bannu **67** J 4
Banská Bystrica **53** G 5
Banyo **91** G 4
Banyuwangi **74** D 5
Banzare Coast **115**
Baoding **70** FG 3
Baoji **70** E 4
Baoqing **71** K 1
Baoshan **70** CD 5
Baotou **70** E 2
Baqen **70** B 4
Ba' qūbah (Iraq) **61** D 2
Barabinsk **63** P 4
Barabinskaya Step' **63** P 5
Baracaldo **56** C 3
Bārah **88** E 6
Barahona **105** H 4
Barakkul' **63** N 5
Baramula **67** J 4
Baran (India) **72** C 2
Barangbarang **75** EF 5
Baranof **98** K 4
Baranovichi **55** J 5
Barão de Capanema **110** E 3
Barão de Melgaco **110** D 3
Barbados **105** K 5
Barcaldine **79** H 3
Barcellona **57** FG 4
Barcelona (Spain) **56** D 3
Barcelona (Venezuela) **109** F 2
Barcelos **109** F 4
Bardawil, Sabkhat al (Egypt) **60** A 3
Bārḍēre **93** G 4
Bardeskan **66** F 3
Barēda **93** J 2
Bareilly **72** C 2
Barentsovo More **62** GJ 1
Barents Sea **114**
Barentu **93** F 1
Bårgå **54** G 2
Barga **72** D 1
Barguzin **68** J 5
Barhaj **72** D 2
Bari **57** G 3
Barīdi, Ra's (Saudi Arabia) **60** B 4
Barīm **89** G 6
Barinas **108** E 2
Baring, Cape **99** O 2
Barisal **73** F 3
Barisan, Pegunungan **74** B 4
Barito, Sungai **74** D 4
Barkā' **89** K 4
Barkam **70** D 4
Barkly Tableland **79** F 2
Barlee, Lake **78** B 4
Barletta **57** G 3
Barmer **72** B 2
Barnaul **63** Q 5
Barnes Ice Cap **101** N 1–2
Barong **70** C 4
Barotseland **94** C 3
Barquisimeto **108** DE 1
Barra (Bahía, Brazil) **111** H 3
Barra (U.K.) **52** B 3
Barracão do Barreto **109** G 5
Barra do Corda **109** J 5
Barragem da Rocha de Galé **56** B 4
Barra Head **52** B 3
Barranca (Peru) **108** C 4
Barranca (Peru) **108** C 6
Barrancabermeja **108** D 2
Barrancas **109** F 2
Barranquilla **108** C 1
Barreiras **111** G 3
Barreirinhas **111** H 1
Barreiro **56** B 4
Barreiros **111** JK 2
Barren **73** F 5
Barren Lands **99** QS 2
Barretos **111** G 5
Barrie **101** LM 7
Barrow (AK, U.S.A.) **98** F 1
Barrow (Argentina) **113** E 6
Barrow (Rep. of Ireland) **52** B 4
Barrow, Point **98** FG 1
Barrow Island **78** A 3
Barsi **72** C 4
Bartica **109** G 2
Bartlesville **103** G 4
Bāruni **72** E 2
Bāsa'īdū (Iran) **61** G 4
Basauri **56** C 3
Basel **57** E 2
Bashi Haixia **71** H 6
Basilan City **75** F 2
Basílio **112** F 5
Baskol' **63** P 5
Basra (Iraq) **61** E 3
Basra (Iraq) **89** H 2
Bassas da India (Reunion) **95** FG 4
Bassein **73** F 4
Basse Terre **105** K 4
Bassinde Rennes **56** C 2
Bass Strait **80** KL 8
Bastak (Iran) **61** G 4
Bastia **57** E 3
Bata **91** F 5
Batagay-Alyta **69** NO 2
Batama (U.S.S.R.) **68** H 5

Batamshinskiy **63** L 5
Batang **70** C 4
Batangas **75** F 1
Batang Hari **74** B 4
Bataysk **59** EF 1
Batemans Bay **79** J 6
Batha **91** H 3
Bathalha **56** B 4
Bathurst (Canada) **101** OP 6
Bathurst (N.S.W., Austr.) **79** H 5
Bathurst, Cape **98** LM 1
Bathurst Inlet **99** PQ 2
Bathurst Inlet **99** Q 2
Bathurst Island (N.T., Austr.) **78** D 1
Bathurst Island (The Arctic) **114**
Batin, Wadi al (Iraq) **61** DE 3
Batkanu **90** B 4
Bātlāq-e Gavkhūnī (Iran) **61** F 2
Batman **59** F 3
Batna **87** G 1
Batoka **94** D 3
Batomga **69** P 4
Baton Rouge **103** H 5
Battambang **73** H 5
Battle Creek **103** J 3
Batu **93** F 3
Batui **75** F 4
Batumi **59** F 2
Batu Puteh, Gunung **74** B 3
Baturité **111** J 1
Baubau **75** F 5
Bauchi **91** F 3
Baures **110** D 3
Bauru **111** FG 5
Baús **111** F 4
Bavaria **53** F 5
Bavispe **102** E 5
Bawdwin **73** G 3
Baxoi **70** C 4
Bayamo **105** G 3
Bayan-Adraga **68** K 6
Bayan-Aul **63** P 5
Bayanbulag **68** G 6
Bayandzurh **68** J 6
Bayanga **92** B 4
Bayan Har Shankou **70** C 4
Bayanhongor **68** H 6
Bayan Obo **70** E 2
Bayâz **66** F 4
Bayāzeh (Iran) **61** G 2
Bayāzeh (Iran) **66** F 4
Bayburt **59** EF 2
Bay City (MI, U.S.A.) **103** K 3
Baydaratskaya Guba **63** N 2
Bay de Verde **101** R 6
Bayern **53** F 5
Bayjī (Iraq) **60** D 2
Bayjī (Iraq) **89** G 2
Baykal'skiy Khrebet **68** J 4–5
Baykit **68** G 3
Bay of Bengal **72–73** EF 4
Bay of Biscay **56** C 2–3
Bay of Fundy **101** O 6–7
Bay of Plenty **82** C 5
Bayonne **56** C 3
Bayovar **108** B 5
Bayram-Ali **67** G 3
Bayreuth **53** F 5
Bayrūt (Lebanon) **60** B 2
Bayrūt (Lebanon) **88** EF 2
Baytown **103** H 6
Bazarnyy Syzgan **62** J 5
Bazaruto National Park **95** F 4
Bazhong **70** E 4
Bear Island **114**
Beata, Cabo **105** H 4
Beatton River **99** NO 4
Beatty **102** C 4
Beaufort (Malaysia) **74** E 2
Beaufort (U.S.A.) **103** K 5
Beaufort Sea **98** JL 1
Beaufort West **94** C 6
Beaumont (TX, U.S.A.) **103** H 5
Beausejour **99** S 5
Beauvais **56** D 2
Beaver (Sask., Can.) **99** Q 5
Beaver (UT, U.S.A.) **102** D 4
Beawar **72** BC 2
Beberibe **111** J 1
Béchar **86** E 2
Bedourie **79** F 3
Be'er Sheva **60** B 3
Be'er Sheva **88** EF 2
Beeville **102** G 6
Bega **79** HJ 6
Begejski Kanal **58** B 1
Begna **55** E 3
Behbehān (Iran) **61** F 3
Behbehān (Iran) **66** E 4
Behshar (Iran) **61** F 1
Bei'an **69** N 6
Beibu Wan **73** J 3
Beida **87** K 2
Beihai **70** E 6
Beijing **71** G 2
Beipiao **71** H 2
Beira **95** F 3
Beirut (Lebanon) **60** B 2
Beirut (Lebanon) **88** EF 2
Bei Shan **70** C 2
Beitbridge **94** DE 4
Beitstad **54** F 3
Beitun **67** M 1
Beja **56** B 4
Bejaïa **87** FG 1
Bekdash **66** E 2
Békéscsaba **58** B 1
Bekopaka **95** G 3
Bela **67** H 5
Belau **75** HJ 2
Bela Vista (Brazil) **110** E 5
Bela Vista (Mozambique) **95** E 5
Belaya Kalitva **59** F 1
Belaya Tserkov **62** F 5–6
Belcher Islands **101** L 4
Belebey **62** K 5
Belém (Amazonas, Brazil) **108** E 4
Belém (Pará, Brazil) **109** J 4
Belén (Colombia) **108** C 3
Belep, Îles **82** B 4
Beleuli **66** F 2
Belfast **52** B 4
Belfield **102** F 2
Belfort **57** E 2
Belgaum **72** BC 4
Belgium **52** DE 4
Belgorod **62** G 5
Belgorod-Dnestrovskiy **58** CD 1
Belgrade **58** B 2
Beli **91** G 4
Belikh (Syria) **60** C 1
Belitung, Pulau **74** C 4
Belize **104** E 4
Belize City **104** E 4
Bel'kachi **69** O 4
Bell **101** LM 5
Bella Bella **99** M 5
Bella Coola **99** M 5
Bellary **72** C 4
Belle Ile **56** C 2
Belleville **102** G 4
Belleville (IL, U.S.A.) **103** J 4
Belleville (Ontario, Can.) **101** M 7
Bellevue (WA, U.S.A.) **102** B 2
Bellin **101** N 3
Bellingham **102** B 2
Bellingshausen **115**
Bellingshausen Sea **115**
Bello **108** C 2
Belluno **57** F 2
Bell Ville **112** D 5
Bellyk **68** F 5
Belmonte **111** J 4
Belmopan **104** E 4
Belogorsk (U.S.S.R.) **69** N 5
Belogor'ye **63** N 3
Belo Horizonte (Minas Gerais, Brazil) **111** H 4–5
Belo Horizonte (Pará, Brazil) **109** H 5
Beloit **103** J 3
Belo Monta **109** H 4
Belorechensk **59** FG 2
Belorussiya **55** J 5
Belovo **63** R 5
Beloyarovo **69** NO 5
Beloye More **62** G 2
Belt'sy **58** C 1
Belush'ya Guba **62** KL 1
Belush'ya Guba **114**
Belyy **62** F 4
Bemidji **103** G 2
Bena Dibile **92** C 5
Benalla **79** H 6
Benares **72** D 2
Bend **102** B 3
Bender Bāyla **93** J 3
Bendery **58** C 1
Bendigo **79** GH 6
Benevento **57** FG 3
Bengal **72** E 3
Bengbu **71** G 4
Benghazi **87** J 2
Bengkulu **74** B 4
Benguela **94** A 2
Beni (Bolivia) **110** C 3
Beni (Zaire) **92** D 4
Benidorm **56** CD 4
Beni Mellal **86** D 2
Benin **90** E 3–4
Benin, Bight of **90** E 4
Benin City **91** EF 4
Beni Ounif **86** E 2
Benjamin Constant **108** D 4
Ben Nevis **52** BC 3
Benson **102** D 5
Bentiaba **94** A 2
Benue **91** F 4
Benxi **71** HJ 2
Beograd **58** B 2
Beraketa **95** H 4
Berati **58** A 2
Berau, Teluk **75** H 4
Berbera **93** H 2
Berbérati **92** B 4
Berchogur **66** FG 1
Berdichev **55** J 6
Berdigestyakh **69** MN 3
Berdyansk **59** E 1
Berekum **90** D 4
Berens River **99** S 5
Berezniki **62** KL 4
Berezovka (Russia, U.S.S.R.) **63** Q 4
Berezovka (Russia, U.S.S.R.) **68** L 4
Berezovo **63** N 3
Berezovskiy **63** LM 5
Bergamo (Italy) **57** EF 2
Bergamo (Turkey) **58** C 3
Bergen (F.R.G.) **53** F 4
Bergen (Norway) **55** DE 3
Bergerac **56** D 3
Bergö **54** H 3
Bergviken **54** G 3
Berhampore **72** E 3
Berhampur **72** DE 4
Bering Land Bridge National Preserve **98** E 2
Beringovskiy **69** XY 3
Bering Strait **98** CD 2–3
Berkakit **69** M 4
Berkeley **102** B 4
Berkner Island **115**
Berlevåg **54** J 1
Berlin **53** F 4
Bermejo (Argentina) **112** D 4
Bermejo (Argentina) **112** C 5
Bermuda Islands **105** K 1
Bern **57** E 2
Bernasconi **113** D 6
Bernburg **53** F 4
Berne **57** E 2
Berner Alpen **57** E 2
Bernina **57** E 2
Bertolínia **111** H 2
Bertoua **91** G 5
Besalampy **95** G 3
Besançon **57** E 2
Besar, Gunung **74** E 4
Beskidy Zachodny **53** GH 5
Beslan **59** F 2
Besna Kobila **58** B 2
Bessarabiya **58** C 1
Bestobe **63** O 5
Beswick **78** E 1
Bethlehem (South Africa) **94** D 5
Béthune **56** D 1
Betong (Thailand) **73** H 6
Bet-Pak-Dala **63** NO 6
Betroka **95** H 4
Beyānlū (Iran) **61** E 1
Beyānlū (Iran) **66** D 3
Bey Dağları **58** CD 3
Beyla **90** C 4
Beyra **93** H 3
Beyşehir Gölü **58** D 3
Béziers **56** D 3

Bhadrakh **72** E 3
Bhadravati **72** C 5
Bhagalpur **72** E 3
Bhamo **73** G 3
Bhandara **72** CD 3
Bharuch **72** B 3
Bhatinda **72** BC 2
Bhatpara **72** E 3
Bhavnagar **72** B 3
Bhilwara **72** BC 2
Bhopal **72** C 3
Bhopalpatnam **72** D 4
Bhuban **72** E 3
Bhubaneswar **72** E 3
Bhumiphol Dam **73** GH 4
Bhusawal **72** C 3
Bhutan **73** F 2
Biak (Indonesia) **75** F 4
Biak (New Guinea) **75** J 4
Biak, Pulau **75** J 4
Biała Podlaska **53** H 4
Białystok **53** H 4
Biankouma **90** C 4
Biaora **72** C 3
Biarritz **56** C 3
Biberach **53** EF 5
Bicuari National Park **94** AB 3
Bida **91** F 4
Bidar **72** C 4
Bidzhan **69** O 6
Bié **94** B 2
Biebrza **53** H 4
Biel **57** E 2
Bielefeld **53** E 4
Bielsko-Biała **53** G 5
Bien Hoa **73** J 5
Bienville, Lac **101** N 4
Bifoum **91** G 6
Big Bend National Park **102** F 6
Biger **68** G 6
Bighorn River **102** E 2
Bight of Bangkok **73** H 5
Bight of Benin **90** E 4
Bigi **92** C 4
Big Spring **102** F 5
Big Trout Lake **100** K 5
Bihać **57** G 3
Bihar **72** DE 2
Bihar **72** E 3
Bijapur **72** C 4
Bijeljina **57** G 3
Bijiang **70** C 5
Bikaner **72** B 2
Bikar **82** C 2
Bikin **69** O 6
Bikini **82** B 2
Bilaspur **72** D 3
Bilbao **56** C 3
Bili **92** D 4
Billings **102** E 2
Bilma, Grand Erg de **91** GH 2
Biloela **79** J 3
Bilogora **57** G 2
Biloxi **103** J 5
Binaiya, Gunung **75** G 4
Binder **68** K 6
Bindura **95** E 3
Bingara **79** J 4
Binghamton **103** L 3
Binjai **74** A 3
Binnaway **79** H 5
Bintan, Pulau **74** B 3
Bintulu **74** D 3
Bira **69** P 6
Birao **92** C 2
Biratnagar **72** E 2
Bi'r Bū Zurayyq **87** K 3
Bi'r Fu'ād **88** D 2
Birjand **66** F 4
Birkat Nasser (Egypt) **60** A 5
Birkenhead **52** C 4
Birksgate Range **78** DE 4
Bîrlad **58** C 1
Birmingham (AL, U.S.A.) **103** J 5
Birmingham (U.K.) **52** C 4
Bir Moghreim **86** C 3
Bi'r Nasīf (Saudi Arabia) **60** C 4
Birnie **82** D 3
Birnin Kebbi **91** EF 3
Birnin Kudu **91** F 3
Birobidzhan **69** O 6
Bir Ounane **90** D 1
Bir Rhoraffa **87** G 2
Bi'r Safājah (Egypt) **60** AB 4
Bi'r Shalatayn **88** F 4
Birsilpur **72** B 2
Birsk **62** L 4
Biru **70** B 4
Biscad **58** B 1
Biscoe Islands **115**
Bishop's Falls **101** Q 6
Biskra **87** G 2
Bismarck **102** F 2
Bismarck Archipelago **80–81** EF 2
Bismarck Range **80** DE 2–3
Bismarck Sea **80** EF 2
Bissau **90** A 3
Bistrița **58** BC 1
Bitchana **93** F 2
Bitkiné **91** H 3
Bitlis **59** F 3
Bitola **58** B 2
Bitterfontein **94** B 6
Bitter Lake (Egypt) **60** A 3
Bitterroot Range **102** D 2–3
Biu **91** G 3
Biyang **70** F 4
Biysk **63** R 5
Bizerta → Banzart **87** GH 1
Bjerkvik **54** G 2
Bjesnica **58** A 2
Björkö **54** H 3
Björnöya **114**
Blackall **79** GH 3
Blackburn, Mount **98** HJ 3
Black Hills **102** F 3
Blackpool **52** C 4
Black River Falls **103** H 3
Black Sea **59** DE 2
Blackwell **102** G 4
Blåfjellhatten **54** F 3
Blagoevgrad **58** B 2
Blagoveshchensk **69** NO 5
Blaine **103** H 2
Blantyre **95** E 3
Blåskavlen **54** E 3
Blåvands Huk **55** E 4
Blekinge **55** FG 4
Blenheim **82** C 5
Blida **87** F 1
Bloemfontein **94** CD 5
Blois **56** D 2
Blönduós **54** AB 2
Bloomington (IL, U.S.A.) **103** J 3
Bloomington (IN, U.S.A.) **103** J 4
Bloomington (MN, U.S.A.) **103** H 3
Blosseville Coast **114**
Bluefields **104** F 5
Blue Ridge **103** KL 4
Bluff Knoll **78** B 5
Blumenau **112** FG 4
Blythe **102** D 5
Blytheville **103** J 4
Bo **90** B 4
Boa Vista (Cape Verde) **90** B 6
Boa Vista (Roraima, Brazil) **109** F 3
Bobai **70** EF 6
Bobo Dioulasso **90** D 3
Bobruysk **55** J 5
Boby, Pic **95** H 4
Boca del Rio **102** E 6
Bôca do Acre **108** E 5
Bocage Vendéen **56** C 2
Bocaiúva **111** H 4
Boca Raton **103** L 6
Bochum **53** E 4
Bodaybo **68** K 4
Bodélé **91** H 2
Boden **54** H 2
Bodensee **57** E 2
Bodö **54** F 2
Bo Duc **73** J 5
Boende **92** C 5
Boffa **90** B 3
Boggeragh Mountains **52** B 4
Bogor **74** C 5
Bogoroditsk **62** G 5
Bogotá **108** D 3
Bogra **72** E 2–3
Boguchany **68** G 4
Bogué **86** C 5
Bo Hai **71** GH 3
Bohemia **53** F 5
Böhmerwald **53** F 5
Bohol **75** F 2
Bohol Sea **75** F 2
Boiaçu **109** F 4
Boise **102** C 3
Boise City **102** F 4
Bojnūrd **66** F 3
Bojuro **112** F 5
Bokatola **92** B 5
Boké **90** B 3
Boknafjorden **55** E 4
Bokora Game Reserve **92** E 4
Bokpyin **74** A 1
Bokungu **92** C 5
Bolan Pass **67** H 5
Bole (China) **67** L 2
Bole (Ghana) **90** D 4
Bolesławiec **53** G 4
Bolgatanga **90** D 3
Boli **71** K 1
Bolia **92** B 5
Bolívar (Argentina) **113** D 6
Bolívar (Colombia) **108** C 3
Bolivia **110** CD 4
Bollon **79** H 4
Bologna **57** F 3
Bologoye **62** F 4
Bologur **69** O 3
Bolombo **92** C 5
Bolsena, Lago di **57** F 3
Bol'shaya Glushitsa **62** K 5
Bol'sheretsk **69** T 5
Bol'shezemel'skaya Tundra **62** KM 2
Bolshoy Kavkaz **59** F 2
Bol'shoy Nimnyr **69** MN 4
Bol'shoy Shantar, Ostrov **69** P 4–5
Bolsón de Mapimi **104** B 2
Bolton **52** C 4
Bolu **59** D 2
Bolzano **57** F 2
Boma **91** G 7
Bombay **72** B 4
Bomberai **75** H 4
Bom Jesus **111** H 2
Bom Jesus da Lapa **111** H 3
Bömlo **55** DE 4
Bomongo **92** B 4
Bom Retiro **112** G 4
Bona, Mount **98** J 3
Bonaparte Archipelago **78** C 1
Bonavista Bay **101** R 6
Bondo **92** C 4
Bondowoso **74** D 5
Bonete, Cerro **112** C 4
Bongor **91** H 3
Bonifacio, Strait of **57** E 3
Bonin Islands **65** R 7
Bonito **110** E 5
Bonn **53** E 4
Bonners Ferry **102** C 2
Bonobono **74** E 2
Boola **90** C 4
Boothby, Cape **115**
Boothia Peninsula **99** T 1
Bophuthatswana **94** C 5
Boquillagas del Carmen **104** B 2
Bor (Yugoslavia) **58** B 2
Bora-Bora **83** EF 4
Borah Peak **102** D 3
Borås **55** F 4
Borasambar **72** D 3
Borāzjān (Iran) **61** F 3
Borāzjān (Iran) **66** E 5
Borba **109** G 4
Bordeaux **56** CD 3
Bordertown **79** G 6
Bordj Fly Sainte Marie **86** E 3
Bordj Messouda **87** G 2
Börgefjellet **54** F 2
Borisoglebsk **62** H 5
Borisov **55** J 5
Borispol **62** F 5
Bo River **92** D 3
Borja (Peru) **108** C 4
Borja (Yugoslavia) **58** A 2
Borkou **91** H 2
Borlänge **55** FG 3
Borneo **74** DE 3
Bornholm **55** F 5
Bornu **91** G 3
Borohoro Shan **67** L 2
Boroko **75** F 3
Borolgustakh **68** M 2
Borovichi **62** FG 4

Borroloola **79** F 2
Börselv **54** HJ 1
Borsippa (Iraq) **60** D 2
Boru **69** Q 1
Borūjen (Iran) **61** F 3
Borūjerd (Iran) **61** E 2
Borzya **68** L 5
Bōsāso **93** H 2
Bose **70** E 6
Boshan **71** G 3
Boshnyakovo **69** Q 6
Boshuslän **55** F 4
Bosna **57** G 3
Bosporus **58** C 2
Bossangoa **92** B 3
Bossembele **92** B 3
Bossemptélé II **92** B 3
Bossier City **103** H 5
Bostandyk **62** J 6
Boston (MA, U.S.A.) **103** MN 3
Botletle **94** C 4
Botoşani **58** C 1
Bo Trach **73** J 4
Botswana **94** CD 4
Botucatu **111** G 5
Bouaflé **90** C 4
Bouaké **90** D 4
Bouar **92** B 3
Bou Arfa **86** E 2
Boubandjida **91** GH 4
Boubandjida National Park **91** GH 4
Boucle de Baoulé, Parc National de la **90** C 3
Bou Djéhiba **90** D 2
Bougainville **81** G 3
Bougainville Reef **79** H 2
Bou Garfa **86** D 3
Bougouni **90** C 3
Bouïra **87** F 1
Bou Izakarn **86** D 3
Boulanouar **86** B 4
Boulder **78** C 5
Boulder **102** F 3
Boulia **79** F 3
Boulouli **90** C 2
Bouna **90** D 4
Boundiali **90** C 4
Boundou **90** B 3
Boun Neua **73** H 3
Bountiful **102** D 3
Bounty Islands **115**
Bourem **90** D 2
Bourg **57** E 2
Bourges **56** D 2
Bourgogne **57** DE 2
Bou Rjeima **86** C 5
Bourke **79** H 4–5
Bournemouth **52** C 4
Bou Saâda **87** F 1
Bouvet Island **115**
Bowen (Argentina) **112** C 5
Bowen (Australia) **79** H 2
Bowling Green **103** J 4
Bowman **102** F 2
Bowman Bay **101** MN 2
Boxing **71** G 3
Boyabo **92** B 4
Boyne **52** B 4
Boyuibe **110** D 5
Bozok Platosu **59** DE 3
Brač **57** G 3
Bradenton **103** K 6
Bradford (U.K.) **52** C 4
Bradshaw **78** E 2
Brady **102** G 5
Braga **56** B 3
Bragança (Brazil) **109** J 4
Bragança (Portugal) **56** B 3
Bragina **69** X 3
Brahmaputra **73** F 2
Brai **101** M 2
Brăila **58** C 1
Bräk **87** H 3
Brampton **101** L 7
Brandberg **94** A 4
Brandenburg **53** F 4
Brandon **99** S 5–6
Brandvlei **94** BC 6
Brantford **101** L 7
Brasil, Planalto do **111** H 4
Brasiléia **110** C 3
Brasília **111** G 4
Braşov **58** C 1
Brassey, Mount **78** E 3
Bratislava **53** G 5
Bratsk **68** H 4
Bratskoye Vodokhranilishche **68** H 4
Bratslav **58** C 1
Bratul Chilia **58** C 1
Braunschweig **53** F 4
Brawley **102** CD 5
Brazil **110–111** EG 3
Brazo Casoquiare **108** E 3
Brazzaville **91** GH 6
Brčko **57** G 3
Brecknock, Península **113** B 9
Breda **52** D 4
Bredbyn **54** G 3
Breiðafjörður **54** A 2
Brejo (Maranhão, Brazil) **111** H 1
Brekken **54** F 3
Bremangerlandet **54** D 3
Bremen **53** E 4
Bremerhaven **53** E 4
Brenner **57** F 2
Brescia **57** F 2
Brest (France) **56** C 2
Bretagne **56** C 2
Breves **109** H 4
Brevoort Island **101** P 3
Brewster, Kap **114**
Brewton **103** J 5
Brezhnev **62** K 4
Bridgeport (CT, U.S.A.) **103** M 3
Bridger Peak **102** E 3
Bridgetown (Australia) **78** B 5
Bridgetown (Barbados) **105** KL 5
Brighton **52** D D 4
Brindisi **57** G 3
Brisbane **79** J 4
Bristol **52** C 4
Bristol Bay **98** EF 4
Bristol Channel **52** C D 4
British Columbia **99** MN 4–5
Britstown **94** C 6
Brive **56** D 2
Brno **53** G 5
Broadus **102** EF 2
Broadview **99** R 5
Brochet **99** R 4
Broken Hill **79** G 5
Brokhovo **69** ST 4
Brokopondo **109** G 3
Brookings (S.D., U.S.A.) **103** G 3
Brooks Range **98** FH 2
Brookton **78** B 5
Broome **78** C 2
Browne Range Nature Reserve **78** CD 3
Brownfield **102** F 5
Brownsville **103** G 6
Brownwood **102** G 5
Bruce, Mount **78** B 3
Bruce Crossing **103** J 2
Brugge **52** D 4
Brumado **111** H 3
Brunei **74** D 2
Brusilovka **62** KL 5
Brusque **112** G 4
Bruxelles **52** D 4
Bryan **103** G 5
Bryan Coast **115**
Bryansk **62** F 5
Bryanskoye **59** G 2
Brzeg **53** G 4
Būbīyān (Kuwait) **61** E 3
Būbīyān (Kuwait) **89** H 3
Bucaramanga **108** D 2
Buchanan **90** B 4
Bucharest → Bucureşti **58** C 2
Buckingham Bay **79** F 1
Buckland **98** EF 2
Buco Zau **91** G 6
Bu Craa **86** C 3
Budapest **58** AB 1
Budennovsk **59** F 2
Búðardalur **54** A 2
Buenaventura (Colombia) **108** C 3
Buenaventura (Mexico) **102** E 6
Buenavista **102** E 7
Buenos Aires **112** DE 5–6
Buenos Aires, Lago **113** B 8
Buffalo (N.Y., U.S.A.) **103** L 3
Buffalo (OK, U.S.A.) **102** G 4
Buffalo (S.D., U.S.A.) **102** F 2
Buffalo (WY, U.S.A.) **102** E 3
Buffalo Lake **99** OP 3
Buffalo Narrows **99** Q 4
Bug **53** H 4
Buga **108** C 3
Bugorkan **68** J 3
Bugöynes **54** J 2
Bugt **69** M 6
Bugul'ma **62** K 5
Buhayrat al Asad **59** E 3
Buhayrat al Asad (Syria) **60** C 1–2
Bujumbura **92** D 5
Buka **81** F 3
Buka **82** B 3
Bukadaban Feng **70** B 3
Bukavu **92** D 5
Bukhara **67** G 3
Bukit Gandadiwata **75** EF 4
Bukit Kambuno **75** EF 4
Bukit Masurai **74** B 4
Bukittinggi **74** AB 3–4
Bukoba **92** E 5
Bukukun **68** K 6
Būl, Kūh-e (Iran) **61** F 3
Bulawayo **94** D 3–4
Buldana **72** C 3
Bulgan **68** H 6
Bulgaria **58** C 2
Bullahâr **93** G 2
Bulo Berde **93** H 4
Bulungu **92** B 5
Bumba **92** C 4
Bumbulan **75** F 3
Bunbury **78** B 5
Bunda **92** E 5
Bundaberg **79** J 3
Bunda Bunda **79** G 3
Bundesrepublik Deutschland **53** EF 5
Bundooma **78** E 3
Bunia **92** DE 4
Buorkhaya, Guba **69** O 1
Buorkhaya, Mys **69** O 1
Buqayq (Saudi Arabia) **61** E 4
Buran **63** R 6
Bura'o **93** H 3
Burayda (Saudi Arabia) **60** D 4
Buraydah **89** G 3
Burdur **58** D 3
Burdwan **72** E 3
Bureinskiy, Khrebet **69** O 5
Bureya **69** O 5
Burgakhcha **69** Q 3
Burgas **58** C 2
Burgaski zaliv **58** C 2
Burgeo **101** Q 6
Burgersdorp **94** D 6
Burgfjället **54** FG 3
Burgos (Mexico) **104** C 3
Burgos (Spain) **56** C 3
Burhanpur **72** C 3
Burin Peninsula **101** QR 6
Burkhala **69** RS 3
Burkina **90** DE 3
Burlington (CO, U.S.A.) **102** F 4
Burlington (IA, U.S.A.) **103** H 3
Burlington (N.Y., U.S.A.) **103** M 3
Burma **73** FG 3
Burmantovo **63** M 3
Burnie **80** L 9
Burns **102** C 3
Burnu **58** D 3
Burqin **67** M 1
Burra (South Australia) **79** F 5
Bursa **58** C 2
Bur Sa'id (Egypt) **60** A 3
Būr Sūdān **88** F 5
Buru **75** G 4
Burundi **92** DE 5
Buşayrah (Syria) **60** C 2
Būshehr (Iran) **61** F 3
Būshehr (Iran) **66** E 5
Bushman Land **94** BC 5
Businga **92** C 4
Busira **92** B 5
Buskerud **55** E 3
Busu Melo **92** C 4
Butang Group **73** G 6
Butaritari **82** C 2

Butembo **92** D 4
Butha Qi **69** M 6
Butte **102** D 2
Butt of Lewis **52** B 3
Button Bay **99** T 4
Button Islands **101** P 3
Butuan **75** G 2
Bu Tu Suay **73** J 5
Buy **62** H 4
Büyük Ağrı Dağı **59** F 3
Buzachi, Poluostrov **66** E 1–2
Buzău **58** C 1
Buzuluk **62** K 5
Byblos **88** F 2
Byblos (Lebanon) **60** B 2
Bydgoszcz **53** G 4
Bygdeå **54** H 3
Bygdeträsket **54** GH 3
Byglandsfjord **55** E 4
Bykovo **62** J 3
Bykovskiy **69** NO 1
Bylot Island **114**
Byrd Station **115**
Byro **78** B 4
Byske **54** H 3
Byskeälven **54** GH 2
Bytom **53** G 4
Byuchennyakh **69** QR 3

C

Caaguazu **112** E 4
Cáatingas **111** GH 2–3
Caazapa **112** E 4
Cabanatuan **75** J 1
Cabezas **110** D 4
Cabimas **108** D 1
Cabinda **91** G 6–7
Cabo Barbas **86** B 4
Cabo Beata **105** H 4
Cabo Bojador **86** BC 3
Cabo Catoche **104** E 3
Cabo Corrientes (Colombia) **108** C 2
Cabo das Correntes **95** F 4
Cabo de Ajo **56** C 3
Cabo de Creus **56** D 3
Cabo de Finisterre **56** B 3
Cabo de Formentor **56** D 3
Cabo de Gata **56** C 4
Cabo de Hornos **113** CD 10
Cabo de la Nao **56** D 4
Cabo Delgado **95** G 2
Cabo de Palos **56** C 4
Cabo de Salinas **56** D 4
Cabo de Santa Maria (Mozambique) **95** EF 5
Cabo de Santa Maria (Portugal) **56** B 4
Cabo de São Roque **111** JK 2
Cabo de São Vicente **56** B 4
Cabo dos Bahías **113** CD 8
Cabo Frio **111** H 5
Cabo Gracias a Dios **104** F 4–5
Cabo Norte **109** J 3
Cabo Orange **109** H 3
Cabo Ortegal **56** B 3
Caborca **102** D 5
Cabo San Antonio (Argentina) **113** E 6
Cabo San Antonio (Cuba) **104** EF 3
Cabo San Diego **113** C 9
Cabo San Lucas **102** E 7
Cabo Santa Elena **104** E 5
Cabo Trafalgar **56** B 4
Cabot Strait **101** Q 6
Cabo Verde **90** AB 6
Cabrera **56** D 4
Cabrera, Sierra de la **56** B 3
Cabruta **108** E 2
Caçador **112** F 4
Čačak **58** AB 2
Caceres (Brazil) **110** E 4
Cáceres (Spain) **56** B 4
Cachi, Nevado de **110** C 5
Cachimbo **109** H 5
Cachimbo, Serra do **109** G 5
Cachoeira **111** J 3
Cachoeira Alta **111** F 4
Cachoeira do Sul **112** F 5
Cachoeiro de Itapemirim **111** HJ 5
Caconda **94** B 2
Cacula **94** A 2
Cadi, Sierra del **56** D 3
Cadiz (Philippines) **75** F 1
Cádiz (Spain) **56** B 4
Cadiz, Golfo de **56** B 4
Caen **56** C 2
Caetite **111** H 3
Cagayan de Oro **75** F 2
Cagayan Islands **75** F 2
Cagliari **57** E 4
Caguas **105** J 4
Caia **95** EF 3
Caibarién **105** G 3
Caico **111** J 2
Caicos Islands **105** H 3
Cailloma **110** B 4
Cairns **79** H 2
Cairo **88** E 2
Caiundo **94** B 3
Cajamarca **108** C 5
Cajazeiras **111** J 2
Cajuapara **109** J 4
Calabar **91** F 4
Calabozo **108** E 2
Calabria **57** G 4
Calabro, Apennino **57** G 4
Calafate **113** B 9
Calais **52** D 4
Calama (Chile) **110** C 5
Calamar **108** D 3
Calamian Group **75** E 1
Cala Ratjada **56** D 4
Calatayud **56** C 3
Calatrava, Campo de **56** C 4
Calbayog **75** FG 1
Calçoene **109** H 3
Calcutta **72** E 3
Caldas **108** C 2
Caldera **112** B 4
Caleta Olivia **113** C 8
Calgary **99** P 5
Cali **108** C 3
Calicut **72** BC 5
California **102** BC 4
California, Golfo de **102** DE 5–7
Calilegua **110** CD 5
Callao **110** A 3
Caltanissetta **57** F 4
Calvi **57** E 3
Camagüey **105** G 3
Camaná **110** B 4
Camapuã **111** F 4
Camaquã **112** F 5
Camarat, Cap **57** E 3
Camargo **110** C 5
Camarones (Argentina) **113** CD 7
Camaxilo **94** B 1
Cambodia **73** HJ 5
Cambrai **56** D 1
Cambrian Mountains **52** C 4
Cambridge **52** D 4
Cambridge (MA, U.S.A.) **103** MN 3
Cambridge Bay **99** QR 2
Cameia National Park **94** C 2
Cameron **103** H 2
Cameroon **91** FG 4
Cameroon, Mont **91** F 5
Cametá **109** HJ 4
Camiranga **109** J 4
Camiri **110** D 5
Camocim **111** H 1
Camooweal (Queensland, Austr.) **79** F 2
Camorta **73** F 6
Campana, Isla **113** A 8
Campbell Island **115**
Campbellton **101** O 6
Camp Century **114**
Campeche **104** D 4
Campeche **104** DE 4
Campeche, Bahia de **104** CD 4
Campidano **57** E 4
Campina Grande **111** J 2
Campinas **111** G 5
Campo **91** F 5
Campo Corral **108** DE 2
Campo de Calatrava **56** C 4
Campo Formoso **111** H 3
Campo Gallo **112** D 4
Campo Grande **111** F 5
Campo Maior **111** H 1
Campos **111** GH 3–4
Campos **111** H 5
Cam Ranh **73** JK 5
Camrose **99** P 5
Ca Na **74** C 1
Canada **98–101**
Canadian River **102** F 4
Çanakkale **58** C 2
Canakkale Boğazı **58** C 2–3
Canal de la Mona **105** J 4
Canal do Norte **109** H 3
Canal du Midi **56** D 3
Canale de Sicilia **57** F 4
Canale di Malta **57** F 4
Cananea **102** DE 5
Canary Islands **86** B 3
Canaveral, Cape **103** KL 6
Canavieiras **111** J 4
Canberra **79** H 6
Canchas **112** BC 4
Candeias **111** J 3
Candelaria **104** D 4
Canéla (Goiás,Brazil) **111** H 3
Cangamba **94** C 2
Cangombé **94** B 2
Cangyuan **70** C 6
Cangzhou **71** G 3
Canindé (Ceará, Brazil) **111** J 1
Çankırı **59** D 2
Cannanore **72** BC 5
Cannes **57** E 3
Canning Basin **78** C 2
Cann River **79** H 6
Canoas **112** F 4
Canora **99** R 5
Canosa **57** G 3
Canso **101** P 6
Cantabrian Mountains **56** BC 3
Cantaura **109** F 2
Canterbury Bight **82** C 5
Can Tho **73** J 6
Canto do Buriti **111** H 2
Canton (China) **70** F 6
Canton (OH, U.S.A.) **103** K 3
Capanema **109** J 4
Capão Bonito **111** G 5
Cap Camarat **57** E 3
Cap Corse **57** E 3
Cap de Fer **87** G 1
Cap de Gaspé **101** P 6
Cap de la Hague **56** C 2
Cap-de-la-Madeleine **101** N 6
Cape Adare **115**
Cape Agulhas **94** C 6
Cape Ann **115**
Cape Arid **78** C 5
Cape Arid National Park **78** C 5
Cape Arnhem **79** F 1
Cape Baring **99** O 2
Cape Bathurst **98** LM 1
Cape Bauld **101** QR 5
Cape Boothby **115**
Cape Breton Island **101** Q 6
Cape Canaveral **103** KL 6
Cape Catastrophe **79** F 5–6
Cape Chapman **99** U 2
Cape Charles (VA, U.S.A.) **103** L 4
Cape Chelyuskin **114**
Cape Chidley **101** P 3
Cape Churchill **99** T 4
Cape Coast **90** DE 4
Cape Cod **103** N 3
Cape Columbine **94** B 6
Cape Comorin **72** C 6
Cape Cretin **80** E 3
Cape Croker **78** E 1
Cape Cross **94** A 4
Cape d'Ambre, Cape Bobraomby **95** HJ 2
Cape Darnley **115**
Cape Dennison **115**
Cape Dorchester **101** M 2
Cape du Couedic **79** F 6
Cape Dyer **101** P 2
Cape Engaño **75** J 1
Cape Farewell **81** Q 9
Cape Farewell **82** C 5
Cape Fear **103** L 5
Cape Finniss **78** E 5
Cape Flattery (WA, U.S.A.) **102** AB 2
Cape Freels **101** R 6
Cape Fria **94** A 3
Cape Grim **80** K 9
Cape Harrison **101** Q 5

Cape Hatteras **103** LM 4
Cape Henrietta Maria **101** L 4
Cape Herluf Trolle **101** T 3
Cape Horn **113** CD 10
Cape Howe **79** J 6
Cape Jaffa **79** F 6
Cape Kellett **99** M 1
Cape Krusenstern National Monument **98** E 2
Cape Lambert **81** F 2
Cape Lambton **99** MN 1
Cape Leeuwin **78** A 5
Cape Lévêque **78** C 2
Capelinha **111** H 4
Cape Lisburne **98** D 2
Cape Londonderry **78** D 1
Cape Lookout **103** L 5
Cape Low **99** UV 3
Cape Maria van Diemen **81** PQ 7
Cape Melville(Queensland, Austr.) **79** GH 1
Cape Mendocino **102** AB 3
Cape Mercy **101** P 3
Cape Meredith **113** D 9
Cape Mohican **98** CD 3
Cape Morris Jesup **114**
Cape Naturaliste **78** A 5
Cape Negrais **73** F 4
Cape Newenham **98** DE 4
Cape Norvegia **115**
Cape of Good Hope **94** B 6
Cape Otway **79** G 6
Cape Palmas **90** C 5
Cape Poinsett **115**
Cape Prince Alfred **99** M 1
Cape Prince of Wales **98** D 2
Cape Providence **80** OP 10
Cape Province **94** CD 6
Cape Race **101** R 6
Cape Raper **101** O 2
Cape Ray **101** Q 6
Cape Rodney (Papua New Guinea) **80** E 4
Cape Sable (Canada) **101** O 7
Cape Sable (FL, U.S.A.) **103** K 6
Cape Saint Francis **94** CD 6
Cape Saint George (Papua New Guinea) **81** F 2–3
Cape Saint Lucia **95** E 5
Cape San Blas **103** J 6
Cape Scott **78** D 1
Cape Smith **101** LM 3
Cape Town **94** B 6
Cape Van Diemen **78** D 1
Cape Verde **90** AB 6
Cape Wessel **79** F 1
Cape Wrath **52** BC 3
Cape Yakataga **98** J 4
Cape York **79** G 1
Cape York Peninsula (Queensland, Austr.) **79** G 1
Cape Zhelaniya **114**
Cap Ferret **56** C 3
Cap-Haïtien **105** H 3–4
Cap Hopes Advance **101** O 3
Capitán Arturo Prat **115**
Cap Lopez **91** F 6
Cap Masoala **95** J 3
Capo Carbonara **57** E 4
Capo Circeo **57** F 3
Capo Gallo **57** F 4
Capoompeta **79** J 4
Capo Palinuro **57** FG 4
Capo Passero **57** G 4
Capo San Marco **57** E 4
Capo Santa Maria di Leuca **57** G 4
Capo Spartivento **57** E 4
Capo Testa **57** E 3
Capri **57** F 3
Capricorn Channel **79** J 3
Caprivi Game Park **94** C 3
Caprivi Strip **94** C 3
Cap Saint-André **95** G 3
Cap Sainte-Marie, Cap Vohimena **95** GH 5
Cap Timiris **86** B 5
Cap Vert **90** A 3
Cap Wolstenholme **101** M 3
Caquetá **108** D 4
Caracal **58** B 2
Caracarai **109** F 3
Caracas **108** E 1
Carahue **113** B 6
Carajás, Serra dos **109** H 4–5
Caratinga **111** H 4
Carauari **108** E 4
Carazinho **112** F 4
Carballo **56** B 3
Carbonara, Capo **57** E 4
Carbonia **57** E 4
Carcassonne **56** D 3
Cárdenas (Cuba) **105** F 3
Cardiff **52** C 4
Cardigan **52** C 4
Careiro **109** G 4
Carey, Lake **78** C 4
Caribbean Sea **105** GJ 4
Caribou Mountains (Alb., Can.) **99** O 4
Carinhanha **111** H 3
Cariparé **111** G 3
Caritianas **109** F 5
Carletonville **94** D 5
Carlisle **52** C 4
Carnarvon (Australia) **78** A 3
Carnarvon (S. Africa) **94** C 6
Carnegie **78** C 4
Carnegie, Lake **78** C 4
Car Nicobar **73** F 6
Carnot **92** B 3
Carolina **109** J 5
Caroline (Kiribati) **83** EF 3
Caroline Islands **82** AB 2
Carondelet **82** D 3
Carpathians **58** BC 1
Carpaţii Meridionali **58** B 1–2
Carpentaria Gulf of **79** F 1
Carpina **111** J 2
Carrick-on-Shannon **52** B 4
Carrillo **104** B 2
Carrizal (Colombia) **108** D 1
Carrizozo **102** E 5
Çarşamba **59** D 3
Carson City **102** C 4
Cartagena (Colombia) **108** C 1
Cartagena (Spain) **56** C 4
Cartago (Costa Rica) **104** F 6
Caruaru **111** J 2
Carvoeiro **109** F 4
Casablanca **86** D 2
Casbas **113** D 6
Cascade Range **102** B 2–3
Cascavel **111** F 5
Caserta **57** F 3
Casey **115**
Casino **79** J 4
Casma **108** C 5
Casper **102** E 3
Caspian Sea **66** DE 2–3
Cassiar Mountains **98** M 4
Cassino (Italy) **57** F 3
Castanhal **109** J 4
Castaño **112** C 5
Castellón **56** CD 4
Castelo de Vide **56** B 4
Castelvetrano **57** F 4
Castilla (Chile) **112** B 4
Castilla (Peru) **108** BC 5
Castilla la Nueva **56** C 3–4
Castilla la Vieja **56** C 3
Castillos **112** F 5
Castlegar **99** O 6
Castor **99** P 5
Castres **56** D 3
Castries (Saint Lucia) **105** K 5
Castro (Chile) **113** B 7
Catalão **111** G 4
Cataluna **56** D 3
Çatalzeytin **59** D 2
Catamarca **112** CD 4
Catanduanes **75** FG 1
Catanduva **111** G 5
Catania **57** G 4
Catanzaro **57** G 4
Catastrophe, Cape **79** F 6
Catbalogan **75** FG 1
Cateel **75** G 2
Catinzaco **112** C 4
Cat Island **105** GH 3
Catoche, Cabo **104** E 3
Catrilo **113** D 6
Catrimani **109** F 3
Catwick Islands **73** J 5–6
Caucasus Mountains **59** F 2
Cauquenes **113** B 6
Caura **109** F 2
Cavalcante **111** G 3
Caxias (Amazonas, Brazil) **108** D 4
Caxias (Maranhão, Brazil) **111** H 1
Caxias do Sul **112** FG 4
Caxito **94** A 1
Cayenne **109** H 3
Cayman Islands **105** FG 4
Ceará **111** HJ 1
Ceballos **104** B 2
Cebollar **112** C 4
Cebu **75** F 2
Čechy **53** F 4
Cedar Falls **103** H 3
Cedar Lake **99** RS 5
Cedar Rapids **103** H 3
Cedros, Isla **102** C 6
Celaya **104** B 3
Celebes **75** EF 4
Celebes Sea **75** F 3
Celje **57** FG 2
Celle **53** F 4
Celtic Sea **52** B 4
Central, Cordilera (Colombia) **108** C 2–3
Central, Cordillera (Peru) **108** C 5
Central African Republic **92** BC 3
Central Arctic District **99** PR 1
Central Kalahari Game Reserve **94** C 4
Central Makran Range **67** GH 5
Centralno Tungusskoye Plato **68** GH 3–4
Central Range (Papua New Guinea) **80** D 2–3
Cereal **99** P 5
Ceres (Brazil) **111** FG 4
Cerf **93** J 6
Cerro Aconcagua **112** BC 5
Cerro Agua Caliente **104** A 2
Cerro Ángel **104** B 3
Cerro Blanco **102** E 6
Cerro Bonete **112** C 4
Cerro Champaquí **112** D 5
Cerro Chirripó **104** F 6
Cerro de la Encantada **102** CD 5
Cerro del Toro **112** C 4
Cerro de Pasco **110** A 3
Cerro de Tocorpuri **110** C 5
Cerro Galán **112** C 4
Cerro Grande **104** B 3
Cerro Las Casilas **102** E 7
Cerro Las Minas **104** E 4–5
Cerro Marahuaca **108** E 3
Cerro Mariquita **104** C 3
Cerro Mohinora **102** E 6
Cerro Murallón **113** B 8
Cerro Nuevo Mundo **110** C 5
Cerro Ojos del Salado **112** C 4
Cerro San Valentín **113** B 8
Cerro Ventana **102** E 7
Cerro Yavi **108** E 2
Cerro Yucuyácua **104** C 4
Cerro Yumari **108** E 3
Cesano **57** F 3
České Budějovice **53** F 5
Českézemě **53** G 5
Ceuta **86** D 1
Ceva-i-Ra **82** C 4
Cévennes **56** D 3
Ceyhan (Turkey) **59** E 3
Ceyhan (Turkey) **59** E 3
Ceyhan (Turkey) **60** B 1
Ceylanpınar (Turkey) **60** C 1
Chaca **110** B 4
Chachapoyas **108** C 5
Chad **91** HJ 3
Chad, Lake **91** G 3
Chādegān (Iran) **61** F 2
Chadobets **68** GH 4
Chagai Hills **67** G 5
Chagda **69** O 4
Chagdo Kangri **72** D 1
Chaghcharān **67** GH 4
Chagos Archipelago **65** F 7
Chagyl **66** F 2
Chahah Burjak **67** G 4
Chah Bahār **67** G 5
Chaiyaphum **73** H 4
Chakari **94** D 3
Chake Chake **93** FG 6
Chakhansur **67** G 4
Chala **110** B 4

Chalbi Desert **93** F 4
Chalhuanca **110** B 3
Challapata **110** C 4
Châlons-sur-Marne **57** D 2
Chalon-sur-Saône **57** DE 2
Chālūs (Iran) **61** F 1
Chaman **67** H 4
Chamba (India) **72** C 1
Chambery **57** E 2
Chamical **112** C 5
Chamoli **72** CD 1
Champagne **57** DE 2
Champaquí, Cerro **112** D 5
Champdoré, Lac **101** O 4
Chana Liang **71** J 1
Chañaral **112** B 4
Chanco **113** B 6
Chandigarh **72** C 1
Chandler **101** P 6
Chandmanĭ **70** C 1
Chandpur **73** F 3
Chandrapur **72** C 3–4
Chanf **67** G 5
Changara **95** E 3
Changchun **71** J 2
Changde **70** F 5
Changji **67** M 2
Chang Jiang **70–71** EG 4
Changling **71** H 2
Changsha **70** F 5
Changwu **70** E 3
Changzhi **70** F 3
Channel Islands (U.K.) **52** C 5
Channel Islands (U.S.A.) **102** C 5
Chaoyang **70** G 6
Chaoyang **71** GH 2
Chapayev-Zheday **68** L 3–4
Chapleau **100** L 6
Chapman, Cape **99** U 2
Chapoma **62** GH 2
Chapra **72** DE 2
Chara **68** L 4
Charagua **110** D 4
Charcot Island **115**
Chard **99** P 4
Chardzhou **67** G 3
Chari **91** H 3
Charity **109** G 2
Charkabozh **62** K 2
Charleroi **52** DE 4
Charlesbourg **101** N 6
Charles Peak **78** C 5
Charleston (S.C., U.S.A.) **103** L 5
Charleston (W.V., U.S.A.) **103** K 4
Charleville **79** H 4
Charlotte **103** KL 4
Charlottesville **103** L 4
Charlottetown **101** P 6
Charlton (Australia) **79** G 6
Charlton (Canada) **101** LM 5
Charters Towers **79** H 2–3
Chartres **56** D 2
Charyshskoye **63** Q 5
Chasel'ka **63** Q 2
Chatanga **68** K 6
Châteauroux **56** D 2
Châtellerault **56** CD 2
Chatham (New Zealand) **81** S 9
Chatham (New Zeeland) **82** D 5
Chatham (Ontario, Can.) **103** K 3
Chattanooga **103** J 5
Chaumont **57** DE 2
Chau Phu **73** HJ 5
Chaves (Brazil) **109** H 4
Chaves (Portugal) **56** B 3
Chayatyn, Khrebet **69** P 5
Chaykovskiy **62** KL 4
Chazhegovo **62** K 3
Cheb **53** F 4
Cheboksary **62** J 4
Cheduba **73** F 4
Chegga (Algeria) **87** G 2
Chegytun **98** C 2
Cheju **71** J 4
Cheju-do **71** J 4
Chekhov **69** Q 6
Chekunda **69** O 5
Chekuyevo **62** G 3
Chelforó **113** C 6
Chelkar **66** F 1
Chełm **53** H 4
Chelmuzhi **62** G 3
Chelyabinsk **63** M 4
Chelyuskin, Cape **114**
Chenachane **86** E 3
Chengde **71** G 2
Chengdu **70** DE 4
Chenxi **70** EF 5
Chenzhou **70** F 5
Chepen **108** C 5
Chepes **112** C 5
Cherbourg **56** C 2
Cherchell **87** F 1
Cheremkhovo **68** H 5
Cherepovets **62** G 4
Cherkassy **62** EF 6
Cherkessk **59** F 2
Chernigov **62** EF 5
Chernovtsy **58** C 1
Chernyakhovsk **55** H 5
Chernyshevskiy **68** K 3
Chernyye Zemli **59** G 1
Chernyy Ostrov **68** F 3
Cherskogo, Khrebet **69** P 1–2
Chervonograd **55** H 5
Chervonoznamenka **58** CD 1
Chesapeake Bay Bridge-Tunnel **103** LM 4
Chesterfield Inlet **99** TU 3
Chesterfield Inlet **99** TU 3
Chesterfield Islands **82** B 4
Chetumal **104** E 4
Cheulik **69** P 2
Cheyenne **102** F 3
Chhatarpur **72** C 3
Chiang Kham **73** H 4
Chiang Mai **73** G 4
Chiang Rai **73** G 4
Chiang Saen **73** H 3
Chiapas **104** D 4
Chiavari **57** E 3
Chiayi **71** H 6
Chiba **71** M 3
Chibagalakh **69** PQ 2
Chibit **63** R 5
Chibougamau **101** N 6
Chicago **103** J 3
Chicapa **94** C 1
Chichagof **98** K 4
Chicheng **71** G 2
Chiclayo **108** B 5
Chico (Chile) **113** C 7
Chicoutimi **101** N 6
Chidley, Cape **101** P 3
Chifeng **71** G 2
Chiganak **63** O 6
Chigorodó **108** C 2
Chigubo **95** E 4
Chihli, Gulf of **71** GH 3
Chihuahua **102** EF 6
Chik Ballapur **72** C 5
Chikhacheva **69** R 1
Chilabombwe **94** D 2
Childress **102** F 5
Chile **113** B 5–6
Chilete **108** C 5
Chilipa de Alvarez **104** C 4
Chillán **113** B 6
Chiloé, Isla de **113** B 7
Chilpancingo **104** BC 4
Chilwa, Lago **95** F 3
Chimbay **66** F 2
Chimborazo **108** C 4
Chimbote **108** C 5
Chimkent **67** H 2
Chin **73** F 3
China **70** DF 4
Chinandega **104** E 5
Chincha Alta **110** A 3
Chindu **70** C 4
Chindwin **73** FG 3
Chinese Wall **70** E 3
Chingola **94** D 2
Chinguetti **86** C 4
Chinju **71** J 4
Chipata **95** E 2
Chirchik **67** HJ 2
Chiriguaná **108** D 2
Chiriquí, Golfo de **108** B 2
Chishui **70** E 5
Chita **68** K 5
Chitado **94** A 3
Chitato **94** C 1
Chitina **98** HJ 3
Chitipa **95** E 1
Chitral **67** J 3
Chittagong **73** F 3
Chittaurgarh **72** BC 3
Chittoor **72** C 5
Chivasso **57** E 2
Chivay **110** B 4
Chizha **62** H 2
Chkalovo **63** O 5
Chobe National Park **94** C 3
Choele Choel **113** CD 6
Choggia **57** F 2
Choiseul **81** G 3
Choiseul **82** B 3
Chojnice **53** G 4
Cholet **56** C 2
Choluteca **104** E 5
Chomutov **53** F 4
Chona **68** J 3
Chon Buri **73** H 5
Ch'ŏngjin **71** JK 2
Ch'ŏngju **71** J 3
Chongqing **70** E 5
Chŏnju **71** J 3
Chonos, Archipiélago de los **113** AB 7–8
Chon Thanh **73** J 5
Ćhorzów **53** G 4
Chosica **110** A 3
Chos Malal **113** BC 6
Chotanagpur **72** DE 3
Chott Melrhir **87** G 2
Choum **86** C 4
Choybalsan **68** K 6
Christchurch (New Zeeland) **81** QR 9
Christmas Island **74** C 6
Chubut **113** C 7
Chudskoye Ozero **55** J 4
Chukar **68** L 3
Chukchi Sea **98** CD 2
Chukchi Sea **114**
Chuken **69** P 6
Chukotsk Peninsula **114**
Chukotsk Range **114**
Chulak-Kurgan **67** HJ 2
Chulasa **62** J 3
Chula Vista **102** C 5
Chulym **63** QR 4
Chulym **68** F 4
Chumikan **69** OP 5
Chumphon **73** GH 5
Ch'unch'ŏn **71** J 3
Chuquibamba **110** B 4
Chuquicamata **110** C 5
Chur **57** E 2
Churchill (Man., Can.) **99** ST 4
Churchill (Man., Can.) **99** T 4
Churchill, Cape **99** T 4
Churchill Falls **101** P 5
Churchill Lake **99** Q 4
Churchill Mountains **115**
Churu **72** C 2
Churuguara **108** E 1
Churún Merú **109** F 2
Chusovoy **63** L 4
Chusovskoy **62** L 3
Chute-des-Passes **101** NO 6
Chutes de Katende (Katende Falls) **92** C 6
Chutes de Livingstone (Livingstone Falls) **92** A 6
Chutes Ngaliema (Stanley Falls) **92** D 4
Chuxiong **70** D 5
Chuyengo **68** HJ 3
Cianjur **74** C 5
Cícero Dantas **111** J 3
Ciechanów **53** H 4
Ciego de Ávila **105** G 3
Ciénaga **108** D 1
Cienfuegos **105** F 3
Cieza **56** C 4
Cihanbeyli Platosu **59** D 3
Cilo Dağı **59** F 3
Cimarron River **102** G 4
Çimen Dağı **59** E 3
Cîmpia Bărăganului **58** C 1–2
Cîmpia Burnazului **58** C 2
Cîmpina **58** C 1
Cinca **56** D 3
Cincinatti **103** K 4
Cinto, Monte **57** E 3
Circeo, Capo **57** F 3
Circle (AK, U.S.A.) **98** J 2
Cirebon **74** C 5
Cirque Mountain **101** P 4
Ciskei **94** D 6

Citta del Vaticano **57** F 3
Ciudad Acuña **104** B 2
Ciudad Bolívar **109** F 2
Ciudad Camargo **102** E 6
Ciudad del Carmen **104** D 4
Ciudad de Rio Grande **104** B 3
Ciudad Guayana **109** F 2
Ciudad Guzmán **104** B 4
Ciudad Hidalgo **104** BC 4
Ciudad Juárez **102** E 5
Ciudad Madero **104** C 3
Ciudad Mante **104** C 3
Ciudad Obregón **102** E 6
Ciudad Río Bravo **104** C 2
Ciudad-Rodrigo **56** B 3
Ciudad Valles **104** C 3
Ciudad Victoria **104** C 3
Civitanova Marche **57** F 3
Civitavecchia **57** F 3
Cizre (Turkey) **59** F 3
Cizre (Turkey) **60** D 1
Claire, Lake **99** P 4
Claire Coast **115**
Clanwilliam **94** BC 6
Clarke Range **79** H 2–3
Clarksburg **103** KL 4
Clarksville **103** J 4
Clay Belt **100** LM 5
Clearwater **103** K 6
Clermont **79** H 3
Clermont-Ferrand **56** D 2
Cleveland (OH, U.S.A.) **103** K 3
Cleveland, Mount **102** D 2
Clinton **99** N 5
Clinton-Colden Lake **99** Q 3
Cloncurry **79** FG 3
Clorinda **112** E 4
Cloud Peak **102** E 3
Clovis **102** F 5
Cluj-Napoca **58** B 1
Cmi Drim **58** B 2
Cnossus **58** C 3
Coahuila **104** B 2
Coal River **99** M 4
Coari **109** F 4
Coast Mountains **98–99** LM 4–5
Coast of Labrador **101** QP 4–5
Coast Range (Queensland, Austr.) **79** J 4
Coast Range (U.S.A.) **102** B 3–4
Coats Island **99** V 3
Coats land **115**
Coatzacoalcos **104** D 4
Cobar **79** H 5
Cobija **110** C 3
Cobquecura **113** B 6
Coburg **53** F 4
Cocachacra **110** B 4
Cochabamba **110** CD 4
Cochin **72** C 6
Cochrane (Chile) **113** B 8
Cocklebiddy **78** D 5
Coco Islands (Burma) **73** F 5
Codó **111** H 1
Cody **102** E 3
Coetivy **93** JK 6
Coeur d'Alene **102** C 2
Coff's Harbour **79** J 5
Coihaique **113** B 8
Coimbatore **72** C 5
Coimbra **56** B 3
Cojimies **108** B 3
Cojutepeque **104** E 5
Colatina **111** HJ 4
Cold Bay **98** E 5
Col de Perthus **56** D 3
Colesberg **94** D 6
Colima **104** B 4
Collier Bay **78** C 2
Collier Ranges National Park **78** B 3
Collines du Perche **56** D 2
Collinson Peninsula **99** R 1–2
Cololo, Nevado **110** C 4
Colombo **72** C 6
Colón (Cuba) **105** F 3
Colón (Panamá) **108** C 2
Colón, Archipiélago de **108** B 6
Colona **78** E 5
Colonia Las Heras **113** C 8
Colorado (Argentina) **113** D 6
Colorado (U.S.A.) **102** EF 4
Colorado Plateau **102** DE 4
Colorado River (AZ, U.S.A.) **102** D 5
Colorado River (TX, U.S.A.) **103** G 5–6
Colorado Springs **102** F 4
Columbia (MO, U.S.A.) **103** H 4
Columbia (S.C., U.S.A.) **103** K 5
Columbia (WA, U.S.A.) **102** BC 2
Columbia, Mount **99** O 5
Columbia Falls **102** D 2
Columbia Mountains **99** NO 5
Columbia Plateau **102** C 3
Columbine, Cape **94** B 6
Columbus (IN, U.S.A.) **103** J 4
Columbus (MS, U.S.A.) **103** K 5
Columbus (OH, U.S.A.) **103** K 4
Columbus (TX, U.S.A.) **103** G 6
Colville Lake **99** MN 2
Comalcalco **104** DE 4
Comandante Luis Piedrabuena **113** CD 8–9
Combarbala **112** B 5
Combermere Bay **73** F 4
Committee Bay **99** U 2
Como **57** E 2
Comodoro Rivadavia **113** C 8
Comorin, Cape **72** C 6
Comoros **95** G 2
Compiègne **56** D 2
Conakry **90** B 4
Conceição do Araguaia **109** HJ 5
Concepción (Bolivia) **110** D 4
Concepción (Chile) **113** B 6
Concepción (Paraguay) **110** E 5
Concepción del Oro **104** B 3
Concepción del Uruguay **112** E 5
Concord **103** M 3
Concórdia (Amazonas, Brazil) **108** E 4
Concordia (Argentina) **112** E 5
Condon **102** C 2
Conejo **102** D 7
Congo **91** H 6
Connaught **52** B 4
Connecticut **103** M 3
Conrad **102** D 2
Conselheiro Lafaiete **111** H 5
Con Son **73** J 6
Constanța **58** C 2
Constantine **87** G 1
Contamana **108** D 5
Contwoyto Lake **99** PQ 2
Conway Reef → Ceva-i-Ra **82** C 4
Cook **78** E 5
Cook, Mount **82** C 5
Cook, Strait **82** C 5
Cookes Peak **102** E 5
Cook Inlet **98** G 3
Cook Islands **82** E 3
Cook Mountains **115**
Cook Strait **81** QR 9
Cooktown **79** H 2
Copenhagen **55** F 4
Copiapó **112** BC 4
Copperbelt **94** D 2
Coqên **72** E 1
Coquimbo **112** B 5
Coral Harbour **99** UV 3
Coral Sea **81** H 3
Coral Sea **82** B 3–4
Coral Sea Islands Territory **79** HJ 1–2
Corcaigh **52** B 4
Cordillera Cantábrica **56** BC 3
Cordillera Central (Colombia) **108** C 2–3
Cordillera Central (Peru) **108** C 5
Cordillera Central (Philippines) **75** J 1
Cordillera Occidental (Colombia) **108** C 2–3
Cordillera Occidental (Peru) **110** BC 3–4
Cordillera Oriental (Bolivia) **110** CD 3–5
Cordillera Oriental (Colombia) **108** CD 2–3
Cordillera Real (Ecuador) **108** C 4
Córdoba (Argentina) **112** D 5
Córdoba (Mexico) **104** C 4
Córdoba (Spain) **56** BC 4
Corfu **58** AB 3
Corigliano Calabro **57** G 4
Corinth (Greece) **58** B 3
Corinto **111** H 4
Cork (Rep. of Ireland) **52** B 4
Çorlu **58** C 2
Cornelio **102** D 6
Cornélio Procópio **111** F 5
Corner Brook **101** Q 6
Cornwall (Ontario, Can.) **101** M 6
Coro **108** DE 1
Coroatá **111** H 1
Corocoro **110** C 4
Coromandel Coast **72** D 5
Coromandel Peninsula **81** R 8
Coronation Gulf **99** P 2
Coronel **113** B 6
Coronel Fabriciano **111** H 4
Coronel Oviedo **112** E 4
Coronel Pringles **113** D 6
Coropuna, Nevado **110** B 4
Corpus Christi **103** G 6
Corrente (Piauí, Brazil) **111** GH 3
Correntes, Cabo das **95** F 4
Correntina **111** GH 3
Corrientes (Argentina) **112** E 4
Corrientes, Cabo (Colombia) **108** C 2
Corse **57** E 3
Corse, Cap **57** E 3
Corsica **57** E 3
Çoruh **59** F 2
Çoruh Dağları **59** F 2
Çorum **62** E 2
Corumbá (Mato Grosso do Sul, Brazil) **110** E 4
Corunna **56** B 3
Corvallis **102** B 3
Cosenza **57** G 4
Cosmoledo Group **93** H 6
Costa Blanca **56** C 4
Costa Brava **56** D 3
Costa de la Luz **56** B 4
Costa del Azahar **56** D 3
Costa del Sol **56** C 4
Costa de Mosquitos **104** F 5
Costa Dorada **56** D 3
Costa Rica **104** EF 6
Costa Verde **56** B 3
Cotabato **75** F 2
Cotagaita **110** CD 5
Coteau du Missouri **102** FG 2
Côte d'Argent **56** C 3
Côte d'Azur **57** E 3
Cotonou **90** E 4
Cotopaxi **108** C 4
Cottbus **53** F 4
Cotulla **102** G 6
Council Bluffs **103** GH 3
Courland **55** H 4
Coventry **52** C 4
Covington (TN, U.S.A.) **103** JK 4
Cowell **79** F 5
Cowra **79** H 5
Coxim **111** F 4
Cox's Bazar **73** F 3
Cradock **94** D 6
Craiova **58** B 2
Crakow **53** H 4–5
Cranbrook (Western Australia) **78** B 5
Crary Mountains **115**
Cratéus **111** HJ 2
Crato (Ceará, Brazil) **111** J 2
Crawford **102** F 3
Creil **56** D 2
Cremona **57** F 2
Cres **57** F 3
Crescent City **102** AB 3
Crete **58** C 3
Creus, Cabo de **56** D 3
Creuse **56** D 2
Criciúma **112** G 4

Crimea **59** D 1
Cristmas Island **83** E 2
Cristóbal, Colón Pico **108** D 1
Croatia **57** G 2
Crockett **103** GH 5
Croker, Cape **78** E 1
Croker Island **78** E 1
Crooked Island **105** H 3
Crooked Island Passage **105** GH 3
Crookston **103** G 2
Cross, Cape **94** A 4
Crotone **57** G 4
Crowell **102** G 5
Crown Prince Frederik Island **99** U 2
Crowsnest Pass **99** OP 6
Cruz Alta **112** F 4
Cruz del Eje **112** CD 5
Cruzeiro do Oeste **111** F 5
Cruzeiro do Sul **108** D 5
Cruz Grande (Mexico) **104** C 4
Crystal Brook **79** F 5
Cuamba **95** F 2
Cuando Cubango **94** BC 3
Cuango **94** B 1
Cuanza **94** B 1–2
Cuanza Norte **94** AB 1
Cuanza Sul **94** AB 2
Cuauhtémoc **102** E 6
Cuba **105** FG 3
Cubango **94** B 3
Cucurpe **102** D 5
Cúcuta **108** D 2
Cuddalore **72** CD 5
Cuddapah **72** C 5
Cudi Dağı **59** F 3
Cuenca (Ecuador) **108** C 4
Cuenca (Spain) **56** C 3–4
Cuencamé de Ceniceros **104** B 3
Cuiabá **110** E 4
Cuito Cuanavale **94** B 3
Cu Lao Hon **73** JK 5
Culiacán **102** E 7
Cumaná **109** F 1
Cumbal **108** C 3
Cumberland **103** L 4
Cumberland Peninsula **101** OP 2
Cumberland Plateau **103** JK 4
Cumberland Sound **101** OP 2–3
Cunani **109** H 3
Cunene **94** A 3
Cunene **94** B 3
Cuneo **57** E 3
Cunnamulla **79** H 4
Cupica **108** C 2
Curaçao, Isla **108** E 1
Curacautin **113** B 6
Curdimurka **79** F 4
Curicó **113** B 5–6
Curimatá **111** H 2–3
Curitiba **112** FG 4
Curtis **82** D 5
Curtis Island **79** J 3
Curuça **109** J 4
Curumu **109** H 4
Curupuru **109** K 4
Curvelo **111** H 4
Cushing, Mount **99** M 4
Cuttack **72** E 3
Cuvette **91** H 6
Cuxhaven **53** E 4
Cuya **110** B 4
Cuyo Islands **75** F 1
Cuzco **110** B 3
Cyangugu **92** D 5
Cyclades **58** BC 3
Cypress Hills **99** PQ 6
Cyprus **59** D 3
Cyprus **60** AB 2
Cyrenaica **87** JK 3
Czechoslovakia **53** G 5
Częstochowa **53** GH 4

D

Dabat **93** F 2
Dabbāgh, Jabal (Saudi Arabia) **60** B 4
Dabola **90** B 3
Dacca **72** E 3
Dadali **82** B 3
Dadanawa **109** G 3
Daet **75** F 1
Dafeng **71** H 4
Dagabur **93** G 3
Dagana (Chad) **91** H 3
Dagi **69** Q 5
Dagur **70** C 3
Dahabān **66** B 6
Da Hinggan Ling **71** GH 1–2
Dahlak Archipelago **93** FG 1
Dahongliutan **67** KL 3
Dahra (Senegal) **90** AB 2
Dahūk (Iraq) **60** D 1
Dahūk (Iraq) **66** C 3
Daintree River National Park **79** G 2
Dairen **71** H 3
Daitō-shotō **71** K 5
Dajarra **79** F 3
Dakar **90** A 3
Dakha **72** F 3
Dakhla **86** B 4
Dakovica **58** B 2
Dala **94** BC 2
Dalälven **55** G 3
Dalaman **58** C 3
Dalandzadgad **70** DE 2
Dalarna **55** F 3
Da Lat **73** J 5
Dalby **79** J 4
Dali **70** D 5
Dallas **103** G 5
Dall Lake **98** E 3
Dalmā' (United Arab Emirates) **61** F 4
Dal'negorsk **71** L 2
Dal'nerechensk **71** KL 1
Dal'nyaya **69** Q 6
Daloa **90** C 4
Dalsland **55** F 4
Dalstroy **69** P 3
Daltonganj **72** DE 3
Dalwallinu **78** B 5
Daly River **78** E 1
Daly Waters **78** E 2
Daman **72** B 3
Damanhūr **88** DE 2
Damara **92** B 3
Damaraland **94** B 4
Damascus **88** F 2
Damascus (Syria) **60** B 2
Damāvand (Iran) **61** F 2
Dāmghan (Iran) **61** FG 1
Damoh **72** C 3
Dampier **78** B 3
Danakil Plain **93** G 2
Danané **90** C 4
Da Nang **73** J 4
Danba **70** D 4
Dandarah **88** E 3
Dandong **71** H 2–3
Danghe Nanshan **70** CD 3
Dangjin Shankou **70** BC 3
Dangshan **71** G 4
Danmark **55** E 4
Danmarks Havn **114**
Dan Sai **73** H 4
Danube **58** C 1
Danville (VA, U.S.A.) **103** L 4
Dan Xian **70** E 7
Dao Xian **70** F 5
Dapoli **72** B 4
Da Qaidam **70** C 3
Dar'ā (Syria) **60** B 2
Dar'ā (Syria) **88** F 2
Dārāb **66** E 5
Dārāb (Iran) **61** G 3
Daraj (Iran) **87** H 2
Dāran (Iran) **61** F 2
Dārān (Iran) **66** DE 4
Darāw (Egypt) **60** A 4
Darband **66** F 4
Darbhanga **72** E 2
Dardanelles **58** C 3
Dar el Beida **86** C 2
Dar es Salaam **93** F 6
Dārfūr **88** C 6
Darganata **67** G 2
Dargaville **81** Q 8
Darién **108** C 2
Darjeeling **72** E 2
Darlag **70** CD 4
Darling Downs **79** H 4
Darling Range **78** B 5
Darling River **79** G 5
Darlington (U.K.) **52** C 4
Darmstadt **53** E 5
Darnah **87** K 2
Darnley, Cape **115**
Dar Rounga **92** C 2–3
Dartmoor **52** C 4
Dartmouth **101** P 7
Darvaza **66** F 2
Darweshan **67** G 4
Darwin (Australia) **78** E 1
Daryācheh-ye Bakhtegān (Iran) **61** FG 3
Daryācheh-ye Namak (Iran) **61** F 2
Daryācheh-ye Orūmīyeh (Iran) **61** D 1
Daryācheh-ye Orūmīyeh (Iran) **66** CD 3
Daryācheh-ye Tashk (Iran) **61** FG 3
Daryācheh-ye Tashk (Iran) **89** J 3
Daryā-ye Māzandarān **66** E 3
Dasht-e Kavīr (Iran) **61** FG 2
Dasht-e Kavīr (Iran) **66** EF 4
Dasht-e Lūt (Iran) **61** G 2
Dasht e Lut (Iran) **66** F 4
Dasht-e Naomid **66–67** G 4
Date **71** M 2
Datia **72** C 2
Datong **70** F 2
Datong **70** D 3
Datta **69** Q 6
Dāuarzan **66** F 3
Daugava **55** H 4
Daugav'pils **55** J 4
Daung Kyun **73** G 5
Dauphin **99** R 5
Dauphiné **57** E 3
Dauphin Lake **99** S 5
Daurskoye **68** F 4
Davangere **72** C 5
Davao **75** G 2
Dāvar Panāh **67** G 5
Dāvarzan (Iran) **61** G 1
Davenport **103** HJ 3
David **108** B 2
Davis (Antarctica) **115**
Davis (CA, U.S.A.) **102** B 4
Davis Inlet **101** P 4
Davis Sea **115**
Davis Strait **101** Q 2
Dawḥat as Salwā (Bahrain) **61** F 4
Dawson **98** K 3
Dawson Creek **99** N 4
Dawu **70** D 4
Dayangshu **69** M 6
Dayong **70** EF 5
Dayr az Zawr (Syria) **60** C 2
Dayr az Zawr (Syria) **89** FG 1
Dayrūt **88** DE 3
Dayton **103** K 4
Daytona Beach **103** KL 6
Dazhu **70** E 4
Dazjā (Iran) **61** G 2
De Aar **94** C 6
Dead Sea **88** EF 2
Dead Sea (Jordan) **60** B 3
Deán Funes **112** CD 5
Dease Lake **98** L 4
Dease Strait **99** Q 2
Death Valley **102** C 4
Death Valley National Monument **102** C 4
Débo, Lac **90** D 2
Deboyne Island **81** F 4
Debra Birhan **93** F 3
Debra Markos **93** F 2
Debra Zeit **93** F 3
Debrecen **58** B 1
Decatur (AL, U.S.A.) **103** J 5
Decatur (IL, U.S.A.) **103** J 4
Deccan **72** CD 3–5
Decepción **115**
Dechang **70** D 5
Dédougou **90** D 3
Dedza **95** E 2
Deering, Mount **78** D 3
Deer Lake **101** Q 6
Dêgê **70** C 4
de Gras, Lac **99** P 3
Deh Bīd (Iran) **61** F 3
Deh Bīd (Iran) **66** E 4
Dehdez (Iran) **61** F 3
Dehlorān **66** D 4
Dehra Dun **72** C 1
Deh Shū **67** G 4
Dej **58** B 1

De Kalb **103** J 3
Delaware **103** M 4
Del Campillo **112** D 5
Del City **102** G 4
Delegate **79** H 6
Delgado, Cabo **95** G 2
Delgerhaan **68** HJ 6
Delgerhet **70** F 1
Delgertsogt **70** E 1
Delhi **72** C 2
Deličal Dağı **58** C 2–3
Delicias **102** E 6
Delījān (Iran) **61** F 2
Delījān (Iran) **66** E 4
Delphi **58** B 3
Delta Dunării **58** CD 1
Delta Junction **98** HJ 3
Demavend, Mount (Iran) **61** F 2
Demba **92** C 6
Dembia **92** C 3
Dempo, Gunung **74** B 4
Dem'yanovka **63** N 5
Dem'yanskoye **63** N 4
Denali National Park and Preservative **98** GH 3
Denau **67** H 3
Den Helder **52** D 4
Denison (TX, U.S.A.) **103** G 5
Denizli **58** C 3
Denkou **70** E 2
Denmark **55** E 4
Denmark Strait **114**
Dennison, Cape **115**
Denpasar **74** D 5
Denton **103** G 5
D'Entrecasteaux Islands **81** F 3
D'Entrecasteaux Islands **82** B 3
Denver **102** F 4
Deogarh **72** D 3
Deoghar **72** E 3
Deolali **72** B 4
Depósita **109** F 3
Deqing **70** F 6
Derbent **66** D 2
Derby (Australia) **78** C 2
Derby (U.K.) **52** C 4
Derdap **58** B 2
Dergachi **62** J 5
Dermott **103** H 5
Derudeb **88** F 5
Deryabino **63** Q 1
Derzhavinsk **63** N 5
Désappointement, Îles du **83** F 3
Desengaño, Punta **113** C 8
Desierto de Atacama **110** C 5
Desierto de Sechura **108** B 5
Des Moines **103** H 3
Desolación, Isla **113** AB 9
Desrouches, Île **93** J 6
Dessau **53** F 4
Dessye **93** FG 2
Detroit **103** K 3
Détroit de Jaques-Cartier **101** P 6
Détroit d'Honguedo **101** OP 6
Deutsche Bucht **53** E 4
Deutsche Demokratische Republik (D.D.R.) **53** F 4
Deva **58** B 1
Devil's Island **109** H 2
Devils Lake **102** G 2
Devon Island **114**
Devonport **82** A 5
Devonport (Tasmania, Austr.) **80** L 9
Devrez **59** D 2
Deyang **70** D 4
Dezfūl (Iran) **61** E 2
Dezfūl (Iran) **66** D 4
Dez Gerd (Iran) **61** F 3
Dezhou **71** G 3
Dhahab (Egypt) **60** B 3
Dhamār **89** G 6
Dhamtari **72** D 3
Dharwar **72** B 4
Dhaulagiri **72** D 2
Dhelfoí **58** B 3
Dhíavlos Zakínthou **58** B 3
Dhirfis Óros **58** B 3
Dhoraji **72** B 3
Dhule **72** B 3
Diable, Île du **109** H 2
Diaca **95** F 2
Diamantina (Minas Gerais, Brazil) **111** H 4
Diamantina (Queensland, Austr.) **79** G 3
Diamantina Lakes **79** G 3
Diamond Jenness Peninsula **99** OP 1
Dianjiang **70** E 4
Dibrugarh **73** FG 2
Dicle **66** C 3
Didiéni **90** C 3
Didyma **58** C 3
Diéma **90** C 3
Dieppe **56** D 2
Dihang **70** C 5
Dijlāh (Iraq) **61** D 2
Dijon **57** E 2
Dıkmen Dağı **59** D 2
Dikson **114**
Dilaram **67** G 4
Di Linh **74** C 1
Dilj **57** G 2
Dilling **88** D 6
Dilolo **94** C 2
Dimashq (Syria) **60** B 2
Dimashq (Syria) **88** F 2
Dimbokro **90** D 4
Dimitrovgrad (Bulgaria) **58** C 2
Dimitrovgrad (U.S.S.R.) **62** JK 5
Dimona (Israel) **60** B 3
Dinagat **75** G 1
Dinajpur **72** E 2
Dinara Planina **57** G 3
Dinder National Park **88** F 6
Dindigul **72** C 5
Dingbian **70** E 3
Dingxi **70** DE 3
Dingxian **70** FG 3
Dinokwe **94** D 4
Dionísio Cerqueira **112** F 4
Diourbel **90** A 3
Dipkarpas (Cyprus) **60** B 2
Dipolog **75** F 2
Diré **90** D 2
Diredawa **93** G 3
Dirico **94** C 3
Dirk Hartog Island **78** A 4
Disappointment, Lake **78** C 3
Dishnā (Egypt) **60** A 4
Disko **114**
Disko Bugt **114**
Disna **55** J 4
District of Fort Smith **99** P 3
District of Inuvik **98** LM 2
District of Keewatin **99** SU 2–3
Distrito Federal **111** G 4
Diu **72** B 3
Dīvāndareeh (Iran) **61** E 1
Divinopolis **111** GH 5
Divo **90** C 4
Dixon Entrance **98** L 5
Diyālā (Iraq) **61** D 2
Diyarbakır **59** F 3
Djanet **87** G 4
Djelfa **87** F 2
Djibouti **93** G 2
Djibouti **93** G 2
Djougou **90** E 4
Dneprodzerzhinsk **59** D 1
Dnepropetrovsk **59** E 1
Dneprovskiy Liman **58** D 1
Dnestr **58** C 1
Doba (Chad) **91** H 4
Dobreta Turnu Severin **58** B 2
Dobrogea **58** C 2
Dobrowolski **115**
Dobrudžansko Plato **58** C 2
Dodecanese **58** C 3
Dodge City **102** F 4
Dodoma **93** FG 6
Dogger Bank **52** D 4
Dogondoutchi **91** EF 3
Doguéraoua **91** F 3
Doğu Karadeniz Dağlari **59** EF 2
Doha (Qatar) **61** F 4
Doha (Qatar) **89** J 4
Dohad **72** B 3
Doi Inthanon **73** G 4
Doilungdêqen **73** F 1–2
Dôle **57** E 2
Dolo **93** G 4
Dolores (Argentina) **113** E 6
Dolphin and Union Strait **99** OP 2
Doma Peaks **80** D 3
Dom Aquino **111** F 4
Dominica **105** K 4
Dominican Republic **105** J 3–4
Dompu **75** E 5
Don (U.S.S.R.) **62** H 6
Don Benito **56** B 4
Dondo (Mozambique) **95** EF 3
Dondra Head **72** D 6
Donegal Bay **52** B 4
Donegal Mountains **52** B 4
Donetsk **59** E 1
Donetskiy Kryazh **59** EF 1
Dongara **78** B 4
Dongchuan **70** D 5
Dongfang **70** E 7
Dong Hai **71** HJ 5
Dongning **71** JK 2
Dongo (Angola) **94** B 2
Dongoura **90** BC 3
Dongping **71** G 3
Dongsheng **70** EF 3
Dongting Hu **70** F 5
Dong Ujimqin Qi **71** G 1
Dongxiang **70** FG 5
Dönna **54** F 2
Doramarkog **70** C 4
Dordrecht **52** D 4
Dori **90** D 3
Dornogovĭ **70** EF 2
Döröö Nuur **68** F 6
Dortmund **53** E 4
Dosso **90** E 3
Dothan **103** J 5
Douala **91** FG 5
Douentza **90** D 3
Douglas (AZ, U.S.A.) **102** E 5
Douglas (U.K.) **52** C 4
Douglas (WY, U.S.A.) **102** EF 3
Doumbouene **91** J 3
Dourados **111** F 5
Douro **56** B 3
Dover (U.K.) **52** D 4
Dovrefjell **54** E 3
Dowlatābād **66** F 5
Dow Rūd (Iran) **61** E 2
Dow Sar (Iran) **61** E 2
Drakensberg (Lesotho) **94** D 5–6
Drake Passage **115**
Drake Strait **113** CD 10
Dráma **58** B 2
Drammen **55** F 4
Drau **57** F 2
Drava **57** G 2
Dresden **53** F 4
Dreux **56** D 2
Drini **58** B 2
Drumheller **99** P 5
Drummondville **101** N 6
Druzhnaya **115**
Druzhnaya II **115**
Dryden **100** J 6
Drysdale River National Park **78** D 2
Dschang **91** F 4
Duaringa **79** HJ 3
Dubawnt Lake **99** R 3
Dubayy (United Arab Emirates) **61** G 4
Dubbo **79** H 5
Dublin (Rep. of Ireland) **52** B 4
Dubna **62** G 4
Dubno **55** J 5
Dubovskoye **59** F 1
Dubrovitsa **55** J 5
Dubrovnik **57** G 3
Dubrovnoye **63** NO 4
Dubuque **103** H 3
Duc de Gloucester, Îles du **83** F 4
Ducie **83** G 4
du Couedic, Cape **79** F 6
Dudhi **72** D 3
Dudinka **63** R 2
Dudley **52** C 4
Duékoué **90** C 4
Duero **56** C 3
Duff Islands **82** C 3
Dugi Otok **57** F 3
Duisburg **52** E 4

Duitama **108** D 2
Dukān (Iraq) **61** D 2
Dukhān (Qatar) **61** F 4
Dukou **70** D 5
Dukwe **94** D 4
Dulan **70** C 3
Dulga-Kyuyel' **68** K 3
Duluth **103** H 2
Dūmā (Syria) **60** B 2
Dumaguete **75** F 2
Dumfries **52** C 3
Dumont d'Urville **115**
Dumpu **82** A 3
Dumyāt **88** E 2
Duna **58** A 1
Dunántúl **58** A 1
Dunaujváros **58** A 1
Dunav **58** B 2
Dunbar (Australia) **79** G 2
Dunbar (U.K.) **52** C 3
Dundalk **52** B 4
Dundalk Bay **52** B 4
Dundas Peninsula **99** P 1
Dundee (U.K.) **52** C 3
Dundgovĭ **70** E 1
Dunedin **81** Q 10
Dunedin **82** C 6
Dunhua **71** J 2
Dunhuang **70** B 2
Dunkerque **56** D 1
Dunkwa **90** D 4
Dún Laoghaire **52** B 4
Dunmarra **78** E 2
Dunqulah al 'Ordi **88** DE 5
Duolun **71** G 2
Durack Range **78** D 2
Dura Europos (Syria) **60** C 2
Durance **57** E 3
Durango (CO, U.S.A.) **102** E 4
Durango (Mexico) **104** AB 3
Duratón **56** C 3
Durban **95** E 5
Durg **72** D 3
Durgapur (India) **72** E 3
Durham (N.C., U.S.A.) **103** L 4
Durmā (Saudi Arabia) **61** E 4
Ḍurmā (Saudi Arabia) **66** D 6
Duroy **68** L 5
Durresi **58** A 2
D'Urville Sea **115**
Dushan **70** E 5
Dushanbe **67** H 3
Düsseldorf **52** E 4
Dutch Harbor **98** D 5
Duwayhin **66** E 6
Duye **92** D 4
Düzce **58** D 2
Dvina, Severnaya **62** H 3
Dwarka **72** A 3
Dyadmo **68** J 4
Dyrhólaey **54** B 3
Dyurmen'tobe **67** GH 1
Dzerzhinsk **62** H 4
Dzhagdy, Khrebet **69** O 5
Dzhalinda **69** M 5
Dzhambul **67** J 2
Dzhankoy **59** D 1
Dzhanybek **62** J 6
Dzhelinde **68** K 1
Dzhetygara **63** M 5
Dzhezkazgan **63** N 6
Dzhigudzhak **69** ST 3
Dzhirgatal' **67** J 3
Dzhugdzhur, Khrebet **69** OP 4
Dzhunkun **68** K 3
Dzhusaly **67** GH 1

E

Eagle (Seychelles) **98** J 3
Eagle Pass **102** FG 6
Eagle Peak **102** BC 3
East Antarctica **115**
East Cape **81** R 8
East China Sea **71** HJ 5
Easter Island **83** H 4
Eastern Ghats **72** CD 3–5
East Falkland **113** E 9
East London **94** CD 6
Eastmain **101** M 5
East Point **103** JK 5
Eastport **103** N 3
East Siberian Sea **114**
Eau Claire **103** H 3
Eauripik **82** A 2
Ebe **69** Q 3
Eberswalde **53** F 4
Eboli **57** G 3
Ebolowa **91** G 5
Ebon **82** C 2
Ebyakh **69** S 2
Ech Cheliff **87** F 1
Echmiadzin **59** F 2
Echo Bay **99** O 2
Écija **56** B 4
Ecuador **108** B 4
Edéa **91** FG 5
Edel Land **78** A 4
Edgeöya **114**
Edinburgh **52** C 3
Edirne **58** C 2
Edmonds **102** B 2
Edmonton **99** OP 5
Edremit **58** C 3
Edward, Lake **92** D 5
Edwards Plateau **102** FG 5–6
Efaté **81** J 5
Efate **82** C 4
Efes **58** C 3
Egersund **55** E 4
Egilsstaðir **54** C 2
Eglab Dersa **86** E 3
Egmont, Mount **81** Q 8
Eğridir Gölü **58** D 3
Egvekinot **98** B 2
Egypt **60** A 4
Egypt **88** DE 4
Eiao **83** F 3
Eidfjord **55** E 3
Eifel **52** E 4
Eights Coast **115**
Eighty Mile Beach **78** BC 2
Eire **52** B 4
Eirunepé **108** D 5
Eisenach **53** F 4
Eisenhüttenstadt **53** FG 4
Ejin Qi **70** D 2
Ekibastuz **63** P 5
Ekoli **92** C 5
Ekwan **100** L 5
El Aaiún **86** C 3
El Adeb Larache **87** G 3
El Alamo **102** C 5
Elat (Israel) **60** B 3
Elat (Israel) **88** EF 3
Elâzığ **59** E 3
Elba **57** F 3
El'ban **69** P 5
El Banco **108** D 2
Elbasani **58** B 2
El Bayadh **87** F 2
Elbe **53** F 4
Elbeyli (Turkey) **59** E 3
Elbeyli (Turkey) **60** B 1
Elbląg **53** G 4
Elbrus **59** F 2
'El Būr **93** H 4
Elburz Mountains (Iran) **61** F 1
Elburz Mountains (Iran) **66** EF 3
El Cajon **102** C 5
El Cerro **110** D 4
Elche **56** C 4
El Cuy **113** C 6
Elda **56** C 4
'El Ḍēre **93** H 4
El Difícil **108** D 2
El Diviso **108** C 3
El Djouf **86** CD 4
El Dorado (AR, U.S.A.) **103** H 5
Eldorado (Argentina) **112** EF 4
El Dorado (KS, U.S.A.) **103** G 4
El Dorado (Mexico) **102** E 7
El Dorado (Venezuela) **109** F 2
Eldoret **92** EF 4
Elektrostal' **62** GH 4
Elemi Triangle **92** EF 4
El Encanto **108** D 4
Elephant Island **115**
Elesbão Veloso **111** H 2
El Escorial **56** C 3
Eleuthera Island **105** G 2
El Fasher **88** CD 6
El Ferrol del Candillo **56** B 3
El'gakan **69** M 4
Elghena **93** F 1
El Goléa **87** F 2
Elgon, Mount **92** EF 4
'El Ḥamurre **93** H 3
El Homr **87** F 3
Elisenvaara **54** JK 3
Elista **59** F 1
Elizabeth **79** F 5
El Jadida **86** D 2
Ełk **53** H 4
Elk City **102** G 4
El Kharga → Al Khārijah **88** DE 3
Elkhart **103** J 3
Elko **102** C 3
Ellef Ringnes Island **114**
Ellensburg **102** BC 2
Ellesmere Island **114**
Ellice Islands **82** C 3
Elliot (Australia) **78** E 2
Elliot (South Africa) **94** D 6
Elliot, Mount **79** H 2
Ellsworth Land **115**
Ellsworth Mountains **115**
El Maestrazgo **56** CD 3
El Maitén **113** B 7
El Medo **93** G 3
El Messir **91** H 2
Elmhurst **103** J 3
Elmira **103** L 3
El Mirador **104** DE 4
El Mreiti **86** D 4
El Obeid **88** DE 6
El Oued **87** G 2
El Paso **102** E 5
El Progreso **104** E 4
El Puerto **102** D 6
El Puerto de Santa Maria **56** B 4
El Salvador **104** DE 5
El Sueco **102** E 6
El Tigre (Venezuela) **109** F 2
El Tránsito **112** B 4
El Tunal **112** D 3–4
Eluru **72** D 4
El Valle **108** C 2
Elvas **56** B 4
Elvira **108** D 5
Ely (NV, U.S.A.) **102** D 4
Emamrud (Iran) **61** G 1
Emamshar **66** F 3
Emba **66** F 1
Embalse de Alcántara **56** B 4
Embalse de Almendra **56** B 3
Embalse del Ebro **56** C 3
Embalse de Mequinenza **56** C 3
Embarcación **110** D 5
Embarras Portage **99** P 4
Emden **53** E 4
Emel'dzak **69** N 4
Emerald **79** H 3
Emi **68** G 5
Emi Koussi **91** HJ 2
Empalme **102** D 6
Empedrado (Argentina) **112** E 4
Ems **53** E 4
Encarnación **112** E 4
Enda Salassie **93** F 2
Ende **75** F 5
Enderbury **82** D 3
Enderby Land **115**
Endicott Mountains **98** GH 2
Engaño, Cape **75** J 1
Engel's **62** J 5
Enggano, Pulau **74** B 5
England **52** D 4
English Channel **52** BC 4–5
Engozero **54** K 2
Enid **102** G 4
Eniwetok **82** B 2
Enkan **69** Q 4
Enköping **55** G 4
Enmore **109** G 2
Ennadai **99** R 3
Ennedi **91** J 2
Enontekiö **54** H 2
Enrekang **75** EF 4
Enschede **53** E 4
Ensenada **102** C 5
Enshi **70** EF 4
Entebbe **92** E 4
Entre Rios (Pará, Brazil) **109** H 5
Enugu **91** F 4
Enugu Ezike **91** F 4
Enurmino **98** C 2
Envigado **108** CD 2
Envira **108** D 5
Épernay **56** D 2

Ephesus **58** C 3
Epi **81** J 5
Épinal **57** E 2
Équateur **92** BC 4
Equatoria **92** DE 3–4
Equatorial Guinea **91** F 5
Erbil **89** G 1
Erbil (Iraq) **60** D 1
Érd **58** A 1
Erechim **112** F 4
Ereentsav **68** L 6
Ereğli (Turkey) **59** D 3
Erenhot **70** F 2
Eresma **56** C 3
Erfurt **53** F 4
Erg Brusset **91** FG 2
Erg Chech **86** E 3–4
Erg de Ténéré **91** FG 2
Erg Iguidi **86** DE 3
Ergun He **68** M 5
Ergun Zuoqi **69** M 5
Eriba **88** F 5
Eric **101** O 5
Erie **103** K 3
Erie, Lake **103** K 3
'Erigâbo **93** H 2
Erikub **82** C 2
Erimbet **67** G 2
Eritrea **93** FG 2
Ermelo **94** DE 5
Ernest Legouvé **83** E 5
Erode **72** C 5
Erongo **94** B 4
Erongo Mountains **94** B 4
Erozionnyy **69** R 2
Errego **95** F 3
Erromanga **82** C 4
Erromango **81** J 5
Ertai **67** N 1
Erzgebirge **53** F 4
Erzincan **59** E 3
Erzurum **59** F 3
Erzurum-Kars Yaylâsı **59** F 2
Esbjerg **55** E 4
Escanaba **103** J 2
Eschan **69** R 3
Escondido **102** C 5
Escuintla **104** D 5
Esfahan (Iran) **61** F 2
Esfahān (Iran) **66** E 4
Eskilstuna **55** G 4
Eskimo Point **99** T 3
Eskişehir **58** D 3
Eslamabad (Iran) **61** E 2
Eslöv **55** F 4
Esmeralda, Isla **113** A 8
Esmeraldas **108** BC 3
España **56** C 4
Esperance Bay **78** C 5
Esperanza (Antarctica) **115**
Espinal (Bolivia) **110** E 4
Espinal (Colombia) **108** D 3
Espinar **110** B 3
Espírito Santo **111** HJ 4
Espiritu Santo **81** J 5
Espiritu Santo **82** BC 4
Esplanada **111** J 3
Espoo (Esbo) **55** H 3–4
Esquel **113** B 7
Essaouira **86** CD 2
Essen **53** E 4
Essendon, Mount **78** C 3
Estados, Isla de los **113** D 9
Estância **111** J 3
Estelí **104** E 5
Esteros **110** D 5
Estevan **99** R 6
Estoniya **55** HJ 4
Estrecho de Gibraltar **56** B 4
Estrecho de le Maire **113** CD 9–10
Estrecho de Magallanes **113** B 9
Estrêla, Serra de (Portugal) **56** B 3
Estremadura **56** B 4
Estrondo, Serra do **109** J 5
Esztergom **58** A 1
Ethiopia **93** FG 3
Ethiopian Plateau **93** FG 3
Etna **57** FG 4
Etosha Namib Desert Park **94** B 3
Etosha Pan **94** B 3
Eugene **102** B 3
Eugenia, Punta **102** C 6
Eugmo **54** H 3
Eungella National Park **79** HJ 3
Euphrates (Iraq) **59** FG 2–4
Euphrates (Iraq) **60** C 2
Eureka (CA, U.S.A.) **102** B 3
Everest, Mount **72** E 2
Everett **102** B 2
Everett Mountains **101** O 3
Everglades National Park **103** K 6
Évora **56** B 4
Evreux **56** D 2
Evvoia **58** B 3
Ewasse **81** F 3
Executive Committee Range **115**
Exeter **52** C 4
Exmouth (Australia) **78** A 3
Extremadura **56** B 4
Eyre **78** D 5
Eyre Peninsula **79** F 5
Eysturoy **52** A 1
Ezop, Gora **69** S 3

F

Fabala **90** C 4
Fabriano **57** F 3
Fada **91** J 2
Faenza **57** F 3
Faeroe Islands **52** A 1
Făgăraş **58** BC 1
Fairbanks **98** GH 3
Fair Isle **52** C 3
Fairmont (W.V., U.S.A.) **103** L 4
Fairview **79** G 2
Faisalabad **67** J 4
Faizabad (Afghanistan) **67** J 3
Faizabad (India) **72** D 2
Fakaina **83** F 4
Fakaofo **82** D 3
Fakarava **83** F 4
Faku **71** H 2
Falagh **92** E 3
Falkenberg **55** F 4
Falkland Islands **113** DE 9
Falkland Sound **113** DE 9
Fallon **102** C 4
Fall River **103** M 3
Falls City **103** G 3
Falmouth **52** B 4
Falster **55** G 4
Falun **55** G 3
Famagusta (Cyprus) **59** D 3
Fana **90** C 3
Fangataufa **83** F 4
Fangzheng **71** JK 1
Faraday **115**
Faradje **92** D 4
Farafangana **95** H 4
Farah **67** G 4
Farallon de Medinilla **82** A 1
Farallon de Pajaros **82** A 1
Faranah **90** B 3
Faraulep **82** A 2
Farewell, Cape **81** Q 9
Fargo (N.D., U.S.A.) **102** G 2
Faridpur **72** E 3
Färjestaden **55** G 4
Farmington (N.M., U.S.A.) **102** E 4
Fårö **55** G 4
Faro **109** G 4
Faro (Portugal) **56** B 4
Farquhar Group **93** J 6
Fārs (Iran) **61** F 3
Fartak, Ra's **89** J 5
Fasā (Iran) **61** F 3
Fasano **57** G 3
Fastov **62** E 6
Fataka **82** C 3
Fatehgarh **72** CD 2
Făurei **58** C 1
Faxaflói **54** A 3
Faxälven **54** G 3
Faya-Largeau **91** HJ 2
Fayetteville (AR, U.S.A.) **103** H 4
Fayetteville (N.C., U.S.A.) **103** KL 5
Faysh Khābur (Iraq) **60** D 1
Fayu **82** B 2
Fazilka **72** B 1
Fdérik **86** C 4
Fear, Cape **103** L 5
Feathertop, Mount **79** H 6
Federal Republic of Germany **53** E 4
Federated States of Micronesia **82** AB 2
Fehmarn **53** F 4
Feijó **108** D 5
Feira de Santana **111** J 3
Feklistova, Ostrov **69** P 4–5
Felipe Carrillo Puerto **104** E 4
Fengcheng **71** HJ 2
Fengjie **70** EF 4
Fengqing **70** CD 6
Fengshui Shan **69** M 5
Feni Islands **81** F 2
Fenoarivo Atsinanana **95** HJ 3
Fensfjorden **54** DE 3
Fenyang **70** F 3
Feodosiya **59** DE 1
Fer, Cap de **87** G 1
Ferfer **93** H 3
Fergana **67** J 2
Fergus Falls **103** G 2
Fergusson **81** F 3
Ferjukot **54** A 3
Ferkéssédougou **90** C 4
Fernando de Noronha Island **107** G 3
Fernandópolis **111** F 5
Fernando Póo → Bioko **91** F 5
Ferrara **57** F 3
Ferreira Gomes **109** H 3
Fès **86** E 2
Fethiye **58** C 3
Fezzan **87** HJ 3
Fianarantsoa **95** H 4
Fierras **54** G 2
Fiji **82** C 4
Fiji Islands **82** C 4
Filadélfia (Paraguay) **110** E 5
Filchner Ice Shelf **115**
Fimbul Ice Shelf **115**
Fimi **92** B 5
Findlay **103** K 3
Finisterre, Cabo de **56** B 3
Finke **78** E 4
Finke, Mount **78** E 5
Finke Gorge National Park **78** E 3
Finland **54** J 3
Finland, Gulf of **55** H 4
Finnmark **54** H 2
Finnmarksvidda **54** H 2
Finnsnes **54** G 2
Finnveden **55** F 4
Finspång **55** G 4
Fiordland National Park **80** P 9–10
Fırat **59** E 3
Firenze **57** F 3
Firminy **56** D 2
Firozabad **72** CD 2
Firth of Forth **52** C 3
Fīrūzābād **66** E 5
Fīrūz Kūh (Iran) **61** F 2
Fisher Strait **99** UV 3
Fishguard **52** B 4
Fiskenæsset **101** R 3
Fitzcarrald **110** B 3
Fitzgerald River National Park **78** B 5
Fitzroy Crossing **78** CD 2
Fitzroy River (Queensland, Austr.) **79** HJ 3
Fitzroy River (Western Australia) **78** C 2
Fizi **92** D 5
Flagstaff **102** D 4
Flamenco (Chile) **112** B 4
Flåsjön **54** G 3
Flattery, Cape (WA, U.S.A.) **102** AB 2
Flensburg **53** E 4
Flinders Chase National Park **79** F 6
Flinders Passage **79** H 2
Flinders Range **79** F 5
Flinders Ranges National Park **79** FG 5
Flinders River **79** G 2
Flin Flon **99** R 5
Flint (Kiribati) **83** E 3
Flint (MI, U.S.A.) **103** K 3
Flisa **55** F 3

Floraville (Queensland, Austr.) **79** F 2
Florence (AL, U.S.A.) **103** J 5
Florence (Italy) **57** F 3
Florencia **108** CD 3
Flores (Guatemala) **104** E 4
Flores (Indonesia) **75** F 5
Flores, Laut **75** E 5
Floriano **111** H 2
Floriano Pleixotc **108** E 5
Florianópolis **112** G 4
Florida (Cuba) **105** G 3
Florida (U.S.A.) **103** KL 6
Floridablanca **108** D 2
Florida Keys **103** L 6–7
Fluk **75** G 4
Fly River **80** D 3
Foci del Po **57** F 3
Focşani **58** C 1
Foggia **57** G 3
Fogo (Cape Verde) **90** B 7
Foleyet **100** L 6
Folkstone **52** D 4
Fond du Lac (WI, U.S.A.) **103** J 3
Fonte Boa **108** E 4
Fonte do Pau-d'Agua **110** E 3
Fonualei **82** D 4
Forbes **79** H 5
Forêt d'Ecouves **56** C 2
Forín Linares **110** D 5
Forkas **90** E 3
Forli **57** F 3
Formentera **56** D 4
Formentor, Cabo de **56** D 3–4
Formosa (Goiás, Brazil) **111** G 4
Formosa (Taiwan) **71** H 6
Formosa, Serra **111** EF 3
Formosa Strait **71** GH 5–6
Formoso (Argentina) **112** E 4
Fornæs **55** F 4
Forrest **78** D 5
Forsayth **79** G 2
Forsnäs **54** G 2
Forssa **55** H 3
Fortaleza (Ceará, Brazil) **111** J 1
Fort Chimo **101** NO 4
Fort Chipewyan **99** PQ 4
Fort Collins **102** EF 3
Fort-de-France **105** K 5
Fort Dodge **103** H 3
Fort Frances **100** J 6
Fort Franklin **99** N 2
Fort George **101** M 5
Forth, Firth of **52** C 3
Fortin Coronel Eugenio Garay **110** D 5
Fortín Ingavi **110** DE 4
Fortín Madrejón **110** E 5
Fortín Ravelo **110** D 4
Fortín Suárez Arana **110** D 4
Fort Lauderdale **103** L 6
Fort Liard **99** N 3
Fort Mackay **99** P 4
Fort McMurray **99** P 4
Fort Miribel **87** F 3
Fort Morgan **102** F 3
Fort Myers **103** K 6
Fort Nelson **99** N 4
Fort Norman **99** M 3
Fort Peck Dam **102** E 2
Fort Peck Lake **102** E 2
Fort Pierce **103** KL 6
Fort Portal **92** DE 4
Fort Providence **99** O 3
Fort Randell Dam **102** FG 3
Fort Resolution **99** P 3
Fort Rupert **101** M 5
Fort Saint John **99** N 4
Fort Severn **100** K 4
Fort Shevchenko **66** E 2
Fort Simpson **99** N 3
Fort Smith (OK, U.S.A.) **103** H 4–5
Fort Stockton **102** F 5
Fortune Bay **101** Q 6
Fort Vermilion **99** O 4
Fort Wayne **103** J 3
Fort Wellington **109** G 2
Fort William **52** BC 3
Fort Worth **102** G 5
Forveaux Strait **82** C 6
Foshan **70** F 6
Fosna **54** F 3
Foso **90** D 4
Fossano **57** E 3
Fossil Bluff **115**
Fougamou **91** G 6
Fougères **56** C 2
Fouladou **90** AB 3
Foumban **91** G 4
Fourmies **56** D 1
Four Mountains, Islands of **98** CD 5
Fouta Djallon **90** B 3
Fouta Ferlo **90** B 2
Foveaux Strait **80** P 10
Fowlers Bay **78** E 5
Fowlers Bay **78** E 5
Foxe Basin **99** VW 2
Foxe Channel **101** M 3
Foxe Peninsula **101** M 3
Fox Islands **98** D 5
Foz do Breu **108** D 5
Franca **111** G 5
France **56** CD 2
Franceville **91** G 6
Francisco de Orellana (Ecuador) **108** C 4
Francisco Escárcega **104** D 4
Francistown **94** D 4
Francs Peak **102** E 3
Frankfurt am Main **53** E 4
Franklin Mountains **99** MN 2–3
Franklin Strait **99** S 1
Fransisco de Orellana (Peru) **108** D 4
Franz Josef Land **114**
Fraser **99** N 5
Fraser or Great Sandy Island **79** J 4
Fraser Plateau **99** N 5
Fredericia **55** EF 4
Fredericton **101** O 6
Frederik IX-Land **101** R 2
Frederiksdal **101** S 3
Frederikshavn **55** EF 4
Frederiksh✕b **101** R 3
Frederik VI-Coast **114**
Fredrika **54** G 3
Fredrikstad **55** F 4
Freetown **90** B 4
Freiburg **53** E 5
Fréjus **57** E 3
French Guiana **109** H 3
French Polynesia **83** EF 4
Fresnillo **104** B 3
Fresno **102** BC 4
Freycinet Peninsula **80** L 9
Fria, Cape **94** A 3
Friesland **52–53** E 4
Frio, Cabo **111** H 5
Frisian Islands **52** E 4
Frobisher Bay **101** O 3
Frobisher Lake **99** Q 4
Frolovo **62** H 6
Fronteiras **111** H 2
Front Range **102** E 3–4
Fröya **54** E 3
Frunze **67** J 2
Fu'an **71** G 5
Fuding **71** H 5
Fuerte Olimpo **110** E 5
Fuerteventura **86** C 3
Fujian **71** G 5
Fujin **69** O 6
Fukui **71** L 3
Fukuoka **71** JK 4
Fukushima **71** LM 2
Fukushima **71** M 3
Fukuyama **71** K 3–4
Funafuti **82** CD 3
Funchal **86** B 2
Funiu Shan **70** F 4
Funtua **91** F 3
Fuqing **71** GH 5
Furancungo **95** E 2
Furmanovka **67** J 2
Furmanovo **62** JK 6
Furneaux Group **80** L 9
Furneaux Group **82** A 5
Fürth **53** F 5
Fusagasugá **108** D 3
Fushun **71** HJ 2
Fusong **71** J 2
Futuna (Vanuatu) **82** C 4
Futuna (Wallis and Futuna) **82** D 3
Fuxin **71** H 2
Fuyang **70** G 4
Fuyuan (China) **70** D 5
Fuyun **67** M 1
Fuzhou **71** GH 5
Fyn **55** F 4

G

Gabela **94** A 2
Gabès **87** H 2
Gabon **91** FG 6
Gaborone **94** CD 4
Gabriel Strait **101** O 3
Gach Sārān (Iran) **61** F 3
Gadag **72** C 4
Gadame **92** E 3
Gadsden **103** J 5
Gaeta **57** F 3
Gaferut **82** A 2
Gagnoa **90** C 4
Gagnon **101** O 5
Gahkom **61** G 3
Gaimán **113** C 7
Gainesville (FL, U.S.A.) **103** K 6
Gairdner, Lake **79** F 5
Gakarosa **94** C 5
Gakona **98** H 3
Galán, Cerro **112** C 4
Galanino **68** F 4
Galápagos Islands **108** B 6
Galathea Deep **82** D 5
Galaţi **58** C 1
Galatina **57** G 3
Galdhöpiggen **54** E 3
Galena **98** F 3
Galesburg **103** HJ 3
Galicia (Poland) **53** H 5
Galicia (Spain) **56** B 3
Galimyy **69** ST 3
Gālka'yo **93** H 3
Galle **72** CD 6
Gallinas, Punta **108** D 1
Gällivare **54** H 2
Gallo, Capo **57** F 4
Gallup **102** E 4
Galole **93** F 5
Galveston **103** H 6
Galvez **112** D 5
Galway **52** B 4
Gamba (Gabon) **91** F 6
Gambia **90** AB 3
Gambier Islands **83** FG 4
Gamboma **91** H 6
Gamboola **79** G 2
Gamvik **54** J 1
Ganāveh **66** E 5
Ganāveh (Iran) **61** F 3
Gandadiwata, Bukit **75** EF 4
Gandhi Sagar Dam **72** C 3
Gandía **56** CD 4
Ganetti **88** E 5
Ganga **72** E 2
Ganga, Mouths of the **72–73** EF 3
Gangan **113** C 7
Gangapur **72** C 2
Gangdisê Shan **72** DE 1
Ganges **72** E 3
Ganina Gar' **68** F 4
Gannett Peak **102** E 3
Gansu **70** DE 3
Ganta **90** C 4
Ganzhou **70** FG 5
Gao **90** D 2
Gao'an **70** FG 5
Gaona **112** D 4
Gaoping **70** F 3
Gaoua **90** D 3
Gaoual **90** B 3
Gaozhou **70** EF 6
Gap **57** E 3
Garanhuns **111** J 2
Garbokaray **68** G 5
Garbosh, Kūh-e (Iran) **61** EF 2
Garda, Lago di **57** F 2
Gardaneh-ye Āvej (Iran) **61** E 2
Gardaneh-ye Kandovān (Iran) **61** F 1
Gardaneh-ye Khāneh Sorkh (Iran) **61** G 3
Gardemoen **55** F 3
Gargano, Promontorio del **57** G 3
Garissa **93** FG 5
Garmisch-Partenkirchen **53** F 5

Garmsar (Iran) 61 F 2
Garmsar (Iran) 66 E 3
Garonne,56 D 3
Garoua (Cameroon) 91 G 4
Garoua Boulai 91 GH 4
Garöwe 93 H 3
Garri, Kūh-e (Iran) 61 E 2
Garry Lake 99 R 2
Garwa 72 D 3
Gary 103 J 3
Garze 70 C 4
Gascogne 56 CD 3
Gascoyne Junction 78 B 3–4
Gashagar 91 G 3
Gashua 91 G 3
Gaspé 101 OP 6
Gassi Touil 87 G 2
Gastello, Iméni 69 R 3
Gästrikland 55 G 3
Gata, Sierra de 56 B 3
Gatchina 55 JK 4
Gates of the Arctic National Park and Preserve 98 G 2
Gauhati 73 F 2
Gauja 55 H 4
Gausta 55 E 4
Gavanka 69 T 4
Gávdhos 58 B 4
Gave de Pau 56 C 3
Gävle 55 G 3
Gävlebukten 55 G 3
Gaya (India) 72 E 3
Gayndah 79 J 4
Gaza Strip 60 AB 3
Gazelle Peninsula 81 F 2
Gaziantep (Turkey) 59 E 3
Gaziantep (Turkey) 60 B 1
Gaziantep Yaylası 59 E 3
Gazimurskiy Zavod 68 L 5
Gazıpaşa (Turkey) 60 A 1
Gbarnga 90 C 4
Gdańsk 53 G 4
Gdynia 53 G 4
Gearhart Mountain 102 B 3
Gedi 93 F 5
Gediz 58 C 3
Geelong 79 G 6
Geigar 88 E 6
Gejiu 70 D 6
Gela 57 F 4
Gelendzhik 59 E 2
Gelsenkirchen 53 E 4
Gemena 92 B 4
Gemsbok National Park 94 C 4–5
General Acha 113 D 6
General Alvear (Argentina) 113 C 6
General Belgrano II 115
General Belgrano III 115
General Bernardo O'Higgins 115
General Madariaga 113 E 6
General Pico 113 D 6
General Roca 113 C 6
General San Martin 115
General Santos 75 G 2
Genève 57 E 2
Gengma 70 C 6
Genoa 57 E 3
Genova 57 E 3
Genova, Golfo di 57 E 3
Gent 52 D 4
George (Quebec, Can.) 101 O 4
Georgetown (Gambia) 90 B 3
Georgetown (Guyana) 109 G 2
George Town (Malaysia) 74 AB 2
Georgetown (Queensland, Austr.) 79 G 2
George Town (Tasmania, Austr.) 82 A 5
George V Coast 115
George VI Sound 115
Georgia (U.S.A.) 103 K 5
Georgia (U.S.S.R.) 59 F 2
Georgian Bay 101 L 6
Georgiu-Dezh 62 G 5
Georgiyevka 63 Q 6
Georgiyevsk 59 F 2
Georg von Neumayer 115
Gera 53 F 4
Geraldton (Western Australia) 78 A 4
Gerãs, Serra do 56 B 3
Gerasimovka 63 O 4
German Democratic Republic 53 F 4
Germi (Iran) 61 G 2
Gerona 56 D 3
Gêrzê 72 D 1
Gesoa 80 D 3
Getafe 56 C 3
Getz Ice Shelf 115
Geyik Dağı 59 D 3
Ghadāmis 87 G 2
Ghana 90 D 4
Ghanzi 94 C 4
Ghardaïa 87 F 2
Gharib, Ra's (Egypt) 60 A 3
Gharyān 87 H 2
Ghazzah 60 B 3
Gheorghe Gheorghiu-Dej 58 C 1
Ghimbi 92 F 3
Ghudāf, Wādī al (Iraq) 60 D 2
Gibraltar 56 B 4
Gibraltar, Estrecho de 56 BC 4
Gibraltar, Strait of 56 B 4
Gibson Desert 78 C 3
Gifu 71 L 3
Giglio 57 F 3
Gijon 56 B 3
Gila Bend 102 D 5
Gila River 102 D 5
Gilbert Islands 82 C 2–3
Gilbert River 79 G 2
Gilbert River 79 G 2
Gilbués 109 J 5
Giles 78 D 4
Gilgandra 79 H 5
Gillam 99 T 4
Gillette 102 E 3
Gingin 78 B 5
Ginir 93 G 3
Gioia 57 G 3
Giresun 59 E 2
Girne (Cyprus) 59 D 3
Girne (Cyprus) 60 A 2
Gironde 56 C 2
Gisborne 81 R 8
Gisborne 82 C 5
Gitarama 92 DE 5
Giuba → Juba 93 G 4
Giza 88 DE 3
Gizhiga 69 U 3
Gizhiginskaya Guba 69 T 3
Gjiri i Vlorë 58 A 2
Gjögur 54 B 2
Gjövik 55 F 3
Glacier Bay National Park and Preserve 98 K 4
Gladstone 79 J 3
Glasgow (U.K.) 52 C 3
Glazov 62 K 4
Glen Canyon National Recreation Area 102 D 4
Glendale 102 D 5
Glendive 102 F 2
Glenhope 81 Q 9
Glennallen 98 H 3
Glenrothes 52 C 3
Glenwood Springs 102 E 4
Glittertind 54 E 3
Gliwice 53 G 4
Głogów 53 G 4
Gloucester (MA, U.S.A.) 103 MN 3
Gloucester (U.K.) 52 C 4
Glubokoye 55 J 4
Glukhov 62 F 5
Goa 72 B 4
Gobabis 94 B 4
Gobi 70 EF 2
Gochas 94 B 4
Godār-e Sorkh (Iran) 61 G 2
Godar-i-Shah 67 G 5
Godavari 72 D 4
Gods Lake 99 T 5
Godthåb 101 R 3
Godwar 72 B 2
Goéland, Lac au 101 M 5–6
Goiânia 111 FG 4
Goiás 111 G 3
Goiás 111 F 4
Goksu 59 D 3
Göksu (Turkey) 59 E 3
Goksu (Turkey) 60 A 1
Golan Heights 60 B 2
Golcuk 58 C 2
Gold Coast 90 DE 5
Gold Coast (Australia) 79 J 4
Golden Hinde 99 M 6
Goldsboro 103 L 4
Goldsworthy 78 BC 3
Golets Skalistyy, Gora 69 O 4
Golf de Lion 56–57 D 2
Golfe de Saint-Malo 56 C 2
Golfito 104 F 6
Golfo de Cadiz 56 B 4
Golfo de California 102 DE 5–7
Golfo de Chiriquí 108 B 2
Golfo de Guayaquil 108 B 4
Golfo de Honduras 104 E 4
Golfo de los Mosquitos 108 B 2
Golfo de Panamá 108 C 2
Golfo de Penas 113 AB 8
Golfo de Tehuantepec 104 CD 4
Golfo de Valencia 56 D 4
Golfo de Venezuela 108 D 1
Golfo di Genova 57 E 3
Golfo di Salerno 57 F 3
Golfo di Squillace 57 G 4
Golfo di Taranto 57 G 3
Golfo San Jorge 113 C 8
Golfo San Matías 113 D 7
Gölgeli Dağları 58 C 3
Golmud 70 B 3
Golovin 98 E 3
Golovnino 71 MN 2
Golubovka 63 O 5
Goma 92 D 5
Gombe 91 G 3
Gomel 62 F 5
Gomera 86 B 3
Goméz Palacio 104 B 2
Gonābād 66 F 4
Gonaïves 105 H 4
Gonam 69 O 4
Gonâve, Ile de la 105 H 4
Gonbad-e Qābus 66 EF 3
Gonda 72 D 2
Gondar 93 F 2
Gondia 72 CD 3
Gongbo' gyamda 70 BC 5
Gonghe 70 D 3
Gongpoquan 70 C 2
Good Hope, Cape of 94 B 6
Goodnews Bay 98 E 4
Goondiwindi 79 HJ 4
Goose Bay 101 P 5
Gora Denezhkin Kamen' 63 LM 3
Gora Ezop 69 S 3
Gora Fisht 59 E 2
Gora Golets-Inyaptuk 68 K 4
Gora Golets-Skalistyy 68 LM 4
Gora Golets Skalistyy 69 O 4
Gora Kamen 68 FG 2
Gora Khil'mi 69 S 1
Gora Khoydype 63 N 2
Gorakhpur 72 D 2
Gora Kovriga 62 J 2
Gora Kuytun 63 R 6
Gora Medvezh'ya 69 P 6
Gora Munku-Sardyk 68 GH 5
Gora Nelkuchan 69 P 3
Gora Pobeda 69 R 2
Gora Sokhor 68 J 5
Gora Syuge-Khaya 69 OP 2
Gora Taklaun 69 Q 3
Gora Tel'pos-Iz 63 LM 3
Gora Yamantau 63 L 5
Góra Zamkowa 53 H 4
Gorda 102 B 4
Gordion 59 D 3
Gordon (WI, U.S.A.) 103 H 2
Gordon Downs 78 D 2
Gorgān (Iran) 61 G 1
Gorgān (Iran) 66 E 3
Gori 59 F 2
Gorki 63 N 2
Gor'kiy 62 H 4
Görlitz 53 F 4
Gorlovka 59 E 1
Gorna Oryakhovitsa 58 C 2
Gorno-Altaysk 63 QR 5
Gornozavodsk 69 Q 6
Gornyak 63 Q 5
Goroka 80 E 3
Goroka 82 A 3
Goromay 69 Q 5

Gorongosa **95** E 3
Gorongosa National Park **95** EF 3
Gorontalo **75** F 3
Gory Byrranga **68** GH 1
Goryn' **55** J 5
Gory Putorana **68** FH 2
Gory Ulutau **67** H 1
Gorzów Wielkopolski **53** G 4
Goshogawara **71** LM 2
Gossi **90** D 2
Göta kanal **55** F 4
Götaland **55** FG 4
Göteborg **55** F 4
Gothenburg (Sweden) **55** F 4
Gotland **55** G 4
Gotska Sandön **55** GH 4
Göttingen **53** EF 4
Goulburn **79** H 5
Goulimime **86** C 3
Gouré **91** G 3
Gourma **90** E 3
Gourma-Rarous **90** D 2
Gouro **91** H 2
Gove Peninsula **79** F 1
Governador Valadares **111** H 4
Goya **112** E 4
Gozo **57** F 4
Graaff Reinet **94** C 6
Gračac **57** G 3
Gradaús, Serra dos **109** H 5
Grafton **79** J 4
Graham (Br. Col., Can.) **98** L 5
Graham Land **115**
Grahamstown **94** D 6
Grain Coast **90** BC 4–C 5
Grajaú **109** J 5
Grampian Mountains **52** C 3
Granada (Nicaragua) **104** E 5
Granada (Spain) **56** C 4
Granby **101** N 6
Gran Canaria **86** BC 3
Gran Chaco **110** D 5
Grand Bassam **90** D 4
Grand Canyon **102** D 4
Grand Canyon National Park **102** D 4
Grand Coulee Dam **102** C 2
Grande, Bahía **113** C 9
Grande Comore **95** GH 2
Grande Prairie **99** NO 4
Grand Erg de Bilma **91** GI 2
Grand Erg Occidental **86–87** EF 2–3
Grand Erg Oriental **87** G 2–3
Grand Forks **102** G 2
Grandin, Lake **99** O 3
Grand Island **102** G 3
Grand Junction **102** E 4
Grand Marais (MN, U.S.A.) **103** HJ 2
Grand Passage **81** H 5
Grand Rapids (Man., Can.) **99** S 5
Grand Rapids (MI, U.S.A.) **103** JK 3
Grand Rapids (MN, U.S.A.) **103** H 2
Grand Teton **102** D 3
Granite City **103** J 4
Granite Peak (MT, U.S.A.) **102** E 2
Granite Peakh (NV., U.S.A.) **102** C 3
Granja **111** H 1
Granön **54** G 3
Gran Sasso d'Italia **57** F 3
Grants Pass **102** B 3
Granville Lake **99** R 4
Gräsö **55** G 3
Grave, Pointe de **56** C 2
'S-Gravenhage **52** D 4
Gravina **57** G 3
Grayling **103** K 3
Graz **57** FG 2
Great Artesian Basin **79** G 3–4
Great Australian Bight **78** DE 5
Great Barrier **82** C 5
Great Barrier Island **81** R 8
Great Barrier Reef **79** H 1–2
Great Basin **102** C 3–4
Great Bear Lake **99** NO 2
Great Dividing Range **79** HJ 3–4
Greater Antilles **105** GH 4
Great Exuma Island **105** G 3
Great Falls **102** D 2
Great Fisher Bank **52** D 3
Great Inagua Island **105** H 3
Great Indian Desert **72** B 2
Great Karroo **94** C 6
Great Nicobar **73** F 6
Great Plains **99** OQ 4–5
Great Plains **102** FG 2–4
Great Salt Lake **102** D 3
Great Salt Lake Desert **102** D 3
Great Sandy Desert **78** C 3
Great Slave Lake **99** P 3
Great Victoria Desert **78** DE 4
Greece **58** B 3
Greeley (CO, U.S.A.) **102** F 3
Green Bay (WI, U.S.A.) **103** J 3
Green Coast **115**
Green Islands (Papua New Guinea) **82** B 3
Greenland **114**
Greenland Sea **114**
Greenock **52** BC 3
Green River (Papua New Guinea) **80** D 2
Green River (UT, U.S.A.) **102** DE 4
Green River (WY, U.S.A.) **102** DE 3
Greensboro (GA, U.S.A.) **103** K 5
Greensboro (N.C., U.S.A.) **103** L 4
Greenvale (Queensland, Austr.) **79** GH 2
Greenville (Liberia) **90** C 5
Greenville (MS, U.S.A.) **103** HJ 5
Greenville (S.C., U.S.A.) **103** K 5
Gregory, Lake (South Australia) **79** F 4
Gregory Range **79** G 2
Greifswald **53** F 4
Grenada **105** K 5
Grenoble **57** E 2
Greymouth **81** Q 9
Grey Range **79** G 4
Grim, Cape **80** K 9
Grimsby **52** CD 4
Grímsey **54** B 2
Grimshaw **99** O 4
Grímsstaðir **54** B 2
Grimstad **55** E 4
Grindavik **54** A 3
Griquatown **94** C 5
Grmeč **57** G 3
Grodno **55** H 5
Gröndalen **54** F 3
Grong **54** F 3
Groningen (Netherlands) **52** E 4
Groote Eylandt **79** F 1
Grootfontein **94** B 3
Groot Vloer **94** BC 5
Groot Winter Berg **94** D 6
Grosseto **57** F 3
Group, Actaeon **83** F 4
Groznyy **59** G 2
Grudziądz **53** G 4
Grünau **94** B 5
Gruñidera **104** B 3
Gruziya **59** F 2
Grytviken **115**
Guadalajara (Mexico) **104** B 3
Guadalajara (Spain) **56** C 3
Guadalcanal **81** G 3
Guadalcanal **82** B 3
Guadalquivir **56** C 4
Guadalupe **56** B 4
Guadalupe (Mexico) **104** C 2
Guadalupe, Isla de **102** C 6
Guadalupe, Sierra de **56** B 4
Guadeloupe (Lesser Antilles) **105** KL 4
Guadeloupe Passage **105** K 4
Guadiana **56** B 4
Guajará Mirim **110** CD 3
Gualeguaychú **112** E 5
Guam **82** A 2
Guaminí **113** D 6
Guanare **108** E 2
Guandacol **112** C 4
Guangde **71** GH 4
Guangdong **70** F 6
Guanghua **70** F 4
Guangshan **70** G 4
Guangxi Zhuangzu Zizhiqu **70** EF 6
Guangyuan **70** E 4
Guangzhou **70** F 6
Guantánamo **105** H 3
Guan Xian **70** D 4
Guapí **108** C 3
Guaporé (Rondônia, Brazil) **110** D 3
Guaqui **110** C 4
Guarapuava **112** F 4
Guarda **56** B 3
Guardal **56** C 4
Guarenas **108** E 1
Guasave **102** E 6
Guasipati **109** F 2
Guatemala **104** DE 4
Guatemala City **104** DE 5
Guaviare **108** E 3
Guayabal **108** E 2
Guayaquil **108** C 4
Guayaquil, Golfo de **108** B 4
Guayaramerin **110** C 3
Guaymallén **112** C 5
Guba (U.S.S.R.) **62** F 3
Guba (Zaire) **94** D 2
Guba Buorkhaya **69** NO 1
Gubakha **63** L 4
Gubkin **62** G 5
Gudermes **59** G 2
Gudur **72** CD 5
Guelta Zemmur **86** C 3
Guéné **90** E 3
Güera **86** B 4
Guéra **91** H 3
Guéréda **91** J 3
Guernsey **52** C 5
Guerrero **104** BC 4
Gügerd, Küh-e (Iran) **61** F 2
Gughe **93** F 3
Guguan **82** A 1
Guiana Highlands **109** FH 3
Guiding **70** E 5
Guidjiba (Ngaoundéré) **91** G 4
Guijá **95** E 4
Guildford **52** C 4
Guilin **70** F 5
Guinan **70** D 3
Guinea **90** BC 3
Guinea, Gulf of **91** EF 5
Guinea-Bissau **90** AB 3
Guinea Equatorial **91** F 5
Güines **105** F 3
Guiratinga **111** F 4
Guisanbourg **109** H 3
Guixi **71** G 5
Gui Xian **70** EF 6
Guiyang **70** E 5
Guizhou **70** E 5
Gujarat **72** B 3
Gujranwala **67** J 4
Gujrat **67** J 4
Gulbarga **72** C 4
Gulf of Aden **89** H 6
Gulf of Alaska **98** HJ 4
Gulf of Boothia **99** T 1
Gulf of Bothnia **54** GH 3
Gulf of Carpentaria **79** F 1
Gulf of Chihli **71** GH 3
Gulf of Guinea **91** EF 5
Gulf of Khambhat **72** B 3–4
Gulf of Kutch **72** A 3
Gulf of Maine **103** N 3
Gulf of Mannar **72** C 6
Gulf of Martaban **73** G 4
Gulf of Mexico **104** DE 2
Gulf of Oman **66** F 5–6
Gulf of Papua **80** DE 3
Gulf of Riga **55** H 4
Gulf of Saint Lawrence **101** P 6
Gulf of Sirt **87** J 2
Gulf of Suez **60** A 3
Gulf of Thailand **73** H 5
Gulf of Tonkin **73** J 3–4
Gulf of Venice **57** F 2–3
Gulfport **103** J 5
Gulf Saint Vincent **79** F 5–6
Gulgong **79** HJ 5
Gulin **70** E 5

Gulistan **67** H 2
Gulu **92** E 4
Guna (India) **72** C 3
Güneydoğu Toros lar **59** EF 3
Gungu **92** B 6
Guntur **72** CD 4
Gunung Abong Abong **74** A 3
Gunung Besar **74** E 4
Gunung Binaiya **75** G 4
Gunung Dempo **74** B 4
Gunung Kerinci **74** B 4
Gunung Kinabalu **74** E 2
Gunung Kwoka **75** H 4
Gunung Leuser **74** A 3
Gunung Lokilalaki **75** F 4
Gunung Maling **75** F 3
Gunung Mulu **74** DE 3
Gunung Mutis **75** F 5
Gunung Saran **74** D 4
Gunung Sorikmerapi **74** A 3
Gunung Tahan **74** B 3
Guoyang **70** G 4
Gurban Obo **70** F 2
Gurbantünggüt Shamo **67** M 1–2
Gurgan (Iran) **61** G 1
Gürlevik Daği **59** E 3
Gurskoye **69** P 5
Gurupá **109** H 4
Gurupí (Goiás, Brazil) **111** G 3
Gurvanbulag **68** HJ 6
Gur'yev **66** E 1
Gusau **91** F 3
Guyana **109** G 3
Guyenne **56** C 3
Guzar **67** H 3
Güzelhisar **58** C 3
Gwalior **72** C 2
Gwelo **94** D 3
Gya La **72** DE 2
Gyangzê **72** E 2
Gydanskiy Poluostrov **63** P 1–2
Gympie **79** J 4
Gyöngyös **58** B 1
Györ **58** A 1
Gypsum Point **99** OP 3
Gyula **58** B 1

H

Haanja Kõrgustik **55** J 4
Ha'apai Group **82** D 4
Haapsalu **55** H 4
Haarlem **52** D 4
Habay (Alb., Can.) **99** O 4
Hābbāniyah (Iraq) **60** D 2
Hachinohe **71** M 2
Ḥadd, Ra's al **89** KL 4
Hadejia **91** F 3
Hadejia **91** G 3
Hadera (Israel) **60** B 2
Hadilik **67** M 3
Hadley Bay **99** Q 1
Ḥaḍramawt **89** H 5
Ḥafar al Bāṭin **89** H 3
Ḥafīrat al 'Aydā (Saudi Arabia) **60** C 4
Ḥafīrat al 'Aydā (Saudi Arabia) **89** F 3
Ḥafīt (Oman) **61** G 4–5
Hāfūn, Ra's **93** J 2
Hagemeister **98** E 4
Hagfors **55** F 3
Hague, Cap de la **56** C 2
Haicheng **71** H 2
Haifa (Israel) **60** B 2
Haifa (Israel) **88** E 2
Haifeng **70** G 6
Haikang **70** EF 6
Haikou **70** F 6–7
Ḥā'il (Saudi Arabia) **60** C 4
Ḥā'il (Saudi Arabia) **89** G 3
Hailar **68** L 6
Hailin **71** J 2
Hailun **69** N 6
Hailuoto **54** H 2
Hainan Dao **70** F 7
Haines **98** K 4
Haines Junction **98** K 3
Hai Phong **73** J 3
Haïti **105** H 4
Ḥajārah, Ṣaḥrā' al **89** GH 2–H 3
Hājjīābād **66** F 5
Hajjīābād-e Māsīleh (Iran) **61** F 2
Hakkâri Dağlari **59** F 3
Hakodate **71** M 2
Halab (Syria) **60** B 1
Ḥalab (Syria) **88** F 1
Ḥalā'ib **88** F 4
Ḥalbā (Lebanon) **60** B 2
Halden **55** F 4
Hale, Mount **78** B 4
Ḥalī **89** G 5
Halifax **101** P 7
Hall **98** C 3
Halland **55** F 4
Hallat' Ammār (Saudi Arabia) **60** B 3
Ḥallat 'Ammār (Saudi Arabia) **66** B 5
Hall Beach **99** V 2
Halle **53** F 4
Halley Bay **115**
Hallingskarvet **55** E 3
Hall Islands **82** B 2
Hall Peninsula **101** O 3
Halls Creek **78** D 2
Halmahera, Laut **75** G 4
Halmstad **55** F 4
Hälsingeskogen **54** G 3
Hälsingland **54** G 3
Halti **54** H 2
Hālūl (Qatar) **61** F 4
Hamadān (Iran) **61** E 2
Hamadān (Iran) **66** DE 4
Hamāh (Syria) **60** B 2
Hamāh (Syria) **88** F 1
Hamamatsu **71** L 4
Hamar **55** F 3
Hamburg **53** F 4
Häme **54** HJ 3
Hämeenlinna (Tavastehus) **54** HJ 3
Hamelin Pool **78** A 4
Hamersley Range **78** B 3
Hamersley Range National Park **78** B 3
Hamhŭng **71** J 2–3
Hami **70** B 2
Hamilton (New Zealand) **81** R 8
Hamilton (Ontario, Can.) **101** M 7
Hamilton (Victoria, Austr.) **79** G 6
Hamm **53** E 4
Hammar, Hawr al (Iraq) **61** E 3
Hammond (IN, U.S.A.) **103** J 3
Hammur Koke **93** F 3
Hampden **81** Q 10
Hamrin, Jabal (Iraq) **60–61** D 2
Hamuku **75** HJ 4
Hanak (Saudi Arabia) **60** B 4
Ḥanak (Saudi Arabia) **66** B 5
Hanang **92** EF 5
Hanceville **99** N 5
Hanchuan **70** F 4
Handan **70** F 3
Handeni **93** F 6
Hanegev (Israel) **60** B 3
Hanggin Houqi **70** E 2
Hangu (China) **71** G 3
Hangzhou **71** H 4
Hankoniemi **55** H 4
Hannover (F.R.G.) **53** E 4
Hanöbukten **55** FG 4
Ha Noi **73** HJ 3
Hanover (South Africa) **94** C 6
Hanover, Islas **113** AB 9
Hanstholm **55** E 4
Hao **83** F 4
Haparanda **54** H 2
Hara **68** J 6
Ḥaraḍh (Saudi Arabia) **61** E 4
Ḥaraḍh (Saudi Arabia) **66** D 6
Harar **93** G 3
Harare **95** E 3
Hararge **93** GH 3
Harazé **91** J 4
Harbin **71** J 1
Hardangerfjorden **55** E 3–4
Hardangerjökulen **55** E 3
Hardangervidda **55** E 3
Hardin **102** E 2
Hargeysa **93** G 3
Hari, Batang **74** B 4
Ḥarib **89** H 6
Hari Kurk **55** H 4
Ḥārim **60** B 1
Härjedalen **54** F 3
Harlingen (TX, U.S.A.) **103** G 6
Härnösand **54** G 3
Harrat al ʿUwayrid (Saudi Arabia) **60** B 4
Harrat Ithnayn (Saudi Arabia) **60** C 4
Harrat Khaybar (Saudi Arabia) **60** C 4
Harrington Harbour **101** Q 5
Harrisburg **103** L 3
Harrismith **94** DE 5
Harrison, Cape **101** Q 5
Harrison Bay **98** G 1
Harsvik **54** E 3
Hartford **103** M 3
Hartlepool **52** C 4
Hartz Mountains National Park **80** KL 9
Har Us Nuur **68** F 6
Harvey (N.D., U.S.A.) **102** G 2
Haryana **72** C 2
Harz **53** F 4
Hasalbag **67** K 3
Hassan **72** C 5
Hassi Bel Guebbour **87** G 3
Hassi Messaoud **87** G 2
Hastings (NE, U.S.A.) **102** G 3
Hastings (New Zealand) **81** R 8
Hat Hin **73** H 3
Ha Tinh **73** J 4
Hattiesburg **103** J 5
Hatutu **83** F 3
Hat Yai **73** H 6
Hauberg Mountains **115**
Haugesund **55** DE 4
Haukipudas **54** J 2
Hauraki Gulf **81** QR 8
Haut Atlas **86** DE 2
Hauterive **101** O 6
Haut-Zaïre **92** CD 4
Havana **105** F 3
Havern **54** G 3
Havre **102** E 2
Havre-Saint-Pierre **101** P 5
Hawaii **83** E 1
Hawaiian Islands **83** E 1
Ḥawallī (Kuwait) **61** E 3
Hawke Harbour **101** Q 5
Hawr al Hammar (Iraq) **61** E 3
Hawrān, Wādī (Iraq) **60** C 2
Hawr as Sʿadīyah (Iraq) **61** E 2
Hay (N.S.W., Austr.) **79** G 5
Hay River (N.W.T., Can.) **99** O 3
Hayyā **88** F 5
Hazarajat **67** H 4
Hazar Gölü **59** E 3
Hearst **100** L 6
Hebei **71** G 3
Hebel **79** H 4
Hebi **70** F 3
Hebrides, Inner **52** B 3
Hebrides, Outer **52** B 3
Hebron (Newfoundl., Can.) **101** P 4
Hecate Strait **98** L 5
Hechi **70** E 6
Hechuan **70** E 4–5
Hedmark **54** F 3
Hefa (Israel) **60** B 2
Hefa (Israel) **88** E 2
Hefei **71** G 4
Hegang **69** O 6
Heidelberg **53** E 5
Heidenheim **53** F 5
Heilbronn **53** E 5
Heilong Jiang **69** O 6
Heilongjiang **71** JK 1
Heimaey **54** A 3
Heimahe **70** C 3
Hejaz (Saudi Arabia) **60** B 4
Hekla **54** B 3
Helagsfjället **54** F 3
Helena (MT, U.S.A.) **102** D 2
Hellas **58** B 3
Hells Canyon **102** C 2
Helmeringhausen **94** B 5
Helong **71** JK 2
Helsingborg **55** F 4
Helsingör **55** F 4

Helsinki (Helsingfors) **55** J 3–4
Henan **70** F 4
Henbury **78** E 3
Henderson (Pacific Ocean, U.K.) **83** G 4
Hendijan (Iran) **61** E 3
Hengduan Shan **70** CD 5
Heng Xian **70** E 6
Hengyang **70** F 5
Henik Lakes **99** S 3
Henrietta Maria, Cape **101** L 4
Henryetta **103** G 4
Henzada **73** FG 4
Heraklia (Syria) **60** C 1
Heraklia (Syria) **88** F 1
Herat **67** G 4
Herberton **79** H 2
Hereford (U.K.) **52** C 4
Herlen He **68** L 6
Herluf Trolle, Cape **101** T 3
Hermiston **102** C 2
Hermit Islands **82** A 3
Hermon, Mount (Lebanon) **60** B 2
Hermosillo **102** DE 6
Herning **55** E 4
Herzliyya (Israel) **60** B 2
He Xian **70** F 6
Ḥeydarābād (Iran) **61** D 1
Ḥeydarābād (Iran) **61** G 3
Heze **70** FG 3
Hialeah **103** K 6
Hidalgo **104** C 3
Hidalgo del Parral **102** EF 6
Hidcolândia **111** FG 4
Hierro **86** B 3
High Level **99** O 4
High Prairie **99** O 4
Higuerote **108** E 1
Hiiumaa **55** H 4
Hillsboro (TX, U.S.A.) **103** G 5
Hilo **83** E 1
Himachal Pradesh **72** C 1
Ḥimā Ḍarīyah, Jabal (Saudi Arabia) **60** C 4
Hims (Syria) **60** B 2
Hinchinbrook Island **79** H 2
Hindu Kush **67** HJ 3–4
Hinganghat **72** C 3
Hingol **67** H 5
Hinnöya **54** G 2
Hinton **99** O 5
Hirara **71** J 6
Hirfanlı Barajı **59** D 3
Hirhafok **87** G 4
Hirosaki **71** LM 2
Hiroshima **71** K 4
Hirtshals **55** E 4
Hismā (Saudi Arabia) **60** B 3
Hispaniola **105** HJ 4
Hitachi **71** M 3
Hitra **54** E 3
Hiva Oa **83** F 3
Hjälmaren **55** G 4
Hjelmsöya **54** H 1
Hmeenselk **54** H 3
Ho **90** E 4
Hoa Binh **73** HJ 3
Hoachanas **94** B 4
Hoare Bay **101** P 2
Hobart (Tasmania, Austr.) **80** L 9
Hobbs **102** F 5
Hoburgen **55** G 4
Hobyā **93** H 3
Ho Chi Minh **73** J 5
Hodda **93** J 2
Hodeida **89** G 6
Hodh **86** D 5
Hofsá **54** B 2
Hofsjökull **54** B 2
Hōfu **71** K 4
Hoggar **87** F 4
Hohhot **70** F 2
Hoima **92** E 4
Hokitika **82** C 5
Hokkaidō **71** M 2
Hokmābād **66** F 3
Holanda **110** C 3
Holguín **105** G 3
Holland **103** J 3
Hollick-Kenyon Plateau **115**
Hollywood (CA, U.S.A.) **102** C 5
Hollywood (FL, U.S.A.) **103** L 6
Holstebro **55** E 4
Holyhead **52** C 4
Homāyūnshahr **66** E 4
Homāyūnshahr (Iran) **61** F 2
Hombori Tondo **90** D 3
Home Bay **101** O 2
Homosassa **103** K 6
Honavar **72** B 5
Honduras **104** E 5
Hönefoss **55** F 3
Hong Kong **70** FG 6
Hongliuhe **70** BC 2
Hongor **70** F 1
Hongyuan **70** D 4
Honiara **81** G 3
Honjara **82** B 3
Honolulu **83** E 1
Hon Panjang **73** H 6
Honshū **71** KL 3
Hood Point **78** BC 5
Hoover Dam **102** D 4
Hope, Point **98** D 2
Hopes Advance, Cap **101** O 3
Hopin **73** G 3
Hordaland **55** E 3
Horizon Deep **82** D 4
Horlick Mountains **115**
Hormuz, Strait of **61** G 4
Hormuz, Strait of **89** K 3
Horn, Cape **113** CD 10
Hornavan **54** G 2
Hörnefors **54** G 3
Horn Islands **82** D 3
Hornos, Cabo de **113** CD 10
Horn Plateau **99** O 3
Horqin Youyi Qianqi **71** H 1
Horsens **55** EF 4
Horsham **79** G 6
Hosalay **59** D 2
Hose Mountains **74** D 3
Hoseynīyeh (Iran) **61** E 3
Hoseynīyeh (Iran) **66** D 4
Hospet **72** C 4
Hospitalet **56** D 3
Hoste, Isla **113** C 10
Hotagen **54** F 3
Hotan **67** K 3
Hotazel **94** C 5
Hoting **54** G 3
Hot Springs **103** H 5
Hottah Lake **99** O 2
Houma (China) **70** F 3
Houma (LA, U.S.A.) **103** H 6
Houston **103** G 5
Hovd **68** F 6
Hovd **70** D 2
Hövsgöl Nuur **68** H 5
Howe, Cape **79** J 6
Howland (Pacific Ocean, U.S.A.) **82** D 2
Howrah **72** E 3
Hoxud **70** A 2
Hox Xil Shan **70** AB 3–4
Hoy **52** C 3
Hrvatska **57** G 2
Hsinchu **71** H 6
Huacho **108** C 6
Hua Hin **73** GH 5
Huaibin **70** FG 4
Huainan **71** G 4
Huairen **70** F 3
Huajuapan de León **104** C 4
Huallaga **108** C 5
Huambo **94** B 2
Huambo **94** B 2
Huanan **71** K 1
Huancabamba **108** C 5
Huancavelica **110** A 3
Huancayo **110** A 3
Huangchuan **70** G 4
Huang Hai **71** H 3
Huangshi **70** F 4
Huang Xian **71** GH 3
Huangyan **71** H 5
Huangzhong **70** D 3
Huánuco **108** C 5–6
Huara **110** C 4
Huaral **110** A 3
Huaraz **108** C 5
Huarmey **108** C 6
Huascarán, Nevado **108** C 5
Huasco **112** B 4
Huashixia **70** C 3
Huayllay **110** A 3
Hubei **70** F 4
Hubli **72** C 4–5
Huckitta **78** F 3
Hudat **93** F 4
Ḥuddur Hadama **93** G 4
Huder **69** M 6
Hudiksvall **54** G 3
Hudson Bay **100** KL 3–4
Hudson Bay (Sask., Can.) **99** R 5
Hudson River **103** M 3
Hudson's Hope **99** N 4
Hudson Strait **101** NO 3
Hue **73** J 4
Huelva **56** B 4
Huesca **56** C 3
Hughenden **79** G 3
Hugo **103** GH 5
Hŭich'on **71** J 2
Huihe **68** L 6
Huíla (Angola) **94** AB 2
Huila (Colombia) **108** C 3
Huilai **70** G 6
Huili **70** D 5
Huimin **71** G 3
Huize **70** D 5
Hulayfā' (Saudi Arabia) **60** C 4
Huld **70** E 1
Hull **101** M 6
Huma **69** N 5
Humaitá (Amazonas, Brazil) **109** F 5
Humaitá (Paraguay) **112** E 4
Humay **110** A 3
Húnaflói **54** A 2
Hunan **70** F 5
Hunchun **71** K 2
Hunedoara **58** B 1
Hungary **58** A 1
Hŭngnam **71** J 3
Hunjiang **71** J 2
Hunsur **72** C 5
Hunter **82** C 4
Huntington **103** K 4
Huntsville (AL, U.S.A.) **103** J 5
Huntsville (Ontario, Can.) **101** M 6
Huntsville (TX, U.S.A.) **103** GH 5
Hunyuan **70** F 3
Huocheng **67** KL 2
Huon **82** B 4
Huon Gulf **80** E 3
Huo Xian **70** F 3
Huron **102** G 3
Hurst **103** G 5
Husum (F.R.G.) **53** E 4
Hutag **68** H 6
Hutchinson (KS, U.S.A.) **102** G 4
Hvar **57** G 3
Hveragerði **54** A 3
Hyargas Nuur **68** F 6
Hyden **78** B 5
Hyderabad (India) **72** CD 4
Hyderabad (Pakistan) **67** H 5
Hyères, Iles d' **57** E 3
Hyesan **71** J 2
Hyvinkää (Hyvinge) **55** H 3

I

Iaçu **111** H 3
Ialomiţa **58** C 2
Iaripo **109** H 3
Iaşi **58** C 1
Ibadan **91** E 4
Ibagué **108** C 3
Ibaiti **111** FG 5
Ibarra **108** C 3
Iberville, Lac d' **101** N 4
Ibestad **54** G 2
Ibi **91** F 4
Ibitiara **111** H 3
Ibiza **56** D 4
Íbiza **56** D 4
Ibotirama **111** H 3
Ibrīm **88** E 4
Icá (Amazonas, Brazil) **108** E 4
Ica (Peru) **110** A 3
Icana (Amazonas, Brazil) **108** E 3
İçel **59** D 3
Ichera **68** J 4
Ichinskaya Sopka **69** ST 4
Ico **111** J 2
Icy Cape **98** E 1

Idaho **102** CD 3
Idaho Falls **102** D 3
Idfū **88** E 4
Idhān Awbārī **87** H 3
Idhān Murzuq **87** H 4
Ídhi Óros **58** BC 3
Ídhra **58** B 3
Idlib (Syria) **60** B 2
Idlib (Syria) **88** F 1
Idre **54** F 3
Ifalik **82** A 2
Ifanadiana **95** H 4
Ife **91** E 4
Ifjord **54** J 1
Igarka **63** R 2
Iglesias **57** E 4
Ignace **100** J 6
Ignashino **69** M 5
İğneada **58** C 2
Iguaçu **112** F 4
Iguala **104** C 4
Iguassú Falls **112** F 4
Iguatu **111** J 2
Ihosy **95** H 4
Ihtamir **68** H 6
Iivaara **54** J 2
Ijebu Ode **91** EF 4
Ijsselmeer **52** E 4
Ijuí **112** F 4
Ikaría **58** C 3
Ikerre **91** F 4
Ikot Ekpene **91** F 4
Ilaferh **87** F 4
Ilagan **75** J 1
Ilam (Iran) **61** E 2
Ilbenge **69** M 3
Ile-à-la-Crosse **99** Q 4
Ilebo **92** C 5
Île d'Anticosti **101** P 6
Ile de France **56** D 2
Ile de la Gonâve **105** H 4
Île de la Madeleine **101** P 6
Ile de Ré **56** C 2
Ile des Noefs **93** J 6
Ile des Pins **81** J 6
Île des Pins **82** C 4
Ile d'Oléron **56** C 2
Ile d'Ouessant **56** B 2
Île du Diable **109** H 2
Ile d'Yeu **56** C 2
Iles Chesterfield **82** B 4
Îles de Los **90** B 4
Iles d'Hyères **57** E 3
Îles du Désappointement **83** F 3
Îles du Duc de Gloucester **83** F 4
Îles du Roi Georges **83** F 3
Iles Glorienses (Réunion) **95** H 2
Îles Palliser **83** F 4
Ile Tidra **86** B 5
Ilha de Maracá **109** HJ 3
Ilha de Marajó **109** HJ 4
Ilha Grande (Brazil) **108** E 4
Ilha Santa Carolina **95** F 4
Ilhéus **111** J 3
Iliamna **98** G 4
Iliamna Lake **98** F 4
Ilichevsk **58** D 1
Ilimsk **68** H 4
Ilinskiy **69** Q 6
Illapel **112** B 5
Illimani, Nevado **110** C 4
Illinois **103** J 3–4
Illizi **87** G 3
Ilo **110** B 4
Iloilo **75** F 1
Ilots de Bass **83** F 4
Ilubabor **92** EF 3
Ilyichovsk **58** D 1
Ima **68** L 4
Imām al Hamzah (Iraq) **61** D 3
Imandra, Ozero **54** K 2
Imatra **54** J 3
Imbituba **112** G 4
Iméni Gastello **69** R 3
Iméni Mariny **69** QR 3
Imgytskoye Boloto **63** O 4
Imperatriz (Maranhão, Brazil) **109** J 5
Imphal **73** F 3
Imtonzha **69** NO 2
Inagua Island, Great **105** H 3
Inarijarvi **54** J 2
In Azaoua **91** F 1
Ince Burnu **59** D 2
Inch'ŏn **71** J 3
Inchôpe **95** E 3
Independence (MO, U.S.A.) **103** H 4
India **72** CD 3
Indiana **103** J 3
Indianapolis **103** J 4
Indian Harbour **101** Q 5
Indian Ocean **117**
Indias Occidentales **105** H 3
Indigirka **69** R 2
Indigirskaya Nizmennost' **69** QR 2
Indispensable Reefs **82** B 3
Indispensable Strait **81** H 3–4
Indore **72** C 3
Indus **67** H 6
İnegöl **58** C 2
In Gall **91** F 2
Ingoda **68** K 5
Ingrid Christensen Coast **115**
Ingul **59** D 1
Inhambane **95** F 4
Inharrime **95** F 4
Inhumas **111** FG 4
Inirida **108** E 3
Inkerman **79** G 2
Inn **53** F 5
Inner Mongolia **70** E 2–3
Innisfail (Queensland, Austr.) **79** H 2
Innokent'yevka **69** P 6
Innsbruck **57** F 2
Inoucdjouac **101** M 4
In Salah **87** F 3
Insulă Sacalin **58** CD 2
Inta **63** L 2
Intletovy **63** P 3
Inuvik **98** L 2
Invercargill (New Zealand) **80** P 10
Inverness **52** C 3
Investigator Strait **79** F 6
Inya **63** R 5
Iolotan **67** G 3
Iona National Park **94** A 3
Ionian Islands **58** A 3
Ionian Sea **58** A 3
Ionioi Nísoi **58** A 3
Iónion Pélagos **58** AB 3
Íos **58** C 3
Iowa **103** H 3
Iowa City **103** H 3
Ipameri **111** G 4
Ipatinga **111** H 4
Ipiales **108** C 3
Ipiaú **111** J 3
Ípiros **58** B 3
Ipixuna (Amazonas, Brazil) **108** D 5
Ipoh **74** B 3
Iporá **111** F 4
Ipswich (Australia) **79** J 4
Ipswich (U.K.) **52** D 4
Ipu **111** H 1
Iquapé **111** G 5
Iquique **110** B 5
Iquitos **108** D 4
Iracoubo **109** H 2
Irafshan **67** G 5
Iráklion **58** C 3
Iran **61** FG 2
Iran **66** EF 4
Iran, Pegunungan **74** D 3
Irapuato **104** B 3
Iraq **60** D 2
Iraq **89** GH 2
Irbid (Jordan) **60** B 2
Irbit **63** M 4
Irebu **92** B 5
Irecê **111** H 3
Irgiz **67** G 1
Irian Jaya **75** HJ 4
Iriba **91** J 2
Iringa **93** F 6
Iriomote-jima **71** HJ 6
Iriona **104** EF 4
Iriri **109** H 4
Irish Sea **52** BC 4
Irkutsk **68** HJ 5
Iron gate → Portile de Fier **58** B 2
Iron Knob **79** F 5
'Irq al Idrīsī **87** K 4–5
'Irq al Maẓhur (Saudi Arabia) **60** D 4
Irrawaddy **73** G 3–4
Irrawaddy, Mouths of the **73** FG 4
Irtuia **109** J 4
Irtysh **63** N 4
Irtysh **63** O 5
Irún **56** C 3
Isa, Mount **79** F 3
Isabela (Ecuador) **108** B 6
Isangi **92** C 4
Ischia **57** F 3
Iscia Baidoa → Isha Bayḍabo **93** G 4
Iseyin **90** E 4
Isfendiyar Dağlari **59** D 2
Isherton **109** G 3
Ishigaki **71** HJ 6
Ishikhly **66** D 3
Ishim **63** NP 4–5
Ishim **63** O 4
Ishimskaya Step' **63** O 5
Ishinomaki **71** M 3
Išiklar Daği **58** C 2
Isil'kul **63** O 5
Isinga **68** K 5
Isiro **92** D 4
Iskenderun (Turkey) **59** E 3
Iskenderun (Turkey) **60** B 1
Iskenderun (Turkey) **60** B 1
Iskenderun Kßrfezi (Turkey) **59** E 3
Iskitim **63** Q 5
Isla Ángel de la Guarda **102** D 6
Isla Aruba **108** E 1
Isla Campana **113** A 8
Isla Cedros **102** C 6
Isla Curaçao **108** DE 1
Isla de Chiloé **113** B 7
Isla de Cozumel **104** E 3
Isla de Guadelupe **102** C 6
Isla de la Juventud **104** F 3
Isla del Maíz **104** F 5
Isla de los Estados **113** D 9
Isla Desolación **113** AB 9
Isla Esmeralda **113** A 8
Isla Grande de Tierra del-Fuego **113** C 9
Isla Hoste **113** C 10
Islamabad **67** J 4
Isla Malpelo **108** B 3
Island Lake **99** T 5
Islands of Four Mountains **98** CD 5
Isla Santa Inés **113** B 9
Islas Baleares **56** D 3–4
Islas Canarias **86** B 3
Islas Hanover **113** AB 9
Isla Tiburon **102** D 6
Isla Tobago **109** F 1
Isla Trinidad (Trinidad and Tobago) **109** F 1
Islay **52** B 3
Isle of Man **52** C 4
Isle of Wight **52** C 4
Isles of Scilly **52** B 5
Isole Eolie o Lipari **57** F 4
Isole Ponziane **57** F 3
Isosyöte **54** J 2
Isparta **58** D 3
Israel **60** B 3
Israel **88** E 2
Issano **109** G 2
Istanbul **58** C 2
İstanbul Boğazi **58** C 2
Isteren **54** F 3
Isthmus of Kra **73** G 5
Istmo de Tehuantepec **104** D 4
Isto, Mount **98** J 2
Istra **57** F 2
Itaberaba **111** H 3
Itabira **111** H 4
Itabuna **111** J 3
Itagüí **108** C 2
Itaituba **109** G 4
Itajaí **112** G 4
Italia **57** FG 3
Italy **57** F 3
Itambé **111** H 4
Itaperucu Mirim **111** H 1
Itaperuna **111** H 5
Itapetinga **111** J 4
Itapipoca **111** J 1

Itapiranga (Amazonas, Brazil) **109** G 4
Itapiúna **111** J 1
Itarsi **72** C 3
Itaúnas **111** J 4
Itbāy **60** AB 4
Itbāy **88** EF 3–4
Itchen Lake **99** P 2
Iténez **110** D 3
Ithaca **103** L 3
Itháki **58** B 3
Ithnayn, Harat (Saudi Arabia) **60** C 4
Itivdleg **101** R 2
Ituberá (Bahía, Brazil) **111** J 3
Ituiutaba **111** FG 4
Itumbiara **111** FG 4
Iturama **111** F 4
Iturbe **110** C 5
Itzehoe **53** EF 4
Iul'tin **98** B 2
Ivalojoki **54** J 2
Ivanhoe **79** GH 5
Ivano-Frankovsk **62** D 6
Ivanovo **62** H 4
Ivigtut **101** S 3
Ivory Coast **90** CD 4
Ivory Coast **90** CD 5
Ivrea **57** E 2
Iwaki **71** M 3
Iwo **91** E 4
Iwo Jima **65** R 7
Iwŏn **71** J 2
Ixiamas **110** C 3
Izhevsk **62** K 4
İzmir **58** C 3
İzmir Körfezi **58** C 3
İzmit **58** CD 2
Izu-shotō (Japan) **71** M 4–5

J

Jabal Abadab **88** EF 5
Jabal' Abd al' Aziz **59** E 3
Jabal al Bishrī **88** F 1
Jabal al Humara **88** E 5
Jabal al Lawz **88** F 3
Jabal an Nabī Shu'ayb **89** G 5
Jabal as Ḩasāwinah **87** H 3
Jabal ash Shaykh (Lebanon) **60** B 2
Jabal at Tubayq (Saudi Arabia) **60** B 3
Jabal Dabbāgh (Saudi Arabia) **60** B 4
Jabal Dabbāgh (Saudi Arabia) **88** F 3
Jabal Hajhir **93** J 2
Jabal Hamātah (Egypt) **60** B 4
Jabal Hamoyet **88** F 5
Jabal Hamrīn (Iraq) **60–61** D 2
Jabal Ḩimā Ḑarīyah (Saudi Arabia) **60** C 4
Jabal Ḩimā Ḑarīyah (Saudi Arabia) **66** C 6
Jabal Ibrāhīm **89** G 4
Jabal Kātrīna (Egypt) **60** AB 3
Jabal Katul **88** D 6
Jabal Lotuke **92** E 4
Jabal Lubnān (Lebanon) **60** B 2
Jabal Marrah **88** CD 6
Jabal Oda **88** F 4
Jabalpur **72** CD 3
Jabal Şabīr **89** G 6
Jabal Shā'ib al Banāt (Egypt) **60** A 4
Jabal Shammar (Saudi Arabia) **60** CD 4
Jabal Ţuwayq (Saudi Arabia) **61** D 4
Jabālyah (Gaza Strip) **60** B 3
Jablah (Syria) **60** B 2
Jablanica **57** G 3
Jabung, Tanjung **74** B 4
Jacareacanga **109** G 5
Jaciara **111** F 4
Jaciparaná **109** F 5
Jackpot **102** D 3
Jackson (MS, U.S.A.) **103** HJ 5
Jackson (TX, U.S.A.) **103** J 4
Jackson, Mount (Antarctica) **115**
Jacksonville (FL, U.S.A.) **103** K 5
Jacksonville (TX, U.S.A.) **103** GH 5
Jacobabad **67** H 5
Jacobina **111** H 3
Jacona **104** B 3–4
Jadal **91** E 2
J.A.D. Jensens Nunatakker **101** S 3
Jādū **87** H 2
Jaén **56** C 4
Jaffa, Cape **79** F 6
Jaffa → Tel Aviv-Yafo **88** E 2
Jaffna **72** D 6
Jagdalpur **72** D 4
Jaguarão **112** F 5
Jaguarari **111** J 3
Jaguariaíva **111** FG 5
Jaguaribe **111** J 2
Jahrom (Iran) **61** F 3
Jahrom (Iran) **66** E 5
Jaina **104** D 3
Jaipur **72** C 2
Jakarta **74** C 5
Jakobshavn **114**
Jakobstad **54** H 3
Jalaid Qi **71** H 1
Jalapa Enríquez **104** CD 4
Jalgaon **72** BC 3
Jalībah (Iraq) **61** E 3
Jalisco **104** B 3
Jalón **56** C 3
Jaluit **82** C 2
Jalūlā' (Iraq) **61** D 2
Jama **108** B 4
Jamaica **105** G 4
Jamāme **93** G 4
Jamari **109** F 5
Jambi **74** B 4
James **102** G 3
James Bay **101** L 5
James Ross Strait **99** S 1–2
Jamestown (N.D., U.S.A.) **102** G 2
Jamestown (N.Y., U.S.A.) **103** L 3
Jamiltepec **104** C 4
Jammu **67** K 4
Jammu and Kashmir **67** K 4
Jamnagar **72** AB 3
Jamsah (Egypt) **60** A 4
Jamshedpur **72** DE 3
Jämtland **54** F 3
Jandaia **111** FG 4
Jandaq **66** EF 4
Janesville **103** J 3
Janjira **72** B 4
Jan Mayen Island **114**
Janos **102** E 5
Januária **111** H 4
Japan **71** L 3
Japurá **108** E 4
Jarābulus (Syria) **60** C 1
Jaramillo **113** C 8
Jarbah **87** H 2
Jardine River National Park **79** G 1
Jarrahdale **78** B 5
Jarud Qi **71** H 2
Jarvis **83** E 3
Jasikan **90** E 4
Jasper (TX, U.S.A.) **103** H 5
Jasper National Park **99** O 5
Jastrzebie Zdrój **53** G 5
Jászberény **58** AB 1
Jataí **111** F 4
Jatobal **109** HJ 4
Jaú (São Paulo, Brazil) **111** G 5
Jauja **110** A 3
Jawa **74** CD 5
Jaya, Puncak **75** J 4
Jayapura **80** D 2
Jazā' ir Farasān **89** G 5
Jazā' ir Khurīyā Murīya **89** K 5
Jazīrat (Egypt) **60** B 4
Jbel Toubkal **86** D 2
Jeci **95** F 2
Jefferson, Mount (NV, U.S.A.) **102** C 4
Jefferson City **103** H 4
Jēkabpils **55** J 4
Jelenia Góra **53** G 4
Jelgava **55** H 4
Jelow Gir (Iran) **61** E 2
Jequié **111** H 3
Jequitinhonha **111** HJ 4
Jerada **86** E 2
Jeremoabo **111** J 3
Jerez de la Frontera **56** B 4
Jerome **102** CD 3
Jersey **52** C 5
Jerusalem **60** B 3
Jerusalem **88** F 2
Jeypore **72** D 4
Jhang Sadar **67** J 4
Jhansi **72** C 2
Jhelum **67** J 4
Jiamusi **71** K 1
Jiang'an **70** DE 5
Jianghua **70** F 5
Jiangmen **70** F 6
Jiangsu **71** GH 4
Jiangxi **70** FG 5
Jiangyou **70** D 4
Jianyang **71** G 5
Jiaozuo **70** F 3
Jiayu **70** F 5
Jiayuguan **70** C 3
Jiddah **89** FG 4
Jiekkevarre **54** GH 2
Jieyang **70** G 6
Jigzhi **70** D 4
Jijiga **93** G 3
Jilib **93** G 4
Jilin **71** HJ 2
Jimāl, Wādi (Egypt) **60** B 4
Jimma **93** F 3
Jinan **71** G 3
Jincheng **70** F 3
Jingdezhen **71** G 5
Jingning **70** E 3
Jing Xian (Anhui, China) **70** E 5
Jing Xian (Hunan, China) **71** G 4
Jingyuan **70** DE 3
Jinhua **71** GH 5
Jining **71** G 3
Jinja **92** E 4
Jinkouhe **70** D 5
Jinping **70** D 6
Jinsha **70** E 5
Jinsha Jiang **70** D 5
Jinshan **71** H 4
Jin Xian **71** H 3
Jinxiang **71** G 3–4
Jinzhou **71** H 2
Jiparaná **109** F 5
Jipijapa **108** B 4
Jishou **70** EF 5
Jisr ash Shughūr (Syria) **60** B 2
Jiu **58** B 2
Jiujiang **70** G 5
Jiuquan **70** C 3
Jixi **71** K 1
João Pessoa **111** K 2
Jodhpur **72** B 2
Joensuu **54** JK 3
Jōetsu **71** L 3
Johannesburg **94** DE 5
John O'Groat's **52** C 3
Johnsons Crossing **98** L 3
Johnston (Pacific Ocean, U.S.A.) **82** D 1
Johnstown **103** L 3
Johor Baharu **74** B 3
Joinvile **112** G 4
Joinville Island **115**
Jokkmokk **54** H 2
Jolo **75** F 2
Jonesboro **103** HJ 4
Jonglei **92** E 3
Jönköping **55** FG 4
Jonquière **101** N 6
Joplin **103** H 4
Jordan **60** B 2–3
Jordan **60** B 3
Jordan **88** F 2
Jorhat **73** F 2
Jos **91** F 4
Joseph Bonaparte Gulf **78** D 1
Joseph Lake **101** O 5
Jos Sodarso, Pulau **75** J 5
Jostedalsbreen **54** E 3
Jotunheimen **54** E 3
Juan de Nova **95** G 3
Juan Fernández Islands **107** B 6
Juárez **113** E 6
Juàzeiro **111** H 2
Juàzeiro do Norte **111** J 2

Jūbā (Sudan) **92** E 4
Jubayl (Lebanon) **60** B 2
Jubayt **88** F 5
Júcar **56** C 4
Juchitan de Zaragoza **104** D 4
Juiz de Fora **111** H 5
Juktån **54** G 2
Juliaca **110** B 4
Julia Creek **79** G 3
Julianatop **109** G 3
Julianehåb **101** S 3
Jumanggoin **70** C 4
Junagadh **72** B 3
Jun Bulen **71** G 1
Junction **102** G 5
Jundiaí **111** G 5
Juneau **98** L 4
Junee **79** H 5
Junggar Pendi **67** M 1
Junín (Argentina) **112** D 5
Jūniyah (Lebanon) **60** B 2
Jun Xian **70** F 4
Juoksengi **54** H 2
Jura (U.K.) **52** B 3
Jurado **108** C 2
Jurien Bay **78** A 5
Jūrmala **55** H 4
Juruá (Amazonas, Brazil) **108** E 4
Juruena **110** E 3
Juruti **109** G 4
Jutaí (Amazonas, Brazil) **108** E 4
Jutland **55** E 4
Juva **54** J 3
Juventud, Isla de la **104** F 3
Ju Xian **71** G 3
Jūyom (Iran) **61** F 3
Juzur Qarqannah **87** H 2
Jylland **55** EF 4
Jyväskylä **54** J 3

K

Kabaena, Pulau **75** F 5
Kabalo **92** D 6
Kaban'ya **69** P 6
Kabba **91** F 4
Kåbdalis **54** G 2
Kabinda **92** CD 6
Kabīr Kūh (Iran) **61** E 2
Kabir Kūh (Iran) **66** D 4
Kabo **92** B 3
Kabompo **94** C 2
Kabondo Dianda **92** D 6
Kabud Rāhang (Iran) **61** E 2
Kabul **67** HJ 4
Kabwe **94** D 2
Kachikattsy **69** NO 3
Kachin **73** G 2
Kachug **68** J 5
Kadirli **59** E 3
Kadiyevka **59** E 1
Kadoma **94** D 3
Kādugli **88** D 6
Kaduna **91** F 3
Kaédi **86** C 5
Kafue **94** D 3
Kafue National Park **94** D 3
Kafue [River] **94** D 2
Kafura **92** E 5
Kagoshima **71** JK 4
Kagul **58** C 1
Kahemba **92** B 6
Kahoolawe **83** E 1
Kahramanmaras **59** E 3
Kai, Kepulauan **75** H 5
Kaifeng **70** FG 4
Kaikoura **81** Q 9
Kaili **70** E 5
Kailu **71** H 2
Kaimur Range **72** D 3
Kainantu **80** E 3
Kainji Dam **91** EF 4
Kainji Reservoir **91** E 3
Kaintragarh **72** DE 3
Kairouan → Al Qayrawān **87** GH 1
Kaiserslautern **53** E 5
Kai Xian **70** E 4
Kaiyuan **70** D 6
Kajaki Dam **67** H 4
Kakhovka **59** D 1
Kakhovskoye Vodokhranilishche **59** DE 1
Kākī (Iran) **61** F 3
Kakinada **72** D 4
Kakisa **99** O 3
Kaktovik **98** J 1
Kalabagh **67** J 4
Kalach **62** H 5
Kalachinsk **63** OP 4
Kalahari **94** C 4
Kalahari Gemsbok National Park **94** BC 5
Kalai-Khumb **67** J 3
Kalajoki **54** H 3
Kalámai **58** B 3
Kalaong **75** F 2
Kalbarri National Park **78** A 4
Kaldbakur **54** A 2
Kalehe **92** D 5
Kalemie **92** CD 6
Kalevala **54** K 2
Kalewa **73** F 3
Kalga **68** L 5
Kalgoorlie **78** C 5
Kalimantan **74** DE 3
Kalinin **62** FG 4
Kaliningrad **55** H 5
Kalisz **53** G 4
Kalixälven **54** H 2
Kallsjön **54** F 3
Kalmar **55** G 4
Kalmykovo **66** E 1
Kaloko **92** D 6
Kalole **92** D 5
Kalsubai **72** B 4
Kaltag **98** F 3
Kaluga **62** FG 5
Kamaishi **71** M 3
Kamanjab **94** B 3
Kamarān **89** G 5
Kamaria Falls **109** FG 2
Kambal'naya Sopka **69** T 5
Kamchatka **69** T 4
Kamenets-Podolskiy **58** C 1
Kamenjak, Rt **57** F 3
Kamen-na-Obi **63** PQ 5
Kamensk-Ural'skiy **63** M 4
Kamet **72** D 1
Kamina **92** D 6
Kamkaly **67** J 2
Kamloops **99** N 5
Kamnrokan **68** K 4
Kampala **92** E 4–5
Kampar **74** B 3
Kampar, Sungai **74** B 3
Kampot **74** B 1
Kampuchea **73** HJ 5
Kamsack **99** R 5
Kamyshin **62** HJ 5
Kanaaupscow **101** M 5
Kanaga **98** B 5
Kanal **55** E 5
Kananga **92** C 6
Kanangra Boyd National Park **79** HJ 5
Kanazawa **71** KL 3
Kanchipuram **72** CD 5
Kandagach **66** F 1
Kandahar **67** H 4
Kandalaksha **54** K 2
Kandalakshskaya Guba **54** K 2
Kandangan **74** DE 4
Kandavu **82** C 4
Kande **90** E 4
Kandi **90** E 3
Kandy **72** D 6
Kandychan **69** RS 3
Kanem **91** GH 3
Kangalassy **69** N 3
Kangan (Iran) **61** F 4
Kangan (Iran) **66** E 5
Kangān (Iran) **66** F 5
Kangar **74** B 2
Kangaroo Island **79** F 6
Kangāvar (Iran) **61** E 2
Kangchenjunga **72** E 2
Kangding **70** D 5
Kangean, Kepulauan **74** E 5
Kangeeak Point **101** P 2
Kanggye **71** J 2
Kangmar **72** DE 1
Kangnūng **71** JK 3
Kango **91** G 5
Kangping **71** H 2
Kangynin **98** B 2
Kaniama **92** C 6
Kaniet Islands **82** A 3
Kanin **62** K 4
Kankan **90** C 3
Kankesanturai **72** D 5–6
Kankossa **86** C 5
Kanmaw Kyun **73** G 5
Kannapolis **103** K 4
Kano **91** F 3
Kanovlei **94** B 3
Kanpur **72** D 2
Kansas **102** G 4
Kansas City **103** H 4
Kansk **68** FG 4
Kantang **73** G 6
Kantaralak **73** HJ 5
Kantchari **90** E 3
Kanye **94** CD 4
Kaohsiung **71** GH 6
Kaolack **90** A 3
Kaoma **94** C 2
Kaouar **91** G 2
Kapanga **92** C 6
Kapatu **95** E 1
Kap Brewster **114**
Kapchagay **67** K 2
Kap Farvel **101** T 4
Kapfenberg **57** G 2
Kapingamarangi **82** B 2
Kapiri Moposhi **94** DE 2
Kapisigdlit **101** RS 3
Kapona **92** D 6
Kaposvár **58** A 1
Kapsukas **55** H 5
Kapustoye **54** K 2
Kaquencgue **94** C 2
Karabekaul **67** GH 3
Karabük **59** D 2
Karabutak **66** F 1
Karachi **67** H 6
Kara Dağ **59** D 3
Karaga **69** U 4
Karaganda **63** OP 6
Karagüney Dağları **59** DE 2
Karaikkudi **72** C 6
Karaj (Iran) **61** F 2
Karaj (Iran) **66** E 3
Kara-Kala **66** F 3
Karakelong, Pulau **75** G 3
Karakoram **67** JK 3–4
Karakorum Shankou **67** JK 3–4
Karaköse **59** F 3
Karalundi **78** B 4
Karam **68** J 4
Karamagay **67** M 1
Karaman **59** D 3
Karamay **67** LM 1
Karasburg **94** B 5
Kara Sea **114**
Karasjåkka **54** H 2
Karasu (Turkey) **59** F 2–3
Karasu-Aras Dağları **59** F 3
Karasuk **63** P 5
Karatal **63** P 6
Karatau **67** J 2
Karathuri **73** G 5
Karatogay **66** F 1
Karaton **66** E 1
Karaul **63** Q 1
Karaulkel'dy **66** EF 1
Karazhingil **63** O 6
Karbalā' (Iraq) **60** D 2
Karbalā' (Iraq) **89** G 2
Kardhitsa **58** B 3
Kärdla **55** H 4
Karen **73** G 4
Karesuando **54** H 2
Karganay **69** X 2
Kargat **63** Q 4
Kargopol' **62** G 3
Kari **91** G 3
Kariba, Lake **94** D 3
Kariba Dam **94** D 3
Karibib **94** B 4
Karikal **72** CD 5
Karimata, Selat **74** C 4
Karimganj **73** F 2
Karisimbi **92** D 5
Karjala **54** K 3
Karkār **80** E 2
Karkas, Kūh-e (Iran) **61** F 2
Karkinitskiy Zaliv **59** D 1
Karleby **54** H 3
Karlik Shan **70** BC 2
Karl-Marx-Stadt **53** F 4
Karlovac **57** G 2
Karlovy Vary **53** F 4
Karlshamn **55** FG 4
Karlskoga **55** FG 4

Karlskrona **55** G 4
Karlsruhe **53** E 5
Karlstad (MN, U.S.A.) **103** G 2
Karlstad (Sweden) **55** F 4
Karmöy **55** DE 4
Karnataka **72** BC 4
Karong **73** F 2
Karonga **95** E 1
Kárpathos **58** C 3
Kars **59** F 2
Karsakpay **67** H 1
Karshi **67** H 3
Karskiye Vorota, Proliv **62–63** L 1
Karskoye More **63** LM 1
Kars Platosu **59** F 2
Kartal **58** C 2
Kartaly **63** LM 5
Karufa **75** H 4
Karwar **72** B 5
Kasai **92** B 5
Kasai Occidental **92** C 6
Kasai Oriental **92** C 5–6
Kasaji **94** C 2
Kasama **95** E 2
Kasba Lake **99** R 3
Kâshân (Iran) **61** F 2
Kâshân (Iran) **66** E 4
Kashi **67** K 3
Kashken Teniz **63** O 6
Kâshmar **66** F 3
Kasimov **62** H 5
Kaskelen **67** K 2
Kas Kong **73** H 5
Kasongo **92** D 5
Kásos **58** C 3
Kaspiyskiy **59** G 1
Kaspiyskoye More **66** D 1
Kassalâ **88** F 5
Kassándra **58** B 2
Kassel **53** E 4
Kastamonu **59** D 2
Kasungu **95** E 2
Katako-Kombe **92** CD 5
Katangli **69** Q 5
Katawaz **67** H 4
Katerini **58** B 2
Katherine **78** E 1
Katherine Gorge National Park **78** E 1
Kathiawar **72** B 3
Kathīri **89** H 5
Kathmandu **72** E 2
Katihar **72** E 2
Katmai National Park and Preserve **98** G 4
Katowice **53** G H 4
Kātrīna, Jabal (Egypt) **60** AB 3
Katrineholm **55** G 4
Katsina **91** F 3
Kattegat **55** F 4
Katyl'ga **63** P 4
Kauai **83** E 1
Kaufbeuren **53** F 5
Kaunas **55** H 5
Kauno Marios **55** H 5
Kavalerovo **71** KL 2
Kavâlla **58** B 2
Kavar (Iran) **61** F 3
Kavendou, Mont **90** B 3
Kavīr, Dasht-e (Iran) **61** FG 2
Kavir-e Abarqu (Iran) **61** F 3
Kavir-e Namak (Iran) **61** G 1
Kawa **88** E 5
Kawich Peak **102** CD 4
Kawm Umbū **88** E 4
Kawm Umbū (Egypt) **60** A 4
Kaya **90** D 3
Kayah **73** G 4
Kayak (AK, U.S.A.) **98** J 4
Kayala **54** K 3
Kayan **74** E 3
Kayes **90** B 3
Kaynar **63** P 6
Kayseri **59** DE 3
Kazachinskoye **68** J 4
Kazakhskiy Melkosopochnik **63** NP 6
Kazakhstan **67** FH 1
Kazan'**62** JK 4
Kazan Islands (Japan) **65** QR 7
Kazanlŭk **58** C 2
Kazanskoye **63** NO 4
Kazbek **59** F 2
Kaz Dağı **58** C 3
Kâzerūn (Iran) **61** F 3
Kazymskaya **63** N 3
Kazymskiy Mys **63** MN 3
Kazzân ar Ruşayriş **88** E 6
Keams Canyon **102** D 4
Keban Gölü **59** E 3
Kebbi **91** E 3
Kebnekaise **54** G 2
Kediat Idjil **86** C 4
Kediri **74** D 5
Kédougou **90** B 3
Keetmanshoop **94** B 5
Kefa **93** F 3
Kefallinia **58** B 3
Keimoes **94** C 5
Keitele **54** J 3
Keith (South Australia) **79** FG 6
Keketa **80** D 3
Kelang **74** B 3
Keli Hâji Ibrâhīm (Iraq) **61** D 1
Keli Hâji Ibrâhīm (Iraq) **89** H 1
Kelkit **59** E 2
Kellett, Cape **99** M 1
Kellog (U.S.S.R.) **63** R 3
Kellogg (ID, U.S.A.) **102** C 2
Kelloselkä **54** J 2
Kelsey **99** S 4
Kelsey Bay **99** MN 5
Keluang **74** B 3
Kem' **54** K 3
Ké Macina **90** CD 3
Kemerovo **63** QR 4
Kemi **54** HJ 2
Kemijärvi **54** J 2
Kemijoki **54** J 2
Kemkra **69** P 4
Kempendyayi **68** LM 3
Kemps Bay **105** G 3
Kempsey **79** J 5
Kenai **98** G 3–4
Kenai Fjords National Park **98** H 4
Kenai Mountains **98** G 3–4
Kenai Peninsula **98** GH 4
Kencha **69** PQ 3
Kendari **75** F 4
Kenhardt **94** C 5
Kenitra **86** D 2
Keniut **69** X 3
Kenmare (N.D., U.S.A.) **102** F 2
Kennedy Range National Park **78** B 3
Keno Hill **98** L 3
Kenora **100** KJ 6
Kentau **67** H 2
Kent Peninsula **99** Q 2
Kentucky **103** JK 4
Kentucky Lake **103** J 4
Kenya **93** F 4–5
Kenya, Mount **93** F 5
Kepe **54** K 2
Kepulauan Anambas **74** C 3
Kepulauan Aru **75** HJ 5
Kepulauan Babar **75** GH 5
Kepulauan Banggai **75** F 4
Kepulauan Kai **75** H 5
Kepulauan Kangean **74** E 5
Kepulauan Leti **75** G 5
Kepulauan Lingga **74** BC 3–4
Kepulauan Mentawai **74** AB 4
Kepulauan Natuna **74** C 3
Kepulauan Riau **74** B 3
Kepulauan Sangihe **75** G 3
Kepulauan Sula **75** FG 4
Kepulauan Talaud **75** G 3
Kepulauan Tanimbar **75** H 5
Kepulauan Tenggara **75** G 5
Kepulauan Togian **75** F 4
Kepulauan Tukangbesi **75** F 5
Kerama-rettō **71** J 5
Kerch **59** E 1
Kerchenskiy Proliv **59** E 1–2
Kerekhtyakh **69** N 3
Kerema **80** E 3
Kerempe Burnu **59** D 2
Keren **93** F 1
Keret', Ozero **54** K 2
Keriske **69** O 2
Kerki **67** GH 3
Kérkira **58** AB 3
Kérkira **58** AB 3
Kermadec Islands **82** D 4–5
Kermān **66** F 4
Kermanshâh (Iran) **61** E 2
Kermanshah (Iran) **89** H 2
Kermānshâhân (Iran) **61** G 3
Kermānshâhân (Iran) **66** EF 4
Kerme Körfezi **58** C 3
Kerzaz **86** E 3
Kestenga **54** K 2
Ketoy, Ostrov **69** S 6
Keul' **68** H 4
Keurusselkä **54** HJ 3
Kewanee **103** J 3
Keyano **101** N 5
Key West **103** L 7
Kezhma **68** H 4
Khabarovsk **69** P 6
Khabr, Kūh-e (Iran) **61** G 3
Khabur (Syria) **59** F 3
Khabūr (Syria) **60** C 1
Khachmas **66** D 2
Khafjī, Ra's al (Saudi Arabia) **61** E 3
Khaipur **67** H 5
Khairpur **67** J 5
Khakhea **94** C 4
Khakriz **67** GH 4
Khalesavoy **63** PQ 3
Khalīj al 'Agabah **60** B 3
Khalīj al 'Aqabah **88** E 3
Khalīj as Suways **60** A 3
Khalīj as Suways **88** E 3
Khalīj Maşīrah **89** K 5
Khalīj Qâbis **87** H 2
Khálki **58** C 3
Khalkidhiki **58** B 2
Khalkis **58** B 3
Khambhat, Gulf of **72** B 3–4
Khamgaon **72** C 3
Khampa **68** L 3
Khampa **69** M 3
Khamseh (Iran) **61** E 1
Khamseh (Iran) **66** D 3
Khanabad **67** HJ 3
Khandwa **72** C 3
Khandyga **69** P 3
Khanglasy **63** M 3
Khanh Hung **73** HJ 6
Khani **68** M 4
Khánia **58** B 3
Khanpur **67** J 5
Khān Shaykhūn (Syria) **60** B 2
Khantau **67** J 2
Khanty-Mansiysk **63** NO 3
Khanyangda **69** Q 4
Khanyardakh **69** N 3
Khao Lang **73** G 6
Khao Luang **73** G 6
Khao Sai Dao Tai **73** H 5
Khappyrastakh **69** M 4
Khara **68** G 5
Kharagpur **72** E 3
Kharan (Pakistan) **67** GH 5
Kharânaq (Iran) **61** G 2
Kharânaq, Kūh-e (Iran) **61** G 2
Kharik **68** H 5
Khârk (Iran) **61** F 3
Kharkov **62** G 5
Kharoti **67** H 4
Kharstan **69** Q 1
Khasavyurt **59** G 2
Khash (Afghanistan) **67** G 4
Khâsh (Iran) **67** G 5
Khash Desert **67** G 4
Khashm Mishraq **66** D 6
Khaskovo **58** C 2
Khatanga **68** H 1
Khatangskiy Zaliv **68** JK 1
Khataren **69** T 3
Khatyrka **69** X 3
Khawr al Fakkān (United Arab Emirates) **61** G 4
Khawr al Fakkān (United Arab Emirates) **66** F 5
Khaybar (Saudi Arabia) **60** C 4
Khaybar (Saudi Arabia) **66** B 5
Khaybar, Harrat (Saudi Arabia) **60** C 4
Khazzân Jabal al Awliyâ' **88** E 5–6
Khe Bo **73** HJ 4
Khenifra **86** D 2
Kherpuchi **69** P 5
Khersan (Iran) **61** F 3
Kherson **59** D 1
Kheta **68** G 1
Kheta **68** H 1
Kheyrâbâd **66** EF 5
Khibiny **54** K 2

Khíos **58** C 3
Khíos **58** C 3
Khirbat Isriyah (Syria) **60** BC 2
Khmel'nitskiy **62** E 6
Khodzheyli **66** F 2
Khoe **69** P 6
Khok Kloi **73** G 6
Kholmsk **69** Q 6
Khomeyn (Iran) **61** F 2
Khongo **69** S 3
Khon Kaen **73** H 4
Khor Anghar **93** G 2
Khorāsān **66** F 4
Khorat Plateau **73** H 4
Khordogoy **68** L 3
Khoronnokh **68** LM 2
Khorramābād (Iran) **61** E 2
Khorramābād (Iran) **66** D 4
Khorramshahr (Iran) **61** E 3
Khorsābād (Iraq) **60** D 1
Khorsābād (Iraq) **66** C 3
Khosrowābād (Iran) **61** E 3
Khrebet Bureinskiy **69** O 5
Khrebet Chayatyn **69** P 5
Khrebet Cherskogo **69** P 1–2
Khrebet Dzhagdy **69** O 5
Khrebet Dzhugdzhur **69** OP 4
Khrebet Khugdyungda **68** G 2
Khrebet Kolymskiy **69** SU 3
Khrebet Koryakskiy **69** VW 3
Khrebet Nuratau **67** H 2
Khrebet Sette Daban **69** PQ 3–4
Khrebet Suntar Khayata **69** PQ 3
Khrebet Turana **69** O 5
Khudzhakh **69** R 3
Khugdyungda, Khrebet **68** G 2
Khulkhuta **59** G 1
Khulna **72** E 3
Khurayş (Saudi Arabia) **61** E 4
Khurayt **88** D 6
Khurr, Wādī al (Saudi Arabia) **60** C 3
Khurramshahr (Iran) **61** E 3
Khursanīyah (Saudi Arabia) **61** E 4
Khuzdar **67** H 5
Khūzestān (Iran) **61** E 3
Khvāf **66** FG 4
Khvojeh, Kūh-e (Iran) **61** E 2
Khvor (Iran) **61** G 2
Khvormūj (Iran) **61** F 3
Khvoy **66** D 3
Kiambi **92** D 6
Kiantajärvi **54** J 2
Kibangou **91** G 6
Kibwezi **93** F 5
Kichi Kichi **91** H 2
Kidal **90** E 2
Kidira **90** B 3
Kiel **53** F 4
Kielce **53** H 4
Kieta **81** G 3
Kieta **82** B 3
Kiffa (Iraq) **86** C 5
Kifrī (Iraq) **60** D 2
Kigali **92** E 5
Kigilyakh **69** P 1
Kigoma **92** D 5
Kihnu **55** H 4
Kikiakki **63** Q 3
Kikladhes **58** BC 3
Kikori **82** A 3
Kikwit **92** B 6
Kilambé **104** E 5
Kilbuck Mountains **98** F 3
Kilchu **71** J 2
Kil'din, Ostrov **54** K 2
Kili **82** C 2
Kılıç Dağları **58** C 3
Kilimanjaro **93** F 5
Kilindini **93** F 5
Kilis (Turkey) **59** E 3
Kilis (Turkey) **60** B 1
Killarney **52** AB 4
Killarney **52** AB 4
Killeen **102** G 5
Killinek **101** O 3
Killini Óros **58** B 3
Kilmarnock **52** C 3
Kil'mez' **62** K 4
Kilmez **62** K 4
Kilosa **93** F 6
Kilpisjärvi **54** H 2
Kilp-Javr **54** K 2
Kilwa **92** D 6
Kilwa Masoko **93** F 6
Kimball, Mount **98** J 3
Kimbe Bay **81** F 3
Kimberley (South Africa) **94** CD 5
Kimberley (Western Australia) **78** D 2
Kimberley Plateau **78** D 2
Kimch'aek **71** JK 2
Kimito **55** H 3
Kimparana **90** CD 3
Kinabalu, Gunung **74** E 2
Kinchega National Park **79** G 5
Kinda (Zaire) **92** C 6
Kindia **90** B 4
Kindu **92** D 5
King **80** K 8
King Christian IX Land **114**
King Christian X Land **114**
King Frederik VIII Land **114**
Kingissepp (Estoniya, U.S.S.R.) **55** H 4
King Leopold Ranges **78** CD 2
Kingman (AZ, U.S.A.) **102** D 4
Kingman (Pacific Ocean, U.S.A.) **82** E 2
Kingoonya **79** F 5
Kingsmill Group **82** C 3
King Sound **78** C 2
Kings Peak (UT, U.S.A.) **102** DE 3
Kingsport **103** K 4
Kingston (Canada) **101** M 7
Kingston (Jamaica) **105** G 4
Kingston (Norfolk Is., Austr.) **82** C 4
Kingston-upon-Hull **52** C 4
Kingstown **105** K 5
Kingsville **102** G 6
King William Island **99** S 2
King Williams Town **94** D 6
Kinkala **91** G 6
Kinmaw **73** F 4
Kinnairds Head **52** C 3
Kinoosao **99** R 4
Kinshasa **92** B 5
Kipaka **92** D 5
Kipushi **94** D 2
Kirakira **82** B 3
Kirbey **68** H 2
Kirbey **68** K 2
Kirensk **68** J 4
Kirgiziya **67** JK 2
Kirgiz Step' **66–67** FH 1
Kiribati **82** DE 3
Kırıkhan **59** E 3
Kırıkhan (Turkey) **60** B 1
Kırıkkale **59** D 3
Kirillovka **59** E 1
Kirimati **83** E 2
Kirishi **55** K 4
Kirkenes **54** J 2
Kirkjubæjarklaustur **54** B 3
Kırklareli **58** C 2
Kirkpatrick, Mount **115**
Kirksville **103** H 3
Kirkūk (Iraq) **60** D 2
Kirkūk (Iraq) **89** GH 1
Kirkwall **52** C 3
Kirkwood (MO, U.S.A.) **103** H 4
Kirov **62** JK 4
Kirov **62** FG 5
Kirovabad **66** D 2
Kirovakan **59** FG 2
Kirovo Chepetsk **62** K 4
Kirovograd **59** D 1
Kirovsk **54** K 2
Kırşehir **59** D 2–3
Kiruna **54** H 2
Kisangani **92** D 4
Kishinev **58** C 1
Kisii **92** E 5
Kısılırmak **59** D 2
Kiska **98** A 5
Kislovodsk **59** F 2
Kismāyu **93** G 5
Kisoro **92** DE 5
Kissidougou **90** BC 4
Kisumu **92** E 5
Kita **90** C 3
Kitakyushū **71** JK 4
Kitale **92** F 4
Kitami **71** M 2
Kitchener **101** L 7
Kitgum **92** E 4
Kíthira **58** B 3
Kíthnos **58** B 3
Kitwe **94** D 2
Kiunga (Papua New Guinea) **80** D 3
Kivak **98** C 3
Kivijärvi **54** HJ 3
Kiviõli **55** J 4
Kivu **92** D 5
Kiyev **62** F 5
Kizel **63** L 4
Kızıl Dağ (Turkey) **59** D 3
Kızıl Dağ (Turkey) **60** A 1
Kızılırmak **62** E 3
Kizlyar **59** G 2
Kizlyarskiy Zaliv **59** G 2
Kizyl-Arvat **66** F 3
Kizyl-Atrek **66** E 3
Klagenfurt **57** FG 2
Klaipėda **55** H 4
Klamath Falls **102** B 3
Klarälven **55** F 3
Klerksdorp **94** D 5
Klintsy **62** F 5
Klit **55** E 4
Kłodzko **53** G 4
Klotz, Lac **101** NO 3
Kluane National Park **98** K 3
Klukhorskiy Pereval **59** F 2
Klyuchr **69** U 4
Knosós **58** C 3
Knox Coast **115**
Knoxville (TN, U.S.A.) **103** K 4
Knud Rasmussen Land **114**
Kōbe **71** KL 3–4
København **55** F 4
Kobenni **86** CD 5
Koblenz **53** E 4
Koboldo **69** O 5
Kobrin **55** H 5
Kobroor, Pulau **75** H 5
Kobuk **98** F 2
Kobuk Valley National Park **98** F 2
Koca Çal **59** D 3
Kocaeli **58** CD 2
Kocasu **58** C 3
Koch **101** M 2
Ko Chang **73** H 5
Kōchi **71** K 4
Kochikha **68** G 1
Kodi **75** E 5
Kodiak **98** G 4
Kodiak Island **98** G 4
Kodima **62** H 3
Kodžha Balkan **58** C 2
Kōes **94** B 5
Koforidua **90** D 4
Kohistan **67** J 3
Kohlu **67** H 5
Kohtla-Järve **55** J 4
Kokalaat **67** GH 1
Kokand **67** HJ 2
Kokchetav **63** N 5
Kokkola **54** H 3
Kokomo **103** J 3
Kokpekty **63** Q 6
Koksoak **101** O 4
Kokstad **94** D 6
Koktuma **63** Q 6
Ko Kut **73** H 5
Kola **54** K 2
Kolai **67** J 3
Kola Peninsula **62** G 2
Kolar **72** C 5
Kolar Gold Fields **72** C 5
Kolbachi **69** M 5
Kolbio **93** G 5
Kolding **55** E 4
Kolesovo **69** S 1
Kolhapur **72** B 4
Koli **54** J 3
Kolkasrags **55** H 4
Kollumúli **54** C 2
Köln **53** E 4
Kołobrzeg **53** G 4
Kolombangara **81** G 3
Kolomna **62** GH 4
Kolomyya **58** C 1
Kolpakovsky **69** T 5
Kolpashevo **63** QR 4
Koluton **63** N 5
Kolwezi **94** D 2

Kolyma **69** TU 2
Kolymskaya **69** UV 2
Kolymskaya Nizmennost' **69** ST 2
Kolymskiy, Khrebet **69** SU 3
Kolymskoye Nagor'ye **69** S 3
Kolyvan' **63** Q 5
Komandorski Islands **65** TU 4
Komandorskije Ostrova **65** TU 4
Komárno **53** G 5
Komba **92** C 4
Kombolchia **93** FG 2
Komelek **69** O 3
Kommunarsk **59** E 1
Komoé, Parc National de la **90** D 4
Komotini **58** C 2
Kompas Berg **94** C 6
Kompong Cham **73** J 5
Kompong Chhnang **73** HJ 5
Kompong Som **73** H 5
Kompot **75** F 3
Komsomol'sk-na-Amure **69** P 5
Kona **90** D 3
Kondakova **69** T 2
Kondinin **78** B 5
Kondoa **93** F 5
Kondon **69** P 5
Kondut **78** B 5
Konevo**62** GH 3
Kong Frederik VI-Kyst **101** T 3
Kongola **94** C 3
Kongolo **92** D 6
Kongor **92** E 3
Konin **53** G 4
Konkan **72** B 4
Konkudera **68** K 4
Konosha **62** H 3
Konotop **62** F 5
Konstantinovka **59** E 1
Konstanz **53** E 5
Kontagora **91** F 3
Kontcha **91** G 4
Kontiomäki **54** J 3
Konya **59** D 3
Konya Ovası **59** D 3
Kooch Bihar **72** E 2
Kootenay National Park **99** OP 5
Kópasker **54** B 2
Kopeysk **63** M 5
Ko Phangan **73** H 6
Ko Phuket **73** G 6
Köping **55** G 4
Koppang **54** F 3
Korba **72** D 3
Korça **58** B 2
Korčula **57** G 3
Kordestān (Iran) **61** E 2
Kordestan (Iran) **89** H 1
Kord Küy (Iran) **61** G 1
Korea Strait **71** J 4
Korenovsk **59** E 1
Korfovskiy **69** P 6
Korhogo **90** C 4
Korinthiakos Kólpos **58** B 3
Kórinthos **58** B 3
Koriolei **93** G 4
Kōriyama **71** M 3
Korkodon **69** ST 3
Korla **67** M 2
Kormakiti Bur (Cyprus) **60** A 2
Koro (Fiji) **82** C 4
Köroğlu Dağları **59** D 2
Korosten **55** J 5
Koro Toro **91** H 2
Korovin Volcano **98** C 5
Korsakov **69** Q 6
Korsfjorden **55** DE 3
Korshunovo **68** K 4
Koryakskiy Khrebet **69** VW 3
Koryresk **69** TU 4
Kos **58** C 3
Kosa Fedotova **59** E 1
Košice **53** H 5
Kosŏng **71** J 3
Kosovska Mitrovica **58** B 2
Kossou, Lac de **90** CD 4
Kostino **63** R 2
Kostroma **62** H 4
Koszalin **53** G 4
Kota **72** C 2
Kotabumi **74** BC 4
Kota Kinabalu **74** DE 2
Kotel'nich **62** J 4
Kotel'nikovo **59** F 1
Kotel'nyy, Ostrov **69** P 1
Kotikovo **69** QR 6
Kotka **55** J 3
Kotlas **62** J 3
Kotlik **98** E 3
Kotovsk **58** CD 1
Kotu Group **82** D 4
Kotuy **68** H 1
Kotzebue Sound **98** E 2
Koudougou **90** D 3
Koulen **73** HJ 5
Koumac **81** H 6
Koumbi-Saleh **86** D 5
Koundara **90** B 3
Koundian **90** B 3
Koungheul **90** AB 3
Kourou **109** H 2
Koutous **91** FG 3
Kouvola **54** J 3
Kova **68** H 4
Kovac **58** A 2
Kovel' **55** H 5
Kovrizhka **69** U 3
Kovrov **62** GH 4
Kowloon **70** FG 6
Kowt-e-Ashrow **67** H 4
Koyuk **98** E 2
Koyukuk **98** F 2
Koyukuk **98** F 2
Kozáni **58** B 2
Kozlu **59** D 2
Kra, Isthmus of **73** G 5
Kragujevac **58** B 2
Kraljevo **58** B 2
Kramfors **54** G 3
Kranj **57** F 2
Krasino **62** K 1
Krasnaya Yaranga **98** C 2
Kraśnik **53** H 4
Krasnodar **59** EF 1–2
Krasnogorsk **69** Q 6
Krasnoje Selo **55** JK 4
Krasnokamsk **62** KL 4
Krasnotur'insk **63** M 4
Krasnoural'sk **63** M 4
Krasnovodsk **66** E 2
Krasnoyarsk **68** F 4
Krasnoyarskiy **63** L 5
Krasnyy Chikoy **68** J 5
Krasnyy Luch **59** E 1
Kremenchug **62** FG 6
Kresti **62** F 4
Krestovka **62** K 2
Krestovskaye **69** P 4
Kresty **68** E 1
Kribi **91** F 5
Krichev **62** F 5
Krishna **72** C 4
Kristiansand **55** E 4
Kristianstad **55** F 4
Kristiansund **54** E 3
Kristineberg **54** G 2
Kristinehamn **55** F 4
Kristinestad (Kristiinankaupunki) **54** H 3
Kríti **58** B 3
Kritikón Pélagos **58** BC 3
Krivoy Rog **59** D 1
Krk **57** F 2
Krnov **53** G 4
Krokom **54** F 3
Kronotsi **69** U 5
Kronotskaya Sopka **69** TU 5
Kronshtadt **55** J 4
Kroonstad **94** D 5
Kropotkin **59** F 1
Krosno **53** H 5
Krotoszyn **53** G 4
Kruger National Park **95** E 4
Krugersdorp **94** D 5
Krung Thep **73** H 5
Kruševac **58** B 2
Krutinka **63** O 4
Kryazh Kula **69** O 2
Krym (Ukraine, U.S.S.R.) **59** D 1
Krymsk **59** E 1
Krymskiye Gory **59** D 2
Ksabi **86** E 3
Ksar Chellala **87** F 1
Ksar el Boukhari **87** F 1
Ksar Torchane **86** C 4
Ksen'yevka **68** L 5
Kuala Lumpur **74** B 3
Kuala Terengganu **74** B 2
Kuamut **74** E 2
Kuantan **74** B 3
Kuban' **59** E 1–2
Kubenskoye, Ozero **62** G 4
Kudus **74** D 5
Kudymkar **62** KI 4
Kufstein **57** F 2
Kūh-e 'Alīābād (Iran) **61** F 2
Kūh-e Alījūq (Iran) **61** F 3
Kūh-e Alvano (Iran) **61** E 2
Kūh-e Būl (Iran) **61** F 3
Kūh-e Dīnār (Iran) **61** F 3
Kūh-e Dinar (Iran) **66** E 4
Kūh-e Garbosh (Iran) **61** EF 2
Kūh-e Garri (Iran) **61** E 2
Kūh-e Gūgerd (Iran) **61** F 2
Kūh-e Karkas (Iran) **61** F 2
Kūh-e Khabr (Iran) **61** G 3
Kūh-e Khāīz (Iran) **61** F 3
Kūh-e Kharānaq (Iran) **61** G 2
Kūh-e Khvojeh (Iran) **61** E 2
Kūh-e Khvojeh (Iran) **66** D 3
Kūh-e Kūkalār (Iran) **61** F 3
Kūh-e Masāhīm (Iran) **61** G 3
Kūh-e Safīd (Iran) **61** E 2
Kūh-e Sorkh (Iran) **61** G 2
Kūhestak **66** F 5
Kūh-e Tābask (Iran) **61** F 3
Kūhhā-ye Qorūd (Iran) **61** F 2–3
Kūhhā-ye-Sabalān **66** D 3
Kūhha ye Zagros (Iran) **61** EF 2–F 3
Kuikkavaara **54** J 3
Kui Nua **74** AB 1
Kuito **94** B 2
Kuivaniemi **54** J 2
Kujani Game Reserve **90** D 4
Kuji **71** M 2
Kula Kangri **73** F 2
Kulakshi **66** EF 1
Kulaneh **67** G 5
Kul'chi **69** P 5
Kulgera **78** E 4
Kulinda **68** J 3
Kullen **55** F 4
Kul'sary **66** E 1
Kulundinskaya Step' **63** P 5
Kulyab **67** HJ 3
Kuma (Russia, U.S.S.R.) **59** G 2
Kumai, Teluk **74** D 4
Kumamoto **71** K 4
Kumanovo **58** B 2
Kumasi **90** D 4
Kumba **91** F 5
Kumbakonam **72** CD 5
Kumdah **89** H 4
Kumertau **62** KL 5
Künas **67** L 2
Kunda Hills **72** C 5
Kunduz **67** H 3
Kunene **94** A 3
Kunes **54** J 1
Kungälv **55** F 4
Kungrad **66** F 2
Kungu **92** B 4
Kungur **62** L 4
Kunlun Shan **67** KM 3
Kunlun Shankou **70** B 3
Kunming **70** D 5
Kunsan **71** J 3
Kuntuk **69** R 4
Kununurra **78** D 2
Kuop **82** B 2
Kuopio **54** J 3
Kuoqiang **70** A 3
Kuorboaivi **54** J 2
Kuoyka **68** LM 1
Kupang **75** F 6
Kupashi **71** N 2
Kupreanof **98** L 4
Kupyansk **62** G 6
Kuqa **67** L 2
Kura **59** G 2
Kurashiki **71** K 3–4
Kurdufān **88** DE 6
Kŭrdžhali **58** C 2
Kure **71** K 4
Kurgan **63** N 4
Kurgan-Tyube **67** H 3
Kuria **82** C 2
Kuria Muria Islands **89** K 5
Kurilovka **62** J 5

Kuril'skiye Ostrova (U.S.S.R) **69** RS 6
Kurmuk **88** E 6
Kurnool **72** C 4
Kursk **62** G 5
Kurşunlu Dağı **59** E 3
Kuruman **94** C 5
Kuruman **94** C 5
Kurunegala **72** D 6
Kurupka **98** C 3
Kurzeme **55** H 4
Kuşada Körfezi **58** C 3
Kusaie **82** B 2
Kushchevskaya **59** E 1
Kushiro **71** MN 2
Kushka **67** G 3
Kushmurun **63** MN 5
Kuskokwim **98** E 3
Kuskokwim Bay **98** E 4
Kuskokwim Mountains **98** FG 3
Kustanay **63** M 5
Kūstī **88** E 6
Kut (Iran) **61** E 3
Kütahya **58** C 3
Kutai, Sungai **74** E 4
Kutaisi **66** C 2
Kutch **72** AB 3
Kutch, Gulf of **72** A 3
Kutch, Rann of **72** AB 3
Kutno **53** G 4
Kuvango **94** B 2
Kuwait **61** E 3
Kuwait **89** H 3
Kuwait (Kuwait) **61** E 3
Kuybyshev **62** K 5
Kuybyshev **63** PQ 4
Kuybyshevo **69** R 6
Kuygan **63** O 6
Kūysanjaq **66** C 3
Kuytun, Gora **63** R 6
Kuyucuk Dağı **58** D 3
Kuyumba **68** G 3
Kuz'mouka **68** F 4
Kuznetsk **62** J 5
Kvænangen **54** H 1
Kvalöy **54** G 2
Kvalöya **54** H 1
Kvarner **57** F 2–3
Kvarnerič **57** F 3
Kverkfjol **54** B 3
Kvichak Bay **98** F 4
Kvikkjokk **54** G 2
Kvinesdal **55** E 4
Kviteseid **55** E 4
Kwajalein **82** C 2
Kwakoegron **109** G 2
Kwangju **71** J 3
Kwethluk **98** E 3
Kwoka, Gunung **75** H 4
Kyakhta **68** J 5
Kyancutta **79** F 5
Kyaukme **73** G 3
Kyeintali **73** F 4
Kyle of Lochalsh **52** B 3
Kynnefjell **55** F 4
Kyoga, Lake **92** E 4
Kyōto **71** KL 3
Kyrbykan **69** N 3
Kyren **68** H J 5
Kyrgyday **69** M 3
Kyrta **62** L 3
Kyrynniky **68** L 3
Kyshtovka **63** P 4
Kyshtym **63** M 4
Kystatam **68** M 2
Kytalyktakh **69** OP 2
Kyuekh-Bulung **68** KL 2
Kyushe **66** F 1
Kyūshū **71** K 4
Kyustendil **58** B 2
Kyusyur **69** N 1
Kyzas **63** RS 5
Kyzultau **63** O 6
Kyzyl **68** FG 5
Kyzyldyykan **67** H 1
Kyzylkum, Peski **67** G 2
Kyzyltau **67** J 2
Kyzyluy **67** H 1
Kzyl-Orda **67** H 2
Kzyltu **63** O 5

L

La Banda **112** D 4
Labbezenga **90** E 2
Labé (Guinea) **90** B 3
Labengke, Pulau **75** F 4
Labinsk **59** F 2
Labrador **101** NP 4
Labrador City **101** O 5
Labrador Sea **101** QR 4
Lábrea **109** F 5
Labuhanbajo **75** EF 5
Labytnangi **63** N 2
Lac Alaotra **95** H 3
Lac Albanel **101** N 5
Lac à l'Eau-Claire **101** MN 4
La Carlota **112** D 5
Lac au Goéland **101** M 5–6
Lac Bienville **101** N 4
Laccadive Islands **72** B 5
Lac Caniapiscau **101** O 5
Lac Champdoré **101** O 4
Lac Débo **90** CD 2
Lac de Gras **99** P 3
Lac de Kossou **90** CD 4
Lac d'Iberville **101** N 4
La Ceiba (Honduras) **104** E 4
Lacepede Bay **79** F 6
Lachlan River **79** GH 5
La Chorrera **108** BC 2
Lac Klotz **101** NO 3
Lac la Martre **99** O 3
Lac la Ronge **99** R 4
Lac Léman **57** E 2
Lac Mai-Ndombe **92** B 5
Lac Maunoir **99** MN 2
Lac Minto **101** N 4
Lac Mistassini **101** N 5
Lac Moero **92** D 6
Lac Naocócane **101** N 5
La Coronilla **112** F 5
La Coruña **56** B 3
La Crosse **103** H 3
La Cruz (Mexico) **102** E 7
Lac Sakami **101** M 5
Lac Seul **100** J 5
Lac Upemba **92** D 6
La Digue **93** K 5
Ladoga, Lake **54** K 3
La Dorada **108** D 2
Ladozhskoye Ozero **54** K 3
Ladysmith **94** D 5
Lae (Marshall Is.) **82** C 2
Lae (Papua New Guinea) **80** E 3
Læsö **55** F 4
La Estrada **56** B 3
Lafayette (IN, U.S.A.) **103** J 3
Lafayette (LA, U.S.A.) **103** H 5–6
Lafia **91** F 4
Lafiagi **91** EF 4
La Fría **108** D 2
Lagarto **111** J 3
Laghouat **87** F 2
Lagoa dos Patos **112** F 5
Lago Agrio **108** C 4
Lagoa Mangueira **112** F 5
Lagoa Mirim **112** F 5
Lago Buenos Aires **113** B 8
Lago Cabora Bassa **95** E 3
Lago Chilwa **95** F 3
Lago de Maracaibo **108** D 1–2
Lago de Nicaragua **104** EF 5
Lago de Poopó **110** C 4
Lago di Bolsena **57** F 3
Lago Maggiore **57** E 2
Lago O'Higgins **113** B 8
Lago Posadas **113** B 8
Lago Rogagua **110** C 3
Lagos (Nigeria) **90** E 4
Lago Titicaca **110** C 4
Lago Viedma **113** B 8
La Grande **102** C 2
La Gran Sabana **109** F 2–3
Laguna **112** G 4
Laguna Madre (TX, U.S.A.) **103** G 6
Laguna Mar Chiquita **112** D 5
Laguna Merín **112** F 5
Lagunas (Chile) **110** BC 5
Lagunas (Peru) **108** C 5
Lagune Ndogo **91** G 6
Lagune Nkomi **91** F 6
Lagunillas **110** D 4
La Habana **105** F 3
Lāhījān **66** E 3
Lāhījān (Iran) **61** F 1
Lahore **67** J 4
Lahti **54** J 3
Lai **91** H 4
Lainioälven **54** H 2
Lajes (Santa Catarina, Brazil) **112** FG 4
La Junta (Bolivia) **110** D 4
La Junta (Mexico) **102** E 6
Lake Abaya **93** F 3
Lake Abitibi **101** M 6
Lake Albert (Zaire/Uganda) **92** E 4
Lake Amadeus **78** E 3
Lake Argyle **78** D 2
Lake Athabasca **99** Q 4
Lake Austin **78** B 4
Lake Ballard **78** C 4
Lake Bangweulu **94** D 2
Lake Barlee **78** B 4
Lake Carey **78** C 4
Lake Carnegie **78** C 4
Lake Chad **91** G 3
Lake Charles **103** H 5
Lake City (FL, U.S.A.) **103** K 5
Lake Claire **99** P 4
Lake Clark National Park and Preserve **98** FG 3
Lake Dall, **98** E 3
Lake Disappointment **78** C 3
Lake Edward **92** D 5
Lake Erie **103** K 3
Lake Eyasi **92** E 5
Lake Eyre **79** F 4
Lake Eyre Basin **79** F 4
Lake Francis Case **102** FG 3
Lake Gairdner **79** F 5
Lake Grandin **99** O 3
Lake Gregory (South Australia) **79** FG 4
Lake Huron **103** K 3
Lake Itchen, **99** P 2
Lake Kariba **94** D 3
Lake Kivu **92** D 5
Lake Kyoga **92** E 4
Lakeland **103** K 6
Lake Lefroy **78** C 5
Lake Mackay **78** D 3
Lake Malawi (Lake Nyasa) **95** EF 2
Lake Manitoba **99** S 5
Lake Maurice **78** E 4
Lake Mc Leod **78** A 3
Lake Melville **101** Q 5
Lake Michigan **103** J 3
Lake Moore **78** B 4
Lake Mweru **92** D 6
Lake Nash **79** F 3
Lake Nasser (Egypt) **60** A 5
Lake Nasser (Egypt) **88** E 4
Lake Natron **93** F 5
Lake Nipigon **100** K 6
Lake Nipissing **101** LM 6
Lake Nyesa **95** EF 2
Lake Oahe **102** FG 2
Lake of the Ozarks **103** H 4
Lake of the Woods **100** H 6
Lake Okeechobee **103** K 6
Lake Ontario **103** L 3
Lake Powell **102** DE 4
Lake Rebecca **78** C 4–5
Lake River **101** L 5
Lake Rukwa **92** E 6
Lake Saint Lucia **95** E 5
Lake Sakakawea **102** F 2
Lake Stefanie **93** F 4
Lake Superior **103** J 2
Lake Tana **93** F 2
Lake Tanganyika **92** DE 6
Lake Taupo **81** R 8
Lake Torrens **79** F 5
Lake Turkana (Lake Rudolf) **93** F 4
Lake Victoria **92** E 5
Lake Volta **90** DE 4
Lake Winnipeg **99** S 5
Lake Winnipegosis **99** RS 5
Lakewood (CO, U.S.A.) **102** E 4
Lakon **81** J 4
Lakon **82** C 3
Lakonikos Kólpos **58** B 3
Lakselv **54** J 1–2
Lakshadweep **72** B 5
Lalara **91** G 5
Lâleli Geçidi **59** E 3
La Ligua **112** B 5
La Linea **56** B 4
Lalitpur **72** C 3
La Loche **99** Q 4

La Mancha **56** C 4
La Manche **52** CD 4
Lamar **102** F 4
La Mariscala **112** F 5
La Marmora **57** E 4
Lamarque **113** C 6
Lamas **108** C 5
Lambaréné **91** F 6
Lambayeque **108** B 5
Lambert, Cape **81** F 2
Lambert Glacier **115**
Lamberts Bay **94** B 6
La Merced **112** C 4
Lamezia Terme **57** G 4
Lamía **58** B 3
Lamington National Park **79** J 4
La Montaña **110** B 2–3
La Mosquitia **104** F 4–5
Lamotrek **82** A 2
Lampang **73** G 4
Lamu **93** G 5
Lancang **70** C 6
Lancaster **52** C 4
Lancaster (CA, U.S.A.) **102** C 5
Lanciano **57** F 3
Land's End **52** B 4
Landshut **53** F 5
Landskrona **55** F 4
Landsort **55** G 4
Landsortsdjupet **55** G 4
Langjökull **54** AB 3
Langkon **74** E 2
Langöya **54** F 2
Langry **69** Q 5
Lang Son **73** J 3
Langzhong **70** E 4
Lansing (MI, U.S.A.) **103** JK 3
Lantini **57** G 4
Lanzarote **86** C 3
Lanzhou **70** DE 3
Laoag **75** J 1
Laon **56** D 2
La Oroya **110** A 3
Laos **73** HJ 4
Laouni **87** G 4
Lapa **112** G 4
La Palma (Canary Islands) **86** B 3
La Palma (Panamá) **108** C 2
La Paragua **109** F 2
La Paz (Argentina) **112** C 5
La Paz (Argentina) **112** E 5
La Paz (Bolivia) **110** C 4
La Paz (Mexico) **102** D 7
La Perouse Strait **71** M 2
La Piedad **104** B 3
Lapland **54** H 2
La Plata **112** E 5–6
Lappajärvi **54** H 3
Lappi **54** J 2
Laptev Sea **114**
Lapua **54** H 3
L'Aquila **57** F 3
Lâr (Iran) **61** G 4
Larache **86** D 1
Laramie Mountains **102** E 3
Larantuka **75** F 5
Laredo (TX, U.S.A.) **102** G 6
Lârestân **66** EF 5
Lârestân (Iran) **61** G 4
La Ribera **56** C 3
La Rioja (Argentina) **112** C 4
La Rioja (Spain) **56** C 3
Lárisa **58** B 3
Larkana **67** H 5
Larlomkriny **63** O 4
Larnaca (Cyprus) **60** A 2
Larne **52** B 4
La Rochelle **56** C 2
La Roche-sur-Yon **56** C 2
La Romana **105** J 4
La Ronge **99** Q 4
Larrey Point **78** B 2
Larsen Ice Shelf **115**
La Salina **102** D 5
Lâs 'Ânôd **93** H 3
Las Cejas **112** D 4
Lâs Dâred **93** H 2
La Serena (Chile) **112** B 4
La Serena (Spain) **56** B 4
La Seyne-sur-Mer **57** E 3
Las Flores **113** E 6
Lâsh-e Joveyn **67** G 4
Lashio **73** G 3
Lashkar Gâh **67** GH 4
Las Lajas **113** BC 6
Las Palmas **86** BC 3
La Spezia **57** EF 3
Las Plumas **113** C 7
Las Tablas **108** B 2
Las Vegas (NV, U.S.A.) **102** C 4
Latady Island **115**
Latakia (Syria) **60** B 2
Lätäseno **54** H 2
Latgales Augstiene **55** J 4
Latviya **55** J 4
Laughlin Peak **102** F 4
Lau Group **82** D 4
Lauhanvuori **54** H 3
Launceston **82** A 5
Launceston (Tasmania, Austr.) **80** L 9
La Unión (Chile) **113** B 7
Laurentian Scarp **101** M 6
Lauria **57** G 3
Lausanne **57** E 2
Laut, Pulau **74** E 4
Laut Arafura **75** HJ 5
Laut Bali **74** E 5
Laut Banda **75** GH 5
Laut Flores **75** E 5
Laut Halmahera **75** G 4
Laut Jawa **74** CD 4
Laut Seram **75** G 4
Laut Sulawesi **75** EF 3
Laut Timor **75** GH 5
Laval (France) **56** C 2
Laval (Quebec, Can.) **101** N 6
Lâvân (Iran) **61** F 4
La Vega **105** H 4
Lavka Integralsoyuza **69** VW 2
Lawra **90** D 3
Lawton **102** G 5
Laydennyy, Mys **62** J 2
La Zarca **104** B 2
Lazarev **69** Q 5
Lâzeh (Iran) **61** F 4
Leavenworth **103** GH 4
Lebanon **88** EF 2
Lebanon (Lebanon) **60** B 2
Lebanon (PA, U.S.A.) **103** L 3
Lebedin **62** F 5
Lebu **113** B 6
Lebyazh'ye **63** P 5
Lecce **57** G 3
Lechang **70** F 5
Le Creusot **57** D 2
Leeds **52** C 4
Leeuwarden **52** DE 4
Leeward Islands (French Polynesia) **83** E 4
Leeward Islands (West Indies) **105** K 4
Leganés **56** C 3
Legaspi **75** F 1
Legnago **57** F 2
Legnano **57** E 2
Legnica **53** G 4
Legune **78** D 2
Le Havre **56** CD 2
Leicester **52** C 4
Leichardt River (Queensland, Austr.) **79** F 2
Leiden **52** DE 4
Leipzig **53** F 4
Leiyang **70** F 5
Leka **54** F 2
Lékana **91** G 6
Leksozero, Ozero **54** K 3
Leleque **113** B 7
Le Maire, Estrecho de **113** CD 9–10
Léman, Lac **57** E 2
Le Mans **56** D 2
Le Mars **103** G 3
Lemieux Islands **101** P 3
Lemmenjoki **54** J 2
Lemmon **102** F 2
Lemoro **75** F 4
Lena **68** J 4
Lendery **62** F 3
Leninabad **67** HJ 2–3
Leninakan **59** F 2
Leningrad **55** K 4
Leningradskaya **115**
Leninogorsk **62** K 5
Leninogorsk **63** Q 5
Leninsk-Kuznetskiy **63** QR 5
Len'ki **63** Q 5
Lenkoran' **66** D 3
Lensk **68** K 3
León **56** B 3
Leon (Mexico) **104** B 3
León (Nicaragua) **104** E 5
León (Spain) **56** B 3
Leonardville **94** B 4
Leonora **78** C 4
Leopold and Astrid Coast **115**
Leorla **70** A 2
Lepsy **63** P 6
Le Puy **56** D 2
Lerfroy, Lake **78** C 5
Lérida (Colombia) **108** D 3
Lérida (Spain) **56** D 3
Leronotski **69** V 4
Léros **58** C 3
Lerum **55** F 4
Lerwick **52** C 2
Leskovac **58** B 2
Les Landes **56** C 3
Lesnaya **69** U 4
Lesosibirsk **68** F 4
Lesotho **94** D 5
Lesozavodsk **71** KL 1
L'Esperance Rock **82** D 5
Lesser Antilles **105** K 4–5
Lesser Slave Lake **99** OP 4
Lestijoki **54** H 3
Lésvos **58** C 3
Leszno **53** G 4
Lethbridge **99** P 6
Lethem **109** G 3
Leti, Kepulauan **75** G 5
Leticia **108** D 4
Letsok-aw Kyun **73** G 5
Leuser, Gunung **74** A 3
Levante, Riviera di **57** E 3
Levis **101** N 6
Levkás **58** B 3
Lewis **52** B 3
Lewiston (ID, U.S.A.) **102** C 2
Lewiston (ME, U.S.A.) **103** N 3
Lexington **103** K 4
Lhari **70** B 4
Lhasa **73** F 2
Lhazhong **72** E 1
Liancheng **70** G 5
Lianjiang **70** EF 6
Lian Xian **70** F 6
Lianyin **69** M 5
Lianyungang **71** GH 4
Liao He **71** H 2
Liaoning **71** H 2
Liaoyuan **71** HJ 2
Liard **99** N 3
Liard River **99** M 4
Liberal **102** F 4
Liberia **90** BC 4
Liberia (Costa Rica) **104** E 5
Libya **87** HK 3
Libyan Desert **88** CD 3–4
Licata **57** F 4
Lichinga **95** F 2
Lida (U.S.S.R.) **55** J 5
Lidköping **55** F 4
Liechtenstein **57** EF 2
Liege **52** E 4
Lieksa **54** K 3
Lienart **92** D 4
Lienz **57** F 2
Liepāja **55** H 4
Lievestuoreenjärvi **54** J 3
Lifou **81** J 6
Ligurian Sea **57** E 3
Lihir Group **82** B 3
Lihou Reef and Cays **79** J 2
Lijiang **70** D 5
Likasi **94** D 2
Likiep **82** C 2
Likouala **91** H 5
Lille **56** D 1
Lilongwe **95** E 2
Lima (OH, U.S.A.) **103** K 3
Lima (Peru) **110** A 3
Lima (Portugal) **56** B 3
Limassol (Cyprus) **59** D 4
Limassol (Cyprus) **60** A 2
Limay Mahuida **113** C 6
Limerick **52** B 4
Limfjorden **55** E 4
Limningen **54** F 3
Límnos **58** C 3
Limoeiro **111** JK 2
Limoges **56** D 2
Limon (CO, U.S.A.) **102** F 4

Limón (Costa Rica) **104** F 5
Limousin **56** D 2
Limpopo **95** E 4
Linakamen **54** K 2
Linares (Chile) **113** B 6
Linares (Mexico) **104** C 3
Linares (Spain) **56** C 4
Lincang **70** CD 6
Lincoln (NE, U.S.A.) **103** G 3
Lincoln (U.K.) **52** C 4
Lincoln Sea **114**
Lindau **53** EF 5
Linden **109** G 2
Lindesnes **55** E 4
Lindi (Tanzania) **93** F 6–7
Line Islands **83** E 2–3
Linfen **70** F 3
Lingayen **75** H 1
Lingga, Kepulauan **74** B 3–4
Lingomo **92** C 4
Lingyuan **71** G 2
Linhares **111** J 4
Linhe **70** E 2
Linhpa **73** G 2
Linjanti **94** C 3
Linköping **55** G 4
Linkou **71** JK 1
Linosa **57** F 4
Lins **111** G 5
Lintao **70** D 3
Linxi **71** G 2
Linxia **70** D 3
Linyi (Shandong, China) **71** G 3
Linz **57** F 2
Lipa **75** F 1
Lipari **57** G 4
Lipetsk **62** GH 5
Lipin Bor **62** G 3
Lisala **92** C 4
Lisboa **56** B 4
Lisbon (Portugal) **56** B 4
Lisburn **52** B 4
Lisburne, Cape **98** D 2
Lishui **71** GH 5
Lisichansk **62** G 6
Lisieux **56** D 2
Lithinon, Ákra **58** B 4
Lithuania **55** H 4
Litke **69** Q 5
Litovko **69** P 6
Little Abaco Island **105** G 2
Little Andaman **73** F 5
Little Colorado River **102** D 4
Little Desert National Park **79** G 6
Little Grand Rapids **99** ST 5
Little Nicobar **73** FG 6
Little Rock **103** H 5
Litva **55** H 4
Liuzhou **70** EF 6
Livengood **98** H 2
Liverpool **52** C 4
Livingston (MT, U.S.A.) **102** DE 2
Livingstone **94** D 3
Livingstone Falls **91** G 7
Livoniya **55** J 4
Livorno **57** EF 3
Liwale **93** F 6
Liwonde **95** F 2–3
Li Xian **70** D 4
Li Xian **70** F 5
Lizard **52** BC 5
Lizarda **109** J 5
Ljubeli **57** F 2
Ljungby **55** F 4
Ljusnan **54** F 3
Llallaqua **110** C 4
Llano Estacado **102** F 5
Llanos **108** DE 2–3
Llanos de Moxos **110** CD 4
Llullaillaco, Volcán **110** C 5
Lobito **94** A 2
Locarno **57** E 2
Loch Lomond **52** C 3
Loch Ness **52** C 3
Lockhart River Mission **79** G 1
Lod (Israel) **60** B 3
Lodja **92** C 5
Lodwar **92** F 4
Łodz **53** G 4
Lofoten **54** F 2
Logan, Mount **98** J 3
Logroño **56** C 3
Lohjanjärvi **55** H 3
Lohjanselkä **55** H 3
Loholoho **75** F 4
Loire, Val de **56** D 2
Loja **108** C 4
Lokan tekojärvi **54** J 2
Lokilalaki, Gunung **75** F 4
Lökken (Norway) **54** E 3
Lokshak **69** O 5
Loks Land **101** P 3
Lolland **55** F 5
Lomami **92** C 4–5
Loma Mountains **90** B 4
Lomas **110** B 4
Lomas de Zamora **112** DE 6
Lomblen, Pulau **75** F 5
Lombok **74** E 5
Lomé **90** E 4
Lomonosov **55** J 4
Lompoc **102** B 5
Łomz'a **53** H 4
Loncoche **113** B 6
London **101** L 7
London (U.K.) **52** CD 4
Londonderry (Chile) **113** B 10
Londonderry (U.K.) **52** B 3
Londonderry, Cape **78** D 1
Londrina **111** F 5
Long Beach (CA, U.S.A.) **102** C 5
Long Beach (WA, U.S.A.) **102** AB 2
Long Island (Papua New Guinea) **80** E 2–3
Long Island (The Bahamas) **105** GH 3
Longjiang **69** M 6
Longlac **100** K 6
Longmont **102** E 3
Long Range Mountaines **101** Q 5–6
Longreach **79** G 3
Long Valley **102** D 5
Longview (TX, U.S.A.) **103** GH 5
Longview (WA, U.S.A.) **102** B 2
Longxi **70** D 3
Long Xian **70** E 4
Long Xuyen **73** J 5
Longyan **70** G 5
Longzhou **70** E 6
Lookout, Cape **103** L 5
Lopatka **69** T 5
Lop Buri **73** H 5
Lopcha **69** M 4
Lop Nur **70** B 2
Lopphavet **54** H 1
Lopydino **62** K 3
Lorca **56** C 4
Lord Howe Island **79** K 5
Lordsburg **102** E 5
Lorestan (Iran) **61** E 2
Lorestan (Iran) **89** H 2
Loreto **102** D 6
Loreto (Colombia) **108** D 4
Loreto (Maranhão, Brazil) **109** JK 5
Lorient **56** C 2
Lorraine **57** E 2
Los Alamos **102** E 4
Los Angeles **102** BC 5
Los Ángeles (Chile) **113** B 6
Losap **82** B 2
Los Blancos **110** D 5
Los Gatos **102** B 4
Lošinj **57** F 3
Los Lagos **113** B 6
Los Lavaderos **104** C 3
Los Mochis **102** E 6
Lospalos **75** G 5
Los Teques **108** E 1
Lost Trail Pass **102** D 2
Los Vilos **112** B 5
Lot **56** D 3
Lota **113** B 6
Lotta **54** J 2
Loubomo **91** G 6
Louga **90** A 2
Louisiade Archipelago **79** J 1
Louisiana **103** H 5
Louis Trichardt **94** D 4
Louisville **103** J 4
Loukhi **62** F 2
Loum **91** FG 5
Lövånger **54** H 3
Lovech **58** B 2
Lovelock **102** C 3
Loviisa **55** J 3
Lovozero **54** L 2
Low, Cape **99** UV 3
Lowa **92** D 5
Lowell **103** M 3
Lower California **102** D 6
Lowestoft **52** D 4
Loyalty Islands **81** J 6
Loyalty Islands **82** C 4
Loyoro **92** E 4
Luacano **94** C 2
Lualaba **92** D 5
Luanda **94** A 1
Luando **94** B 2
Luando **94** B 2
Luando Reserve **94** B 2
Luang Prabang **73** H 4
Luangwa **95** E 2
Luangwa Valley Game Reserve **95** E 2
Luanshya **94** D 2
Luapala **94** D 2
Luba **91** F 5
Lubalo **94** B 1
Lubang Islands **75** EF 1
Lubango **94** A 2
Lubao **92** D 6
Lubbock **102** F 5
Lübeck **53** F 4
Lubefu **92** CD 5
Lublin **53** H 4
Lubnān, Jabal (Lebanon) **60** B 2
Lubny **62** F 6
Lubumbashi **94** D 2
Lucas **110** E 3
Lucea **105** G 4
Lucena (Spain) **56** C 4
Lučenec **53** G 5
Lucera **57** G 3
Lucero **102** E 5
Lüchun **70** D 6
Lucknow **72** D 2
Lucusse **94** C 2
Lüda **71** H 3
Ludhiana **72** BC 1
Ludogorie **58** C 2
Ludvika **55** G 3
Ludwigshafen **53** E 5
Luebo **92** C 6
Lüeyang **70** E 4
Lufeng **70** G 6
Luga **55** J 4
Lugano **57** E 2
Luganville **82** C 4
Lugenda **95** F 2
Lugnvik **54** G 3
Lugo **56** B 3
Lugoj **58** B 1
Lugovoy **67** J 2
Luhuo **70** D 4
Luiana **94** C 3
Luimneach **52** B 4
Luís Correia **111** H 1
Luiza **92** C 6
Lukashkin Yar **63** PQ 3
Lukolela (Congo) **92** B 5
Luleå **54** H 2
Luleälven **54** H 2
Lüleburgaz **58** C 2
Lumbala Kaquengue **94** C 2
Lumbala N'guimbo **94** C 2
Lumding **73** F 2
Lumsden **80** P 10
Lunda Norte **94** BC 1
Lunda Sul **94** C 2
Lundazi **95** E 2
Lüneburg **53** EF 4
Lunkho **67** J 3
Luochuan **70** E 3
Luofu **92** D 5
Luoisiade **82** B 3
Luoyang **70** F 4
Luoyuan **71** GH 5
Lupane **94** D 3
Lupeni **58** B 1
Luputa **92** C 6
Lūq **93** G 4
Lusaka **94** D 3
Lusambo **92** C 5
Lushui **70** C 5
Lusk **102** F 3
Lūt, Dasht-e (Iran) **61** G 2
Luton **52** C 4
Lutsk **55** J 5

Luxembourg **52** DE 5
Luxi **70** C 6
Luxi **70** D 6
Luxor (Egypt) **60** A 4
Luza **62** J 3
Luza **62** J 3
Luzern **57** E 2
Luzhai **70** E 6
Luzhou **70** E 5
Luzhskaya Vozvyshennost' **55** HJ 4
L'vovka **63** P 4
Lyakhovskiye Ostrova **69** P 1
Lynchburg **103** L 4
Lynd **79** G 2
Lynn Lake **99** RS 4
Lynx Lake **99** Q 3
Lyon **57** E 2
Łyso Gory **53** H 4
Lyubertsy **62** G 4

M

Ma'ān (Jordan) **60** B 3
Maarianhamina (Mariehamn) **55** H 3–4
Ma'arrat an Nu'mān (Syria) **59** E 3–4
Ma'arrat an Nu'mān (Syria) **60** B 2
Maastricht **52** E 4
Mabaruma **109** G 2
Mabote **95** E 4
Ma'būs Yūsuf **87** K 3
Macadam Plains **78** B 4
Macaíba **111** J 2
Macao **70** F 6
Macapá **109** H 3
Macará (Peru) **108** C 4
Macas **108** C 4
Macau **111** J 2
Macauley **82** D 4–5
Macdonnell Ranges **78** E 3
Maceió **111** JK 2
Macerata **57** F 3
Machala **108** C 4
Machevna **69** W 3
Machilipatnam **72** D 4
Machupicchu **110** B 3
Macia **95** E 5
Mackay, Lake **78** D 3
Mackenzie **98** LM 2
Mackenzie Bay **98** K 2
Mac Kenzie Bay **115**
Mackenzie King Island **114**
Mackenzie Mountains **98–99** LM 2–3
Mackenzie River **79** H 3
Mackinaw City **103** K 2
Macocola **94** B 1
Macomia **95** FG 2
Mâcon (France) **57** DE 2
Macon (GA, U.S.A.) **103** K 5
Macquarie Island **115**
Mac Robertson Land **115**
Madagascar **95** H 3
Madā'in Şāliḥ **66** B 5
Madang **80** E 3
Madang **82** A 3
Madaoua **91** F 3
Madd, Ra's Abū (Saudi Arabia) **60** B 4
Madeira (Brazil) **109** F 4–5
Madeira (Portugal) **86** B 2
Madeleine, Île de la **101** P 6
Madeniyet **63** P 6
Madetkoski **54** J 2
Madhya Pradesh **72** CD 3
Madimba **92** B 5
Madingo-Kayes **91** G 6
Madison (WI, U.S.A.) **103** HJ 3
Madiun **74** D 5
Madoi **70** C 4
Madrakah **66** BC 6
Madrakah, Ra's al **89** K 5
Madras (India) **72** D 5
Madre de Dios **110** C 3
Madre Oriental, Sierra **104** BC 2–3
Madrid **56** C 3
Madrona, Sierra **56** C 4
Madura, Pulau **74** D 5
Madurai **72** C 6
Madyan (Saudi Arabia) **60** B 4
Maebashi **71** L 3
Maevatanana **95** H 3
Maéwo **81** J 5
Mafeteng **94** D 5
Mafia Island **93** G 6
Magadan **69** S 4
Magallanes, Estrecho de **113** B 9
Magangue **108** D 2
Magaria **91** F 3
Magdagachi **69** N 5
Magdalena (Colombia) **108** D 1–2
Magdeburg **53** F 4
Magellan, Strait of **113** BC 9
Mageröya **54** J 1
Maggiore, Lago **57** E 2
Magnitogorsk **63** L 5
Magyarország **58** A 1
Mahābād (Iran) **61** D 1
Mahābād (Iran) **66** D 3
Mahabharat Range **72** E 2
Mahabo **95** GH 4
Mahadday Wêyne **93** H 4
Mahajan **72** B 2
Mahajanga **95** H 3
Mahalapye **94** D 4
Mahanoro **95** H 3
Maharashtra **72** BC 4
Maha Sarakham **73** H 4
Mahatsanary **95** G 5
Mahbés **86** CD 3
Mahbubnagar **72** C 4
Mahd adh Dhahab **66** C 6
Maḥḍah (Oman) **61** G 4
Mahdia (Guyana) **109** G 2
Mahenge **93** F 6
Mahesana **72** B 3
Mahia Peninsula **81** R 8
Mahkene **54** F 3
Mahmūdābād (Iran) **61** F 1
Mahmud-Raqi **67** H 4
Mahón **56** D 4
Mahuva **72** B 3
Maiana **82** C 2
Maiduguri **91** G 3
Maimana **67** GH 3
Mai-Ndombe, Lac **92** B 5
Maine **103** N 2
Mainland (Orkney Is., U.K.) **52** C 3
Mainland (Shetland Is., U.K.) **52** C 2
Maintirano **95** G 3
Mainz **53** E 5
Maio **90** B 6
Maipú (Argentina) **113** E 6
Maipuco **108** D 4
Maitengwe **94** D 4
Maitland (N.S.W., Austr.) **79** J 5
Maíz, Isla del **104** F 5
Majuro **82** C 2
Makale (Ethiopia) **93** FG 2
Makambako **92** EF 6
Makarikari **94** CD 4
Makarikha **63** LM 2
Makarov **69** Q 6
Makat **66** E 1
Makaw **70** C 5
Makedhonía **58** B 2
Makedonia **58** B 2
Makeyevka **59** E 1
Makgadikgadi Pan **94** CD 4
Makhachkala **66** D 2
Makinsk **63** O 5
Makkah **89** G 4
Makó **58** B 1
Makokou **91** G 5
Makran **66–67** G 5
Makri **72** D 4
Maksimovka **71** L 1
Mākū **59** F 3
Makurdi **91** F 4
Makushino **63** N 4
Makuyuni **93** F 5
Makwa **82** BC 3
Malabar Coast **72** BC 5–6
Malabo **91** F 5
Malacca, Strait of **74** B 3
Málaga **56** C 4
Malagasy Republic **95** H 3
Malaimbandy **95** H 4
Malaita **81** H 3
Malaita **82** B 3
Malakāl **92** E 3
Malakula **81** J 5
Malang **74** D 5
Malanje **94** B 1
Malao **81** J 5
Mälaren **55** G 4
Malargue **113** C 6
Malaspina (Argentina) **113** C 7
Malatya **59** E 3
Malatya Dağları **59** E 3
Malawi **95** E 2
Malāwi (Iran) **61** E 2
Malawi, Lake **95** EF 2
Malawi National Park **95** E 2
Malaybalay **75** FG 2
Malāyer (Iran) **61** E 2
Malaysia **74** BD 2
Malden **83** E 3
Maldives **72** B 6
Maldonado **112** F 5
Malegaon **72** BC 3
Malei **95** F 3
Malek **92** E 3
Malekula **82** C 4
Maleyevo **68** G 4
Malhada **111** H 3
Mali **90** CD 2–3
Mali Kyun **73** G 5
Malindi **93** G 5
Maling, Gunung **75** F 3
Malin Head **52** B 3
Mallaig **52** B 3
Mallani **72** B 2
Mallery Lake **99** S 3
Mallorca **56** D 4
Malmö **55** F 4
Maloelap **82** C 2
Malozemel'skaya Tundra **62** JK 2
Malpelo, Isla **108** B 3
Malta **57** F 4
Malta (MT, U.S.A.) **102** E 2
Maluku **75** G 4
Maluku, Laut **75** G 3
Malung **55** F 3
Maly Kavkaz **59** FG 2
Malyy Lyakhovskiy, Ostrov **69** Q 1
Malyy Yenisey **68** FG 5
Mama **68** K 4
Mamagota **81** FG 3
Mambasa **92** D 4
Mambéré **92** B 3–4
Mamoré **110** C 3
Mamou **90** B 3
Mamuju **75** E 4
Mamuno **94** C 4
Man **90** C 4
Manacapuru **109** F 4
Manado **75** F 3
Managua **104** E 5
Manaka **81** Q 9
Manakara **95** H 4
Manama (Bahrain) **61** F 4
Mananara **95** H 3
Manapouri **82** C 6
Manas (China) **67** M 2
Manaus **109** FG 4
Manchester **52** C 4
Manchuria **71** HJ 2
Máncora **108** B 4
Mand (Iran) **61** F 3
Mandalay **73** G 3
Mandal-Ovoo **70** D 2
Mandasor **72** B 3
Mandera **93** G 4
Mandeville **105** G 4
Mandiana **90** C 3
Mandimba **95** F 2
Mandji **91** G 6
Mandla **72** CD 3
Mandor **74** C 3
Mandvi **72** A 3
Manfredonia **57** G 3
Manga (Minas Gerais, Brazil) **111** H 3
Manga (Niger/Chad) **91** GH 3
Mangaia **83** E 4
Mangalore **72** B 5
Mangnai **70** B 3
Mangoky **95** G 4
Mangole, Pulau **75** G 4
Mangueira, Lagoa **112** F 5
Mangut **68** K 6
Manhan **68** F 6
Manhattan **103** G 4
Manicaland **95** E 3

Manicore **109** F 5
Manicouagan **101** O 5
Maniganggo **70** CD 4
Manihi **83** F 3
Manipur **73** F 3
Manisa **58** C 3
Manistique **103** J 2
Manitoba **99** S 5
Manitoba, Lake **99** S 5
Manitowoc **103** J 3
Manizales **108** C 2
Manjil (Iran) **61** E 1
Mankato **103** H 3
Manlay **70** E 2
Manmad **72** BC 3
Mannheim **53** E 4–5
Manning **99** O 4
Manoa **108** E 5
Manono **92** D 6
Manra **82** D 3
Manresa **56** D 3
Mansa **94** D 2
Mansel Island **101** L 3
Mansfield (OH, U.S.A.) **103** K 3
Manta **108** B 4
Mantecal **108** E 2
Mantova **57** F 2
Manú **110** B 3
Manuae **83** E 4
Manuangi **83** F 4
Manuel Urbano **108** DE 5
Manukau **82** C 5
Manus **80** E 2
Manus **82** A 3
Manychskaya Vpadina **59** F 1
Manyoni **92** E 6
Manzanillo (Cuba) **105** G 3
Manzanillo (Mexico) **104** B 4
Manzhouli **68** L 6
Manzil Bū Ruqaybah **87** G 1
Manzurka **68** J 5
Mao **105** H 4
Maoke, Pegunungan **75** J 4
Maoming **70** F 6
Mapaga **75** EF 4
Mapai **95** E 4
Mapi **75** J 5
Maple Creek **99** Q 6
Mapuera **109** G 4
Maputo **95** E 5
Maquela do Zombo **94** B 1
Maquinchao **113** C 7
Maraá **108** E 4
Marabá **109** HJ 5
Maracá, Ilha de **109** HJ 3
Maracaibo **108** D 1
Maracaibo, Lago de **108** D 1–2
Maracaju **111** F 5
Maracay **108** E 1
Marādah **87** J 3
Maradi **91** F 3
Marāgheh **66** D 3
Marahuaca, Cerro **108** E 3
Marajó, Ilha de **109** HJ 4
Maramba **94** D 3
Marānd **66** D 3
Maranhão (Brazil) **111** GH 2
Marañón **108** C 4
Marão, Serra do **56** B 3
Marathon (Ontario, Can.) **100** K 6
Marawī (Sudan) **88** E 5
Marbella **56** C 4
March (Austria) **57** G 2
Marche **57** F 3
Marche, Plateaux de la **56** D 2
Mar Chiquita, Laguna **112** D 5
Mar del Plata **113** E 6
Mardin **59** F 3
Mardin Eşigi **59** F 3
Maré **81** J 6
Maré **82** C 4
Marēg **93** H 4
Marganets **59** D 1
Margaret River (Western Australia) **78** A 5
Margaritovo **71** KL 2
Margilan **67** J 2
Margyang **72** E 1–2
Mari (Burma) **73** G 2
Mari (Papua New Guinea) **80** D 3
Maria (Tuamotu Is.) **83** F 4
Maria (Tubai Is.) **83** E 4
Mariana Islands **82** A 1
Marianao **105** F 3
Maria Theresa (Pacific Ocean) **83** E 5
Mariato, Punta **108** B 2
Maria van Diemen, Cape **81** Q 7
Maribor **57** FG 2
Maricourt **101** N 3
Marie Byrd Land **115**
Mariental **94** B 4
Mariestad **55** F 4
Marietta **103** JK 5
Mariinsk **63** R 4
Mariinskoye **69** Q 5
Marília **111** G 5
Maringa (Paraná, Brazil) **111** F 5
Mariny, Iméni **69** R 3
Marion (IN, U.S.A.) **103** J 3
Marion (OH, U.S.A.) **103** K 3
Marion Reef **79** J 2
Mariu **80** D 3
Marīyyah (United Arab Emirates) **61** F 5
Märjamaa **55** HJ 4
Marka **93** GH 4
Markha **68** M 3
Marko **54** G 2
Markovo **63** R 3
Marlin **103** G 5
Marmara **58** C 2
Marmara, Sea of **58** C 2
Marmara Denizi **58** C 2
Marmaris **58** C 3
Marne **56** D 2
Maroa **108** E 3
Maroni **109** H 3
Maroua **91** GH 3
Marovoay **95** H 3
Marowijne **109** H 3
Marquadah **59** F 3
Marquesas Islands **83** F 3
Marquette **103** J 2
Marrakech **86** D 2
Marree **79** F 4
Marrero **103** HJ 6
Marrupa **95** F 2
Marsa al' Alam (Egypt) **60** B 4
Marsa al 'Alam (Egypt) **88** EF 3
Marsabit National Reserve **93** F 4
Marsala **57** F 4
Marsa 'Umm Ghayj (Egypt) **60** B 4
Marseille **57** E 3
Marsfjllet **54** G 2
Marshall Islands **82** BC 2
Marshalltown **103** H 3
Marsh Harbour **105** G 2
Marta **57** F 3
Martaban, Gulf of **73** G 4
Martigues **57** DE 3
Martinique **105** K 5
Martinique Passage **105** K 5
Martin Vaz Islands **107** H 5
Martre, Lac la **99** O 3
Marutea **83** F 4
Mary **67** G 3
Maryborough (Queensland, Austr.) **79** J 4
Maryland **103** L 4
Marystown **101** QR 6
Maryville **103** H 3
Masāhīm, Kūh-e (Iran) **61** G 3
Masai Steppe **93** F 5
Masaka **92** E 5
Masākin **87** H 1
Masan **71** J 3
Masasi **95** F 2
Masaya **104** E 5
Masbate **75** F 1
Mascarene Islands **95** K 6
Maseru **94** D 5
Mashhad **66** FG 3
Mashīz (Iran) **61** G 3
Mashīz (Iran) **66** F 5
Mashonaland **95** E 3
Masindi **92** E 4
Maşīrah **89** K 4
Masjed Soleymān (Iran) **61** E 3
Masjed Soleymān (Iran) **66** D 4
Maskanah (Syria) **60** B 2
Masoala, Cap **95** J 3
Masohi **75** G 4
Mason City **103** H 3
Masqat **89** K 4
Massachusetts **103** M 3
Massafra **57** G 3
Massangena **95** E 4
Massau **81** EF 2
Massava **63** M 3
Massawa **93** FG 1
Masset **98** L 5
Massif Central **56** D 2–3
Massif du Pelvoux **57** E 2
Massif du Tsaratanana **95** H 2
Massinga **95** F 4
Masteksay **66** E 1
Mastuj **67** J 3
Mastung **67** H 5
Mastūrah **66** B 6
Masvingo **95** E 4
Maşyāf (Syria) **60** B 2
Matabeleland **94** D 3–4
Matadi **92** A 6
Matagalpa **104** E 5
Matagami **101** M 6
Matagorda Island **103** G 6
Mataiva **83** F 3
Matam **90** B 2
Matara (Sri Lanka) **72** CD 6
Matarani **110** B 4
Mataranka **78** E 1
Matatiele **94** D 6
Matatila Dam **72** C 2
Mata-Utu **82** D 3
Matay **63** P 6
Matehuala **104** B 3
Matera **57** G 3
Mathura **72** C 2
Matla **72** E 3
Mato Grosso **110–111** EF 3
Mato Grosso (Mato Grosso, Brazil) **110** E 3
Matozinhos **56** B 3
Mátra **58** A 1
Matrūh **88** D 2
Matsudo **71** M 3
Matsue **71** K 3
Matsuyama **71** K 4
Matterhorn(NV., U.S.A.) **102** CD 3
Matterhorn (Switzerland) **57** E 2
Matthew **82** C 4
Matu **74** D 3
Matua, Ostrov **69** S 6
Maturín **109** F 2
Matyushkinskaya **63** PQ 4
Maubeuge **56** D 1
Maués **109** G 4
Maui **83** E 1
Mauke **83** E 4
Maun **94** C 4
Mauna Kea **83** E 1
Maunoir, Lac **99** MN 2
Maupihaa **83** E 4
Mauralasan **74** E 3
Maurice, Lake **78** E 4
Mauritania **86** BD 5
Mauritius **95** K 5
Mavasjaure **54** G 2
Mawson **115**
Mawson Coast **115**
Maxcanu **104** D 3
Mayaguana Island **105** H 3
Mayagüez **105** J 4
Mayāmey (Iran) **61** G 1
Mayd **93** H 2
Maydān (Iraq) **61** D 2
Maykop **59** F 2
Maymakan **69** P 4
Mayna **68** F 5
Maynas **108** C 4
Mayo, Mountains of **52** B 4
Mayor-Krest **69** Q 2
Mayotte **95** H 2
May Pen **105** G 4
Maysk **63** P 4
Mayumba **91** FG 6
Mayya **69** O 3
Mazabuka **94** D 3
Mazar **67** K 3
Mazar-i-Sharif **67** H 3
Mazatenango **104** D 5
Mazatlán **104** A 3

Mazomeno **92** D 5
Mazong Shan **70** C 2
Mazowsze **53** H 4
Mazury **53** H 4
Mbabane **95** E 5
Mbakaou Reservoir **91** G 4
Mbala (Zambia) **95** E 1
Mbale **92** E 4
Mbalmayo **91** G 5
Mbamba Bay **95** E 2
Mbandaka **92** B 4
Mbanga **91** FG 5
M'banza Congo **94** AB 1
Mbanza-Ngungu **92** B 6
Mbeya **92** E 6
Mbinda **91** G 6
Mbini **91** F 5
Mbokou **92** D 3
Mbour **90** A 3
Mbuji-Mayi **92** CD 6
McAllen **102** G 6
McCammon **102** D 3
McComb **103** H 5
McCook **102** F 3
McKean **82** D 3
McKeesport **103** L 3
McKinley, Mount **98** G 3
Mc Leod, Lake **78** A 3
M'Clintock Channel **99** R 1
M'Clure Strait **99** O 1
Mc Murdo **115**
Mc Murdo Sound **115**
Meadow Lake **99** Q 5
Meaux **56** D 2
Mecca **89** G 4
Mecklenburg **53** F 4
Mecklenburger Bucht **53** F 4
Medan **74** A 3
Medanosa, Punta **113** CD 8
Medellín **108** CD 2
Medelpad **54** G 3
Medford **102** B 3
Medgidia **58** C 2
Mediaş **58** B 1
Medicine Bow **102** E 3
Medicine Hat **99** P 5
Medigan **63** R 5
Medina **89** G 4
Medina (Saudi Arabia) **60** C 4
Mediterranean Sea **56** CE 4
Mednogorsk **63** L 5
Medvezhiy Var **68** F 1
Meekatharra **78** B 4
Meerut **72** C 2
Mega (Ethiopia) **93** F 4
Mega (Indonesia) **75** H 4
Megasani Hill **72** E 3
Meghalaya **73** F 2
Megra **62** H 2
Meguinenza, Embalse de **56** CD 3
Mehrīz (Iran) **61** G 3
Meiganga **91** G 4
Meissen **53** F 4
Mei Xian **70** G 6
Mejillones **110** BC 5
Mékambo **91** G 5
Meknès **86** D 2
Mekong **73** HJ 4–5
Mekong, Mouths of the **73** J 6
Mekongga, Gunung **75** F 4
Melaka **74** B 3
Melanesia **81** FJ 2–3
Melanesia **82** BC 3
Melbourne **79** G 6
Melbourne (FL, U.S.A.) **103** KL 6
Melchor Ocampo **104** B 4
Melendiz Dağı **59** D 3
Meletsk **68** F 4
Meleuz **62** KL 5
Melfort **99** QR 5
Melilla **86** E 1
Melimoyo, Monte **113** B 7
Melitopol' **59** E 1
Melo **112** F 5
Meltaus **54** H 2
Melun **56** D 2
Melville **99** R 5
Melville, Cape **79** G 1
Melville, Lake **101** Q 5
Melville Bay **114**
Melville Hills **99** N 2
Melville Island **78** E 1
Melville Island **114**
Melville Peninsula **99** UV 2
Melyuveyem **69** W 3
Memmingen **53** EF 5
Memphis (Egypt) **88** E 3
Memphis (TN, U.S.A.) **103** J 4
Mena **62** F 5
Ménaka **90** E 2
Mendoza (Argentina) **112** C 5
Mendoza (Peru) **108** C 5
Mengcheng **71** G 4
Mengene Dağı **59** F 3
Menghai **70** CD 6
Mengzi **70** D 6
Menihek Lakes **101** O 5
Meningie **79** FG 6
Menkere **68** M 2
Menongue **94** B 2
Menorca **56** D 3
Mentawai, Kepulauan **74** A 4
Mentese **58** C 3
Menyuan **70** D 3
Menza **68** J 6
Menzies **78** C 4
Menzies, Mount **115**
Mepistskaro **59** F 2
Meppen **53** E 4
Meråker **54** F 3
Merano **57** F 2
Merced **102** BC 4
Mercedes (Argentina) **112** E 4
Mercedes (Argentina) **112** C 5
Mercedes (Uruguay) **112** E 5
Merchants Bay **101** P 2
Mercy, Cape **101** P 3
Meredith, Cape **113** D 9
Merefa **62** G 6
Merenga **69** ST 3
Mergui **73** G 5
Mergui Archipelago **73** G 5
Meriç **58** C 2
Mérida (Mexico) **104** DE 3
Mérida (Spain) **56** B 4
Mérida (Venezuela) **108** D 2
Meridian **103** J 5
Mérignac **56** C 2
Merikarvia **54** H 3
Merín, Laguna **112** F 5
Merredin **78** B 5
Merritt Island **103** KL 6
Merseburg **53** F 4
Mersin (Turkey) **59** D 3
Mersin (Turkey) **60** B 1
Meru Game Reserve **93** F 4–5
Merzifon **59** E 2
Mesabi Range **103** H 2
Mesopotamia **89** GH 2
Mesopotamia (Iraq) **60–61** D 2–3
Messina (Italy) **57** FG 4
Messiniakós Kolpós **58** B 3
Messo **63** P 2
Mesters Vig **114**
Meta **108** DE 2
Meta Incognita Peninsula **101** O 3
Metairie **103** H 5–6
Metán **112** D 4
Metangula **95** EF 2
Metemma **92** F 2
Metéora-monastery **58** B 3
Metlakatla **98** L 4
Metu **92** F 3
Metz **57** E 2
Meuse **57** E 2
Mexicali **102** CD 5
Mexican Hat **102** E 4
Mexico **104** AB 2
Mexico, Gulf of **104** DE 2
México City **104** BC 4
Meymeh (Iran) **61** F 2
Mezen' **62** H 2
Mezhdurechenskiy **63** N 4
Miami (FL, U.S.A.) **103** K 6
Miami Beach **103** L 6
Miāndowāb (Iran) **61** D 1
Mīaneh (Iran) **61** E 1
Miāneh (Iran) **89** H 1
Mianyang **70** DE 4
Miarinarivo **95** H 3
Miazz **63** LM 5
Michigan **103** JK 2–3
Michigan, Lake **103** J 3
Michoacán **104** B 4
Michurinsk **62** G 5
Micronesia **82** BC 3
Middelburg (South Africa) **94** DE 5
Middelburg (South Africa) **94** D 6
Middle Andaman **73** F 5
Midi, Canal du **56** D 3
Midland **102** F 5
Midland (MI, U.S.A.) **103** JK 3
Midžor **58** B 2
Miekojärvi **54** HJ 2
Mielec **53** H 4
Mieres **56** B 3
Migiurtinia **93** HJ 2
Mijdaḥah **89** H 6
Mikha Tskhakaya **59** F 2
Mikhaylovgrad **58** B 2
Mikhaylovka **62** H 5
Mikinai **58** B 3
Mikindani **95** FG 2
Mikino **69** U 3
Míkonos **58** C 3
Milagro **108** C 4
Milan **57** E 2
Milando Reserve **94** B 1
Milange **95** F 3
Milano **57** E 2
Milâs **58** C 3
Milazzo **57** FG 4
Milcan Tepe **59** E 3
Mildura **79** G 5
Mile **70** D 6
Miles **79** HJ 4
Miles City **102** EF 2
Milford Haven **52** B 4
Milgun **78** B 3–4
Mili **82** C 2
Milk River **102** E 2
Millau **56** D 3
Millevaches, Plateau de **56** D 2
Mílos **58** B 3
Milparinka **79** G 4
Milwaukee **103** J 3
Mina **68** F 5
Mīnā' 'Abd Allāh (Kuwait) **61** E 3
Mīnā' 'Abd Allāh (Kuwait) **66** D 5
Minahassa Peninsula **75** F 3
Minas (Uruguay) **112** F 5
Mīnā' Sa'ūd (Saudi Arabia) **61** E 3
Minas Gerais **111** GH 4
Minas Novas **111** H 4
Minatitlán **104** D 4
Minbya **73** F 3
Mincha **112** B 5
Mindanao **75** FG 2
Mindelo **90** B 6
Mindoro **75** F 1
Mindoro Strait **75** EF 1
Mineiros **111** F 4
Mineral'nyye Vody **59** F 2
Minerva Reefs **82** D 4
Minfeng **67** L 3
Mingary **79** G 5
Mingechaur **66** D 2
Mingshui **71** J 1
Mingteke **67** K 3
Minho **56** B 3
Ministro João Alberto **111** F 3
Minna **91** F 4
Minneapolis (KS, U.S.A.) **102** G 4
Minneapolis (MN, U.S.A.) **103** GH 3
Minnesota **103** GH 2
Minot **102** F 2
Minqin **70** D 3
Minqing **71** G 5
Minsin **73** G 2
Minsk **55** J 5
Minto (Fed. States of Micronesia) **82** B 2
Minto, Lac **101** N 4
Minusinsk **68** F 5
Min Xian **70** D 4
Miquelon **101** M 6
Mirabad **67** G 4
Miramichi Bay **101** P 6
Miranda **110** E 5
Miranda de Ebro **56** C 3
Miri **74** D 3
Miriam Vale **79** J 3
Mirim, Lagoa **112** F 5
Mirnyy **115**
Mirpur Khas **67** H 5
Mirtóon Pélagos **58** B 3

Mirzapur **72** D 2–3
Mish'āb, Ra's al (Saudi Arabia) **61** E 3
Mishan **71** K 1
Miskolc **58** AB 1
Misool, Pulau **75** H 4
Misr **60** A 4
Mişr **88** DE 4
Mişrātah **87** H 2
Mişrātah, Ra's **87** J 2
Mississippi **103** HJ 5
Mississippi Delta **103** J 6
Mississippi River **103** H 5
Missoula **102** D 2
Missouri **103** H 4
Missouri River **102–103** GH 3–4
Mistassini, Lac **101** MN 5
Misti, Volcán **110** B 4
Misty Fjords National Monument **98** L 4
Mitchell **102** G 3
Mitchell River **79** G 2
Mitilini **58** C 3
Mitra **91** F 5
Mitú **108** D 3
Mitumba, Monts **92** D 5–6
Miyako **71** M 3
Miyakonojō **71** K 4
Miyako-rettō **71** H 6
Miyaly **66** E 1
Mizdah **87** H 2
Mizen Head **52** AB 4
Mizoram **73** F 3
Mizuho **115**
Mizusawa **71** M 3
Mjölby **55** G 4
Mjösa **55** F 3
Mkata **93** F 6
Mkomazi **93** F 5
Mkomazi Game Reserve **93** F 5
Mkushi **94** DE 2
Mladá Boleslav **53** FG 4
Mljet **57** G 3
Moab **102** E 4
Moamba **95** E 5
Moba **92** D 6
Mobaye **92** C 4
Mobile **103** J 5
Mobridge **102** F 2
Moçambique **95** G 3
Mochudi **94** D 4
Mocímboa da Praia **95** G 2
Moctezuma **102** E 6
Moctezuma **104** B 3
Mocuba **95** F 3
Modena (Italy) **57** F 3
Modena (NV., U.S.A.) **102** D 4
Moero, Lac **92** D 6
Mogadouro, Serra do **56** B 3
Mogaung **73** G 2
Mogilev **55** JK 5
Mogilev Podol'skiy **58** C 1
Mogogh **92** E 3
Mogoyn **68** G 6
Mogoytui **68** KL 5
Moguqi **69** M 6
Mohe **69** M 5
Moheli **95** G 2
Mohikan, Cape **98** D 3
Mohon Peak **102** D 5
Mohoro **93** F 6
Mohtar-Lam **67** H 4
Mointy **63** O 6
Mo i Rana **54** F 2
Mojave Desert **102** C 4
Mojiang **70** D 6
Mokp'o **71** J 4
Mokra Gora **58** AB 2
Moldava **58** C 1
Moldaviya **58** C 1
Moldefjorden **54** E 3
Mole Game Reserve **90** D 4
Molepolole **94** CD 4
Mollendo **110** B 4
Molodechno **55** J 5
Molodezhnaya **115**
Molokai **83** E 1
Molopo **94** C 5
Mombasa **93** FG 5
Mombetsu **71** M 2
Momboyo **92** B 5
Monaco **57** E 3
Monaghan **52** B 4
Monapo **95** G 2
Monarch Mountain **99** M 5
Monasterio de Montserrat **56** D 3
Monastery of Saint Catherine (Egypt) **60** AB 3
Monchegorsk **54** K 2
Mönchen-Gladbach **52** E 4
Monclova **104** B 2
Moncton **101** O 6
Mondo **91** H 3
Mondragone **57** F 3
Monfalcone **57** F 2
Monga **92** C 4
Mong Hpayak **73** G 3
Monghyr **72** E 2–3
Mongolia **68** GJ 6
Mongolo **68** J 2
Mongu **94** C 3
Mönhhaan **70** F 1
Monkira **79** G 3
Monou **91** J 2
Monreal del Campo **56** C 3
Monroe (LA, U.S.A.) **103** H 5
Monroe (MI, U.S.A.) **103** K 3
Monrovia **90** B 4
Mons **52** D 4
Mont Afao **87** G 3
Montague **98** H 4
Montana **102** DE 2
Montauban **56** D 3
Montbeliard **57** E 2
Mont Blanc **57** E 2
Mont Cameroon **91** F 5
Montceau-les-Mines **56** D 2
Mont-de-Marsan **56** C 3
Monte Alegre **109** H 4
Monte Binga **95** E 3
Monte Carlo **57** E 3
Monte Cinto **57** E 3
Monte Claros **111** H 4
Montecristi **105** H 3–4
Montecristo **57** F 3
Monte Cristo **110** D 3
Monte d'Oro **57** E 3
Montego Bay **105** G 4
Montejinnie **78** E 2
Monte Melimoyo **113** B 7
Montemoreos **104** C 2
Monte Negro Falls **94** A 3
Montepuez **95** F 2
Monte Quemado **112** D 4
Monterado **74** C 3
Monterey **102** B 4
Monteria **108** C 2
Montero **110** D 4
Monterrey **104** B 2
Montes Altos **109** J 5
Montes de Toledo **56** C 4
Montesilvano **57** F 3
Montes Universales **56** C 3
Montevideo **112** EF 5–6
Montgomery **103** J 5
Monti di Ala **57** E 3
Mont Kavendou **90** B 3
Mont Lozére **56** D 3
Montluçon **56** D 2
Mont Panié **81** H 6
Mont Pelat **57** E 3
Montpelier (VT, U.S.A.) **103** M 3
Montpéllier **56** D 3
Montréal **101** N 6
Montreux **57** E 2
Montrose **102** E 4
Monts d'Aubrac **56** D 3
Montserrat **105** K 4
Monts Mitumba **92** D 5–6
Monts Nimba **90** C 4
Monts Notre-Dame **101** O 6
Monts Otish **101** N 5
Monts Tamgak **91** F 2
Monts Timétrine **90** DE 2
Mont Tahat **87** G 4
Mont Tembo **91** G 5
Mont Ventoux **57** E 3
Monza **57** E 2
Moonie **79** J 4
Mooraberree **79** G 4
Moore, Lake **78** B 4
Moorhead **103** G 2
Moorlands **79** FG 6
Moose Jaw **99** Q 5
Moosonee **101** L 5
Mopti **90** D 3
Moquegua **110** BC 4
Mora (Sweden) **55** F 3
Moradabad **72** CD 2
Moramanga **95** H 3
Morane **83** F 4
Moratuwa **72** CD 6
Morava (Czechoslovakia) **53** G 5
Morava (Western Australia) **78** B 4
Morava (Yugoslavia) **58** B 2
Morawhanna **109** G 2
Moray Firth **52** C 3
Moree **79** H 4
More Laptevykh **68** MN 1
Morelia **104** B 4
Morena, Sierra **56** BC 4
Moreno (Peru) **108** C 5
Möre og Romsdal **54** E 3
Moresby **98** L 5
Mori (China) **70** B 2
Morioka **71** M 3
Mornington Island (Queensland, Austr.) **79** F 2
Morobe **82** A 3
Morocco **86** D 2
Morogoro **93** F 6
Moro Gulf **75** F 2
Morombe **95** G 4
Mörön **68** H 6
Morón (Cuba) **105** G 3
Morón (Spain) **56** B 4
Morón (Venezuela) **108** E 1
Morondava **95** G 4
Moroni **95** G 2
Moroshechnoye **69** T 4
Morotai, Pulau **75** G 3
Morozovsk **59** F 1
Morro de Môco **94** AB 2
Mors **55** E 4
Morshansk **62** H 5
Mörsil **54** F 3
Mortlock Islands **82** B 2
Morwell **79** H 6
Moselle **57** E 2
Moshi **93** F 5
Mosjöen **54** F 2
Moskal'vo **69** Q 5
Moskenesöya **54** F 2
Moskva **62** FG 4
Mosquera **108** C 3
Mosquitos, Costa de **104** F 5
Mosquitos, Golfo de los **108** B 2
Moss **55** F 4
Mosselbaai **94** C 6
Mossendjo **91** G 6
Mossoró **111** J 2
Mostaganem **86** EF 1
Mostar **57** G 3
Mosul **89** G 1
Motala **55** G 4
Motihari **72** DE 2
Motril **56** C 4
Motykleyka **69** RS 4
Moudjéria **86** C 5
Moul **91** G 2
Moulins **56** D 2
Moulmein **73** G 4
Moundou **91** H 4
Mount Adam **113** DE 9
Mountains of Mayo **52** B 4
Mount Aspiring **80** P 9
Mount Augustus **78** B 3
Mount Balbi **81** F 3
Mount Bangeta **80** E 3
Mount Blackburn **98** HJ 3
Mount Bona **98** J 3
Mount Brassey **78** E 3
Mount Bruce **78** B 3
Mount Brukkaros **94** B 5
Mount Carter **79** G 1
Mount Cleveland **102** D 2
Mount Columbia **99** O 5
Mount Cook **81** Q 9
Mount Cushing **99** M 4
Mount Dalrymple **79** H 3
Mount Deering **78** D 3
Mount Demavend (Iran) **61** F 2
Mount Douglas **79** H 3
Mount Egmont **81** Q 8
Mount Elbert **102** E 4
Mount Elgon **92** EF 4
Mount Elliot (Queensland, Austr.) **79** H 2
Mount Essendon **78** C 3
Mount Everest **72** E 2

Mount Feathertop **79** H 6
Mount Finke **78** E 5
Mount Forel **114**
Mount Gambier **79** FG 6
Mount Godwin Austin **67** K 3
Mount Hale (Western Australia) **78** B 4
Mount Hermon (Lebanon) **60** B 2
Mount Hood **102** B 2–3
Mount Hutton **79** H 4
Mount Isa **79** F 3
Mount Isto **98** J 2
Mount Jackson (Antarctica) **115**
Mount Jackson (Australia) **78** BC 5
Mount Jefferson (NV, U.S.A.) **102** C 4
Mount Kenya **93** F 5
Mount Kimball **98** J 3
Mount Kirkpatrick **115**
Mount Livermore **102** F 5
Mount Logan **98** J 3
Mount Magnet **78** B 4
Mount Marcus Baker **98** H 3
Mount McKinley **98** G 3
Mount Menzies **115**
Mount Morgan **79** J 3
Mount Mowbullan **79** J 4
Mount Nurri **79** H 5
Mount Nyiru **93** F 4
Mount Oglethorpe **103** K 5
Mount Olympus **102** AB 2
Mount Omatako **94** B 4
Mount Ord **78** D 2
Mount Ossa **80** L 9
Mount Ossa **82** A 5
Mount Pulog **75** J 1
Mount Queen Bess **99** N 5
Mount Rainier **102** B 2
Mount Ratz **98** L 4
Mount Robson **99** NO 5
Mount Roosevelt **99** M 4
Mount Shasta **102** B 3
Mount Shenton **78** C 4
Mount Sir James MacBrian **98** M 3
Mount Sunflower **102** F 4
Mount Tama **94** A 2
Mount Taylor **102** E 4
Mount Victoria (Burma) **73** F 3
Mount Vsevidof **98** D 5
Mount Waddington **99** MN 5
Mount Whitney **102** C 4
Mount Wilhelm **80** D 3
Mount Wilson **102** E 4
Mount Wrightson **102** D 5
Moura **109** F 4
Moussoro **91** H 3
Mouths of the Amazon **109** J 3
Mouths of the Danube **58** CD 1–2
Mouths of the Ganges **72–73** EF 3
Mouths of the Irrawaddy **73** FG 4
Mouths of the Mekong **73** J 5–6
Mouths of the Orinoco **109** FG 2
Movas **102** E 6
Mowbullan, Mount **79** J 4
Moxico **94** BC 2
Moxos, Llanos de **110** CD 4
Moyale **93** F 4
Moyobamba **108** C 5
Mozambique **95** EF 3
Mozambique Channel **95** FG 2–4
Mozdok **59** FG 2
Mozharka **68** F 5
Mozyr' **55** J 5
Mpanda **92** E 6
Mpika **95** E 2
Msata **93** F 6
Mtsensk **62** G 5
Mtwara **95** G 2
Muang Nan **73** H 4
Muang Ngao **73** GH 4
Muang Phrae **73** H 4
Muang Ubon **72** H 4
Muar **74** B 3
Muaraenim **74** B 4
Muara Teweh **74** D 4
Mubarak (Iran) **61** G 4
Mubi **91** G 3
Muchinga Escarpment **95** E 2
Mucojo **95** G 2
Mudanjiang **71** JK 2
Muddy Gap **102** E 3
Mufulira **94** D 2
Muganskaya Step' **66** D 3
Muhagiriya **88** D 6
Muhammad, Ra's (Egypt) **60** B 4
Muḥammad Qawl **88** F 4
Mühlhausen **53** F 4
Mühlig-Hofmann Mountains **115**
Muhulu **92** D 5
Mui Bai Bung **73** H 6
Muite **95** F 2
Mukachevo **58** B 1
Mukur **66** EF 1
Mukur (Afghanistan) **67** H 4
Mulan **71** J 1
Mulanje **95** F 3
Mulata **93** G 3
Mulchén **113** B 6
Mulegé **102** D 6
Mulgrave Island **80** D 4
Mulhacén **56** C 4
Mulhouse **57** E 2
Mull **52** B 3
Mullaittivu **72** D 6
Mullaley **79** HJ 5
Muller, Pegunungan **74** D 3
Mullet Peninsula **52** A 4
Mullewa (Western Australia) **78** B 4
Mulligan River **79** F 4
Mulobezi **94** D 3
Multan **67** J 5
Multanovy **63** O 3
Mulu, Gunung **74** DE 3
Mulym'ya **63** N 3
Mumra **66** D 1
Muna, Pulau **75** F 5
München **53** F 5
Muncie **103** JK 3
Mundar **69** R 2
Munday **102** G 5
Münden **53** E 4
Munhango **94** B 2
Munich **53** F 5
Munkhafaḍ al Qaṭṭārah **88** D 3
Munster **52** B 4
Münster **53** E 4
Muntii Rodnei **58** B 1
Munugudzhak **69** TU 3
Munzur Silsilesi **59** EF 3
Muojärvi **54** J 2
Muong Hiem **73** H 3
Muong Khoua **73** H 3
Muong Sing **73** H 3
Mupa National Park **94** B 3
Mura **57** G 2
Murallón, Cerro **113** B 8
Murana **75** H 4
Muranga **93** F 5
Murashi **62** J 4
Murat (Turkey) **59** F 3
Murchison River **78** AB 4
Murcia **56** C 4
Murdo **102** FG 3
Mureş **58** B 1
Muriaé **111** H 5
Murilo **82** B 2
Murjek **54** H 2
Murmansk **54** K 2
Murmashi **54** K 2
Murom **62** H 4
Muromtsevo **63** P 4
Muroran **71** M 2
Murray Bridge **79** F 6
Murray River **79** G 5
Murrumbidgee River **79** H 5
Murta **68** F 5
Murukta **68** H 2
Mururoa **83** F 4
Murwara **72** D 3
Murwara **72** D 3
Muş **59** F 3
Musala **58** B 2
Musan **71** JK 2
Musandam Peninsula (Oman) **61** G 4
Muscat **89** K 4
Musgrave **79** G 1
Musgrave Ranges **78** E 4
Mushāsh al 'Ashāwī (Saudi Arabia) **61** E 4
Mūsiān (Iran) **61** E 2
Muskegon **103** JK 3
Muskogee **103** GH 4
Mussende **94** B 2
Mustafa **69** P 3
Mūṭ (Egypt) **88** D 3
Mutanda **94** D 2
Mutarara **95** F 3
Mutare **95** E 3
Mutoray **68** H 3
Mutshatsha **94** CD 2
Mutsu-wan **71** M 2
Mu Us Shamo **70** E 3
Muynak **66** F 2
Muzaffarnagar **72** CD 2
Muzaffarpur **72** DE 2
Muzhi **63** M 2
Muztag **67** L 3
Muztag **67** M 3
Mvomero **93** F 6
Mwanza (Tanzania) **92** E 5
Mweka **92** C 5
Mwinilunga **94** CD 2
Myakit **69** S 3
Myaundzha **69** R 3
Mycenae **58** B 3
Myingyan **73** G 3
Myitkyina **73** G 2
Myitta **73** G 5
Myittha **73** G 3
Mymensingh **73** F 3
Mýrdalsjökull **54** B 3
Myrtle Beach **103** L 5
Mys Aniva **69** Q 6
Mys Buorkhaya **69** O 1
Mys Duga-Zapadnaya **69** R 4
Mys Kanin Nos **62** H 2
Mys Kril'on **69** Q 6
Mys Kronotskiy **69** U 4–5
Mys Kurgalski **55** J 4
Mys Laydennyy **62** J 2
Mys Lopatka **69** T 5
Mys Navarin **69** X 3
Mys Olyutorskiy **69** VW 4
Mysore **72** C 5
Mysovaya **69** T 2
Mys Peschanyy **66** E 2
Mys Pitsunda **59** F 2
Mys Sarych **59** D 2
Mys Shipunskiy **69** TU 5
Mys Svatoy Nos **69** P 1
Mys Svyatoy Nos **62** GH 2
Mys Taran **55** GH 4–5
Mys Tarkhankut **59** D 1
Mys Taygonos **69** U 3
Mys Terpeniya **69** QR 6
Mys Tolstoy **69** T 4
Mys Uengan **63** MN 1
Mys Yelizavety **69** Q 5
Mys Yuzhnyy **69** ST 4
My Tho **73** J 5

N

Naandi **92** D 3
Naba **73** G 3
Na Baek **73** H 4
Nabk al Gharbī (Saudi Arabia) **60** B 3
Nābul **87** H 1
Nābulus (Westbank) **60** B 2
Nachana **72** B 2
Nadiad **72** B 3
Nador **86** E 1
Nadym **63** O 2
Nærbö **55** E 4
Næstved **55** F 4
Naftshahr (Iran) **61** D 2
Nafuce **91** F 3
Nafūd al 'Urayq (Saudi Arabia) **60** D 4
Nafūd as Sirr **66** CD 5–6
Nafūd as Surrah **66** C 6
Naga **75** F 1
Naga Hills **73** FG 2
Nagaland **73** FG 2
Nagano **71** L 3
Nagaoka **71** L 3
Nagasaki **71** J 4
Nagaur **72** B 2
Nagda **72** C 3
Nagercoil **72** C 6
Nago **71** J 5

Nagornyy **69** N 4
Nagoya **71** L 4
Nagpur **72** C 3
Nagqu **70** B 4
Nagykanizsa **58** A 1
Naha **71** J 5
Nahanni National Park
99 M, N 3
Nahariyya (Israel) **60** B 2
Nahāvand (Iran) **61** E 2
Nahāvand (Iran) **66** D 4
Nahr an Nīl (Egypt) **60** A 4
Nahr an Nīl (Egypt) **88** E 3
Nain **101** P 4
Nā'īn (Iran) **61** F 2
Nairobi **93** F 5
Najafābād (Iran) **61** F 2
Najafābād (Iran) **66** DE 4
Najd (Saudi Arabia) **60** CD 4
Najd (Saudi Arabia) **89** G 3–4
Najin **71** K 2
Najrān **89** GH 5
Nakhichevan' **66** CD 3
Nakhodka **71** K 2
Nakhon Ratchasima **73** H 5
Nakhon Sawan **73** G 4
Nakhon Si Thammarat
73 GH 6
Nakina **100** K 5
Nakuru **93** F 5
Nalayh **68** J 6
Nal'chik **59** F 2
Nālūt **87** H 2
Namak, Kavir-e (Iran) **61** G 1
Namanga **93** F 5
Namangan **67** J 2
Namapa **95** G 2
Namaqualand **94** B 5
Namatanai **81** F 2
Nambour **79** J 4
Nam Can **73** J 6
Nam Dinh **73** HJ 3
Nametil **95** F 3
Namib Desert **94** AB 4–5
Namib Desert Park **94** AB 4
Namibe **94** A 3
Namibe Reserve **94** A 3
Namibia **94** AB 4
Namjagbarwa Feng **70** C 5
Namkham **73** G 3
Namlea **75** G 4
Namling **72** E 2
Namoi River **79** H 5
Namoluk **82** B 2
Namonuito **82** A 2
Namorik **82** C 2
Nampala **90** C 2
Nampula **95** FG 3
Namru **72** D 1
Namsang **73** G 3
Namsen **54** F 2–3
Namsos **54** F 3
Namtsy **69** NO 3
Namu **82** C 2
Namuli **95** F 3
Namur **52** E 4
Namy **69** O 2
Nancha **69** NO 6
Nanchang **70** G 5
Nanchong **70** E 4
Nancy **57** E 2
Nanda Devi **72** D 1
Nander **72** C 4
Nandyal **72** C 4
Nanfeng **70** G 5
Nanga Parbat **67** J 3–4
Nangatayap **74** D 4
Nangong **70** FG 3
Nang Xian **70** B 5
Nanjiang **70** E 4
Nanjing **71** GH 4
Nan Ling **70** EF 5
Nanning **70** E 6
Nanping (Fujian, China)
71 G 5
Nanping (Gansu, China)
70 DE 4
Nansei-shotō **71** J 5
Nantes **56** C 2
Nanton **99** P 5
Nantong **71** H 4
Nanumanga **82** C 3
Nanumea **82** C 3
Nanuque **111** HJ 4
Nanyang **70** F 4
Nanyuki **93** F 4
Nanzhang **70** F 4
Naococane, Lac **101** NO 5
Napata **88** E 5
Napier **81** R 8
Napier **82** C 5
Napier Mountains **115**
Naples (Italy) **57** F 3
Napo (Peru) **108** D 4
Napoli **57** F 3
Nara (Japan) **71** L 4
Nara (Mali) **90** C 2
Naranjos **104** C 3
Narasun **68** K 5
Narathiwat **73** H 6
Narayanganj **73** F 3
Narbonne **56** D 3
Nares Strait **114**
Narew **53** H 4
Narmada **72** C 3
Närpes (Närpiö) **54** H 3
Narrabri **79** HJ 5
Narrogin **78** B 5
Narsinghgarh **72** C 3
Narssaq **101** S 3
Narva **55** J 4
Narvik **54** G 2
Narwietooma **78** E 3
Naryn **68** G 5
Näsåker **54** G 3
Nashville **103** JK 4
Näsijärvi **54** H 3
Nasik **72** B 3
Nāşir **92** E 3
Nassau (The Bahamas)
105 G 2
Nasser, Birkat **88** E 4
Nasser, Birkat (Egypt) **60** A 5
Nasser, Lake (Egypt) **60** A 5
Nässjö **55** FG 4
Nata **94** D 4
Natal (Brazil) **111** JK 2
Natal (South Africa) **94–95** E 5
Natashquan **101** P 5
Natchez **103** H 5
Natitingou **90** E 3
Natividade **111** G 3
Natkyizin **73** G 5
Natron, Lake **93** F 5
Natuna, Kepulauan **74** C 3
Naturaliste, Cape **78** A 5
Naupe **108** C 5
Nauru **81** J 2
Nauru **82** C 3
Naushki **68** J 5
Nauta **108** D 4
Navarino **113** C 10
Navarra **56** C 3
Navia (Spain) **56** B 3
Navojoa **102** DE 6
Navolok**62** G 3
Nawabshah **67** H 5
Náxos **58** C 3
Nayarit **104** B 3
Nāy Band (Iran) **61** F 4
Nāy Band, Ra's-e (Iran) **61** F 4
Nayoro **71** M 2
Nazaré **56** B 4
Nazareth (Peru) **108** C 5
Nazca **110** A 3
Naze **71** J 5
Nazerat (Israel) **60** B 2
Nazilli **58** C 3
Ndali **90** E 4
Ndélé **92** C 3
Ndendé **91** G 6
N'Djamena **91** H 3
Ndola **94** D 2
Neagh, Lough **52** B 4
Néapolis **58** B 3
Near Islands **98** A 5
Nebit-Dag **66** E 3
Nebolchi **62** F 4
Nebraska **102** FG 3
Nechako Reservoir **99** M 5
Necochea **113** E 6
Nédéley **91** H 2
Nedong **73** F 2
Neftelensk **68** J 4
Nefteyugansk **63** O 3
Negage **94** AB 1
Negelli **93** F 3
Negombo **72** C 6
Negonengo **83** F 4
Negra, Punta **108** B 5
Negrais, Cape **73** F 4
Negritos **108** B 4
Negros **75** F 1–2
Nehāvand (Iran) **61** E 2
Nehe **69** MN 6
Neijiang **70** DE 5
Nei Monggol Zizhiqu **70** DG 2
Neiva **108** CD 3
Nejd (Saudi Arabia) **60** CD 5
Nekemt **93** F 3
Nelemnoye **69** S 2
Nel'kan **69** P 4
Nelkuchan, Gora **69** P 3
Nellore **72** D 5
Nel'ma **69** P 6
Nelson (New Zealand) **81** Q 9
Nelson (New Zeeland) **82** C 5
Nelson Island **98** D 3
Nelspruit **95** E 5
Néma **86** D 5
Nemunas **55** H 4
Nemuro **71** N 2
Nendo **81** J 4
Nenjiang **69** MN 6
Nepa **68** J 4
Nepal **72** DE 2
Nepeña **108** C 5
Nerchinsk **68** L 5
Nerekhta **62** H 4
Neringa-Nida **55** H 4
Neriquinha **94** C 3
Nesbyen **55** E 3
Néstos **58** B 2
Netanya (Israel) **60** B 2
Netherlands **52** D–E 4
Netherlands Antilles **105** K 4
Netherlands Antilles **108** E 1
Nettilling Lake **101** NO 2
Nettuno **57** F 3
Neuchâtel **57** E 2
Neuquén **113** C 6
Nevada (U.S.A.) **102** C 4
Nevada, Sierra (Spain) **56** C 4
Nevado Ausangate **110** B 3
Nevado Cololo **110** C 4
Nevado Coropuna **110** B 4
Nevado de Cachi **110** C 5
Nevado de Colima **104** B 4
Nevado Huascarán **108** C 5
Nevado Illimani **110** C 4
Nevado Sajama **110** C 4
Nevado Salluyo **110** C 3
Nevado Yerupajá **110** A 3
Never **69** M 5
Nevers **56** D 2
Nevinnomyssk **59** F 2
Nevşehir **59** D 3
Nev'yansk **63** M 4
New Albany **103** J 4
New Amsterdam **109** G 2
Newark (N.J., U.S.A.) **103** M 3
Newark (OH, U.S.A.) **103** K 3
New Bedford **103** M 3
New Bern **103** L 4
New Britain **81** F 3
New Brunswick (Canada)
101 O 6
Newburgh (N.Y., U.S.A.)
103 LM 3
New Caledonia **81** H 6
Newcastle (N.S.W., Austr.)
79 J 5
Newcastle (WY, U.S.A.)
102 EF 3
Newcastle-upon-Tyne **52** C 3
Newcastle Waters **78** E 2
New England **103** MN 3
Newenham, Cape **98** DE 4
Newfoundland **101** PQ 5
Newfoundland **101** QR 6
New Georgia **81** G 3
New Glasgow **101** P 6
New Guinea **75** J 4
New Hanover **81** F 2
New Hanover **82** B 3
New Haven **103** M 3
New Hebrides **81** J 5
New Hebrides **82** C 4
New Iberia **103** H 6
New Ireland **81** F 2
New Ireland **82** AB 3
New Liskeard **103** K 2
Newman **78** B 3
New Meadows **102** C 2
New Mexico **102** E 5
New Orleans **103** J 5–6
New Plymouth **81** Q 8
New Plymouth **82** C 5

Newport (OR, U.S.A.) **102** AB 3
Newport (U.K.) **52** C 4
Newport Beach **102** C 5
New Providence Island **105** G 3
Newry (N.T., Austr.) **78** D 2
New Siberian Islands **114**
New South Wales **79** GH 5
New Stuvahok **98** F 4
Newtonabbey **52** B 4
New York (N.Y., U.S.A.) **103** M 3
New York (U.S.A.) **103** L 3
New Zealand **81** RS 9
New Zealand **82** C 5
Neya **62** H 4
Neyriz (Iran) **61** G 3
Neyshâbūr **66** F 3
Nezhin **62** F 5
Ngamiland **94** C 3
Ngamring **72** E 2
Ngangla Ringco **72** DE 1
Nganglong Kangri **72** D 1
Ngatik **82** B 2
Ngidinga **92** B 6
Ngoc Linh **73** J 4
Ngoko **91** H 5
Ngoring **70** C 3
Nguara **91** H 3
Nhambiquara **110** E 3
Nha Trang **73** JK 5
Niagara Falls **103** L 3
Niamey **90** E 3
Niamtougou **90** E 3
Niangara **92** D 4
Nia-Nia **92** D 4
Nianzishan **69** M 6
Nias, Pulau **74** AB 3
Niassa **95** F 2
Nicaragua **104** EF 5
Nicaragua, Lago de **104** EF 5
Nice **57** E 3
Nichalakh **69** QR 1
Nicobar Islands **73** F 6
Nicocli **108** C 2
Nicosia (Cyprus) **59** D 3
Nicosia (Cyprus) **60** A 2
Nicoya, Península de **104** E 6
Nicuadala **95** F 3
Nidelva **55** E 4
Niedersachsen **53** EF 4
Niedre Tauern **57** F 2
Niellé **90** C 3
Niemba **92** D 6
Nieuw Amsterdam **109** H 2
Nieuw Nickerie **109** G 2
Nieuwoudtville **94** BC 6
Niğde **59** DE 3
Niger **91** FG 2
Niger (River) **91** F 4
Niger Delta **91** F 5
Nigeria **91** EG 4
Nihau **83** E 1
Nihiru **83** F 4
Niigata **71** L 3
Nijmegen **52** E 4
Nikel **54** K 2
Nikk **90** E 4
Nikolayev **58** D 1
Nikolayevka **63** N 5
Nikolayevsk-na-Amure **69** PQ 5
Nikoleyeva **55** JK 4
Nikol'sk **62** J 4
Nikol'skiy **67** H 1
Nikopol **59** D 1
Nīkpey (Iran) **61** E 1
Nikšic **58** A 2
Nikumaroro **82** D 3
Nile (Egypt) **60** A 4
Nimba, Monts **90** C 4
Nimbe **91** F 5
Nimes **56** D 3
Nimule **92** E 4
Nincheng **71** G 2
Ninety Mile Beach **79** H 6
Nineveh (Iraq) **60** D 1
Nineveh (Iraq) **89** G 1
Ningbo **71** H 5
Ningde **71** G 5
Ningdu **70** G 5
Ningxia Huizu Zizhiqu **70** E 3
Ninigo Group **82** A 3
Niokolo Koba, Parc National du **90** B 3
Nioro du Sahel **90** C 2
Niort **56** C 2
Niout **86** D 5
Nipigon **100** K 6
Nipigon, Lake **100** K 6
Nipissing, Lake **101** LM 6
Nippur **89** H 2
Nis **58** B 2
Nisāb (S. Yemen) **89** H 6
Nísoi **58** B 3
Niterói **111** H 5
Nitiya **69** P 4
Nitiya **69** P 4
Nitra **53** G 5
Niuafo'ou **82** D 4
Niuato Putapu **82** D 4
Niue **82** D 4
Niugini **81** E 4
Niulakita **82** C 3
Niutao **82** C 3
Nizamabad **72** C 4
Nizhneangarsk **68** JK 4
Nizhne-Ozernaya **69** UV 4
Nizhneudinsk **68** G 5
Nizhnevartovskoye **63** PQ 3
Nizhneye Karelina **68** J 4
Nizhniy Pyandzh **67** H 3
Nizhniy Tagil **63** M 4
Nizhnyaya Omka **63** O 4
Nizhnyaya Poyma **68** G 4
Nizhnyaya Tunguska **68** F 3
Nizhnyaya Voch' **62** K 3
Nizhnyava Zolotitsa (Nizhnyaya) **62** H 2
Nizina Podlaska **53** H 4
Nizip (Turkey) **60** B 1
Nizip (Turkey) **89** F 1
Njunes **54** G 2
Njutånger **54** G 3
Nkayi **91** G 6
Nkhata Bay **95** E 2
Nkolabona **91** G 5
Nkomi, Lagune **91** F 6
Nkongsamba **91** G 4–5
Nkurenkuru **94** B 3
Noatak National Preserve **98** F 2
Noefs, Ile des **93** J 6
Nogales **102** DE 5
Nogayskiye Step' **59** G 2
Noginsk **62** G 4
Nokrek Peak **73** F 2
Nomad **82** A 3
Nome **98** D 3
Nonacho Lake **99** Q 3
Nong Khai **73** H 4
Nonouti **82** C 3
Nordaustlandet **114**
Nordfriesische Inseln **53** E 3–4
Norðoyar **52** A 1
Nordkapp **54** J 1
Nordkinn **54** J 1
Nord-Kvaloy **54** G 1
Nordland **54** EF 2
Nordostrundingen **114**
Nordöyane **54** E 3
Nordreisa **54** H 2
Nord-Tröndelag **54** F 3
Nordvik **68** K 1
Norfolk (NE, U.S.A.) **102** G 3
Norfolk (VA, U.S.A.) **103** L 4
Norfolk Islands **82** C 4
Norge **54** EF 2
Nori **63** O 2
Noril'sk **63** R 2
Norman **102** G 4
Normanby Island **79** J 1
Normandie **56** CD 2
Normanton **79** G 2
Norra Storfjället **54** G 2
Norrbotten **54** GH 2
Norrköping **55** G 4
Norrland **54** FG 3
Norrtälje **55** G 4
Norseman **78** C 5
Norsjö (Sweden) **54** G 3
Norsk **69** O 5
Norte, Canal do **109** H 3
Northam (Australia) **78** B 5
Northampton (U.K.) **52** C 4
North Andaman **73** F 5
North Battleford **99** Q 5
North Bay **101** M 6
North Bend **102** AB 3
North Cape (New Zealand) **82** C 5
North Carolina **103** L 4
North Cascades National Park **102** BC 2
North Channel (U.K.) **52** B 3–4
North Dakota **102** FG 2
Northeast Cape **98** D 3
Northeast Providence Channel **105** G 2
Northern Cook Islands **82** E 3
Northern Indian Lake **99** S 4
Northern Ireland **52** B 4
Northern Mariana Islands **82** B 1
Northern Territory **78** E 2–3
North Fork Pass **98** K 3
North Geomagnetic Pole **114**
North Highlands **102** BC 4
North Island **81** Q 8
North Island **82** C 5
North Korea **71** K 2
North Lakhimpur **73** F 2
North Las Vegas **102** C 4
North Little Rock **103** H 5
North Magnetic Pole **114**
North Minch **52** B 3
North Platte **102** F 3
North Platte **102** F 3
North Point **80** L 8
North Pole **114**
North Sea **52** D 3
North Slope **98** FH 2
North Uist **52** B 3
Northumberland Islands **79** J 3
Northumberland Strait **101** P 6
North West Cape **78** A 3
North West Highlands **52** BC 3
Northwest Territories (Canada) **99** NT 2
Norton Sound **98** DE 3
Norvegia, Cape **115**
Norway **54** F 2
Norwegian Sea **54** DE 2–3
Norwich **52** D 4
Noshiro **71** L 2
Nosovaya **62** K 2
Nosratābād **66** F 5
Nossob **94** BC 5
Nosy-Bé **95** H 2
Noteć **53** G 4
Nótioi Sporádhes **58** C 3
Notodden **55** E 4
Noto-hantō **71** L 3
Notre Dame Bay **101** QR 6
Nottingham (Ontario, Can.) **101** MN 3
Nottingham (U.K.) **52** C 4
Nouadhibou **86** B 4
Nouakchott **86** B 5
Nouméa **81** J 6
Nouméa **82** C 4
Nouvelle-Calédonie **81** H 6
Nouvelle Calédonie **82** B 4
Nova Cruz **111** JK 2
Nova Iguaçu **111** H 5
Nova Mambone **95** F 4
Novara **57** E 2
Nova Scotia **101** OP 7
Nova Vida **110** D 3
Novaya Kakhovka **59** D 1
Novaya Kazanka **62** J 6
Novaya Zemlya **62** KL 1
Novaya Zemlya **114**
Novgorod **55** K 4
Novgorodka **55** J 4
Novi Ligure **57** E 3
Novillero **104** A 3
Novi Pazar (Yugoslavia) **58** AB 2
Novi Sad **58** A 1
Novoaltaysk **63** QR 5
Novobiryusinskiy **68** G 4
Novograd-Volynskiy **55** J 5
Novo Hamburgo **112** FG 4
Novokazalinsk **67** G 1
Novokocherdyk **63** M 5
Novokuznetsk **63** R 5
Novolazarevskaya **115**
Novomoskovsk **62** G 5
Novopavlovskoye **68** K 5
Novopokrovskaya **59** F 1
Novopolotsk **55** J 4

Novorossiysk **59** E 2
Novorybnoye **68** HJ 1
Novoshakhtinsk **62** H 6
Novosibirsk **63** QR 4
Novosibirskiye Ostrova → New Siberian Islands **61** QR 2
Novotroitskoye **67** JK 2
Novoyeniseysk **68** FG 4
Novoye Ust'ye **69** Q 4
Novvy Bug **59** D 1
Novy Uzen' **66** E 2
Novyy Karymkary **63** N 3
Novyy Port **63** O 2
Novyy Tanguy **68** H 4
Nowa Sól **53** FG 4
Nowbarān (Iran) **61** E 2
Nowdesheh (Iran) **61** E 2
Nowdesheh (Iran) **66** D 3
Nowgong **73** F 2
Nowra **79** J 5
Now Shahr (Iran) **61** F 1
Nowy Sacz **53** H 5
Nsukka **91** F 4
Ntui **91** G 5
Nuatja **90** E 4
Nūbiyah **88** DE 5
Nueltin Lake **99** S 3
Nueva Esperanza **110** CD 4
Nueva Galia **113** CD 6
Nueva Gerona **104** F 3
Nueva León **104** BC 2
Nueva Lubecka **113** BC 7
Nueva Rosita **104** B 2
Nueve de Julio **113** D 6
Nuevo Casas Grandes **102** E 5
Nuevo Laredo **104** BC 2
Nuevo Mundo, Cerro **110** C 5
Nuevo Rocafuerte **108** C 4
Nugāl **93** H 3
Nuguria Islands **82** B 3
Nui **82** C 3
Nukey Bluff **79** F 5
Nukhayb (Iraq) **60** D 2
Nukhayb (Iraq) **66** C 4
Nuku'alofa **82** D 4
Nukufetau **82** C 3
Nuku Hiva **83** F 3
Nukulaelae **82** D 3
Nukumanu Islands **82** B 3
Nukunau **82** C 3
Nukunonu **82** D 3
Nukuoro **82** B 2
Nukus **66** FG 2
Nullarbor Plain **78** DE 5
Numan **91** G 4
Numbulwar Mission **78** EF 1
Numfor, Pulau **75** H 4
Numto **63** O 3
Nungnain Sum **71** G 1
Nunivak Island **98** D 3–4
Nunlygran **98** B 2
Nuntherungie **79** G 5
Nunyamo **98** C 2
Nuoro **57** E 3
Nuqrah (Saudi Arabia) **60** C 4
Nuqrah (Saudi Arabia) **66** C 5
Nuratau, Khrebet **67** H 2
Nuremberg **53** F 5
Nurhak Daği **59** E 3
Nūrī **88** E 5
Nuristan **67** J 3
Nürnberg **53** F 5
Nurri, Mount **79** H 5
Nushki **67** H 5
Nutak **101** P 4
Nuupas **54** J 2
Nuwaybi'al Muzayyinah (Egypt) **60** B 3
Nyabéssan **91** G 5
Nyakanazi **92** E 5
Nyaksimvol' **63** M 3
Nyala **88** CD 6
Nyamlell **92** D 3
Nyandoma **62** H 3
Nyasa, Lake **95** EF 2
Nyazepetrovsk **63** L 4
Nyda **63** O 2
Nyika Plateau **95** E 2
Nyima **72** E 1
Nyiregyháza **58** B 1
Nyiru, Mount **93** F 4
Nyköbing (Denmark) **55** F 5
Nyköping (Sweden) **55** G 4
Nylstroom **94** D 4
Nymagee **79** H 5
Nyurba **68** L 3
Nzega **92** E 5
Nzérékoré **90** C 4

O

Oahe, Lake **102** F 2
Oahe Dam **102** F 3
Oahu **83** E 1
Oakbank **79** G 5
Oakland (CA, U.S.A.) **102** B 4
Oakley **102** F 4
Oak Ridge **103** K 4
Oates Coast **115**
Oaxaca **104** C 4
Oaxaca de Juárez **104** C 4
Oba **100** L 6
Obala **91** G 5
Oban (U.K.) **52** B 3
Obeh **67** G 4
Óbidos **109** GH 4
Obihiro **71** M 2
Obil'noye **59** FG 1
Obluch'ye **69** O 6
Obodovka **58** C 1
Obruk Platosu **59** D 3
Obskaya Guba **63** O 1–2
Ocala **103** K 6
Ocaña (Colombia) **108** D 2
Occidental, Cordillera (Colombia) **108** C 2–3
Oconee River **103** K 5
Odawara **71** L 3–4
Ödemiş **58** C 3
Odendaalsrus **94** D 5
Odense **55** EF 4
Oder **53** F 4
Odessa (TX, U.S.A.) **102** F 5
Odessa (U.S.S.R.) **58** D 1
Odienné **90** C 4
Odorheiu Secuiesc **58** C 1
Odra **53** FG 4
Odzala National Park **91** GH 5
Oeiras **111** H 2
Oeno **83** G 4
Offenbach **53** E 4–5
Oficina **109** F 2
Ogaden **93** GH 3
Ōgaki **71** L 3
Ogallala **102** F 3
Ogbomosho **91** EF 4
Ogden **102** D 3
Ogilvie Mountains **98** JK 2
Oglat Beraber **86** E 2
Ogoki **100** K 5
Ogooué **91** G 6
Ograzden **58** B 2
O'Higgins, Lago **113** B 8
Ohio **103** K 3
Ohio River **103** K 4
Ohopoho **94** A 3
Ohrid **58** B 2
Oiapoque **109** H 3
Ōita **71** K 4
Ojo de Agua **112** D 4
Ojos del Salado, Cerro **112** C 4
Okaba **75** J 5
Okahandja **94** B 4
Okak Islands **101** P 4
Okapa **80** E 3
Okara **67** J 4
Okavango **94** C 3
Okavango Swamp **94** C 3
Okavarumendu **94** B 4
Okayama **71** K 3–4
Okeanskoye **69** T 5
Okeechobee, Lake **103** K 6
Okha (U.S.S.R.) **69** Q 5
Okhotsk **69** Q 4
Okhotskiy Perevoz **69** P 3
Okhotskoye More **69** QS 4
Okinawa-jima **71** JK 5
Oki-shotō **71** K 3
Oklahoma **102–103** G 4
Oklahoma City **103** G 4
Okondja **91** G 6
Okstindan **54** F 2
Oktemberyan **59** F 2
Oktyabrskiy **62** KL 5
Oktyabr'skiy (U.S.S.R.) **68** F 5
Oktyabr'skiy (U.S.S.R.) **69** N 4
Oktyabr'skoye **63** N 3
Öland **55** G 4
Olanga **54** JK 2
Olavarría **113** DE 6
Olbia **57** E 3
Old Bahama Channel **105** G 3
Oldenburg **53** E 4
Oleaborg **54** J 3
Olenegorsk **54** K 2
Olenëk **68** M 1
Olenëk **68** K 2
Olenëkskiy Zaliv **68** LM 1
Olenevod **69** WX 3
Oléron, Ile d' **56** C 2
Ölgiy **68** F 6
Olifants **95** E 4
Olimarao **82** A 2
Olimbia **58** B 3
Olimbos**58** B 2–3
Olinda **111** K 2
Ollagüe, Volcán **110** C 5
Olmos **108** C 5
Olomouc **53** G 5
Olonets **54** K 3
Oloyskiye Gorg **69** U 2
Oloyskiye Gory **69** U 2
Olsztyn **53** H 4
Olt **58** B 2
Olympia (N.A, U.S.A.) **102** B 2
Olympia → Olimbia (Greece) **58** B 3
Olympus **58** B 3
Olympus, Mount **102** B 2
Olyutorka **69** V 3
Olyutorskiy **69** VW 3
Omaha **103** G 3
Oman **61** G 5
Oman **89** JK 4–5
Oman, Gulf of **66** F 5–6
Oman, Gulf of **89** K 4
Omatako, Mount **94** B 4
Omboué **91** F 6
Omchali **66** E 2
Ömnögovĭ **70** DE 2
Omolon **69** T 2
Omolon **69** U 2
Omsk **63** O 4
Omutinskiy **63** N 4
Omutninsk **62** K 4
Onawa **103** G 3
Ondangwa **94** B 3
Ondo **91** E 4
Öndörhaan **68** K 6
Onega **62** G 3
Onega**62** G 3
Ongole **72** D 4
Onilahy **95** G 4
Onitsha **91** F 4
Onkuchakh **68** KL 2
Ono-i-Lau Islands **82** CD 4
Onon **68** L 5
Onotoa **82** C 3
Onslow **78** B 3
Ontario (OR, U.S.A.) **102** C 3
Ontario, Lake **103** L 3
Ontojärvi **54** J 3
Ontong Java **82** B 3
Oodnadatta **79** F 4
Ooldea **78** E 5
Oostende **52** D 4
Opasatika **100** L 6
Opis (Iraq) **60** D 2
Opobo **91** F 5
Opole **53** G 4
Oporto **56** B 3
Oppland **54** E 3
Oradea **58** B 1
Oran **86** E 1
Orange (France) **57** D 3
Orange (TX, U.S.A.) **103** H 5
Orange, Cabo **109** H 3
Orange Free State **94** D 5
Oranje **94** B 5
Orapa **94** D 4
Ora Tyube **67** H 3
Orcadas **115**
Ord, Mount **78** D 2
Ord River **78** D 2
Ordu **59** E 2
Ordynskoye **63** Q 5
Ordzhonikidze **59** FG 2
Örebro **55** FG 4
Oregon **102** BC 3
Orel **62** G 5
Orem **102** D 3
Orenburg **62** K 5
Orense **56** B 3
Öresund **55** F 4
Organ Peak **102** E 5
Orgeyev **58** C 1

Orhon Gol **68** HJ 6
Oriental, Cordillera (Bolivia) **110** CD 3–5
Oriental, Cordillera (Colombia) **108** CD 2–3
Orihuela **56** C 4
Orillia **101** M 7
Orinduik **109** F 3
Orinoco (Colombia) **108** E 3
Orinoco (Venezuela) **108** E 2
Orissa **72** DE 3
Orissaare **55** H 4
Oristano **57** E 3–4
Orivesi **54** J 3
Oriximiná **109** G 4
Orizaba **104** C 4
Orkanger **54** E 3
Orkney (South Africa) **94** D 5
Orkney Islands **52** C 3
Orlando **103** K 6
Orléans **56** D 2
Ormara **67** GH 5
Ormoc **75** FG 1
Ornö **55** G 4
Örnsköldsvik **54** G 3
Oro, Monte d' **57** E 3
Orocué **108** D 3
Oroluk **82** B 2
Orona **82** D 3
Oroqen Zizhiqi **69** M 5
Oroquieta **75** F 2
Oroville (WA, U.S.A.) **102** C 2
Orsa **54** F 3
Orsa Finnmark **54** F 3
Orsha **55** JK 5
Orsk **63** L 5
Ortegal, Cabo **56** B 3
Orto-Ayan **69** NO 1
Ortonville **103** G 2
Orūmīyeh **59** F 3
Oruro **110** C 4
Osa **68** H 5
Ōsaka **71** L 4
Osakarovka **63** O 5
Osceola **103** H 3
Osen **54** F 3
Osh **67** J 2
Oshakati **94** AB 3
Oshkosh **103** J 3
Oshogbo **91** EF 4
Oshtoran Kūh (Iran) **61** E 2
Oshtoran Kūh (Iran) **89** HJ 2
Osijek **57** G 2
Osinovka **63** Q 6
Oskarshamn **55** G 4
Oskoba **68** H 3
Oslo **55** F 4
Oslofjorden **55** F 4
Osmanabad **72** C 4
Osmaneli **58** D 2
Osmaniye (Turkey) **59** E 3
Osmaniye (Turkey) **60** B 1
Osnabrück **53** E 4
Osorno **113** B 7
Osoyoos **99** O 6
Ost Berlin **55** F 5
Österdalälven **54** F 3
Österdalen **54** F 3
Östergötland **55** G 4
Östersund **54** FG 3
Östhavet **54** JK 1
Ostrava **53** G 5
Ostroda **53** GH 4
Ostrołeka **53** H 4
Ostrov (Russia, U.S.S.R.) **55** J 4
Ostrova Chernyye Brat'ya **69** S 6
Ostrov Beringa **65** T 4
Ostrov Bol'shoy Begichev **68** KL 1
Ostrov Bol'shoy Shantar **69** P 4–5
Ostrov Feklistova **69** P 4–5
Ostrov Iturup **69** R 6–7
Ostrov Ketoy **69** S 6
Ostrov Kil'din **54** KL 2
Ostrov Kolguyev **62** J 2
Ostrov Kotel'nyy **69** P 1
Ostrov Malyy Lyakhovskiy **69** Q 1
Ostrov Matua **69** S 6
Ostrovnoye (U.S.S.R.) **69** U 2
Ostrovnoye (U.S.S.R.) **69** TU 5
Ostrov Onekotan **69** ST 6
Ostrov Paramushir **69** ST 5
Ostrov Rasshua **69** S 6
Ostrov Shiashkotan **69** S 6
Ostrov Simushir **69** S 6
Ostrov Urup **69** S 6
Ostrov Vaygach **63** L 1–2
Ostrov Zav'yalova **69** RS 4
Ostrowiec Świetokrzyski **53** H 4
Ostrow Wielkopolski **53** G 4
Ōsumi-shotō **71** JK 4
Otaru **71** M 2
Otavalo **108** C 3
Otavi **94** B 3
Otepää Kõrgustik **55** J 4
Otjozondu **94** B 4
Otradnoye **69** T 5
Ottawa **101** MN 6
Ottawa River **101** M 6
Ottumwa **103** H 3
Otway, Cape **79** G 6
Otwock **53** H 4
Ouachita Mountains **103** GH 5
Ouadane **86** C 4
Ouadda **92** C 3
Ouaddaï **91** J 3
Ouad Naga **86** BC 5
Ouagadougou **90** DE 3
Ouahigouya **90** D 3
Oualam **90** E 3
Ouanda-Djallé **92** C 3
Ouangolodougou **90** D 4
Ouargla **87** G 2
Ouarzazate **86** D 2
Oubangui **91** H 5
Oudtshoorn **94** C 6
Oued Zem **86** D 2
Ouessant, Ile de **56** B 2
Ouesso **91** H 5
Ouezzane **86** DE 2
Ouham **91** H 4
Oujda **86** E 2
Oulu **54** J 2
Oulujärvi **54** J 3
Oum Chalouba **91** J 2
Oum Hadjer **91** H 3
Ounianga **91** J 2
Ouricuri **111** J 2
Ourinhos **111** G 5
Outapi **94** A 3
Outjo **94** B 4
Outokumpu **54** J 3
Ouvéa **81** J 6
Ouyen **79** G 5–6
Ovalle **112** B 5
Ovamboland **94** AB 3
Oviedo (Spain) **56** B 3
Owensboro **103** J 4
Owerri **91** F 4
Owo **91** F 4
Oxford **52** C 4
Oyem **91** G 5
Oyo (Nigeria) **90** E 4
Oyón **110** A 3
Oysurdakh **69** S 2
Ozamiz **75** F 2
Ozark Plateau **103** H 4
Ózd **58** B 1
Ozernovskiy **69** T 5
Ozero Balkhash **63** OP 6
Ozero Baykal **68** J 5
Ozero Chervonoye **55** J 5
Ozero Dadynskoye **59** FG 1
Ozero Il'men **55** K 4
Ozero Imandra **54** K 2
Ozero Keret' **54** K 2
Ozero Kubenskoye **62** G 4
Ozero Leksozero **54** K 3
Ozero Manych Gudilo **59** F 1
Ozero Nyuk **54** K 3
Ozero Osvejskoje **55** J 4
Ozero Pyaozero **54** K 2
Ozero Sasykkol' **63** Q 6
Ozero Segozero **54** K 3
Ozero Seletyteniz **63** O 5
Ozero Sevan **59** G 2
Ozero Syamozero **54** K 3
Ozero Taymyr **68** H 1
Ozero Tengiz **63** N 5
Ozero Verkhneye Kuyto **54** K 3
Ozero Zaysan **63** Q 6

P

Paarl **94** B 6
Paavola **54** J 3
Pacaraima, Sierra **109** F 3
Pacasmayo **108** BC 5
Pachiza **108** C 5
Pachuca **104** C 3–4
Pacific Ocean **116**
Padang **74** B 4
Padang, Pulau **74** B 3
Padangpanjang **74** AB 4
Padangsidempuan **74** A 3
Paddle Prairie **99** O 4
Paderborn **53** E 4
Padilla **110** D 4
Padova **57** F 2
Padre Island **103** G 6
Paducah **103** J 4
Pag **57** FG 3
Pagan **82** A 1
Pago-Pago **82** D 3
Pagri **72** E 2
Päijänne **54** J 3
Paisley **52** BC 3
Paita **108** B 4–5
Pakin **82** B 2
Pakistan **67** H 5
Pakokku **73** FG 3
Pak Phanang **73** H 6
Pakse **73** J 4
Pakwach **92** E 4
Palacios **103** G 6
Palangkaraya **74** D 4
Palanpur **72** B 3
Palapye **94** D 4
Palatka **69** RS 3
Palauk **73** G 5
Palaw **73** G 5
Palawan **74–75** E 2
Palawan Passage **74–75** E 1–2
Palca **110** C 4
Palembang **74** BC 4
Palencia **56** C 3
Palenque **104** D 4
Palermo **57** F 4
Palestine **60** B 2–3
Paletwa **73** F 3
Pali **72** B 2
Paljakka **54** J 3
Palk Strait **72** C 5–6
Pallastunturit **54** H 2
Palliser, Cape **81** R 9
Palma (Spain) **56** D 4
Pal Malmal **81** F 3
Palmares **111** JK 2
Palmar Sur **104** F 6
Palma Soriano **105** G 3
Palm Bay **103** KL 6
Palmeira dos Indios **111** J 2
Palmeirais (Piauí, Brazil) **111** H 2
Palmer (Antarctica) **115**
Palmer Archipelago **115**
Palmer Land **115**
Palmerston **82** E 4
Palmerston North **81** R 9
Palmerston North **82** C 5
Palmira **108** C 3
Palmyra (Pacific Ocean, U.S.A.) **82** E 2
Palmyra (Syria) **60** C 2
Palmyra (Syria) **88** F 2
Palmyras Point **72** E 3
Palo Alto **102** B 4
Paloich **88** E 6
Palopo **75** F 4
Palo Santo **112** E 4
Paltamo **54** J 3
Palu (Indonesia) **75** E 4
Palu (Turkey) **59** EF 3
Pamekasan **74** D 5
Pamir **67** JK 3
Pamlico Sound **103** L 4
Pampa **102** F 4
Pampas (Argentina) **112–113** D 5–6
Pamplona (Spain) **56** C 3
Pan, Tierra del **56** B 3
Panaji **72** B 4
Panama **108** C 2
Panamá, Golfo de **108** C 2
Panama Canal **108** B 2
Panama City (FL, U.S.A.) **103** J 5
Panay **75** F 1
Pandamatenga **94** D 3
Pandharpur **72** BC 4
Pandivere Kõrgustik **55** J 4

Panevežys **55** HJ 4
Panggoe **82** B 3
Panjao **67** H 4
Panjgur **67** G 5
Panorama **111** F 5
Pantanal de São Lourénço **110** E 4
Pantanal do Río Negro **110** E 4
Pantelleria **57** F 4
Pan Xian **70** DE 5
Paoua **92** B 3
Pápa **58** A 1
Papeete **83** F 4
Papenburg **53** E 4
Papey **54** C 3
Paphos **59** D 4
Paphos (Cyprus) **60** A 2
Papua, Gulf of **80** DE 3
Papua New Guinea **80** E 2–3
Papua New Guinea **82** AB 3
Pará (Brazil) **109** GH 5
Parabel **63** Q 4
Paracatu **111** G 4
Paracel Islands **73** K 4
Paraguai **110** E 5
Paraguarí **112** E 4
Paraguay **110** DE 5
Paraguay **112** E 4
Paraíba **111** J 2
Parakou **90** E 4
Paramaribo **109** GH 2
Paramirim **111** H 3
Paraná (Argentina) **112** DE 5
Paraná (Brazil) **111** F 5
Paranaguá **112** G 4
Paranam **109** G 2
Paranavai **111** F 5
Parangaba **111** J 1
Paraoa **83** F 4
Paratinga **111** H 3
Parbig **63** Q 4
Parc National de la Boucle De Baoule **90** C 3
Parc National de la Komoé **90** D 4
Parc National de Sinianka-Minia **91** H 3
Parc National de Taï **90** C 4
Parc National de Wonga Wongué **91** F 6
Parc National de Zakouma **91** H 3
Parc National du Bamingui-Bangoran **92** BC 3
Parc National du Niokolo Koba **90** B 3
Parcs Nationaux du "W" **90** E 3
Pardo **111** H 4
Pardubice **53** G 4
Parecis, Serra dos **110** D 3
Parepare **75** E 4
Parima, Sierra **109** F 3
Parinari **108** D 4
Pariñas, Punta **108** B 4
Parintins **109** G 4
Paris (France) **56** D 2
Paris (TX, U.S.A.) **103** G 5
Parkano **54** H 3
Parker **102** D 5
Parkersburg **103** K 4
Parlakimidi **72** D 4
Parlakote **72** D 4
Parma (Italy) **57** F 3
Parnaíba (Brazil) **111** H 1
Parnaíba (Brazil) **111** H 1
Parnamirim **111** J 2
Parnarama **111** H 2
Parnassós Óros **58** B 3
Pärnu **55** H 4
Parpaillon **57** E 3
Parral **113** B 6
Parry Islands **114**
Parry Peninsula **99** MN 2
Partille **55** F 4
Partizansk **71** K 2
Paryang **72** D 2
Parys **94** D 5
Pasadena **102** C 5
Pascagoula **103** J 5
Pas de Calais **52** D 4
Pasni **67** G 5
Paso de Indios **113** C 7
Paso del Limay **113** BC 7
Paso de los Libres **112** E 4
Paso de los Vientos **105** H 3–4
Paso de San Francisco **112** C 4
Paso Río Mayo **113** B 8
Passau **53** F 5
Passo Fundo **112** F 4
Passos **111** G 5
Pasto **108** C 3
Pastos Bons **111** H 2
Patagonia **113** BC 7–9
Patan (India) **72** B 3
Patan (Nepal) **72** DE 2
Paterson **103** LM 3
Pathankot **72** C 1
Patiala **72** C 1–2
Pativilca **108** C 6
Patkaglik **67** M 3
Patna **72** E 2
Patnagarh **72** D 3
Patos **111** J 2
Patos, Lagoa dos **112** F 5
Patos de Minas **111** G 4
Pátrai **58** B 3
Patras **58** B 3
Patrïkos Kólpos **58** B 3
Patrocínio **111** G 4
Pau **56** C 3
Pau d'Arco **109** J 5
Paulina Peak **102** B 3
Paulistana **111** H 2
Paulo Afonso **111** J 2
Pauls Valley **103** G 5
Pavlodar **63** P 5
Pavlof Volcano **98** E 4
Pavlovka **63** O 5
Paxson **98** H 3
Payakumbuh **74** B 3–4
Paynes Find**78** B 4
Paysandú **112** E 5
Payturma **68** F 1
Pazardžik **58** B 2
Peace River **99** NO 4
Peace River **99** P 4
Peaked Mountain **103** N 2
Pearl **103** J 5
Peary Land **114**
Pebane **95** F 3
Pebas **108** D 4
Peć **58** B 2
Pechora **62** K 2
Pechorskoye More **62** KL 2
Pecos **102** F 5
Pecos Plains **102** F 5
Pecos River **102** F 5
Pécs **58** A 1
Pedernales (Venezuela) **109** F 2
Pedro Afonso **109** J 5
Pedro de Valdivia **110** BC 5
Pedro Juan Caballero **110** E 5
Peera Peera Poolanna Lake **79** F 4
Pegu **73** G 4
Pegunungan Barisan **74** B 4
Pegunungan Maoke **75** J 4
Pegunungan Muller **74** D 3
Pegunungan Schwaner **74** D 4
Pegu Yoma **73** G 3–4
Pehuajó **113** D 6
Peixe (Goiás, Brazil) **111** G 3
Pekalongan **74** CD 5
Pekanbaru **74** B 3
Pekin **103** HJ 3
Peking **71** G 3
Pelat, Mont **57** E 3
Pelješac **57** G 3
Pelly **98** L 3
Pelly Bay **99** U 2
Pelly Crossing **98** K 3
Pelly Mountains **98** L 3
Peloponnese **58** B 3
Pelopónnisos **58** B 3
Pelotas (Río Grande do Sul, Brazil) **112** F 5
Pelvoux, Massif du **57** E 3
Pemangkat **74** C 3
Pematangsiantar **74** A 3
Pemba (Mozambique) **95** G 2
Pemba Island (Tanzania) **93** FG 6
Pembina **102** G 2
Penas, Golfo de **113** AB 8
Pendembu **90** B 4
Penedo **111** J 3
Penglai **71** GH 3
Península Brecknock **113** B 9
Península de Nicoya **104** E 6
Península de Taitao **113** AB 8
Península Valdés **113** D 7
Péninsule de Gaspé **101** OP 6
Peninsule d'Ungava **101** MN 4
Penisola Salentina **57** G 3
Penninechain (U.K.) **52** C 4
Pennsylvania **103** L 3
Penny Ice Cap **101** O 2
Penong **78** E 5
Penrhyn **83** E 3
Pensacola **103** J 5
Pensacola Mountains **115**
Pentecoste **82** C 4
Pentecôte **81** J 5
Penza **62** H 5
Penzhinskaya Guba **69** U 3
Penzhinskiy Khrebet **69** U 3
Peoria **103** J 3
Perche, Collines du **56** D 2
Pereira **108** C 3
Pereval Yablonitse **58** BC 1
Pergamino **112** D 5
Pergamon **58** C 3
Périgueux **56** CD 2
Perm **62** L 4
Pernambuco **111** J 2
Perpignan **56** D 3
Perryville **98** F 4
Persepolis (Iran) **61** F 3
Perseverancia **110** D 3
Persia **61** F 2
Persia **66** EF 4
Persian Gulf **61** F 4
Persian Gulf → The Gulf **89** J 3
Perth (Australia) **78** B 5
Perth (U.K.) **52** C 3
Perthus, Col de **56** D 3
Peru **108** C 5
Perugia **57** F 3
Pervomaysk (Ukraine, U.S.S.R.) **58** D 1
Pervomayskiy **62** H 3
Pervoural'sk **63** L 4
Pesaro **57** F 3
Pescara **57** F 3
Peschanyy, Mys **66** E 2
Peshawar **67** J 4
Peski Karakumy **66–67** FG 3
Peski Kyzylkum **67** GH 2
Peski Sary Ishikotrau **63** P 6
Peski Taukum **67** JK 2
Pessac **56** C 3
Petaluma **102** B 4
Petare **108** E 1
Petauke **95** E 2
Petén **104** DE 4
Peterborough (Ontario, Can.) **101** M 7
Peterborough (South Australia) **79** F 5
Peter I Island **115**
Petersburg (VA, U.S.A.) **103** L 4
Petites Pyrénées **56** D 3
Petorca **112** B 5
Petra **88** F 2
Petra Azul **111** H 4
Petrel **115**
Petrila **58** B 1
Petrodvorets **55** J 4
Petrolina **111** H 2
Petropavlovsk **63** NO 4–5
Petropavlovsk-Kamchatskiy **69** ST 5
Petrópolis **111** H 5
Petrova Gora **57** G 2
Petrovsk **62** J 5
Petrovsk-Zabaykal'skiy **68** J 5
Petrozavodsk **62** FG 3
Peureulak **74** A 3
Pevek **114**
Pforzheim **53** E 5
Phalodi **72** B 2
Phaltan **72** BC 4
Phatthalung **73** H 6
Phenix City **103** J 5
Phet Buri **73** G 5
Philadelphia **103** M 4
Philae **88** E 4
Philippines **75** G 1
Phillipsburg **102** G 4

Phitsanulok **73** H 4
Phnom Aural **74** B 1
Phnom Penh **73** H 5
Phoenix (AZ, U.S.A.) **102** D 5
Phoenix Islands **82** D 3
Phuket **73** G 6
Phuoc Le **73** J 5
Phu Set **73** J 4
Phu Vinh **73** J 5–6
Piacenza **57** EF 2–3
Piara Açu **109** H 5
Piatra Neamţ **58** C 1
Piauí **111** H 2
Pibor Post **92** E 3
Picardie **56** D 2
Pic Boby **95** H 4
Pichanal **110** D 5
Pichilemu **113** B 5
Pickle Lake **100** J 5
Pico Cristóbal Colón **108** D 1
Pico de Aneto **56** D 3
Pico Rondón **109** F 3
Picos **111** H 2
Pico Tamacuarí **108** E 3
Pidurutalagala **72** D 6
Piedras Negras **104** B 2
Piedra Sola **112** E 5
Pielinen **54** J 3
Pierre **102** FG 3
Piešťány **53** G 5
Pietarsaari **54** H 3
Pietermaritzburg **94** DE 5
Pietersburg **94** D 4
Pigué **113** D 6
Pihtipudas **54** J 3
Pikelot **82** A 2
Pikhtovka **63** Q 4
Pik Pobedy **67** KL 2
Piła (Poland) **53** G 4
Pilão Arcado **111** H 3
Pilar (Alagoas, Brazil) **111** J 2
Pilar (Paraguay) **112** E 4
Pilcomayo **110** DE 5
Pilot Peak **102** D 3
Pil'tun **69** Q 5
Pim **63** O 3
Pimenta Bueno **110** D 3
Pimental (Brazil) **109** G 4
Pimentel (Peru) **108** B 5
Pinaki **83** F 4
Pínar del Rio **104** EF 3
Pindaíba **111** F 3
Pindaré Mirim **109** J 4
Pindhos Óros **58** B 2–3
Pine Bluff **103** H 5
Pine Island Bay **115**
Pine Pass **99** N 4
Pinerolo **57** E 2–3
Pinetown **95** E 5
Pingdingshan **70** FG 4
Pingdu **71** H 3
Pingelap **82** B 2
Pingle **70** EF 6
Pingliang **70** E 3
Pingluo **70** E 3
Pingquan **71** G 2
Pingtung **71** H 6
Pingwu **70** DE 4
Pingxiang (China) **70** E 6
Pingxiang (Jiangxi, China) **70** F 5
Pingyang **71** H 5
Pingyao **70** F 3
Pinheiro **109** J 4
Pinnaroo **79** G 6
Pinrang **75** E 4
Pins, Île des **82** C 4
Pinsk **55** J 5
Pinyug **62** J 3
Piotrków Trybunalski **53** G 4
Piracicaba **111** G 5
Piracuruca **111** H 1
Piraiévs **58** B 3
Pirapora **111** H 4
Pires do Río **111** G 4
Pirin **58** B 2
Piripiri **111** H 1
Pirot **58** B 2
Piru **75** G 4
Pisa **57** F 3
Pisac **110** B 3
Pisagua **110** B 4
Pisco **110** A 3
Písek **53** F 5
Pishan **67** K 3
Pitalito **108** C 3
Pitcairn **83** G 4
Piteå **54** H 2
Piteşti **58** B 2
Pit-Gorodoko **68** FG 4
Pitkyaranta **54** K 3
Pitt **82** D 5
Pittsburgh (PA, U.S.A.) **103** L 3
Pium **111** G 3
Pjorga **54** B 3
Placentia Bay **101** QR 6
Placetas **105** G 3
Plaine des Flandres **56** D 1
Planalto Central **111** G 4
Planalto do Brasil **111** H 4
Planalto do Mato Grosso **110–111** EF 3–4
Plasencia **56** B 3–4
Plateau de Millevaches **56** D 2
Plateau du Djado **91** G 1
Plateau du Tademaït **87** F 3
Plateau Laurentien **101** NQ 5
Plateau of Tibet **72** DE 1
Plateaux **91** GH 6
Plateaux de la Marche **56** D 2
Plato Ustyurt **66** EF 2
Platte River **102** FG 3
Plaza Huincul **113** C 6
Pleasanton **102** G 6
Pleiku **73** J 5
Plentywood **102** EF 2
Pleven **58** BC 2
Ploče **57** G 3
Płock **53** GH 4
Ploieşti **58** C 2
Plovdiv **58** B 2
Plymouth (U.K.) **52** C 4
Plzeň **53** F 5
Po (Italy) **57** F 3
Pobedy, Pik **67** KL 2
Pocatello **102** D 3
Pocklington Reef **81** G 4
Poconé **110** E 4
Poços de Caldas **111** G 5
Podgornoye **63** Q 4
Podgornyy **69** R 6
Podol'sk **62** G 4
Podosinovets **62** J 3
Podresovo **63** N 4
Pod'yelanka **68** H 4
Pofadder **94** BC 5
Pogibi **69** Q 5
Pohjanmaa **54** J 3
Poinsett, Cape **115**
Point Arena **102** B 4
Point Barrow **98** FG 1
Point Conception **102** B 5
Point Culver **78** CD 5
Point D'Entrecasteaux **78** AB 5
Pointe-à-Pitre **105** K 4
Pointe de Grave **56** C 2
Pointe de Penmarch **56** BC 2
Pointe Louis-XIV **101** L 5
Pointe Noire **91** G 6
Point Hope **98** D 2
Point Lake **99** P 2
Poitiers **56** D 2
Poitou **56** CD 2
Pojeierze Pomorskie **53** G 4
Pojezierze Mazurskie **53** H 4
Pokrovsk **69** N 3
Pola de Siero **56** B 3
Poland **53** G 4
Polar Plateau **115**
Polatlı **59** D 3
Pole of Inaccessibility **115**
Polesie Lubelskie **53** H 4
Polgovskoye **63** N 4
Polist' **55** K 4
Pollensa **56** D 4
Polotsk **55** J 4
Polska **53** G 4
Polson **102** D 2
Poltava **62** FG 6
Poluostrov Buzachi **66** F 1
Poluostrov Kamchatka **69** S 4–5
Poluostrov Kanin **62** HJ 2
Poluostrov Kol'skiy **62** G 2
Poluostrov Koni **69** S 4
Poluostrov Rybachiy **54** K 2
Poluostrov Taymyr **68** FH 1
Poluostrov Yamal **63** NO 1
Polyarnik **98** B 2
Polyarnyy Ural **63** MN 2
Polynesia **83** EG 2–4
Pombal (Bahía, Brazil) **111** J 3
Pomerania **53** FG 4
Pomio **82** B 3
Pommersche Bucht **53** F 4
Pomona **102** C 5
Pompei **57** F 3
Pompeyevka **69** O 6
Ponape **82** B 2
Ponca City **103** G 4
Ponce **105** J 4
Pondicherry **72** CD 5
Ponente, Rivera di **57** E 3
Ponferrada **56** B 3
Ponoy **62** H 2
Ponta da Baleia **111** J 4
Ponta do Padrão **94** A 1
Ponta Grossa **112** F 4
Ponta Porã **111** EF 5
Ponte Nova **111** H 5
Pontevedra **56** B 3
Pontianak **74** C 4
Pontine Mountains **59** EF 2
Poochera **78** E 5
Pool **91** H 6
Poole **52** C 4
Poopó **110** C 4
Poopó, Lago de **110** C 4
Poorman **98** F 3
Popayán **108** C 3
Poplar Bluff **103** H 4
Popokabaka **92** B 6
Popondetta **80** E 3
Porangatu **111** FG 3
Porbandar **72** A 3
Porco **110** C 4
Pori (Björneborg) **54** H 3
Porirua **81** R 9
Porjus **54** H 2
Porlamar **109** F 1
Porpoise Bay **115**
Porsangerhalvöya **54** HJ 1
Porsgrunn **55** EF 4
Portage la-Prairie **99** S 5
Port Alberni **99** N 6
Port Alice **99** M 5
Port Arthur (Tasmania, Austr.) **80** L 9
Port Arthur (TX, U.S.A.) **103** H 6
Port Augusta **79** F 5
Port au Prince **105** H 4
Port Blair **73** F 5
Port Blandford **101** R 6
Port Darwin (Falkland Is., U.K.) **113** E 9
Port Darwin (N.T., Austr.) **78** DE 1
Port Elizabeth **94** D 6
Port Gentil **91** F 6
Port Harcourt **91** F 4–5
Port Hardy **99** M 5
Port Hedland **78** B 3
Port Hope Simpson **101** QR 5
Port Huron **103** K 3
Port Keats **78** DE 1
Port Láirge **52** B 4
Portland (ME, U.S.A.) **103** N 3
Portland (OR, U.S.A.) **102** B 2
Portland (Victoria, Austr.) **79** G 6
Portlaoise **52** B 4
Port Lincoln **79** F 5
Port Loko **90** B 4
Port-Louis (Mauritius) **95** K 6
Port Moller **98** E 4
Port Moresby **80** E 3
Port Moresby **82** A 3
Port Nelson **99** T 4
Port Nolloth **94** B 5
Port-Nouveau-Québec **101** OP 4
Pôrto Alegre (Río Grande do Sul, Brazil) **112** FG 5
Porto Amboim **94** A 2
Pôrto Artur **111** F 3
Pôrto de Moz **109** H 4
Pôrto Esperidião **110** E 4
Port of Spain **109** F 1
Pôrto Grande **109** H 3
Pôrto Jofre **110** E 4
Pörtom **54** H 3
Pôrto Murtinho **110** E 5
Pôrto Nacional **111** G 3
Porto Novo (Benin) **90** E 4
Pôrto Santana **109** H 4

Pôrto Santo **86** B 2
Pôrto Seguro **111** J 4
Pôrto Valter **108** D 5
Porto-Vecchio **57** E 3
Pôrto Velho **109** F 5
Portoviejo **108** BC 4
Portree **52** B 3
Port Said (Egypt) **60** A 3
Port Said (Egypt) **88** E 2
Port Saint Johns **94** DE 6
Port Saunders **101** Q 5
Portsmouth (N.H., U.S.A.) **103** MN 3
Portsmouth (OH, U.S.A.) **103** K 4
Portsmouth (U.K.) **52** C 4
Portsmouth (VA, U.S.A.) **103** L 4
Portugal **56** B 3
Portugalete **56** C 3
Port Wakefield **79** F 5
Porvenir **113** BC 9
Posadas **112** E 4
Posht-e Badam (Iran) **61** G 2
Positos **110** D 5
Posse **111** G 3
Postavy **55** J 4
Poste-de-la-Baleine **101** M 4
Poste Maurice Cortier **87** F 4
Postmasburg **94** C 5
Posto Cunambo **108** CD 4
Potapovo **63** R 2
Potenza **57** G 3
Potgietersrus **94** D 4
Poti (Gruziya, U.S.S.R.) **59** F 2
Potiskum **91** G 3
Potosi (Bolivia) **110** C 4
Potrerillos **112** BC 4
Potsdam **53** F 4
Pou Bia **73** H 4
Povenets **62** F 3
Póvoa de Varzim **56** B 3
Powell, Lake **102** D 4
Požarevac **58** B 2
Poza Rica de Hidalgo **104** C 3
Poznan **53** G 4
Pozo Almonte **110** C 5
Prado **111** J 4
Praha → Prague **53** FG 4–5
Praia **90** B 7
Prainha **109** FG 5
Praslin **93** K 5
Prato **57** F 3
Praya **74** E 5
Prepansko jezero **58** B 2
Presidencia Roque Sáenz-Peña **112** D 4
Presidente Dutra **111** H 2
Presidente Prudente **111** F 5
Presnogor'kovka **63** N 5
Preston (U.K.) **52** C 4
Pretoria **94** D 5
Priazovskaya Vozvyshennost' **59** E 1
Pribilof Islands **98** D 4
Příbram **53** F 5
Prichernomorskaya Nizmennost' **59** D 1
Prieska **94** C 5
Prikaspiyskaya Nizmennost **66** DE 1
Prikubanskaya Nizmennost' **59** E 1
Prilep **58** B 2
Priluki **62** H 3
Primavera **115**
Primeira Cruz **111** H 1
Primorsk **55** J 3
Primorsko-Akhtarsk **59** E 1
Prince Albert **99** Q 5
Prince Albert Mountains **115**
Prince Albert National Park **99** Q 5
Prince Albert Peninsula **99** O 1
Prince Albert Sound **99** OP 1
Prince Charles Island **101** LM 2
Prince Charles Mountains **115**
Prince Edward Island (Canada) **101** P 6
Prince Edward Islands (Antarctica) **115**
Prince George **99** N 5
Prince of Wales Island (AK, U.S.A.) **98** L 4
Prince of Wales Island (Canada) **99** S 1
Prince of Wales Island (Queensland, Austr.) **79** G 1
Prince of Wales Strait **99** O 1
Prince Patrick Island **114**
Prince Rupert **98** L 5
Princess Astrid Coast **115**
Princess Charlotte Bay **79** G 1
Princess Martha Coast **115**
Princess Ragnhild Coast **115**
Princess Royal Island **98** M 5
Prince William Sound **98** H 3
Príncipe **91** F 5
Pripet Marshes **55** J 5
Pristina **58** B 2
Prizren **58** B 2
Prokhladnyy **59** F 2
Prokhorkino **63** P 4
Prokop'yevsk **63** R 5
Proliv Karskiye Vorota **62–63** L 1
Proliv Nevel'skogo **69** Q 5
Prome **73** G 4
Promontoire Portland **101** LM 4
Promontorio del Gargano **57** G 3
Propria **111** J 3
Protochnoye **63** N 3
Provence **57** E 3
Providence (R.I., U.S.A.) **103** M 3
Providence, Cape **80** P 10
Prudhoe Bay **98** H 1
Prut **58** C 1
Prydz Bay **115**
Przheval'sk **67** K 2
Pshish **59** E 2
Pskov **55** J 4
Pskovskoye Ozero **55** J 4
Ptich **55** J 5
Pucallpa **108** D 5
Pucheng **71** G 5
Pudasjärvi **54** J 2
Puebla **104** C 4
Pueblo **102** F 4
Pueblo Hundido **112** C 4
Puelches **113** CD 6
Puente Alto **112** BC 5
Puente-Genil **56** C 4
Puerto Aisén **113** B 8
Puerto Angel **104** C 4
Puerto Asis **108** C 3
Puerto Ayacucho **108** E 2
Puerto Baquerizo Moreno **108** B 6
Puerto Barrios **104** E 4
Puerto Cabello **108** E 1
Puerto Cabezas **104** F 5
Puerto Carreño **108** E 2
Puerto Chicama **108** BC 5
Puerto Coig **113** C 9
Puerto Colombia **108** C 1
Puerto Cortés **104** E 4
Puerto Cumarebo **108** E 1
Puerto Deseado **113** CD 8
Puerto de Somport **56** C 3
Puerto de Villatoro **56** B 3
Puerto Escondido **104** C 4
Puerto Esperanza **112** F 4
Puerto Estrella **108** D 1
Puerto Heath **110** C 3
Puerto Juárez **104** E 3
Puerto la Cruz **109** F 1
Puerto Leguizamo **108** D 4
Puerto Lempira **104** F 4
Puerto Limón **108** D 3
Puertollano **56** C 4
Puerto Madryn **113** C 7
Puerto Magdalena **102** D 7
Puerto Maldonado **110** C 3
Puerto Montt **113** B 7
Puerto Natales **113** B 9
Puerto Nuevo **108** E 2
Puerto Padilla **110** B 3
Puerto Páez **108** E 2
Puerto Patillos **110** B 5
Puerto Patiño **110** C 4
Puerto Plata **105** HJ 4
Puerto Portillo **108** D 5
Puerto Princesa **75** E 2
Puerto Rico (Argentina) **112** F 4
Puerto Rico (U.S.A.) **105** J 4
Puerto Rondón **108** D 2
Puerto Siles **110** C 3
Puerto Suárez **110** E 4
Puerto Vallarta **104** AB 3
Puerto Varas **113** B 7
Puerto Verlarde **110** D 4
Puerto Villamizar **108** D 2
Puerto Villazón **110** D 3
Puerto Wilches **108** D 2
Puerto Williams **113** BC 9–10
Pugachev **62** JK 5
Pukapuka (Cook Is.) **82** DE 3
Pukapuka (French Polynesia) **83** F 3
Pukaruha **83** FG 4
Pukatawagan **99** RS 4
Pukch'ŏng **71** J 2
Puksoozero **62** H 3
Pula **57** F 3
Pulap **82** A 2
Pulau Alor **75** F 5
Pulau Bacan **75** G 4
Pulau Bangka **74** C 4
Pulau Belitung **74** C 4
Pulau Biak **75** J 4
Pulau Bintan **74** B 3
Pulau Enggano **74** B 5
Pulau Jos Sodarso **75** J 5
Pulau Kabaena **75** F 5
Pulau Kai Besar **75** H 5
Pulau Karakelong **75** G 3
Pulau Kobroor **75** H 5
Pulau Labengke **75** F 4
Pulau Laut **74** E 4
Pulau Lomblen **75** F 5
Pulau Madura **74** D 5
Pulau Mangole **75** G 4
Pulau Misool **75** H 4
Pulau Morotai **75** G 3
Pulau Muna **75** F 5
Pulau Nias **74** A 3
Pulau Numfor **75** H 4
Pulau Padang **74** B 3
Pulau Roti **75** F 6
Pulau Salawati **75** H 4
Pulau Selaru **75** H 5
Pulau Selayar **75** F 5
Pulau Siberut **74** A 4
Pulau Simeulue **74** A 3
Pulau Taliabu **75** F 4
Pulau Trangan **75** H 5
Pulau Waigeo **75** H 3
Pulau Wetar **75** G 5
Pulau Wokam **75** H 5
Pulau Yamdena **75** H 5
Pulau Yapen **75** J 4
Puławy **53** H 4
Pullman **102** C 2
Pulog, Mount **75** J 1
Pulozero **54** K 2
Pulusuk **82** A 2
Puna de Atacama **110** C 5–6
Puncak Jaya **75** J 4
Pune **72** B 4
Punjab **67** J 4
Punjab **72** BC 1
Punkaharju **54** J 3
Puno **110** B 4
Punta Alta **113** D 6
Punta Arenas **113** B 9
Punta Desengaño **113** C 8
Punta Eugenia **102** C 6
Punta Fijo **108** D 1
Punta Gallinas **108** D 1
Punta Gorda (Belize) **104** E 4
Punta Gorda (Nicaragua) **104** F 5
Punta Mariato **108** B 2
Punta Medanosa **113** CD 8
Punta Negra **108** B 5
Punta Pariñas **108** B 4
Punta Prieta **102** D 6
Puntarenas **104** EF 6
Punta Rieles **110** E 5
Puqi **70** F 5
Pur **63** P 2
Purdy Islands **82** A 3
Purnia **72** E 2
Purus **109** F 4
Puruvesi **54** J 3
Pusan **71** JK 3
Pushchino **69** T 5
Pushkin **55** K 4
Pushkino **62** J 5
Pustoretsk **69** U 3
Putao **73** G 2

Putorana, Gory **68** FH 2
Putumayo **108** D 4
Puulavesi **54** J 3
Puyang **70** G 3
Puy de Sancy **56** D 2
Puyo **108** C 4
Pweto **92** D 6
Pyaozero, Ozero **54** K 2
Pyatigorsk **59** F 2
Pyatistennoy **69** TU 2
Pyawbwe **73** G 3
Pyhäjoki **54** HJ 3
Pyhätunturi **54** J 2
Pyinmana **73** G 4
P'yŏngyang **71** HJ 3
Pyrénées **56** CD 3
Pyshchug **62** J 4

Q

Qābis **87** H 2
Qā'emshahr (Iran) **61** F 1
Qafşah **87** G 2
Qagcaka **72** D 1
Qahremānshahr (Iran) **61** E 2
Qaidam Pendi **70** BC 3
Qala-Nau **67** G 3
Qālat **67** H 4
Qal' at Dīzah (Iraq) **61** D 1
Qal'at Şāliḥ (Iraq) **61** E 3
Qal' at Sukkar (Iraq) **61** E 3
Qalīb ash Shuyūkh (Kuwait) **61** E 3
Qamalung **70** CD 4
Qamdo **70** C 4
Qaminis **87** J 2
Qanāt as Suways (Egypt) **60** A 3
Qapqal **67** L 2
Qarah Dagh **59** F 3
Qardo **93** H 3
Qasr-e Shīrīn (Iran) **61** DE 2
Qasr-e Shīrīn (Iran) **66** D 4
Qaşr Farāfirah **88** D 3
Qatar **61** F 4
Qatar **89** J 3
Qatrūyeh (Iran) **61** G 3
Qāyen **66** F 4
Qayyārah (Iraq) **60** D 2
Qazvīn **66** DE 3
Qeshm [ö] (Iran) **61** G 4
Qeshm [ort] (Iran) **61** G 4
Qeys (Iran) **61** F 4
Qezel Owzan (Iran) **61** E 1
Qezi'ot (Israel) **60** B 3
Qian'an **71** H 2
Qiaowan **70** C 2
Qidong **71** H 4
Qiemo **67** M 3
Qift (Egypt) **60** A 4
Qijiang **70** E 5
Qijiaojing **70** B 2
Qila Saifullah **67** H 4
Qilian Shan **70** CD 3
Qimen **71** G 5
Qinā (Egypt) **60** A 4
Qina, Wādī (Egypt) **60** A 4
Qingdao **71** H 3
Qinggang **71** HJ 1
Qinghai **70** C 3
Qinghai Hu **70** D 3
Qingjiang (Jiangsu, China) **71** GH 4
Qingjiang (Jiangxi, China) **70** FG 5
Qing Zang Gaoyuan **72** DE 1
Qinhuangdao **71** GH 3
Qinling Shan **70** E 4
Qinzhou **70** E 6
Qionghai **70** F 7
Qionglai **70** D 4
Qiqiar **68** M 5
Qiqihar **69** MN 6
Qira **67** L 3
Qirjat Yam (Israel) **60** B 2
Qitai **70** AB 2
Qitaihe **71** K 1
Qiyang **70** F 5
Qog Ul **71** G 2
Qolleh-ye Damāvand (Iran) **61** F 2
Qolleh-ye Damāvand (Iran) **66** E 3
Qom (Iran) **61** F 2
Qom (Iran) **66** E 4
Qomsheh (Iran) **61** F 2–3
Qomsheh (Iran) **66** E 4
Qorud, Kuhha-ye (Iran) **61** F 2–3
Qoşbeh-ye Naşşār (Iran) **61** E 3
Qotbābād (Iran) **61** G 4
Qotbābād (Iran) **66** F 5
Quang Ngai **73** J 4
Quanhov **70** E 5
Quan Phu Quoc **73** H 5
Quanzhou (Fujian, China) **71** GH 6
Qu'Appelle **99** R 5
Quartu Sant' Elena **57** E 4
Qūchān **66** F 3
Québec **101** MO 5
Québec **101** N 6
Quebracho Coto **112** D 4
Queen Charlotte Islands **98** KL 5
Queen Charlotte Sound **98** LM 5
Queen Elizabeth Islands **114**
Queen Fabiola Mountains **115**
Queen Mary Coast **115**
Queen Maud Gulf **99** R 2
Queen Maud Land **115**
Queen Maud Mountains **115**
Queensland **79** GH 3
Queenstown (South Africa) **94** D 6
Queenstown (Tasmania, Austr.) **80** L 9
Quelimane **95** F 3
Quembo **94** B 2
Que Que **94** D 3
Querétaro **104** BC 3
Queshan **70** F 4
Quesnel **99** N 5
Quetta **67** H 4
Quevedo **108** C 4
Quezaltenango **104** DE 5
Quibala **94** B 2
Quibdó **108** C 2
Quiçama National Park **94** A 1–2
Quiculungo **94** B 1
Quillabamba **110** B 3
Quillacollo **110** C 4
Quillaicillo **112** B 5
Quillota **112** B 5
Quilon **72** C 6
Quimilí **112** D 4
Quimper **56** C 2
Quincy **103** H 4
Quines **112** C 5
Qui Nhon **73** JK 5
Quintana Roo **104** E 3–4
Quito **108** C 4
Quixadá **111** J 1
Qujing **70** D 5
Qulansiyah **93** J 2
Qulbān Layyah (Iraq) **61** E 3
Qulbān Layyah (Iraq) **66** D 5
Qurnat aş Şawdā' (Lebanon) **60** B 2
Qūs (Egypt) **60** A 4
Qusaybah **66** C 4
Qusum **70** B 5
Qu Xian **71** GH 5

R

Raab **57** G 2
Raahe **54** H 3
Rába (Hungary) **58** A 1
Raba (Indonesia) **75** E 5
Rabak **88** E 6
Rabat (Morocco) **86** D 2
Rabaul **82** B 3
Rabyānah **87** K 4
Rach Gia **73** HJ 5–6
Racine **103** J 3
Radhanpur **72** B 3
Radisson **101** M 5
Radom **53** H 4
Radomsko **53** G 4
Rae **99** O 3
Ra's-e Nāy Band (Iran) **61** F 4
Raevavae **83** F 4
Rafaela **112** D 5
Rafah **60** B 3
Rafha' (Saudi Arabia) **60** D 3
Rafḥā' (Saudi Arabia) **89** G 3
Rafsanjān (Iran) **61** G 3
Raga **92** D 3
Rahimyar Khan **67** J 5
Raiatea **83** E 4
Raichur **72** C 4
Raiganj **72** E 2
Raigarh **72** D 3
Rainbow Peak **102** C 3
Rainier, Mount **102** B 2
Rainy Lake **100** J 6
Raipur **72** D 3
Rajada **111** H 2
Rajahmundry **72** D 4
Rajakoski **54** J 2
Rajapalaiyam **72** C 6
Rajasthan **72** BC 2
Rajgarh **72** C 3
Rajkot **72** AB 3
Raj Nandgaon **72** D 3
Rajshahi **72** E 3
Rakahanga **82** E 3
Rakitnoye **55** J 5
Rakulka **62** HJ 3
Raleigh **103** L 4
Ralik Chain **82** C 2
Ramādah **87** H 2
Ramapo Deep **65** R 6
Ramea **101** Q 6
Rāmhormoz (Iran) **61** E 3
Ramlat Hagolan **60** B 2
Ramlat Rabyānah **87** JK 4
Rampur **72** CD 2
Ramree **73** F 4
Ramsgate **52** D 4
Rancagua **112** B 5
Ranchi **72** DE 3
Randers **55** F 4
Randijaure **54** G 2
Rangoon **73** FG 4
Rangpur **72** E 2
Rankin Inlet **99** T 3
Rann of Kutch **72** AB 3
Rantauprapat **74** AB 3
Ranua **54** J 2
Raoul **82** D 4
Rapa **83** F 4
Rapa Nui **83** H 4
Rapid City **102** F 3
Raraka **83** F 4
Rarotonga **83** E 4
Ra's Abū Madd (Saudi Arabia) **60** B 4
Ra's Abū Qumayyis (United Arab Emirates) **61** F 4
Ra's al Abyad (Saudi Arabia) **60** BC 5
Ra's al Abyaḍ (Tunisia) **87** G 1
Ra's al Khafjī (Saudi Arabia) **61** E 3
Ra's al Khaymah (United Arab Emirates) **61** G 4
Ra's al Madrakah **89** K 5
Ra's al Mish'āb (Saudi Arabia) **61** E 3
Ra's ash Shaykh (Saudi Arabia) **60** B 3
Ra's Asir **93** J 2
Ra's as Saffānīyah (Saudi Arabia) **61** E 3
Ra's aṭ Ṭīb **87** H 1
Ra's az Zawr (Saudi Arabia) **61** E 4
Ra's Ba'labakk (Syria) **60** B 2
Ra's Banās (Egypt) **60** B 5
Ra's Banās (Egypt) **88** F 4
Ra's Barīdī (Saudi Arabia) **60** B 4
Ras Dashan **93** F 2
Ra's Fartak **89** J 5
Ra's Ghārib (Egypt) **60** A 3
Ra's Hāfūn **93** J 2
Rasht **66** D 3
Raskoh **67** GH 5
Ra's Mişrātah **87** J 2
Ra's Muhammad (Egypt) **60** B 4
Rasshua, Ostrov **69** S 6
Rasskazovo **62** H 5
Rastigaissa **54** J 1
Råstojaure **54** H 2
Ratak Chain **82** C 2
Ratangarh **72** B 2
Rat Buri **73** G 5
Rat Islands **98** A 5
Ratlam **72** BC 3
Ratnagiri **72** B 4
Ratnapura **72** D 6
Ratta **63** Q 3
Raufarhöfn **54** BC 2
Raukela **72** DE 3

Raúl Leoni, Represa **109** F 2
Rauma (Raumo) (Finland) **54** H 3
Raupelyan **98** C 2
Ravahere **83** F 4
Ravânsar (Iran) **61** E 2
Râvar (Iran) **61** G 3
Râvar (Iran) **66** F 4
Ravenna **57** F 3
Ravenshoe (Queensland, Austr.) **79** GH 2
Râwah **66** C 4
Rawaki **82** D 3
Rawalpindi **67** J 4
Rawândūz **66** C 3
Rawlinna **78** D 5
Rawlins **102** E 3
Rawson **113** D 7
Raychikhinsk **69** NO 6
Raymond **102** B 2
Râzân (Iran) **61** E 2
Razdan **59** F 2
Razgrad **58** C 2
Ré, Ile de **56** C 2
Reading **52** C 4
Real, Cordillera **108** C 4
Realico **112** D 5
Reao **83** G 4
Rebbenesöy **54** G 1
Rebecca, Lake **78** C 5
Reboly **62** F 3
Recife **111** K 2
Récifs d'Entrecasteaux **82** B 4
Reconquista **112** DE 4
Red Bluff **102** B 3
Red Deer **99** P 5
Red Deer River (Alb., Can.) **99** P 5
Redding **102** B 3
Redenção da Gurguéia **111** H 2
Red Lake **100** J 5
Redoubt Volcano **98** G 3
Red River (LA, U.S.A.) **103** H 5
Red River (MN, U.S.A.) **103** G 2
Red Sea **60** B 4
Red Sea **89** FG 4–5
Red Water **99** P 5
Reef Islands **82** BC 3
Regensburg **53** F 5
Reggane **86** EF 3
Reggio di Calabria **57** G 4
Reggio nell'Emilia **57** EF 3
Reghin **58** B 1
Regina **99** R 5
Regina **109** H 3
Registan **67** GH 4
Rehoboth **94** B 4
Reims **56** D 2
Reina Adelaida, Archipiélago de la **113** A 9
Reindeer Lake **99** R 4
Reinoksfjellet **54** G 2
Reitoru **83** F 4
Rekinniki **69** U 3
Reliance **99** Q 3
Remansão **109** HJ 4
Remanso **111** H 2
Rembang **74** D 5
Renascença **108** E 4
Renfrew **101** M 6
Rengo **112** B 5
Rennell **81** H 4
Rennell **82** B 3
Rennes **56** C 2
Rennie Lake **99** Q 3
Reno **102** BC 4
Renton **102** B 2
Replot **54** H 3
Represa Raúl Leoni **109** F 2
Republic of Ireland **52** B 4
Repulse Bay **99** U 2
Requena **108** D 5
Réservoir Baskatong **101** MN 6
Réservoir Cabonga **101** M 6
Réservoir Decelles **101** M 6
Réservoir Gouin **101** MN 6
Réservoir Pipmouacan **101** N 6
Reshteh-ye Kūhhā-ye Alborz (Iran) **61** F 1
Reshteh-ye Kūhhā-ye Alborz (Iran) **66** E 3
Resistencia **112** DE 4
Reşiţa **58** B 1
Resolution Island **101** P 3
Réunion **95** HK 6
Reus **56** D 3
Revilla Gigedo Islands **97** G 8
Rewari **72** C 2
Rey (Iran) **61** F 2
Rey (Iran) **66** E 3
Reykjahlíð **54** B 2
Reykjanes **54** A 3
Reykjavik **54** A 3
Reynosa **104** C 2
Rezé **56** C 2
Rēzekne **55** J 4
Rhein **52** E 4
Rhinelander **103** J 2
Rhinmal **72** B 2
Rhodes **58** C 3
Rhodope Mts **58** BC 2
Rhondda **52** C 4
Rhône **57** D 3
Rías Altas **56** B 3
Rías Bajas **56** B 3
Riau, Kepulauan **74** B 3
Ribeirão Prêto **111** G 5
Riberalta **110** C 3
Richard's Bay **95** E 5
Richland **102** C 2
Richmond (Queensland, Austr.) **79** G 3
Richmond (VA, U.S.A.) **103** L 4
Richmond Hill **101** LM 7
Riding Mountain National Park **99** RS 5
Rietavas **55** H 4
Riga **55** H 4
Rihand Dam **72** D 3
Riiser-Larsen Ice Shelf **115**
Riiser-Larsen Peninsula **115**
Rijau **91** F 3
Rijeka **57** F 2
Riley **102** CD 3
Rimatara **83** E 4
Rimini **57** F 3
Rimnicu Sărat **58** C 1
Rîmnicu Vîlcea **58** B 1–2
Rimouski **101** O 6
Rinchinlhümbe **68** G 5
Rinconada **110** C 5
Ringgold Isles **82** D 4
Ringvassöy **54** G 2
Ríobamba **108** C 4
Río Branco (Acre, Brazil) **108** E 5
Río Branco (Roraima, Brazil) **109** F 3
Río Bravo del Norte **102** EF 5–6
Río Chico (Argentina) **113** C 8
Río Claro **111** G 5
Río Colorado (Argentina) **113** D 6
Río Cuarto **112** CD 5
Rio das Mortes **111** F 3
Río de Janeiro **111** H 5
Río de la Plata **112** E 5–6
Rio de Oro **86** BC 4
Río Gallegos **113** C 9
Rio Grande **102** G 6
Río Grande (Argentina) **113** C 9
Río Grande (Bahía, Brazil) **111** H 3
Río Grande (Brazil) **111** G 4–5
Río Grande (Río Grande do Sul, Brazil) **112** F 5
Rio Grande de Santiago **104** B 3
Río Grande do Norte **111** J 2
Río Grande do Sul **112** EF 4
Río Grande o'Guapay **110** D 4
Rioja **108** C 5
Río Lagartos **104** E 3
Riom **56** D 2
Río Mulatos **110** C 4
Río Negro (Argentina) **113** D 6–7
Río Negro (Brazil) **109** F 4
Ríosucio **108** C 2
Río Turbio Mines **113** B 9
Río Verde (Goiás, Brazil) **111** F 4
Río Verde de Mato Grosso **111** F 4
Ritzville **102** C 2
Rivadavia (Chile) **112** BC 4
Rivas **104** E 5
Rivera (Argentina) **113** D 6
Rivera (Uruguay) **112** E 5
Riverside **102** C 5
Riviera di Levante **57** E 3
Riviera di Ponente **57** E 3
Rivoli **57** E 2
Riwoqê **70** C 4
Riyâdh (Saudi Arabia) **61** E 4
Riyadh (Saudi Arabia) **89** H 4
Rize **59** F 2
Rizhao **71** GH 3
Rizhskiy Zaliv **55** H 4
Rjuven **55** E 4
Rkiz **86** B 5
Roanne **56** D 2
Roan Plateau **102** E 4
Robât-e Khân (Iran) **61** G 2
Robert Butte **115**
Robinson River **79** F 2
Robore **110** E 4
Robson, Mount **99** NO 5
Rocha **112** F 5
Rocha de Galé, Barragem da **56** B 4
Rochefort **56** C 2
Rocher River **99** P 3
Rocher Thomasset **83** F 3
Rochester (MN, U.S.A.) **103** H 3
Rochester (N.Y., U.S.A.) **103** L 3
Rockefeller Plateau **115**
Rockford **103** J 3
Rockhampton **79** HJ 3
Rock Hill **103** K 5
Rock Island **103** H 3
Rockport (CA, U.S.A.) **102** B 4
Rock Springs **102** E 3
Rocky Mount **103** L 4
Rocky Mountains **97** FH 4–6
Rocky Mountains **100** MQ 4–6
Rodeo (Mexico) **104** B 2
Rodez **56** D 3
Ródhos **58** C 3
Ródhos **58** C 3
Rodina **68** FG 4
Rodney, Cape (Papua New Guinea) **80** E 4
Rodopi **58** BC 2
Roebourne **78** B 3
Roebuck Bay **78** C 2
Roes Welcome Sound **99** U 2–3
Rogagua, Lago **110** C 3
Rogaland **55** E 4
Rogers Peak **102** D 4
Rohtak **72** C 2
Rolla (N.D., U.S.A.) **102** G 2
Rolleston **79** H 3
Roma (Queensland, Austr.) **79** H 4
Roma (Rome) **57** F 3
Romaine **101** P 5
Roman **58** C 1
Romania **58** BC 1
Romanovka **68** K 5
Romans-sur-Isère **57** E 2
Rome (Italy) **57** F 3
Rome (OR, U.S.A.) **102** C 3
Romny **62** F 5
Romsdal **54** E 3
Roncador, Serra do **111** F 3
Ronda (Spain) **56** C 4
Rondane **54** EF 3
Rondón, Pico **109** F 3
Rondônia **110** D 3
Rondonia **110** D 3
Rondonópolis **111** F 4
Rongan **70** E 5
Ronge, Lac la **99** R 4
Rongelap **82** C 2
Rongerik **82** C 2
Rongjiang **70** E 5
Rong Xian **70** F 6
Rönne **55** F 4
Ronneby **55** G 4
Ronne Ice Shelf **115**
Roosevelt, Mount **99** M 4
Roosevelt Island **115**
Roper River **78** E 1
Roraima (Brazil) **109** F 3
Roraima (Venezuela) **109** F 2
Röros **54** F 3
Rosario (Argentina) **112** D 5

Rosário (Maranhão, Brazil) **111** H 1
Rosario (Mexico) **104** A 3
Rosario, Bahía **102** C 6
Rosario de Lerma **112** C 4
Roseau **105** K 4
Roseburg **102** B 3
Rosenheim **53** F 5
Rosetown **99** Q 5
Rosignol **109** G 2
Roşiori de Vede **58** C 2
Roskilde **55** F 4
Roslavl' **62** F 5
Rossano **57** G 4
Ross Ice Shelf **115**
Ross Island **115**
Rosslare **52** B 4
Rosso **86** B 5
Rossosh **62** GH 5
Ross River **98** L 3
Ross Sea **115**
Rostock **53** F 4
Rostov **62** G 4
Rostov-na-Donu **59** EF 1
Roswell **102** EF 5
Rota **82** A 2
Rothera **115**
Roti, Pulau **75** F 6
Rotorua **81** R 8
Rotterdam **52** D 4
Rotuma **82** C 3
Rouen **56** D 2
Rovaniemi **54** J 2
Rovdino **62** H 3
Rovereto **57** F 2
Rovigo **57** F 2
Rovno **55** J 5
Rowley **101** M 2
Roxas (Philippines) **75** F 1
Roy Hill **78** C 3
Rozhdestvenskoye **62** J 4
Roztocze **53** H 4
Rtishchevo **62** H 5
Rt Ploča **57** G 3
Ruacana Falls **94** AB 3
Ruaha National Park **92** E 6
Ruapehu **81** R 8
Rubtsovsk **63** Q 5
Ruby **98** G 3
Rudall River National Park **78** C 3
Rudbar **67** G 4–5
Rudnyy **63** M 5
Rufiji **93** F 6
Rufino **112** D 5
Rufisque **90** A 3
Rügen **53** F 4
Ruhr **53** E 4
Ruijin **70** G 5
Rujm al Mudhari **66** B 4
Rukwa, Lake **92** E 6
Rumādah **89** G 6
Rum Jungle **78** E 1
Rumphi **95** E 2
Rundu **94** B 3
Rungwa **92** E 6
Rupert (Quebec, Can.) **101** M 5
Rurrenabaque **110** C 3
Rurutu **83** E 4
Rusakovo **69** U 4
Ruse **58** C 2
Rushan (U.S.S.R.) **67** J 3
Russas **111** J 1
Russkaya (Antarctica) **115**
Russkaya (U.S.S.R.) **71** L 1
Rustavi **59** G 2
Rustenburg **94** D 5
Rutenga **95** E 4
Ruvuma **95** FG 2
Ruwenzori National Park **92** DE 5
Ruzayevka **62** H 5
Ružomberok **53** GH 5
Rwanda **92** DE 5
Ryazan' **62** GH 5
Ryazhsk **62** GH 5
Rybachiy, Poluostrov **54** K 2
Rybach'ye **67** K 2
Rybnik **53** G 4
Rybnitsa **58** C 1
Ryn Peski **62** J 6
Ryukyu Islands **71** J 5
Rzeszów **53** H 4

S

Sa'ādatābād (Iran) **61** F 3
Sa'ādatābād (Iran) **66** E 4
Saalfeld **53** F 4
Saarbrücken **53** E 5
Saaremaa **55** H 4
Saariselkä **54** J 2
Šabac **58** A 2
Sabadell **56** D 3
Sabah **74** E 2
Sabanalarga **108** C 1
Sabaya **110** C 4
Sabhā (Libya) **87** H 3
Sabinas **104** B 2
Sabkhat al Bardawīl (Egypt) **60** A 3
Sable, Cape (Canada) **101** O 7
Sable, Cape (FL., U.S.A.) **103** K 6
Sable Island **101** P 7
Sabonkafi **91** F 3
Sabrina Coast **115**
Sabzevār **66** F 3
Sachsen **53** F 4
Sachs Harbour **99** N 1
Sacramento **102** BC 4
Sacramento Mountains **102** E 5
Sacramento Valley **102** B 3–4
Şa'dah **89** G 5
Sad Bi'Ar (Syria) **60** B 2
Saddlede **54** F 3
Sa Dec **74** C 1
Sadiya **73** G 2
Sad Kharv (Iran) **61** G 1
Sadon **66** C 2
Sado-shima **71** L 3
Sæböl **54** A 2
Şafāqis **87** GH 2
Saffānīyah, Ra's as (Saudi Arabia) **61** E 3
Safi **86** D 2
Safīd, Kūh-e (Iran) **61** E 2
Safonovo (U.S.S.R.) **62** J 2
Safonovo (U.S.S.R.) **62** F 4
Safonovo (U.S.S.R.) **69** X 3
Şafwān (Iraq) **61** E 3
Şafwān (Iraq) **66** D 5
Saga (China) **72** DE 2
Sagaing **73** FG 3
Sagar **72** C 3
Sagastyr **69** N 1
Sage **102** D 3
Saglouc **101** M 3
Sagres **56** B 4
Sagua la Grande **105** G 3
Sagunto **56** C 4
Sagwon **98** GH 2
Sahagún (Colombia) **108** CD 2
Sahara **86–87** HK 4
Saharanpur **72** C 2
Sahiwal **67** J 4
Sahlābad **66** F 4
Saḥrā' al Hajārah (Iraq) **60–61** D 3
Saḥrā' al Ḥajārah (Iraq) **89** GH 2–H 3
Sahuayo de Diaz **104** B 4
Sa'īdābād (Iran) **61** G 3
Sa'īdābād (Iran) **66** F 5
Said Bundas **92** CD 3
Saigon **73** JK 5
Saihan Toroi **70** CD 2
Saiki **71** KL 4
Saimaa **54** J 3
Saindak **67** G 5
Sāīn Dezh (Iran) **61** E 1
Saint Alban's (Newfoundl., Can.) **101** QR 6
Saint-André, Cap **95** G 3
Saint Anthony **101** QR 5
Saint Arnaud **79** G 6
St. Austell **52** BC 4
Saint-Brieuc **56** C 2
Saint Cloud **103** GH 2
Saint Croix **105** JK 4
Saint-Denis (France) **56** D 2
Saint-Denis (Réunion) **95** HK 6
Saint-Dizier **57** E 2
Saint-Elie **109** H 3
Saintes **56** C 2
Sainte-Thérèse **101** N 6
Saint-Étienne **56** D 2
Saint Francis, Cape **94** CD 6
St. Gallen **57** E 2
Saint George (Queensland, Austr.) **79** H 4
Saint George (UT, U.S.A.) **102** D 4
Saint George, Cape (Papua New Guinea) **81** F 2
Saint-Georges **101** NO 6
Saint George's **105** K 5
Saint George's Channel **52** B 4
Saint George's Channel (Papua New Guinea) **81** F 2–3
Saint Helena **84** B 6
Saint Jean **101** N 6
Saint Jérôme **101** N 6
Saint-John **101** O 6
Saint John's (Antigua) **105** K 4
Saint Johns (AZ, U.S.A.) **102** E 5
Saint John's (Canada) **101** R 6
Saint Joseph (MO, U.S.A.) **103** H 4
Saint Kitts-Nevis **105** K 4
Saint Lawrence Island **98** C 3
Saint Lawrence River **101** O 6
Saint Léonard **101** O 6
Saint Louis (MO, U.S.A.) **103** HJ 4
Saint-Louis (Senegal) **90** A 2
Saint Lucia **105** K 5
Saint Lucia, Lake **95** E 5
Saint-Malo **56** C 2
Saint Marys **80** L 9
St. Marys (AK, U.S.A.) **98** E 3
Saint Matthias Group **81** EF 2
Saint Matthias Group **82** B 3
St. Moritz **57** F 2
Saint-Nazaire **56** C 2
Saint Paul (MN, U.S.A.) **103** H 3
Saint-Paul (Réunion) **95** HK 6
St. Peter and St. Paul Rocks **107** G 2
Saint Petersburg **103** K 6
Saint Pierre et Miquelon **101** Q 6
Saint-Quentin **56** D 1–2
Saint-Thomas (Ontario, Can.) **101** L 7
Saint Vincent **105** K 5
Saint Vincent, Gulf **79** F 6
Saint Vincent Passage **105** K 5
Saipan **82** A 1
Sajama, Nevado **110** C 4
Sakākah (Saudi Arabia) **60** C 3
Sakākah (Saudi Arabia) **66** C 4–5
Sakami, Lac **101** M 5
Sakaraha **95** G 4
Sakarya **58** D 2
Sakata **71** L 3
Såkevare **54** G 2
Sakhalin **69** QR 5
Sakhalinskiy Zaliv **69** Q 5
Sakht Sar (Iran) **61** F 1
Saksaul'skiy **67** G 1
Salaca **55** HJ 4
Salada **104** B 2
Salado **112** D 4
Salado **113** C 6
Salaga **90** D 4
Salālah (Oman) **89** J 5
Salamá **104** D 4
Salamanca (Spain) **56** B 3
Salamat **91** J 3
Salar de Atacama **110** C 5
Salar de Uyuni **110** C 5
Salavat **62** KL 5
Salaverry **108** C 5
Salawati, Pulau **75** H 4
Sala y Gómes **83** H 4
Saldanha **94** B 6
Sale (Australia) **79** H 6
Salé (Morocco) **86** D 2
Şāleḥābād (Iran) **61** E 2
Salekhard **63** N 2
Salem (India) **72** C 5
Salem (OR, U.S.A.) **102** B 3
Salerno **57** F 3
Saletekri **72** D 3
Salida **102** E 4
Salihli **58** C 3
Salina (KS, U.S.A.) **102** G 4
Salina (UT, U.S.A.) **102** D 4

Salinas (CA, U.S.A.) **102** B 4
Salinas (Ecuador) **108** B 4
Salinas de Hidalgo **104** B 3
Salinas Grandes **112** CD 4–5
Salinópolis **109** J 4
Salisbury (Canada) **101** MN 3
Salling **55** E 4
Salluyo, Nevado **110** C 3
Salmas **59** F 3
Salmon Mountains **102** B 3
Salon-de-Provence **57** E 3
Salonga National Park **92** C 5
Salonica **58** B 2
Salpausselkä **54** J 3
Salsbruket **54** F 3
Sal'sk **59** F 1
Salso **57** F 4
Salta **110** CD 5
Saltdalselva **54** G 2
Saltillo **104** B 2–3
Salt Lake (Queensland, Austr.) **79** F 3
Salt Lake City **102** D 3
Salto (Uruguay) **112** E 5
Salt Range **67** J 4
Salumbar **72** B 3
Salvador (Brazil) **111** J 3
Salwā (Qatar) **61** F 4
Salwā (Qatar) **89** J 4
Salwá Baḥrī (Egypt) **60** A 4
Salween **73** G 4
Salzach **57** F 2
Salzburg **57** F 2
Salzgitter **53** F 4
Samagaltay **68** G 5
Samak, Tanjung **74** C 4
Samangan **67** H 3
Samar **75** G 1
Samarkand **67** H 3
Sāmarrā' (Iraq) **60** D 2
Samarskoye **63** Q 6
Samaūma **108** E 5
Sambaliung **74–75** E 3
Sambalpur **72** DE 3
Sambava **95** J 2
Sambor (Kampuchea) **74** C 1
S. Ambrosio Island **107** C 5
Samfya **94** DE 2
Samka **73** G 3
Sam Neua **73** H 3
Samoa Islands **82** D 3
Samokov **58** B 2
Sámos **58** C 3
Samothraki **58** C 2
Sampit **74** D 4
Samsang **72** D 1
Samsun **59** E 2
Samthar **72** C 2
Samus' **63** QR 4
Samut Prakan **73** H 5
Samut Songkhram **73** H 5
San'ā' **89** GH 5
Sanae **115**
Sanaga **91** G 5
Sanandaj (Iran) **61** E 2
Sanandaj (Iran) **66** D 3
San Andrés **105** F 5
San Andrés Tuxtla **104** CD 4
San Angelo **102** F 5
San Antonia de Cortés **104** E 4–5
San Antonio (Chile) **112** B 5
San Antonio (TX., U.S.A.) **102** G 6
San Antonio, Cabo (Argentina) **113** E 6
San Antonio, Cabo (Cuba) **104** EF 3
San Antonio Oeste **113** D 7
Sanāw **89** J 5
San Bernardino **102** C 5
San Bernardo (Chile) **112** BC 5
San Borja **110** C 3
San Carlos (Nicaragua) **104** F 5
San Carlos (Philippines) **75** F 1
San Carlos de Bariloche **113** BC 7
San Carlos del Zulia **108** D 2
San Casme **112** E 4
San Cristóbal (Argentina) **112** D 5
San Cristóbal (Dominican Rep.) **105** HJ 4
San Cristobal (Solomon Is.) **81** H 4
San Cristobal (Solomon Is.) **82** B 3
San Cristóbal (Venezuela) **108** D 2
San Cristobal, Isla **108** B 6
San Cristóbal de las Casas **104** D 4
Sancti Spíritus **105** G 3
Sand **55** E 4
Sandakan **74** E 2
Sandaré **90** B 3
Sandefjord **55** EF 4
Sand Hills **102** F 3
San Diego **102** C 5
San Diego, Cabo **113** C 9
San Dimitri Point **57** F 4
Sandnes **55** DE 4
Sandoa **92** C 6
Sandon **59** F 2
San Dona di Piave **57** F 2
Sandoy **52** A 1
Sandviken **55** G 3
Sandykachi **67** G 3
Sandy Lake **100** J 5
San Felípe (Chile) **112** B 5
San Felípe (Colombia) **108** E 3
San Felipe (Venezuela) **108** E 1
San Fernando (Chile) **113** B 5
San Fernando (Mexico) **104** C 3
San Fernando (Spain) **56** B 4
San Fernando (Trinidad and Tobago) **109** F 1
San Fernando de Apure **108** E 2
San Fernando de Atabapo **108** E 3
San Francisco (Argentina) **112** D 5
San Francisco (CA., U.S.A.) **102** B 4
San Francisco, Paso de **112** C 4
San Francisco del Rincón **104** B 3
San Francisco de Macorís **105** HJ 4
Sangar **69** N 3
Sangatolon **69** R 3
Sangha **91** GH 5
Sangihe, Kepulauan **75** G 3
Sangli **72** BC 4
San Gregorio (Chile) **113** B 9
Sanhe **68** M 5
San Ignacio (Bolivia) **110** C 3
San Ignacio (Bolivia) **110** D 4
San Ignacio (Paraguay) **112** E 4
Sanikiluaq **101** M 4
San Isidro (Argentina) **112** DE 5
San Jacinto **108** C 2
San Javier (Bolivia) **110** D 4
Sanjawi **67** H 4
San Joaquín **110** D 3
San Joaquin River **102** BC 4
San Jorge, Golfo **113** C 8
San Jose (CA, U.S.A.) **102** B 4
San José (Costa Rica) **104** F 6
San José de Chiquitos **110** DE 4
San José de Jáchal **112** C 5
San José del Cabo **102** E 7
San José del Guaviare **108** D 3
San José de Mayo **112** E 5
San Juan (Argentina) **112** C 5
San Juan (Dominican Rep.) **105** H 4
San Juan (Peru) **110** A 4
San Juan (Puerto Rico) **105** J 4
San Juan Bautista Tuxtepec **104** C 4
San Juan del Norte **104** F 5
San Julián **113** C 8
San Justo **112** D 5
Sankt Gotthard-Pass **57** E 2
Sankt Pölten **57** G 2
Sankt Veit an der Glan **57** F 2
Sankuru **92** C 5
San Lorenzo (Ecuador) **108** C 3
Sanlúcar de Barrameda **56** B 4
San Lucas, Cabo **102** E 7
San Luis (Argentina) **112** C 5
San Luís (Venezuela) **108** E 1
San Luis Obispo **102** B 4
San Luis Potosi **104** BC 3
San Luis Rio Colorado **102** D 5
San Marino **57** F 3
San Martín (Colombia) **108** D 3
San Martín de los Andes **113** BC 7
San Mateo **102** B 4
San Matías **110** E 4
San Matías, Golfo **113** D 7
San Miguel (Bolivia) **110** D 3
San Miguel (El Salvador) **104** E 5
San Miguel de Allende **104** BC 3
San Miguel de Huachi **110** C 4
San Miguel del Padrón **105** FG 3
San Miguel de Tucumán **112** C 4
Sannār **88** E 6
San Nicolás (Argentina) **112** DE 5
San Nicolás (Mexico) **104** B 2
Sannikova **114**
Sanok **53** H 5
San Onofre **108** C 2
San Pablo (Argentina) **113** C 9
San Pedro (Argentina) **110** D 5
San Pedro (Mexico) **104** B 2
San Pedro (Paraguay) **110** E 5
San Pedro de Arimena **108** D 3
San Pedro Sula **104** E 4
San Quintin **102** C 5
San Rafael (Argentina) **112** C 5
San Remo **57** E 3
San Salvador (El Salvador) **104** E 5
San Salvador (Watling Is.) **105** GH 3
San Salvador de Jujuy **110** C 5
Sansanding **90** C 3
San Sebastian (Argentina) **113** C 9
San Sebastián (Spain) **56** C 3
San Severo **57** G 3
Santa Ana (CA, U.S.A.) **102** C 5
Santa Ana (El Salvador) **104** DE 5
Santa Ana (Mexico) **102** D 5
Santa Ana (Solomon Is.) **81** H 4
Santa Barbara (CA, U.S.A.) **102** B 5
Santa Bárbara do Sul **112** F 4
Santa Catalina (Chile) **112** C 4
Santa Catarina (Brazil) **112** FG 4
Santa Clara (CA, U.S.A.) **102** B 4
Santa Clara (Cuba) **105** F 3
Santa Clara (Mexico) **102** E 6
Santa Clotilde **108** D 4
Santa Cruz (Argentina) **113** C 9
Santa Cruz (Bolivia) **110** D 4
Santa Cruz (CA, U.S.A.) **102** B 4
Santa Cruz, Isla (Ecuador) **108** B 6
Santa Cruz de Mudela **56** C 4
Santa Cruz de Tenerife **86** BC 3
Santa Cruz do Sul **112** F 4
Santa Cruz Islands (Solomon Is.) **81** J 4
Santa Elena **108** B 4
Santa Fé (Argentina) **112** DE 5
Santa Fe (N.M., U.S.A.) **102** EF 4
Santa Filomena **109** J 5
Santa Helena **109** JK 4

Santa Inés, Isla **113** B 9
Santa Isabel **82** B 3
Santa Isabel (Argentina) **113** C 6
Santa Isabel (Solomon Is.) **81** G 3
Santa Maria (CA., U.S.A.) **102** B 4
Santa Maria (Portugal) **86** A 1
Santa María (Río Grande do Sul, Brazil) **112** F 4
Santa Maria, Cabo de **56** B 4
Santa Maria di Leuca, Capo **57** G 4
Santa Maria dos Marmelos **109** F 5
Santa Marta **108** D 1
Santana do Livramento **112** EF 5
Santander (Colombia) **108** C 3
Santander (Spain) **56** C 3
Sant' Antioco **57** E 4
Santarém **109** H 4
Santa Rita (Colombia) **108** D 3
Santa Rita (Venezuela) **108** E 2
Santa Rosa (Argentina) **113** CD 6
Santa Rosa (CA, U.S.A.) **102** B 4
Santa Rosa (N.M., U.S.A.) **102** F 5
Santa Rosa (Río Grande do Sul, Brazil) **112** F 4
Santa Rosalia **102** D 6
Santa Sylvina **112** DE 4
Santa Teresa (Goiás, Brazil) **111** G 3
Santiago (Chile) **112** BC 5
Santiago (Haiti) **105** HJ 4
Santiago (Panamá) **108** B 2
Santiago, Cerro **105** F 6
Santiago da Cacém **56** B 4
Santiago de Compostela **56** B 3
Santiago de Cuba **105** G 4
Santiago del Estero **112** CD 4
Santo André **111** G 5
Santo Ângelo **112** F 4
Santo Antão **90** A 6
Santo António de Jesus **111** HJ 3
Santo Antônio do Icá **108** E 4
Santo Domingo (Dominican Rep.) **105** J 4
Santo Domingo (Mexico) **102** D 6
Santos **111** G 5
Santo Tomás (Nicaragua) **104** F 5
Santo Tomé de Guayana **109** F 2
San Valentín, Cerro **113** B 8
São Borja **112** E 4
São Carlos (São Paulo, Brazil) **111** G 5
São Domingos **111** G 3
São Felix **111** F 3
São Felix do Xingu **109** H 5
São Francisco (Brazil) **111** HJ 2
São Francisco do Sul **112** G 4
São João **111** G 5
São João del Rei **111** GH 5
São João do Piauí **111** H 2
São José do Río Prêto **111** FG 5
São José dos Campos **111** FG 5
São Leopoldo **112** FG 4
São Luís (Maranhão, Brazil) **111** H 1
São Mateus **111** J 4
São Miguel **86** A 1
São Miguel do Araguaia **111** FG 3
Saône **57** D 2
São Nicolau **90** B 6
São Paulo **111** FG 5
São Paulo **111** G 5
São Paulo de Olivença **108** E 4
São Raimundo Nonato **111** H 2
São Romão (Minas Gerais, Brazil) **111** G 4
São Roque, Cabo de **111** HJ 2
São Sebastião (São Paulo, Brazil) **111** GH 5
São Tiago **90** B 6
São Tomé (São Tomé) **91** F 5
São Tomé and Principe **91** F 5
São Vicente (Cape Verde) **90** A 6
São Vicente (São Paulo, Brazil) **111** G 5
São Vicente, Cabo de **56** B 4
Sape (Indonesia) **75** E 5
Sapele **91** F 4
Sapporo **71** LM 2
Sapulut **74** E 3
Sāqand (Iran) **61** G 2
Saqqez (Iran) **61** E 1
Sara Buri **73** H 5
Sarafjagār (Iran) **61** F 2
Sarajevo **57** G 3
Saraktash **62** L 5
Saralzhin **66** E 1
Saran' **63** O 6
Saran, Gunung **74** D 4
Saranpaul' **63** M 3
Saransk **62** J 5
Sarapul **62** KL 4
Sarasota **103** K 6
Saratok **74** D 3
Saratov **62** HJ 5
Sarawak **74** D 3
Saraya **59** E 3
Sārāya (Syria) **60** B 2
Sarco **112** B 4
Sar Dasht (Iran) **61** D 1
Sardegna **57** E 3
Sardinia **57** E 3
Sarek National Park **54** G 2
Sarektjåkkå **54** G 2
Sargasso Sea **105** JK 2
Sargodha **67** J 4
Sarh **91** H 4
Sārī **66** E 3
Sarigan **82** A 1
Sarıoğlan **59** E 3
Sarīr Tibistī **87** J 4
Sariwon **71** HJ 3
Sarkand **63** P 6
Sarmi **75** J 4
Sarmiento **113** C 8
Sarnia **100–101** L 7
Saroako **75** F 4
Saronikos Kólpos **58** B 3
Saros Kőrfezi **58** C 2
Saroto **63** NO 2
Sarpinskaya Nizmennost' **59** G 1
Sartyn'ya **63** M 3
Sarva **58** A 2
Sarvestān (Iran) **61** F 3
Saryassiya **67** H 3
Saryg-Sep **68** G 5
Sary-Ozek **67** K 2
Sary-Tash **67** J 3
Sasaram **72** D 3
Sasebo **71** J 4
Saskatchewan **99** Q 5
Saskatoon **99** Q 5
Saskylakh **68** KL 1
Sason Dağları **59** F 3
Sasovo **62** H 5
Sassari **57** E 3
Sassuolo **57** F 3
Sastre **112** D 5
Sasykkol', Ozero **63** Q 6
Satara (U.S.S.R.) **69** NO 2
Satawal **82** A 2
Satawan **82** B 2
Satipo **110** B 3
Satka **63** L 4
Satna **72** D 3
Satpura Range **72** BC 3
Sattahip **74** B 1
Satu Mare **58** B 1
Sauce **112** E 5
Sauda Nathil (Saudi Arabia) **61** F 4
Saudi Arabia **60–61** CD 4
Saudi Arabia **89** GH 4
Sault Sainte Marie **100** L 6
Saumarez Reef **79** J 3
Saurimo **94** BC 1
Sava **58** AB 2
Savai'i **82** D 3
Savannah **103** K 5
Savannakhet **73** HJ 4
Savant Lake **100** JK 5
Save (Mozambique) **95** E 4
Sāveh (Iran) **61** F 2
Sāveh (Iran) **66** E 3
Savo **54** J 3
Savoie **57** E 2
Savonselkä **54** J 3
Sawākin **88** F 5
Sawbā **92** E 3
Sawdirī **88** D 6
Sawhāj **88** E 3
Sawu Laut **75** F 5
Sayan Vostochnyy **68** G 5
Saydā (Lebanon) **60** B 2
Sayḥūt **89** J 5
Saynshand **70** F 2
Saywūn **89** H 5
Sazin **67** J 3
Sbaa **86** E 3
Scafell Pike **52** C 4
Scaife Mountains **115**
Scammon Bay **98** DE 3
Scarborough **52** C 4
Schefferville **101** O 5
Schenectady **103** M 3
Schleswig **53** EF 4
Schleswig-Holstein **53** E 4
Schouten Islands **80** DE 2
Schwaner, Pegunungan **74** D 4
Schwarzwald **53** E 5
Schwatka Mountains **98** F 2
Schwedt **53** F 4
Schweinfurt **53** F 4
Schwenningen **53** E 5
Schwerin **53** F 4
Sciacca **57** F 4
Scicli **57** F 4
Scilly, Isles of **52** B 5
Scoresby Sound **114**
Scoresbysund **114**
Scotia Sea **115**
Scotland **52** C 3
Scott (Antarctica) **115**
Scott, Cape**98** LM 5
Scott, Cape (N.T., Austr.) **78** D 1
Scott Island **115**
Scottsdale (AZ., U.S.A.) **102** D 5
Scottsdale (Tasmania, Austr.) **80** L 9
Seabra **111** H 3
Sea of Azov **59** E 1
Sea of Crete **58** BC 3
Sea of Japan **71** KL 3
Sea of Marmara → Marmara Denizi **58** C 2
Seattle **102** B 2
Sebastián Vizcaino, Bahía **102** D 6
Sebkha Azzel Matti **86** EF 3
Sebkha Mekerrhane **87** F 3
Sebkha Oumm ed Droûs Telli **86** CD 4
Sebkha Tah **86** C 3
Sebkhet Oumm ed Droûs-Guebli **86** C 4
Sechura **108** B 5
Sechura, Desierto de **108** B 5
Sedan **57** D 2
Seddenga **88** DE 4
Seeheim **94** B 5
Sefadu **90** B 4
Sefrou **86** E 2
Segesta **57** F 4
Segezha **54** K 3
Ségou **90** C 3
Segovia **56** C 3
Segozero, Ozero **54** K 3
Segre (Spain) **56** D 3
Seguam **98** C 5
Seguin **102** G 6
Segura **56** C 4
Seiland **54** H 1
Seine **56** D 2
Seke **92** E 5
Sekkemo **54** H 2
Sekoma **94** C 4
Sekondi-Takoradi **90** D 5
Selaru, Pulau **75** H 5
Selassi **75** H 4
Selatan, Tanjung **74** D 4
Selat Karimata **74** C 4

Selat Mentawai **74** A 4
Selat Salue Timpaus **75** F 4
Selawik **98** F 2
Selayar, Pulau **75** F 5
Seldovia **98** G 4
Selemdzhinsk **69** O 5
Selenge **68** HJ 6
Selenge (Zaire) **92** B 5
Selgon **69** P 6
Selinunte **57** F 4
Selizharovo **62** F 4
Selkirk Mountains **99** O 5–6
Selma (AL, U.S.A.) **103** J 5
Selous Game Reserve **93** F 6
Selvagens, Ilhas **86** B 2
Selvânâ **59** F 3
Selvas **108–109** EF 5
Selwyn Lake **99** R 3–4
Selwyn Mountains **98** LM 3
Semarang **74** D 5
Sembé **91** G 5
Semiozernoye **63** M 5
Semipalatinsk **63** Q 5
Semisopochnoi **98** AB 5
Semitau **74** D 3
Semmering **58** A 1
Semnān (Iran) **61** F 2
Semnān (Iran) **66** E 3
Semporna **75** E 3
Senador Pompeu **111** HJ 2
Sena Madureira **108** E 5
Sendai **71** M 3
Sêndo **70** C 4
Senegal **90** AB 3
Sénégal (River) **90** B 2
Senftenberg **53** F 4
Senhor do Bonfim **111** H 3
Senja **54** G 2
Senjavin Grop**82** B 2
Senneterre **101** M 6
Sens **56** D 2
Senta **58** A 1
Sentinel Peak **99** N 5
Seoni **72** C 3
Seoul **71** J 3
Sepik **82** A 3
Sepik River **80** D 2
Sept-Îles **101** O 5
Şerafettin Dağları **59** F 3
Serakhs **67** G 3
Seram **75** G 4
Seram, Laut **75** GH 4
Serang **74** C 5
Serdobsk **62** HJ 5
Seremban **74** B 3
Serengeti National Park **92** EF 5
Sergino **63** N 3
Sergipe **111** J 3
Seroglazovka **59** G 1
Serov **63** M 4
Serowe **94** D 4
Serpa **56** B 4
Serpukhov **62** G 5
Serra Acarai **109** G 3
Serra Bonita **111** G 4
Serra da Estrêla (Portugal) **56** B 3
Serra do Cachimbo **109** G 5
Serra do Estrondo **109** J 5
Serra do Marao **56** B 3
Serra do Mogadouro **56** B 3
Serra do Navio **109** H 3
Serra do Roncador **111** F 3
Serra dos Carajás **109** H 4–5
Serra dos Gradaús **109** H 5
Serra dos Parecis **110** D 3
Serra do Tombador **110** E 3
Serra Formosa **111** EF 3
Serrai **58** B 2
Serra Talhada **111** J 2
Serrezuela **112** C 5
Serrinha **111** J 3
Serrota **56** BC 3
Seruai **75** J 4
Serule **94** D 4
Sesfontein **94** A 3
Sesheke **94** CD 3
Sesibi **88** DE 4
Seskarö **54** H 2
Sestroretsk **55** JK 3
Séte **56** D 3
Sete Lagoas **111** H 4
Sétif **87** G 1
Settat **86** D 2
Sette Daban, Khrebet **69** P 3
Setúbal **56** B 4
Setúbal, Baía de **56** B 4
Seumanyam **74** A 3
Sevarujo **110** C 4
Sevastopol' **59** D 2
Sever **69** V 3
Severnaya Dvina **62** H 3
Severnaya Zemlya **114**
Severnoye **63** P 4
Severn River (Ontario, Can.) **100** K 4
Severnyy Anyuyskiy Khrebet **69** UW 2
Severodvinsk**62** G 3
Severomorsk **54** KL 2
Severo Sibirskaya Nizmennost' **68** FK 1
Sevier Desert **102** D 4
Sevilla **56** B 4
Sevrey **70** D 2
Seward (AK, U.S.A.) **98** H 3
Seward (NE, U.S.A.) **102** G 3
Seward Peninsula **98** E 2
Sewell **112** BC 5
Seychelles **93** JK 5
Seyhan **59** E 3
Seymchan **69** S 3
Sfax **87** GH 2
S. Félix Island **107** B 5
Shaanxi **70** EF 4
Shaba **92** CD 6
Shache **67** K 3
Shackleton Ice Shelf **115**
Shackleton Range **115**
Shaddādī (Syria) **59** F 3
Shaddādī (Syria) **60** C 1
Shadrinsk **63** MN 4
Shaffhausen **57** E 2
Shahdol **72** D 3
Shaḥḥāt **87** K 2
Shahjahanpur **72** CD 2
Shahmīrzad (Iran) **61** F 2
Shahr Kord (Iran) **61** F 2
Shahr Kord (Iran) **66** E 4
Shahtinsk **63** O 6
Shā'ib al Banāt, Jabal (Egypt) **60** A 4
Sha'īb Hasb (Saudi Arabia) **60** D 3
Sha'īb Nisāh (Saudi Arabia) **61** E 4
Shakhrisyabz **67** H 3
Shakhterskiy **69** XY 3
Shakhty **59** F 1
Shaki **90** E 4
Shaktinsk **67** J 2
Shalgiya **63** O 6
Shalkar **62** K 5
Shām, Jabal ash (Oman) **89** K 4
Shamattawa **99** T 4
Shambe **92** E 3
Shāmīyah **60** C 2
Shammar, Jabal (Saudi Arabia) **60** CD 4
Shamrock **102** F 4
Shams (Iran) **61** G 3
Shan **73** G 3
Shandan **70** D 3
Shandī **88** E 5
Shandong **71** GH 3
Shandong Bandao **71** H 3
Shangcheng **70** FG 4
Shangdu **70** F 2
Shanghai **71** H 4
Shanghang **70** G 5–6
Shangqiu **70** G 4
Shangrao **71** G 5
Shangzhi **71** J 1–2
Shanh **68** H 6
Shankou **70** B 2
Shannon **52** B 4
Shannon, Mouth of the **52** A 4
Shanshan **70** B 2
Shantarskiye Ostrova **69** P 4
Shantou **70** G 6
Shanxi **70** F 3
Shaoguan **70** F 6
Shaowu **71** G 5
Shaoxing **71** GH 5
Shaoyang **70** F 5
Shaqrā' **89** H 6
Sharāf **66** C 4
Shark Bay **78** A 4
Sharm ash Shaykh (Egypt) **60** AB 4
Shary **66** C 5
Shashamanna **93** F 3
Shashi **70** F 4
Shasta, Mount **102** B 3
Shatt al Arab (Iraq) **61** E 3
Shatt al 'Arab (Iraq) **89** H 2
Shaṭṭ al Jarīd **87** G 2
Shaviklde **59** G 2
Shawinigan **101** N 6
Shaybārā (Saudi Arabia) **60** B 4
Shaykh, Ra's ash **60** B 3
Shaykh Ṣa'd (Iraq) **61** E 2
Shaykh 'Uthmān **89** H 6
Shchara **55** J 5
Shchel'yayur **62** KL 2
Shchuchinsk **63** N 5
Sheboygan **103** J 3
Shedin Peak **99** M 4
Sheffield **52** C 4
Shekhawati **72** C 2
Sheki **66** D 2
Shelburne **101** OP 7
Shelby **102** D 2
Sheldon Point **98** D 3
Shelikof Strait **98** G 4
Shellharbour **79** J 5
Shenandoah National Park **103** L 4
Shendam **91** F 4
Shenmu **70** F 3
Shenton, Mount **78** C 4
Shenyang **71** HJ 2
Shepetovka **55** J 5
Sherbro Island **90** B 4
Sherbrooke **101** N 6
Sheridan **102** E 3
Sherridon **99** RS 4
Shevchenko **66** E 2
Shevli **69** O 5
Sheya **68** L 3
Sheyang **71** H 4
Sheyenne River **102** G 2
Shibarghan **67** GH 3
Shibazhan **69** MN 5
Shīb Kūh (Iran) **61** F 3–4
Shijiazhuang **70** FG 3
Shikarpur **67** H 5
Shikoku **71** K 4
Shilka **68** L 5
Shilkan **69** R 4
Shilla **72** C 1
Shillong **73** F 2
Shimanovsk **69** N 5
Shimizu **71** L 4
Shimoga **72** BC 5
Shingshal **67** JK 3
Shiping **70** D 6
Shipunovo **63** Q 5
Shiquanhe **72** C 1
Shirabad **67** H 3
Shirase Glacier **115**
Shīrāz (Iran) **61** F 3
Shīrāz (Iran) **66** E 5
Shire **95** E 3
Shirikrabat **67** G 2
Shīr Kūh (Iran) **61** FG 3
Shir Kuh (Iran) **66** E 4
Shishaldin Volcano **98** DE 5
Shishou **70** F 5
Shiveluch, Sopka **69** U 4
Shivpuri **72** C 2
Shizuoka **71** L 4
Shkodra **58** AB 2
Sholapur **72** C 4
Shoptykul' **63** P 5
Shorawak **67** H 4–5
Shoshone **102** D 3
Shoshoni **102** E 3
Shouguang **71** G 3
Showa **115**
Show Low **102** DE 5
Shqiperia **58** AB 2
Shreveport **103** H 5
Shrewsbury **52** CD 4
Shuangliao **71** H 2
Shuangyashan **71** K 1
Shucheng **71** G 4
Shuicheng **70** DE 5
Shule **67** K 3
Shumagin Islands **98** F 4–5
Shumerlya **62** J 4
Shuo Xian **70** F 3
Shurinda **68** K 4

Shūshtar **66** D 4
Shūshtar (Iran) **61** E 2
Shuwak **88** F 6
Siahan Range **67** GH 5
Siah-Chashmeh **59** F 3
Siargao **75** G 2
Šiauliai **55** H 4
Sibay **63** L 5
Šibenik **57** G 3
Siberut, Pulau **74** A 4
Sibirskoe, Sredne **68** FK 2–3
Sibirskoye Nizmennost' **63** NQ 3
Sibiti **91** G 6
Sibiu **58** B 1
Sibolga **74** A 3
Sibsagar **73** FG 2
Sibu **74** D 3
Sibuyan Sea **75** F 1
Sicasica **110** C 4
Sichote-Alin **69** P 6
Sichuan **70** CE 4
Sicilia **57** F 4
Sicilia, Canale de **57** F 4
Sicily **57** F 4
Sicuani **110** B 3
Siderno **57** G 4
Sidi-bel-Abbès **86** EF 1–2
Sidon (Lebanon) **60** B 2
Siedlce **53** H 4
Siegen **53** E 4
Siena **57** F 3
Sierra Colorada **113** C 7
Sierra de Alcaraz **56** C 4
Sierra de Aracena **56** B 4
Sierra de Gata **56** B 3
Sierra de Gredos **56** B 3
Sierra de Guadarrama **56** C 3
Sierra de Gúdar **56** C 3
Sierra de la Cabrera **56** B 3
Sierra del Cadí **56** D 3
Sierra Leone **90** B 4
Sierra Madre (Mexico) **104** D 4
Sierra Madre del Sur **104** BC 4
Sierra Madre Oriental **104** BC 2–3
Sierra Madrona **56** C 4
Sierra Mojada **104** B 2
Sierra Morena **56** BC 4
Sierra Nayarit **104** B 3
Sierra Nevada (CA., U.S.A.) **102** BC 3–4
Sierra Nevada (Spain) **56** C 4
Sierra Pacaraima **109** F 3
Sierra Parima **109** F 3
Sierra Vizcaíno **102** D 6
Sífnos **58** B 3
Sighetu Marmaţiei **58** B 1
Signy Island **115**
Siguiri **90** C 3
Siirt (Turkey) **59** F 3
Sikar **72** C 2
Sikasso **90** C 3
Sikerin **69** Q 2
Sikkim **72** E 2
Siktyakh **69** N 2
Silchar **73** F 3
Silesia **53** G 4
Silet **87** F 4
Silifke (Turkey) **59** D 3
Silifke (Turkey) **60** AB 1
Siliguri **72** E 2
Silistra **58** C 2
Siljan **55** FG 3
Silkleborg **55** E 4
Siltou **91** H 2
Silver City **102** E 5
Sil'yeyaki **69** Q 1
Simanggang **74** D 3
Simav **58** C 2–3
Simenga **68** J 3
Simeulue, Pulau **74** A 3
Simferopol' **59** D 2
Simla **72** C 1
Simojärvi **54** J 2
Simplicio Mendes **111** H 2
Simpson Desert **79** F 3
Simpson Desert National Park **79** F 4
Simrishamn **55** FG 4
Sīnā' (Egypt) **60** A 3
Sīnā' (Egypt) **88** E 3
Sinai (Egypt) **60** A 3
Sināwan **87** H 2
Sincelejo **108** C 2
Sind **67** H 5
Sinda **69** P 6
Singapore **74** B 3
Singaraja **74** E 5
Singida **92** E 5
Singleton **79** J 5
Sinianka-Minia, Parc National du **91** H 3
Sinjaja **55** J 4
Sinjār (Iraq) **59** F 3
Sinjār (Iraq) **60** C 1
Sinkiang Uighur **67** L 3
Sinnamary **109** H 2
Sinop **59** E 2
Sinskoye **69** N 3
Sintang **74** D 3
Sinŭiju **71** HJ 3
Sioux City **103** G 3
Sioux Falls **103** G 3
Siping **71** H 2
Sipiwesk **99** S 4
Siple Station **115**
Siracusa **57** G 4
Sir Edward Pellew Group **79** F 2
Sireniki **98** BC 3
Siret **58** C 1
Sīrgān **67** G 5
Sirino **57** G 3
Sir James MacBrian, Mount **98** M 3
Sirsa **72** C 2
Sirt **87** J 2
Sisak **57** G 2
Sisophon **73** H 5
Sisseton **102** G 2
Sistema Iberico **56** C 3
Sistemas Béticos **56** C 4
Sistig-Khem **68** G 5
Sitapur **72** D 2
Sittwe **73** F 3
Sivaki **69** N 5
Sivas **59** E 3
Sivash **59** DE 1
Siverek **59** E 3
Sīwah **88** D 3
Siwalik Range **72** CD 1–2
Siwan **72** D 2
Si Xian **71** G 4
Sjælland **55** F 4
Sjövegan **54** G 2
Skagen **55** F 4
Skagern **55** F 4
Skagerrak **55** EF 4
Skagway **98** K 4
Skåne **55** F 4
Skarsöy **54** E 3
Skarstind **54** E 3
Skarźysko-Kamienna **53** H 4
Skeldon **109** G 2
Skeleton Coast Park **94** A 3
Skellefteå **54** H 3
Skellefteälven **54** G 2
Skien **55** E 4
Skierniewice **53** H 4
Skiftet **55** H 3
Skikda **87** G 1
Skikotsu **71** N 2
Skíros **58** B 3
Skjoldungen **101** T 3
Sklad **68** M 1
Skópelos **58** B 3
Skopi **58** C 3
Skopje **58** B 2
Skövde **55** F 4
Skye **52** B 3
Slantsy **55** J 4
Śląsk **53** G 4
Slatina **58** B 2
Slave Coast **90** E 4
Slave River **99** P 3–4
Slavgorod **63** P 5
Slavonski Brod **57** G 2
Slavuta **55** J 5
Slavyansk **62** G 6
Sligo **52** B 4
Sliven **58** C 2
Slobodka **58** C 1
Slobodskoy **62** K 4
Slonim **55** J 5
Slovakia **53** H 5
Slovechno **55** J 5
Slovensko **53** H 5
Sluch' **55** J 5
Słupsk **53** G 4
Slutsk **55** J 5
Småland **55** G 4
Smallwood Réservoir **101** P 5
Smidovich **114**
Smirnykh **69** Q 6
Smith **99** P 4
Smokey Dome **102** CD 3
Smoky Cape **79** J 5
Smoky Hill River **102** FG 4
Smöla **54** E 3
Smolensk **62** F 5
Smooth Rock Falls **101** L 6
Snake River **102** C 2
Snezhnoye **69** W 2
Snoul **74** C 1
Snowdon **52** C 4
Snowdrift **99** PQ 3
Sobolevo **69** T 5
Sobral **111** HJ 1
Sochi **59** E 2
Society Islands **83** EF 4
Socorro (N.M., U.S.A.) **102** E 5
Sodankylä **54** J 2
Soddu **93** F 3
Söderhamn **54** G 3
Södermanland **55** G 4
Södertälje **55** G 4
Sofia → Sofiya **58** B 2
Sofiya **58** B 2
Sofiysk **69** O 5
Sofiysk **69** PQ 5
Sofporog **54** K 2
Sogamoso **108** D 2
Sogndalsfjöra **54** E 3
Sogn og Fjordane **54** E 3
Sog Xian **70** B 4
Söke **58** C 3
Sokhor, Gora **68** J 5
Sokodé **90** E 4
Sokółka **53** H 4
Sokolov **53** F 4
Sokosti **54** J 2
Sokoto **91** EF 3
Solberg **54** G 3
Soldatovo **69** V 3
Soledad (Colombia) **108** D 1
Soligorsk **55** J 5
Solikamsk **62** KL 4
Sol'-Iletsk **62** L 5
Solimões **108** E 4
Solitaire **94** B 4
Solomon Islands **81** G 3
Solomon Islands **82** B 3
Solomon Islands **82** BC 3
Solomon Sea **81** F 3
Solomon Sea **82** B 3
Solov'yevsk **68** L 5
Solyanka **68** M 3
Somalia **93** GH 3–4
Somerset (Australia) **79** G 1
Somme **56** D 1
Sonakh **69** P 5
Songea **95** F 2
Song Hong **73** H 3
Songhua Jiang **71** J 1
Songkhla **73** H 6
Songnim **71** J 3
Songo **95** E 3
Sonid Youqi **70** F 2
Sonid Zuoqi **70** F 2
Sonmiani Bay **67** H 5
Sonneberg **53** F 4
Sonoita **102** D 5
Sonoma Peak **102** C 3
Sonora (Mexico) **102** D 6
Sonoran Desert **102** D 5
Sonqor **66** D 4
Sonqor (Iran) **61** E 2
Sonsonate **104** DE 5
Sopka Shiveluch **69** U 4
Sopochnaya Karga **68** DE 1
Sopron **58** A 1
Sopur **67** J 4
Sora **57** F 3
Soria **56** C 3
Sorikmerapi, Gunung **74** A 3
Sorkh, Kūh-e (Iran) **61** G 2
Sorkheh (Iran) **61** F 2
Sor Mertvyy Kultuk **66** E 1
Sorong **75** H 4
Soroti **92** E 4
Söröya **54** H 1
Sör Rondane Mountains **115**
Sorsatunturi **54** J 2
Sorsele **54** G 2

Sorsogon **75** F 1
Sortavala **54** K 3
Sör-Tröndelag **54** F 3
Sosnogorsk **62** KL 3
Sosnovyy Bor **63** Q 3
Sosyka **59** EF 1
Sotra **55** D 3
Sotsial **63** P 6
Souanké **91** GH 5
Soudan **79** F 3
Sŏul **71** HJ 3
Soumenselkä **54** H 3
Soure **109** J 4
Souris River **99** R 6
Sousa **111** J 2
Sousse → Sūsah (Tunisia) **87** H 1
South Africa **94** BD 6
Southampton **52** C D 4
Southampton Island **99** UV 3
South Andaman **73** F 5
South Australia **78–79** E 4
South Bend (IN, U.S.A.) **103** JK 3
South Bend (WA, U.S.A.) **102** B 2
South Carolina **103** K 5
South China Sea **74** CD 2
South Dakota **102** FG 3
South East Cape **80** L 9
Southend **99** R 4
Southend-on-Sea **52** D 4
Southern Alps **82** C 5
Southern Cook Islands **83** E 4
Southern Cross **78** B 5
Southern Uplands **52** C 3
Southern Yemen **89** HJ 5–6
South Geomagnetic Pole **115**
South Georgia **115**
South Island **80** P 9
South Island **82** C 5
South Korea **71** JK 3
South Magnetic Pole **115**
South Orkney Islands **115**
South Platte River **102** F 3
South Pole **115**
South Sandwich Islands **115**
South Saskatchewan **99** PQ 5
South Shetland Islands **115**
South Shields **52** C 3
South Uist **52** B 3
South Wellesley Islands (Queensland, Austr.) **79** FG 2
Southwest Cape **80** P 10
Soven **112** C 5
Sovetsk **62** J 4
Sovetskaya Gavan' **69** PQ 6
Sovetskaya Rechka **63** QR 2
Soya Strait **65** R 5
Sozimskiy **62** K 4
Spain **56** BC 4
Spanish Town **105** G 4
Spartanburg **103** K 5
Spartí **58** B 3
Spassk Dal'niy **71** K 2
Spearfish **102** F 3
Spence Bay **99** T 2
Spencer Gulf **79** F 5
Spicer Islands **101** M 2
Spitsbergen **114**
Split **57** G 3
Spokane **102** C 2
Spooner **103** H 2
Springbok **94** B 5
Springdale (AR, U.S.A.) **103** H 4
Springfield (CO, U.S.A.) **102** F 4
Springfield (IL, U.S.A.) **103** HJ 4
Springfield (MA, U.S.A.) **103** M 3
Springfield (MO, U.S.A.) **103** H 4
Springfield (OR, U.S.A.) **102** B 3
Springs **94** D 5
Squillace, Golfo di **57** G 4
Srbija **58** B 2
Sredinnyy Khrebet **69** TU 4–5
Sredna Gora **58** BC 2
Srednekolymsk **69** S 2
Sredne Sibirskoye Plosko-gor'ye **68** FK 2–3
Sredniy **69** S 4
Srednyaya Itkana **69** U 3
Sremska Mitrovica **58** A 1–2
Srikakulam **72** DE 4
Sri Lanka (Ceylon) **72** D 6
Srinagar **67** K 4
Staaten River National Park **79** G 2
Stadlandet **54** D 3
Stafford **52** C 4
Stalowa Wola **53** H 4
Stamford (CT, U.S.A.) **103** M 3
Standerton **94** D 5
Stanke Dimitrov **58** B 2
Stanley (Falkland Is., U.K.) **113** E 9
Stanley Falls **92** D 4
Stanley Mission **99** R 4
Stanovka **63** O 4
Stanovoy Khrebet **68** LN 4
Stanovoy Nagor'ye **68** KL 4
Stara Planina **58** BC 2
Staraya Russa **55** K 4
Staraya Vorpavla **63** N 3
Stara Zagora **58** C 2
Starbuck **83** E 3
Stargard Szczecinski **53** G 4
Starodub **62** F 5
Starogard Gdanski **53** G 4
Staryy Oskol **62** G 5
Staten Island **113** D 9–10
Stavanger **55** DE 4
Stavropol' **59** F 1
Stavropolka **63** N 5
Stavropol'skaya Vozvyshen-nost' **59** F 1
Steen River **99** O 4
Stefanie, Lake **93** F 4
Stefansson Island **99** Q 1
Steinkopf **94** B 5
Stellenbosch **94** BC 6
Stenon **58** C 3
Stepanakert **66** D 3
Sterlitamak **62** KL 5
Steubenville **103** K 3
Stevenson Entrance **98** G 4
Stewart (AK, U.S.A.) **98** M 4
Stewart (Canada) **98** KL 3
Stewart (New Zealand) **80** P 10
Stewart Crossing **98** K 3
Stewart Island **82** B 3
Stewart Island (New Zeeland) **80** P 10
Steyr **57** F 2
Stillwater **103** G 4
Stip **58** B 2
Stirling Range National Park **78** B 5
Stjördal **54** F 3
Stockholm **55** G 4
Stockton **102** BC 4
Stockton Plateau **102** F 5
Stöde **54** G 3
Stoke-on-Trent **52** C 4
Stokksnes **54** BC 3
Stony Rapids **99** Q 4
Stony River **98** FG 3
Storån **54** G 3
Storavan **54** G 2
Stord **55** E 4
Storkerson Peninsula **99** Q 1
Stornoway **52** B 3
Storsjßn **54** F 3
Storuman **54** G 2
Storvigelen **54** F 3
Stöttingfjället **54** G 3
Strait of Belle Isle **101** Q 5
Strait of Bonifacio **57** E 3
Strait of Dover **52** D 4
Strait of Gibraltar **56** B 4
Strait of Hormuz **61** G 4
Strait of Hormuz **89** K 3
Strait of Magellan **113** BC 9
Strait of Malacca **74** B 3
Straits of Florida **103** KL 6–7
Stralsund **53** F 4
Strand **94** B 6
Stranraer **52** B 4
Strasbourg **57** E 2
Stratford (TX, U.S.A.) **102** F 4
Straubing **53** F 5
Streaky Bay **78** E 5
Strelka-Chunya **68** H 3
Stretto de Messina **57** G 4
Streymoy **52** A 1
Strömsund **54** G 3
Stung Treng **73** J 5
Sturt Desert **79** G 4
Sturt National Park **79** G 4
Stuttgart **53** E 5
Styr' **55** J 5
Subayhah **66** B 5
Suceava **58** C 1
Sucre **110** D 4
Sudan **88** DE 6
Sudbury **101** L 6
Suddie **109** G 2
Sudety **53** G 4
Suðuroy **52** A 1
Suez (Egypt) **60** A 3
Suez Canal (Egypt) **60** A 3
Şuḩār **89** K 4
Sühbaatar **70** F 1
Suhl **53** F 4
Suide **70** EF 3
Suining **71** G 4
Suir **62** F 3
Suizhong **71** H 2
Sukaraja **74** D 4
Sukhana **68** L 2
Sukhona **62** H 4
Sukhumi **59** F 2
Sukkertoppen **101** R 2
Sukkur **67** H 5
Suksukan **69** S 3
Sula, Kepulauan **75** FG 4
Sulaimāniya (Iraq) **61** D 2
Sulaimāniya (Iraq) **66** CD 3
Sulaiman Range **67** H 4–5
Sulanheer **70** E 2
Sulawesi **75** EF 4
Sulawesi, Laut **75** F 3
Sulb **88** DE 4
Sulima **90** B 4
Sulitjelma **54** G 2
Sullana **108** BC 4
Sultan Dağları **58–59** D 3
Sulu Archipelago **75** EF 2–3
Sulu Sea **75** EF 2
Sumarokovo **63** R 3
Sumatera **74** AB 3–4
Sumaúma **109** G 5
Šumava **53** F 5
Sumba **75** EF 5
Sumbawa **74** E 5
Sumbawanga **92** E 6
Sumbe **94** A 2
Sümber **70** E 1
Sumburgh Head **52** C 3
Sumgait **66** DE 2
Summel (Iraq) **59** F 3
Summel (Iraq) **60** D 1
Summit Lake **99** N 4
Sumperk **53** G 5
Sumter **103** L 5
Sumy **62** G 5
Suna **92** EF 6
Sunderland **52** C 4
Sündıren Dağları **58** D 3
Sundsvall **54** G 3
Sunflower, Mount **102** F 4
Sungai Barito **74** D 4
Sungai Kampar **74** B 3
Sungai Kutai **74** E 4
Sungai Mamberamo **75** J 4
Sunnan **54** F 3
Sunndalsfjorden **54** E 3
Suntar Khayata, Khrebet **69** PQ 3
Suokonmäki **54** H 3
Suolahti **54** J 3
Suomenselkä **54** J 3
Suomi **54** J 3
Suoyarvi **62** F 3
Superior (WI, U.S.A.) **103** H 2
Süphan Dağı **59** F 3
Suquṭrā **93** J 2
Şūr (Lebanon) **60** B 2
Surabaya **74** D 5
Surakarta **74** CD 5
Surat (India) **72** B 3
Surat (Queensland, Austr.) **79** H 4
Suratgarh **72** B 2
Surat Thani **73** GH 6
Surendranagar **72** AB 3
Surgut **63** O 3
Surgutikha **63** R 3
Surin **73** H 5
Surinam **109** G 3

Sūrīyah **60** BC 2
Sūrīyah **88** F 2
Surud Ad **93** H 2
Survey Pass **98** FG 2
Susa (Iran) **61** E 2
Susques **110** C 5
Susuman **69** R 3
Sutlej **67** J 4–5
Sutton (AK, U.S.A.) **98** H 3
Sutun'ya **69** NO 2
Suva **82** C 4
Suva Gora **58** B 2
Suva Planina **58** B 2
Suvorov **82** E 3
Suwałki **53** H 4
Suways, Qanat as (Egypt) **60** A 3
Suwon **71** J 3
Suzhou **71** GH 4
Suzun **63** Q 5
Svalbard **114**
Svartisen **54** F 2
Svealand **55** FG 4
Sveg **54** F 3
Svendborg **55** F 4–5
Sverdlovsk **63** M 4
Sverige **54** G 3
Svetlogorsk (Belorussiya, U.S.S.R.) **55** J 5
Svetlograd **59** F 1
Svetlyy **69** N 4
Svetozarevo **58** B 2
Svobodnyy **69** N 5
Swain Reefs **79** J 3
Swains **82** D 3
Swakopmund **94** A 4
Swan River **99** R 5
Swansea **52** C 4
Swaziland [Ngwane] **95** E 5
Sweden **54** G 3
Swellendam **94** C 6
Świdnik **53** H 4
Swift Current **99** Q 5
Swinoujście **53** FG 4
Switzerland **57** E 2
Syadaykharvuta **63** OP 2
Syalakh **69** MN 2
Syangannakh **69** R 2
Syðri-Hagangur **54** B 2
Sydney (Canada) **101** Q 6
Sydney (N.S.W., Austr.) **79** J 5
Syktyvkar **62** JK 3
Sylhet **73** F 3
Syracuse (N.Y., U.S.A.) **103** L 3
Syr-Dar'ya **67** H 2
Syria **60** BC 2
Syria **88** F 2
Syrian Desert **60** C 2
Syuge-Khaya, Gora **69** P 2
Syurkum **69** Q 5
Syzran **62** J 5
Szczecin **53** F 4
Szczecinek **53** G 4
Szeged **58** A 1
Székesféhérvár **58** A 1
Szekszárd **58** A 1
Szentes **58** AB 1
Szolnok **58** B 1
Szombathely **58** A 1

T

Taarom **79** HJ 4
Tabacal **110** D 5
Tabaqah (Syria) **60** C 2
Ţabaqah (Syria) **66** B 3
Tabarqah **59** E 3
Tabas (Iran) **61** G 2
Tabasco **104** D 4
Tabatinga **108** E 4
Tabelbala **86** E 3
Tabelbalet **87** G 3
Tabeng **73** HJ 5
Tabiteuea **82** C 3
Tabla **90** E 3
Table Mountain **94** B 6
Tábor (Czechoslovakien) **53** F 5
Tabor (U.S.S.R.) **69** R 1
Tabora **92** E 6
Tabou **90** C 5
Tabrīz **66** D 3
Tabuaeran **83** E 2
Tabūk (Saudi Arabia) **60** B 3
Tabūk (Saudi Arabia) **88** F 3
Tacheng **67** L 1
Tacloban **75** F 1
Tacna **110** B 4
Tacoma **102** B 2
Tacuarembó **112** EF 5
Tademaït, Plateau du **87** F 3
Tadoule Lake **99** S 4
Tadzhikistan **67** HJ 3
Taegu **71** J 3
Taejŏn **71** J 3
Tagama **91** F 2
Taganrog **59** E 1
Taganrogskiy Zaliv **59** E 1
Tagounite **86** D 3
Taguatinga **111** G 3
Taguenout Haggueret **90** D 1
Tagula Island **79** J 1
Tahan, Gunung **74** B 3
Tahat, Mont **87** G 4
Tahiti **83** EF 4
Tahoe, Lake **102** C 4
Tahoua **91** EF 3
Tahrūd **66** F 5
Tahtali Dağlari **59** E 3
Tahuata **83** F 3
Taibus Qi **70** FG 2
Taichung **71** H 6
Tailai **71** H 1
Taimba **68** G 3
Tainan **71** GH 6
Taipei **71** H 6
Taiping (Malaysia) **74** B 3
Taipu **111** J 2
Taitao, Península de **113** AB 8
Taitung **71** H 6
Taivalkoski **54** J 2
Taiwan **71** H 6
Taiyuan **70** F 3
Ta'izz **89** G 6
Tajito **102** D 5
Tájo **56** B 4
Tajrīsh (Iran) **61** F 2
Tajrīsh (Iran) **66** E 3
Tajumulco, Volcán **104** D 4
Tak **73** G 4
Takāb (Iran) **61** E 1
Takāb (Iran) **66** D 3
Takamatsu **71** KL 4
Takatshwane **94** C 4
Takeo **74** B 1
Takestan (Iran) **61** E 1
Takhta-Bazar **67** G 3
Takht-e Soleiman (Iran) **61** F 1
Takijuq Lake **99** P 2
Takla Landing **99** M 4
Takla Makan **67** L 3
Taklaun, Gora **69** Q 3
Taklimakan Shamo **67** LM 3
Takua Pa **74** A 2
Talak **91** EF 2
Talakan **69** O 6
Talandzha **69** O 6
Talara **108** B 4
Talaud, Kepulauan **75** G 3
Talavera de la Reina **56** C 3–4
Talawdī **88** E 6
Talaya (U.S.S.R.) **68** G 4
Talaya (U.S.S.R.) **69** S 3
Talca **113** B 6
Talcahuano **113** B 6
Taldy-Kurgan **63** PQ 6
Talence **56** C 3
Tālesh **66** D 3
Taliabu, Pulau **75** FG 4
Talimardzhan **67** H 3
Taliqan **67** HJ 3
Taliwang **74** E 5
Talkalakh (Syria) **60** B 2
Talkeetna Mountains **98** H 3
Tall Afar (Iraq) **60** D 1
Tallahassee **103** K 5
Tall aş Şuwār (Syria) **60** C 2
Tallinn **55** J 4
Tall Kayf (Iraq) **60** D 1
Tall Kūshik (Syria) **60** C 1
Talo **93** F 2
Taltal **112** B 4
Tama, Mount **94** A 2
Tamale **90** D 4
Tamanrasset **87** G 4
Tamaulipas **104** C 3
Tambacounda **90** B 3
Tambalan **74** E 3
Tambisan **75** E 2
Tambo (Queensland, Austr.) **79** H 3
Tambov **62** H 5
Tamch **68** F 6
Tamchaket **86** C 5
Tame **108** D 2
Tamel Aike **113** BC 8
Tamgak, Monts **91** F 2
Tamil Nadu **72** C 5
Tampa **103** K 6
Tampere (Tammerfors) **54** H 3
Tampico **104** C 3
Tamu **73** F 3
Tamworth (N.S.W., Austr.) **79** J 5
Tana **81** J 5
Tana (Kenya) **93** F 5
Tana (Norway) **54** J 1
Tana (Vanuatu) **82** C 4
Tana, Lake **93** F 2
Tanaga **98** A 5
Tanami **78** DE 2
Tanami Desert **78** E 2
Tanami Desert Wildlife Sanctuary **78** E 3
Tanana **98** G 2
Tanana River **98** H 3
Tanch'ŏn **71** JK 2
Tandaho **93** G 2
Tandil **113** E 6
Tane-ga-shima **71** K 4
Tanga **93** F 5–6
Tanganyika, Lake **92** DE 6
Tang-e Karam (Iran) **61** F 3
Tanger **86** D 1
Tanggula Shan **70** AB 4
Tanggula Shankou **70** B 4
Tanghe **70** F 4
Tangmai **70** C 4
Tangshan **71** G 3
Tangyuan **71** J 1
Tanimbar, Kepulauan **75** H 5
Tanjung, Jabung **74** C 4
Tanjung Api **74** C 3
Tanjungbalai **74** AB 3
Tanjung Samak **74** C 4
Tanjung Selatan **74** D 4
Tanjungselor **74** E 3
Tanjung Vals **75** J 5
Tannu Ola **68** F 5
Ţanţā **88** E 2
Tan Tan **86** C 3
Tanzania **92** EF 6
Tao'an **71** H 1–2
Taolanaro **95** H 5
Taoudenni **90** D 1
Taoyuan **71** H 5
Tapachula **104** D 5
Tapajós **109** GH 4
Tapurucuara **108** E 4
Taquari **110** E 4
Taquari **111** F 4
Tara (U.S.S.R.) **63** OP 4
Tarābulus (Lebanon) **60** B 2
Ţarābulus (Lebanon) **88** EF 2
Ţarābulus (Libya) **87** HJ 2
Taracua **108** E 3
Tarakan **74** E 3
Tarakki **67** H 4
Taranto **57** G 3
Taranto, Golfo di **57** G 3–4
Tarapoto **108** C 5
Tarasovo **62** J 2
Tarata (Peru) **110** C 4
Tarauacá **108** D 5
Tarawa **82** C 2
Tarbes **56** D 3
Taree **79** J 5
Tareya **68** F 1
Ţarīf (United Arab Emirates) **61** F 4
Tarija **110** D 5
Tarim Liuchang **70** A 2
Tarin Kowt **67** GH 4
Tarko-Zale **63** PQ 3
Tarkwa **90** D 4
Tarlac **75** J 1
Tarma **110** A 3
Tarn **56** D 3
Tarnobrzeg **53** H 4
Tarnów **53** H 4
Taroudant **86** D 2
Tarragona **56** D 3
Tarrasa **56** D 3
Tarsū Mūsā **87** J 4

Tarsus (Turkey) **60** B 1
Tart **70** B 3
Tartagal **110** D 5
Tartu **55** J 4
Tartus (Syria) **60** B 2
Ṭarṭus (Syria) **88** F 2
Tarutung **74** A 3
Tashakta **63** R 6
Tashauz **66** F 2
Tashk, Daryācheh-ye (Iran) **61** FG 3
Tashkent **67** H 2
Tashtagol **63** R 5
Tasman Bay **81** Q 9
Tasmania **80** KL 9
Tasmania **82** A 5
Tasman Sea **80** NO 8
Tasman Sea **82** B 5
Tassili N-Ajjer **87** G 3
Tas-Tumus **69** O 1
Tasūj **59** G 3
Tatabánya **58** A 1
Tatakoto **83** F 4
Tatarbunary **58** C 1
Tatarsk **63** P 4
Tatarskiy Proliv **69** Q 6
Tatry **53** H 5
Taubaté **111** GH 5
Taumaturgo **108** D 5
Taunggon **73** G 3
Taungup **73** F 4
Taunton **52** C 4
Tauranga **81** R 8
Tauranga **82** C 5
Taurus Mountains (Turkey) **60** A 1
Taurus Mountains → Toros Dağ-lari **59** DE 3
Tavatuma **69** T 3
Tavda **63** N 4
Taverner Bay **101** N 2
Tavolara **57** E 3
Tavoy **73** G 5
Tawau **74** E 3
Tawitawi Group **75** F 2
Ṭawūq (Iraq) **60** D 2
Tawzar **87** G 2
Taxco de Alarcón **104** BC 4
Taxkorgan **67** K 3
Tayga **63** QR 4
Taylor **98** DE 2
Taymā' (Saudi Arabia) **60** C 4
Taymā' (Saudi Arabia) **66** B 5
Taymyr **68** F 2
Taymyr, Ozero **68** H 1
Tayshet **68** G 4
Taytay **75** E 1
Taz **63** P 2
Taza **86** E 2
Tāzah Khurmātū (Iraq) **60** D 2
Tazovskij **63** P 2
Tbilisi **59** FG 2
Tcholliré **91** G 4
Teba **75** J 4
Tébessa **87** G 1
Tebingtinggi **74** A 3
Tebingtinggi **74** B 4
Tebulos Mta **59** G 2
Tecer Dağlari **59** E 3
Tecka **113** B 7
Tecomán **104** B 4
Tecuci **58** C 1
Tedzhen **66** FG 3
Teeside **52** C 4
Tefé **109** F 4
Tegal **74** C 5
Tegre **93** FG 2
Tegucigalpa **104** E 5
Tegyul'te-Tërde **69** O 3
Teheran → Tehrān **66** DE 3
Tehrān **66** DE 3
Tehuacán **104** C 4
Teiga Plateau **88** D 5
Tejo **56** B 4
Tekeli **67** K 2
Tekes **67** L 2
Tekirdağ **58** C 2
Telanaipura **74** B 4
Tel Aviv-Yafo (Israel) **60** B 2–3
Tel Aviv-Yafo (Israel) **88** E 2
Telegraph Creek **98** LM 4
Telemaco Borba **111** FG 5
Telemark **55** E 4
Telén **113** C 6
Teles Pires **109** G 5
Teli **68** F 5
Tell al 'Amārna **88** E 3
Tello **112** C 5
Telok Anson **74** B 3
Tel'pos-Iz, Gora **63** L 3
Telukbatang **74** CD 4
Teluk Berau **75** H 4
Teluk Bone **75** F 4
Teluk Cendrawasih **75** HJ 4
Teluk Kumai **74** D 4
Teluk Tomini **75** F 4
Témacine **87** G 2
Tematangi **83** F 4
Tembenchi **68** G 3
Tembo **92** B 6
Tembo, Mont **91** G 5
Temirtau **63** O 5
Temiscaming **101** M 6
Temoe **83** G 4
Tempa **114**
Temple **103** G 5
Temuco **113** B 6
Tena **108** C 4
Tenali **72** D 4
Tenasserim **73** G 4–5
Tenere **91** FG 1–2
Ténéré, Erg de **91** G 2
Tenerife **86** B 3
Ténès **87** F 1
Tengchong **70** C 5
Tenggara, Kepulauan **75** G 5
Tengiz, Ozero **63** N 5
Teniente Marsh **115**
Teniente Matienzo **115**
Tenke (U.S.S.R.) **68** L 3
Tennant Creek **78** EF 2
Tennessee **103** J 4
Tenojoki **54** J 2
Teófilo Otoni **111** H 4
Tepatitlán **104** B 3
Tepic **104** AB 3
Teraina **83** E 2
Teramo **57** F 3
Tercan **59** F 3
Terceira **86** A 1
Terek **59** G 2
Teresina **111** H 2
Teressa **73** F 6
Terhazza **86** D 4
Termez **67** H 3
Terni **57** F 3
Ternopol' **62** E 6
Terpugovo **63** N 4
Terrace **98** M 5
Terracina **57** F 3
Terracy Bay **100** K 6
Tessalit **90** E 1
Tessenei **93** F 2
Testa, Capo **57** E 3
Tete **95** E 3
Tétouan **86** D 1
Tetovo **58** B 2
Tevere **57** F 3
Teverya (Israel) **60** B 2
Têwo **70** D 4
Texarkana **103** H 5
Texas (U.S.A.) **102** FG 5
Texas City **103** G 6
Teya **68** F 3
Teykovo **62** GH 4
Teyuareh **67** G 4
Tezpur **73** F 2
Thailand **73** GH 4
Thailand, Gulf of **73** H 5
Thakhek **73** HJ 4
Thames **52** C 4
Thana **72** B 4
Thangoo **78** C 2
Thanh Hoa **73** HJ 4
Thanjavur **72** CD 5
Thap Sakae **73** GH 5
Thar Desert **72** B 2
Thargomindah **79** G 4
Tharthār, Wādī ath (Iraq) **60** D 2
Thásos **58** BC 2
Thaton **73** G 4
The Alps **57** EF 2
The Bahamas **105** GH 2–3
Thebes (Egypt) **60** A 4
Thebes (Egypt) **88** E 3
The Everglades **103** K 6
The Gambia **90** A 3
The Granites **78** DE 3
The Granites **78** DE 3
The Gulf **61** EF 3–4
The Gulf **89** J 3
The Hague **52** D 4
Thehran (Iran) **61** F 2
The Johnston Lakes **78** BC 5
The Pas **99** R 5
Thermaïkos Kólpos **58** B 2–3
Thessalía **58** B 3
Thessaloníki **58** B 2
The Wash **52** D 4
Thiès **90** A 3
Thimphu **72** E 2
Thio (Ethiopia) **93** G 2
Thio (New Caledonia) **81** J 6
Thíra **58** C 3
Thompson **99** S 4
Thompson Falls **102** CD 2
Thon Buri **73** GH 5
Thonon **57** E 2
Thraki **58** BC 2
Thrakion Pélagos **58** BC 2
Three Forks **102** D 2
Three Kings Islands **81** PQ 7
Three Kings Islands **82** C 5
Three Pagodas Pass **73** G 4
Thule **114**
Thunder Bay (Canada) **100** K 6
Thung Song **73** GH 6
Thurston Island **115**
Thy **55** E 4
Tiandong **70** E 6
Tiangua **111** H 1
Tianjin **71** G 3
Tianjun **70** CD 3
Tianmen **70** F 4
Tiantai **71** H 5
Tiaret **87** F 1
Tiber **57** F 3
Tibesti **91** H 1
Tibet **72** E 1
Tichla **86** B 4
Tidjkdja **86** C 5
Tidra, Ile **86** B 5
Tieli **71** J 1
Tielongtan **67** K 4
Tientsin **71** G 3
Tierra de Campos **56** BC 3
Tierra del Fuego, Isla Grande de **113** C 9
Tierra del Pan **56** B 3
Tigil **69** T 4
Tigris (Iraq) **60** D 2
Tigris (Iraq) **61** D 2
Tiguent **86** B 5
Tihāmat **89** G 5
Tijuana **102** C 5
Tikal **104** E 4
Tikhoretsk **59** F 1
Tikhvin **62** FG 4
Tilburg **52** DE 4
Tilichiki **69** V 3
Tillabéri **90** E 3
Tillamook **102** B 2
Timanskiy Kryazh **62** J 2–K 3
Timaru **81** Q 9
Timaru **82** C 5
Timashevskaya **59** EF 1
Timbauba **111** J 2
Timétrine **90** D 2
Timétrine, Monts **90** D 2
Timia **91** F 2
Timir-Atakh-Tas **69** S 2
Timişoara **58** B 1
Timkapaul' **63** M 3
Timmins **101** L 6
Timmoudi **86** E 3
Timor **75** G 5
Timor, Laut **75** G 6
Timote **113** D 6
Tinaca Point **75** G 2
Tindouf **86** D 3
Tinfouchy **86** DE 3
Tingmiarmiut **101** T 3
Tingri **72** E 2
Tinian **82** A 2
Tini Wells **88** C 6
Tinogasta **112** C 4
Tínos **58** C 3
Tinsukia **73** G 2
Ti-n Zaouâtene **87** F 4
Tirān (Egypt) **60** B 4
Tirana **58** AB 2
Tiraspol' **58** CD 1
Tire **58** C 3
Tirgovişte **58** C 1–2
Tîrgu Jiu **58** B 1
Tîrgu Mureş **58** BC 1

Tîrnâveni **58** B 1
Tirol **57** F 2
Tirso **57** E 3
Tiruchchirappalli **72** CD 5
Tirunelveli **72** C 6
Tirupati **72** CD 5
Tiruvannamalai **72** C 5
Tisdale **99** R 5
Tisza **58** B 1
Tiszántúl **58** B 1
Titicaca, Lago **110** C 4
Titograd **58** A 2
Titovo Užice **58** AB 2
Titov Veles **58** B 2
Titusville **103** K 6
Tiveden **55** F 4
Tizatlan **104** C 4
Tizimín **104** E 3
Tiznit **86** CD 3
Tjåhumas **54** G 2
Tkhach **59** F 2
Tkvarcheli **59** F 2
Tlemcen **86** E 2
Toamasina **95** HJ 3
Tobago, Isla **109** F 1
Toba & Kakar Ranges **67** H 4
Tobermorey **79** F 3
Tobol **63** N 4
Tobol **63** M 5
Tobol'sk **63** NO 4
Tobseda **62** K 2
Tocantinia **109** J 5
Tocantins **109** J 4
Tocapilla **110** B 5
Tocorpuri, Cerro de **110** C 5
Togiak **98** E 4
Togian, Kepulauan **75** F 4
Togni **88** F 5
Togo **90** E 4
Togtoh **70** F 2
Togyz **67** G 1
Tohma **59** E 3
Toijala **54** H 3
Tok (AK, U.S.A.) **98** J 3
Tokara-rettō **71** J 4–5
Tokat **59** E 2
Tokelau Islands **82** D 3
Tokko **68** L 4
Tokmak (U.S.S.R.) **59** E 1
Tokmak (U.S.S.R.) **67** K 2
Toksun **67** M 2
Toktogul **67** J 2
Toku-no-shima **71** J 5
Tokur **69** O 5
Tokushima **71** KL 4
Tōkyō **71** L 3
Tolbukhin **58** C 2
Toledo(OH, U.S.A.) **103** K 3
Toledo (Spain) **56** C 4
Toledo, Montes de **56** C 4
Tolga (Norway) **54** F 3
Toli **67** L 1
Toliara **95** G 4
Tolima **108** CD 3
Toltén **113** B 6
Toluca **104** BC 4
Tol'yatti **62** J 5
Tomakomai **71** M 2
Tomaszów Mazowiecki **53** H 4
Tomatlán **104** AB 4
Tombador, Serra do **110** E 3
Tombigbee River **103** J 5
Tombouctou **90** D 2
Tomé **113** B 6
Tomelloso **56** C 4
Tomini, Teluk **75** F 4
Tomkinson Ranges **78** D 4
Tomma **54** F 2
Tommot **69** N 4
Tompa **68** JK 4
Tomsk **63** R 4
Tonantins **108** E 4
Tondano **75** G 3
Tonekābon (Iran) **61** F 1
Tonekābon (Iran) **66** E 3
Tonga **82** D 4
Tonga (Sudan) **92** E 3
Tonga Islands **82** D 4
Tongariro National Park **81** QR 8
Tongatapu Group **82** D 4
Tongchuan **70** E 3
Tonghai **70** D 6
Tonghe **71** J 1
Tonghua **71** J 2
Tongliao **71** H 2
Tongoy **112** B 5
Tongren (Guizhou, China) **70** E 5
Tongren (Qinghai, China) **70** D 3
Tongtian He **70** C 4
Tongyu **71** H 2
Tonj **92** D 3
Tonk **72** C 2
Tonle Sap **73** H 5
Tonopah **102** C 4
Tonstad **55** E 4
Toompine **79** G 4
Toowoomba **79** J 4
Topeka **103** G 4
Topolinyy **69** P 3
Topozero, Ozero **54** K 2
Toraya **110** B 3
Torbat-e Heydarīyeh **66** FG 2–3
Torbay **52** C 4
Torbino **62** F 4
Torey **68** H J 5
Tori **92** E 3
Torino **57** E 2
Torneälven **54** H 2
Torneträsk **54** GH 2
Toro, Cerro del **112** C 4
Torom **69** P 5
Toronto **101** M 7
Toropets **62** F 4
Tororo **92** E 4
Toros Dağlari (Turkey) **59** D 3
Toros Dăglari (Turkey) **60** A 1
Torquato Severo **112** F 5
Torrelavega **56** C 3
Torrens, Lake **79** F 5
Torrens Creek **79** H 3
Torrente **56** C 4
Torreón **104** B 2–3
Torres Strait **79** G 1
Torres Strait **80** D 4
Torrington **102** F 3
Tortkuduk **63** O 5
Tortosa **56** D 3
Torud (Iran) **61** G 2
Toruń **53** G 4
Toscana **57** F 3
Tosontsengel **68** G 6
Tostuya **68** K 1
Totma **62** H 4
Totness **109** G 2
Totoras **112** D 5
Totten Glacier **115**
Tottori **71** K 3
Touggourt **87** G 2
Toulon **57** E 3
Toulouse **56** D 3
Toungoo **73** G 4
Touraine **56** D 2
Tourcoing **56** D 1
Tourine **86** C 4
Tours **56** D 2
Towakaima **109** G 2
Townsend **102** D 2
Townsville **79** H 2
Toyama **71** L 3
Toygunen **98** C 2
Toyohashi **71** L 4
Toyota **71** L 3
Trabzon **59** E 2
Trafalgar, Cabo **56** B 4
Trâghan **87** HJ 3
Trang **73** G 6
Trangan, Pulau **75** H 5
Transantarctic Mountains **115**
Transilvania **58** B 1
Transkei **94** D 6
Transtrandsfjällen **54** F 3
Transvaal **94** D 5
Trapani **57** F 4
Traun **57** F 2
Treinta y Tres **112** EF 5
Trelew **113** CD 7
Trelleborg **55** F 4
Tremonton **102** D 3
Trenčín **53** G 5
Trenel **113** D 6
Trenque Lauquen **113** D 6
Trento **57** F 2
Trenton (N.J., U.S.A.) **103** M 3
Trepassey **101** R 6
Tres Arroyos **113** D 6
Tres Cerros **113** C 8
Tres Esquinas **108** CD 3
Três Lagoas **111** F 5
Tres Puentes **112** BC 4
Treviso **57** F 2
Triabunna **80** L 9
Trialetskiy Khrebet **59** F 2
Trichur **72** C 5
Trier **52** E 5
Trieste **57** F 2
Trikala **58** B 3
Trincomalee **72** D 6
Trindade Island **107** G 5
Trinidad (Bolivia) **110** D 3
Trinidad (CA, U.S.A.) **102** B 3
Trinidad (Colombia) **108** D 2
Trinidad (Cuba) **105** G 3
Trinidad (Uruguay) **112** E 5
Trinidad, Isla **109** F 1
Trinidad and Tobago **109** FG 1
Trinity Islands **98** G 4
Trinkitat **88** F 5
Tripoli (Lebanon) **60** B 2
Tripoli (Lebanon) **88** EF 2
Tripoli (Libya) **87** H 2
Tripolitania **87** HJ 2
Tripura **73** F 3
Trivandrum **72** C 6
Trnava **53** G 5
Trobriand or Kiriwina Islands **81** F 3
Trois-Pistoles **101** O 6
Trois Rivières **101** N 6
Troitsk (U.S.S.R.) **63** M 5
Troitsk (U.S.S.R.) **68** F 4
Troitsko-Pechorsk **62** KL 3
Trollhättan **55** F 4
Trollhetta **54** E 3
Tromelin **85** H 6
Troms **54** G 2
Tromsö **54** G 2
Trondheim **54** F 3
Troodos (Cyprus) **59** D 4
Troodos (Cyprus) **60** A 2
Trout Peak **102** E 3
Trout River **101** Q 6
Troy (AL, U.S.A.) **103** J 5
Troy (Turkey) **58** C 3
Troyan **58** BC 2
Troyez **56** D 2
Troy Peak **102** C 4
TrucialCoast **89** KJ 3–4
Trucial Coast (United Arab Emirates) **61** FG 4
Trujillo (Peru) **108** C 5
Trujillo (Venezuela) **108** D 2
Truk Islands **82** B 2
Truro **101** P 6
Trust Territory of the Pacific Islands **82** AB 2
Truth or Consequences (Hot Springs) **102** E 5
Truva **58** C 3
Trysilfjellet **54** F 3
Tsavo National Park **93** F 5
Tselinograd **63** NO 5
Tsenhermandal **68** JK 6
Tsenogora **62** J 3
Tsentralno Tungusskoye Plato **68** H 3–4
Tsetseg **68** F 6
Tsetserleg (Mongolia) **68** G 6
Tsetserleg (Mongolia) **68** H 6
Tshane **94** C 4
Tshesebe **94** D 4
Tshikapa **92** C 6
Tsiafajavona **95** H 3
Tsimlyanskoye Vodokhranilishche **59** F 1
Tsingtao **71** H 3
Tsipanda **69** OP 4
Tsjokkassa **54** HJ 2
Tskhinvali **59** F 2
Tsodilo Hills **94** C 3
Tsuchiura **71** M 3
Tsumeb **94** B 3
Tsumkwe **94** C 3
Tsuruoka **71** L 3
Tuamotu Archipelago **83** FG 4
Tuan **73** H 3
Tuapse **59** E 2
Tuba **68** H 4
Ţubal, Wādī aţ (Iraq) **60** C 2
Tubarão **112** G 4
Tubayq, Jabal at (Saudi Arabia) **60** B 3

Ṭubruq **87** K 2
Tubuaï **83** F 4
Tubuai Islands **83** EF 4
Tucano **111** J 3
Tucavaca **110** E 4
Tucson **102** D 5
Tucumcari **102** F 4
Tucuruí **109** HJ 4
Tufi **82** A 3
Tuguegarao **75** J 1
Tugur **69** P 5
Tukangbesi, Kepulauan **75** F 5
Tuktoyaktuk **98** L 2
Tukzar **67** H 3
Tula (Mexico) **104** C 3
Tula (U.S.S.R.) **62** G 5
Tulancingo **104** C 3–4
Tulbagh **94** B 6
Tulcán **108** C 3
Tulcea **58** C 1
Tulchin **58** C 1
Tuloma **54** K 2
Tulsa **103** GH 4
Tuluá **108** C 3
Tulun **68** H 5
Tumaco **108** C 3
Tumany **69** T 3
Tumat **69** PQ 1
Tumbes **108** B 4
Tumd Youqi **70** F 2
Tumeremo **109** F 2
Tūmū **87** H 4
Tunas **111** G 5
Tunduru **95** F 2
Tunga **91** F 4
Tungsten **98** M 3
Tunguska, Nizhnyaya **68** F 2
Tungus-Khaya **69** N 3
Tūnis **87** G 1
Tunisia **87** GH 1
Tunja **108** D 2
Tununak **98** D 3
Tunxi **71** G 5
Tuöroyri **52** A 1
Tuostakh **69** P 2
Tuotuo Heyan **70** B 4
Tupã **111** F 5
Tupelo **103** J 5
Tupiza **110** C 5
Tuquan **71** H 1
Tura (U.S.S.R.) **68** H 3
Turakh **68** MN 1
Turana, Khrebet **69** O 5
Turanskaya **66** F 2
Turanskaya Nizmennost **66–67** FG 2
Turbo **108** C 2
Tūreh (Iran) **61** E 2
Tureia **83** F 4
Turgay **67** G 1
Turgayskaya Dolina **63** M 5–6
Turgayskaya Stolovaya Strana **63** M 5
Türgen Uul **68** F 6
Tŭrgovishte **58** C 2
Turgutlu **58** C 3
Turhal **59** E 2
Turin **57** E 2–3
Turkana, Lake **93** F 4
Turkestan **67** H 2
Turkey **59** DE 3
Turkey **60** AB 1
Türkiye **59** DE 3
Turkmeniya **66** F 3
Turks and Caicos Islands **105** HJ 3
Turks Islands **105** H 3
Turku (Åbo) **55** H 3
Turnu Măgurele **58** BC 2
Turpan **70** A 2
Tursha **62** J 4
Turukhansk **63** RS 2
Turukta **68** L 3
Tuscaloosa **103** J 5
Tuticorin **72** C 6
Tutonchany **68** FG 3
Tutubu **92** E 6
Tutuila **82** D 3
Tuvalu **82** D 3
Ṭuwayq, Jabal (Saudi Arabia) **61** D 4
Ṭuwayq, Jabal (Saudi Arabia) **89** H 3–4
Tuxpan de Rodríguez Cano **104** C 3
Tuxtla Gutiérrez **104** D 4
Tuz Gölü **59** D 3
Tūz Khurmātū (Iraq) **61** D 2
Tuzla **57** G 3
Tyan'-Shan' **67** JK 2
Tychy **53** G 4
Tygda **69** N 5
Tyler **103** G 5
Tynda **69** M 4
Tyrma **69** O 5
Tyrrhenian Sea **57** F 3–4
Tyubelyakh **69** Q 2
Tyukalinsk **63** O 4
Tyumen' **63** MN 4
Tyungulyu **69** O 3
Tzaneen **94** DE 4

U

Uad el Jat **86** C 3
Ua Huka **83** F 3
Uatumá **109** G 4
Uauá **111** J 2
Uaupés **108** E 4
Ubá **111** H 5
Ubangi **92** B 4
ʿUbayyid, Wādī al (Iraq) **60** CD 2
Ubeda **56** C 4
Uberaba **111** G 4
Uberlândia **111** G 4
Ubolratna Dam **73** H 4
Ubombo **95** E 5
Ubort' **55** J 5
Ucayali **108** D 5
Uch-Aral **63** Q 6
Uch Kuduk **67** GH 2
Udachnaya **68** K 2
Udaipur **72** B 3
Udanna **69** Q 2
Uddevalla **55** F 4
Uddjaure **54** G 2
Udgir **72** C 4
Udine **57** F 2
Udipi **72** B 5
Udon Thani **73** H 4
Udskoye **69** O 5
Udzha **68** L 1
Uele **92** C 4
Uelen **98** C 2
Uelzen **53** F 4
Ufa **62** L 4–5
Ugalla **92** E 6
Ugalla River Game Reserve **92** E 6
Uganda **92** E 4
Uglegorsk **69** Q 6
Ugoyan **69** N 4
Ugulan **69** T 3
Ugumun **68** L 2
Ugun **69** N 4
Uherské Hradiště **53** G 5
Uil **66** E 1
Uis Mine **94** AB 4
Uitenhage **94** DE 6
Ujae **82** C 2
Ujelang **82** B 2
Ujiji **92** D 6
Ujjain **72** C 3
Ujung **75** E 5
Ujung Pandang **75** E 4–5
Uka **69** U 4
Ukelayat **69** WX 3
Ukhta **62** K 3
Ukmergė **55** HJ 4
Ukraina (U.S.S.R.) **58–59** D 1
Ukrainka **54** K 5–6
Uktym **62** J 3
Ukwaa **92** E 3
Ulaanbaatar **68** J 6
Ulaga **69** O 2
Ulan Bator **68** J 6
Ulan-Ude **68** J 5
Ularunda **79** H 4
Ulety **68** K 5
Ulhasnagar **72** B 4
Uliastay **68** G 6
Uliga **82** C 2
Ullapool **52** B 3
Ulovo **69** S 1
Ulsan **71** JK 3
Ulster **52** B 4
Ulu **88** E 6
Uludağ **58** C 3
Ulutau, Gory **67** H 1
Ul'yanovsk **62** J 5
Uma **68** M 5
Uman' **58** D 1
Umanak **114**
Umari **75** J 4
Umba **54** K 2
Umboi **80** E 3
Umbria **57** F 3
Umeå **54** H 3
Umm al Qaywayn (United Arab Emirates) **61** G 4
Umm Durmān **88** E 5
Umm Lajj (Saudi Arabia) **60** B 4
Umm Ruwābah **88** E 6
Umm Urūmah (Saudi Arabia) **60** B 4
Umnak **98** D 5
Umtata **94** D 6
Umuarama **111** F 5
Umvuma **95** E 3
Unaí **111** G 4
Unalakleet **98** E 3
Unalaska **98** D 5
Unayzah (Jordan) **60** B 3
ʿUnayzah (Saudi Arabia) **60** D 4
Ungava Bay **101** O 4
União do Vitória **112** F 4
Unimak **98** E 5
United Arab Emirates **61** FG 5
United Kingdom **52** DC 3
United States **102–103**
Unity **99** Q 5
Universales, Montes **56** C 3
Unst **52** C 2
Uoyan **68** K 4
Upata **109** F 2
Upemba, Lac **92** D 6
Upemba National Park **92** D 6
Upernavik **114**
Upington **94** C 5
Upolu **82** D 3
Upper Red Lake **103** GH 2
Uppland **55** G 3
Uppsala **55** G 4
Urak **69** Q 4
Ural **62** K 5
Ural **66** E 1
Ural Mountains **63** LM 2–4
Ural'sk **62** K 5
Urandangie **79** F 3
Urandi **111** H 3
Uranium City **99** Q 4
Uraricoera **109** F 3
Urayq, Natud al (Saudi Arabia) **60** D 4
Urbano Santos **111** H 1
Uren **62** J 4
Urewera National Park **81** R 8
Urfa (Turkey) **59** E 3
Urfa (Turkey) **60** C 1
Urfa Platosu **59** E 3
Urgench **66** FG 2
Uribia **108** D 1
Uromi **91** F 4
Ur Suq ash Shuyūkh (Iraq) **61** DE 3
Ursus **53** H 4
Uruaçu **111** G 3
Uruapan **104** B 4
Urucará **109** G 4
Uruçuí **111** H 2
Uruguaiana **112** E 4–5
Uruguay **112** EF 5
Urumchi **67** M 2
Ürümqi **67** M 2
Uruqnay **112** E 5
Uryupinsk **62** H 5
Uşak **58** C 3
Usevolozisk **54** K 3
ʾUshayrah (Saudi Arabia) **61** DE 4
Ushuaia **113** C 9
Üsküdar **58** C 2
Ussuriysk **71** K 2
Ust'-Bol'sheretsk **69** ST 5
Ust'-Chayka **68** J 3
Ust'-Ilimsk **68** H 4
Ust-Kada **68** H 5
Ust'-Kamchatsk **69** U 4
Ust'-Kamenogorsk **63** QR 5–6
Ust'-Karenga **68** L 5
Ust'-Karsk **68** L 5
Ust'-Khayryuzovo **69** ST 4
Ust'-Kulom **62** K 3
Ust'-Kut **68** J 4

Ust-Labinsk **59** EF 1
Ust'-Nera **69** Q 3
Ust'-Olenëk **68** LM 1
Ust'-Ozernoye **63** RS 4
Ust'-Pit **68** F 4
Ust'-Port **63** Q 2
Ust'-Sugoy **69** S 3
Ust'-Tatta **69** O 3
Ust'-Tym **63** Q 4
Ust'-Ura **62** H 3
Ust'-Urgal **69** O 5
Ust'-Us **68** F 5
Ust'-Usa **62** L 2
Ust'-Uyskoye **63** M 5
Ustuyurt, Plato **66** F 2
Ust'-Vyyskaya **62** J 3
Ust'Yuribey **63** NO 2
Usu **67** L 2
Usulután **104** E 5
Usumacinta, Rio **104** D 4
Utah **102** D 4
Utah Lake **102** D 4
Utata **68** H J 5
Utës **63** P 5
Utesiki **69** W 2
Utiariti **110** E 3
Utica **103** M 3
Utirik **82** C 2
Utrecht **52** DE E 4
Utrera **56** B 4
Uttyakh **69** O 2
Uuldza **68** K 6
Uusimaa **55** J 3
Uvarovo **62** H 5
Uvinza **92** DE 6
Uvs Nuur **68** F 5
Uwayrid, Harrat al (Saudi Arabia) **60** B 4
Uxituba **109** G 4
Uyaly **67** G 2
Uyandi **69** Q 2
Uyega **69** Q 3
Uyuni **110** C 5
Uyuni, Salar de **110** C 5
Uzbekistan **67** GH 2
Uzbel Shankou **67** J 3
Uzhgorod **58** B 1
Uzhur **63** R 4
Uzunköprü **58** C 2

V

Vaal **94** C 5
Vaasa (Vasa) **54** H 3
Vác **58** A 1
Vacaria **112** FG 4
Vadodara **72** B 3
Vaduz **57** E 2
Vágar **52** A 1
Vaghena **81** G 3
Vairaatea **83** F 4
Vaitupu **82** C 3
Vakarevo **69** W 3
Valachia **58** BC 2
Valcheta **113** C 7
Valday **62** F 4
Val de Loire **56** D 2
Valdepeñas **56** C 4
Valdés, Península **113** D 7
Valdez **98** H 3
Valdivia (Chile) **113** B 6
Val-d'Or **101** M 6
Valdosta **103** K 5
Valença **111** J 3
Valenca do Piauí **111** H 2
Valence **57** DE 2–3
Valencia (Spain) **56** CD 4
Valencia (Venezuela) **108** E 2
Valentine **102** F 3
Valera **108** D 2
Valga **55** J 4
Valjevo **58** AB 2
Valladolid (Mexico) **104** E 3
Valladolid (Spain) **56** C 3
Vall de Uxó **56** C 4
Valle de la Pascua **108** E 2
Valledupar **108** D 1
Valle Grande **110** D 4
Vallenar **112** BC 4
Valletta **57** F 4
Valleyview **99** O 4
Valparaíso (Chile) **112** B 5
Vals, Tanjung **75** J 5
Vammala **54** H 3
Van **59** F 3
Vanavara **68** H 3
Vancouver **99** N 6
Vancouver Island **99** M 6
Vanda **115**
Vanderbijlpark **94** D 5
Vanderhoof **99** N 5
Van Diemen, Cape **78** D 1
Van Diemen Gulf **78** E 1
Vanduzi **95** E 3
Vänern **55** F 4
Van Gölü **59** F 3
Vangunu **81** G 3
Vanikolo Islands **81** J 4
Vanikoro Island **82** C 3
Vankarem **98** B 2
Vannes **56** C 2
Vanoua Lava **81** J 4
Vanoua Lava **82** C 3
Vanrhynsdorp **94** B 6
Vanua Levu **82** C 4
Vanuatu **81** J 5
Vanuatu **82** B 3
Vanzhil'kynak **63** QR 3
Varanasi **72** D 2
Varangerfjorden **54** K 1–2
Varangerhalvöya **54** JK 1
Varaždin **57** G 2
Varberg **55** F 4
Vardofjällen **54** FG 2
Varginha **111** GH 5
Varkaus **54** J 3
Värmland **55** F 4
Varna (Bulgaria) **58** C 2
Värnamo **55** F 4
Varsinais Suomi **55** H 3
Var'yegan **63** P 3
Vashnel **63** N 3
Vasiss **63** O 4
Vassdalsegga **55** E 4
Västerås **55** G 4
Västerbotten **54** G 3
Västergötland **55** F 4
Västervik **55** G 4
Vasto **57** F 3
Västra Granberget **54** H 2
Vasyugan **63** P 4
Vaticano, Citta Del **57** F 3
Vatnajökull **54** B 3
Vatoa **82** D 4
Vättern **55** F 4
Vatyna **69** W 3
Vaughn **102** E 5
Vaupés **108** D 3
Vava'u Group **82** D 4
Växjö **55** FG 4
Vayvida **68** FG 3
Vazhgort **62** J 3
Veadeiros **111** G 3
Vefsna **54** F 2
Vega **54** F 2
Vegreville **99** P 5
Vejle **55** E 4
Velež **57** G 3
Vélez-Málaga **56** C 4
Velikiye Luki **55** K 4
Velikiy Ustyug **62** HJ 3
Veliko Tŭrnovo **58** C 2
Vella Lavella **81** G 3
Vellore **72** CD 5
Velsk **62** H 3
Vel't **62** K 2
Vemor'ye **69** Q 6
Venado Tuerto **112** D 5
Venda **95** E 4
Venezia **57** F 2
Venezuela **108–109** EF 2
Venezuela, Golfo de **108** D 1
Vengerovo **63** P 4
Venice **57** F 2
Venta **55** H 4
Ventoux, Mont **57** E 3
Ventspils **55** H 4
Ventura **102** C 5
Venustiano Carranza **104** D 4
Vera (Argentina) **112** DE 4
Veracruz (Mexico) **104** CD 4
Veraval **72** AB 3
Verbania **57** E 2
Verdalsöra **54** F 3
Verdun **57** E 2
Vereeniging **94** D 5
Verkhn'aya Salda **63** M 4
Verkhneimbatskoye **63** RS 3
Verkhneural'sk **63** LM 5
Verkhnevilyuyskt **68** LM 3
Verkhneye Kuyto,Ozero **54** K 3
Verkhnyaya Amga **69** NO 4
Verkhnyaya Vol'dzha **63** PQ 4
Verkhoyansk **69** O 2
Verkhoyanskiy Khrebet **69** N 2–P 3
Vermilion Bay **100** J 5
Vermont **103** M 3
Verona **57** F 2
Vérroia **58** B 2
Versailles **56** D 2
Vershina **63** M 3
Vershino-Shakhtaminskiye **68** L 5
Vest-Agder **55** E 4
Vesterålen **54** FG 2
Vestfirðir **54** A 2
Vestfjorden **54** F 2
Vestvågöy **54** F 2
Vesuvio **57** F 3
Vetlanda **55** G 4
Vetrenyy **69** R 3
Viacha **110** C 4
Viborg **55** E 4
Vibo Valentia **57** G 4
Vicecommodoro Marambio **115**
Vicenza **57** F 2
Vichada **108** E 3
Vichy **56** D 2
Vicksburg **103** HJ 5
Victoria (Australia) **79** G 6
Victoria (Canada) **99** N 6
Victoria (Chile) **113** B 6
Victoria (Hong Kong) **70** F 6
Victoria (Seychelles) **93** JK 5
Victoria (TX, U.S.A.) **103** G 6
Victoria, Lake **92** E 5
Victoria, Mount **82** A 3
Victoria, Mount (Burma) **73** F 3
Victoria de Durango **104** B 3
Victoria de las Tunas **105** G 3
Victoria Falls **94** D 3
Victoria Island **99** PQ 1
Victoria Land **115**
Victoria River **78** E 2
Victoria Strait **99** R 2
Victoria West **94** C 6
Vicuña Mackenna **112** D 5
Vidin **58** B 2
Vidisha **72** C 3
Vidsel **54** H 2
Viduša **57** G 3
Vidzemes Augstiene **55** J 4
Viedma **113** D 7
Viedma, Lago **113** B 8
Vieng Pou Kha **73** H 3
Vienna (Austria) **57** G 2
Vienne **57** DE 2
Vientiane **73** H 4
Vientos, Paso de los **105** H 3–4
Vierzon **56** D 2
Vietnam **73** JK 5
Vifosa **58** B 2
Vigan **75** J 1
Vigevano **57** E 2
Vigo **56** B 3
Viiala **54** H 3
Vijayawada **72** D 4
Vikna **54** F 3
Vila **81** J 5
Vila **82** C 4
Vila Conceição **109** F 3
Vilanculo **95** F 4
Vila Nova de Gaia **56** B 3
Vila Velha (Amapá, Brazil) **109** H 3
Vila Velha (Espírito Santo, Brazil) **111** HJ 5
Vıldız Dağları **58** C 2
Vilhena **110** D 3
Villa Abecia **110** CD 5
Villa Bella **110** C 3
Villach **57** F 2
Villa Constitución **112** D 5
Villa Coronado **104** B 2
Villa Dolores **112** C 5
Villa Frontera **104** B 2
Villagarcia de Arosa **56** B 3
Villaguay **112** E 5
Villahermosa **104** D 4
Villa Huidobro **112** D 5
Villa Ingavi **110** D 5
Villalonga **113** D 6
Villa María **112** D 5

Villa Mazán **112** C 4
Villa Montes **110** D 5
Villanova y Geltrú **56** D 3
Villa Ocampo **104** AB 2
Villareal de las Enfants **56** CD 4
Villa Regina **113** C 6
Villarreal de los Infantes **56** CD 4
Villarrica (Chile) **113** B 6
Villarrica (Paraguay) **112** E 4
Villatoro, Puerto de **56** B 3
Villa Unión (Argentina) **112** C 4
Villavicencio **108** D 3
Villazón **110** C 5
Villefranche **57** DE 2
Villena **56** C 4
Vilnius **55** J 5
Vilyuy **69** MN 3
Vilyuyskoye Plato **68** J 2
Vilyuyskt **68** M 3
Viña del Mar **112** B 5
Vindhya Range **72** BC 3
Vinh **73** J 4
Vinh Giat **73** JK 5
Vinh Linh **73** J 4
Vinh Loi **73** J 6
Vinkovci **57** G 2
Vinnitsa **62** E 6
Vinson Massif **115**
Virac **75** F 1
Virandozero **62** FG 3
Viranşehir **59** F 3
Virden **99** R 6
Virgem da Lapa **111** H 4
Virginia (South Africa) **94** D 5
Virginia (U.S.A.) **103** L 4
Virginia Beach **103** LM 4
Virginia Falls **99** N 3
Virgin Islands **105** JK 4
Virrat **54** H 3
Virtsu **55** H 4
Virtul Gutii **58** B 1
Visayan Sea **75** F 1
Visby **55** G 4
Viscount Melville Sound **99** P 1
Vishakhapatnam **72** DE 4
Vista Alegre (Roraima, Brazil) **109** F 3
Vistula **53** G 5
Vitebsk **55** K 4
Vitiaz Strait **80** E 3
Viti Levu **82** C 4
Vitim **68** K 4–5
Vitimskoye Ploskogor'ye **68** K 5
Vitória (Espírito Santo, Brazil) **111** HJ 5
Vitória (Pará, Brazil) **109** H 4
Vitoria (Spain) **56** C 3
Vitória da Conquista **111** H 3
Vittorio Veneto **57** F 2
Vivorata **113** E 6
Vizianagaram **72** D 4
Vladimir **62** H 4
Vladimir **71** L 2
Vladimirovka **62** K 5
Vladimir-Volynskiy **55** H 5
Vladivostok **71** K 2
Vlissingen **52** D 4
Vlorë **58** A 2
Vltava **57** F 2
Vogan **90** E 4
Voghera **57** E 2
Voi **93** F 5
Voinjama **90** C 4
Volcán Citlaltépetl **104** C 4
Volcán Llullaillaco **110** C 5
Volcán Miravalles **104** EF 5
Volcán Misti **110** B 4
Volcán Ollagüe **110** C 5
Volcán Popocatéptl **104** C 4
Volcán Tajumulco **104** D 4
Volga **62** J 5
Volgo-Balt (I.V. Lenin) Kanal **62** FG 3
Volgodonsk **59** F 1
Volgograd **62** H 6
Volkhau **54** K 4
Volkhov **55** K 4
Volochayevka **69** O 6
Vologda **62** GH 4
Volokon **68** J 4
Volos **58** B 3
Vol'sk **62** J 5
Volta **90** E 4
Volta, Lake **90** DE 4
Volta Redonda **111** GH 5
Volynskoye Polesye **55** J 5
Volzhsk **62** J 4
Volzhskiy **62** J 6
Vopnafjörður **54** C 2
Vórioi Sporádhes **58** B 3
Vorkuta **63** MN 2
Vormsi **55** H 4
Voronezh **62** GH 5
Voroshilovgrad **59** EF 1
Võrts Järv **55** J 4
Võru **55** J 4
Vosges **57** E 2
Vostochnaya Litsa**62** G 2
Vostochnyy Sayan **68** G 5
Vostok (Antarctica) **115**
Vostok (Kiribati) **83** E 3
Votkinsk **62** K 4
Voyampolka **69** T 4
Vozhega **62** H 3
Voznesensk **58** D 1
Vozvyshennost' Karabil' **67** G 3
Vran **57** G 3
Vranje **58** B 2
Vratsa **58** B 2
Vršac **58** B 1
Vryburg **94** C 5
Vryheid **95** E 5
Vsetin **53** G 5
Vsevidof, Mount **98** D 5
Vsevolozhsk **55** K 3
Vukovar **57** G 2
Vung Tau **73** J 5
Vuoksa **54** J 3
Vyaltsevo **62** H 4
Vyatskiye Polyany **62** K 4
Vyazemskiy **69** OP 6
Vyaz'ma **62** F 4
Vyborg **54** J 3
Vychegda **62** J 3
Vygozero, Ozero **62** G 3
Vyksa **62** H 4
Vyngapur **63** P 3
Vysotsk **55** J 3
V'yuny **63** Q 4

W

"W", Parcs Nationaux, du **90** E 3
Wabowden **99** S 5
Wabrah **66** D 5
Waco (TX, U.S.A.) **103** G 5
Wad **67** H 5
Waddān **87** J 3
Waddington, Mount **99** M 5
Wādi al ʿArabah (Jordan) **60** B 3
Wādī al Bāṭin (Iraq) **61** DE 3
Wādī al Ghudāf (Iraq) **60** D 2
Wādi al Khurr (Saudi Arabia) **60** C 3
Wādī al ʿUbayyid (Iraq) **60** CD 2
Wādī ath Tharthār (Iraq) **60** D 2
Wādī aṭ Ṭubal (Iraq) **60** C 2
Wādī Ḥalfa' **88** E 4
Wādī Ḥawrān (Iraq) **60** C 2
Wādī Jimāl (Egypt) **60** B 4
Wādī Qina (Egypt) **60** A 4
Wadley **103** K 5
Wad Madanī **88** EF 6
Wafrah **66** D 5
Wagga Wagga **79** H 6
Wagin **78** B 5
Wah **67** J 4
Wahai **75** G 4
Wāḥāt al Khārijah **88** E 3–4
Waigeo, Pulau **75** H 4
Waingapu **75** F 5
Wajir **93** G 4
Wakayama **71** L 4
Wake **82** C 1
Wakkanai **71** M 1
Wałbrzych **53** G 4
Waldia **93** F 2
Wales (U.K.) **52** C 4
Walewale **90** D 3
Walgett **79** H 4–5
Wallaroo **79** F 5
Wallis **82** D 3
Wallis and Futuna **82** CD 3
Walnut Ridge **103** H 4
Walvis Bay **94** A 4
Wanaaring **79** G 4
Wanaka **82** C 5
Wandel Sea **114**
Wanganui **81** R 8
Wangka **73** G 5
Wangqing **71** J 2
Wan Hsa-la **73** G 3
Wankie **94** D 3
Wankie National Park **94** D 3
Wanxian **70** E 4
Warangal **72** CD 4
Warbumi **75** H 4
Warburton Mission **78** D 4
Waren **75** J 4
Warner Peak **102** C 3
Warner Robins **103** K 5
Warragul **79** H 6
Warren (MI, U.S.A.) **103** K 3
Warrenton **94** C 5
Warri **91** F 4
Warrnambool **79** G 6
Warrumbungle Range **79** H 5
Warszawa → Warsaw **53** H 4
Warta **53** G 4
Warwick (Queensland, Austr.) **79** J 4
Wasatch Range **102** D 3–4
Washington (D.C., U.S.A.) **103** L 4
Washington (U.S.A.) **102** BC 2
Wasua **80** D 3
Wasum **81** E 3
Watampone **75** F 4
Waterberg **94** B 4
Waterford **52** B 4
Waterloo (IA, U.S.A.) **103** H 3
Waterton Lakes National Park **99** OP 6
Watertown (N.Y., U.S.A.) **103** LM 3
Watheroo **78** B 5
Watrous (Canada) **99** QR 5
Watrous (N.M., U.S.A.) **102** F 4
Watsa **92** D 4
Watson Lake **98** LM 3
Wauchope **79** J 5
Wausau **103** J 3
Wave Hill **78** E 2
Wāw **92** D 3
Wawotobi **75** F 4
Waycross **103** K 5
Wayland **103** K 4
Weagamow Lake **100** J 5
Webbe Shibeli **93** G 3
Weddel Sea **115**
Weichang **71** G 2
Weiden **53** F 5
Weifang **71** GH 3
Weimar **53** F 4
Weining **70** D 5
Weipa **79** G 1
Wejherowo **53** G 4
Welkom **94** D 5
Wellesley Islands (Queensland, Austr.) **79** F 2
Wellington (New Zealand) **81** R 9
Wellington, Isla (Chile) **113** AB 8
Wells (NV, U.S.A.) **102** C 3
Wels **57** F 2
Wendeng **71** H 3
Wenshan **70** DE 6
Wentworth **79** G 5
Wenzhou **71** H 5
Wepener **94** D 5
Weser **53** E 4
Wesleyville **101** R 6
Wessel, Cape **79** F 1
West Antarctica **115**
Westbank **60** B 2
West Berlin **55** F 5
West Cape **82** C 6
Western Australia **78** C 3–4
Western Ghats Kerala **72** BC 4–5
Western Sahara **86** C 4
Western Samoa **82** D 3
West Falkland **113** D 9
West Ice Shelf **115**
Westlock **99** P 5
West Memphis **103** H 4–5

West Palm Beach **103** L 6
West Plains **103** H 4
Westport **81** Q 9
Westport **82** C 5
Westree **101** L 6
West Wirginia **103** K 4
West Wyalong **79** H 5
West Yellowstone **102** D 3
Wetar, Pulau **75** G 5
Wetaskiwin **99** P 5
Wete **93** FG 5
Wewak **80** D 2
Wewak **82** A 3
Weyburn **99** R 6
Whale Cove **99** T 3
Whangarei **81** Q 8
Whangarei **82** C 5
Wheatland **102** F 3
Wheeler Peak (NV, U.S.A.) **102** E 4
Wheeling **103** KL 4
Whitecourt **99** O 5
Whitehaven **52** C 4
Whitehorse **98** KL 3
White Mountain Peak **102** C 4
White Nile **88** E 6
White Pass **98** L 4
White River (Ontario, Can.) **100** L 6
White Russia **55** J 5
Whitewood **79** G 3
Whitmore Mountains **115**
Wholdaia Lake **99** QR 3
Wichita **102** G 4
Wichita Falls **102** G 5
Wick **52** C 3
Wickenburg **102** D 5
Wien **57** G 2
Wiener Neustadt **57** G 2
Wieprz **53** H 4
Wiesbaden **53** E 4
Wilhelm, Mount **80** D 3
Wilhelmshaven **53** E 4
Wilkes-Barre **103** L 3
Wilkes Land **115**
Willcox **102** E 5
Willemstad **108** E 1
Willeroo **78** E 2
Williams (AZ, U.S.A.) **102** D 4
Williams Lake **99** N 5
Williamsport **103** L 3
Williston (South Africa) **94** C 6
Williston (U.S.A.) **102** F 2
Williston Lake **99** N 4
Wilmington (DE, U.S.A.) **103** L 4
Wilmington (N.C., U.S.A.) **103** L 5
Wilowmore **94** C 6
Wilson **103** L 4
Wilson Bluff **78** D 5
Wilsons Promontory **79** H 6
Windhoek **94** B 4
Windsor (Canada) **103** K 3
Windward Islands (French Polynesia) **83** F 4
Windward Islands (Lesser Antilles) **105** L 4–5
Winisk **100** K 4
Winisk River **100** K 5
Winneba **90** D 4
Winnemucca **102** C 3
Winnipeg **99** S 6
Winnipeg **100** KJ 5
Winnipeg, Lake **99** S 5
Winnipegosis, Lake **99** RS 5
Winona **103** H 3
Winslow (AZ., U.S.A.) **102** DE 4
Winslow (Kiribati) **82** D 3
Winston-Salem **103** K 4
Winterthur **57** E 2
Wisconsin **103** HJ 2
Wiseman **98** G 2
Wisła **53** G 4
Wismar **53** F 4
Wittenberg **53** F 4
Wittenberge **53** F 4
Włocławek **53** G 4
Wokam, Pulau **75** H 5
Woleai **82** A 2
Wollastone Lake **99** R 4
Wollaston Lake **99** R 4
Wollaston Peninsula **99** OP 2
Wollongong **79** J 5
Wolverhamton **52** C 4
Wonga Wongué, Parc National de **91** F 6
Wonju **71** J 3
Wŏnsan **71** J 3
Wonthaggi **79** GH 6
Wood Buffalo National Park **99** OP 4
Woodlark **81** F 3
Woodlark **82** B 3
Wood River Lakes **98** F 4
Woodstock (Queensland, Austr.) **79** G 2
Woodward **102** FG 4
Woomera **79** F 5
Wooramel **78** A 4
Worcester (South Africa) **94** BC 6
Worcester (U.K.) **52** C 4
Worchester (MA, U.S.A.) **103** M 3
Worland **102** E 3
Wosi **75** G 4
Wotho **82** BC 2
Wotje **82** C 2
Wrangel Island **114**
Wrangell **98** J 3
Wrangell **98** L 4
Wrangell–Saint Elias National Park and Preserve **98** J 3
Wrigley **99** N 3
Wrocław **53** G 4
Wuchuan **70** E 5
Wudaoliang **70** B 3
Wudu **70** D 4
Wugang **70** F 5
Wugong **70** E 4
Wuhai **70** E 3
Wuhan **70** FG 4
Wuhu **71** G 4
Wüjang **72** D 1
Wukari **91** F 4
Wuliang Shan **70** D 6
Wun Rog **92** D 3
Wuppertal **53** E 4
Wurung **79** G 2
Würzburg **53** F 5
Wutunghliao **70** D 5
Wuvulu **82** A 3
Wuwei **70** D 3
Wuxi **71** H 4
Wuxing **71** H 4
Wuyiling **69** N 6
Wuyuan **70** E 2
Wuzhi Shan **70** E 7
Wuzhong **70** E 3
Wuzhou **70** F 6
Wynbring **78** E 5
Wyndham **78** D 2
Wyoming (U.S.A.) **102** E 3
Wyoming Peak **102** DE 3
Wyperfeld National Park **79** G 6
Wysoczyzna Ciechanowska **53** GH 4

X

Xainza **72** E 1
Xai-Xai **95** E 5
Xambioá **109** J 5
Xangongo **94** AB 3
Xánthi **58** B 2
Xanthos **58** C 3
Xapecó **112** F 4
Xapuri **110** C 3
Xayar **67** L 2
Xenia **103** K 4
Xiaguan **70** D 5
Xiamen **71** G 6
Xi'an **70** EF 4
Xiangfan **70** F 4
Xiangshan **71** H 5
Xiangtan **70** F 5
Xiangyin **70** F 5
Xianju **71** H 5
Xianyang **70** E 4
Xiao'ergou **69** M 6
Xiao Hinggan Ling **69** N 5–6
Xiapu **71** H 5
Xichang **70** D 5
Xigazê **72** E 2
Xiliao He **71** H 2
Ximiao **70** D 2
Xin Barag Zuoqi **68** L 6
Xingcheng **71** GH 2
Xingdi **70** A 2
Xingren **70** E 5
Xingtai **70** F 3
Xingu **109** H 4
Xing Xian **70** EF 3
Xingxingxia **70** C 2
Xingyi **70** D 5–6
Xining **70** D 3
Xinjiang Uygur Zizhiqu **67** KM 2
Xinjin (Liaoning, China) **71** H 3
Xinjin (Sichuan, China) **70** D 4
Xinlitun **69** N 5
Xin Xian **70** F 3
Xinxiang **70** FG 3
Xinyang **70** F 4
Xinyi **71** G 4
Xinyuan **67** L 2
Xique-Xique **111** H 3
Xiushui **70** F 5
Xiuyan **71** H 2
Xiwu **70** C 4
Xixiang **70** E 4
Xizang Zizhiqu **72** DE 1
Xpuhil **104** E 4
Xuanhan **70** E 4
Xuanhua **70** F 2
Xuanwei **70** D 5
Xuchang **70** FG 4
Xuguit Qi **68** LM 6
Xümatang **70** C 4
Xuwen **70** F 6
Xuyong **70** DE 5
Xuzhou **71** G 4

Y

Yablonovyy Khrebet **68** JL 5
Yabrūd (Syria) **60** B 2
Yacuiba **110** D 5
Yadgir **72** C 4
Yagoua **91** GH 3
Yagradagze Shan **70** C 3
Yakima **102** BC 2
Yakmach **67** G 5
Yakoma **92** C 4
Yakrik **67** L 2
Yakumo **71** LM 2
Yakutat **98** K 4
Yakutsk **69** N 3
Yala (Sri Lanka) **72** D 6
Yala (Thailand) **73** H 6
Yalgoo **78** B 4
Yalnızçam Dağları **59** F 2
Yalong Jiang **70** D 4–5
Yalta **59** D 2
Yalutorovsk **63** MN 4
Yamagata **71** LM 3
Yambio **92** D 4
Yambol **58** C 2
Yamburg **63** OP 2
Yamdena, Pulau **75** H 5
Yamoussoukro **90** C 4
Yamuna **72** D 2
Yana **69** P 1
Yan'an **70** E 3
Yanartaş Dağları **58** CD 3
Yanbu' (Saudi Arabia) **60** C 4
Yanbu' (Saudi Arabia) **88** F 4
Yanchang **70** EF 3
Yandrakinot **98** C 2
Yangambi **92** CD 4
Yangjiang **70** F 6
Yangquan **70** F 3
Yangtze Leiang **71** G 4
Yang Xian **70** E 4
Yanhe **70** E 5
Yanhuqu **72** D 1
Yankton **102** G 3
Yano-Indigirskaya Nizmennost **69** PR 1
Yanov Stan **63** Q 2
Yanqi Huizu Zizhixian **67** LM 2
Yanshou **71** J 1
Yanskiy Zaliv **69** OP 1
Yantai **71** H 3
Yaoundé **91** G 5
Yapen, Pulau **75** J 4
Yapura **108** D 4
Yaraka **79** G 3
Yaranga **69** X 3
Yaransk **62** J 4
Yari **108** D 3
Yarlung Zangbo Jiang **70** B 5
Yarmouth **101** O 7
Yaroslavl' **62** G 4
Yarram **79** H 6

Yarroto **63** O 2
Yartsevo **63** RS 3
Yarumal **108** CD 2
Yashkino **69** P 5
Yasnyy **69** N 5
Yaté-Village **81** J 6
Yathkyed Lake **99** S 3
Yatsushiro **71** JK 4
Yavi, Cerro **108** E 2
Yawng-hwe **73** G 3
Ya Xian **70** E 7
Yazd (Iran) **61** G 3
Yazd (Iran) **66** E 4
Yazdān **67** G 4
Yaz-ed Khvāst (Iran) **61** F 3
Yecheng **67** K 3
Yedoma **62** H 3
Yeeda River **78** C 2
Yefremov **62** G 5
Yegorlykskaya **59** F 1
Yei **92** E 4
Yelabuga **62** K 4
Yelets **62** G 5
Yelizarovo **63** N 3
Yelizovo **69** T 5
Yellowhead Pass **99** O 5
Yellowknife **99** P 3
Yellow Sea **71** H 4
Yellowstone National Park **102** D 3
Yellowstone river **102** EF 2
Yelovka **69** U 4
Yelvertoft **79** F 3
Yemanzhelinsk **63** M 5
Yematan (China) **70** C 3
Yematan (China) **70** C 4
Yemen **89** GH 5
Yengisar **67** K 3
Yengo **91** H 5
Yengue **91** F 5
Yenice **59** E 3
Yenisey **63** R 2
Yenisey **68** F 4
Yenisey, Malyy **68** FG 5
Yepoko **63** OP 2
Yercha **69** R 2
Yerema **68** J 3
Yerevan **59** FG 2
Yergeni **59** F 1
Yermak **63** P 5
Yerofey-Pavlovich **69** M 5
Yeropol **69** V 2
Yertom **62** J 3
Yerupajá, Nevado **110** A 3
Yerushalayim **60** B 3
Yerushalayim **88** F 2
Yesil **63** N 5
Yeşilırmak **59** E 2
Yessentuki **59** F 2
Yetman **79** J 4
Yeu, Ile d' **56** C 2
Yevpatoriya **59** D 1
Yeya **59** E 1
Yeysk **59** E 1
Yi'an **69** N 6
Yibin **70** D 5
Yichang **70** F 4
Yichun **69** N 6
Yidu **70** F 4
Yıldız Dağı **59** E 2
Yilehuli Shan **69** MN 5
Yiliang **70** D 6
Yinchuan **70** E 3
Yingde **70** F 6
Yingkou **71** H 2
Yining **67** L 2
Yirga Alem **93** F 3
Yitulihe **69** M 5
Yiyang **70** F 5
Ylikitka **54** J 2
Yllastuntun **54** H 2
Yoboki **93** G 2
Yogyakarta **74** CD 5
Yokohama **71** LM 3–4
Yokosuka **71** LM 3–4
Yokote **71** LM 3
Yola **91** G 4a
Yolombo **92** C 5
Yonago **71** K 3
Yŏngan **71** JK 2
Yongchang **70** D 3
Yong deng **70** D 3
Yongren **70** D 5
Yonkers **103** M 3
Yonne **56** D 2
York (PA, U.S.A.) **103** L 4
York (U.K.) **52** C 4
York (Western Australia) **78** B 5
Yorke Peninsula **79** F 5
Yorkton **99** R 5
Yoshkar Ola **62** J 4
Yŏsu **71** J 4
Young **79** H 5
Youngstown **103** KL 3
Yozgat **59** D 3
Ytyk-Kel' **69** O 3
Yuanping **70** F 3
Yucatán Peninsula **104** E 3–4
Yucheng **71** G 3
Yuci **70** F 3
Yudoma **69** P 4
Yuexi **70** D 5
Yueyang **70** F 5
Yugorskiy Poluostrov **63** M 2
Yugoslavia **57** G 3
Yukagirskoye Ploskogor'ye **69** ST 2
Yukon **98** EF 3
Yukon-Charley Rivers National Preserve **98** J 2–3
Yukon Flats **98** H 2
Yukon Flats National Monument **98** H 2
Yukon Plateau **98** K 3
Yukon River **98** J 2
Yukon Territory **98** KL 3
Yulin (China) **70** EF 6
Yulin (Shaanxi, China) **70** E 3
Yuma (CO, U.S.A.) **102** F 3
Yumari, Cerro **108** E 3
Yumen **70** C 3
Yumenzhen **70** C 2
Yunaska **98** C 5
Yunling Shan **70** C 5
Yunnan **70** D 6
Yunxiao **71** G 6
Yuriby **63** P 1
Yurimaguas **108** C 5
Yurty **69** U 4
Yushan (China) **71** G 5
Yushan (Taiwan) **71** H 6
Yushnoye **69** Q 6
Yuxi **70** D 6
Yu Xian **70** FG 2–3
Yuzhno-Sakhalinsk **69** Q 6
Yuzhnyy Bug **58** CD 1

Z

Zabarjad (Egypt) **60** B 5
Zabol **67** G 4
Zabrze **53** G 4
Zacapu **104** B 4
Zacatecas **104** B 3
Zadar **57** G 3
Zadetkale Kyun **73** G 5
Zadran **67** H 4
Za'faranah (Egypt) **60** A 3
Żag **86** D 3
Zāgheh-ye Bālā (Iran) **61** E 2
Zagorsk **62** G 4
Zagreb **57** G 2
Zagros, Kūhha ye (Iran) **61** EF 2–F 3
Zagros Mountains (Iran) **61** F 3
Zāhedān **67** G 5
Ẓāhirah (Oman) **61** G 5
Zahlah **88** F 2
Zahlah (Lebanon) **60** B 2
Zaire **91** G 6–7
Zaire **92** BD 5
Zaire (Angola) **94** A 1
Zakamensk **68** H J 5
Zakharov **69** O 3
Zākhū **66** C 3
Zákinthos **58** B 3
Zakouma, Parc National de **91** H 3
Zalābiyah (Syria) **60** C 2
Zalaegerszeg **58** A 1
Ẓalim **89** G 4
Zaliv Akademii **69** P 5
Zaliv Kara-Bogaz Gol **66** E 2
Zaliv Shelikhova **69** T 3–4
Zaliv Terpeniya **69** Q 6
Zallah **87** J 3
Zamakh **89** H 5
Zambeze **95** E 3
Zambezi **94** C 2
Zambia **94** D 2
Zamboanga **75** F 2
Zamkowa, Góra **53** H 4
Zamora (Ecuador) **108** C 4
Zamora (Spain) **56** B 3
Zamość **53** H 4
Zanesville **103** K 4
Zanjān **66** D 3
Zanjān (Iran) **61** E 1
Zanthus **78** C 5
Zanul'e **62** K 3
Zanzibar **93** FG 6
Zanzibar Island **93** FG 6
Zaouatallaz **87** G 4
Zaoyang **70** F 4
Zaozernyy **68** FG 4
Zaozhuang **71** G 4
Zapadnaya Dvina **55** J 4
Zapadno **63** OP 3
Zapala **113** B 6
Zaporosh'ye **59** E 1
Zaragoza (Spain) **56** C 3
Zarand (Iran) **61** F 2
Zarand (Iran) **61** G 3
Zarand (Iran) **66** F 4
Zárate **112** E 5
Zaraza **108** E 2
Zard Kūh (Iran) **61** F 2
Zarechensk **54** K 2
Zarghun **67** H 4
Zaria **91** F 3
Zaruma **108** C 4
Zaskar Mountains **67** K 4
Zastron **94** D 6
Zatish'ye **69** T 2
Zatoka Gdańska **53** G 4
Zav'yalova, Ostrov **69** RS 4
Zāwiyat Masūs **87** K 2
Zawr, Ra's az (Saudi Arabia) **61** E 4
Zayü **70** C 5
Zduńska Wola **53** G 4
Zeehan **82** A 5
Zêkog **70** D 4
Zelenoborskiy **54** K 2
Zelenodol'sk **62** JK 4
Zelenokumsk **59** F 2
Zell am See **57** F 2
Žemaičiu Aukštuma **55** H 4
Žemaitija **55** H 4
Zemgale **55** HJ 4
Zemio **92** D 3
Zenica **57** G 3
Zeya **69** N 5
Zêzere **56** B 4
Zhag'yab **70** C 4
Zhailma **63** M 5
Zhaksylyk **63** O 6
Zhanabas **67** H 1
Zhanabek **63** P 6
Zhangjiakou **70** FG 2
Zhangping **71** G 5
Zhangwu **71** H 2
Zhangye **70** CD 3
Zhangzhou **71** G 5–6
Zhangzi **70** F 3
Zhanjiang **70** F 6
Zhantekets **63** Q 6
Zhao'an **70** G 6
Zhaodong **71** HJ 1
Zhaojue **70** D 5
Zhaotong **70** D 5
Zhaoyuan **71** J 1
Zhaozhou **71** HJ 1
Zharkamys **66** F 1
Zharkova **63** R 4
Zharlykamys **63** P 6
Zharma **63** Q 6
Zharyk **63** O 6
Zhdanov **59** E 1
Zhejiang **71** GH 5
Zhelaniya, Cape **114**
Zhel'dyadyr **67** H 1
Zhelezinka **63** P 5
Zheleznodorozhnyy **62** K 3
Zheleznogorsk **62** FG 5
Zhenghe **71** G 5
Zhengzhou **70** F 4
Zhenjiang **71** GH 4
Zhenlai **71** H 1
Zhenning **70** DE 5
Zhenxiong **70** D 5
Zhenyuan **70** E 5
Zhigalovo **68** J 5
Zhijiang **70** E 5
Zhitomir **55** J 5
Zhlatyr **63** P 5
Zhmerinka **58** C 1

Zhongba **72** D 2
Zhongning **70** E 3
Zhongwei **70** DE 3
Zhong Xian **70** E 4
Zhongxiang **70** F 4
Zhoukouzhen **70** FG 4
Zhuanghe **71** H 3
Zhuo Xian **70** G 3
Zhupanovo **69** TU 5
Zhurban **69** N 5
Zhushan **70** EF 4
Zhuzhou **70** F 5
Zibā (Saudi Arabia) **60** B 4
Zielona Góra **53** G 4
Zigong **70** DE 5
Ziguinchor **90** A 3
Zihuatanejo **104** B 4
Zilair **63** L 5
Zile **62** E 2
Žilina **53** G 5
Zima **68** H 5
Zimba **94** D 3
Zimbabwe **94–95** DE 3
Zimbabwe **95** E 4
Zimi **90** B 4
Zimovniki **59** F 1
Zincirli **59** E 3
Zinder **91** F 3
Zlatoust **63** L 4
Zlatoustovsk **69** OP 5
Znamenka **59** D 1
Znojmo **53** G 5
Zoigê **70** D 4
Zolotaya Gora **69** N 5
Zomba **95** F 3
Zonga **92** B 4
Zonguldak **59** D 2
Zorritos **108** B 4
Zrenjanin **58** B 1
Zufār **89** J 5
Zugdidi **59** F 2
Zugspitze **57** F 2
Zújar **56** B 4
Zunyi **70** E 5
Zurbāṭīyah (Iraq) **61** D 2
Zurich **57** E 2
Zurmat **67** H 4
Zuwārah **87** H 2
Zvolen **53** G 5
Zwickau **53** F 4
Żyrardów **53** H 4
Zyryanka **69** S 2
Zyryanovsk **63** Q 6